THE POSTAL SERVICE
GUIDE TO
U.S. STAMPS

UPDATED STAMP VALUES

31ST EDITION

An Imprint of HarperCollins Publishers

HarperCollins books may be purchased for educational, business, or sales
promotional use. For information please write: Special Markets Department,
HarperCollins Publishers Inc., 10 East 53rd Street, New York, NY 10022.

Printed in the United States of America

Library of Congress Cataloging-in-Publication Data has been applied for.

ISBN 0-06-052826-5

04 05 06 07 08 ❖/QWT 10 9 8 7 6 5 4 3 2 1

Table of Contents

The Arts in Stamps

A merican artists, performers, composers, and writers have been celebrated around the world for their cultural contributions. Their style has wielded international influence, and their technical and structural innovations have had an equally great impact. Many distinguished products of the American vision have become classics, and every postage stamp, of course, is a miniature art object. In 2004, the U.S. Postal Service continued to foster this tradition of honoring Americans who loom large in the cultural landscape. Four acclaimed choreographers, George Balanchine, Martha Graham, Agnes de Mille, and Alvin Ailey, were commemorated this year, along with sculptor Isamu Noguchi, writer James Baldwin, composer Henry Mancini, and theater legend Moss Hart. For children of all ages, a beautifully painted block of four stamps highlighted the theme of friendship in the animation of Walt Disney. Also, the man who introduced millions of children to the joys of reading, Theodor Geisel (better known as Dr. Seuss), appeared on a stamp with an appropriately whimsical design. A still life by Martin Johnson Heade, a versatile painter of the 19th century, was featured in the American Treasures series. And lastly, a stamp pane celebrating art of American Indians demonstrated that even when the names of individual creators may be unknown, American artists have produced extraordinarily beautiful objects. As anyone who collects them can testify, stamps offer an artful window on American culture.

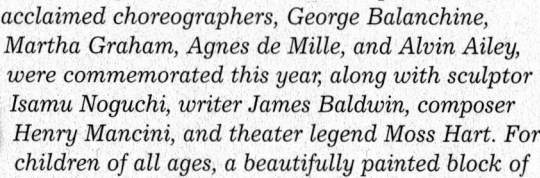

Philately (fi-latt'-eh-lee) is the study of stamps and other postal materials. Stamp collectors are sometimes called philatelists. Collectors often begin by saving stamps from letters, packages, and postcards, sometimes focusing on a favorite subject or theme. They usually start with used stamps and a few inexpensive accessories, such as a small album and a package of stamp hinges.

There are many types of stamps—for example, definitive, commemorative, and special—and formats, such as sheets, booklets, or coils. Stamps may be conventional adhesive ("lick-and-stick") or self-adhesive ("no-lick, peel-and-stick").

Definitive stamps ("regular issues") are the most common. They feature everything from animals to the American flag to historic vehicles. Generally less than an inch square with denominations from one cent to several dollars, they are printed in large quantities, often more than once.

Commemorative stamps—larger and more colorful than definitives—are printed in smaller quantities and typically only once. On sale for a limited period of time, they are issued most often in the prime First-Class rate. They honor people, events, or subjects that are a part of American life and culture.

Special stamps—Christmas, Love, Holiday Celebration, international rate, Priority Mail, and Express Mail—tend to be larger and more colorful. They usually are on sale for a limited time.

Sheet stamps are printed as large press sheets, then trimmed into smaller units called panes, which generally contain twenty stamps. Smaller commemorative panes are often called souvenir sheets. Individual stamps tend to have perforations ("perfs") or die-cut edges on all sides.

Booklet stamps are enclosed in a small folder or issued in a flat unit to be folded by the customer. Most individual booklet stamps have at least one straight edge (no perfs or die cuts).

Coil, or roll, stamps usually have two straight edges on opposite sides. They are issued in coils of a hundred to ten thousand stamps.

Some collectors save envelopes with stamps ("covers"). When collecting "postal history," save the entire envelope if there's something special about the address or return address (a famous place or person, for example), or the postmark (a date or location of some historic significance).

The best way to remove stamps from envelopes is **soaking**. Tear the envelope around the stamp, leaving a small margin. Place it into a pan of warm, not hot, water with the stamp facing down. After a few minutes, the stamp should sink to the bottom. Immediately remove the piece of envelope and wait a few minutes for all adhesive to dislodge from the stamp. Lift the stamp out with your fingers or tongs. Wet stamps are delicate and should be handled carefully.

Place the stamp between two paper towels and put a heavy object, such as a book, on top to keep the stamp from curling as it dries. Leave the stamp overnight. If a stamp still shows signs of adhesive after lengthy soaking, dry it facedown on a single paper towel with nothing touching the back. If necessary, the stamp can be flattened after it has dried.

Many collectors include **First Day Covers** in their collections. These can be purchased directly from the U.S. Postal Service. Or you can buy the stamp yourself, attach it to your own envelope, and send it to the first day Post Office for cancellation. Your local postmaster can help you with this.

There are many types of **stamp albums**. Some feature pictures of the stamps that should be placed on each page. Others have loose-leaf

Seminole doll   USA??

pages to accommodate a growing collection. Computer software can be used to design pages personalizing your collection. A **stock book** has plastic or paper pockets and no pictures of stamps, so you can use it for your collection or to hold duplicate stamps, stamps for trading, and stamps you intend to add to your collection.

When adding stamps to an album, it's best to use a stamp hinge—a small strip of thin material (often glassine) with gum on one side. Unlike tape or glue (which should *never* be used), hinges let you peel the stamp off the page without damaging it. Some collectors use stamp mounts—small, clear plastic sleeves. Although more expensive than hinges, they protect stamps from air, dirt, and moisture.

Collectors use a variety of other materials and accessories. Transparent **glassine envelopes** protect stamps from grease and air. A **stamp catalog** is a reference book (like this one) with illustrations and values of stamps. A **magnifying glass** is useful when examining stamps; **tongs** are used to pick up and move stamps. A **perforation gauge** measures perforations along the edges of stamps. **Watermark fluid** will enhance a watermark, a design or pattern that is pressed into some stamp paper during manufacturing.

When figuring the **value** of a stamp, ask yourself two questions: "How rare is it?" and "What condition is it in?" Stamp catalog prices will give you an idea of the stamp's rarity. However, the stamp may sell at more or less than the catalog price, depending on its condition. Stamp dealers categorize stamps according to their condition. A stamp in **mint condition** is the same as when purchased from the Post Office. Hinge marks on mint stamps can reduce value, which is why stamp mounts are recommended for mint stamps.

In evaluating the condition of a stamp, first look at the front. Are the colors bright or faded? Is the stamp clean, dirty, or stained? Is it torn or creased? A torn stamp is not considered "collectible," but it can be used as a space filler until you get a better one. Are the perforations intact? Has the stamp been canceled? A stamp with a light cancellation is in better condition than one with heavy marks across it.

Is the stamp design centered, crooked, or off to one side? Centering can range from "superb" (perfectly centered on the stamp) to "good" (the design on at least one side is marred somewhat by the perfs). Anything less would be graded "fair" or "poor" and, like torn stamps, should be saved only as space filler. Centering varies widely on older stamps.

An examination of the back of the stamp will reveal whether it has been carelessly treated and thus is less valuable. The values in this book are for used and unused stamps in "very fine" condition.

MARTIN JOHNSON HEADE   USA 37

In addition to buying stamps at the Post Office, check the ads in philatelic newspapers and magazines at your local library. Some publications are listed under Periodicals in this book, and most will send you a free sample on request. There are also many stamp-related sites on the Internet.

In addition to stamps, many philatelists collect **postal stationery**, products with the stamp design printed and/or embossed directly on them. Among these products are **stamped envelopes**, which were first issued in the United States in 1853. More than five hundred million are printed each year. **Stamped postal cards** (or **postal cards**) were first issued in 1873. Several different stamped card designs are issued each year. **Aerogrammes** (also called **air letters**) are designed to be letters and envelopes in one. They are specially stamped, marked for folding, and gummed for sealing.

Other **philatelic collectibles** include:

Plate numbers (including **plate blocks**) appear on or adjacent to stamps. Found most often on sheet stamps, plate blocks are the stamps that have the printing plate numbers in the adjoining selvage, or margin (usually in the corner of the pane). On coils, these numbers appear in the margins of the stamps themselves; collectors often save a **plate number strip** of two or more stamps with the number on the center stamp. On booklets, the plate numbers usually appear on the booklet "tab," which affixes the stamps to the booklet cover.

Booklet panes are panes of stamps affixed in, or as part of, a thin folder to form a booklet. With self-adhesive stamps, a newer convertible booklet format has been created, so that the stamps, liner, and booklet are all one unit. Collectors of booklet panes usually save the entire pane or booklet.

Marginal blocks (including **copyright blocks**) feature marginal inscriptions other than plate numbers. The most common is the copyright block, which features the copyright symbol ©, copyright date, and U.S. Postal Service. All U.S. stamp designs since 1978 are copyrighted.

First Day Covers (FDCs) are envelopes bearing new stamps that have been postmarked on the first day of sale. For each new stamp, the U.S. Postal Service generally selects one location, usually related to the stamp subject, as the place for the first day dedication ceremony and the first day postmark.

First day ceremony programs are given to those who attend first day ceremonies. They contain a list of participants, information on the stamp subject, and the actual stamp attached and postmarked.

Many collectors join **stamp clubs**, a great source for stamps and advice. Ask your local postmaster or librarian about clubs in your area or refer to the Organizations section in this book.

Nature of America: Pacific Coral Reef

Sixth in an educational series, this stamp pane features John D. Dawson's painting of a coral reef near Guam, a U.S. territory in the Pacific.

Date of Issue: January 2, 2004
Place of Issue: Honolulu, HI

Lunar New Year: Year of the Monkey

This is the 12th stamp in the award-winning Lunar New Year series.

Date of Issue: January 13, 2004
Place of Issue: San Francisco, CA

Love: Candy Hearts

This stamp brings to mind childhood exchanges of candy hearts and other tokens of affection.

Date of Issue: January 14, 2004
Place of Issue: Boston, MA

Black Heritage: Paul Robeson

The 27th stamp in the Black Heritage series honors Paul Robeson, remembered for his prodigious talents as a performer and for his commitment to social justice.

Date of Issue: January 20, 2004
Place of Issue: Princeton, NJ

Theodor Seuss Geisel

This issuance honors Theodor Seuss Geisel, better known as the beloved author Dr. Seuss, on the 100th anniversary of his birth.

Date of Issue: March 2, 2004
Place of Issue: La Jolla, CA

Garden Blossoms (Wedding Stamps)

The Postal Service offers these beautiful stamps for weddings and other special occasions.

Date of Issue: March 4, 2004
Place of Issue: New York, NY

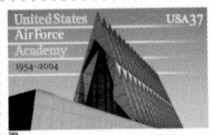

United States Air Force Academy

This stamp marks the 50th anniversary of the establishment of the U.S. Air Force Academy near Colorado Springs, Colorado.

Date of Issue: April 1, 2004
Place of Issue: USAF Academy, CO

Henry Mancini

Henry Mancini was one of the most successful composers in the history of television and film.

Date of Issue: April 13, 2004
Place of Issue: Los Angeles, CA

American Choreographers

Master choreographers George Balanchine, Martha Graham, Agnes de Mille, and Alvin Ailey left a lasting mark on the art of dance.

Date of Issue: May 4, 2004
Place of Issue: Newark, NJ

Lewis & Clark Prestige Booklet

This 32-page booklet commemorating the 200th anniversary of the Lewis and Clark expedition includes two stamp designs: individual portraits of Meriwether Lewis and William Clark.

Date of Issue: May 14, 2004
Place of Issue: Hartford, IL

Lewis & Clark Bicentennial Stamp

This stamp depicts expedition leaders Meriwether Lewis and William Clark surveying the countryside.

Date of Issue: May 14, 2004
Place of Issue: Hartford, IL

Isamu Noguchi

Five works by sculptor Isamu Noguchi appear on a stamp pane commemorating the 100th anniversary of his birth.

Date of Issue: May 18, 2004
Place of Issue: Long Island City, NY

National World War II Memorial

Like the memorial it depicts, this stamp honors the millions of Americans who served overseas and on the home front during World War II.

Date of Issue: May 29, 2004
Place of Issue: Washington, DC

2004 Olympic Games ✻ Athens, Greece

Featuring a stylized depiction of a runner, this issuance celebrates the spirit of athleticism inspired by ancient Greek games.

Date of Issue: June 9, 2004
Place of Issue: Philadelphia, PA

The Art of Disney: Friendship

Issued in partnership with Walt Disney Studios, this set of stamps features animated characters that have become symbols of friendship and good times.

Date of Issue: June 23, 2004
Place of Issue: Anaheim, CA

USS *Constellation*

This issuance marks the 150th anniversary of the launching of the USS *Constellation*, the last entirely sail-powered warship built by the U.S. Navy.

Date of Issue: June 30, 2004
Place of Issue: Baltimore, MD

R. Buckminster Fuller

This stamp honors R. Buckminster Fuller—inventor, architect, engineer, and philosopher—50 years after he patented his geodesic dome.

Date of Issue: July 12, 2004
Place of Issue: Stanford, CA

Literary Arts: James Baldwin

The 20th stamp in the Literary Arts series honors James Baldwin, one of the foremost American writers of the 20th century.

Date of Issue: July 23, 2004
Place of Issue: New York, NY

American Treasures: Martin Johnson Heade

The fourth issuance in the American Treasures series features Martin Johnson Heade's *Giant Magnolias on a Blue Velvet Cloth* (circa 1890).

Date of Issue: August 12, 2004
Place of Issue: Sacramento, CA

ART OF THE AMERICAN INDIAN

Mimbres bowl USA37 | Kutenai parfleche USA37 | Tlingit sculptures USA37 | Ho-Chunk bag USA37 | Seminole doll USA37

    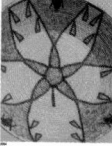

Mississippian effigy USA37 | Acoma pot USA37 | Navajo weaving USA37 | Seneca carving USA37 | Luiseño basket USA37

Art of the American Indian

These ten stamps feature American Indian artifacts dating from around the 11th century to circa 1969.
Date of Issue: August 21, 2004
Place of Issue: Santa Fe, NM

Legends of Hollywood: John Wayne

The tenth stamp in the Legends of Hollywood series honors American film legend John Wayne, known for his portrayals of rugged cowboy characters.
Date of Issue: September 9, 2004
Place of Issue: Los Angeles, CA

Sickle Cell Disease Awareness

The Postal Service continues to raise public awareness about health issues, here focusing on an inherited blood disease.
Date of Issue: September 29, 2004
Place of Issue: Atlanta, GA

C L O U D S C A P E S

Cloudscapes

This educational pane of 15 stamps features photographs of cloud types arranged according to altitude.
Date of Issue: October 4, 2004
Place of Issue: Milton, MA

Holiday Celebrations: Hanukkah

This stamp commemorates Hanukkah, the Jewish holiday that celebrates the rededication of the Temple of Jerusalem almost 2,200 years ago.
Date of Issue: October 15, 2004
Place of Issue: New York, NY

Holiday Ornaments

Four hand-painted Santa Claus ornaments evoke the joys of the winter holiday season.
Date of Issue: November 16, 2004
Place of Issue: New York, NY

Christmas: *Madonna and Child* by Lorenzo Monaco

The 2004 Christmas stamp is a detail of Florentine painter Lorenzo Monaco's *Madonna and Child* (1413), from the collection of the National Gallery of Art.

Date of Issue: October 14, 2004
Place of Issue: New York, NY

Holiday Celebrations: Kwanzaa

The Kwanzaa stamp commemorates an African-American celebration of family, community, and culture.

Date of Issue: October 16, 2004
Place of Issue: Chicago, IL

Moss Hart

This stamp honors the award-winning dramatist and director Moss Hart on the 100th anniversary of his birth.

Date of Issue: October 24, 2004
Place of Issue: New York, NY

Stamped Cards

Columbia University Stamped Card

The U.S. Postal Service commemorates the 250th anniversary of the founding of Columbia University in New York, NY, with the issuance of a stamped card in the Historic Preservation series.

Date of Issue: March 25, 2004
Place of Issue: New York, NY

Harriton House Stamped Card

The U.S. Postal Service commemorates the 300th anniversary of Harriton House in Bryn Mawr, PA, with the issuance of a stamped card in the Historic Preservation series.

Date of Issue: June 10, 2004
Place of Issue: Bryn Mawr, PA

Snowy Egret

This first-class, definitive stamp features an artistic rendering of a snowy egret. Admired for its graceful plumage, the snowy egret is considered one of the most beautiful American birds.
Date of Issue: January 30, 2004
Place of Issue: Norfolk, VA

American Design: Chippendale Chair

Issued as part of the American Design series, this 4-cent definitive stamp features a stylized treatment of a Chippendale chair made in Philadelphia circa 1760.
Date of Issue: March 5, 2004
Place of Issue: New York, NY

Distinguished Americans: Wilma Rudolph

At the 1960 Olympic Games, Wilma Rudolph became the first U.S. woman to win three track-and-field gold medals in one Olympiad. This is the fifth stamp in the Distinguished Americans series.
Date of Issue: July 14, 2004
Place of Issue: Sacramento, CA

American Design: Navajo Jewelry

To be issued as part of the American Design series, this 2-cent definitive features a squash blossom necklace made by a Navajo silversmith.
Date of Issue: August 20, 2004
Place of Issue: Indianapolis, IN

Explanation of Catalog Prices

The United States Postal Service sells only the commemoratives and special issues released during the past few years. Current postal stationery and regular issues remain on sale for longer periods of time. Prices in this book are called "catalog prices" by stamp collectors. Collectors use catalog prices as guidelines when buying or trading stamps. It is important to remember the prices are simply guidelines to the stamp values. Stamp condition is very important in determining the actual value of a stamp.

Prices are Estimated

Listed prices are estimates of how much you can expect to pay for a stamp from a dealer. A 20-cent minimum valuation has been established that represents a fair-market price to have a dealer locate and provide a single stamp to a customer. Dealers may charge less per stamp to provide a group of such stamps, and may charge less for such a single stamp. Similarly, a $1.00 minimum has been established for First Day Covers (FDCs). If you sell a stamp to a dealer, he or she may offer you much less than the catalog price. Dealers pay based on their interest in owning a particular stamp. If they already have a full supply, they may only buy additional stamps at a low price.

Condition Affects Value

The catalog prices are given for unused (mint) stamps and used (canceled) stamps that have been hinged and are in "very fine" condition. Stamps in "superb" condition that have never been hinged may cost more than the listed price. Stamps in less than "fine" condition may cost less.

The prices for used stamps are based on a light cancellation; a heavy cancellation lessens a stamp's value. Canceled stamps may be worth more than uncanceled stamps. This happens if the cancellation is of a special type or for a significant date. Therefore, it is important to study an envelope before removing a stamp and discarding its "cover." Additional information about and examples of stamp conditions can be found in the Introduction to this book.

Sample Listing

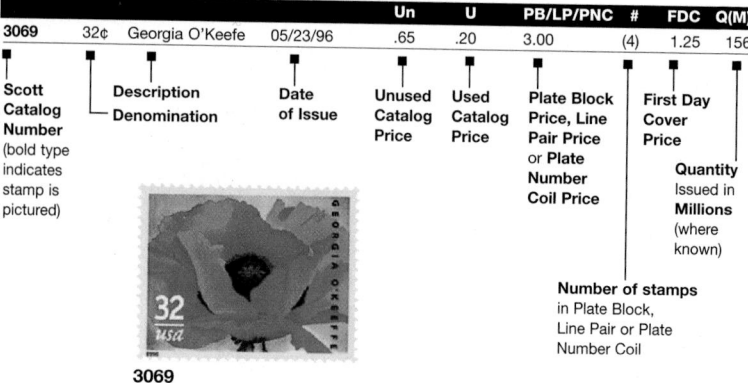

				Un	U	PB/LP/PNC	#	FDC	Q(M)
3069	32¢	Georgia O'Keefe	05/23/96	.65	.20	3.00	(4)	1.25	156

Scott Catalog Number (bold type indicates stamp is pictured)

Description — Denomination

Date of Issue

Unused Catalog Price

Used Catalog Price

Plate Block Price, Line Pair Price or **Plate Number Coil Price**

First Day Cover Price

Quantity Issued in **Millions** (where known)

Number of stamps in Plate Block, Line Pair or Plate Number Coil

3069

Understanding the Listings

■ Prices in **regular type** for single unused and used stamps are taken from the *Scott 2004 Specialized Catalogue of U.S. Stamps & Covers,* whose editors have based these prices on **actual retail values** as they found them in the marketplace. The Scott numbering system for stamps is used in this book. Prices quoted for unused and used stamps are for "very fine" condition, except where "very fine" is not available.

■ Stamp values in *italic* generally refer to items difficult to value accurately.

■ A dash (—) in a value column means the item is known to exist but information is insufficient for establishing a value.

■ The stamp listings contain a number of additions designated "*a*," "*b*," "*c*," etc. These represent recognized variations of stamps as well as errors. These listings are as complete as space permits.

Occasionally, a new stamp or major variation may be inserted by the catalog editors into a series or sequence where it was not originally anticipated. These additions are identified by capital letters "*A*," "*B*" and so forth. For example, a new stamp which logically belonged between 1044 and 1045 is designated 1044A, even though it is entirely different from 1044. The insertion was preferable to a complete renumbering of the series.

■ Prices for Plate Blocks, First Day Covers, American Commemorative Panels and Souvenir Pages are taken from *Scott 2004 Specialized Catalogue of U.S. Stamps & Covers.*

Sample Listing & Variation Listing

			Un	U	PB/LP/PNC	#	FDC	Q(M)
2281	25¢ Honeybee	09/02/88	.45	.20	3.75	(3)	1.25	
a	Imperf. pair		50.00					
b	Black omitted		60.00	—				
d	Pair, imperf. between		1,000.00					

Scott Catalog Number (bold type indicates stamp is pictured)

Description Denomination

Date of Issue

Unused Catalog Price

Used Catalog Price

Plate Block Price, Line Pair Price or **Plate Number** Coil Price

First Day Cover Price

Quantity Issued in **Millions** (where known)

Number of Stamps in Plate Block, Line Pair or Plate Number Coil

2281

Commemorative and Definitive Stamps

1847-1875

1

2

3

4

5

11

12

14

17

Issues of 1847	Un	U
Thin, Bluish Wove Paper,		
July 1, Imperf., Unwmkd.		
1 5¢ Benjamin Franklin	6,250.00	550.00
a 5¢ dark brown	7,250.00	625.00
b 5¢ orange brown	8,000.00	850.00
c 5¢ red orange	17,500.00	5,500.00
Pen cancel		275.00
Double transfer of top and		
bottom frame lines		700.00
Double transfer of top, bottom and		
left frame lines and numerals		3,000.00
2 10¢ George		
Washington	27,500.00	1,350.00
Pen cancel		750.00
Vertical line through second "F"		
of "OFFICE"	—	1,900.00
With "stick pin" in tie, or		
with "harelip"	—	1,900.00
Double transfer in lower		
right "X," or of left and		
bottom frame lines	—	2,000.00
Double transfer in		
"POST OFFICE"	—	2,500.00
Issues of 1875, Reproductions		
of 1 and 2, Bluish Paper, Without Gum		
3 5¢ Franklin	725.00	—
4 10¢ Washington	900.00	—

5¢. On the originals, the left side of the white shirt frill touches the oval on a level with the top of the "F" of "Five." On the reproductions, it touches the oval about on a level with the top of the figure "5."

10¢. On the originals, line of coat points to "T" of TEN and right line of coat points between "T" and "S" of CENTS.

On the reproductions left, line of coat points to right tip of "X" and right line of coat points to center of "S" of CENTS.

On the reproductions, the eyes have a sleepy look, the line of the mouth is straighter, and in the curl of hair near the left cheek is a strong black dot, while the originals have only a faint one.

Issues of 1851-1857, Imperf.		
5 1¢ Franklin, type I	200,000.00	45,000.00
5A 1¢ blue, type Ib	17,500.00	7,000.00
#6-9: Franklin (5), 1851		
6 1¢ blue, type Ia	37,500.00	10,000.00
7 1¢ blue, type II	1,200.00	160.00
Cracked plate	1,450.00	375.00
8 1¢ blue, type III	15,000.00	3,250.00
8A 1¢ blue, type IIIa	4,750.00	1,050.00
9 1¢ blue, type IV	750.00	125.00
Triple transfer,		
one inverted	900.00	175.00

Issues of 1851-1857	Un	U
#10-11, 25-26a all had plates on which at		
least four outer frame lines (and usually much		
more) were recut, adding to their value.		
10 3¢ orange brown		
Washington, type I (11)	3,250.00	110.00
3¢ copper brown	3,750.00	260.00
On part-India paper	—	1,000.00
11 3¢ Washington, type I	275.00	11.00
3¢ deep claret	360.00	19.00
Double transfer,		
"GENTS" for "CENTS"	410.00	50.00
12 5¢ Jefferson, type I	20,000.00	950.00
13 10¢ green Washington,		
type I (14)	16,000.00	800.00
14 10¢ green, type II	4,750.00	200.00
15 10¢ Washington, type III	4,750.00	200.00
16 10¢ green, type IV (14)	30,000.00	1,600.00
17 12¢ Washington	5,500.00	325.00
Issues of 1857-1861, Perf. 15.5		
(Issued in 1857 except #18, 27, 28A, 29,		
30, 30A, 35, 36b, 37, 38, 39)		
#18-24: Franklin (5)		
18 1¢ blue, type I	2,000.00	600.00
19 1¢ blue, type Ia	25,000.00	6,750.00
20 1¢ blue, type II	1,100.00	250.00
21 1¢ blue, type III	13,000.00	2,500.00
22 1¢ blue, type IIIa	2,000.00	500.00
23 1¢ blue, type IV	8,500.00	700.00
24 1¢ blue, type V	175.00	40.00
"Curl" on shoulder	240.00	67.50
"Earring" below ear	600.00	95.00
Long double		
"curl" in hair	300.00	80.00
b Laid paper		1,750.00
#25-26a: Washington (11)		
25 3¢ rose, type I	2,750.00	100.00
Major cracked plate	4,250.00	550.00
26 3¢ dull red, type II	75.00	7.50
3¢ brownish carmine	150.00	18.00
3¢ claret	170.00	23.00
Left or right frame		
line double	110.00	17.50
Cracked plate	750.00	250.00
26a 3¢ dull red, type IIa	225.00	65.00
Double transfer	325.00	135.00
Left frame line double	—	160.00

5
Bust of Benjamin
Franklin.

Detail of **#7, 20** Type II

Lower scrollwork
incomplete (lacks little
balls and lower plume
ornaments). Side orna-
ments are complete.

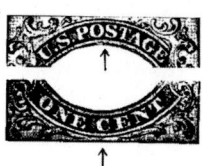

Detail of **#9, 23** Type IV

Similar to Type II, but
outer lines recut top,
bottom or both.

Detail of **#5, 18, 40**
Type I

Has curved, unbroken
lines outside labels.
Scrollwork is substan-
tially complete at top,
forms little balls at
bottom.

Detail of **#8, 21** Type III

Outer lines broken in
the middle. Side orna-
ments are substantially
complete.

Detail of **#8A, 22**
Type IIIa

Outer lines broken top
or bottom but not
both.

Detail of **#24** Type V

Similar to Type III of
1851-57 but with side
ornaments partly cut
away.

Detail of **#6, 19** Type Ia

Same as Type I at bot-
tom but top ornaments
and outer line partly
cut away. Lower scroll-
work is complete.

Detail of **#5a** Type Ib

Lower scrollwork is
incomplete, the little
balls are not so clear.

3¢ Washington Types I-IIa, Series 1851-1857, 1857-1861, 1875

10
Bust of George Washington

Detail of **#10, 11, 25, 41**
Type I

There is an outer frame line
at top and bottom.

Detail of **#26**
Type II

The outer frame line has
been removed at top and
bottom. The side frame lines
were recut so as to be continuous from the top to the
bottom of the plate.

Detail of **#26a**
Type IIa

The side frame lines
extended only to the bot-
tom of the stamp design.

5¢ Jefferson Types I-II, Series 1851-1857, 1857-1861

12
Portrait of
Thomas Jefferson

Detail of **#12, 27-29**
Type I

There are projections on all
four sides.

Detail of **#30-30a**
Type II

The projections at top and
bottom are partly cut away.

10¢ Washington Types I-IV, Series 1851-1857, 1857-1861, 1875

15
Portrait of
George Washington

Detail of **#13, 31, 43**
Type I

The "shells" at the lower
corners are practically
complete. The outer line
below the label is very
nearly complete. The
outer lines are broken
above the middle of the
top label and the "X" in
each upper corner.

Detail of **#14, 32**
Type II

The design is complete at
the top. The outer line at the
bottom is broken in
the middle. The shells are
partly cut away.

Detail of **#15, 33**
Type III

The outer lines are broken
above the top label and
the "X" numerals. The
outer line at the bottom
and the shells are partly
cut away, as in Type II.

Detail of **#16, 34** Type IV

The outer lines have been
recut at top or bottom or
both. Types I, II, III and IV
have complete ornaments
at the sides of the stamps
and three pearls at each
outer edge of the bottom
panel.

Detail of
#35
Type V

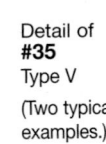

(Two typical
examples.)
Side orna-
ments
slightly cut
away. Outer
lines com-
plete at top

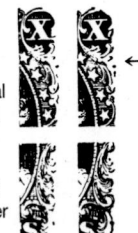

except over right "X." Outer
lines complete at bottom
and shells nearly so.

Issues of 1857-1861	Un	U
Perf. 15.5		
#27-29: Jefferson (12)		
27 5¢ brick red, type I	30,000.00	1,400.00
28 5¢ red brown, type I	5,500.00	900.00
b 5¢ brt. red brn., type I	6,000.00	1,100.00
28A 5¢ Indian red, type I	32,500.00	3,000.00
29 5¢ brown, type I	2,750.00	375.00
Defective transfer	—	—
30 5¢ orange brown, type II	1,200.00	1,150.00
30A 5¢ brown, type II (30)	2,100.00	300.00
b Printed on both sides	4,500.00	4,750.00
#31-35: Washington (15)		
31 10¢ green, type I	18,500.00	1,050.00
32 10¢ green, type II	5,250.00	275.00
33 10¢ green, type III	5,250.00	275.00
"Curl" on forehead or in left "X"	—	350.00
34 10¢ green, type IV	32,500.00	2,250.00
35 10¢ green, type V	275.00	65.00
Small "curl" on forehead	325.00	77.50
"Curl" in "e" or "t" of "Cents"	350.00	90.00
Plate I Outer frame lines complete		
36 12¢ blk. Washington (17), plate I	1,500.00	290.00
Triple transfer	1,800.00	—
36b 12¢ black, plate III	800.00	190.00
Vertical line through rosette	975.00	270.00
37 24¢ gray lilac	1,600.00	350.00
a 24¢ gray	1,600.00	350.00
38 30¢ orange Franklin	1,900.00	450.00
Recut at bottom	2,200.00	575.00
39 90¢ blue Washington	3,000.00	7,500.00
Double transfer at top or bottom	3,250.00	—
Pen cancel		2,500.00

Note: Beware of forged cancellations of #39. Genuine cancellations are rare

Issues of 1875	Un	U
Government Reprints, White Paper Without Gum, Perf. 12		
40 1¢ bright blue Franklin (5)	625.00	
41 3¢ scarlet Wash. (11)	3,250.00	
42 5¢ orange brown Jefferson (30)	1,400.00	
43 10¢ blue green Washington (14)	3,000.00	
44 12¢ greenish black Washington (17)	3,250.00	
45 24¢ blackish violet Washington (37)	3,250.00	
46 30¢ yellow orange Franklin (38)	3,250.00	
47 90¢ deep blue Washington (39)	4,500.00	
48-54 Not assigned		
Issue of 1861, Thin, Semi-Transparent Paper		
#55-62 are no longer considered postage stamps. Many experts consider them to be essays and/or trial color proofs.		
62B 10¢ dark green Washington (58)	7,250.00	1,250.00

30   **37**

38   **39**

40

62B

**Purple Heart
Matted Keepsake**

12" x 16"

This collectible honors the sacrifices of the men and women who defend our nation.

To order this philatelic product call **1-800-STAMP-24** *or visit us online at* **www.usps.com**
Item #108982–$21.95

63   64   65   67

68   69   70   71

72   73   77

Details

Issues of 1861-62, 1861-66, 1867 and 1875

Detail of #63, 86, 92

There is a dash in 63, 86 and 92 added under the tip of the ornament at the right of the numeral in upper left corner.

Detail of #67, 75, 80, 95

There is a leaf in 67, 75, 80 and 95 added to the foliated ornaments at each corner.

Detail of #69, 85E, 90, 97

In 69, 85E, 90 and 97, ovals and scrolls have been added at the corners.

Detail of #64-66, 74, 79, 82-83, 85, 85C, 88, 94

In 64-66, 74, 79, 82-83, 85, 85C, 88 and 94, ornaments at corners have been enlarged and end in a small ball.

Detail of #68, 85D, 89, 96

There is an outer line in 68, 85D, 89 and 96 cut below the stars and an outer line added to the ornaments above them.

Detail of #72, 101

In 72 and 101, parallel lines form an angle above the ribbon containing "U.S. Postage"; between these lines a row of dashes has been added, along with a point of color to the apex of the lower line.

Issues of 1861-1862	Un	U
Perf. 12		
63 1¢ blue Franklin	325.00	35.00
Double transfer	—	47.50
Dot in "U"	350.00	40.00
a 1¢ ultramarine	*2,000.00*	*375.00*
b 1¢ dark blue	750.00	110.00
c Laid paper	—	*4,000*
d Vert. pair, imperf. horizontally		—
e Printed on both sides	—	*4,000.00*
64 3¢ pink Washington	*9,500.00*	850.00
a 3¢ pigeon blood pink	*20,000.00*	*3,500.00*
b 3¢ rose pink	600.00	150.00
65 3¢ rose Washington	130.00	2.50
Cracked plate	—	—
Double transfer	150.00	5.50
b Laid paper	—	500.00
d Vertical pair, imperf. horizontally	*6,000.00*	*750.00*
e Printed on both sides	*11,000.00*	*3,750.00*
f Double impression		*7,500.00*
66 3¢ lake Washington is considered a Trial Color Proof		*2,000.00*
67 5¢ buff Jefferson	*21,000.00*	875.00
68 10¢ yellow green Washington	850.00	50.00
10¢ deep yellow green on thin paper	1,000.00	60.00
Double transfer	975.00	55.00
a 10¢ dark green	975.00	62.50
b Vert. pair, imperf. horizontally		*3,500.00*
69 12¢ blk. Washington	1,700.00	100.00
12¢ intense black	1,750.00	115.00
Double transfer of top or bottom frame line	1,800.00	130.00
Double transfer of top and bottom frame lines	1,850.00	135.00
70 24¢ red lilac Washington	2,500.00	200.00
Scratch under "A" of "POSTAGE"		—
a 24¢ brown lilac	2,250.00	175.00
b 24¢ steel blue	*9,000.00*	800.00
c 24¢ violet	*10,000.00*	1,450.00
d 24¢ grayish lilac	4,500.00	1,450.00
71 30¢ orange Franklin	1,800.00	160.00
a Printed on both sides		—
72 90¢ bl. Washington	3,250.00	425.00
a 90¢ pale blue	3,000.00	425.00
b 90¢ dark blue	3,500.00	650.00
Issues of 1861-1866		
73 2¢ blk. Andrew Jackson	375.00	50.00
Double transfer	425.00	55.00
Major double transfer of top left corner and "POSTAGE"		*12,500.00*
Cracked plate	—	—

Issues of 1861-1866	Un	U
Perf. 12		
#74 3¢ scarlet Washington was not regularly issued and is considered a Trial Color Proof.		
75 5¢ red brown Jefferson (67)	5,000.00	475.00
76 5¢ brown Jefferson (67)	1,400.00	120.00
a 5¢ dark brown	1,400.00	175.00
Double transfer of top or bottom frame line	1,500.00	130.00
77 15¢ blk. Lincoln	2,750.00	160.00
Double transfer	2,850.00	170.00
78 24¢ lilac Washington (70)	2,000.00	175.00
a 24¢ grayish lilac	2,000.00	150.00
b 24¢ gray	2,000.00	150.00
c 24¢ blackish violet	60,000.00	*3,250.00*
d Printed on both sides		—
Grills on U.S. Stamps		
Between 1867 and 1870, postage stamps were embossed with pyramid-shaped grills that absorbed cancellation ink to prevent reuse of canceled stamps.		
Issues of 1867, With Grills		
Grills A, B and with C: Points Up		
A. Grill Covers Entire Stamp		
79 3¢ rose Washington (56)	7,500.00	1,350.00
b Printed on both sides		—
80 5¢ brown Jefferson (57)	—	*130,000.00*
a 5¢ dark brown		*130,000.00*
81 30¢ orange Franklin (61)		*70,000.00*
B. Grill about 18 x 15mm		
82 3¢ rose Washington (56)		*185,000.00*
C. Grill about 13 x 16mm		
83 3¢ rose Washington (56)	5,250.00	1,000.00
Double grill	6,500.00	2,300.00
Grills, D, Z, E, F with Points Down		
D. Grill about 12 x 14mm		
84 2¢ black Jackson (73)	15,000.00	3,500.00
85 3¢ rose Washington (56)	6,500.00	1,000.00
Split grill		1,100.00
Z. Grill about 11 x 14mm		
85A 1¢ blue Franklin (55)		*935,000.00*
85B 2¢ black Jackson (73)	7,500.00	1,200.00
Double transfer	*8,000.00*	1,250.00
85C 3¢ rose Washington (56)	13,500.00	3,500.00
Double grill	15,000.00	
85D 10¢ grn. Washington (58)		*95,000.00*
85E 12¢ blk. Washington (59)	*14,000.00*	1,700.00
Double transfer of top frame line		1,800.00
85F 15¢ black Lincoln (77)		*240,000.00*
E. Grill about 11 x 13mm		
86 1¢ blue Franklin (55)	3,250.00	475.00
a 1¢ dull blue	3,250.00	475.00
Double grill	—	600.00
Split grill	3,400.00	525.00

1867-1875

Issues of 1867	Un	U
With Grills, Perf. 12		
87 2¢ black Jackson (73)	1,600.00	160.00
2¢ intense black	1,700.00	200.00
Double grill	—	—
Double transfer	1,750.00	175.00
88 3¢ rose Washington (65)	900.00	22.50
a 3¢ lake red	1,100.00	40.00
Double grill	—	—
Very thin paper	950.00	25.00
89 10¢ grn. Washington (68)	5,000.00	300.00
Double grill	6,400.00	500.00
90 12¢ blk. Washington (69)	5,000.00	350.00
Double transfer of top		
or bottom frame line	5,250.00	375.00
91 15¢ black Lincoln (77)	10,000.00	625.00
Double grill	—	950.00
F. Grill about 9 x 13mm		
92 1¢ blue Franklin (63)	3,000.00	450.00
a 1¢ pale blue	2,500.00	375.00
Double transfer	3,250.00	500.00
Double grill	—	825.00
93 2¢ black Jackson (73)	500.00	50.00
Double grill	—	180.00
Very thin paper	550.00	57.50
94 3¢ red Washington (65)	425.00	7.50
a 3¢ rose	425.00	7.50
Double grill		—
End roller grill		350.00
Quadruple split grill	750.00	130.00
c Vertical pair,		
imperf. horizontally	1,100.00	
d Printed on both sides	7,500.00	
95 5¢ brown Jefferson (67)	3,500.00	800.00
a 5¢ black brown	4,000.00	1,050.00
96 10¢ yellow green		
Washington (68)	3,250.00	240.00
a 10¢ dark green	3,250.00	240.00
Double transfer	—	—
Quadruple split grill		700.00
97 12¢ blk. Washington (69)	3,250.00	250.00
Double transfer of top		
or bottom frame line	3,600.00	275.00
Triple grill		—
98 15¢ black Lincoln (77)	4,000.00	300.00
Double transfer of		
upper right corner	—	—
Double grill	—	450.00
Quadruple split grill	4,750.00	625.00
99 24¢ gray lilac		
Washington (70)	6,250.00	950.00
100 30¢ orange Franklin (71)	7,000.00	800.00
Double grill	9,250.00	1,650.00
101 90¢ bl. Washington (72)	11,500.00	1,600.00
Double grill	15,500.00	

Issues of 1869-1875	Un	U
Reissue of 1861-1866 Issues,		
Without Grill, Perf. 12		
102 1¢ blue Franklin (63)	900.00	1,200.00
103 2¢ black Jackson (73)	4,000.00	5,500.00
104 3¢ brown red		
Washington (65)	4,000.00	6,750.00
105 5¢ brown Jefferson (67)	3,000.00	2,900.00
106 10¢ grn. Washington (68)	3,250.00	12,500.00
107 12¢ blk. Washington (69)	4,500.00	6,750.00
108 15¢ black Lincoln (77)	4,750.00	9,000.00
109 24¢ deep violet		
Washington (70)	5,750.00	10,000.00
110 30¢ brownish orange		
Franklin (71)	5,750.00	13,500.00
111 90¢ bl. Washington (72)	6,500.00	55,000.00
Issues of 1869, With Grill,		
Hardware Paper		
G. Grill about 9.5 x 9mm		
112 1¢ buff Franklin	825.00	160.00
Double grill	1,250.00	340.00
b Without grill	6,000.00	
113 2¢ br. Post Horse and		
Rider	750.00	85.00
Split grill	900.00	110.00
Double transfer		105.00
114 3¢ Locomotive	300.00	18.00
Triple grill	—	—
Sextuple grill	—	3,250.00
Gray paper	—	95.00
a Without grill	1,500.00	
115 6¢ Washington	3,100.00	210.00
Quadruple split grill	—	825.00
116 10¢ Shield and Eagle	2,500.00	140.00
End roller grill	—	—
117 12¢ S.S. Adriatic	2,600.00	150.00
Split grill	3,100.00	165.00
118 15¢ Landing of Columbus,		
type I	8,250.00	650.00
119 15¢ type II (118)	3,750.00	250.00
b Center inverted	415,000.00	15,000.00
c Center double, one inverted		80,000.00
120 24¢ Declaration of		
Independence	8,000.00	750.00
b Center inverted	285,000.00	15,000.00
121 30¢ Shield, Eagle		
and Flags	7,500.00	550.00
Double grill	—	1,100.00
b Flags inverted	275,000.00	67,500.00
122 90¢ Lincoln	10,000.00	2,300.00
Split grill	—	—
Issues of 1875, Reissue of 1869 Issue,		
Without Grill, Hard White Paper, Perf. 12		
123 1¢ buff (112)	500.00	325.00
124 2¢ brown (113)	700.00	500.00
125 3¢ blue (114)	5,500.00	22,500.00
126 6¢ blue (115)	1,900.00	2,100.00

112

113

114

115

116

117

118

120

121

122

Details

15¢ Landing of Columbus, Types I-III, Series 1869-1875

Detail of **#118** Type I
Picture unframed.

Detail of **#119** Type II
Picture framed.

#129 Type III
Same as Type I but
without fringe of
brown shading lines
around central
vignette.

134   **135**   **136**   **137**

138   **139**   **140**   **141**

142   **143**   **144**

156   **157**   **158**

Details

Detail of **#134, 145**   Detail of **#135, 146**   Detail of **#136, 147**

Detail of **#156, 167, 182, 192**   Detail of **#157, 168, 178, 180, 183, 193**   Detail of **#158, 169, 184, 194**

1¢. In the pearl at the left of the numeral "1" there is a small crescent.   2¢. Under the scroll at the left of "U.S." there is a small diagonal line. This mark seldom shows clearly.   3¢. The under part of the upper tail of the left ribbon is heavily shaded.

	Issues of 1875	Un	U
127	10¢ yellow (116)	2,000.00	1,750.00
128	12¢ green (117)	2,750.00	2,750.00
129	15¢ brown and blue, type III (118)	1,900.00	1,150.00
a	Imperf. horizontally	6,000.00	7,000
130	24¢ grn. & violet (120)	2,250.00	1,600.00
131	30¢ bl. & carmine (121)	3,000.00	2,500.00
132	90¢ car. & black (122)	5,000.00	5,500.00
	Issue of 1880, Reissue of 1869, Soft Porous Paper		
133	1¢ buff (112)	350.00	225.00
a	1¢ brown orange, issued without gum	240.00	200.00
	Issues of 1870-1871		
	With Grill, White Wove Paper, No Secret Marks		
	H. Grill about 10 x 12mm		
134	1¢ Franklin	2,300.00	150.00
	End roller grill		675.00
135	2¢ Jackson	1,200.00	70.00
136	3¢ Washington	725.00	20.00
	Cracked plate	—	90.00
137	6¢ Lincoln	4,750.00	525.00
	Double grill	—	900.00
138	7¢ Edwin M. Stanton	3,750.00	425.00
139	10¢ Jefferson	5,000.00	675.00
140	12¢ Henry Clay	22,500.00	3,000.00
141	15¢ Daniel Webster	7,500.00	1,200.00
142	24¢ Gen. Winfield Scott	—	6,500.00
143	30¢ Alexander Hamilton	17,000.00	2,800.00
144	90¢ Commodore Perry	15,000.00	1,800.00
	Split grill		1,900.00

	Issues of 1870-1871	Un	U
	Without Grill, White Wove Paper, No Secret Marks		
145	1¢ ultra. Franklin (134)	575.00	15.00
146	2¢ red brn. Jackson (135)	325.00	12.00
147	3¢ grn. Washington (136)	300.00	1.50
148	6¢ carmine Lincoln (137)	850.00	25.00
	6¢ violet carmine	1,000.00	75.00
149	7¢ verm. Stanton (138)	1,000.00	90.00
150	10¢ brown Jefferson (139)	1,250.00	22.50
151	12¢ dull violet Clay (140)	2,250.00	160.00
152	15¢ brt. or. Webster (141)	2,400.00	160.00
153	24¢ purple Scott (142)	1,750.00	140.00
154	30¢ black Hamilton (143)	6,000.00	200.00
155	90¢ carmine Perry (144)	4,500.00	300.00
	Issues of 1873, Without Grill, White Wove Paper, Thin to Thick, Secret Marks		
156	1¢ ultra. Franklin	275.00	3.75
	Paper with silk fibers	—	25.00
f	Imperf. pair	—	550.00
157	2¢ br. Jackson	375.00	17.50
	Double paper	1,000.00	100.00
c	With grill	1,850.00	750.00
158	3¢ gr. Washington	130.00	.60
	olive green	375.00	15.00
	Cracked plate	—	32.50

ROY ACUFF

(1903-1992)

ROY CLAXTON ACUFF, often called the King of Country Music, was one of country music's first true superstars. He helped turn the Grand Ole Opry into the nation's foremost country music institution, and Nashville, Tennessee, into the country music capital of America. When a severe case of sunstroke dashed his dreams of an athletic career, Acuff turned to music and his fiddle. In 1936 Acuff's band made their first recordings, including a version of a traditional song that would become one of Acuff's best known numbers, "The Great Speckled Bird." A February 1938 performance at the Grand Ole Opry earned Acuff national fame and made his band—the Smoky Mountain Boys—Opry regulars. Acuff wrote many of his own songs, but also played and recorded songs by obscure or unknown songwriters. His repertoire included traditional and sacred songs—"Will the Circle Be Unbroken" and "I Saw the Light"—and songs about trains, such as "Wabash Cannonball." Acuff kept his music free from the influence of cowboy or western-style music and his band played primarily acoustic instruments. In 1962, he became the first living member of the Country Music Hall of Fame. ❑

Issues of 1873	Un	U
Without Grill, White Wove Paper,		
Thin to Thick, Secret Marks		
159 6¢ dull pk. Lincoln	425.00	17.50
b With grill	1,800.00	
160 7¢ or. verm. Stanton	1,350.00	80.00
Ribbed paper	—	95.00
161 10¢ br. Jefferson	950.00	20.00
162 12¢ bl. vio. Clay	2,500.00	105.00
163 15¢ yel. or. Webster	2,500.00	125.00
a With grill	5,250.00	
164 24¢ pur. Scott		—
165 30¢ gray blk. Hamilton	3,000.00	110.00
166 90¢ rose carm. Perry	2,750.00	250.00

Issues of 1875, Special Printing, Hard,		
White Wove Paper, Without Gum,		
Secret Marks, Perf. 12		
Although perforated, these stamps were		
usually cut apart with scissors. As a result,		
the perforations are often much mutilated		
and the design is frequently damaged.		
167 1¢ ultra. Franklin (156)	12,500.00	
168 2¢ dk. br. Jackson (157)	5,750.00	
169 3¢ blue green		
Washington (158)	15,000.00	—
170 6¢ dull rose Lincoln (159)	14,500.00	
171 7¢ reddish vermilion		
Stanton (160)	3,500.00	
172 10¢ pale brown		
Jefferson (161)	14,500.00	
173 12¢ dark vio. Clay (162)	5,000.00	

Issues of 1875	Un	U
174 15¢ bright orange		
Webster (163)	14,500.00	
175 24¢ dull pur. Scott (142)	3,500.00	5,000.00
176 30¢ greenish black		
Hamilton (143)	12,000.00	
177 90¢ vio. car. Perry (144)	14,000.00	
Regular Issue, Yellowish Wove Paper,		
Perf. 12		
178 2¢ verm. Jackson (157)	425.00	10.00
c With grill	775.00	
179 5¢ Zachary Taylor, June	600.00	20.00
Cracked plate	—	170.00
Double paper	675.00	
Paper with silk fibers	—	32.50
c With grill	3,000.00	
Special Printing, Hard, White		
Wove Paper, Without Gum		
180 2¢ carmine vermilion		
Jackson (157)	40,000.00	
181 5¢ br. bl. Taylor (179)	95,000.00	
Issues of 1879, Soft, Porous		
Paper, Thin to Thick, Perf. 12		
182 1¢ dark ultramarine		
Franklin (156)	325.00	3.50
183 2¢ verm. Jackson (157)	140.00	3.00
a Double impression	—	5,500.00

JAMES THURBER

(1894-1961)

JAMES THURBER—honored in 1994 in the Postal Service's Literary Arts series—was an artist, humorist, playwright, and cartoonist. Born in Ohio and educated at Ohio State University, Thurber worked as a reporter and in civil service before landing a writing position at *The New Yorker*, where he shared office space—and a keen comic sense—with the brilliant essayist, E. B. White. Thurber's gift for drawing first appeared in a book, *Is Sex Necessary?* written in 1929 by the two staffers. Two years later, Thurber's cartoons featuring menacing women, bewildered men, and large dogs with long ears and sad eyes debuted in *The New Yorker*. In 1933 Thurber left the maga-

zine but continued to be a regular contributor. By 1940 his failing eyesight had begun to limit his drawing; by 1952 he was nearly blind. Thurber's legacy, which includes some 17 books and thousands of cartoons, preserves for today's readers his comic genius that is as hilarious today as it was 50 years ago. The stamp art is a self-portrait. ❑

 159

 160

 161

162

163

 179

Details

Detail of #137, 148

Detail of #138, 149

Detail of #139, 150, 187

Detail of #159, 170, 186, 195

6¢. The first four vertical lines of the shading in the lower part of the left ribbon have been strengthened.

Detail of #160, 171, 196

7¢. Two small semi-circles are drawn around the ends of the lines that outline the ball in the lower righthand corner.

Detail of #161, 172, 188, 197

10¢. There is a small semi-circle in the scroll at the right end of the upper label.

Detail of #140, 151

Detail of #141, 152

Detail of #143, 154, 165, 176

Detail of #162, 173, 198

12¢. The balls of the figure "2" are crescent-shaped.

Detail of #163, 174, 189, 199

15¢. In the lower part of the triangle in the upper left corner two lines have been made heavier, forming a "V." This mark can be found on some of the Continental and American (1879) printings, but not all stamps show it.

Detail of #190

30¢. In the "S" of "CENTS," the vertical spike across the middle section of the letter has been broadened.

205   206   207   208

209   210   211   212

219   220   221   222   223   224

225   226   227   228   229

Details

Issues of 1881-1882, Re-engravings of 1873 Designs

Detail of **#206**

1¢. Upper vertical lines have been deepened, creating a solid effect in parts of background. Upper arabesques shaded.

Detail of **#207**

3¢. Shading at sides of central oval is half its previous width A short horizontal dash has been cut below the "TS" of "CENTS."

Detail of **#208**

6¢. Has three vertical lines instead of four between the edge of the panel and the outside of the stamp.

Detail of **#209**

10¢. Has four vertical lines instead of five between left side of oval and edge of the shield. Horizontal lines in lower part of background strengthened.

	Issues of 1879	Un	U
184	3¢ grn. Washington (158)	110.00	.60
	Double transfer	—	—
	Short transfer	—	6.00
185	5¢ blue Taylor (179)	525.00	12.00
186	6¢ pink Lincoln (159)	1,100.00	22.50
187	10¢ brown Jefferson		
	(139) (no secret mark)	3,250.00	25.00
188	10¢ brown Jefferson		
	(161) (with secret mark)	2,250.00	25.00
	black brown	2,450.00	37.50
	Double transfer		45.00
189	15¢ red or. Webster (163)	350.00	22.50
190	30¢ full blk. Hamilton (143)	1,100.00	65.00
191	90¢ carmine Perry (144)	2,250.00	275.00
	Issues of 1880, Special Printing,		
	Soft Porous Paper, Without Gum, Perf. 12		
192	1¢ dark ultramarine		
	Franklin (156)	27,500.00	
193	2¢ blk. br. Jackson (157)	16,000.00	
194	3¢ blue green		
	Washington (158)	50,000.00	
195	6¢ dull rose		
	Lincoln (159)	35,000.00	
196	7¢ scarlet vermilion		
	Stanton (160)	5,500.00	
197	10¢ deep brown		
	Jefferson (161)	28,500.00	
198	12¢ blk. pur. Clay (162)	8,000.00	
199	15¢ or. Webster (163)	27,500.00	
200	24¢ dk. vio. Scott (142)	7,750.00	
201	30¢ greenish black		
	Hamilton (143)	18,000.00	
202	90¢ dull carmine		
	Perry (144)	25,000.00	
203	2¢ scarlet vermilion		
	Jackson (157)	55,000.00	
204	5¢ dp. bl. Taylor (179)	85,000.00	
	Issues of 1882, Perf. 12		
205	5¢ Garfield, Apr. 10	300.00	9.00
	Special Printing, Soft Porous		
	Paper, Without Gum, Perf. 12		
205C	5¢ gray brown		
	Garfield (205)	40,000.00	
	Issues of 1881-1882, Designs		
	of 1873 Re-engraved		
206	1¢ Franklin, Aug. 1881	85.00	.90
	Double transfer	110.00	6.00
207	3¢ Washington,		
	July 16, 1881	85.00	.55
	Double transfer	—	12.00
	Cracked plate	—	
208	6¢ Lincoln, June 1882	625.00	90.00
a	6¢ deep brown red	550.00	140.00
209	10¢ Jefferson, Apr. 1882	175.00	6.00
	10¢ pur. or. olive brown	190.00	6.50
b	10¢ black brown	1,400.00	200.00

	Issues of 1883	Un	U
210	2¢ Washington, Oct. 1	50.00	.60
	Double transfer	55.00	2.25
211	4¢ Jackson, Oct. 1	300.00	20.00
	Cracked plate	—	
	Special Printing, Soft Porous Paper, Perf. 12		
211B	2¢ pale red brown		
	Washington (210)	450.00	—
c	Horizontal pair,		
	imperf. between	1,900.00	
211D	4¢ deep blue green		
	Jackson (211) no gum	37,500.00	
	Issues of 1887, Perf. 12		
212	1¢ Franklin, June	120.00	2.00
	Double transfer		—
213	2¢ green Washington		
	(210), Sept. 10	50.00	.40
	Double transfer	—	3.25
b	Printed on both sides		—
214	3¢ vermilion Washington		
	(207), Oct. 3	80.00	60.00
	Issues of 1888, Perf. 12		
215	4¢ carmine		
	Jackson (211), Nov.	250.00	20.00
216	5¢ indigo		
	Garfield (205), Feb.	275.00	14.00
217	30¢ orange brown		
	Hamilton (165), Jan.	450.00	120.00
218	90¢ pur. Perry (166),		
	Feb.	1,200.00	250.00
	Issues of 1890-1893, Perf. 12		
219	1¢ Franklin, Feb. 22, 1890	30.00	.60
	Double transfer	—	—
219D	2¢ lake Washington		
	(220), Feb. 22, 1890	250.00	1.75
	Double transfer	—	—
220	2¢ Washington, 1890	25.00	.55
	Double transfer	—	3.25
a	Cap on left "2"	150.00	10.00
c	Cap on both "2s"	625.00	30.00
221	3¢ Jackson, Feb. 22, 1890	85.00	7.50
222	4¢ Lincoln, June 2, 1890	110.00	3.00
	Double transfer	125.00	—
223	5¢ Grant, June 2, 1890	90.00	3.00
	Double transfer	110.00	3.75
224	6¢ Garfield, Feb. 22, 1890	85.00	20.00
225	8¢ Sherman, Mar. 21, 1893	65.00	14.00
226	10¢ Webster,		
	Feb. 22, 1890	200.00	3.75
	Double transfer	—	—
227	15¢ Clay, Feb. 22, 1890	275.00	22.50
	Double transfer	—	—
	Triple transfer	—	
228	30¢ Jefferson,		
	Feb. 22, 1890	425.00	32.50
	Double transfer	—	—
229	90¢ Perry, Feb. 22, 1890	650.00	130.00
	Short transfer at bottom	—	—

Issues of 1893		Un	U	PB	#	FDC	Q(M)
Columbian Exposition Issue, Printed by The American Bank Note Co., Perf. 12							
230 1¢ Columbus in Sight of Land	01/02/93	22.50	.40	325.00	(6)	*6,000.00*	449
Double transfer		27.50	.75				
Cracked plate		90.00					
231 2¢ Landing of Columbus	01/02/93	21.00	.30	275.00	(6)	*11,000.00*	1,464
Double transfer		26.00	.35				
Triple transfer		62.50	—				
Quadruple transfer		95.00					
Broken hat on third							
figure left of Columbus		65.00	.45				
Broken frame line		22.50	.35				
Recut frame lines		22.50	—				
Cracked plate		87.50	—				
232 3¢ *Santa Maria,* Flagship	01/02/93	60.00	15.00	725.00	(6)	*10,000.00*	12
Double transfer		80.00	—				
233 4¢ ultramarine, Fleet	01/02/93	87.50	7.50	1,050.00	(6)	*15,000.00*	19
a 4¢ blue (error)		*19,500.00*	*15,000.00*	*145,000.00*	(4)		
Double transfer		125.00	—				
234 5¢ Columbus Soliciting							
Aid from Queen Isabella	01/02/93	95.00	8.00	1,400.00	(6)	*25,000.00*	35
Double transfer		145.00	—				
235 6¢ Columbus Welcomed							
at Barcelona	01/02/93	85.00	22.50			*20,000.00*	5
a 6¢ red violet		85.00	22.50	1,175.00	(6)		
Double transfer		110.00	30.00				
236 8¢ Columbus Restored to Favor	03/93	75.00	11.00	825.00	(6)		11
Double transfer		87.50	—				
237 10¢ Columbus							
Presenting Natives	01/02/93	140.00	8.00	3,350.00	(6)	*30,000.00*	17
Double transfer		180.00	12.50				
Triple transfer		—					
238 15¢ Columbus							
Announcing His Discovery	01/02/93	240.00	70.00	*3,750.00*	(6)		2
Double transfer		—	—				
239 30¢ Columbus at La Rábida	01/02/93	300.00	90.00	*8,500.00*	(6)		0.6
240 50¢ Recall of Columbus	01/02/93	600.00	180.00	*14,000.00*	(6)		0.2
Double transfer		—	—				
Triple transfer		—	—				
241 $1 Queen Isabella							
Pledging Her Jewels	01/02/93	1,250.00	625.00	*47,500.00*	(6)		0.05
Double transfer		—	—				
242 $2 Columbus in Chains	01/02/93	1,300.00	600.00	*67,500.00*	(6)	*60,000.00*	0.05
243 $3 Columbus Describing							
His Third Voyage	01/02/93	2,000.00	1,050.00				0.03
a $3 olive green		2,000.00	1,050.00	*85,000.00*	(6)		
244 $4 Queen Isabella and							
Columbus	01/02/93	2,750.00	1,300.00				0.03
a $4 rose carmine		2,750.00	1,300.00	*250,000.00*	(6)		
245 $5 Portrait of Columbus	01/02/93	3,100.00	1,600.00	*190,000.00*	(6)		0.03

230

231

232

233

234

235

236

237

238

239

240

241

242

243

244

245

1894

246

248

253

254

255

256

257

258

259

Details

2¢ Washington Types I-III, Series 1894-1898

Triangle of **#248-50, 265** Type I

Horizontal lines of uniform thickness run across the triangle.

Triangle of **#251, 266** Type II

Horizontal lines cross the triangle, but are thinner within than without.

Triangle of **#252, 267, 279B-279Be** Type III

The horizontal lines do not cross the double frame lines of the triangle.

Issues of 1894		Un	U	PB	#

Unwmkd., Perf. 12

Bureau Issues Starting in 1894 and continuing until 1979, the Bureau of Engraving and Printing in Washington produced all U.S. postage stamps except #909-21, 1335, 1355, 1410-18 and 1789. Beginning in 1979, security printers in addition to the Bureau of Engraving and Printing started producing postage stamps under contract with the U.S. Postal Service.

#	Description	Date	Un	U	PB	#
246	1¢ Franklin	10/94	32.50	4.50	450.00	(6)
	Double transfer		40.00	5.50		
247	1¢ blue Franklin (246)	11/94	70.00	2.25	900.00	(6)
	Double transfer		—	3.75		
248	2¢ pink Washington, type I	10/94	27.50	6.00	275.00	(6)
	Double transfer		—	—		
249	2¢ carmine lake, type I (248)	10/94	160.00	5.50	2,250.00	(6)
	Double transfer		—	6.50		
250	2¢ carmine, type I (248)		30.00	2.50		
a	2¢ rose		30.00	4.50		
b	2¢ scarlet		30.00	1.00	375.00	(6)
	Double transfer		—	5.00		
c	Vertical pair, imperf. horizontally		4,500.00			
d	Horizontal pair, imperf. between		2,000.00			
251	2¢ carmine, type II (248)		300.00	11.00	3,250.00	(6)
252	2¢ carmine, type III (248)		130.00	11.00		
a	2¢ scarlet		130.00	11.00	1,900.00	(6)
b	Horizontal pair, imperf. vertically		1,500.00			
c	Horizontal pair, imperf. between		1,750.00			
253	3¢ Jackson	09/94	115.00	10.00	1,400.00	(6)
254	4¢ Lincoln	09/94	150.00	6.00	1,900.00	(6)
255	5¢ Grant	09/94	110.00	7.00	1,200.00	(6)
	Worn plate, diagonal lines missing in oval background		110.00	5.00		
	Double transfer		135.00	6.50		
c	Vertical pair, imperf. horiz.		4,000.00			
256	6¢ Garfield	07/94	185.00	22.50	2,900.00	(6)
a	Vertical pair, imperf. horizontally		1,600.00		14,000.00	(6)
257	8¢ Sherman	03/94	140.00	17.50	1,850.00	(6)
258	10¢ Webster	09/94	300.00	12.50	3,350.00	(6)
	Double transfer		350.00	15.00		
259	15¢ Clay	10/94	325.00	60.00	5,000.00	(6)

	Issues of 1894		Un	U	PB	#
260	50¢ Jefferson	11/94	575.00	135.00	*10,500.00*	(6)
261	$1 Perry, type I	11/94	1,000.00	350.00	*17,500.00*	(6)
261A	$1 black Perry, type II (261)	11/94	2,300.00	750.00	*27,500.00*	(6)
262	$2 James Madison	12/94	3,250.00	1,200.00	*42,500.00*	(6)
263	$5 John Marshall	12/94	5,000.00	2,500.00	*23,500.00*	(3)
	Issues of 1895, Wmkd. (191), Perf. 12					
264	1¢ blue Franklin (246)	04/95	6.50	.50	225.00	(6)
265	2¢ carmine Washington,					
	type I (248)	05/95	30.00	2.80	400.00	(6)
	Double transfer		45.00	6.50		
266	2¢ carmine, type II (248)		30.00	5.00	425.00	(6)
267	2¢ carmine, type III (248)		5.50	.40	190.00	(6)
268	3¢ purple Jackson (253)	10/95	37.50	2.00	675.00	(6)
	Double transfer		45.00	4.50		
269	4¢ dark brown Lincoln (254)	06/95	40.00	3.00	725.00	(6)
	Double transfer		45.00	5.00		
270	5¢ chocolate Grant (255)	06/11/95	37.50	3.00	625.00	(6)
	Double transfer		45.00	4.50		
	Worn plate, diagonal lines					
	missing in oval background		40.00	3.25		
271	6¢ dull brown Garfield (256)	08/95	110.00	7.50	2,750.00	(6)
	Very thin paper		120.00	7.50		
a	Wmkd. USIR		*10,000.00*	*7,500.00*		
272	8¢ violet brown Sherman (257)	07/95	70.00	2.50	975.00	(6)
	Double transfer		85.00	4.00		
a	Wmkd. USIR		*5,000.00*	750.00	*20,000.00*	(3)
273	10¢ dark green Webster (258)	06/95	100.00	2.00	1,750.00	(6)
	Double transfer		125.00	4.50		
274	15¢ dark blue Clay (259)	09/95	240.00	14.00	3,750.00	(6)
275	50¢ orange Jefferson (260)	11/95	300.00	30.00	6,000.00	(6)
a	50¢ red orange		325.00	35.00	6,000.00	(6)
276	$1 black Perry, type I (261)	08/95	650.00	90.00	*14,000.00*	(6)
276A	$1 black Perry, type II (261)	08/95	1,400.00	190.00	*25,000.00*	(6)
277	$2 bright blue Madison (262)	08/95	1,100.00	350.00		
a	$2 dark blue		1,100.00	350.00	*21,000.00*	(6)
278	$5 dark green Marshall (263)	08/95	2,300.00	550.00	*75,000.00*	(6)

260   261

262   263

277

Watermark 191
Double-line
"USPS" in
capital letters;
detail at right.

Details

$1 Perry, Types I-II, Series 1894

Detail of **#261, 276**
Type I

The circles enclosing
$1 are broken.

Detail of **#261A, 276A**
Type I

The circles enclosing
$1 are complete.

Issues of 1897-1903		Un	U	PB	#	FDC	Q(M)
Wmkd. 191, Perf. 12							
279	1¢ deep grn. Franklin (246) 01/98	9.00	.50	185.00	(6)		
	Double transfer	12.00	1.10				
279B	2¢ red Washington, type III (248) 01/98	9.00	.40	200.00	(6)		
c	2¢ rose carmine, type III	250.00	75.00	2,900.00	(6)		
d	2¢ orange red, type III	11.50	.55	220.00	(6)		
e	Booklet pane of 6 04/16/00	425.00	1,250.00				
f	2¢ carmine, type IV	10.00	.50	220.00	(6)		
g	2¢ pink, type IV	14.00	1.00	250.00	(6)		
h	2¢ vermillion, type IV	11.00	.55	235.00	(6)		
i	2¢ brown orange, type IV	100.00	10.00	450.00	(3)		
280	4¢ rose brn. Lincoln (254) 10/98	30.00	2.00				
a	4¢ lilac brown	30.00	2.00				
b	4¢ orange brown	30.00	2.00	625.00	(6)		
	Extra frame line at top	50.00	7.50				
281	5¢ dark blue Grant (255) 03/98	35.00	1.80	650.00	(6)		
	Double transfer	45.00	3.75				
	Worn plate, diagonal lines missing in oval background	40.00	2.00				
282	6¢ lake Garfield (256) 12/98	47.50	5.00	900.00	(6)		
	Double transfer	60.00	7.50				
a	6¢ purple lake	65.00	10.00	1,100.00	(6)		
282C	10¢ brown Webster (258), type I 11/98	190.00	5.00	2,500.00	(6)		
	Double transfer	210.00	8.50				
283	10¢ orange brown Webster (258), type II	135.00	4.50	1,750.00	(6)		
284	15¢ olive grn. Clay (259) 11/98	160.00	10.00	2,100.00	(6)		
Issues of 1898, Trans-Mississippi Exposition Issue, Wmkd. 191, Perf. 12							
285	1¢ Jacques Marquette on the Mississippi 06/17/98	30.00	6.50	325.00	(6)	12,500.00	71
	Double transfer	40.00	7.50				
286	2¢ Farming in the West 06/17/98	27.50	2.50	300.00	(6)	12,500.00	160
	Double transfer	42.50	3.75				
	Worn plate	30.00	3.00				
287	4¢ Indian Hunting Buffalo 06/17/98	140.00	24.00	1,500.00	(6)	27,500.00	5
288	5¢ John Charles Frémont on the Rocky Mountains 06/17/98	140.00	21.00	1,400.00	(6)	17,500.00	8
289	8¢ Troops Guarding Wagon Train 06/17/98	180.00	42.50	2,900.00	(6)	20,000	3
a	Vertical pair, imperf. horizontally	22,500.00		75,000.00	(4)		
290	10¢ Hardships of Emigration 06/17/98	180.00	30.00	3,250.00	(6)	27,500.00	5
291	50¢ Western Mining Prospector 06/17/98	700.00	190.00	26,000.00	(6)	50,000.00	0.5
292	$1 Western Cattle in Storm 06/17/98	1,250.00	600.00	50,000.00	(6)	—	0.06
293	$2 Mississippi River Bridge 06/17/98	2,100.00	1,000.00	150,000.00	(6)		0.06

282C

285

286

287

288

289

290

291

292

293

Details

10¢ Webster Types I-II, Series 1898

Detail of **#282C**
Type I

The tips of the foliate ornaments do not impinge on the white curved line below "TEN CENTS."

Detail of **#283**
Type II

The tips of the ornaments break the curved line below the "E" of "TEN" and the "T" of "CENTS."

294

295

296

297

298

299

300

301

302

303

304

305

306

307

308

309

310

311

312

313

	Issues of 1901-1903		Un	U	PB	#	FDC	Q(M)
	Issues of 1901, Pan-American Exposition Issue, Perf. 12							
294	1¢ Fast Lake Navigation	05/01/01	18.00	3.00	225.00	(6)	4,500.00	91
a	Center inverted		9,500.00	10,000.00	75,000.00	(4)		
295	2¢ Empire State Express	05/01/01	17.50	1.00	225.00	(6)	2,750.00	210
a	Center inverted		42,500.00	17,500.00	400,000.00	(4)		
296	4¢ Electric Automobile	05/01/01	85.00	15.00	2,100.00	(6)		6
a	Center inverted		35,000.00		175,000.00	(4)		
297	5¢ Bridge at Niagara Falls	05/01/01	95.00	14.00	2,250.00	(6)	15,000.00	7
298	8¢ Canal Locks at							
	Sault Ste. Marie	05/01/01	120.00	50.00	4,000.00	(6)		5
299	10¢ Fast Ocean Navigation	05/01/01	160.00	25.00	6,750.00	(6)		5
	Wmkd. (191), Perf. 12 (All issued in 1903 except #300b, 306, 308)							
300	1¢ Franklin	02/03	12.00	.25	210.00	(6)		
	Double transfer		17.50	1.00				
	Worn plate		13.00	.35				
	Cracked plate		14.00	.30				
b	Booklet pane of 6	03/06/07	600.00	12,500.00				
301	2¢ Washington	01/17/03	16.00	.40	250.00	(6)		
	Double transfer		27.50	1.25				
	Cracked plate		—	1.25				
c	Booklet pane of 6	01/24/03	500.00	2,250.00				
302	3¢ Jackson	02/03	55.00	3.50	800.00	(6)		
	Double transfer		77.50	4.75				
	Cracked plate		—	—				
303	4¢ Grant	02/03	60.00	2.30	825.00	(6)		
	Double transfer		77.50	2.75				
304	5¢ Lincoln	01/03	60.00	2.00	825.00	(6)		
305	6¢ Garfield	02/03	72.50	3.50	925.00	(6)		
	6¢ brownish lake		72.50	3.50				
	Double transfer		77.50	4.50				
306	8¢ Martha Washington	12/02	45.00	3.00	750.00	(6)		
	8¢ lavender		55.00	3.75				
307	10¢ Daniel Webster	02/03	70.00	2.80	1,100.00	(6)		
308	13¢ Benjamin Harrison	11/18/02	50.00	9.00	700.00	(6)		
309	15¢ Henry Clay	05/27/03	170.00	7.50	3,250.00	(6)		
	Double transfer		210.00	9.00				
310	50¢ Jefferson	03/23/03	475.00	27.50	7,500.00	(6)		
311	$1 David G. Farragut	06/05/03	750.00	75.00	18,000.00	(6)		
312	$2 Madison	06/05/03	1,200.00	200.00	32,500.00	(6)		
313	$5 Marshall	06/05/03	2,900.00	750.00	110,000.00	(6)		

For listings of #312 and 313 with perf. 10, see #479 and 480.

1903-1908

	Issues of 1906-1908		Un	U	PB/LP	#	FDC	Q(M)
	Imperf. (All issued in 1908 except #314)							
314	1¢ bl. grn. Franklin (300)	10/02/06	18.00	15.00	185.00	(6)		
314A	4¢ brown Grant (303)	04/08	70,000.00	40,000.00				
	#314A was issued imperforated, but all copies were privately perforated at the sides.							
315	5¢ blue Lincoln (304)	05/12/08	240.00	850.00	2,600.00	(6)		
	Coil Stamps, Perf. 12 Horizontally							
316	1¢ bl. grn. pair Franklin (300)	02/18/08	120,000.00	—	200,000.00	(2)		
317	5¢ blue pair Lincoln (304)	02/24/08	15,000.00	—	35,000.00	(2)		
	Coil Stamp, Perf. 12 Vertically							
318	1¢ bl. grn. pair Franklin (300)	07/31/08	14,000.00	—	22,500.00	(2)		
	Issues of 1903, Perf. 12							
319	2¢ Washington	11/12/03	6.00	.25	110.00	(6)		
a	2¢ lake, type I		—	—				
b	2¢ carmine rose, type I		7.50	.40	150.00	(6)		
c	2¢ scarlet, type I		7.00	.30	125.00	(6)		
d	Vertical pair, imperf. horizontally		7,500.00					
e	Vertical pair, imperf. between		1,750.00					
f	2¢ lake, type II		10.00	.30	300.00	(6)		
g	Booklet pane of 6, carmine, type I	12/03/03	125.00	550.00				
h	Booklet pane of 6, carmine, type II		500.00					
i	2¢ carmine, type II		75.00	50.00				
j	2¢ carmine rose, type II		50.00	1.75	1,000.00	(6)		
k	2¢ scarlet, type II		50.00	.65	1,000.00	(6)		
m	Booklet pane of 6, lake		—					
n	Booklet pane of 6, carmine rose		225.00	650.00				
p	Booklet pane of 6, scarlet		185.00	575.00				
q	Booklet pane of 6, lake		300.00	750.00				
	Issues of 1906, Washington (319), Imperf.							
320	2¢ carmine	10/02/06	17.50	17.50	200.00	(6)		
	Double transfer		25.00	21.50				
a	2¢ lake, die II		45.00	40.00	725.00	(6)		
b	2¢ scarlet		18.50	12.50	225.00	(6)		
c	2¢ carmine rose, type I		50.00	40.00				
d	2¢ carmine, type II		125.00	275.00				
	Issues of 1908, Coil Stamp (319), Perf. 12 Horizontally							
321	2¢ carmine pair, type I	02/18/08	360,000.00		—			
	Coil Stamp, Perf. 12 Vertically							
322	2¢ carmine pair, type II	07/31/08	5,500.00	—	15,500.00	(2)		
	Issues of 1904, Louisiana Purchase Exposition Issue, Perf. 12							
323	1¢ Robert R. Livingston	04/30/04	30.00	5.00	275.00	(6)	6,000.00	80
	Diagonal line through left "1"		50.00	12.50				
324	2¢ Thomas Jefferson	04/30/04	27.50	2.00	275.00	(6)	4,750.00	193
325	3¢ James Monroe	04/30/04	90.00	30.00	950.00	(6)	5,000.00	5
326	5¢ William McKinley	04/30/04	95.00	25.00	1,000.00	(6)	22,500.00	7
327	10¢ Map of Louisiana Purchase	04/30/04	175.00	30.00	2,250.00	(6)	24,000.00	4
	Issues of 1907, Jamestown Exposition Issue, Wmkd. (191), Perf. 12							
328	1¢ Captain John Smith	04/26/07	30.00	5.00	275.00	(6)	6,000.00	78
	Double transfer		35.00	6.00				
329	2¢ Founding of Jamestown, 1607	04/26/07	35.00	4.50	375.00	(6)	9,000.00	149
330	5¢ Pocahontas	04/26/07	150.00	30.00	2,750.00	(6)		

319

323

324

325

326

327

328

329

330

Details

2¢ Washington Die I-II, Series 1903

Detail of #319a, 319b, 319g Die I

Detail of #319c, 319f, 319h, 319i Die II

331

332

333

334

335

336

337

338

339

340

341

342

Details

3¢ Washington Types I-IV, Series 1908-1919

Detail of **#333, 345, 359, 376, 389, 394, 426, 445, 456, 464, 483, 493, 501-01b**
Type I

Top line of toga rope is weak and rope shading lines are thin. Fifth line from left is missing. Line between lips is thin.

Detail of **#484, 494, 502, 541** Type II

Top line of toga rope is strong and rope shading lines are heavy and complete. Line between lips is heavy.

Detail of **#529**
Type I

Top row of toga rope is strong but fifth shading line is missing as in Type I. Toga button center shading line consists of two dashes, central dot. "P," "O" of "POSTAGE" are separated by line of color.

Detail of **#530, 535**
Type IV

Top rope shading lines are complete. Second, fourth toga button shading lines are broken in middle, third line is continuous with dot in center. "P," "O" of "POSTAGE" are joined.

	Issues of 1908-1909		Un	U	PB/LP	#
	Wmkd. (191) Perf. 12 (All issued in 1908 except #336, 338-42, 345-47)					
331	1¢ Franklin	12/08	7.25	.40	77.50	(6)
	Double transfer		9.50	.75		
a	Booklet pane of 6	12/02/08	160.00	*450.00*		
b	"China Clay" paper		*1,000.00*			
332	2¢ Washington	11/08	6.75	.35	70.00	(6)
	Double transfer		12.50	—		
	Cracked plate		—	—		
a	Booklet pane of 6	11/16/08	135.00	*400.00*		
333	3¢ Washington, type I	12/08	35.00	3.00	350.00	(6)
a	"China Clay" paper		*1,000.00*		*7,500.00*	(6)
334	4¢ Washington	12/08	42.50	1.50	425.00	(6)
	Double transfer		55.00	—		
a	"China Clay" paper		*1,300.00*			
335	5¢ Washington	12/08	55.00	2.50	550.00	(6)
a	"China Clay" paper		*1,000.00*			
336	6¢ Washington	01/09	65.00	6.50	750.00	(6)
a	"China Clay" paper		*750.00*			
337	8¢ Washington	12/08	50.00	3.00	525.00	(6)
	Double transfer		57.50	—		
a	"China Clay" paper		*1,000.00*			
338	10¢ Washington	01/09	70.00	2.00	800.00	(6)
a	"China Clay" paper		*1,000.00*			
339	13¢ Washington	01/09	42.50	19.00	500.00	(6)
	Line through "TAG" of "POSTAGE"		70.00	—		
a	"China Clay" paper		*1,000.00*		*7,500.00*	(6)
340	15¢ Washington	01/09	70.00	6.50	650.00	(6)
a	"China Clay" paper		*1,000.00*		*9,000.00*	(6)
341	50¢ Washington	01/13/09	350.00	20.00	*7,000.00*	(6)
342	$1 Washington	01/29/09	525.00	100.00	*16,000.00*	(6)
	Imperf.					
343	1¢ green Franklin (331)	12/08	5.00	4.50	47.50	(6)
	Double transfer		11.00	7.00		
344	2¢ carmine Washington (332)	12/10/08	6.00	3.00	77.50	(6)
	Double transfer		12.50	4.00		
	Foreign entry, design of 1¢		*1,250.00*	—		
	#345-47: Washington (333-35)					
345	3¢ deep violet, type I	1809	11.50	20.00	155.00	(6)
	Double transfer		22.50	—		
346	4¢ orange brown	02/25/09	19.00	*22.50*	175.00	(6)
	Double transfer		37.50	—		
347	5¢ blue	02/25/09	36.00	35.00	275.00	(6)
	Cracked plate		—			
	Issues of 1908-1910, Coil Stamps, Perf. 12 Horizontally					
	#350-51, 354-56: Washington (Designs of 334-35, 338)					
348	1¢ green Franklin (331)	12/29/08	37.50	25.00	290.00	(2)
349	2¢ carmine Washington (332)	01/09	80.00	17.50	550.00	(2)
	Foreign entry, design of 1¢		—	*1,750.00*		
350	4¢ orange brown	08/15/10	160.00	140.00	1,250.00	(2)
351	5¢ blue	01/09	175.00	175.00	1,250.00	(2)
	Issues of 1909, Coil Stamps, Perf. 12 Vertically					
352	1¢ green Franklin (331)	01/09	95.00	55.00	750.00	(2)
	Double transfer		—	—		

Issues of 1909			Un	U	PB/LP	#	FDC	Q(M)
	Coil Stamps, Perf. 12 Vertically							
353	2¢ carmine Washington (332)	01/12/09	95.00	15.00	750.00	(2)		
354	4¢ orange brown	02/23/09	220.00	120.00	1,500.00	(2)		
355	5¢ blue	02/23/09	230.00	130.00	1,500.00	(2)		
356	10¢ yellow	01/07/09	2,750.00	2,750.00	13,000.00	(2)		
	Bluish Paper, Perf. 12, #359-66: Washington (Designs of 333-40)							
357	1¢ green Franklin (331)	02/16/09	90.00	100.00	1,000.00	(6)		
358	2¢ carmine Washington (332)	02/16/09	85.00	100.00	975.00	(6)		
	Double transfer		—					
359	3¢ deep violet, type I	1909	2,000.00	2,600.00	22,500.00	(6)		
360	4¢ orange brown	1909	24,000.00		110,000.00	(4)		
361	5¢ blue	1909	5,000.00	12,500.00	75,000.00	(6)		
362	6¢ red orange	1909	1,500.00	5,000.00	16,000.00	(6)		
363	8¢ olive green	1909	27,500.00		125,000.00	(3)		
364	10¢ yellow	1909	1,850.00	5,500.00	32,500.00	(6)		
365	13¢ blue green	1909	3,000.00	2,250.00	30,000.00	(6)		
366	15¢ pale ultramarine	1909	1,450.00	11,000.00	11,000.00	(6)		
	Lincoln Memorial Issue, Wmkd. (191)							
367	2¢ Bust of Abraham Lincoln	02/12/09	5.50	1.75	150.00	(6)	500.00	148
	Double transfer		7.50	2.50				
	Imperf.							
368	2¢ carmine (367)	02/12/09	19.00	20.00	180.00	(6)	12,500.00	1
	Double transfer		42.50	27.50				
	Bluish Paper							
369	2¢ carmine (367)	02/09	210.00	275.00	2,900.00	(6)		0.6
	Alaska-Yukon Pacific Exposition Issue							
370	2¢ Willam H. Seward	06/01/09	8.75	2.00	200.00	(6)	3,000.00	153
	Double transfer		10.50	4.50				
	Imperf.							
371	2¢ carmine (370)	06/09	22.50	22.50	220.00	(6)		0.5
	Double transfer		37.50	27.50				
	Hudson-Fulton Celebration Issue, Wmkd. (191)							
372	2¢ Half Moon & Clermont	09/25/09	12.50	4.75	280.00	(6)	750.00	73
	Double transfer		15.00	5.00				
	Imperf.							
373	2¢ carmine (372)	09/25/09	25.00	25.00	240.00	(6)	7,000.00	0.2
	Double transfer		42.50	30.00				
	Issues of 1910-1911, Wmkd. (190) #376-82: Washington (Designs of 333-38, 340)							
374	1¢ green Franklin (331)	11/23/10	7.00	.25	77.50	(6)		
	Double transfer		14.00	—				
	Cracked plate		—	—				
a	Booklet pane of 6	10/07/10	175.00	200.00				
375	2¢ carmine Washington (332)	11/23/10	7.00	.25	85.00	(6)		
	Cracked plate		—	—				
	Double transfer		12.00	—				
	Foreign entry, design of 1¢		—	1,450.00				
a	Booklet pane of 6	11/30/10	100.00	175.00				
b	2¢ lake		525.00					
376	3¢ deep violet, type I	01/16/11	21.50	2.00	220.00	(6)		

367

370

372

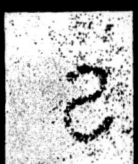

USPS

Watermark 190
Single-line
"USPS"
in capital letters;
detail at right.

397

398

399

400

To order these new stamps and other related philatelic products call 1-800-STAMP-24 or visit us online at www.usps.com

The Art of Disney: Friendship

Issued in partnership with Walt Disney Studios, this set of stamps features animated characters that have become symbols of friendship and good times.

	Issues of 1911		Un	U	PB/LP	#	FDC	Q(M)
	Wmkd. (190), Perf. 12							
377	4¢ brown	01/20/11	32.50	1.00	280.00	(6)		
	Double transfer		—	—				
378	5¢ blue	01/25/11	32.50	.75	325.00	(6)		
	Double transfer		—	—				
379	6¢ red orange	01/25/11	37.50	1.00	500.00	(6)		
380	8¢ olive green	02/08/11	115.00	15.00	1,100.00	(6)		
381	10¢ yellow	01/24/11	105.00	6.00	1,125.00	(6)		
382	15¢ pale ultramarine	03/01/11	275.00	17.50	2,400.00	(6)		
	Issues of 1910, Imperf.							
383	1¢ green Franklin (331)	12/10	2.25	2.00	45.00	(6)		
	Double transfer		6.50	—				
384	2¢ carmine Washington (332)	12/10	3.75	2.50	130.00	(6)		
	Double transfer		7.50	—				
	Rosette plate, crack on head		*150.00*	—				
	Issues of 1910, Coil Stamps, Perf. 12 Horizontally							
385	1¢ green Franklin (331)	11/01/10	40.00	20.00	450.00	(2)		
386	2¢ carmine Washington (332)	11/01/10	75.00	27.50	1,000.00	(2)		
	Issues of 1910-1911, Coil Stamps, Wmkd. (190), Perf. 12 Vertically							
387	1¢ green Franklin (331)	11/01/10	200.00	75.00	900.00	(2)		
388	2¢ carmine Washington (332)	11/01/10	1,050.00	*525.00*	*8,500.00*	(2)		
389	3¢ deep violet Washington, type I (333)	01/24/11	65,000.00	10,000.00	140,000.00	(2)		
	Issues of 1910-1913, Coil Stamps, Perf. 8.5 Horizontally							
390	1¢ green Franklin (331)	12/12/10	5.00	*6.50*	37.50	(2)		
	Double transfer		—	—				
391	2¢ carmine Washington (332)	12/23/10	40.00	15.00	260.00	(2)		
	Coil Stamps, Perf. 8.5 Vertically #394-96: Washington (Designs of 333-35)							
392	1¢ green Franklin (331)	12/12/10	25.00	25.00	200.00	(2)		
	Double transfer		—	—				
393	2¢ carmine Washington (332)	12/16/10	47.50	10.00	300.00	(2)		
394	3¢ deep violet, type I	09/18/11	57.50	55.00	400.00	(2)		
395	4¢ brown	04/15/12	60.00	52.50	425.00	(2)		
396	5¢ blue	03/13	57.50	50.00	400.00	(2)		
	Issues of 1913, Panama Pacific Exposition Issue, Wmkd. (190), Perf. 12							
397	1¢ Vasco Nunez de Balboa	01/01/13	17.50	1.80	175.00	(6)	*5,000.00*	167*
	Double transfer		21.00	2.75				
398	2¢ Pedro Miguel Locks, Panama Canal	01/13	20.00	.75	275.00	(6)		251*
	Double transfer		40.00	2.50				
a	2¢ carmine lake		*1,250.00*					
399	5¢ Golden Gate	01/01/13	80.00	9.50	1,900.00	(6)	*21,000.00*	14*
400	10¢ Discovery of San Francisco Bay	01/01/13	135.00	20.00	2,350.00	(6)	10,000.00	8*
400A	10¢ orange (400)	08/13	210.00	16.00	*11,500.00*	(6)		
	*Includes perf. 10 printing quantities.							

Issues of 1914-1915		Un	U	PB/LP	#
Perf. 10					
401 1¢ green (397)	12/14	27.50	5.50	340.00	(6)
402 2¢ carmine (398)	01/15	75.00	2.50	1,950.00	(6)
403 5¢ blue (399)	02/15	175.00	17.50	4,000.00	(6)
404 10¢ irabge (400)	07/15	875.00	65.00	12,500.00	(6)
Issues of 1912-1914, Wmkd. (190), Perf. 12					
405 1¢ green	02/12	7.00	.25	95.00	(6)
Cracked plate		14.50	—		
Double transfer		8.50	—		
a Vertical pair, imperf. horizontally		1,500.00	—		
b Booklet pane of 6	02/08/12	60.00	75.00		
406 2¢ carmine, type I	02/12	7.00	.25	105.00	(6)
Double transfer		9.00	—		
a Booklet pane of 6	02/08/12	60.00	90.00		
b Double impression		—			
c 2¢ lake		1,750.00	2,750.00		
407 7¢ black	04/14	80.00	12.50	1,200.00	(6)
Imperf. #408-13: Washington (Designs of 405-6)					
408 1¢ green	03/12	1.10	.65	18.00	(6)
Double transfer		2.40	1.00		
Cracked plate		—	—		
409 2¢ carmine, type I	02/12	1.30	.65	35.00	(6)
Cracked plate		14.00	—		
Coil Stamps, Perf. 8.5 Horizontally					
410 1¢ green	03/12	6.00	4.25	30.00	(2)
Double transfer		—	—		
411 2¢ carmine, type I	03/12	10.00	4.00	55.00	(2)
Double transfer		12.50	—		
Coil Stamps, Perf. 8.5 Vertically					
412 1¢ green	03/18/12	25.00	5.50	120.00	(2)
413 2¢ carmine, type I	03/12	50.00	2.00	280.00	(2)
Double transfer		52.50	—		
Perf. 12					
414 8¢ Franklin	02/12	45.00	2.00	475.00	(6)
415 9¢ Franklin	04/14	55.00	13.50	650.00	(6)
416 10¢ Franklin	01/12	45.00	.75	500.00	(6)

405   **406**   **407**   **414**   **415**   **416**

Details

2¢ Washington, Types I-VII, Series 1912-1921

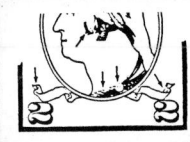

Detail of **#406-06a, 411, 413, 425-25e, 442, 444, 449, 453, 461, 463-63a, 482, 499-99f** Type I

One shading line in first curve of ribbon above left "2" and one in second curve of ribbon above right "2." Toga button has only a faint outline. Top line of toga rope, from button to front of the throat, is very faint. Shading lines of face end in the front of the ear, with little or no joining, to form lock of hair.

Detail of **#482a, 500** Type Ia

Similar to Type I but all lines are shorter.

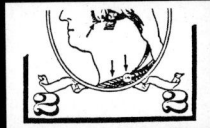

Detail of **#454, 487, 491, 539** Type II

Shading lines in ribbons as in Type I. Toga button, rope and rope shading lines are heavy. Shading lines of face at lock of hair end in strong vertical curved line.

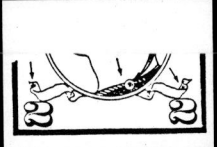

Detail of **#450, 455, 488, 492, 540, 546** Type III

Two lines of shading in curves of ribbons.

Detail of **#526, 532** Type IV

Top line of toga rope is broken. Toga button shading lines form "DID." Line of color in left "2" is very thin and usually broken.

Detail of **#527, 533** Type V

Top line of toga rope is complete. Toga button has five verticle shading lines. Line of color in left "2" is very thin and usually broken. Nose shading dots are as shown.

Detail of **#528, 534** Type Va

Same as Type V except third row from bottom of nose shading dots has four dots instead of six. Overall height of design is $1/3$mm shorter than Type V.

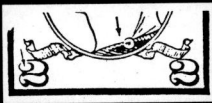

Detail of **#528A, 534A** Type VI

Generally same as Type V except line of color in left "2" is very heavy.

Detail of **#528B, 534B** Type VII

Line of color in left "2" is continuous, clearly defined and heavier than in Type V or Va but not as heavy as Type VI. An additional vertical row of dots has been added to upper lip. Numerous additional dots appear in hair at top of head.

417

418

419

420

421

423

434

After 1915 (from 1916 to date),
all postage stamps, except #519 and 832b,
are on unwatermarked paper.

	Issues of 1912-1914		Un	U	PB	#
417	12¢ Franklin	04/14	50.00	5.00	625.00	(6)
	Double transfer		55.00	—		
	Triple transfer		72.50	—		
418	15¢ Franklin	02/12	85.00	4.50	850.00	(6)
	Double transfer		—	—		
419	20¢ Franklin	04/14	200.00	18.50	2,000.00	(6)
420	30¢ Franklin	04/14	125.00	17.50	1,450.00	(6)
421	50¢ Franklin	08/14	425.00	22.50	10,00.00	(6)
	Wmkd. (191)					
422	50¢ Franklin (421)	02/12/12	250.00	18.50	4,750.00	(6)
423	$1 Franklin	02/12/12	525.00	75.00	12,000.00	(6)
	Double transfer		550.00			
	Issues of 1914-1915, Wmkd. (190), Perf. 10 #424-30: Wash. (Designs of 405-06, 333-36, 407)					
424	1¢ green	09/05/14	2.50	.20	42.50	(6)
	Cracked plate		—	—		
	Double transfer		4.75	—		
	Experimental precancel, New Orleans			—		
c	Vertical pair, imperf. horizontally		2,000.00	1,750.00		
d	Booklet pane of 6		5.25	7.50		
e	As "d", imperf.		1,600.00			
425	2¢ rose red, type I	09/05/14	2.30	.20	27.50	(6)
	Cracked plate		9.50	—		
	Double transfer		—	—		
e	Booklet pane of 6	01/06/14	17.50	25.00		
426	3¢ deep violet, type I	09/18/14	15.00	1.50	200.00	(6)
427	4¢ brown	09/07/14	35.00	1.00	475.00	(6)
	Double transfer		45.00	—		
428	5¢ blue	09/14/14	35.00	1.00	390.00	(6)
429	6¢ red orange	09/28/14	50.00	2.00	525.00	(6)
430	7¢ black	09/10/14	90.00	5.00	950.00	(6)
	#431-33, 435, 437-40: Franklin (414-21, 423)					
431	8¢ pale olive green	09/26/14	37.50	3.00	550.00	(6)
	Double impression		—			
432	9¢ salmon red	10/06/14	50.00	9.00	700.00	(6)
433	10¢ orange yellow	09/09/14	47.50	1.00	825.00	(6)
434	11¢ Franklin	08/11/15	25.00	8.50	240.00	(6)
435	12¢ claret brown	09/10/14	27.50	6.00	290.00	(6)
	Double transfer		35.00	—		
	Triple transfer		40.00	—		
a	12¢ copper red		30.00	7.00	325.00	(6)
436	Not assigned					
437	15¢ gray	09/16/14	135.00	7.25	1,125.00	(6)
438	20¢ ultramarine	09/19/14	220.00	6.00	3,250.00	(6)
439	30¢ orange red	09/19/14	260.00	16.00	4,100.00	(6)
440	50¢ violet	12/10/15	575.00	16.00	15,000.00	(6)

	Issues of 1914		Un	U	PB/LP	#
	Coil Stamps, Perf. 10 Horizontally #441-59: Wash.					
	(Designs of 405-06, 333-35; Flat Press, 18.5-19 x 22mm)					
441	1¢ green	11/14/14	1.00	1.00	8.00	(2)
442	2¢ carmine, type I	07/22/14	10.00	6.00	60.00	(2)
	Coil Stamps, Perf. 10 Vertically					
443	1¢ green	05/29/14	25.00	7.50	155.00	(2)
444	2¢ carmine, type I	04/25/14	40.00	3.00	300.00	(2)
445	3¢ violet, type I	12/18/14	225.00	125.00	1,300.00	(2)
446	4¢ brown	10/02/14	125.00	50.00	750.00	(2)
447	5¢ blue	07/30/14	47.50	27.50	260.00	(2)
	Issues of 1915-1916, Coil Stamps, Perf. 10 Horizontally					
	(Rotary Press, Designs 18.5-19 x 22.5mm)					
448	1¢ green	12/12/15	6.00	4.00	45.00	(2)
449	2¢ red, type I	12/05/15	2,600.00	600.00	*15,000.00*	(2)
450	2¢ carmine, type III	02/16	10.00	5.00	100.00	(2)
451	Not assigned					
	Issues of 1914-1916, Coil Stamps, Perf. 10 Vertically (Rotary Press, Designs 19.5 20 x 22mm)					
452	1¢ green	11/11/14	10.00	3.00	75.00	(2)
453	2¢ carmine rose, type I	07/03/14	150.00	6.00	725.00	(2)
	Cracked plate		—	—		
454	2¢ red, type II	06/15	82.50	10.00	425.00	(2)
455	2¢ carmine, type III	12/15	8.50	1.00	50.00	(2)
456	3¢ violet, type I	02/02/16	240.00	95.00	1,250.00	(2)
457	4¢ brown	02/18/16	25.00	17.50	150.00	(2)
	Cracked plate		35.00	—		
458	5¢ blue	03/09/16	30.00	17.50	180.00	(2)
	Issue of 1914, Horizontal Coil Stamp, Imperf.					
459	2¢ carmine, type I	06/30/14	240.00	*1,100.00*	1,000.00	(2)
	Issues of 1915, Wmkd. 191, Perf. 10					
460	$1 violet black Franklin (423)	02/08/15	850.00	100.00	*12,000.00*	(6)
	Double transfer		900.00	—		
	Perf. 11					
461	2¢ pale carmine red Washington					
	(406), type I	06/17/15	150.00	*300.00*	1,500.00	(6)
	Privately perforated copies of #409 have been made to resemble 461.					
	Issues of 1916-1917, Unwmkd., Perf. 10 #462-69: Wash. (Designs of 405-06, 333-36, 407)					
462	1¢ green	09/27/16	7.00	.35	160.00	(6)
	Experimental precancel, Springfield, MA,					
	or New Orleans, LA			10.00		
a	Booklet pane of 6	10/15/16	9.50	*12.50*		
463	2¢ carmine, type I	09/25/16	4.50	.40	130.00	(6)
	Experimental precancel, Springfield, MA			22.50		
	Double transfer		6.50	—		
a	Booklet pane of 6	10/08/16	95.00	*110.00*		
464	3¢ violet, type I	11/11/16	75.00	17.50	1,350.00	(6)
	Double transfer in "CENTS"		*90.00*	—		
465	4¢ orange brown	10/07/16	45.00	2.50	650.00	(6)
466	5¢ blue	10/17/16	75.00	2.50	950.00	(6)
	Experimental precancel, Springfield, MA			175.00		
467	5¢ carmine (error in plate of 2¢)		550.00	*750.00*		
468	6¢ red orange	10/10/16	95.00	9.00	1,350.00	(6)
	Experimental precancel, Springfield, MA			175.00		
469	7¢ black	10/10/16	130.00	15.00	1,350.00	(6)
	Experimental precancel, Springfield, MA			175.00		

	Issues of 1916-1917		Un	U	PB/LP	#	FDC
	#470-78: Franklin (Designs of 414-16, 434, 417-21, 423)						
470	8¢ olive green	11/13/16	60.00	8.00	600.00	(6)	
	Experimental precancel, Springfield, MA			165.00			
471	9¢ salmon red	11/16/16	60.00	18.50	750.00	(6)	
472	10¢ orange yellow	10/17/16	110.00	2.50	1,350.00	(6)	
473	11¢ dark green	11/16/16	40.00	18.50	360.00	(6)	
	Experimental precancel, Springfield, MA			575.00			
474	12¢ claret brown	10/10/16	55.00	7.50	625.00	(6)	
	Double transfer		65.00	8.50			
	Triple transfer		77.50	11.00			
475	15¢ gray	11/16/16	200.00	16.00	3,000.00	(6)	
476	20¢ light ultramarine	12/05/16	250.00	17.50	3,600.00	(6)	
476A	30¢ orange red		3,450.00	—	40,000	(6)	
477	50¢ light violet	03/02/17	1,100.00	80.00	57,500.00	(6)	
478	$1 violet black	12/22/16	800.00	25.00	13,000.00	(6)	
	Double transfer		825.00	32.50			
479	$2 dark blue Madison (312)	03/22/17	275.00	42.50	4,000.00	(6)	
480	$5 light green Marshall (313)	03/22/17	225.00	40.00	3,100.00 ·	(6)	
	Issues of 1916-1917, Imperf.						
	#481-96: Washington (Designs of 405-06, 333-35)						
481	1¢ green	11/16	1.00	.65	13.00	(6)	
	Double transfer		2.50	1.50			
482	2¢ carmine, type I	12/08/16	1.40	1.25	22.50	(6)	
482A	2¢ deep rose, type Ia			50,000.00			
483	3¢ violet, type I	10/13/17	13.00	7.50	115.00	(6)	
	Double transfer		17.50	—			
484	3¢ violet, type II		10.00	5.00	87.50	(6)	
	Double transfer		12.50	—			
485	5¢ carmine (error in plate of 2¢)	03/17	12,000.00		130.00	(6)	
	Issues of 1916-1922, Coil Stamps, Perf. 10 Horizontally						
486	1¢ green	01/18	.90	.40	4.75	(2)	
	Double transfer		2.25	—			
487	2¢ carmine, type II	11/15/16	13.50	5.00	105.00	(2)	
488	2¢ carmine, type III	1919	2.50	1.75	20.00	(2)	
	Cracked plate		12.00	7.50			
489	3¢ violet, type I	10/10/17	5.00	1.50	32.50	(2)	
	Coil Stamps, Perf. 10 Vertically						
490	1¢ green	11/17/16	.55	.25	3.50	(2)	
	Cracked plate (horizontal)		7.50	—			
	Cracked plate (vertical) retouched		9.00	—			
	Rosette crack		60.00	—			
491	2¢ carmine, type II	11/17/16	2,200.00	750.00	12,000.00	(2)	
492	2¢ carmine, type III		9.50	.40	55.00	(2)	
493	3¢ violet, type I	07/23/17	16.00	3.50	110.00	(2)	
494	3¢ violet, type II	02/04/18	10.00	1.10	75.00	(2)	
495	4¢ orange brown	04/15/17	10.00	4.00	75.00	(2)	
	Cracked plate		25.00	—			
496	5¢ blue	01/15/19	3.50	1.25	30.00	(2)	
497	10¢ orange yellow						
	Franklin (416)	01/31/22	20.00	11.00	140.00	(2)	4,500.00

Issues of 1917-1919		Un	U	PB	#
Perf. 11, #498-507: Washington (Designs of 405-06, 333-36, 407)					
498	1¢ green 03/17	.35	.25	16.50	(6)
	Cracked plate	7.50	—		
a	Vertical pair, imperf. horizontally	600.00			
b	Horizontal pair, imperf. between	325.00			
c	Vertical pair, imperf. between	*450.00*	—		
d	Double impression	250.00	*2,500.00*		
e	Booklet pane of 6 04/06/17	2.50	*2.00*		
f	Booklet pane of 30 09/17	*1,000.00*			
g	Perf. 10 top or bottom	*5,000.00*	—		
499	2¢ rose, type I 03/17	.35	.25	16.50	(6)
	Double transfer	6.00	—		
a	Vertical pair, imperf. horizontally	175.00			
b	Horizontal pair, imperf. vertically	*300.00*	*225.00*		
c	Vertical pair, imperf. between	*850.00*	*225.00*		
e	Booklet pane of 6 03/31/17	4.00	*2.50*		
f	Booklet pane of 30 09/17	*28,000.00*			
g	Double impression	175.00	—		
500	2¢ deep rose, type Ia	275.00	240.00	2,100.00	(6)
	Pair, types I and Ia	*1,275.00*			
501	3¢ light violet, type I 03/17	11.00	.40	125.00	(6)
b	Booklet pane of 6 10/17/17	75.00	*60.00*		
c	Vertical pair, imperf. horizontally, type I	*1,250.00*			
d	Double impression	*2,750.00*	*2,750.00*		
502	3¢ dark violet, type II	14.00	.75	140.00	(6)
b	Booklet pane of 6 02/28/18	60.00	*55.00*		
c	Vertical pair, imperf. horizontally	*500.00*	—		
d	Double impression	625.00	300.00		
e	Perf. 10, top or bottom	*9,500.00*	*6,000.00*		
503	4¢ brown 03/17	10.00	.40	130.00	(6)
504	5¢ blue 03/17	9.00	.35	125.00	(6)
	Double transfer	11.00	—		
505	5¢ rose (error in plate of 2¢)	350.00	550.00		
506	6¢ red orange 03/17	12.50	.40	170.00	(6
507	7¢ black 03/17	27.50	1.25	250.00	(6)
#508-12, 514-18: Franklin (Designs of 414-16, 434, 417-21, 423)					
508	8¢ olive bister 03/17	12.00	.65	170.00	(6)
b	Vertical pair, imperf. between	—	—		
c	Perf. 10 top or bottom		*4,500.00*		
509	9¢ salmon red 03/17	14.00	1.75	140.00	(6)
510	10¢ orange yellow 03/17	17.50	.25	180.00	(6)
511	11¢ light green 05/17	9.00	2.50	125.00	(6)
	Double transfer	12.50	3.25		
512	12¢ claret brown 05/17	9.00	.40	125.00	(6)
a	12¢ brown carmine	10.00	.50		
b	Perf. 10, top or bottom	—	*3,250.00*		
513	13¢ apple green 01/10/19	11.00	6.00	125.00	(6)
	13¢ deep apple green	12.50	6.50		
514	15¢ gray 05/17	37.50	1.50	550.00	(6)
515	20¢ light ultramarine 05/17	45.00	.45	600.00	(6)
	20¢ deep ultramarine	50.00	.55		
b	Vertical pair, imperf. between	*1,500.00*	*1,750.00*		
c	Double impression	*1,250.00*			
d	Perf. 10 at top or bottom	—	*10,000.00*		
516	30¢ orange red 05/17	37.50	1.50	600.00	(6)
a	Perf. 10 top or bottom	*5,000.00*	*5,500.00*		

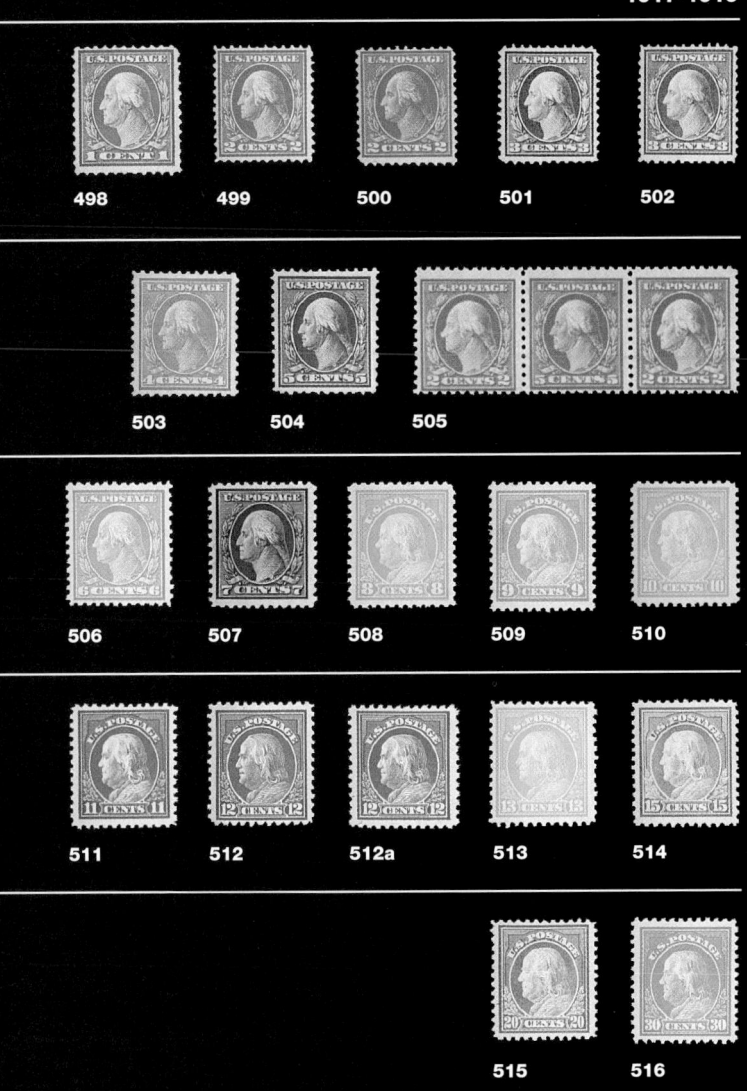

Read about the newest issues in the
"2004 Issues—New U.S. Postage Stamps" section.

517

523

524

*To order this beautiful keepsake and other philatelic products call **1-800-STAMP-24** or visit us online at **www.usps.com***

First Flight Matted Keepsake 14" x 11.5"

This collectible commemorates the first controlled, powered and sustained flight in a heavier-than-air flying machine by Orville and Wilbur Wright on December 17, 1903.

Item #563982-$27.95

	Issues of 1917		Un	U	PB	#	FDC	Q(M)
	Wmkd. (191), Perf. 11							
517	50¢ red violet	05/17	65.00	.75	1,600.00	(6)		
b	Vertical pair, imperf. between							
	and at bottom		—	6,000.00				
c	Perf. 10, top or bottom			10,000.00				
518	$1 violet brown	05/17	50.00	1.50	1,300.00	(6)		
b	$1 deep brown		1,800.00	1,050.00				
519	2¢ carm. Washington (332)	10/10/17	450.00	1,200.00	2,700.00	(6)		
	Privately perforated copies of #344 have been made to resemble #519.							
520-22	Not assigned							
	Issues of 1918, Unwmkd.							
523	$2 Franklin	08/19/18	600.00	240.00	12,000.00	(8)		
524	$5 Franklin	08/19/18	200.00	35.00	4,000.00	(8)		
	Issues of 1918-1920 #525-35: Washington (Designs of 405-06, 333)							
525	1¢ gray green	12/18	2.50	.90	22.50	(6)		
	1¢ Emerald		3.50	1.25				
a	1¢ dark green		6.00	1.75				
c	Horizontal pair, imperf. between		100.00					
d	Double impression		40.00	—				
526	2¢ carmine, type IV	03/06/20	27.50	4.00	240.00	(6)	800.00	
	Gash on forehead		40.00	—				
	Malformed "2" at left		37.50	6.00				
527	2¢ carmine, type V	03/20/20	20.00	1.25	165.00	(6)		
	Line through "2" and "EN"		30.00	—				
a	Double impression		65.00	—				
b	Vertical pair, imperf. horizontally		600.00					
c	Horizontal pair, imperf. vertically		1,000.00	—				
528	2¢ carmine, type Va	05/04/20	9.50	.40	82.50	(6)		
c	Double impression		27.50					
g	Vertical pair, imperf. between		3,500.00					
528A	2¢ carmine, type VI	06/24/20	52.50	2.00	425.00	(6)		
d	Double impression		160.00	—				
f	Vertical pair, imperf. horizontally		—					
h	Vertical pair, imperf. between		1,000.00					
528B	2¢ carmine, type VII	11/03/20	22.50	.75	175.00	(6)		
	Retouched on cheek		400.00	—				
e	Double impression		70.00					
529	3¢ violet, type III	03/18	3.80	.50	60.00	(6)		
a	Double impression		40.00	—				
b	Printed on both sides		1,500.00					
530	3¢ purple, type IV		1.80	.30	18.00	(6)		
	"Blister" under "U.S."		4.75	—				
	Recut under "U.S."		4.75	—				
a	Double impression		30.00	—				
b	Printed on both sides		350.00					
	Imperf.							
531	1¢ green	01/19	9.50	8.00	85.00	(6)		
532	2¢ carmine rose, type IV	03/20	40.00	27.50	325.00	(6)		
533	2¢ carmine, type V	05/04/20	110.00	80.00	1,050.00	(6)		
534	2¢ carmine, type Va	05/25/20	11.00	7.00	105.00	(6)		
534A	2¢ carmine, type VI	07/26/20	45.00	25.00	375.00	(6)		
534B	2¢ carmine, type VII	12/02/20	2,100.00	1,250.00	17,000.00	(6)		
535	3¢ violet, type IV	1918	9.00	5.00	75.00	(6)		
a	Double impression		90.00	—				
	Issues of 1919, Perf. 12.5							
536	1¢ gray green							
	Washington (405)	08/15/19	22.50	20.00	200.00	(6)		
a	Horizontal pair, imperf. vertically		900.00					

	Issues of 1919		Un	U	PB	#	FDC	Q(M)
	Perf. 11							
537	3¢ Allied Victory	03/03/19	10.00	3.25	115.00	(6)	*800.00*	100
	Double transfer		—	—				
a	deep red violet		*1,400.00*	*2,000.00*	10,000.00	(6)		
b	light reddish violet		12.50	4.00	140.00	(6)		
c	red violet		75.00	15.00				
	Issues of 1919, George Washington, Unwmkd., Perf. 11 x 10							
538	1¢ green	06/19	11.00	8.50	110.00	(4)		
	Double transfer		17.50	—				
a	Vertical pair, imperf. horizontally		50.00	*100.00*	900.00	(4)		
539	2¢ carmine rose, type II		2,750.00	*5,250.00*	*17,500.00*	(4)		
540	2¢ carmine rose, type III	06/14/19	13.00	9.50	55.00	(4)		
	Double transfer		22.50	—				
a	Vertical pair, imperf. horizontally		50.00	*100.00*	1,000.00	(4)		
b	Horizontal pair, imperf. vertically		*1,250.00*					
541	3¢ violet, type II	06/19	45.00	30.00	360.00	(4)		
	Issue of 1920, Perf. 10 x 11							
542	1¢ green	05/26/20	14.00	1.50	165.00	(6)	*1,750.00*	
	Issues of 1921, Perf. 10							
543	1¢ green	05/21	.50	.30	14.00	(4)		
	Double transfer		—	—				
	Triple transfer		—	—				
a	Horizontal pair, imperf. between		*1,750.00*					
	Issue of 1922, Perf. 11							
544	1¢ green		*20,000.00*	*3,250.00*				
	Issues of 1921							
545	1¢ green	05/21	200.00	175.00	1,100.00	(4)		
546	2¢ carmine rose, type III	05/21	125.00	*160.00*	775.00	(4)		
	Recut in hair		140.00	*185.00*				
a	Perf. 10 at left		*7,500.00*	*10,000.00*				
	Issue of 1920							
547	$2 Franklin	11/01/20	175.00	40.00	4,000.00	(8)		
	Pilgrim Tercentenary Issue							
548	1¢ The *Mayflower*	12/21/20	4.50	2.25	47.50	(6)	*900.00*	138
	Double transfer		—	—				
549	2¢ Landing of the Pilgrims	12/21/20	6.50	1.60	65.00	(6)	*700.00*	196
550	5¢ Signing of the Compact	12/21/20	40.00	14.00	450.00	(6)	*2,500.00*	11
	Issues of 1922-1925 (See also #581-91, 594-606, 622-23, 631-42, 658-79, 684-87, 692-701, 723)							
551	½¢ Nathan Hale	04/04/25	.30	.20	5.75	(6)	17.50	(4)
	"Cap" on fraction bar		.75	.20				
552	1¢ Franklin	01/17/23	1.50	.20	22.50	(6)	25.00	(2)
	Double transfer		3.50					
a	Booklet pane of 6	08/11/23	7.50	*4.00*				
553	1½¢ Warren G. Harding	03/19/25	2.50	.20	30.00	(6)	30.00	(2)
554	2¢ Washington	01/15/23	1.30	.20	20.00	(6)	37.50	
	Double transfer		2.50	.80				
a	Horizontal pair, imperf. vertically		*300.00*					
b	Vertical pair, imperf. horizontally		*4,000.00*					
c	Booklet pane of 6	02/10/23	6.75	*3.00*				
d	Perf. 10 at top or bottom		*7,000.00*	*5,000.00*				
555	3¢ Lincoln	02/12/23	17.50	1.25	170.00	(6)	35.00	
556	4¢ Martha Washington	01/15/23	19.00	.50	170.00	(6)	60.00	
a	Vertical pair, imperf. horizontally		*10,500.00*					
b	Perf. 10, top or bottom		*3,000.00*	*10,000.00*				
557	5¢ Theodore Roosevelt	10/27/22	19.00	.30	190.00	(6)	*125.00*	
a	Imperf., pair		*1,500.00*					
b	Horizontal pair, imperf. vertically		—					
c	Perf. 10, top or bottom		—	*7,500.00*				

537

547

548

549

550

551

552

553

554

555

556

557

558

559

560

561

562

563

564

565

566

567

568

569

570

571

572

573

Issues of 1922-1923		Un	U	PB	#	FDC
Perf. 11						
558	6¢ Garfield 11/20/22	35.00	1.00	400.00	(6)	225.00
	Double transfer	55.00	2.00			
	Same, recut	55.00	2.00			
559	7¢ McKinley 05/01/23	9.00	.75	80.00	(6)	175.00
	Double transfer	—	—			
560	8¢ Grant 05/01/23	50.00	1.00	575.00	(6)	175.00
	Double transfer	—	—			
561	9¢ Jefferson 01/15/23	14.00	1.25	170.00	(6)	175.00
	Double transfer	—	—			
562	10¢ Monroe 01/15/23	17.50	.35	200.00	(6)	175.00
a	Vertical pair, imperf. horizontally	2,250.00				
b	Imperf., pair	1,500.00				
c	Perf. 10 at top or bottom		5,500.00			
563	11¢ Rutherford B. Hayes 10/04/22	1.40	.60	27.50	(6)	600.00
a	11¢ light bluish green	1.40	.60			
d	Imperf., pair		17,500.00			
564	12¢ Grover Cleveland 03/20/23	6.00	.35	80.00	(6)	175.00
a	Horizontal pair, imperf. vertically	1,750.00				
565	14¢ American Indian 05/01/23	4.00	.90	50.00	(6)	400.00
	Double transfer	—	—			
566	15¢ Statue of Liberty 11/11/22	20.00	.30	275.00	(6)	550.00
567	20¢ Golden Gate 05/01/23	20.00	.30	250.00	(6)	*500.00*
a	Horizontal pair, imperf. vertically	1,500.00				
568	25¢ Niagara Falls 11/11/22	18.00	.75	240.00	(6)	*650.00*
b	Vertical pair, imperf. horizontally	2,000.00				
c	Perf. 10 at one side	5,000.00	11,000.00			
569	30¢ Buffalo 03/20/23	30.00	.60	240.00	(6)	*850.00*
	Double transfer	55.00	—			
570	50¢ Arlington Amphitheater 11/11/22	47.50	.40	575.00	(6)	*1,250.00*
571	$1 Lincoln Memorial 02/12/23	40.00	.65	300.00	(6)	*7,000.00*
	Double transfer	90.00	1.60			
572	$2 U.S. Capitol 03/20/23	77.50	9.00	650.00	(6)	*20,000.00*
573	$5 Head of Freedom,					
	Capitol Dome 03/20/23	120.00	15.00	1,800.00	(8)	*32,500.00*
a	Carmine lake and dark blue	200.00	20.00	2,400.00	(8)	
574	Not assigned					
	Issues of 1923-1925, Imperf.					
575	1¢ green Franklin (552) 03/20/23	7.00	5.00	70.00	(6)	
576	1½¢ yel. brn. Harding (553) 04/04/25	1.40	1.50	20.00	(6)	45.00
577	2¢ carmine Washington (554)	1.50	1.25	25.00	(6)	
	Issues of 1923, Perf. 11 x 10					
578	1¢ green Franklin (552) 1923	95.00	*160.00*	800.00	(4)	
579	2¢ carmine Washington (554) 1923	85.00	*140.00*	600.00	(4)	
	Recut in eye	*110.00*	*150.00*			
	Issues of 1923-1926, Perf. 10 (See also #551-73, 622-23, 631-42, 658-79, 684-87, 692-701, 723)					
580	Not assigned					
581	1¢ green Franklin (552) 04/21/23	11.00	.75	125.00	(4)	*6,000.00*
582	1½¢ brn. Harding (553) 03/19/25	5.50	.65	45.00	(4)	40.00
	Pair with full horiz. gutter between	*160.00*				
583	2¢ carm. Wash. (554) 04/14/24	3.00	.30	37.50	(4)	
a	Booklet pane of 6 08/27/26	95.00	*85.00*			1,800.00
584	3¢ violet Lincoln (555) 08/01/25	32.50	3.00	275.00	(4)	55.00
585	4¢ yellow brown Martha					
	Washington (556) 03/25	19.00	.65	230.00	(4)	55.00
586	5¢ blue T. Roosevelt (557) 12/24	19.00	.40	240.00	(4)	57.50
587	6¢ red orange Garfield (558) 03/25	9.25	.60	110.00	(4)	60.00
588	7¢ black McKinley (559) 05/29/26	13.50	6.25	125.00	(4)	70.00

1923-1929

	Issues of 1925-1926		Un	U	PB/LP	#	FDC	Q(M)
	Perf. 11 x 10							
589	8¢ olive grn. Grant (560)	05/29/26	30.00	4.50	250.00	(4)	72.50	
590	9¢ rose Jefferson (561)	05/29/26	6.00	2.50	60.00	(4)	72.50	
591	10¢ orange Monroe (562)	06/08/25	70.00	.50	475.00	(4)	95.00	
592-93	Not assigned							
	Issues of 1923, Perf. 11							
594	1¢ green Franklin (552),							
	design 19.75 x 22.25mm	1923	*16,000.00*	6,750.00				
595	2¢ carmine Washington (554),							
	design 19.75 x 22.25mm	1923	300.00	*350.00*	2,100.00	(4)		
596	1¢ green Franklin (552),							
	design 19.25 x 22.5mm	1923		120,000.00				
	Issues of 1923-1929, Coil Stamps, Perf. 10 Vertically							
597	1¢ green Franklin (552)	07/18/23	.30	.20	2.25	(2)	*600.00*	
	Gripper cracks or double transfer		2.60	1.00				
598	1¼¢ brown Harding (553)	03/19/25	1.00	.20	4.75	(2)	60.00	
599	2¢ carmine Washington							
	(554), type I	01/23	.40	.20	2.30	(2)	*1,500.00*	
	Double transfer		1.90	1.00				
	Gripper cracks		2.30	2.00				
599A	2¢ carmine Washington							
	(554), type II	03/29	125.00	11.00	675.00	(2)		
600	3¢ violet Lincoln (555)	05/10/24	7.25	.20	25.00	(2)	80.00	
601	4¢ yellow brown							
	M. Washington (556)	08/05/23	4.50	.35	30.00	(2)		
602	5¢ dark blue T. Roosevelt (557)	03/05/24	1.75	.20	10.00	(2)	85.00	
603	10¢ orange Monroe (562)	12/01/24	4.00	.20	26.50	(2)	100.00	
	Coil Stamps, Perf. 10 Horizontally							
604	1¢ yel. grn. Franklin (552)	07/19/24	.35	.20	3.75	(2)	90.00	
605	1¼¢ yel. brn. Harding (553)	05/09/25	.35	.20	3.50	(2)	70.00	
606	2¢ carmine Washington (554)	12/31/23	.35	.20	2.60	(2)	125.00	
607-09	Not assigned							
	Issues of 1923, Harding Memorial Issue, Perf. 11							
610	2¢ blk. Warren Gamaliel Harding	09/01/23	.65	.25	20.00	(6)	30.00	1,459
	Double transfer		1.75	.50				
a	Horizontal pair, imperf. vertically		2,500.00					
	Imperf.							
611	2¢ blk. Harding (610)	11/15/23	5.75	4.00	70.00	(6)	90.00	0.8
	Perf. 10							
612	2¢ blk. Harding (610)	09/12/23	17.50	1.75	300.00	(4)	100.00	100
	Perf. 11							
613	2¢ black Harding (610)	1923		42,500.00				
	Issues of 1924, Huguenot-Walloon Tercentary Issue, May 1							
614	1¢ Ship *Nieu Nederland*	01/05/24	2.75	3.25	40.00	(6)	40.00	51
615	2¢ Walloons' Landing							
	at Fort Orange (Albany)	01/05/24	5.00	2.25	55.00	(6)	55.00	78
	Double transfer		12.00	3.50				
616	5¢ Huguenot Monument to							
	Jan Ribault at							
	Duval County, Florida	01/05/24	22.50	13.00	225.00	(6)	80.00	6

599   610

614   615   616

Details

2¢ Washington, Types I-II, Series 1923-1929

Detail of **#599, 634**
Type I

No heavy hair lines at top
center of head.

Detail of **#599A, 634A**
Type II

Three heavy hair lines at
top center of head.

617

618

619

620

621

622

623

627

628

629

630

	Issues of 1925		Un	U	PB	#	FDC	Q(M)
	Lexington-Concord Issue, Perf. 11							
617	1¢ Washington at Cambridge	04/04/25	2.50	2.50	40.00	(6)	35.00	16
618	2¢ "The Birth of Liberty,"							
	by Henry Sandham	04/04/25	5.00	4.00	55.00	(6)	37.50	27
619	5¢ "The Minute Man,"							
	by Daniel Chester French	04/04/25	20.00	13.00	200.00	(6)	85.00	5
	Line over head		42.50	19.00				
	Norse-American Issue							
620	2¢ Sloop *Restaurationen*	05/18/25	4.00	3.00	180.00	(8)	25.00	9
621	5¢ Viking Ship	05/18/25	12.50	11.00	525.00	(8)	40.00	2
	Issues of 1925-1926 (See also #551-79, 581-91, 594-606, 631-42, 658-79, 684-87, 692-701, 723)							
622	13¢ Benjamin Harrison	01/11/26	12.50	.75	145.00	(6)	22.50	
623	17¢ Woodrow Wilson	12/28/25	14.00	.30	160.00	(6)	27.50	
624-26	Not assigned							
	Issues of 1926							
627	2¢ Independence							
	Sesquicentennial Exposition	05/10/26	3.00	.50	37.50	(6)	10.00	308
628	5¢ John Ericsson Memorial	05/29/26	6.50	3.25	75.00	(6)	30.00	20
629	2¢ Alexander Hamilton's Battery	10/18/26	2.25	1.70	35.00	(6)	6.25	41
a	Vertical pair, imperf. between		—					
	International Philatelic Exhibition Souvenir Sheet							
630	2¢ Battle of White Plains,							
	sheet of 25 with selvage							
	inscription (629)	10/18/26	375.00	450.00			1,500.00	0.1
	Dot over first "S" of "States"		400.00	475.00				
	Imperf. (See also #551-79, 581-91, 594-606, 622-23, 658-79, 684-87, 692-701, 723)							
631	1½¢ yellow brown							
	Harding (553)	08/27/26	1.90	1.70	62.50	(4)	35.00	
	Issues of 1926-1934, Perf. 11 x 10.5 (See also #551-73, 575-79, 581-91, 594-606, 622-23, 631-42, 684-87, 692-701, 723)							
632	1¢ green Franklin (552)	06/10/27	.20	.20	2.00	(4)	45.00	
	Pair with full vertical gutter between		150.00	—				
	Cracked plate		—	—				
a	Booklet pane of 6	11/02/27	5.50	*4.00*			*3,250.00*	
b	Vertical pair, imperf. between		*3,500.00*	*125.00*				
c	Horizontal pair, imperf. between		*7,500.00*					
633	1½¢ yellow brown							
	Harding (553)	05/17/27	1.90	.20	62.50	(4)	45.00	
634	2¢ carmine Washington							
	(554), type I	12/10/26	.20	.20	2.60	(4)	47.50	
	Pair with full vertical gutter between		200.00					
b	2¢ carmine lake, type I		—	—	—	(4)		
c	Horizontal pair, imperf. between		*7,000.00*					
d	Booklet pane of 6	02/25/27	1.50	*1.50*				
634A	2¢ carmine Washington							
	(554), type II	12/28/27	350.00	13.50	2,000.00	(4)		
	Pair with full vertical or							
	horizontal gutter between		1,000.00	—				
635	3¢ violet Lincoln (555)	02/03/27	.40	.20	13.50	(4)	47.50	
a	3¢ bright violet Lincoln	02/07/34	.20	.20	6.00	(4)	25.00	
	Gripper cracks		3.25	2.00				
636	4¢ yellow brown Martha							
	Washington (556)	05/17/27	2.10	.20	75.00	(4)	50.00	
	Pair with full vertical gutter between		*200.00*					
637	5¢ dark blue Theodore							
	Roosevelt (557)	03/24/27	2.10	.20	14.00	(4)	50.00	
	Pair with full vertical gutter between		*275.00*					

1927-1931

Issues of 1927-1931		Un	U	PB/LB	#	FDC	Q(M)
Perf. 11 x 10.5							
638	6¢ red orange Garfield (558) 07/27/27	2.10	.20	14.00	(4)	57.50	
	Pair with full vert. gutter between	200.00					
639	7¢ black McKinley (559) 03/24/27	2.10	.20	14.00	(4)	57.50	
a	Vertical pair, imperf.						
	between	325.00	100.00				
640	8¢ olive green Grant (560) 06/10/27	2.10	.20	14.00	(4)	67.50	
641	9¢ orange red Jefferson (561) 1931	2.10	.20	13.00	(4)	72.50	
642	10¢ orange Monroe (562) 02/03/27	3.50	.20	20.00	(4)	90.00	
	Double transfer	—	—				
Perf. 11							
643	2¢ Vermont Sesquicentennial 08/03/27	1.40	.80	37.50	(6)	6.00	40
644	2¢ Burgoyne at Saratoga 08/03/27	3.75	2.10	32.50	(6)	12.50	26
Issues of 1928							
645	2¢ Valley Forge 05/26/28	1.05	.50	25.00	(6)	4.00	101
Perf. 11 x 10.5							
646	2¢ Battle of Monmouth/						
	Molly Pitcher 10/20/28	1.10	1.10	35.00	(4)	15.00	10
	Wide spacing, vertical pair	50.00	—				
Hawaii Sesquicentennial Issue							
647	2¢ Washington (554) 08/13/28	4.50	4.50	135.00	(4)	15.00	6
	Wide spacing, vertical pair	125.00					
648	5¢ Theodore Roosevelt (557) 08/13/28	12.50	13.50	275.00	(4)	22.50	1
Aeronautics Conference Issue, Perf. 11							
649	2¢ Wright Airplane 12/12/28	1.25	.80	10.00	(6)	7.00	51
650	5¢ Globe and Airplane 12/12/28	5.00	3.25	47.50	(6)	10.00	10
	Plate flaw "prairie dog"	27.50	12.50				
Issues of 1929							
651	2¢ George Rogers Clark 02/25/29	.65	.50	9.50	(6)	6.00	17
	Double transfer	4.25	2.25				
652	Not assigned						
Perf. 11 x 10.5							
653	½¢ olive brown						
	Nathan Hale (551) 5/25/29	.20	.20	1.60	(4)	27.50	
Electric Light's Golden Jubilee Issue, Perf. 11							
654	2¢ Thomas Edison's First Lamp 06/05/29	.70	.70	22.50	(6)	10.00	32
Perf. 11 x 10.5							
655	2¢ carmine rose (654) 06/11/29	.65	.20	35.00	(4)	80.00	210
Coil Stamp, Perf. 10 Vertically							
656	2¢ carmine rose (654) 06/11/29	14.00	1.75	65.00	(2)	90.00	133
Perf. 11							
657	2¢ Sullivan Expedition 06/17/29	.70	.60	22.50	(6)	4.00	51
a	2¢ lake	350.00	—				

643

644

645

646

647

648

649

650

651

654

657

658

669

680

681

682

683

684

685

Issues of 1929		Un	U	PB/LP	#	FDC	Q(M)
#658-68 overprinted "Kans.," Perf. 11 x 10.5							
(See also #551-73, 575-79, 581-91, 594-606, 622-23, 631-42, 684-87, 692-701, 723)							
658	1¢ Franklin	05/01/29	2.50	2.00	35.00	(4)	50.00	13
a	Vertical pair, one without overprint		375.00					
659	1½¢ brown Harding (553)	05/01/29	4.00	2.90	50.00	(4)	52.50	8
	Wide spacing, pair		70.00					
660	2¢ carmine Washington (554)	05/01/29	4.50	1.00	47.50	(4)	52.50	87
661	3¢ violet Lincoln (555)	05/01/29	22.50	15.00	210.00	(4)	60.00	3
662	4¢ yellow brown Martha Washington (556)	05/01/29	22.50	9.00	210.00	(4)	62.50	2
663	5¢ deep blue T. Roosevelt (557)	05/01/29	14.00	9.75	150.00	(4)	80.00	3
664	6¢ red orange Garfield (558)	05/01/29	32.50	18.00	450.00	(4)	90.00	1
665	7¢ black McKinley (559)	05/01/29	30.00	27.50	500.00	(4)	100.00	1
666	8¢ olive green Grant (560)	05/01/29	105.00	70.00	775.00	(4)	125.00	2
667	9¢ light rose Jefferson (561)	05/01/29	16.00	11.25	225.00	(4)	140.00	1
668	10¢ orange yel. Monroe (562)	05/01/29	25.00	12.00	350.00	(4)	175.00	3
	#669-79 overprinted "Nebr."							
669	1¢ Franklin	05/01/29	4.00	2.25	50.00	(4)	50.00	8
a	Vertical pair, one without overprint		—					
670	1½¢ brown Harding (553)	05/01/29	3.75	2.50	52.50	(4)	50.00	9
671	2¢ carmine Washington (554)	05/01/29	3.75	1.30	42.50	(4)	55.00	73
672	3¢ violet Lincoln (555)	05/01/29	15.00	12.00	165.00	(4)	65.00	2
673	4¢ yellow brown Martha Washington (556)	05/01/29	21.00	15.00	250.00	(4)	75.00	2
	Wide spacing, pair		120.00					
674	5¢ deep blue T. Roosevelt (557)	05/01/29	20.00	15.00	275.00	(4)	75.00	2
675	6¢ red orange Garfield (558)	05/01/29	47.50	24.00	525.00	(4)	100.00	1
676	7¢ black McKinley (559)	05/01/29	25.00	18.00	300.00	(4)	100.00	0.8
677	8¢ olive green Grant (560)	05/01/29	35.00	25.00	400.00	(4)	125.00	1
678	9¢ light rose Jefferson (561)	05/01/29	42.50	27.50	525.00	(4)	140.00	0.5
679	10¢ orange yel. Monroe (562)	05/01/29	125.00	22.50	950.00	(4)	175.00	2
	Warning: Excellent forgeries of the Kansas and Nebraska overprints exist.							
	Perf. 11							
680	2¢ Battle of Fallen Timbers	09/14/29	.80	.80	22.50	(6)	3.50	29
681	2¢ Ohio River Canalization	10/19/29	.70	.65	15.00	(6)	3.50	33
	Issues of 1930							
682	2¢ Mass. Bay Colony	04/08/30	.60	.50	22.50	(6)	3.50	74
683	2¢ Gov. Joseph West and Chief Shadoo, a Kiowa	04/10/30	1.20	1.20	40.00	(6)	3.50	25
	Perf. 11 x 10.5							
684	1½¢ Warren G. Harding	12/01/30	.35	.20	1.75	(4)	4.50	
	Pair with full horizontal gutter between		175.00					
	Pair with full vertical gutter between		—					
685	4¢ William H. Taft	06/04/30	.90	.25	13.50	(4)	6.00	
	Gouge on right "4"		2.10	.60				
	Recut right "4"		2.10	.65				
	Pair with full horizontal gutter between		—					
	Coil Stamps, Perf. 10 Vertically							
686	1½¢ brn. Harding (684)	12/01/30	1.80	.20	6.50	(2)	5.00	
687	4¢ brown Taft (685)	09/18/30	3.25	.45	13.00	(2)	20.00	

1930-1932

	Issues of 1930		Un	U	PB	#	FDC	Q(M)
	Perf. 11							
688	2¢ Battle of Braddock's Field	07/09/30	1.00	.85	30.00	(6)	4.00	26
689	2¢ Gen. von Steuben	09/17/30	.55	.55	20.00	(6)	4.00	66
a	Imperf., pair		2,750.00		12,500.00	(6)		
	Issues of 1931							
690	2¢ General Pulaski	01/16/31	.30	.25	10.00	(6)	4.00	97
691	Not assigned							
	Perf. 11 x 10.5 (See also #551-73, 575-79, 581-91, 594-606, 622-23, 631-42, 658-79, 684-87, 723)							
692	11¢ light bl. Hayes (563)	09/04/31	2.60	.25	14.00	(4)	100.00	
	Retouched forehead		20.00	1.00				
693	12¢ brown violet Cleveland (564)	08/25/31	5.50	.20	25.00	(4)	100.00	
694	13¢ yellow green Harrison (622)	09/04/31	2.00	.25	14.00	(4)	100.00	
695	14¢ dark blue American Indian (565)	09/08/31	3.75	.30	26.00	(4)	100.00	
696	15¢ gray Statue of Liberty (566)	08/27/31	8.00	.25	37.50	(4)	125.00	
	Perf. 10.5 x 11							
697	17¢ black Wilson (623)	07/25/31	4.50	.25	37.50	(4)	2,750.00	
698	20¢ carmine rose Golden Gate (567)	09/08/31	8.25	.25	37.50	(4)	325.00	
	Double transfer		20.00	—				
699	25¢ blue green Niagara Falls (568)	07/25/31	8.50	.25	45.00	(4)	2,000.00	
700	30¢ brown Buffalo (569)	09/08/31	15.00	.25	67.50	(4)	300.00	
	Cracked plate		26.00	.85				
701	50¢ lilac Arlington Amphitheater (570)	09/04/31	37.50	.25	180.00	(4)	425.00	
	Perf. 11							
702	2¢ "The Greatest Mother"	05/21/31	.25	.20	1.90	(4)	3.00	99
a	Red cross omitted		40,000.00					
703	2¢ Yorktown	10/19/31	.40	.25	2.25	(4)	3.50	25
a	2¢ lake and black		4.50	.75				
b	2¢ dark lake and black		450.00		2,250.00	(4)		
c	Pair, imperf. vertically		5,000.00		—	(6)		
	Issues of 1932, Washington Bicentennial Issue, Perf. 11 x 10.5							
704	½¢ Portrait by Charles W. Peale	01/01/32	.20	.20	6.00	(4)	5.00 (4)	88
	Broken circle		.75	.20				
705	1¢ Bust by Jean Antoine Houdon	01/01/32	.20	.20	4.50	(4)	4.00 (2)	1,266
706	1½¢ Portrait by Charles W. Peale	01/01/32	.40	.20	15.00	(4)	4.00 (2)	305
707	2¢ Portrait by Gilbert Stuart	01/01/32	.20	.20	1.50	(4)	4.00	4,222
	Gripper cracks		1.75	.65				
708	3¢ Portrait by Charles W. Peale	01/01/32	.55	.20	17.50	(4)	4.00	456
709	4¢ Portrait by Charles P. Polk	01/01/32	.25	.20	5.50	(4)	4.00	151
	Broken bottom frame line		1.50	.50				
710	5¢ Portrait by Charles W. Peale	01/01/32	1.60	.20	16.50	(4)	4.00	171
	Cracked plate		5.25	1.10				
711	6¢ Portrait by John Trumbull	01/01/32	3.25	.20	52.50	(4)	4.00	112
712	7¢ Portrait by John Trumbull	01/01/32	.25	.20	9.00	(4)	4.00	83
713	8¢ Portrait by Charles B.J.F. Saint Memin	01/01/32	2.75	.50	50.00	(4)	4.50	97
	Pair, full vert. gutter between		—					
714	9¢ Portrait by W. Williams	01/01/32	2.40	.20	35.00	(4)	4.50	76
715	10¢ Portrait by Gilbert Stuart	01/01/32	10.00	.20	90.00	(4)	4.50	147

688   **689**   **690**

702   **703**

704   **705**   **706**

707   **708**   **709**

710   **711**   **712**

713   **714**   **715**

716   **717**   **718**   **719**   **720**

724   **725**   **726**

727   **728**   **729**

730

731   **732**   **733**

Issues of 1932		Un	U	PB/LP	#	FDC	Q(M)
Olympic Winter Games Issue, Perf. 11							
716	2¢ Ski Jumper	01/25/32	.40	.20	10.00	(6)	6.00	51
	Recut		3.50	1.50				
	Colored "snowball"		25.00	5.00				
Perf. 11 x 10.5							
717	2¢ Arbor Day	04/22/32	.20	.20	6.00	(4)	4.00	100
Olympic Summer Games Issue, Perf. 11 x 10.5							
718	3¢ Runner at Starting Mark	06/15/32	1.40	.20	11.50	(4)	6.00	168
	Gripper cracks		4.25	.75				
719	5¢ Myron's Discobolus	06/15/32	2.20	.20	20.00	(4)	8.00	53
	Gripper cracks		4.25	1.00				
720	3¢ Washington	06/16/32	.20	.20	1.30	(4)	7.50	
	Pair with full vertical or horizontal gutter between		200.00					
	Recut lines on face		2.00	.75				
b	Booklet pane of 6	07/25/32	35.00	12.50			100.00	
c	Vertical pair, imperf. between		1,250.00	1,250.00				
Coil Stamp, Perf. 10 Vertically							
721	3¢ deep violet (720)	06/24/32	2.75	.20	10.00	(2)	15.00	
	Recut lines around eyes		—	—				
Coil Stamp, Perf. 10 Horizontally							
722	3¢ deep violet (720)	10/12/32	1.50	.35	6.25	(2)	15.00	
Coil Stamp, Perf. 10 Vertically (See also #551-73, 575-79, 581-91, 594-606, 622-23, 631-42, 684-87, 692-701)							
723	6¢ deep orange Garfield (558)	08/18/32	11.00	.30	60.00	(2)	15.00	
Perf. 11							
724	3¢ William Penn	10/24/32	.35	.20	8.00	(6)	3.25	49
a	Vertical pair, imperf. horizontally		—					
725	3¢ Daniel Webster	10/24/32	.40	.25	16.50	(6)	3.25	49
Issues of 1933							
726	3¢ Georgia Settlement	02/12/33	.35	.20	10.00	(6)	3.25	61
Perf. 10.5 x 11							
727	3¢ Peace of 1783	04/19/33	.20	.20	3.75	(4)	3.50	73
Century of Progress Issue							
728	1¢ Restoration of Fort Dearborn	05/25/33	.20	.20	1.90	(4)	3.00 (3)	348
	Gripper cracks		2.00	—				
729	3¢ Federal Building at Chicago	05/25/33	.20	.20	2.40	(4)	3.00	480
American Philatelic Society Issue Souvenir Sheets, Without Gum, Imperf.							
730	1¢ sheet of 25 (728)	08/25/33	27.50	27.50			100.00	0.4
a	Single stamp from sheet		.75	.50			3.25 (3)	11
731	3¢ sheet of 25 (729)	08/25/33	25.00	25.00			100.00	0.4
a	Single stamp from sheet		.65	.50			3.25	11
Perf. 10.5 x 11							
732	3¢ National Recovery Act	08/15/33	.20	.20	1.50	(4)	3.25	1,978
	Gripper cracks		1.50	—				
	Recut at right		2.00					
Perf. 11							
733	3¢ Byrd Antarctic Expedition II	10/09/33	.50	.50	12.00	(6)	10.00	5
	Double transfer		2.75	1.00				
734	5¢ General Tadeusz Kosciuszko	10/13/33	.55	.25	27.50	(6)	4.50	45
a	Horizontal pair, imperf. vertically		2,250.00	25,000.00	(8)			

Issues of 1934		Un	U	PB	#	FDC	Q(M)
National Stamp Exhibition Issue Souvenir Sheet, Without Gum, Imperf.							
735	3¢ Byrd sheet of 6 (733)	02/10/34	12.50	10.00			40.00	0.8
a	Single stamp from sheet		2.00	1.65			5.00	4
	Perf. 11							
736	3¢ Maryland Tercentenary	03/23/34	.20	.20	6.00	(6)	1.60	46
	Double transfer		—	—				
	Mothers of America Issue, Perf. 11 x 10.5							
737	3¢ Portrait of his Mother,							
	by James A. McNeill Whistler	05/02/34	.20	.20	1.00	(4)	1.60	193
	Perf. 11							
738	3¢ deep violet (737)	05/02/34	.20	.20	4.25	(6)	1.60	15
739	3¢ Wisconsin Tercentenary	07/07/34	.20	.20	2.90	(6)	1.10	64
a	Vert. pair, imperf. horizontally		350.00					
b	Horiz. pair, imperf. vertically		525.00		2,000.00	(6)		
	National Parks Issue, Unwmkd.							
740	1¢ El Capitan, Yosemite							
	(California)	07/16/34	.20	.20	1.00	(6)	2.25	84
	Recut		1.50	.50				
a	Vertical pair, imperf.							
	horizontally, with gum		1,300.00					
741	2¢ Grand Canyon (Arizona)	07/24/34	.20	.20	1.25	(6)	2.25	74v
	Double transfer		1.25	—				
a	Vertical pair, imperf.							
	horizontally, with gum		475.00					
b	Horizontal pair, imperf.							
	vertically, with gum		600.00					
742	3¢ Mt. Rainier, and Mirror Lake,							
	(Washington)	08/03/34	.20	.20	1.75	(6)	2.50	95
a	Vertical pair, imperf.							
	horizontally, with gum		700.00					
743	4¢ Cliff Palace, Mesa Verde							
	(Colorado)	09/25/34	.35	.40	7.00	(6)	2.25	19
a	Vertical pair, imperf.							
	horizontally, with gum		1,000.00					
744	5¢ Old Faithful, Yellowstone							
	(Wyoming)	07/30/34	.70	.65	8.75	(6)	2.25	30
a	Horizontal pair, imperf.							
	vertically, with gum		600.00					
745	6¢ Crater Lake (Oregon)	09/05/34	1.10	.85	15.00	(6)	3.00	16
746	7¢ Great Head, Acadia							
	Park (Maine)	10/02/34	.60	.75	10.00	(6)	3.00	15
a	Horizontal pair, imperf.							
	vertically, with gum		725.00					
747	8¢ Great White Throne,							
	Zion Park (Utah)	09/18/34	1.60	1.50	15.00	(6)	3.25	15
748	9¢ Glacier National Park							
	(Montana)	08/27/34	1.50	.65	14.00	(6)	3.50	17
749	10¢ Great Smoky Mountains							
	(North Carolina)	10/08/34	3.00	1.25	22.50	(6)	6.00	18
	American Philatelic Society Issue Souvenir Sheet, Imperf.							
750	3¢ sheet of 6 (742)	08/28/34	30.00	27.50			40.00	0.5
a	Single stamp from sheet		3.50	3.25			3.25	3
	Trans-Mississippi Philatelic Exposition Issue Souvenir Sheet							
751	1¢ sheet of 6 (740)	10/10/34	12.50	12.50			35.00	0.7
a	Single stamp from sheet		1.40	1.60			3.25 (3)	4

735

736

737

739

740

741

742

744

743

745

746

747

748

749

750

751

Examples of Special Printing Position Blocks

Gutter Block 752

Centerline Block 754

Line Block 756

Arrow Block 763

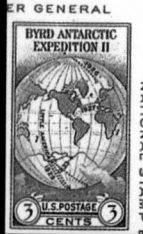

Cross-Gutter Block 768

Issues of 1935		Un	U	PB	#	FDC	Q(M)
Special Printing (#752-71), Without Gum, Perf. 10.5 x 11							
752	3¢ violet Peace of 1783 (727)	03/15/35	.20	.20	22.50	(4)	5.00	3
Perf. 11								
753	3¢ blue Byrd Expedition II (733)	03/15/35	.50	.45	17.50	(6)	6.00	2
Imperf.								
754	3¢ dp. vio. Whistler's Mother (737)	03/15/35	.60	.60	15.00	(6)	6.00	2
755	3¢ deep violet Wisconsin (739)	03/15/35	.60	.60	15.00	(6)	6.00	2
756	1¢ green Yosemite (740)	03/15/35	.20	.20	4.00	(6)	6.00	3
757	2¢ red Grand Canyon (741)	03/15/35	.25	.25	5.75	(6)	6.00	3
	Double transfer		—					
758	3¢ deep violet Mt. Rainier (742)	03/15/35	.50	.45	14.00	(6)	6.00	2
759	4¢ brown Mesa Verde (743)	03/15/35	.95	.95	20.00	(6)	6.50	2
760	5¢ blue Yellowstone (744)	03/15/35	1.50	1.40	25.00	(6)	6.50	2
	Double transfer		—					
761	6¢ dark blue Crater Lake (745)	03/15/35	2.40	2.25	37.50	(6)	6.50	2
762	7¢ black Acadia (746)	03/15/35	1.50	1.40	30.00	(6)	6.50	2
	Double transfer		—					
763	8¢ sage green Zion (747)	03/15/35	1.60	1.50	37.50	(6)	7.50	2
764	9¢ red orange Glacier (748)	03/15/35	1.90	1.75	42.50	(6)	7.50	2
765	10¢ gray black Smoky Mts. (749)	03/15/35	3.75	3.50	50.00	(6)	7.50	2
766	1¢ yellow grn. (728), pane of 25	03/15/35	25.00	25.00			250.00	0.1
a	Single stamp from pane		.70	.50			5.50 (3)	2
767	3¢ violet (729), pane of 25	03/15/35	23.50	23.50			250.00	0.09
a	Single stamp from pane		.60	.50			5.50	2
768	3¢ dark blue (733), pane of 6	03/15/35	20.00	15.00			250.00	0.3
a	Single stamp from pane		2.80	2.40			6.50	2
769	1¢ green (740), pane of 6	03/15/35	12.50	11.00			250.00	0.3
a	Single stamp from pane		1.85	1.80			4.00	2
770	3¢ deep violet (742), pane of 6	03/15/35	30.00	24.00			250.00	0.2
a	Single stamp from pane		3.25	3.10			5.00	1
771	16¢ dark blue Great Seal of U.S.	03/15/35	2.40	2.40	50.00	(6)	12.50	1

For perforate variety, see #CE2.

A number of position pieces can be collected from the panes or sheets of the 1935 Special Printing issues, including horizontal and vertical gutter (#752, 766-70) or line (#753-65, 771) blocks of four (HG/L and VG/L), arrow-and-guideline blocks of four (AGL) and crossed-gutter or centerline blocks of four (CG/L). Pairs sell for half the price of blocks of four. Arrow-and-guideline blocks are top or bottom only.

	HG/L	VG/L	AGL	CG/L		HG/L	VG/L	AGL	CG/L
752	5.75	9.50		50.00	762	4.25	3.75	8.25	14.00
753	2.25	25.00	52.50	67.50	763	3.75	4.75	11.00	17.50
754	1.75	1.40	3.00	7.25	764	5.00	4.50	10.50	22.50
755	1.75	1.40	3.00	7.25	765	9.00	10.50	24.00	30.00
756	.45	.55	1.25	3.00	766	5.50	7.00		15.00
757	.70	.55	1.25	3.50	767	5.25	6.75		15.00
758	1.40	1.25	2.75	5.25	768	7.50	9.00		20.00
759	2.75	2.25	4.75	8.50	769	6.00	9.00		15.00
760	3.50	4.25	9.00	15.00	770	12.50	11.00		30.00
761	6.50	5.50	12.50	20.00	771	6.50	5.50	12.50	60.00

Issues of 1935		Un	U	PB	#	FDC	Q(M)
Perf. 11 x 10.5							
Beginning with #772, unused values are for never-hinged stamps.							
772	3¢ Connecticut Tercentenary 04/26/35	.20	.20	1.75	(4)	10.00	71
	Defect in cent design	1.00	.25				
773	3¢ California Pacific						
	International Expo 05/29/35	.20	.20	1.10	(4)	10.00	101
	Pair with full vertical gutter between	—					
	Perf. 11						
774	3¢ Boulder Dam 09/30/35	.20	.20	1.65	(6)	10.00	74
	Perf. 11 x 10.5						
775	3¢ Michigan Centenary 11/01/35	.20	.20	1.25	(4)	10.00	76
	Issues of 1936						
776	3¢ Republic of Texas 03/02/36	.20	.20	1.10	(4)	17.50	124
	Perf. 10.5 x 11						
777	3¢ Rhode Island Tercentenary 05/04/36	.20	.20	1.10	(4)	9.00	67
	Pair with full gutter between	200.00					
	Third International Philatelic Exhibition Issue Souvenir Sheet, Imperf.						
778	Sheet of 4 different stamps						
	(#772, 773, 775 and 776) 05/09/36	1.75	1.75			13.00	3
a-d	Single stamp from sheet	.40	.35				3
779-81	Not assigned						
	Perf. 11 x 10.5						
782	3¢ Arkansas Statehood 06/15/36	.25	.20	1.25	(4)	12.00	73
783	3¢ Oregon Territory 07/14/36	.20	.20	1.10	(4)	8.50	74
	Double transfer	1.00	.50				
784	3¢ Susan B. Anthony 08/26/36	.20	.20	.75	(4)	12.00	270
	Period missing after "B"	.75	.25				

THE ADVENTURES OF HUCKLEBERRY FINN

When Huckleberry Finn runs away from his drunk and abusive father and Jim runs away from slavery in Mark Twain's *The Adventures of Huckleberry Finn*, the two begin a voyage together on a raft on the Mississippi River. Twain's tale of their epic journey is filled with the sights and sounds of the river and of the varied people Huck and Jim encounter along the way. The tale is also a trip through the complex moral issues of slavery, cruelty, friendship, and loyalty. By the time *Huckleberry Finn* was published in 1884, Twain had come to believe that slavery was wrong, but the book's characters reflect the many facets of that complicated issue through their words and actions. Considered by many to be Twain's finest book, *The Adventures of*

Huckleberry Finn was one of four classic American children's books honored by the Postal Service in 1993. The other books were *Rebecca of Sunnybrook Farm*, *Little House on the Prairie*, and *Little Women*. ❑

772

773

774

775

776

777

778

782

783

784

785

786

787

788

789

790

791

792

793

794

795

796

798

799

800

801

802

	Issues of 1936-1937		Un	U	PB	#	FDC	Q(M)
	Army Issue, Perf. 11 x 10.5							
785	1¢ George Washington, Nathanael Greene and Mount Vernon	12/15/36	.20	.20	.85	(4)	6.00	105
	Pair with full vertical gutter between		—					
786	2¢ Andrew Jackson, Winfield Scott and The Hermitage	01/15/37	.20	.20	.85	(4)	6.00	94
787	3¢ Generals Sherman, Grant and Sheridan	02/18/37	.20	.20	1.25	(4)	6.00	88
788	4¢ Generals Robert E. Lee and "Stonewall" Jackson and Stratford Hall	03/23/37	.30	.20	8.00	(4)	6.00	36
789	5¢ U.S. Military Academy at West Point	05/26/37	.60	.25	8.50	(4)	6.00	37
	Navy Issue							
790	1¢ John Paul Jones, John Barry, *Bon Homme Richard* and *Lexington*	12/15/36	.20	.20	.85	(4)	6.00	105
791	2¢ Stephen Decatur, Thomas MacDonough and *Saratoga*	01/15/37	.20	.20	.75	(4)	6.00	92
792	3¢ David G. Farragut and David D. Porter, *Hartford* and *Powhatan*	02/18/37	.20	.20	1.00	(4)	6.00	93
793	4¢ Admirals William T. Sampson, George Dewey and Winfield S. Schley	03/23/37	.30	.20	9.00	(4)	6.00	35
794	5¢ Seal of U.S. Naval Academy and Naval Cadets	05/26/37	.60	.25	9.00	(4)	6.00	37
	Issues of 1937							
795	3¢ Northwest Territory Ordinance	07/13/37	.20	.20	1.10	(4)	9.00	85
	Perf. 11							
796	5¢ Virginia Dare and Parents	08/18/37	.20	.20	6.50	(6)	11.00	25
	Society of Philatelic Americans Issue Souvenir Sheet, Imperf.							
797	10¢ blue green (749)	08/26/37	.60	.40			10.00	5
	Perf. 11 x 10.5							
798	3¢ Constitution Sesquicentennial	09/17/37	.20	.20	1.40	(4)	9.00	100
	Territorial Issues, Perf. 10.5 x 11							
799	3¢ Hawaii	10/18/37	.20	.20	1.25	(4)	10.00	78
	Perf. 11 x 10.5							
800	3¢ Alaska	11/12/37	.20	.20	1.25	(4)	10.00	77
	Pair with full gutter between		—					
801	3¢ Puerto Rico	11/25/37	.20	.20	1.25	(4)	10.00	81
802	3¢ Virgin Islands	12/15/37	.20	.20	1.25	(4)	10.00	76
	Pair with full vertical gutter between		275.00					

1938-1939

	Issues of 1938-1939		Un	U	PB	#	FDC
	Presidential Issue, Perf. 11 x 10.5 (#804b, 806b, 807a issued in 1939, 832b in 1951, 832c in 1954, rest in 1938; see also 839-51)						
803	½¢ Benjamin Franklin	05/19/38	.20	.20	.40	(4)	3.00
804	1¢ George Washington	04/25/38	.20	.20	.25	(4)	3.00
	Pair with full vertical gutter between		160.00	—			
b	Booklet pane of 6	01/27/39	2.00	.50			
805	1½¢ Martha Washington	05/05/38	.20	.20	.20	(4)	3.00
	Pair with full horizontal gutter between		175.00				
b	Horizontal pair, imperf. between		160.00	25.00			
806	2¢ John Adams	06/03/38	.20	.20	.30	(4)	3.00
	Recut at top of head		3.00	1.50			
b	Booklet pane of 6	01/27/39	4.75	.85			15.00
807	3¢ Thomas Jefferson	06/16/38	.20	.20	.25	(4)	3.00
a	Booklet pane of 6	01/27/39	8.50	2.00			17.50
b	Horizontal pair, imperf. between		1,500.00	—			
c	Imperf., pair		2,500.00				
808	4¢ James Madison	07/01/38	.75	.20	3.50	(4)	3.00
809	4½¢ The White House	07/11/38	.20	.20	1.50	(4)	3.00
810	5¢ James Monroe	07/21/38	.20	.20	1.00	(4)	3.00
811	6¢ John Quincy Adams	07/28/38	.20	.20	1.00	(4)	3.00
812	7¢ Andrew Jackson	08/04/38	.25	.20	1.25	(4)	3.00
813	8¢ Martin Van Buren	08/11/38	.30	.20	1.40	(4)	3.00
814	9¢ William H. Harrison	08/18/38	.30	.20	1.40	(4)	3.00
	Pair with full vertical gutter between		—				
815	10¢ John Tyler	09/02/38	.25	.20	1.25	(4)	3.00
816	11¢ James K. Polk	09/08/38	.65	.20	3.00	(4)	5.00
817	12¢ Zachary Taylor	09/14/38	.90	.20	4.00	(4)	5.00
818	13¢ Millard Fillmore	09/22/38	1.25	.20	7.00	(4)	5.00
819	14¢ Franklin Pierce	10/06/38	.90	.20	4.50	(4)	5.00
820	15¢ James Buchanan	10/13/38	.40	.20	1.90	(4)	5.00
821	16¢ Abraham Lincoln	10/20/38	.90	.25	5.00	(4)	6.00
822	17¢ Andrew Johnson	10/27/38	.85	.20	4.50	(4)	6.00
823	18¢ Ulysses S. Grant	11/03/38	1.75	.20	8.75	(4)	6.00
824	19¢ Rutherford B. Hayes	11/10/38	1.25	.35	6.25	(4)	6.00
825	20¢ James A. Garfield	11/10/38	.70	.20	3.50	(4)	7.00
826	21¢ Chester A. Arthur	11/22/38	1.25	.20	7.50	(4)	7.00
827	22¢ Grover Cleveland	11/22/38	1.00	.40	9.50	(4)	8.00
828	24¢ Benjamin Harrison	12/02/38	3.50	.20	15.00	(4)	8.00
829	25¢ William McKinley	12/02/38	.60	.20	3.00	(4)	8.00
830	30¢ Theodore Roosevelt	12/08/38	3.50	.20	15.00	(4)	9.00
831	50¢ William Howard Taft	12/08/38	5.00	.20	22.50	(4)	12.50

803

804

805

806

807

808

809

810

811

812

813

814

815

816

817

818

819

820

821

822

823

824

825

826

827

828

829

830

831

832

833

834

835

836

837

838

852

853

854

855

856

857

858

Issues of 1938-1954			Un	U	PB/LP	#	FDC	Q(M)
Perf. 11								
832	$1 Woodrow Wilson	08/29/38	6.50	.20	31.50	(4)	50.00	
a	Vertical pair, imperf. horizontally		1,600.00					
b	Watermarked "USIR" (1951)		210.00	65.00	—	(4)		
c	$1 red violet and black	08/31/54	6.00	.20	30.00	(4)	25.00	
d	As "c," vert. pair, imperf. horiz.		1,500.00					
e	Vertical pair, imperf. between		2,750.00					
f	As "c," vert. pair, imperf. between		8,500.00					
833	$2 Warren G. Harding	09/29/38	18.00	3.75	90.00	(4)	100.00	
834	$5 Calvin Coolidge	11/17/38	90.00	3.00	400.00	(4)	160.00	
a	$5 red, brown and black		3,000.00	7,000.00				
Issues of 1938, Perf. 11 x 10.5								
835	3¢ Constitution Ratification	06/21/38	.25	.20	3.50	(4)	15.00	73
Perf. 11								
836	3¢ Swedish-Finnish Tercentenary	06/27/38	.20	.20	2.50	(6)	15.00	59
Perf. 11 x 10.5								
837	3¢ Northwest Territory	07/15/38	.20	.20	6.50	(4)	15.00	66
838	3¢ Iowa Territorial Centennial	08/24/38	.20	.20	6.00	(4)	15.00	47
	Pair with full vertical gutter between		—					
Issues of 1938-39, Coil Stamps, Perf. 10 Vertically								
839	1¢ green Washington (804)	01/20/39	.30	.20	1.40	(2)	4.75	
840	1½¢ bister brn.							
	Martha Washington (805)	01/20/39	.30	.20	1.50	(2)	4.75	
841	2¢ rose carmine							
	John Adams (806)	01/20/39	.40	.20	1.75	(2)	4.75	
842	3¢ deep violet Jefferson (807)	01/20/39	.50	.20	2.00	(2)	4.75	
	Gripper cracks		—					
	Thin, translucent paper		2.50	—				
843	4¢ red violet Madison (808)	01/20/39	7.50	.40	27.50	(2)	5.00	
844	4½¢ dark gray							
	White House (809)	01/20/38	.70	.40	5.00	(2)	5.00	
845	5¢ bright blue Monroe (810)	01/20/39	5.00	.35	27.50	(2)	5.00	
846	6¢ red orange							
	John Quincy Adams (811)	01/20/39	1.10	.20	7.50	(2)	6.50	
847	10¢ brown red Tyler (815)	01/20/39	11.00	.50	42.50	(2)	9.00	
Coil Stamps, Perf. 10 Horizontally								
848	1¢ green Washington (804)	01/27/39	.85	.20	2.75	(2)	5.00	
849	1½¢ bister brn.							
	Martha Washington (805)	01/27/39	1.25	.30	4.50	(2)	5.00	
850	2¢ rose carmine							
	John Adams (806)	01/27/39	2.50	.40	6.50	(2)	5.00	
851	3¢ deep violet Jefferson (807)	01/27/39	2.25	.35	6.25	(2)	5.50	
Perf. 10.5 x 11								
852	3¢ Golden Gate Exposition	02/18/39	.20	.20	1.25	(4)	15.00	114
853	3¢ New York World's Fair	04/01/39	.20	.20	1.75	(4)	15.00	102
Perf. 11								
854	3¢ Washington's Inauguration	04/30/39	.40	.20	3.50	(6)	15.00	73
Perf. 11 x 10.5								
855	3¢ Baseball	06/12/39	1.75	.20	7.50	(4)	35.00	81
Perf. 11								
856	3¢ Panama Canal	08/15/39	.25	.20	3.25	(6)	17.50	68
Perf. 10.5 x 11								
857	3¢ Printing	09/25/39	.20	.20	1.00	(4)	14.00	71
Perf. 11 x 10.5								
858	3¢ 50th Anniversary of Statehood							
	(Montana, North Dakota, South							
	Dakota, Washington)	11/02/39	.20	.20	1.10	(4)	12.50	67

1940

Issues of 1940		Un	U	PB	#	FDC	Q(M)
Famous Americans Issue, Perf. 10.5 x 11							
Authors							
859	1¢ Washington Irving	01/29/40	.20	.20	.95	(4)	3.00	56
860	2¢ James Fenimore Cooper	01/29/40	.20	.20	.95	(4)	3.00	53
861	3¢ Ralph Waldo Emerson	02/05/40	.20	.20	1.25	(4)	3.00	53
862	5¢ Louisa May Alcott	02/05/40	.30	.20	8.25	(4)	4.00	22
863	10¢ Samuel L. Clemens (Mark Twain)	02/13/40	1.65	1.20	32.50	(4)	8.00	13
Poets							
864	1¢ Henry W. Longfellow	02/16/40	.20	.20	1.75	(4)	3.00	52
865	2¢ John Greenleaf Whittier	02/16/40	.20	.20	1.75	(4)	3.00	52
866	3¢ James Russell Lowell	02/20/40	.20	.20	2.25	(4)	3.00	52
867	5¢ Walt Whitman	02/20/40	.35	.20	9.00	(4)	4.00	22
868	10¢ James Whitcomb Riley	02/24/40	1.75	1.25	30.00	(4)	6.00	12
Educators							
869	1¢ Horace Mann	03/14/40	.20	.20	1.90	(4)	3.00	52
870	2¢ Mark Hopkins	03/14/40	.20	.20	1.25	(4)	3.00	52
871	3¢ Charles W. Eliot	03/28/40	.20	.20	2.25	(4)	3.00	52
872	5¢ Frances E. Willard	03/28/40	.40	.20	9.00	(4)	4.00	21
873	10¢ Booker T. Washington	04/07/40	1.25	1.10	27.50	(4)	10.00	14
Scientists							
874	1¢ John James Audubon	04/08/40	.20	.20	.95	(4)	3.00	59
875	2¢ Dr. Crawford W. Long	04/08/40	.20	.20	.95	(4)	3.00	58
876	3¢ Luther Burbank	04/17/40	.20	.20	1.10	(4)	3.00	58
877	5¢ Dr. Walter Reed	04/17/40	.25	.20	5.00	(4)	4.00	24
878	10¢ Jane Addams	04/26/40	1.10	.85	16.00	(4)	6.00	15
Composers							
879	1¢ Stephen Collins Foster	05/03/40	.20	.20	1.00	(4)	3.00	57
880	2¢ John Philip Sousa	05/03/40	.20	.20	1.00	(4)	3.00	58
881	3¢ Victor Herbert	05/13/40	.20	.20	1.10	(4)	3.00	56
882	5¢ Edward A. MacDowell	05/13/40	.40	.20	9.25	(4)	4.00	21
883	10¢ Ethelbert Nevin	06/10/40	3.75	1.35	32.50	(4)	6.00	13
Artists							
884	1¢ Gilbert Charles Stuart	09/05/40	.20	.20	1.00	(4)	3.00	54
885	2¢ James A. McNeill Whistler	09/05/40	.20	.20	.95	(4)	3.00	54
886	3¢ Augustus Saint-Gaudens	09/16/40	.20	.20	1.00	(4)	3.00	55
887	5¢ Daniel Chester French	09/16/40	.50	.20	8.00	(4)	4.00	22
888	10¢ Frederic Remington	09/30/40	1.75	1.25	20.00	(4)	6.00	14
Inventors							
889	1¢ Eli Whitney	10/07/40	.20	.20	1.90	(4)	3.00	48
890	2¢ Samuel F.B. Morse	10/07/40	.20	.20	1.10	(4)	3.00	53
891	3¢ Cyrus Hall McCormick	10/14/40	.25	.20	1.75	(4)	3.00	54
892	5¢ Elias Howe	10/14/40	1.10	.30	12.50	(4)	4.00	20
893	10¢ Alexander Graham Bell	10/28/40	11.00	2.00	65.00	(4)	8.00	14

859	860	861	862	863
864	865	866	867	868
869	870	871	872	873
874	875	876	877	878
879	880	881	882	883
884	885	886	887	888
889	890	891	892	893

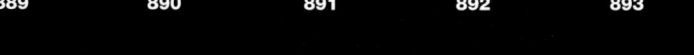

894

895

896

897

898

899

900

901

902

903

904

905

906

907

908

	Issues of 1940		Un	U	PB	#	FDC	Q(M)
894	3¢ Pony Express	04/03/40	.25	.20	2.75	(4)	10.00	46
	Perf. 10.5 x 11							
895	3¢ Pan American Union	04/14/40	.20	.20	2.75	(4)	7.00	48
	Perf. 11 x 10.5							
896	3¢ Idaho Statehood	07/03/40	.20	.20	1.75	(4)	7.00	51
	Perf. 10.5 x 11							
897	3¢ Wyoming Statehood	07/10/40	.20	.20	1.50	(4)	7.00	50
	Perf. 11 x 10.5							
898	3¢ Coronado Expedition	09/07/40	.20	.20	1.50	(4)	7.00	61
	National Defense Issue							
899	1¢ Statue of Liberty	10/16/40	.20	.20	.45	(4)	4.25	
	Cracked plate		3.00					
	Gripper cracks		3.00					
a	Vertical pair, imperf. between		650.00	—				
b	Horizontal pair, imperf. between		35.00	—				
	Pair with full vertical gutter between		200.00					
900	2¢ 90mm Antiaircraft Gun	10/16/40	.20	.20	.45	(4)	4.25	
a	Horizontal pair, imperf. between		40.00	—				
	Pair with full vertical gutter between		275.00					
901	3¢ Torch of Enlightenment	10/16/40	.20	.20	.60	(4)	4.25	
a	Horizontal pair, imperf. between		27.50	—				
	Pair with full vertical gutter between		—					
	Perf. 10.5 x 11							
902	3¢ Thirteenth Amendment	10/20/40	.20	.20	3.00	(4)	10.00	44
	Issue of 1941, Perf. 11 x 10.5							
903	3¢ Vermont Statehood	03/04/41	.20	.20	1.75	(4)	10.00	55
	Issues of 1942							
904	3¢ Kentucky Statehood	06/01/42	.20	.20	1.10	(4)	5.50	64
905	3¢ Win the War	07/04/42	.20	.20	.40	(4)	5.50	
	Pair with full vertical or horizontal gutter between		175.00					
b	3¢ purple		—	500.00				
906	5¢ Chinese Resistance	07/07/42	.85	.20	9.00	(4)	12.00	21
	Issues of 1943							
907	2¢ Allied Nations	01/14/43	.20	.20	.30	(4)	5.50	1,700
	Pair with full vertical or horizontal gutter between		225.00					
908	1¢ Four Freedoms	02/12/43	.20	.20	.60	(4)	5.50	1,200

VISIT US ONLINE AT **THE POSTAL STORE**

AT **WWW.USPS.COM**

OR CALL **1-800-STAMP-24**

Issues of 1943-1944		Un	U	PB	#	FDC	Q(M)
Overrun Countries Issue, Perf. 12							
909	5¢ Poland 06/22/43	.20	.20	3.50*	(4)	5.00	20
910	5¢ Czechoslovakia 07/12/43	.20	.20	2.75*	(4)	4.00	20
911	5¢ Norway 07/27/43	.20	.20	1.30*	(4)	4.00	20
912	5¢ Luxembourg 08/10/43	.20	.20	1.20*	(4)	4.00	20
913	5¢ Netherlands 08/24/43	.20	.20	1.20*	(4)	4.00	20
914	5¢ Belgium 09/14/43	.20	.20	1.10*	(4)	4.00	20
915	5¢ France 09/28/43	.20	.20	1.25*	(4)	4.00	20
916	5¢ Greece 10/12/43	.35	.25	9.00*	(4)	4.00	15
917	5¢ Yugoslavia 10/26/43	.25	.20	4.25*	(4)	4.00	15
918	5¢ Albania 11/09/43	.20	.20	4.25*	(4)	4.00	15
919	5¢ Austria 11/23/43	.20	.20	3.50*	(4)	4.00	15
920	5¢ Denmark 12/07/43	.20	.20	5.25*	(4)	4.00	15
921	5¢ Korea 11/02/44	.20	.20	4.50*	(4)	5.00	15
	"KORPA" plate flaw	17.50	12.50				
*Instead of plate numbers, the selvage is inscribed with the name of the country.							
Issues of 1944, Perf. 11 x 10.5							
922	3¢ Transcontinental Railroad 05/10/44	.20	.20	1.40	(4)	9.00	61
923	3¢ Steamship 05/22/44	.20	.20	1.25	(4)	7.50	61
924	3¢ Telegraph 05/24/44	.20	.20	.90	(4)	7.50	61
925	3¢ Philippine 09/27/44	.20	.20	1.10	(4)	7.50	50
926	3¢ Motion Pictures 10/31/44	.20	.20	.90	(4)	7.50	53

THE WIZARD OF OZ

The Wizard of Oz, MGM's beloved and spectacular musical, premiered on August 17, 1939, at Grauman's Chinese Theater in Hollywood. Sixty-five years later, it remains an all-time favorite movie classic, watched by millions of children and adults every year. Starring 16-year-old Judy Garland, the movie won an Oscar for "Over the Rainbow"—the wistful song by Harold Arlen and E.Y. Harburg—which Garland continued to sing throughout her career. The movie is based on a children's story written by L. Frank Baum in 1900. Dorothy, a little girl living in Kansas, is swept away by a tornado and wakes up in Oz. A dream sequence takes Dorothy on adventures with her pals—the Scarecrow, the Tin Man, and the Cowardly Lion—as they travel to see the Wizard of Oz. The movie was honored by the Postal Service along with *Gone With The Wind*, *Beau Geste*, and *Stagecoach* in the 1990 Classic Films issue. ❑

909

910

911

912

913

914

915

916

917

918

919

920

921

922

923

924

925

926

927

928

929

930

931

932

933

934

935

936

937

938

939

940

941

942

943

944

945

946

947

	Issues of 1945		Un	U	PB	#	FDC	Q(M)
	Perf. 11 x 10.5							
927	3¢ Florida Statehood	03/03/45	.20	.20	.50	(4)	7.50	62
928	5¢ United Nations Conference	04/25/45	.20	.20	.45	(4)	7.50	76
	Perf. 10.5 x 11							
929	3¢ Iwo Jima (Marines)	07/11/45	.20	.20	.55	(4)	14.00	137
	Issues of 1945-1946, Franklin D. Roosevelt Issue, Perf. 11 x 10.5							
930	1¢ Roosevelt and Hyde Park Residence	07/26/45	.20	.20	.25	(4)	3.50	128
931	2¢ Roosevelt and "The Little White House" at Warm Springs, Ga.	08/24/45	.20	.20	.45	(4)	3.50	67
932	3¢ Roosevelt and White House	06/27/45	.20	.20	.45	(4)	3.50	134
933	5¢ Roosevelt, Map of Western Hemisphere and Four Freedoms	01/30/46	.20	.20	.45	(4)	3.50	76
934	3¢ Army, Sept. 28	09/28/45	.20	.20	.45	(4)	8.00	128
935	3¢ Navy	10/27/45	.20	.20	.55	(4)	8.00	136
936	3¢ Coast Guard	11/10/45	.20	.20	.45	(4)	8.00	112
937	3¢ Alfred E. Smith	11/26/45	.20	.20	.40	(4)	2.50	309
	Pair with full vertical gutter between	—						
938	3¢ Texas Statehood	12/29/45	.20	.20	.40	(4)	7.50	171
	Issues of 1946							
939	3¢ Merchant Marine	02/26/46	.20	.20	.45	(4)	8.00	136
940	3¢ Veterans of World War II	05/09/46	.20	.20	.40	(4)	8.00	260
941	3¢ Tennessee Statehood	06/01/46	.20	.20	.45	(4)	3.00	132
942	3¢ Iowa Statehood	08/03/46	.20	.20	.40	(4)	3.00	132
943	3¢ Smithsonian Institution	08/10/46	.20	.20	.35	(4)	3.00	139
944	3¢ Kearny Expedition	10/16/46	.20	.20	.30	(4)	3.00	115
	Issues of 1947, Perf. 10.5 x 11							
945	3¢ Thomas A. Edison	02/11/47	.20	.20	.35	(4)	3.25	157
	Perf. 11 x 10.5							
946	3¢ Joseph Pulitzer	04/10/47	.20	.20	.35	(4)	3.00	120
947	3¢ Postage Stamps Centenary	05/17/47	.20	.20	.30	(4)	3.00	127

PAUL LAURENCE DUNBAR

(1872-1906)

Born in Dayton, Ohio, the son of former slaves, PAUL LAURENCE DUNBAR was the first African American to gain national recognition as a poet. Known particularly for his poems written in dialect (which he called "minors"), Dunbar also wrote poems in standard English ("majors") as well as short stories, novels, librettos, plays, songs, and essays. By age 14 some of his poems had been published in the *Dayton Herald*. In 1893 Dunbar self-published his first book of poetry. In 1895 a favorable review in *Harper's Weekly* of his second poetry collection, *Majors and Minors*, led to a 6-month reading tour in England. On his return to the United States and after a brief internship at the Library of Congress, he returned to Ohio. Although his health was deteriorating, Dunbar nevertheless continued to write poems— *Lyrics of Love and Laughter* (1903) and *Howdy, Honey, Howdy* and *Lyrics of Sunshine and Shadow* (both in 1905)—and short stories: *Folks From Dixie* and *The Heart of Happy Hollow*. Dunbar was honored by the Postal Service in the 1975 American Arts issue. ❑

1947-1948

Issues of 1947		Un	U	PB	#	FDC	Q(M)
Centenary International Philatelic Exhibition Issue Souvenir Sheet, Imperf.							
948	Souvenir sheet of 2						
	stamps (#1-2) 05/19/47	.55	.45			3.50	10
a	5¢ single stamp from sheet	.20	.20				
b	10¢ single stamp from sheet	.25	.25				
	Perf. 11 x 10.5						
949	3¢ Doctors 06/09/47	.20	.20	.30	(4)	6.50	133
950	3¢ Utah Settlement 07/24/47	.20	.20	.30	(4)	1.00	132
951	3¢ U.S. Frigate *Constitution* 10/21/47	.20	.20	.35	(4)	6.00	131
	Perf. 10.5 x 11						
952	3¢ Everglades National Park 12/05/47	.20	.20	.35	(4)	3.00	122
	Issues of 1948						
953	3¢ Dr. G.W. Carver 01/05/48	.20	.20	.45	(4)	2.50	122
	Perf. 11 x 10.5						
954	3¢ California Gold 01/24/48	.20	.20	.30	(4)	1.50	131
955	3¢ Mississippi Territory 04/07/48	.20	.20	.50	(4)	1.50	123
956	3¢ Four Chaplains 05/28/48	.20	.20	.50	(4)	5.00	122
957	3¢ Wisconsin Statehood 05/29/48	.20	.20	.35	(4)	1.00	115
958	5¢ Swedish Pioneer 06/04/48	.20	.20	.45	(4)	1.00	64
959	3¢ Progress of Women 07/19/48	.20	.20	.30	(4)	1.00	118
	Perf. 10.5 x 11						
960	3¢ William Allen White 07/31/48	.20	.20	.40	(4)	1.00	78
	Perf. 11 x 10.5						
961	3¢ U.S.-Canada Friendship 08/02/48	.20	.20	.30	(4)	1.00	113
962	3¢ Francis Scott Key 08/09/48	.20	.20	.40	(4)	1.00	121
963	3¢ Salute to Youth 08/11/48	.20	.20	.30	(4)	1.00	78
964	3¢ Oregon Territory 08/14/48	.20	.20	.35	(4)	1.00	52
	Perf. 10.5 x 11						
965	3¢ Harlan F. Stone 08/25/48	.20	.20	.60	(4)	1.00	54
966	3¢ Palomar Observatory 08/30/48	.20	.20	.95	(4)	3.00	61
a	Vertical pair, imperf. between	525.00					
	Perf. 11 x 10.5						
967	3¢ Clara Barton 09/07/48	.20	.20	.30	(4)	2.75	58

EDWARD G. ROBINSON

(1893-1973)

EDWARD G. ROBINSON, the sixth actor honored by the U.S. Postal Service in the Legends of Hollywood series, appeared in some 90 films, including *Double Indemnity* (1944), *Key Largo* (1948), and *The Ten Commandments* (1956). Born Emanuel Goldenberg in Romania, Robinson immigrated to the United States with his family when he was a young boy. In 1913 he began his professional acting career, working in theater for many years before eventually moving into film. Best remembered for his classic portrayals of gangsters in *Little Caesar* (1931) and several other films, Robinson's versatile acting career included numerous roles in film and television. Shortly before he died, Robinson received an Academy Award for lifetime achievement in films. A respected actor, he is also remembered as a philanthropist, humanitarian, and art collector. ❏

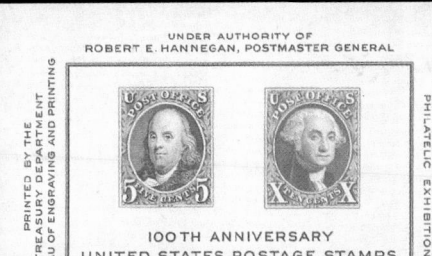

948

949

950

951

952

953

954

955

956

957

958

959

960

961

962

963

964

965

966

967

1948-1950

968

969

970

971

972

973

974

975

976

977

978

979

980

981

982

983

984

985

986

987

988

	Issues of 1948		Un	U	PB	#	FDC	Q(M)
968	3¢ Poultry Industry	09/09/48	.20	.20	.40	(4)	1.50	53
	Perf. 10.5 x 11							
969	3¢ Gold Star Mothers	09/21/48	.20	.20	.40	(4)	1.50	77
	Perf. 11 x 10.5							
970	3¢ Fort Kearny	09/22/48	.20	.20	.40	(4)	1.50	58
971	3¢ Volunteer Firemen	10/04/48	.20	.20	.50	(4)	7.00	56
972	3¢ Indian Centennial	10/15/48	.20	.20	.45	(4)	1.00	58
973	3¢ Rough Riders	10/27/48	.20	.20	.45	(4)	1.00	54
974	3¢ Juliette Gordon Low	10/29/48	.20	.20	.40	(4)	6.00	64
	Perf. 10.5 x 11							
975	3¢ Will Rogers	11/04/48	.20	.20	.45	(4)	1.50	67
976	3¢ Fort Bliss	11/05/48	.20	.20	1.00	(4)	2.50	65
	Perf. 11 x 10.5							
977	3¢ Moina Michael	11/09/48	.20	.20	.45	(4)	1.00	64
978	3¢ Gettysburg Address	11/19/48	.20	.20	.50	(4)	1.75	63
	Perf. 10.5 x 11							
979	3¢ American Turners	11/20/48	.20	.20	.30	(4)	1.25	62
980	3¢ Joel Chandler Harris	12/09/48	.20	.20	.55	(4)	1.25	57
	Issues of 1949, Perf. 11 x 10.5							
981	3¢ Minnesota Territory	03/03/49	.20	.20	.30	(4)	2.00	99
982	3¢ Washington and Lee University	04/12/49	.20	.20	.30	(4)	2.00	105
983	3¢ Puerto Rico Election	04/27/49	.20	.20	.30	(4)	2.00	109
984	3¢ Annapolis Tercentenary	05/23/49	.20	.20	.30	(4)	2.00	107
985	3¢ Grand Army of the Republic	08/29/49	.20	.20	.40	(4)	2.00	117
	Perf. 10.5 x 11							
986	3¢ Edgar Allan Poe	10/07/49	.20	.20	.45	(4)	2.50	123
	Thin outer frame line at top, inner frame line missing		6.00					
	Issues of 1950, Perf. 11 x 10.5							
987	3¢ American Bankers	01/03/50	.20	.20	.40	(4)	2.00	131
	Perf. 10.5 x 11							
988	3¢ Samuel Gompers	01/27/50	.20	.20	.30	(4)	1.00	128

TENNESSEE WILLIAMS

(1911-1983)

American playwright TENNESSEE WILLIAMS—born Thomas Lanier Williams in Mississippi—was a published writer before he was twenty. In his 40-year career, he wrote more than 70 plays as well as screenplays, novels, poems, essays, and short stories. He once said that he wrote, not for success, but out of "biological necessity." Known for introducing previously taboo subjects such as homosexuality and nymphomania to the American theater, Williams enjoyed his first major success and won his first New York Drama Critics Circle award in 1944 with the autobiographical *The Glass Menagerie*. In 1947, *A Streetcar Named Desire* brought Williams the first of two Pulitzer Prizes—the second was awarded to *Cat On A Hot Tin Roof* in 1955. The characters he created—Stanley Kowalski, Blanche Dubois, Big Daddy, Maggie the Cat—embodied strong emotions and captivated theater audiences. He is considered by many as America's greatest dramatist after Eugene O'Neill. ❏

Issues of 1950		Un	U	PB	#	FDC	Q(M)
National Capital Sesquicentennial Issue, Perf. 10.5 x 11, 11 x 10.5							
989	3¢ Statue of Freedom on Capitol Dome	04/20/50	.20	.20	.30	(4)	1.00	132
990	3¢ Executive Mansion	06/12/50	.20	.20	.40	(4)	1.00	130
991	3¢ Supreme Court	08/02/50	.20	.20	.30	(4)	1.00	131
992	3¢ U.S. Capitol	11/22/50	.20	.20	.40	(4)	1.00	130
	Gripper cracks		1.00	.50				
Perf. 11 x 10.5							
993	3¢ Railroad Engineers	04/29/50	.20	.20	.40	(4)	3.00	122
994	3¢ Kansas City, MO	06/03/50	.20	.20	.40	(4)	1.00	122
995	3¢ Boy Scouts	06/30/50	.20	.20	.50	(4)	6.00	132
996	3¢ Indiana Territory	07/04/50	.20	.20	.50	(4)	1.00	122
997	3¢ California Statehood	09/09/50	.20	.20	.30	(4)	2.00	121
Issues of 1951							
998	3¢ United Confederate Veterans	05/30/51	.20	.20	.35	(4)	1.50	119
999	3¢ Nevada Settlement	07/14/51	.20	.20	.30	(4)	1.00	112
1000	3¢ Landing of Cadillac	07/24/51	.20	.20	.30	(4)	1.00	114
1001	3¢ Colorado Statehood	08/01/51	.20	.20	.30	(4)	1.00	114
1002	3¢ American Chemical Society	09/04/51	.20	.20	.40	(4)	1.50	117
1003	3¢ Battle of Brooklyn	12/10/51	.20	.20	.30	(4)	1.00	116
Issues of 1952							
1004	3¢ Betsy Ross	01/02/52	.20	.20	.35	(4)	1.00	116
1005	3¢ 4-H Club	01/15/52	.20	.20	.50	(4)	3.00	116
1006	3¢ B&O Railroad	02/28/52	.20	.20	.45	(4)	2.00	113
1007	3¢ American Automobile Association	03/04/52	.20	.20	.40	(4)	1.50	117

GARRY WINOGRAND

(1928-1984)

I photograph to find out what something will look like photographed. Thus GARRY WINOGRAND explained his lifelong relationship with photography. Early in his career in the 1950s, Winogrand worked as a magazine photojournalist and advertising photographer. In the 1960s he took to the streets of New York where he photographed his subjects—women, demonstrations, zoo animals—with a wide-angle lens, often framing his subjects at unusual angles. Winogrand's photographs were published in four books—including *The Animals* (1969), *Women are Beautiful* (1975), and *Stock Photographs* (1980)—and exhibited at New York's Museum of Modern Art where his 1977 solo exhibit and photography book carried the same title: *Public Relations.*

Garry Winogrand 1928-1984

In 2002 he was one of 20 important and influential photographers honored by the Postal Service in Masters of American Photography. The photograph reproduced on Winogrand's stamp is typical of his whimsical view of contemporary urban life: the random mixing of pedestrians, their chance gestures, and the interactions of men and women. ❑

989

990

991

992

993

994

995

996

997

998

999

1000

1001

1002

1003

1004

1005

1006

1007

1008

1009

1010

1011

1012

1013

1014

1015

1016

1017

1018

1019

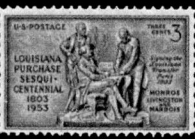
1020

1021

1022

1023

1024

1025

1026

1027

1028

1029

Issues of 1952		Un	U	PB	#	FDC	Q(M)
1008 3¢ NATO	04/04/52	.20	.20	.30	(4)	1.00	2,900
1009 3¢ Grand Coulee Dam	05/15/52	.20	.20	.30	(4)	1.00	115
1010 3¢ Arrival of Lafayette	06/13/52	.20	.20	.45	(4)	1.00	113
Perf. 10.5 x 11							
1011 3¢ Mt. Rushmore Memorial	08/11/52	.20	.20	.35	(4)	1.00	116
Perf. 11 x 10.5							
1012 3¢ Engineering	09/06/52	.20	.20	.45	(4)	1.00	114
1013 3¢ Service Women	09/11/52	.20	.20	.30	(4)	1.50	124
1014 3¢ Gutenberg Bible	09/30/52	.20	.20	.30	(4)	1.00	116
1015 3¢ Newspaper Boys	10/04/52	.20	.20	.30	(4)	1.00	115
1016 3¢ International Red Cross	11/21/52	.20	.20	.30	(4)	1.50	136
Issues of 1953							
1017 3¢ National Guard	02/23/53	.20	.20	.30	(4)	1.00	115
1018 3¢ Ohio Statehood	03/02/53	.20	.20	.45	(4)	1.00	119
1019 3¢ Washington Territory	03/02/53	.20	.20	.30	(4)	1.00	114
1020 3¢ Louisiana Purchase	04/30/53	.20	.20	.50	(4)	1.00	114
1021 5¢ Opening of Japan	07/14/53	.20	.20	.65	(4)	1.25	89
1022 3¢ American Bar Association	08/24/53	.20	.20	.30	(4)	4.50	115
1023 3¢ Sagamore Hill	09/14/53	.20	.20	.35	(4)	1.00	116
1024 3¢ Future Farmers	10/13/53	.20	.20	.30	(4)	1.00	115
1025 3¢ Trucking Industry	10/27/53	.20	.20	.30	(4)	1.25	124
1026 3¢ General George S. Patton, Jr.	11/11/53	.20	.20	.40	(4)	2.00	115
1027 3¢ New York City	11/20/53	.20	.20	.35	(4)	1.00	116
1028 3¢ Gadsden Purchase	12/30/53	.20	.20	.30	(4)	1.00	116
Issue of 1954							
1029 3¢ Columbia University	01/04/54	.20	.20	.30	(4)	1.00	119

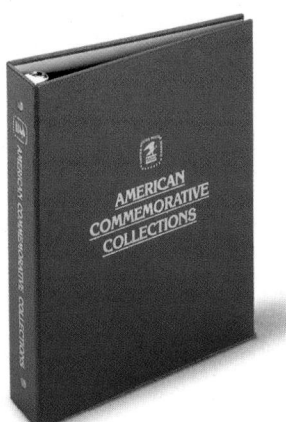

American Commemorative Collections Binder

You'll find this binder is a great way to keep your panels and sheets in mint condition.

Item #880600–American Commemorative Collections Binder $21.95

To order, call **1-800 STAMP-24** or
visit us online at **www.usps.com**

Issues of 1954-1967			Un	U	PB	#	FDC
Liberty Issue, Perf. 11 x 10.5							
1030	½¢ Benjamin Franklin	10/20/55	.20	.20	.35	(4)	1.00
1031	1¢ George Washington	03/56	.20	.20	.25	(4)	
	Pair with full vertical or						
	horizontal gutter between		150.00				
b	Wet printing		.20	.20	.25	(4)	1.00
	Perf. 10.5 x 11						
1031A	1¼¢ Palace of the Governors	06/17/60	.20	.20	.45	(4)	1.00
1032	1½¢ Mt. Vernon	02/22/56	.20	.20	1.75	(4)	1.00
	Perf. 11 x 10.5						
1033	2¢ Thomas Jefferson	09/15/54	.20	.20	.25	(4)	1.00
	Pair with full vertical or						
	horizontal gutter between		—				
1034	2½¢ Bunker Hill Monument and						
	Massachusetts Flag	06/17/59	.20	.20	.50	(4)	1.00
1035	3¢ Statue of Liberty	06/24/54	.20	.20	.25	(4)	
a	Booklet pane of 6	06/30/54	4.00	1.25			3.50
b	Tagged	07/06/66	.30	.25	5.50	(4)	40.00
c	Imperf., pair		2,000.00				
d	Horizontal pair, imperf. between		—				
e	Wet printing	06/24/54	.20	.20	.35	(4)	1.00
f	As "a," untagged		5.00	1.50			
g	As "a," vertical imperf. between		5,000.00				
1036	4¢ Abraham Lincoln	11/19/54	.20	.20	.35	(4)	
a	Booklet pane of 6	07/31/58	2.75	1.25			4.00
b	Tagged	11/02/63	.60	.40	8.50	(4)	50.00
	Perf. 10.5 x 11						
1037	4½¢ The Hermitage	03/16/59	.20	.20	.65	(4)	1.00
	Perf. 11 x 10.5						
1038	5¢ James Monroe	12/02/54	.20	.20	.45	(4)	1.00
	Pair with full vertical gutter between		200.00				
1039	6¢ Theodore Roosevelt	11/18/55	.25	.20	1.25	(4)	
a	Wet printing	11/18/55	.40	.20	2.00	(4)	1.00
1040	7¢ Woodrow Wilson	01/10/56	.20	.20	1.00	(4)	1.00
	Perf. 11						
1041	8¢ Statue of Liberty	04/09/54	.25	.20	2.00	(4)	1.00
a	Carmine double impression		575.00				
1042	8¢ Statue of Liberty, redrawn	03/22/58	.20	.20	.90	(4)	1.00
	Perf. 11 x 10.5						
1042A	8¢ Gen. John J. Pershing	11/17/61	.20	.20	.90	(4)	1.25
	Perf. 10.5 x 11						
1043	9¢ The Alamo	06/14/56	.30	.20	1.30	(4)	1.25
1044	10¢ Independence Hall	07/04/56	.30	.20	1.40	(4)	1.00
b	Tagged	07/06/66	.25	.20	1.10	(4)	40.00
d	Tagged	07/06/66	2.00	1.00	35.00	(4)	
	Perf. 11						
1044A	11¢ Statue of Liberty	06/15/61	.30	.20	1.50	(4)	1.25
c	Tagged	01/11/67	2.00	1.60	35.00	(4)	40.00

1031A

1030   **1031**

1032

1033   **1034**

1037

1035   **1036**

1038   **1039**   **1040**

1041   **1042**   **1042A**

1043   **1044**

1044A

1045

1046

1047

1048

1049

1050

1051

1052

1053

	Issues of 1955-1968		Un	U	PB/LP	#	FDC
	Perf. 11 x 10.5						
1045	12¢ Benjamin Harrison	06/06/59	.35	.20	1.50	(4)	1.25
a	Tagged	1968	.35	.20	4.00	(4)	40.00
1046	15¢ John Jay	12/12/58	.60	.20	3.00	(4)	1.25
a	Tagged	07/06/66	1.10	.50	13.00	(4)	40.00
	Perf. 10.5 x 11						
1047	20¢ Monticello	04/13/56	.40	.20	1.75	(4)	1.25
	Perf. 11 x 10.5						
1048	25¢ Paul Revere	04/18/58	1.10	.75	4.75	(4)	1.25
1049	30¢ Robert E. Lee	09/21/55	.70	.20	4.00	(4)	
a	Wet printing	09/21/55	1.10	.75	5.00	(4)	2.00
1050	40¢ John Marshall	04/58	1.50	.20	7.50	(4)	
a	Wet printing	09/24/55	2.25	.25	12.50	(4)	2.00
1051	50¢ Susan B. Anthony	04/58	1.50	.20	7.00	(4)	
a	Wet printing	08/25/55	1.75	.20	11.00	(4)	6.00
1052	$1 Patrick Henry	10/58	4.50	.20	19.00	(4)	
a	Wet printing	10/07/55	5.25	1.00	22.50	(4)	10.00
	Perf. 11						
1053	$5 Alexander Hamilton	03/19/56	60.00	6.75	260.00	(4)	50.00
	Issues of 1954-1980, Coil Stamps, Perf. 10 Vertically						
1054	1¢ dark green						
	Washington (1031)	08/57	.20	.20	1.00	(2)	
b	Imperf., pair		2,500.00	—			
c	Wet printing	10/08/54	.35	.20	1.75	(2)	1.00
	Coil Stamp, Perf. 10 Horizontally						
1054A	1¼¢ turquoise Palace						
	of the Governors (1031A)	06/17/60	.20	.20	2.25	(2)	1.00
	Coil Stamps, Perf. 10 Vertically						
1055	2¢ rose carmine						
	Jefferson (1033)	05/57	.35	.20	.80	(2)	
a	Tagged	05/06/68	.20	.20	.75	(2)	32.50
b	Imperf., pair (Bureau precanceled)			550.00			
c	As "a," imperf., pair		600.00				
d	Wet printing	10/22/54	.40	.20	3.50	(2)	1.00
1056	2½¢ gray blue						
	Bunker Hill (1034)	09/09/59	.35	.25	3.50	(2)	2.00
1057	3¢ deep violet Statue of						
	Liberty (1035)	10/56	.35	.20	.80	(2)	
a	Imperf., pair		1,750.00	—	2,750.00	(2)	
b	Tagged	06/26/67	1.00	.50	25.00	(2)	
c	Wet printing	07/20/54	.35	.20	2.75	(2)	1.00
1058	4¢ red violet Lincoln (1036)	07/31/58	.50	.20	2.50	(2)	1.00
a	Imperf., pair		120.00	120.00	200.00	(2)	
b	Wet printing (Bureau precanceled)		27.50	.50	375.00	(2)	
	Coil Stamp, Perf. 10 Horizontally						
1059	4½¢ blue green						
	The Hermitage (1037)	05/01/59	1.50	1.20	14.00	(2)	1.75
	Coil Stamp, Perf. 10 Vertically						
1059A	25¢ green Revere (1048)	02/25/65	.50	.30	2.00	(2)	1.25
b	Tagged	04/03/73	.80	.20	3.25	(2)	40.00
	Dull finish gum	1980	1.25		5.00	(2)	
c	Imperf., pair		55.00		100.00	(2)	

Issues of 1954			Un	U	PB	#	FDC	Q(M)
	Perf. 11 x 10.5							
1060	3¢ Nebraska Territory	05/07/54	.20	.20	.30	(4)	1.00	116
1061	3¢ Kansas Territory	05/31/54	.20	.20	.30	(4)	1.00	114
	Perf. 10.5 x 11							
1062	3¢ George Eastman	07/12/54	.20	.20	.30	(4)	1.00	128
	Perf. 11 x 10.5							
1063	3¢ Lewis and Clark Expedition	07/28/54	.20	.20	.35	(4)	1.00	116
	Issues of 1955, Perf. 10.5 x 11							
1064	3¢ Pennsylvania Academy of the Fine Arts	01/15/55	.20	.20	.45	(4)	1.00	116
	Perf. 11 x 10.5							
1065	3¢ Land-Grant Colleges	02/12/55	.20	.20	.30	4)	1.25	120
1066	8¢ Rotary International	02/23/55	.20	.20	.95	(4)	2.25	54
1067	3¢ Armed Forces Reserve	05/21/55	.20	.20	.30	(4)	1.00	176
	Perf. 10.5 x 11							
1068	3¢ New Hampshire	06/21/55	.20	.20	.50	(4)	1.50	126
	Perf. 11 x 10.5							
1069	3¢ Soo Locks	06/28/55	.20	.20	.30	(4)	1.00	122
1070	3¢ Atoms for Peace	07/28/55	.20	.20	.35	(4)	1.00	134
1071	3¢ Fort Ticonderoga	09/18/55	.20	.20	.30	(4)	1.00	119
	Perf. 10.5 x 11							
1072	3¢ Andrew W. Mellon	12/20/55	.20	.20	.35	(4)	1.00	112

CARY GRANT

(1904-1986) One of the silver screen's most beloved actors, CARY GRANT charmed audiences as a debonair leading man, bringing wit and sophistication to his roles in more than 70 movies. Born Archibald Leach in Bristol, England, he joined a troupe of performers and came with them to the United States in 1920. He performed on the vaudeville circuit, on Broadway, and on screen in *Singapore Sue*, a one-reel film released in 1932. That same year, using the screen name Cary Grant, he appeared in his first feature film, *This is the Night*. In 1942, he became a U.S. citizen legally changing his name to Cary Grant.

Best known for starring in romantic comedies such as *An Affair to Remember* (1957), Grant was often teamed with Hollywood's most prominent leading ladies, including Katharine Hepburn in *The Philadelphia Story* (1940), Grace Kelly in *To Catch a Thief* (1955), and Audrey Hepburn in *Charade* (1963). In 1941 he played an enigmatic villain in the Alfred Hitchcock film *Suspicion* and went on to star in other Hitchcock films, including *Notorious* (1946) and *North by Northwest* (1959). At the 42nd Academy Awards in 1970, Frank Sinatra presented Grant with a special Oscar "for his unique mastery of the art of screen acting." In 1999, when the American Film Institute announced the 50 greatest American screen legends, Grant was second among the men. ❑

1060

1061

1062

1063

1064

1065

1066

1067

1068

1069

1070

1071

1072

1073

1074

1075

1076

1077

1078

1079

1080

1081

1082

1083

1084

1085

	Issues of 1956		Un	U	PB	#	FDC	Q(M)
1073	3¢ Benjamin Franklin	01/17/56	.20	.20	.40	(4)	1.00	129
	Perf. 11 x 10.5							
1074	3¢ Booker T. Washington	04/05/56	.20	.20	.40	(4)	1.50	121
	Fifth International Philatelic Exhibition Issues Souvenir Sheet, Imperf.							
1075	Statue of Liberty Sheet of 2 stamps							
	(1035, 1041)	04/28/56	2.00	2.00			5.00	3
a	3¢ (1035), single stamp from sheet		.80	.80				
b	8¢ (1041), single stamp from sheet		1.00	1.00				
	Perf. 11 x 10.5							
1076	3¢ New York Coliseum and Columbus Monument	04/30/56	.20	.20	.30	(4)	1.00	120
	Wildlife Conservation Issue							
1077	3¢ Wild Turkey	05/05/56	.20	.20	.35	(4)	1.50	123
1078	3¢ Pronghorn Antelope	06/22/56	.20	.20	.35	(4)	1.50	123
1079	3¢ King Salmon	11/09/56	.20	.20	.35	(4)	1.50	109
	Perf. 10.5 x 11							
1080	3¢ Pure Food and Drug Laws	06/27/56	.20	.20	.50	(4)	1.00	113
	Perf. 11 x 10.5							
1081	3¢ Wheatland	08/05/56	.20	.20	.30	(4)	1.00	125
	Perf. 10.5 x 11							
1082	3¢ Labor Day	09/03/56	.20	.20	.30	(4)	1.00	118
	Perf. 11 x 10.5							
1083	3¢ Nassau Hall	09/22/56	.20	.20	.50	(4)	1.00	122
	Perf. 10.5 x 11							
1084	3¢ Devils Tower	09/24/56	.20	.20	.30	(4)	1.00	118
	Pair with full horizontal gutter between		—					
	Perf. 11 x 10.5							
1085	3¢ Children's Stamp	12/15/56	.20	.20	.30	(4)	1.00	101

FREDERICK LAW OLMSTED

(1822-1903)

FREDERICK LAW OLMSTED—known today as the father of landscape architecture—was determined to create environments that would not only soothe the human mind, but also provide opportunities for people from many walks of life to meet. In diverse landscapes such as parkways, residential communities, and academic campuses, Olmsted managed to combine active spaces for physical pursuits with more passive places for visual and emotional gratification. Perhaps his most famous work is New York City's Central Park. In 1858, the plan submitted by Olmsted and co-designer Calvert Vaux won the competition to design the park.

Olmsted's commitment to complement urban areas with the beauty of natural settings is apparent throughout the 843-acre park. Other well-known projects include the U.S. Capitol grounds in Washington, D.C., the Stanford University campus in northern California, and George Vanderbilt's Biltmore Estate near Asheville, North Carolina. Olmsted was also instrumental in preserving places like Yosemite Valley for future generations. The stamp issued in his honor in 1999 features a detail of a portrait by John Singer Sargent and fragments of the plans for Central Park, Brooklyn's Prospect Park, and the Buffalo, New York, park system. ❑

Issues of 1957		Un	U	PB	#	FDC	Q(M)
1086 3¢ Alexander Hamilton	01/11/57	.20	.20	.30	(4)	1.00	115
Perf. 10.5 x 11							
1087 3¢ Polio	01/15/57	.20	.20	.30	(4)	1.50	187
Perf. 11 x 10.5							
1088 3¢ Coast and Geodetic Survey	02/11/57	.20	.20	.30	(4)	1.00	115
1089 3¢ American Institute of Architects	02/23/57	.20	.20	.30	(4)	1.25	107
Perf. 10.5 x 11							
1090 3¢ Steel Industry	05/22/57	.20	.20	.30	(4)	1.00	112
Perf. 11 x 10.5							
1091 3¢ International Naval Review- Jamestown Festival	06/10/57	.20	.20	.30	(4)	1.00	118
1092 3¢ Oklahoma Statehood	06/14/57	.20	.20	.35	(4)	1.00	102
1093 3¢ School Teachers	07/01/57	.20	.20	.35	(4)	2.00	102
Perf. 11							
1094 4¢ Flag	07/04/57	.20	.20	.35	(4)	1.00	84
Perf. 10.5 x 11							
1095 3¢ Shipbuilding	08/15/57	.20	.20	.45	(4)	1.00	126
Champion of Liberty Issue, Perf. 11							
1096 8¢ Bust of Ramon Magsaysay on Medal	08/31/57	.20	.20	.85	(4)	1.25	39
Plate block of 4, ultramarine # omitted		—					
Perf. 10.5 x 11							
1097 3¢ Marquis de Lafayette	09/06/57	.20	.20	.30	(4)	1.00	123
Perf. 11							
1098 3¢ Wildlife Conservation	11/22/57	.20	.20	.35	(4)	1.25	174
Perf. 10.5 x 11							
1099 3¢ Religious Freedom	12/27/57	.20	.20	.30	(4)	1.00	114
Issues of 1958							
1100 3¢ Gardening-Horticulture	03/15/58	.20	.20	.30	(4)	1.00	123
1101-03 Not assigned							
Perf. 11 x 10.5							
1104 3¢ Brussels Universal and International Exhibition	04/17/58	.20	.20	.30	(4)	1.00	114
1105 3¢ James Monroe	04/28/58	.20	.20	.30	(4)	1.00	120
1106 3¢ Minnesota Statehood	05/11/58	.20	.20	.30	(4)	1.00	121
Perf. 11							
1107 3¢ International Geophysical Year	05/31/58	.20	.20	.35	(4)	1.00	126
Perf. 11 x 10.5							
1108 3¢ Gunston Hall	06/12/58	.20	.20	.30	(4)	1.00	108

1086

1087

1088

1089

1090

1091

1092

1093

1094

1095

1096

1097

1098

1099

1100

1104

1105

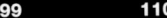

1106

1107

1108

1109

1110

1111

1112

1113

1114

1115

1116

1117

1118

1119

1120

1121

1122

1123

1124

1125

1126

1127

1128

1129

1130

1131

	Issues of 1958		Un	U	PB	#	FDC	Q(M)
	Perf. 10.5 x 11							
1109	3¢ Mackinac Bridge	06/25/58	.20	.20	.30	(4)	1.00	107
	Champion of Liberty Issue							
1110	4¢ Bust of Simon Bolivar on							
	Medal	07/24/58	.20	.20	.35	(4)	1.25	115
	Perf. 11							
1111	8¢ Bust of Bolivar on Medal	07/24/58	.20	.20	1.25	(4)	1.25	39
	Plate block of four, ocher # only		—					
	Perf. 11 x 10.5							
1112	4¢ Atlantic Cable	08/15/58	.20	.20	.35	(4)	1.00	114
	Issues of 1958-1959, Abraham Lincoln Sesquicentennial Issue, Perf. 10.5 x 11							
1113	1¢ Portrait by George Healy	02/12/59	.20	.20	.25	(4)	1.00	120
1114	3¢ Sculptured Head by							
	Gutzon Borglum	02/27/59	.20	.20	.40	(4)	1.00	91
	Perf. 11 x 10.5							
1115	4¢ Lincoln and Stephen Douglas							
	Debating, by Joseph							
	Boggs Beale	08/27/58	.20	.20	.60	(4)	1.00	114
1116	4¢ Statue in Lincoln Memorial							
	by Daniel Chester French	05/30/59	.20	.20	.40	(4)	1.00	126
	Champion of Liberty Issue, Perf. 10.5 x 11							
1117	4¢ Bust of Lajos Kossuth on							
	Medal	09/19/58	.20	.20	.30	(4)	1.25	120
	Perf. 11							
1118	8¢ Bust of Kossuth on Medal	09/19/58	.20	.20	1.10	(4)	1.25	44
	Perf. 10.5 x 11							
1119	4¢ Freedom of the Press	09/22/58	.20	.20	.30	(4)	1.00	118
	Perf. 11 x 10.5							
1120	4¢ Overland Mail	10/10/58	.20	.20	.30	(4)	1.00	125
	Perf. 10.5 x 11							
1121	4¢ Noah Webster	10/16/58	.20	.20	.40	(4)	1.00	114
	Perf. 11							
1122	4¢ Forest Conservation	10/27/58	.20	.20	.30	(4)	1.00	156
	Perf. 11 x 10.5							
1123	4¢ Fort Duquesne	11/25/58	.20	.20	.35	(4)	1.00	124
	Issues of 1959							
1124	4¢ Oregon Statehood	02/14/59	.20	.20	.30	(4)	1.00	120
	Champion of Liberty Issue, Perf. 10.5 x 11							
1125	4¢ Bust of José de San Martin							
	on Medal	02/25/59	.20	.20	.30	(4)	1.25	133
a	Horizontal pair, imperf. between		1,500.00					
	Perf. 11							
1126	8¢ Bust of San Martin							
	on Medal	02/25/59	.20	.20	.90	(4)	1.25	45
	Perf. 10.5 x 11							
1127	4¢ NATO	04/01/59	.20	.20	.30	(4)	1.00	122
	Perf. 11 x 10.5							
1128	4¢ Arctic Explorations	04/06/59	.20	.20	.40	(4)	1.00	131
1129	8¢ World Peace Through							
	World Trade	04/20/59	.20	.20	.85	(4)	1.00	47
1130	4¢ Silver Centennial	06/08/59	.20	.20	.30	(4)	1.00	123
	Perf. 11							
1131	4¢ St. Lawrence Seaway	06/26/59	.20	.20	.35	(4)	1.25	126
	Pair with full horizontal gutter between		—					

	Issues of 1959		Un	U	PB	#	FDC	Q(M)
1132	4¢ 49-Star Flag	07/04/59	.20	.20	.40	(4)	1.00	209
1133	4¢ Soil Conservation	08/26/59	.20	.20	.35	(4)	1.00	121
	Perf. 10.5 x 11							
1134	4¢ Petroleum Industry	08/27/59	.20	.20	.40	(4)	1.50	116
	Perf. 11 x 10.5							
1135	4¢ Dental Health	09/14/59	.20	.20	.40	(4)	3.50	118
	Champion of Liberty Issue, Perf. 10.5 x 11							
1136	4¢ Bust of Ernst Reuter on Medal	09/29/59	.20	.20	.30	(4)	1.25	112
	Perf. 11							
1137	8¢ Bust of Reuter on Medal	09/29/59	.20	.20	.90	(4)	1.25	43
	Perf. 10.5 x 11							
1138	4¢ Dr. Ephraim McDowell	12/03/59	.20	.20	.40	(4)	1.25	115
a	Vertical pair, imperf. between		450.00					
b	Vertical pair, imperf. horizontally		350.00					
	Issues of 1960-1961, American Credo Issue, Perf. 11							
1139	4¢ Quotation from Washington's Farewell Address	01/20/60	.20	.20	.40	(4)	1.00	126
1140	4¢ Benjamin Franklin Quotation	03/31/60	.20	.20	.40	(4)	1.00	125
1141	4¢ Thomas Jefferson Quotation	05/18/60	.20	.20	.45	(4)	1.00	115
1142	4¢ Francis Scott Key Quotation	09/14/60	.20	.20	.50	(4)	1.00	122
1143	4¢ Abraham Lincoln Quotation	11/19/60	.20	.20	.50	(4)	1.00	121
	Pair with full horizontal gutter between		—					
1144	4¢ Patrick Henry Quotation	01/11/61	.20	.20	.50	(4)	1.00	113
	Issues of 1960							
1145	4¢ Boy Scouts	02/08/60	.20	.20	.45	(4)	4.00	139
	Olympic Winter Games Issue, Perf. 10.5 x 11							
1146	4¢ Olympic Rings and Snowflake	02/18/60	.20	.20	.40	(4)	1.00	124
	Champion of Liberty Issue							
1147	4¢ Bust of Thomas Masaryk on Medal	03/07/60	.20	.20	.30	(4)	1.25	114
a	Vertical pair, imperf. between		3,250.00					
	Perf. 11							
1148	8¢ Bust of Masaryk on Medal	03/07/60	.20	.20	.95	(4)	1.25	44
a	Horizontal pair, imperf. between		—					
	Perf. 11 x 10.5							
1149	4¢ World Refugee Year	04/07/60	.20	.20	.30	(4)	1.00	113
	Perf. 11							
1150	4¢ Water Conservation	04/18/60	.20	.20	.35	(4)	1.00	122
	Perf. 10.5 x 11							
1151	4¢ SEATO	05/31/60	.20	.20	.35	(4)	1.00	115
a	Vertical pair, imperf. between		140.00					

1132

1133

1134

1135

1136

1137

1138

1139

1140

1141

1142

1143

1144

1145

1146

1147

1148

1149

1150

1151

1152

1153

1154

1155

1156

1157

1158

1159

1160

1161

1162

1163

1164

1165

1166

1167

1168

1169

1170

1171

1172

1173

Issues of 1960		Un	U	PB	#	FDC	Q(M)
Perf. 11 x 10.5							
1152 4¢ American Woman	06/02/60	.20	.20	.30	(4)	1.25	111
Perf. 11							
1153 4¢ 50-Star Flag	07/04/60	.20	.20	.30	(4)	1.00	153
Perf. 11 x 10.5							
1154 4¢ Pony Express	07/19/60	.20	.20	.55	(4)	1.50	120
Perf. 10.5 x 11							
1155 4¢ Employ the Handicapped	08/28/60	.20	.20	.30	(4)	1.50	118
1156 4¢ 5th World Forestry Congress	08/29/60	.20	.20	.30	(4)	1.00	118
Perf. 11							
1157 4¢ Mexican Independence	09/16/60	.20	.20	.30	(4)	1.00	112
1158 4¢ U.S.-Japan Treaty	09/28/60	.20	.20	.35	(4)	1.00	125
Champion of Liberty Issue, Paderewski, Perf. 10.5 x 11							
1159 4¢ Bust of Ignacy Jan Paderewski on Medal	10/08/60	.20	.20	.30	(4)	1.25	120
Perf. 11							
1160 8¢ Bust of Paderewski on Medal	10/08/60	.20	.20	.90	(4)	1.25	43
Perf. 10.5 x 11							
1161 4¢ Sen. Robert A. Taft Memorial	10/10/60	.20	.20	.45	(4)	1.00	107
Perf. 11 x 10.5							
1162 4¢ Wheels of Freedom	10/15/60	.20	.20	.30	(4)	1.00	110
Perf. 11							
1163 4¢ Boys' Clubs of America	10/18/60	.20	.20	.30	(4)	1.00	124
1164 4¢ First Automated Post Office	10/20/60	.20	.20	.30	(4)	1.00	124
Champion of Liberty Issue, Perf. 10.5 x 11							
1165 4¢ Bust of Gustaf Mannerheim on Medal	10/26/60	.20	.20	.30	(4)	1.25	125
Perf. 11							
1166 8¢ Bust of Mannerheim on Medal	10/26/60	.20	.20	.80	(4)	1.25	42
1167 4¢ Camp Fire Girls	11/01/60	.20	.20	.55	(4)	2.50	116
Champion of Liberty Issue, Perf. 10.5 x 11							
1168 4¢ Bust of Giusseppe Garibaldi on Medal	11/02/60	.20	.20	.30	(4)	1.25	126
Perf. 11							
1169 8¢ Bust of Garibaldi on Medal	11/02/60	.20	.20	.85	(4)	1.25	43
Perf. 10.5 x 11							
1170 4¢ Sen. Walter F. George Memorial	11/05/60	.20	.20	.45	(4)	1.00	124
1171 4¢ Andrew Carnegie	11/25/60	.20	.20	.35	(4)	1.00	120
1172 4¢ John Foster Dulles Memorial	12/06/60	.20	.20	.35	(4)	1.00	117
Perf. 11 x 10.5							
1173 4¢ Echo I-Communications for Peace	12/15/60	.20	.20	.65	(4)	2.50	124

Issues of 1961		Un	U	PB	#	FDC	Q(M)
Champion of Liberty Issue, Perf. 10.5 x 11							
1174	4¢ Bust of Gandhi on Medal 01/26/61	.20	.20	.30	(4)	1.25	113
Perf. 11							
1175	8¢ Bust of Gandhi on Medal 01/26/61	.20	.20	1.00	(4)	1.25	42
1176	4¢ Range Conservation 02/02/61	.20	.20	.40	(4)	1.00	111
Perf. 10.5 x 11							
1177	4¢ Horace Greeley 02/03/61	.20	.20	.45	(4)	1.00	99
Issues of 1961-1965, Civil War Centennial Issue, Perf. 11 x 10.5							
1178	4¢ Fort Sumter 04/12/61	.25	.20	1.10	(4)	4.00	101
1179	4¢ Shiloh 04/07/62	.20	.20	.75	(4)	4.00	125
Perf. 11							
1180	5¢ Gettysburg 07/01/63	.20	.20	.85	(4)	4.00	80
1181	5¢ The Wilderness 05/05/64	.20	.20	.60	(4)	4.00	125
1182	5¢ Appomattox 04/09/65	.25	.20	1.40	(4)	4.00	113
a	Horizontal pair, imperf. vertically	4,500.00					
1183	4¢ Kansas Statehood 05/10/61	.20	.20	.35	(4)	1.00	106
Perf. 11 x 10.5							
1184	4¢ Sen. George W. Norris 07/11/61	.20	.20	.40	(4)	1.00	111
1185	4¢ Naval Aviation 08/20/61	.20	.20	.35	(4)	1.00	117
	Pair with full vertical gutter between	150.00					
Perf. 10.5 x 11							
1186	4¢ Workmen's Compensation 09/04/61	.20	.20	.35	(4)	1.00	121
	With plate # inverted			.60	(4)		
Perf. 11							
1187	4¢ Frederic Remington 10/04/61	.20	.20	.40	(4)	1.25	112
Perf. 10.5 x 11							
1188	4¢ Republic of China 10/10/61	.20	.20	.45	(4)	5.50	111
1189	4¢ Naismith-Basketball 11/06/61	.20	.20	.50	(4)	6.50	109
Perf. 11							
1190	4¢ Nursing 12/28/61	.20	.20	.50	(4)	10.00	145
Issues of 1962							
1191	4¢ New Mexico Statehood 01/06/62	.20	.20	.30	(4)	1.50	113
1192	4¢ Arizona Statehood 02/14/62	.20	.20	.30	(4)	1.50	122
1193	4¢ Project Mercury 02/20/62	.20	.20	.35	(4)	3.00	289
1194	4¢ Malaria Eradication 03/30/62	.20	.20	.30	(4)	1.00	120
Perf. 10.5 x 11							
1195	4¢ Charles Evans Hughes 04/11/62	.20	.20	.30	(4)	1.00	125

1174

1175

1176

1177

1178

1179

1180

1181

1182

1183

1184

1185

1186

1187

1188

1189

1190

1191

1192

1193

1194

1195

1196

1197

1198

1199

1200

1201

1202

1203

1204

1205

1206

1207

1208

1209

1213

1230

1231

1232

1233

1234

Issues of 1962		Un	U	PB/LP	#	FDC	Q(M)
Perf. 11							
1196 4¢ Seattle World's Fair	04/25/62	.20	.20	.30	(4)	1.00	147
1197 4¢ Louisiana Statehood	04/30/62	.20	.20	.50	(4)	1.00	119
Perf. 11 x 10.5							
1198 4¢ Homestead Act	05/20/62	.20	.20	.30	(4)	1.00	123
1199 4¢ Girl Scout Jubilee	07/24/62	.20	.20	.30	(4)	5.00	127
Pair with full vertical gutter between		250.00					
1200 4¢ Sen. Brien McMahon	07/28/62	.20	.20	.40	(4)	1.00	131
1201 4¢ Apprenticeship	08/31/62	.20	.20	.30	(4)	1.00	120
Perf. 11							
1202 4¢ Sam Rayburn	09/16/62	.20	.20	.30	(4)	1.50	121
1203 4¢ Dag Hammarskjold	10/23/62	.20	.20	.30	(4)	1.00	121
1204 4¢ black, brown and yellow (yellow inverted), Dag Hammarskjold, special printing	11/16/62	.20	.20	1.10	(4)	5.00	40
Christmas Issue							
1205 4¢ Wreath and Candles	11/01/62	.20	.20	.30	(4)	1.10	862
1206 4¢ Higher Education	11/14/62	.20	.20	.35	(4)	1.25	120
1207 4¢ Winslow Homer	12/15/62	.20	.20	.45	(4)	1.25	118
a Horizontal pair, imperf. between		6,750.00					
Issues of 1963-1966							
1208 5¢ Flag over White House	01/09/63	.20	.20	.40	(4)	1.00	
Pair with full horizontal gutter between		—					
a Tagged	08/25/66	.20	.20	2.00	(4)	30.00	
b Horizontal pair, imperf. between		1,500.00					
Issues of 1962-1966, Perf. 11 x 10.5							
1209 1¢ Andrew Jackson	03/22/63	.20	.20	.20	(4)	1.00	
Pair with full vertical gutter between		—					
a Tagged	07/06/66	.20	.20	.40	(4)	30.00	
1210-12 Not assigned							
1213 5¢ George Washington	11/23/62	.20	.20	.40	(4)	1.00	
a Booklet pane of 5 + label		3.00	2.00			4.00	
b Tagged	10/28/63	.50	.20	4.50	(4)	30.00	
c As "a," tagged	10/28/63	2.00	1.50			100.00	
1214-24 Not assigned							
Coil Stamps, Perf. 10 Vertically							
1225 1¢ green Jackson (1209)	05/31/63	.20	.20	2.00	(2)	1.00	
a Tagged	07/06/66	.20	.20	.75	(2)	30.00	
1226-28 Not assigned							
1229 5¢ dark blue gray Washington (1213)	11/23/62	1.10	.20	3.50	(2)	1.00	
a Tagged	10/28/63	1.40	.20	6.50	(2)	30.00	
b Imperf., pair		450.00		1,250.00	(2)		
Issues of 1963, Perf. 11							
1230 5¢ Carolina Charter	04/06/63	.20	.20	.40	(4)	1.00	130
1231 5¢ Food for Peace-Freedom from Hunger	06/04/63	.20	.20	.40	(4)	1.00	136
1232 5¢ West Virginia Statehood	06/20/63	.20	.20	.40	(4)	1.00	138
1233 5¢ Emancipation Proclamation	08/16/63	.20	.20	.50	(4)	1.75	132
1234 5¢ Alliance for Progress	08/17/63	.20	.20	.40	(4)	1.00	136

	Issues of 1963		Un	U	PB	#	FDC	Q(M)
1235	5¢ Cordell Hull	10/05/63	.20	.20	.50	(4)	1.00	131
	Perf. 11 x 10.5							
1236	5¢ Eleanor Roosevelt	10/11/63	.20	.20	.45	(4)	1.00	133
	Perf. 11							
1237	5¢ The Sciences	10/14/63	.20	.20	.40	(4)	1.25	130
1238	5¢ City Mail Delivery	10/26/63	.20	.20	.50	(4)	1.25	128
a	Tagged omitted		7.50					
1239	5¢ International Red Cross	10/29/63	.20	.20	.50	(4)	1.50	119
	Christmas Issue							
1240	5¢ National Christmas Tree and White House	11/01/63	.20	.20	.50	(4)	1.25	1,300
	Pair with full horizontal gutter between		—					
a	Tagged	11/02/63	.65	.50	5.00	(4)	60.00	
1241	5¢ John James Audubon, (See also #C71)	12/07/63	.20	.20	.45	(4)	1.25	175
	Issues of 1964, Perf. 10.5 x 11							
1242	5¢ Sam Houston	01/10/64	.20	.20	.45	(4)	1.75	126
	Perf. 11							
1243	5¢ Charles M. Russell	03/19/64	.20	.20	.40	(4)	1.25	128
	Perf. 11 x 10.5							
1244	5¢ New York World's Fair	04/22/64	.20	.20	.45	(4)	1.25	146
	Perf. 11							
1245	5¢ John Muir	04/29/64	.20	.20	.45	(4)	1.50	120
	Perf. 11 x 10.5							
1246	5¢ President John Fitzgerald Kennedy Memorial	05/29/64	.20	.20	.60	(4)	2.25	512
	Perf. 10.5 x 11							
1247	5¢ New Jersey Settlement	06/15/64	.20	.20	.50	(4)	1.00	124
	Perf. 11							
1248	5¢ Nevada Statehood	07/22/64	.20	.20	.40	(4)	1.00	123
1249	5¢ Register and Vote	08/01/64	.20	.20	.45	(4)	1.25	453
	Perf. 10.5 x 11							
1250	5¢ Shakespeare	08/14/64	.20	.20	.40	(4)	1.50	123
1251	5¢ Doctors William and Charles Mayo	09/11/64	.20	.20	.60	(4)	2.75	123
	Perf. 11							
1252	5¢ American Music	10/15/64	.20	.20	.40	(4)	1.50	127
a	Blue omitted		1,000.00					
1253	5¢ Homemakers	10/26/64	.20	.20	.40	(4)	1.00	121

2004 Commemorative Stamp Yearbook

1236

1237

1235

1239

1240

1238

1241

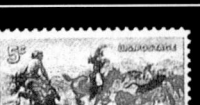

1243

1244

1242

1245

1246

1247

1248

1249

1252

1253

1250

1251

1254   1255

1258

1259

1260

1256   1257 1257b

1261

1262

1263

1264

1265

1266

1267

1268

1269

1270

1271

1272

1273

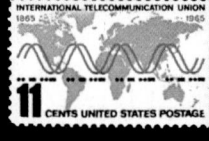

1274

1275

1276

	Issues of 1964		Un	U	PB	#	FDC	Q(M)
	Christmas Issue, Perf. 11							
1254	5¢ Holly	11/09/64	.25	.20			1.00	352
a	Tagged		.60	.50				
1255	5¢ Mistletoe	11/09/64	.25	.20			1.00	352
a	Tagged		.60	.50				
1256	5¢ Poinsettia	11/09/64	.25	.20			1.00	352
a	Tagged		.60	.50				
1257	5¢ Sprig of Conifer	11/09/64	.25	.20			1.00	352
a	Tagged		.60	.50				
b	Block of four, #1254-57		1.00	1.00	1.10	(4)	3.00	
c	As "b," tagged		2.50	2.25	5.50	(4)	57.50	
	Perf. 10.5 x 11							
1258	5¢ Verrazano-Narrows Bridge	11/21/64	.20	.20	.45	(4)	1.00	120
	Perf. 11							
1259	5¢ Fine Arts	12/02/64	.20	.20	.40	(4)	1.00	126
	Perf. 10.5 x 11							
1260	5¢ Amateur Radio	12/15/64	.20	.20	.60	(4)	5.00	122
	Issues of 1965, Perf. 11							
1261	5¢ Battle of New Orleans	01/08/65	.20	.20	.60	(4)	1.00	116
1262	5¢ Physical Fitness-Sokol	02/15/65	.20	.20	.50	(4)	1.25	115
1263	5¢ Crusade Against Cancer	04/01/65	.20	.20	.40	(4)	2.50	120
	Perf. 10.5 x 11							
1264	5¢ Winston Churchill Memorial	05/13/65	.20	.20	.40	(4)	1.25	125
	Perf. 11							
1265	5¢ Magna Carta	06/15/65	.20	.20	.40	(4)	1.00	120
	Corner block of four, black PB# omitted		—					
1266	5¢ International Cooperation							
	Year-United Nations	06/26/65	.20	.20	.40	(4)	1.00	115
1267	5¢ Salvation Army	07/02/65	.20	.20	.40	(4)	2.00	116
	Perf. 10.5 x 11							
1268	5¢ Dante Alighieri	07/17/65	.20	.20	.40	(4)	1.00	115
1269	5¢ President Herbert Hoover							
	Memorial	08/10/65	.20	.20	.45	(4)	1.00	115
	Perf. 11							
1270	5¢ Robert Fulton	08/19/65	.20	.20	.40	(4)	1.00	116
1271	5¢ Florida Settlement	08/28/65	.20	.20	.45	(4)	1.00	117
a	Yellow omitted		350.00					
1272	5¢ Traffic Safety	09/03/65	.20	.20	.45	(4)	1.00	114
1273	5¢ John Singleton Copley	09/17/65	.20	.20	.50	(4)	1.00	115
1274	11¢ International							
	Telecommunication Union	10/06/65	.35	.20	2.25	(4)	1.10	27
1275	5¢ Adlai E. Stevenson Memorial	10/23/65	.20	.20	.40	(4)	1.00	128
	Christmas Issue							
1276	5¢ Angel with Trumpet							
	(1840 Weather Vane)	11/02/65	.20	.20	.40	(4)	1.00	1,140
a	Tagged	11/15/65	.75	.25	5.50	(4)	42.50	
1277	Not assigned							

Issues of 1965-1978			Un	U	PB	#	FDC
Prominent Americans Issue, Perf. 11 x 10.5, 10.5 x 11 (See also #1299, 1303-05C)							
1278	1¢ Thomas Jefferson	01/12/68	.20	.20	.20	(4)	1.00
a	Booklet pane of 8	01/12/68	1.00	.75			2.50
b	Bklt. pane of 4 + 2 labels	05/10/71	.80	.60			11.50
c	Untagged (Bureau precanceled)		6.25	1.25			
d	Tagging omitted		3.50	—			
1279	1¼¢ Albert Gallatin	01/30/67	.20	.20	6.00	(4)	1.00
1280	2¢ Frank Lloyd Wright	06/08/66	.20	.20	.25	(4)	1.00
	Pair with full vertical gutter between		—				
a	Booklet pane of 5 + label	01/08/68	1.25	.80			3.50
b	Untagged (Bureau precanceled)		1.35	.40			
c	Booklet pane of 6	05/07/71	1.00	.75			15.00
d	Tagging omitted		3.50	—			
1281	3¢ Francis Parkman	09/16/67	.20	.20	.25	(4)	1.00
a	Untagged (Bureau precanceled)		3.00	.75			
b	Tagging omitted		4.50	—			
1282	4¢ Abraham Lincoln	11/19/65	.20	.20	.40	(4)	1.00
a	Tagged	12/01/65	.20	.20	.55	(4)	30.00
	Pair with full horizontal gutter between		—				
1283	5¢ George Washington	02/22/66	.20	.20	.50	(4)	1.00
a	Tagged	02/23/66	.20	.20	.60	(4)	30.00
1283B	5¢ redrawn	11/17/67	.20	.20	.50	(4)	1.00
	Dull finish gum		.20		1.40	(4)	
d	Untagged (Bureau precanceled)		13.25	1.00			
1284	6¢ Franklin D. Roosevelt	01/29/66	.20	.20	.60	(4)	1.00
a	Tagged	12/29/66	.20	.20	.80	(4)	30.00
b	Booklet pane of 8	12/28/67	1.50	1.00			2.75
c	Booklet pane of 5 + label	01/09/68	1.50	1.00			100.00
1285	8¢ Albert Einstein	03/14/66	.20	.20	.85	(4)	2.50
a	Tagged	07/06/66	.20	.20	.85	(4)	30.00
1286	10¢ Andrew Jackson	03/15/67	.20	.20	1.00	(4)	1.00
b	Untagged (Bureau precanceled)		57.50	1.75			
1286A	12¢ Henry Ford	07/30/68	.25	.20	1.00	(4)	1.50
c	Untagged (Bureau precanceled)		4.75	1.00	145.00	(4)	
1287	13¢ John F. Kennedy	05/29/67	.30	.20	1.50	(4)	1.75
a	Untagged (Bureau precanceled)		5.95	1.00	100.00	(4)	
b	Tagging omitted		12.50	—			
1288	15¢ Oliver Wendell Holmes	03/08/68	.30	.20	1.25	(4)	1.00
a	Untagged (Bureau precanceled)		.75	.75	29.50	(4)	
d	Type II		.55	.20	8.00	(4)	
f	As "d", tagging omitted		5.00	—			
Booklet Stamp, Perf. 10							
1288B	15¢ magenta, tagged						
	(1288), Single from booklet		.35	.20			1.00
c	Booklet pane of 8	06/14/78	2.80	1.75			3.00
e	As "c," vert. imperf. between		—				
Perf. 11 x 10.5, 10.5 x 11							
1289	20¢ George C. Marshall	10/24/67	.40	.20	1.75	(4)	1.10
a	Tagged	04/03/73	.40	.20	1.75	(4)	30.00
1290	25¢ Frederick Douglass	02/14/67	.55	.20	2.25	(4)	2.50
a	Tagged	04/03/73	.45	.20	2.00	(4)	30.00
b	Magenta		25.00	—	150.00		
1291	30¢ John Dewey	10/21/68	.65	.20	2.90	(4)	1.75
a	Tagged	04/03/73	.50	.20	2.25	(4)	30.00
1292	40¢ Thomas Paine	01/29/68	.80	.20	3.25	(4)	1.75
a	Tagged	04/03/73	.65	.20	2.75	(4)	30.00
1293	50¢ Lucy Stone	08/13/68	1.00	.20	4.25	(4)	2.50
a	Tagged	04/03/73	.80	.20	3.50	(4)	30.00

1278   1279

1281

1280   1282

1283   1283B

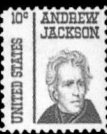

1284

1285   1286   1286A

1287   1288   1289   1290

1291

1292   1293

1294

1295

1305

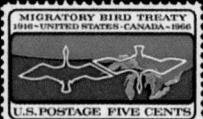

1306

1307

1308

1309

1310

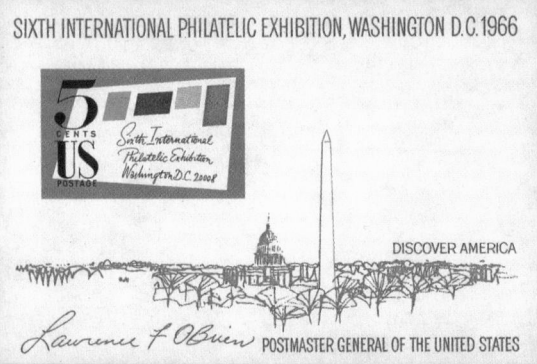

1311

1312

1313

1314

	Issues of 1966-1973		Un	U	PB/LP	#	FDC	Q(M)
	Perf. 11 x 10.5, 10.5 x 11							
1294	$1 Eugene O'Neill	10/16/67	2.25	.20	10.00	(4)	6.00	
a	Tagged	04/03/73	1.65	.20	6.75	(4)	50.00	
1295	$5 John Bassett Moore	12/03/66	10.00	2.25	42.50	(4)	40.00	
a	Tagged	04/03/73	8.50	2.00	35.00	(4)	90.00	
1296	Not assigned							
	Issues of 1967-1975, Coil Stamps, Perf. 10 Horizontally							
1297	3¢ violet Parkman (1281)	11/04/75	.20	.20	.45	(2)	1.00	
a	Imperf., pair		30.00		55.00	(2)		
b	Untagged (Bureau precanceled)		1.05	.25	62.50	(2)		
c	As "b," imperf., pair		295.00	—	25.00	(2)		
1298	6¢ Franklin D. Roosevelt (1284)	12/28/67	.20	.20	1.10	(2)	1.00	
a	Imperf., pair		2,000.00					
b	Tagging omitted		3.00					
	Issues of 1966-1981, Coil Stamps, Perf. 10 Vertically (See also #1279-96)							
1299	1¢ green Jefferson (1278)	01/12/68	.20	.20	.25	(2)	1.00	
a	Untagged (Bureau precanceled)		8.00	1.75	295.00	(2)		
b	Imperf., pair		30.00	—	60.00	(2)		
1300-02	Not assigned							
1303	4¢ blk. Lincoln (1282)	05/28/66	.20	.20	.75	(2)	1.00	
a	Untagged (Bureau precanceled)		8.75	.75	250.00	(2)		
b	Imperf., pair		750.00		1,900.00	(2)		
1304	5¢ bl. Washington (1283)	09/08/66	.20	.20	.40	(2)	1.00	
a	Untagged (Bureau precanceled)		6.50	.65	195.00	(2)		
b	Imperf., pair		175.00		400.00	(2)		
e	As "a," imperf. pair			375.00	850.00	(2)		
1304C	5¢ redrawn (1283B)	1981	.20	.20	1.25	(2)		
d	Imperf., pair		750.00					
1305	6¢ gray brown Roosevelt	02/28/68	.20	.20	.55	(2)	1.00	
a	Imperf., pair		75.00		130.00	(2)		
b	Untagged (Bureau precanceled)		20.00	1.00	675.00	(2)		
1305E	15¢ magenta, Type I (1288)	06/14/78	.25	.20	1.10	(2)	1.00	
	Dull finish gum		.60		3.50	(2)		
f	Untagged (Bureau precanceled)		37.50	37.50	1,350.00	(2)		
g	Imperf., pair		30.00		75.00	(2)		
h	Pair, imperf. between		200.00		550.00	(2)		
i	Type II, dull gum		.60	.20	2.75	(2)		
j	Type II, dull gum, imperf., pair		85.00		290.00	(2)		
1305C	$1 dull purple Eugene O'Neill (1294)	01/12/73	2.00	.40	5.50	(2)	4.00	
d	Imperf., pair		2,250.00		4,000.00	(2)		
	Issues of 1966, Perf. 11							
1306	5¢ Migratory Bird Treaty	03/16/66	.20	.20	.40	(4)	1.75	117
1307	5¢ Humane Treatment of Animals	04/09/66	.20	.20	.40	(4)	1.25	117
1308	5¢ Indiana Statehood	04/16/66	.20	.20	.50	(4)	1.00	124
1309	5¢ American Circus	05/02/66	.20	.20	.50	(4)	2.00	131
	Sixth International Philatelic Exhibition Issue							
1310	5¢ Stamped Cover	05/21/66	.20	.20	.40	(4)	1.00	122
	Souvenir Sheet, Imperf.							
1311	5¢ Stamped Cover (1310) and Washington, D.C., Scene	05/23/66	.20	.20			1.10	15
	Perf. 11							
1312	5¢ The Bill of Rights	07/01/66	.20	.20	.45	(4)	1.75	114
	Perf. 10.5 x 11							
1313	5¢ Poland's Millennium	07/30/66	.20	.20	.45	(4)	1.25	128
	Perf. 11							
1314	5¢ National Park Service	08/25/66	.20	.20	.45	(4)	1.00	120
a	Tagged	08/26/66	.30	.25	2.00	(4)	35.00	

	Issues of 1966		Un	U	PB	#	FDC	Q(M)
1315	5¢ Marine Corps Reserve	08/29/66	.20	.20	.45	(4)	1.50	125
a	Tagged		.30	.20	2.00	(4)	35.00	
b	Black and bister omitted		16,000.00					
1316	5¢ General Federation of							
	Women's Clubs	09/12/66	.20	.20	.45	(4)	1.25	115
a	Tagged	09/13/66	.30	.20	2.00	(4)	35.00	
	American Folklore Issue							
1317	5¢ Johnny Appleseed and							
	Apple	09/24/66	.20	.20	.45	(4)	1.00	124
a	Tagged	09/26/66	.30	.20	2.00	(4)	35.00	
1318	5¢ Beautification of America	10/05/66	.20	.20	.45	(4)	1.00	128
a	Tagged		.30	.20	2.00	(4)	35.00	
1319	5¢ Great River Road	10/21/66	.20	.20	.60	(4)	1.00	128
a	Tagged	10/22/66	.30	.20	2.00	(4)	35.00	
1320	5¢ Savings Bond-Servicemen	10/26/66	.20	.20	.45	(4)	1.00	116
a	Tagged	10/27/66	.30	.20	1.75	(4)	35.00	
b	Red, dark bl. and blk. omitted		4,250.00					
c	Dark blue omitted		8,500.00					
	Christmas Issue							
1321	5¢ Madonna and Child,							
	by Hans Memling	11/01/66	.20	.20	.40	(4)	1.00	1,174
a	Tagged	11/02/66	.30	.20	1.50	(4)	35.00	
1322	5¢ Mary Cassatt	11/17/66	.20	.20	.60	(4)	1.00	114
a	Tagged		.30	.25	1.75	(4)	35.00	
	Issues of 1967							
1323	5¢ National Grange	04/17/67	.20	.20	.40	(4)	1.00	121
a	Tagging omitted		6.00	—				
1324	5¢ Canada Centenary	05/25/67	.20	.20	.40	(4)	1.00	132
a	Tagging omitted		6.00	—				
1325	5¢ Erie Canal	07/04/67	.20	.20	.40	(4)	1.00	119
a	Tagging omitted		11.00	—				
1326	5¢ Search for Peace	07/05/67	.20	.20	.40	(4)	1.00	122
a	Tagging omitted		5.00	—				
1327	5¢ Henry David Thoreau	07/12/67	.20	.20	.50	(4)	1.00	112
1328	5¢ Nebraska Statehood	07/29/67	.20	.20	.40	(4)	1.00	117
a	Tagging omitted		7.50	—				
1329	5¢ Voice of America	08/01/67	.20	.20	.40	(4)	2.00	112
a	Tagging omitted		15.00	—				
	American Folklore Issue							
1330	5¢ Davy Crockett	08/17/67	.20	.20	.60	(4)	1.25	114
a	Vertical pair, imperf. between		6,000.00					
b	Green omitted		—					
c	Black and green omitted		—					
e	Tagging omitted		6.00	—				
	Accomplishments in Space Issue							
1331	5¢ Space-Walking Astronaut	09/29/67	.50	.20			3.00	60
b	Tagging omitted		15.00	—				
1332	5¢ Gemini 4 Capsule							
	and Earth	09/29/67	.50	.20	2.50	(4)	3.00	60
a	Tagging omitted		15.00	—				
b	Pair, #1331-1332		1.10	1.25				
c	As "b", Tagging omitted		40.00	—				
1333	5¢ Urban Planning	10/02/67	.20	.20	.50	(4)	1.00	111
1334	5¢ Finland Independence	10/06/67	.20	.20	.50	(4)	1.00	111

1315

1316

1317

1318

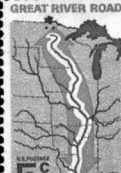

1319

1320

1321

1322

1323

1324

1325

1326

1327

1328

1329

1330

1331   1332   1332b

1333

1334

1335

1336

1345

1346

1347

1348

1349

1350

1337

1338

1351

1352

1353

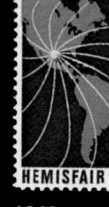

1339   **1340**

1341   **1342**

1354

1354a

1343   **1344**

	Issues of 1967		Un	U	PB	#	FDC	Q(M)
	Perf. 12							
1335	5¢ Thomas Eakins	11/02/67	.20	.20	.50	(4)	1.40	114
	Christmas Issue, Perf. 11							
1336	5¢ Madonna and Child,							
	by Hans Memling	11/06/67	.20	.20	.40	(4)	1.25	1,209
a	Tagging omitted		5.00	—				
1337	5¢ Mississippi Statehood	12/11/67	.20	.20	.60	(4)	1.00	113
a	Tagging omitted		6.00	—				
	Issues of 1968-1971							
1338	6¢ Flag over White House							
	(design 19 x 22mm)	01/24/68	.20	.20	.45	(4)	1.00	
k	Vertical pair, imperf. between		500.00					
m	Tagging omitted		4.00	—				
	Coil Stamp, Perf. 10 Vertically							
1338A	6¢ dk bl, rd and grn (1338)	05/30/69	.20	.20	.30	(2)	1.00	
b	Imperf., pair		500.00					
q	Tagging omitted		8.50	—				
	Perf. 11 x 10.5							
1338D	6¢ dark blue, red and green							
	(1338, design 18.25 x 21mm)	08/07/70	.20	.20	2.60	(20)	1.00	
e	Horizontal pair, imperf. between		175.00					
n	Tagging omitted		5.00	—				
1338F	8¢ dk bl, rd and slt grn (1338)	05/10/71	.20	.20	3.00	(20)	1.00	
i	Imperf., vertical pair		45.00					
j	Horizontal pair, imperf. between		55.00					
o	Tagging omitted		6.50	—				
	Coil Stamp, Perf. 10 Vertically							
1338G	8¢ dk bl, rd and slt grn (1338)	05/10/71	.20	.20	.40	(2)	1.00	
h	Imperf., pair		55.00					
r	Tagging omitted		6.00	—				
	Issues of 1968, Perf. 11							
1339	6¢ Illinois Statehood	02/12/68	.20	.20	.60	(4)	1.00	141
1340	6¢ HemisFair '68	03/30/68	.20	.20	.50	(4)	1.00	144
a	White omitted		1,250.00					
1341	$1 Airlift	04/04/68	2.00	1.25	8.50	(4)	7.00	
	Pair with full horizontal gutter between			—				
1342	6¢ Support Our Youth-Elks	05/01/68	.20	.20	.50	(4)	1.00	147
a	Tagging omitted		7.50	—				
1343	6¢ Law and Order	05/17/68	.20	.20	.50	(4)	2.00	130
1344	6¢ Register and Vote	06/27/68	.20	.20	.50	(4)	1.00	159
	Historic Flag Issue							
1345	6¢ Ft. Moultrie Flag, 1776	07/04/68	.40	.25			3.00	23
1346	6¢ Ft. McHenry (U.S.)							
	Flag, 1795-1818	07/04/68	.30	.25			3.00	23
1347	6¢ Washington's							
	Cruisers Flag, 1775	07/04/68	.25	.25			3.00	23
1348	6¢ Bennington Flag, 1777	07/04/68	.25	.25			3.00	23
1349	6¢ Rhode Island Flag, 1775	07/04/68	.25	.25			3.00	23
1350	6¢ First Stars and							
	Stripes, 1777	07/04/68	.25	.25			3.00	23
1351	6¢ Bunker Hill Flag, 1775	07/04/68	.25	.25			3.00	23
1352	6¢ Grand Union Flag, 1776	07/04/68	.25	.25			3.00	23
1353	6¢ Philadelphia Light Horse							
	Flag, 1775	07/04/68	.25	.25			3.00	23
1354	6¢ First Navy Jack, 1775	07/04/68	.25	.25			3.00	23
a	Strip of 10, #1345-54		2.75	3.25	6.00	(20)	12.50	

	Issues of 1968		Un	U	PB	#	FDC	Q(M)
	Perf. 12							
1355	6¢ Walt Disney	09/11/68	.30	.20	1.40	(4)	25.00	153
a	Ocher omitted		600.00	—				
b	Vertical pair, imperf. horizontally		700.00					
c	Imperf., pair		600.00					
d	Black omitted		1,500.00					
e	Horizontal pair, imperf. between		4,750.00					
f	Blue omitted		1,750.00					
g	Tagging omitted		15.00	—				
	Perf. 11							
1356	6¢ Father Marquette	09/20/68	.20	.20	.60	(4)	1.00	133
	American Folklore Issue							
1357	6¢ Pennsylvania Rifle, Powder Horn, Tomahawk, Pipe and Knife	09/26/68	.20	.20	.50	(4)	1.25	130
1358	6¢ Arkansas River Navigation	10/01/68	.20	.20	.50	(4)	1.00	132
1359	6¢ Leif Erikson	10/09/68	.20	.20	.50	(4)	1.00	129
	Perf. 11 x 10.5							
1360	6¢ Cherokee Strip	10/15/68	.20	.20	.60	(4)	1.00	125
a	Tagging omitted		6.00	—				
	Perf. 11							
1361	6¢ John Trumbull	10/18/68	.20	.20	.60	(4)	2.00	128
1362	6¢ Waterfowl Conservation	10/24/68	.20	.20	.65	(4)	1.25	142
a	Vertical pair, imperf. between		525.00	—				
b	Red and dark blue omitted		900.00					
	Christmas Issue							
1363	6¢ Angel Gabriel, from "The Annunciation," by Jan Van Eyck	11/01/68	.20	.20	2.00	(10)	1.25	1,411
a	Untagged	11/02/68	.20	.20	2.00	(10)	10.00	
b	Imperf., pair (tagged)		225.00					
c	Light yellow omitted		65.00					
d	Imperf., pair (untagged)		290.00					
1364	6¢ American Indian	11/04/68	.20	.20	.70	(4)	1.25	125
	Issues of 1969, Beautification of America Issue							
1365	6¢ Capitol, Azaleas and Tulips	01/16/69	.25	.20			1.00	48
1366	6¢ Washington Monument, Potomac River and Daffodils	01/16/69	.25	.20			1.00	48
1367	6¢ Poppies and Lupines along Highway	01/16/69	.25	.20			1.00	48
1368	6¢ Blooming Crabapple Trees Lining Avenue	01/16/69	.25	.20			1.00	48
a	Block of 4, #1365-68		1.00	1.75	1.25	(4)	4.00	
1369	6¢ American Legion	03/15/69	.20	.20	.45	(4)	1.00	149
	American Folklore Issue							
1370	6¢ "July Fourth" by Grandma Moses	05/01/69	.20	.20	.50	(4)	1.10	139
a	Horizontal pair, imperf. between		225.00	—				
b	Black and Prussian blue omitted		800.00					
c	Tagging omitted		7.50	—				
1371	6¢ Apollo 8	05/05/69	.20	.20	.65	(4)	2.25	187
1372	6¢ W.C. Handy	05/17/69	.20	.20	.65	(4)	2.25	126
a	Tagging omitted		7.50	—				
1373	6¢ California Settlement	07/16/69	.20	.20	.45	(4)	1.00	144
1374	6¢ John Wesley Powell	08/01/69	.20	.20	.60	(4)	1.00	136
a	Tagging omitted		7.50	—				
1375	6¢ Alabama Statehood	08/02/69	.20	.20	.60	(4)	1.00	151

1356

1357

1355

1358

1360

1361

1359

1365

1366

1362

1363

1364

1367

1368

1368a

1372

1369

1370

1371

1376   **1377**

1378   **1379**   **1379a**

1380

1381   **1382**

1383

1384

1384 Precancel

1385

1386

1387   **1388**

1391

1389   **1390**   **1390a**

1392

	Issues of 1969		Un	U	PB	#	FDC	Q(M)
	Botanical Congress Issue, Perf. 11							
1376	6¢ Douglas Fir (Northwest)	08/23/69	.35	.20			1.50	40
1377	6¢ Lady's Slipper (Northeast)	08/23/69	.35	.20			1.50	40
1378	6¢ Ocotillo (Southwest)	08/23/69	.35	.20			1.50	40
1379	6¢ Franklinia (Southeast)	08/23/69	.35	.20			1.50	40
a	Block of 4, #1376-79		1.50	2.50	1.75	(4)	5.00	
	Perf. 10.5 x 11							
1380	6¢ Dartmouth College Case	09/22/69	.20	.20	.50	(4)	1.00	130
	Perf. 11							
1381	6¢ Professional Baseball	09/24/69	.65	.20	2.90	(4)	12.00	131
a	Black omitted		1,100.00					
1382	6¢ Intercollegiate Football	09/26/69	.20	.20	1.00	(4)	6.50	139
1383	6¢ Dwight D. Eisenhower	10/14/69	.20	.20	.50	(4)	1.00	151
	Christmas Issue, Perf. 11 x 10.5							
1384	6¢ Winter Sunday in Norway, Maine	11/03/69	.20	.20	1.40	(10)	1.25	1,710
	Precanceled		.50	.20				
b	Imperf., pair		1,000.00					
c	Light green omitted		22.50					
d	Light green and yellow omitted		950.00	—				
e	Yellow omitted		2,250.00					
f	Tagging omitted		5.00	—				
	Precanceled versions issued on an experimental basis in four cities whose names appear on the stamps: Atlanta, GA; Baltimore, MD; Memphis, TN; and New Haven, CT.							
	Perf. 11							
1385	6¢ Hope for the Crippled	11/20/69	.20	.20	.50	(4)	1.25	128
1386	6¢ William M. Harnett	12/03/69	.20	.20	.55	(4)	1.00	146
	Issues of 1970, Natural History Issue							
1387	6¢ American Bald Eagle	05/06/70	.20	.20			1.50	50
1388	6¢ African Elephant Herd	05/06/70	.20	.20			1.50	50
1389	6¢ Tlingit Chief in Haida Ceremonial Canoe	05/06/70	.20	.20			1.50	50
1390	6¢ Brontosaurus, Stegosaurus and Allosaurus from Jurassic Period	05/06/70	.20	.20			1.50	50
a	Block of 4, #1387-90		.55	.80	.70	(4)	4.00	
1391	6¢ Maine Statehood	07/09/70	.20	.20	.60	(4)	2.00	172
	Perf. 11 x 10.5							
1392	6¢ Wildlife Conservation	07/20/70	.20	.20	.50	(4)	1.00	142

	Issues of 1970-1974		Un	U	PB/LP	#	FDC	Q(M)
1393	6¢ Dwight D. Eisenhower	08/06/70	.20	.20	.45	(4)	1.00	
a	Booklet pane of 8		1.50	.75			3.00	
b	Booklet pane of 5 + label		1.50	.75			1.50	
c	Untagged (Bureau precanceled)		12.75	3.00	175.00	(4)		
	Perf. 10.5 x 11							
1393D	7¢ Benjamin Franklin	10/20/72	.20	.20	.60	(4)	1.00	
e	Untagged (Bureau precanceled)		4.25	1.00	52.50	(4)		
f	Tagging omitted		4.00	—				
	Perf. 11							
1394	8¢ Eisenhower	05/10/71	.20	.20	.60	(4)	1.00	
	Pair with full vertical gutter between		—					
a	Tagging omitted		4.00	—				
	Perf. 11 x 10.5							
1395	8¢ deep claret Eisenhower							
	1394), Single from booklet		.20	.20			1.00	
a	Booklet pane of 8	05/10/71	1.80	1.25			2.50	
b	Booklet pane of 6	05/10/71	1.25	1.10			2.50	
c	Booklet pane of 4 + 2							
	labels	01/28/72	1.65	1.00			2.25	
d	Booklet pane of 7 +							
	label	01/28/72	1.90	1.10			2.25	
1396	8¢ U.S. Postal Service	07/01/71	.20	.20	2.00	(12)	1.00	
1397	14¢ Fiorello H. LaGuardia	04/24/72	.25	.20	1.15	(4)	1.00	
a	Untagged (Bureau precanceled)		145.00	17.50				
1398	16¢ Ernie Pyle	05/07/71	.30	.20	1.25	(4)	1.50	
a	Untagged (Bureau precanceled)		22.50	5.00	95.00	(4)		
1399	18¢ Dr. Elizabeth Blackwell	01/23/74	.35	.20	1.50	(4)	1.25	
1400	21¢ Amadeo P. Giannini	06/27/73	.40	.20	1.65	(4)	1.50	
	Coil Stamps, Perf. 10 Vertically							
1401	6¢ dark blue gray Eisenhower							
	(1393)	08/06/70	.20	.20	.50	(2)	1.00	
a	Untagged (Bureau precanceled)		19.50	3.00	525.00	(2)		
b	Imperf., pair		2,000.00		—	(2)		
1402	8¢ deep claret Eisenhower							
	(1394)	05/10/71	.20	.20	.60	(2)	1.00	
a	Imperf., pair		45.00		70.00	(2)		
b	Untagged (Bureau precanceled)		6.75	.75	185.00	(2)		
c	Pair, imperf. between		6,250.00					
1403-04	Not assigned							
	Issues of 1970, Perf. 11							
1405	6¢ Edgar Lee Masters	08/22/70	.20	.20	.50	(4)	1.00	138
a	Tagging omitted		30.00	—				
1406	6¢ Woman Suffrage	08/26/70	.20	.20	.50	(4)	1.00	135
1407	6¢ South Carolina Settlement	09/12/70	.20	.20	.55	(4)	1.00	136
1408	6¢ Stone Mountain Memorial	09/19/70	.20	.20	.50	(4)	1.00	133
1409	6¢ Ft. Snelling	10/17/70	.20	.20	.50	(4)	1.00	135
	Anti-Pollution Issue, Perf. 11 x 10.5							
1410	6¢ Save Our Soil							
	Globe and Wheat Field	10/28/70	.25	.20			1.25	40
1411	6¢ Save Our Cities							
	Globe and City Playground	10/28/70	.25	.20			1.25	40
1412	6¢ Save Our Water							
	Globe and Bluegill Fish	10/28/70	.25	.20			1.25	40
1413	6¢ Save Our Air							
	Globe and Seagull	10/28/70	.25	.20			1.25	40
a	Block of 4, #1410-13		1.10	1.50	2.25	(10)	4.00	

1393

1393D

1394

1396

1397

1398

1399

1400

1405

1406

1407

1408

1409

1410   1411

1412   1413   1413a

1414

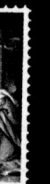

1414a

1415   1416

1417   1418   1418b

1419

1420

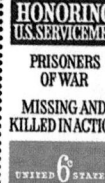

1421   1422   1422a

1423

1424

1425

1426

1427   1428

1429   1430   1430a

Issues of 1970		Un	U	PB	#	FDC	Q(M)
Christmas Issue, Perf. 10.5 x 11							
1414 6¢ Nativity, by Lorenzo Lotto	11/05/70	.20	.20	1.10	(8)	1.25	639*
a	Precanceled	.20	.20	1.90	(8)	7.50	358
b	Black omitted	525.00					
c	As "a," blue omitted	1,500.00					
d	Type II	.20	.20	2.75	(8)		
e	Type II, precanceled	.25	.20	4.00	(8)		

#1414a-18a were furnished to 68 cities. Unused prices are for copies with gum and used prices are for copies with or without gum but with an additional cancellation.

*Includes #1414a.

		Un	U	PB	#	FDC	Q(M)
Perf. 11 x 10.5							
1415 6¢ Tin and Cast-iron Locomotive	11/05/70	.30	.20			1.50	122
a	Precanceled	.75	.20				110
b	Black omitted	2,500.00					
1416 6¢ Toy Horse on Wheels	11/05/70	.30	.20			1.50	122
a	Precanceled	.75	.20				110
b	Black omitted	2,500.00					
c	Imperf., pair		4,000.00				
1417 6¢ Mechanical Tricycle	11/05/70	.30	.20			1.50	122
a	Precanceled	.75	.20				110
b	Black omitted	2,500.00					
1418 6¢ Doll Carriage	11/05/70	.30	.20			1.50	122
a	Precanceled	.75	.20				110
b	Block of 4, #1415-18	1.25	1.75	3.00	(8)	5.50	
c	Block of 4, #1415a-18a	3.25	3.75	6.25	(8)	15.00	
d	Black omitted	2,500.00					
Perf. 11							
1419 6¢ United Nations	11/20/70	.20	.20	.50	(4)	1.00	128
	Pair with full horizontal gutter between	—					
1420 6¢ Landing of the Pilgrims	11/21/70	.20	.20	.50	(4)	1.00	130
a	Orange and yellow omitted	900.00					
Disabled American Veterans and Servicemen Issue							
1421 6¢ Disabled American Veterans Emblem	11/24/70	.20	.20			2.00	67
1422 6¢ U.S. Servicemen	11/24/70	.20	.20			2.00	67
a	Attached pair, #1421-22	.30	.40	1.00	(4)	3.00	
Issues of 1971							
1423 6¢ American Wool Industry	01/19/71	.20	.20	.50	(4)	1.00	136
a	Tagging omitted	11.00	—				
1424 6¢ Gen. Douglas MacArthur	01/26/71	.20	.20	.60	(4)	1.50	135
1425 6¢ Blood Donor	03/12/71	.20	.20	.50	(4)	1.00	131
a	Tagging omitted	11.00	—				
Perf. 11 x 10.5							
1426 8¢ Missouri Statehood	05/08/71	.20	.20	2.00	(12)	1.00	161
Wildlife Conservation Issue, Perf. 11							
1427 8¢ Trout	06/12/71	.20	.20			1.25	44
1428 8¢ Alligator	06/12/71	.20	.20			1.25	44
1429 8¢ Polar Bear and Cubs	06/12/71	.20	.20			1.25	44
1430 8¢ California Condor	06/12/71	.20	.20			1.25	44
a	Block of 4, #1427-30	.80	1.00	.90	(4)	3.00	
b	As "a," light green and dark green omitted from #1427-28	4,500.00					
c	As "a," red omitted from #1427, 1429-30	7,500.00					

1971

	Issues of 1971		Un	U	PB	#	FDC	Q(M)
1431	8¢ Antarctic Treaty	06/23/71	.20	.20	.65	(4)	1.00	139
a	Tagging omitted		9.00					
	American Revolution Bicentennial Issue							
1432	8¢ Bicentennial Commission							
	Emblem	07/04/71	.20	.20	.85	(4)	1.00	138
a	Gray and black omitted		500.00					
b	Gray omitted		900.00					
1433	8¢ John Sloan	08/02/71	.20	.20	.70	(4)	1.00	152
a	Tagging omitted		—					
	Space Achievement Decade Issue							
1434	8¢ Earth, Sun and Landing							
	Craft on Moon	08/02/71	.20	.20				88
a	Tagging omitted		30.00				2.00	
1435	8¢ Lunar Rover and							
	Astronauts	08/02/71	.20	.20	.65	(4)		88
a	Tagging omitted		30.00					
b	Pair #1434-1435		.40	.45				
c	As "b", tagging omitted		—					
d	As "b", blue & red omitted		1,500.00					
1436	8¢ Emily Dickinson	08/28/71	.20	.20	.65	(4)	1.00	143
a	Black and olive omitted		700.00					
b	Pale rose omitted		7,500.00					
1437	8¢ San Juan, Puerto Rico	09/12/71	.20	.20	.65	(4)	1.00	149
a	Tagging omitted		9.00					
	Perf. 10.5 x 11							
1438	8¢ Prevent Drug Abuse	10/04/71	.20	.20	1.00	(6)	1.00	139
1439	8¢ CARE	10/27/71	.20	.20	1.25	(8)	1.00	131
a	Black omitted		4,750.00					
b	Tagging omitted		5.00					
	Historic Preservation Issue, Perf. 11							
1440	8¢ Decatur House,							
	Washington, D.C.	10/29/71	.20	.20			1.25	43
1441	8¢ Whaling Ship *Charles W. Morgan*,							
	Mystic, Connecticut	10/29/71	.20	.20			1.25	43
1442	8¢ Cable Car, San Francisco	10/29/71	.20	.20			1.25	43
1443	8¢ San Xavier del Bac Mission,							
	Tucson, Arizona	10/29/71	.20	.20			1.25	43
a	Block of 4, #1440-43		.75	1.00	.90	(4)	3.00	
b	As "a," black brown omitted		2,100.00					
c	As "a," ocher omitted		—					
d	As "a," tagging omitted		65.00					
	Christmas Issue, Perf. 10.5 x 11							
1444	8¢ Adoration of the Shepherds,							
	by Giorgione	11/10/71	.20	.20	1.80	(12)	1.25	1,074
a	Gold omitted		500.00					
1445	8¢ Partridge in a Pear Tree	11/10/71	.20	.20	1.80	(12)	1.25	980

1431

1432

1433

1434   1435   1435b

1436

1437

1438

1439

1440   1441

1442   1443   1443a

1444

1445

1446   **1447**

1448   **1449**

1452

1450   **1451**   **1451a**

1454

1453

1456   **1457**

1455

1458   **1459**   **1459a**

1460   **1461**   **1462**

1463

Issues of 1972		Un	U	PB	#	FDC	Q(M)
1446	8¢ Sidney Lanier	02/03/72	.20	.20	.65	(4)	1.00	137
a	Tagging omitted		15.00					
	Perf. 10.5 x 11							
1447	8¢ Peace Corps	02/11/72	.20	.20	1.00	(6)	1.00	150
a	Tagging omitted		5.00					
	National Parks Centennial Issue (See also #C84)							
1448	2¢ Ship at Sea	04/05/72	.20	.20				43
1449	2¢ Cape Hatteras Lighthouse	04/05/72	.20	.20				43
1450	2¢ Laughing Gulls on Driftwood	04/05/72	.20	.20				43
1451	2¢ Laughing Gulls and Dune	04/05/72	.20	.20				43
a	Block of 4, #1448-51		.25	.45	.50	(4)	2.00	
b	As "a," black omitted		2,250.00					
1452	6¢ Performance at Wolf Trap Farm, Shouse Pavilion	06/26/72	.20	.20	.55	(4)	1.00	104
a	Tagging omitted		11.00					
1453	8¢ Old Faithful, Yellowstone	03/01/72	.20	.20	.70	(4)	1.00	164
a	Tagging omitted		15.00					
1454	15¢ View of Mount McKinley in Alaska	07/28/72	.30	.20	1.30	(4)	1.00	54

Note: Beginning with this National Parks Centennial issue, the USPS began to offer stamp collectors first day cancellations affixed to 8" x 101/2" souvenir pages. The pages are similar to the stamp announcements that have appeared on Post Office bulletin boards beginning with Scott #1132. See "Souvenir Pages" listed in the back of this book (see Table of Contents)

1455	8¢ Family Planning	03/18/72	.20	.20	.65	(4)	1.00	153
a	Yellow omitted		1,000.00					
c	Dark brown missing		9,500.00					
d	Tagging omitted		—					
	American Bicentennial Issue, Perf. 11 x 10.5							
1456	8¢ Glass Blower	07/04/72	.20	.20			1.00	50
1457	8¢ Silversmith	07/04/72	.20	.20			1.00	50
1458	8¢ Wigmaker	07/04/72	.20	.20			1.00	50
1459	8¢ Hatter	07/04/72	.20	.20			1.00	50
a	Block of 4, #1456-59		.65	.90	.80	(4)	2.50	
	Olympic Games Issue, (See also #C85)							
1460	6¢ Bicycling and Olympic Rings	08/17/72	.20	.20	1.25	(10)	1.00	67
	Cylinder flaw (broken red ring)		10.00					
1461	8¢ Bobsledding and Olympic Rings	08/17/72	.20	.20	1.60	(10)	1.00	180
a	Tagging omitted		7.50					
1462	15¢ Running and Olympic Rings	08/17/72	.30	.20	3.00	(10)	1.00	46
1463	8¢ Parent Teachers Association	09/15/72	.20	.20	.65	(4)	1.00	180

Issues of 1972		Un	U	PB	#	FDC	Q(M)
Wildlife Conservation Issue, Perf. 11							
1464 8¢ Fur Seals	09/20/72	.20	.20			1.50	50
1465 8¢ Cardinal	09/20/72	.20	.20			1.50	50
1466 8¢ Brown Pelican	09/20/72	.20	.20			1.50	50
1467 8¢ Bighorn Sheep	09/20/72	.20	.20			1.50	50
a Block of 4, #1464-67		.65	.90	.75	(4)	3.00	
b As "a," brown omitted		4,000.00					
c As "a," green and blue omitted		4,500.00					
d As "a," red & brown omitted		4,000.00					

Note: With this Wildlife Conservation issue the USPS introduced the "American Commemorative Series" Stamp Panels. Each panel contains a block of four or more mint stamps with text and background illustrations. See pages 493-497 for a complete listing.

		Un	U	PB	#	FDC	Q(M)
1468 8¢ Mail Order Business	09/27/72	.20	.20	1.75	(12)	1.00	185
Perf. 10.5 x 11							
1469 8¢ Osteopathic Medicine	10/09/72	.20	.20	1.00	(6)	1.50	162
American Folklore Issue, Perf. 11							
1470 8¢ Tom Sawyer Whitewashing a Fence, by Norman Rockwell	10/13/72	.20	.20	.65	(4)	1.50	163
a Horizontal pair, imperf. between		4,500.00					
b Red and black omitted		1,700.00					
c Yellow and tan omitted		2,400.00					
Christmas Issue, Perf. 10.5 x 11							
1471 8¢ Angels from "Mary, Queen of Heaven" by the Master of the St. Lucy Legend	11/09/72	.20	.20	1.75	(12)	1.00	1,003
a Pink omitted		140.00					
b Black omitted		4,000.00					
1472 8¢ Santa Claus	11/09/72	.20	.20	1.75	(12)	1.00	1,017
Perf. 11							
1473 8¢ Pharmacy	11/10/72	.20	.20	.65	(4)	8.00	166
a Blue and orange omitted		750.00					
b Blue omitted		2,100.00					
c Orange omitted		2,100.00					
1474 8¢ Stamp Collecting	11/17/72	.20	.20	.65	(4)	1.25	167
a Black omitted		575.00					
Issues of 1973, Perf. 11 x 10.5							
1475 8¢ Love	01/26/73	.20	.20	1.00	(6)	2.00	320
American Bicentennial Issue, Perf. 11							
1476 8¢ Printer and Patriots Examining Pamphlet	02/16/73	.20	.20	.65	(4)	1.00	166
1477 8¢ Posting a Broadside	04/13/73	.20	.20	.65	(4)	1.00	163
Pair with full horizontal gutter between		—					
1478 8¢ Postrider	06/22/73	.20	.20	.65	(4)	1.00	159
1479 8¢ Drummer	09/28/73	.20	.20	.65	(4)	1.00	147
Boston Tea Party							
1480 8¢ British Merchantman	07/04/73	.20	.20			1.00	49
1481 8¢ British Three-Master	07/04/73	.20	.20			1.00	49
1482 8¢ Boats and Ship's Hull	07/04/73	.20	.20			1.00	49
1483 8¢ Boat and Dock	07/04/73	.20	.20			1.00	49
a Block of 4, #1480-83		.65	.90	.75	(4)	3.00	
b As "a," blk. (engraved) omitted		1,400.00					
c As "a," blk. (lithographed) omitted		1,200.00					

1464 1465

1468

1466 1467 1467a

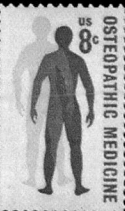

1469 1470

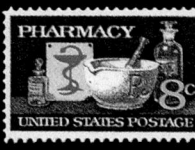

1471 1472

1473

1474

1475 1476 1477

1478 1479

1480

1481

1482 1483

1483a

1484   **1485**

1486   **1487**

1488

1489   **1490**   **1491**   **1492**   **1493**

Nearly 27 billion U.S. stamps are sold yearly to carry your letters to every corner of the world.	Mail is picked up from nearly a third of a million local collection boxes, as well as your mailbox.	More than 87 billion letters and packages are handled yearly—almost 300 million every delivery day.	The People in your Postal Service handle and deliver more than 500 million packages yearly.	Thousands of machines, buildings, and vehicles must be operated and maintained to keep your mail moving.
People Serving You	People Serving You	People Serving You	People Serving You	People Serving You

1494   **1495**   **1496**   **1497**   **1498**

The skill of sorting mail manually is still vital to delivery of your mail.	Employees use modern, high-speed equipment to sort and process huge volumes of mail in central locations.	Thirteen billion pounds of mail are handled yearly by postal employees as they speed your letters and packages.	Our customers include 54 million urban and 12 million rural families, plus 9 million businesses.	Employees cover 4 million miles each delivery day to bring mail to your home or business.
People Serving You	People Serving You	People Serving You	People Serving You	People Serving You

Issues of 1973		Un	U	PB	#	FDC	Q(M)
American Arts Issue, Perf. 11							
1484 8¢ George Gershwin and Scene							
from "Porgy and Bess"	02/28/73	.20	.20	1.75	(12)	1.00	139
a Vertical pair, imperf. horizontally		225.00					
1485 8¢ Robinson Jeffers, Man and Children							
of Carmel with Burro	08/13/73	.20	.20	1.75	(12)	1.00	128
a Vertical pair, imperf. horizontally		250.00					
1486 8¢ Henry Ossawa Tanner,							
Palette and Rainbow	09/10/73	.20	.20	1.75	(12)	2.50	146
1487 8¢ Willa Cather, Pioneer Family							
and Covered Wagon	09/20/73	.20	.20	1.75	(12)	1.00	140
a Vertical pair, imperf. horizontally		275.00					
1488 8¢ Nicolaus Copernicus	04/23/73	.20	.20	.65	(4)	1.25	159
a Orange omitted		1,000.00					
b Black omitted		900.00					
Postal Service Employees Issue, Perf. 10.5 x 11							
1489 8¢ Stamp Counter	04/30/73	.20	.20			1.00	49
1490 8¢ Mail Collection	04/30/73	.20	.20			1.00	49
1491 8¢ Letter Facing on Conveyor	04/30/73	.20	.20			1.00	49
1492 8¢ Parcel Post Sorting	04/30/73	.20	.20			1.00	49
1493 8¢ Mail Canceling	04/30/73	.20	.20			1.00	49
1494 8¢ Manual Letter Routing	04/30/73	.20	.20			1.00	49
1495 8¢ Electronic Letter Routing	04/30/73	.20	.20			1.00	49
1496 8¢ Loading Mail on Truck	04/30/73	.20	.20			1.00	49
1497 8¢ Mail Carrier	04/30/73	.20	.20			1.00	49
1498 8¢ Rural Mail Delivery	04/30/73	.20	.20			1.00	49
a Strip of 10, #1489-98		1.75	2.00	3.25	(20)	5.00	
b As "a," tagging omitted		—					

#1489-98 were the first United States postage stamps to have printing on the back.

(See also 1559-62.)

DOROTHY PARKER

(1893-1967)

DOROTHY PARKER, who wrote short stories, poems, plays, essays, book reviews, and screenplays, found writing difficult. "I can't write five words but that I change seven," she admitted. A major figure at the Algonquin Round Table, an intellectual and literary group that met daily at New York's Algonquin Hotel in the 1920s, Parker was noted for her sharp humor and wit. The daughter of a Jewish merchant and a Scottish schoolteacher, she considered herself an outsider with a "mongrel" background. Her writing often addressed the pretensions and inequities of society. She embraced many radical causes including the Sacco and Vanzetti trial during the 1920s and was called before the House Un-American Activities Committee in the 1950s. When she died, she left her papers to the National

Association for the Advancement of Colored People. A popular and widely published writer and one of the most successful women writers of her time, she perhaps is best remembered for her oft-quoted, "Men seldom make passes/At girls who wear glasses." Parker was honored by the Postal Service in 1992 as a Literary Arts issue. ❑

1973-1974

	Issues of 1973		Un	U	PB	#	FDC	Q(M)
	Perf. 11							
1499	8¢ Harry S. Truman	05/08/73	.20	.20	.75	(4)	1.25	157
	Progress in Electronics Issue, (See also #C86)							
1500	6¢ Marconi's Spark Coil and Gap	07/10/73	.20	.20	.55	(4)	1.00	53
1501	8¢ Transistors and Printed Circuit Board	07/10/73	.20	.20	.70	(4)	1.00	160
a	Black omitted		450.00					
b	Tan and lilac omitted		1,100.00					
1502	15¢ Microphone, Speaker, Vacuum Tube, TV Camera Tube	07/10/73	.30	.20	1.30	(4)	1.00	39
a	Black omitted		1,350.00					
1503	8¢ Lyndon B. Johnson	08/27/73	.20	.20	1.90	(12)	1.00	153
a	Horizontal pair, imperf. vertically		350.00					
	Issues of 1973-1974, Rural America Issue							
1504	8¢ Angus and Longhorn Cattle, by F.C. Murphy	10/05/73	.20	.20	.65	(4)	1.00	146
a	Green and red brown omitted		950.00					
b	Vertical pair, imperf. between		—					
1505	10¢ Chautauqua Tent and Buggies	08/06/74	.20	.20	.85	(4)	1.00	151
1506	10¢ Wheat Fields and Train	08/16/74	.20	.20	.85	(4)	1.00	141
a	Black and blue omitted		700.00					
	Issues of 1973, Christmas Issue, Perf. 10.5 x 11							
1507	8¢ Small Cowper Madonna, by Raphael	11/07/73	.20	.20	1.75	(12)	1.00	885
	Pair with full vertical gutter between		—					
1508	8¢ Christmas Tree in Needlepoint	11/07/73	.20	.20	1.75	(12)	1.00	940
	Pair with full horizontal gutter between		—					
a	Vertical pair, imperf. between		300.00					
	Issues of 1973-1974, Perf. 11 x 10.5							
1509	10¢ 50-Star and 13-Star Flags	12/08/73	.20	.20	4.25	(20)	1.00	
a	Horizontal pair, imperf. between		50.00	—				
b	Blue omitted		175.00	—				
c	Imperf., pair		900.00					
d	Horizontal pair, imperf. vertically		1,000.00					
e	Tagging omitted		9.00					
1510	10¢ Jefferson Memorial	12/14/73	.20	.20	.85	(4)	1.00	
a	Untagged (Bureau precanceled)		4.00	1.00	50.00	(4)		
b	Booklet pane of 5 + label		1.65	.90			2.25	
c	Booklet pane of 8		1.65	1.00			2.50	
d	Booklet pane of 6	08/05/74	5.25	1.75			3.00	
e	Vertical pair, imperf. horizontally		525.00					
f	Vertical pair, imperf. between		700.00					
g	Tagging omitted		5.00					

1499

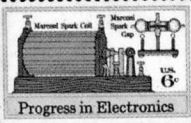

1500

1501

1502

1503

1504

1505

1506

1507

1508

1509

1510

1974

1511

1518

1525

1526

1527

1528

1529

1530   **1531**   **1532**   **1533**

1537a

1534   **1535**   **1536**   **1537**

Issues of 1973-1974		Un	U	PB/LP	#	FDC	Q(M)
1511 10¢ ZIP Code	01/04/74	.20	.20	1.75	(8)	1.00	
Pair with full horizontal gutter between		—					
a Yellow omitted		65.00					
1512-17 Not assigned							
Coil Stamps, Perf. 10 Vertically							
1518 6.3¢ Liberty Bell	10/01/74	.20	.20	.80	(2)	1.00	
a Untagged (Bureau precanceled)		.35	.20	1.65	(2)		
b Imperf., pair		210.00		550.00	(2)		
c As "a," imperf., pair			100.00	250.00	(2)		
1519 10¢ red and blue Flags (1509)	12/08/73	.20	.20			1.00	
a Imperf., pair		37.50					
1520 10¢ blue Jefferson Memorial							
(1510)	12/14/73	.25	.20	.75	(2)	1.00	
a Untagged (Bureau precanceled)		5.50	1.25	185.00	(2)		
b Imperf., pair		40.00		70.00	(2)		
1521-24 Not assigned							
Issues of 1974, Perf. 11							
1525 10¢ Veterans of Foreign Wars	03/11/74	.20	.20	.85	(4)	1.25	149
Perf. 10.5 x 11							
1526 10¢ Robert Frost	03/26/74	.20	.20	.85	(4)	1.00	145
Perf. 11							
1527 10¢ Expo '74 World's Fair	04/18/74	.20	.20	2.50	(12)	1.00	135
Perf. 11 x 10.5							
1528 10¢ Horse Racing	05/04/74	.25	.20	3.50	(12)	3.00	156
a Blue omitted		875.00					
b Red omitted		—					
Perf. 11							
1529 10¢ Skylab	05/14/74	.20	.20	.85	(4)	1.50	164
a Vertical pair, imperf. between		—					
Universal Postal Union Issue							
1530 10¢ Michelangelo, from "School							
of Athens," by Raphael	06/06/74	.20	.20			1.00	24
1531 10¢ "Five Feminine Virtues,"							
by Hokusai	06/06/74	.20	.20			1.00	24
1532 10¢ "Old Scraps," by							
John Fredrick Peto	06/06/74	.20	.20			1.00	24
1533 10¢ "The Lovely Reader,"							
by Jean Etienne Liotard	06/06/74	.20	.20			1.00	24
1534 10¢ "Lady Writing Letter,"							
by Gerard Terborch	06/06/74	.20	.20			1.00	24
1535 10¢ Inkwell and Quill, from							
"Boy with a Top," by Jean-Baptiste							
Simeon Chardin	06/06/74	.20	.20			1.00	24
1536 10¢ Mrs. John Douglas,							
by Thomas Gainsborough	06/06/74	.20	.20			1.00	24
1537 10¢ Don Antonio Noriega,							
by Francisco de Goya	06/06/74	.20	.20			1.00	24
a Block of 8, #1530-37		1.75	1.60	3.50	(16)	4.00	
b As "a," imperf. vertically		7,000.00					

	Issues of 1974		Un	U	PB	#	FDC	Q(M)
	Mineral Heritage Issue, Perf. 11							
1538	10¢ Petrified Wood	06/13/74	.20	.20			1.00	42
a	Light blue and yellow omitted		—					
1539	10¢ Tourmaline	06/13/74	.20	.20			1.00	42
a	Light blue omitted		—					
b	Black and purple omitted		—					
1540	10¢ Amethyst	06/13/74	.20	.20			1.00	42
a	Light blue and yellow omitted		—					
1541	10¢ Rhodochrosite	06/13/74	.20	.20			1.00	42
a	Block of 4, #1538-41		.80	.90	.90	(4)	2.75	
b	As "a," light blue and							
	yellow omitted		1,900.00					
c	Light blue omitted		—					
d	Black and red omitted		—					
1542	10¢ First Kentucky Settlement-							
	Ft. Harrod	06/15/74	.20	.20	.85	(4)	1.00	156
a	Dull black omitted		750.00					
b	Green, black and blue omitted		3,000.00					
c	Green omitted		—					
d	Green and black omitted		—					
e	Tagging omitted		—					
	American Bicentennial Issue, First Continental Congress							
1543	10¢ Carpenters' Hall	07/04/74	.20	.20			1.00	49
1544	10¢ "We Ask but for Peace,							
	Liberty and Safety"	07/04/74	.20	.20			1.00	49
1545	10¢ "Deriving Their Just Powers							
	from the Consent of							
	the Governed"	07/04/74	.20	.20			1.00	49
1546	10¢ Independence Hall	07/04/74	.20	.20			1.00	49
a	Block of 4, #1543-46		.80	.90	.90	(4)	2.75	
1547	10¢ Energy Conservation	09/23/74	.20	.20	.85	(4)	1.00	149
a	Blue and orange omitted		850.00					
b	Orange and green omitted		600.00					
c	Green omitted		825.00					
	American Folklore Issue							
1548	10¢ Headless Horseman							
	and Ichabod Crane	10/10/74	.20	.20	.85	(4)	1.50	157
1549	10¢ Retarded Children	10/12/74	.20	.20	.85	(4)	1.00	150
a	Tagging omitted		7.50					
	Christmas Issue, Perf. 10.5 x 11							
1550	10¢ Angel from Perussis							
	Altarpiece	10/23/74	.20	.20	2.10	(10)	1.00	835
	Perf. 11 x 10.5							
1551	10¢ "The Road-Winter," by							
	Currier and Ives	10/23/74	.20	.20	2.50	(12)	1.00	883
a	Buff omitted		35.00					
	Precanceled Self-Adhesive, Imperf.							
1552	10¢ Dove Weather Vane atop							
	Mount Vernon	11/15/74	.20	.20	4.25	(20)	1.50	213
	Issues of 1975, American Arts Issue, Perf. 10.5 x 11							
1553	10¢ Benjamin West,							
	Self-Portrait	02/10/75	.20	.20	2.10	(10)	1.00	157
	Perf. 11							
1554	10¢ Paul Laurence Dunbar							
	and Lamp	05/01/75	.20	.20	2.10	(10)	1.50	146
a	Imperf., pair		1,300.00					
1555	10¢ D.W. Griffith and							
	Motion-Picture Camera	05/27/75	.20	.20	.85	(4)	1.00	149
a	Brown omitted		625.00					

1538

1539

1540

1541 1541a

1542

1543 1544

1545 1546 1546a

1547

1548

Retarded Children Can Be Helped

1549

1550

1551

1552

1553

1554

1555

1975

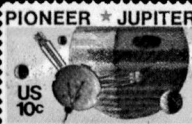

1556

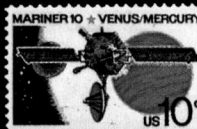

1557

1558

1559

1560

1561

YOUTHFUL HEROINE
On the dark night of April 26, 1777, 16-year-old Sybil Ludington rode her horse "Star" alone through the Connecticut countryside rallying her father's militia to repel a raid by the British on Danbury.

GALLANT SOLDIER
The conspicuously courageous actions of black foot soldier Salem Poor at the Battle of Bunker Hill on June 17, 1775, earned him citations for his bravery and leadership ability.

FINANCIAL HERO
Businessman and broker Haym Salomon was responsible for raising most of the money needed to finance the American Revolution and later to save the new nation from collapse.

1562

FINANCIAL HERO
Businessman and broker Haym Salomon was responsible for raising most of the money needed to finance the American Revolution and later to save the new nation from collapse.

1563

1564

1565　　**1566**　　**1569**

1567　　**1568**　**1568a**

1570　　　　　　**1570a**

Issues of 1975		Un	U	PB	#	FDC	Q(M)
Space Issues, Perf. 11							
1556 10¢ Pioneer 10 Passing							
Jupiter	02/28/75	.20	.20	.85	(4)	1.25	174
a	Red and yellow omitted	1,400.00					
b	Blue omitted	950.00					
c	Tagging omitted	9.00					
1557 10¢ Mariner 10, Venus							
and Mercury	04/04/75	.20	.20	.85	(4)	1.25	159
a	Red omitted	450.00					
b	Ultramarine and bister omitted	2,000.00					
c	Tagging omitted	9.00					
1558 10¢ Collective Bargaining	03/13/75	.20	.20	1.75	(8)	1.00	153
Imperfs. of #1558 exist from printer's waste							
American Bicentennial Issue Perf. 11 x 10.5							
1559 8¢ Sybil Ludington							
Riding Horse	03/25/75	.20	.20	1.50	(10)	1.00	63
a	Back inscription omitted	210.00					
1560 10¢ Salem Poor Carrying							
Musket	03/25/75	.20	.20	2.10	(10)	1.50	158
a	Back inscription omitted	210.00					
1561 10¢ Haym Salomon							
Figuring Accounts	03/25/75	.20	.20	2.10	(10)	1.00	167
a	Back inscription omitted	210.00					
b	Red omitted	250.00					
1562 18¢ Peter Francisco							
Shouldering Cannon	03/25/75	.35	.20	3.60	(10)	1.00	45
Battle of Lexington & Concord, Perf. 11							
1563 10¢ "Birth of Liberty,"							
by Henry Sandham	04/19/75	.20	.20	2.50	(12)	1.00	144
a	Vertical pair, imperf. horizontally	425.00					
Battle of Bunker Hill							
1564 10¢ "Battle of Bunker							
Hill," by John Trumbull	06/17/75	.20	.20	2.50	(12)	1.00	140
Military Uniforms							
1565 10¢ Soldier with Flintlock							
Musket, Uniform Button	07/04/75	.20	.20			1.00	45
1566 10¢ Sailor with Grappling							
Hook, First Navy Jack, 1775	07/04/75	.20	.20			1.00	45
1567 10¢ Marine with Musket,							
Full-Rigged Ship	07/04/75	.20	.20			1.00	45
1568 10¢ Militiaman with							
Musket, Powder Horn	07/04/75	.20	.20			1.00	45
a	Block of 4, #1565-68	.85	.90	2.50	(12)	2.50	
Apollo Soyuz Space Issue							
1569 10¢ Apollo and Soyuz							
after Link-up and Earth	07/15/75	.20	.20			5.00	81
Pair with full horizontal gutter between		—					
1570 10¢ Spacecraft before Link-up,							
Earth and Project Emblem	07/15/75	.20	.20			3.00	81
a	Attached pair, #1569-70	.45	.40	2.50	(12)		
b	As "a", tagging omitted	30.00	—				
c	As "a," vertical pair,						
	imperf. horizontally	2,150.00					

	Issues of 1975		Un	U	PB	#	FDC	Q(M)
	Perf. 11 x 10.5							
1571	10¢ International Women's Year	08/26/75	.20	.20	1.30	(6)	1.00	146
	Postal Service Bicentennial Issue							
1572	10¢ Stagecoach and							
	Trailer Truck	09/03/75	.20	.20			1.00	42
1573	10¢ Old and New Locomotives	09/03/75	.20	.20			1.00	42
1574	10¢ Early Mail Plane and Jet	09/03/75	.20	.20			1.00	42
1575	10¢ Satellite for Mailgrams	09/03/75	.20	.20			1.00	42
a	Block of 4, #1572-75		.85	.90	2.50	(12)	2.50	
b	As "a," red "10¢" omitted		9,500.00					
	Perf. 11							
1576	10¢ World Peace Through Law	09/29/75	.20	.20	.85	(4)	1.25	147
a	Tagging omitted		8.00					
	Banking and Commerce Issue							
1577	10¢ Engine Turning, Indian Head							
	Penny and Morgan Silver Dollar	10/06/75	.25	.20			1.00	73
1578	10¢ Seated Liberty Quarter, $20							
	Gold Piece and Engine Turning	10/06/75	.25	.20			1.00	73
a	Attached pair, #1577-78		.50	.40	1.20	(4)	1.75	
b	Brown and blue omitted		2,000.00					
c	As "a," brn., blue and yel. omitted		2,500.00					
	Christmas Issue							
1579	(10¢) Madonna and Child,							
	by Domenico Ghirlandaio	10/14/75	.20	.20	2.50	(12)	1.00	739
a	Imperf., pair		90.00					
	Plate flaw ("d" damaged)		5.00	—				
	Perf. 11.2							
1580	(10¢) Christmas Card,							
	by Louis Prang, 1878	10/14/75	.20	.20	2.50	(12)	1.00	879
a	Imperf., pair		90.00					
c	Perf. 10.9		.25	.20	3.50	(12)		
	Perf. 10.5 x 11.3							
1580B	(10¢) Christmas Card,							
	by Louis Prang, 1878		.65	.20	15.00	(12)		
	Issues of 1977-1981, Americana Issue, Perf. 11 x 10.5 (Designs 18.5 x 22.5mm; #1590-90a, 17.5 x 20mm; see also 1606, 1608, 1610-19, 1622-23, 1625, 1811, 1813, 1816)							
1581	1¢ Inkwell & Quill	12/08/77	.20	.20	.25	(4)	1.00	
a	Untagged (Bureau precanceled)		4.50	1.50	22.50	(4)		
d	Tagging omitted		4.50					
1582	2¢ Speaker's Stand	12/08/77	.20	.20	.25	(4)	1.00	
a	Untagged (Bureau precanceled)		4.50	1.50	22.50	(4)		
b	Cream paper, dull gum, *1981*		.20	.20	.25	(4)		
c	Tagging omitted		4.50					
1583	Not assigned							
1584	3¢ Early Ballot Box	12/08/77	.20	.20	.30	(4)	1.00	
a	Untagged (Bureau precanceled)		.75	.50				
b	Tagging omitted		7.50					
1585	4¢ Books, Bookmark, Eyeglasses	12/08/77	.20	.20	.40	(4)	1.00	
a	Untagged (Bureau precanceled)		1.05	.75	13.50	(4)		
1586-89	Not assigned							
	Booklet Stamp							
1590	9¢ Capitol Dome, single (1591)							
	from booklet (1623a)	03/11/77	.45	.20			1.00	
	Booklet Stamp, Perf. 10							
1590A	Single (1591) from booklet (1623c)		20.00	15.00				
	#1590 is on white paper; #1591 is on gray paper.							

1572 **1573**

1571

1574 **1575** **1575a**

1576

1577 **1578** **1578a**

1581 **1582**

1579 **1580**

1584 **1585**

1591

1592

1593

1594

1595

1596

1597

1599

1603

1604

1605

1606

1608

1610

1611

1612

Issues of 1975-1981		Un	U	PB/LP	#	FDC
Americana Issue, Perf. 11 x 10.5						
1591 9¢ Capitol Dome	11/24/75	.20	.20	.85	(4)	1.00
a Untagged (Bureau precanceled)		1.75	1.00	50.00	(4)	
b Tagging omitted		5.00				
1592 10¢ Contemplation of Justice	11/17/77	.20	.20	.90	(4)	1.00
a Untagged (Bureau precanceled)		9.50	5.00	95.00	(4)	
b Tagging omitted		7.50				
1593 11¢ Printing Press	11/13/75	.20	.20	.90	(4)	1.00
a Tagging omitted		4.00				
1594 12¢ Torch, Statue of Liberty	04/08/81	.25	.20	1.60	(4)	1.00
a Tagging omitted		5.00				
1595 13¢ Liberty Bell, single from booklet		.30	.20			1.00
a Booklet pane of 6	10/31/75	2.25	*1.00*			2.00
b Booklet pane of 7 + label		2.25	*1.00*			2.75
c Booklet pane of 8		2.25	*1.00*			2.50
d Booklet pane of 5 + label	04/02/76	1.75	*1.00*			2.25
e Vertical pair, imperf. between		*800.00*				
Perf. 11						
1596 13¢ Eagle and Shield	12/01/75	.25	.20	3.25	(12)	1.00
a Imperf., pair		*50.00*	—			
b Yellow omitted		*160.00*				
d Line perforated		*27.50*	—	375.00	(12)	
1597 15¢ Ft. McHenry Flag	06/30/78	.30	.20	1.90	(6)	1.00
a Imperf., pair		*20.00*				
b Gray omitted		*600.00*				
d Tagging omitted		3.00				
Booklet Stamp, Perf. 11 x 10.5						
1598 15¢ Ft. McHenry Flag (1597), single from booklet		.40	.20			1.00
a Booklet pane of 8	06/30/78	4.25	*.80*			2.50
1599 16¢ Head, Statue of Liberty	03/31/78	.35	.20	1.90	(4)	1.00
1600-02 Not assigned						
1603 24¢ Old North Church	11/14/75	.50	.20	2.25	(4)	1.00
a Tagging omitted		7.50				
1604 28¢ Ft. Nisqually	08/11/78	.55	.20	2.40	(4)	1.00
Dull finish gum		1.10		10.00	(4)	
1605 29¢ Sandy Hook Lighthouse	04/14/78	.60	.20	3.00	(4)	1.50
Dull finish gum		2.00		15.00	(4)	
1606 30¢ Morris Township School No.2	08/27/79	.55	.20	2.40	(4)	1.25
a Tagging omitted		15.00				
1607 Not assigned						
Perf. 11						
1608 50¢ Iron "Betty" Lamp	09/11/79	.85	.20	3.75	(4)	1.50
a Black omitted		*300.00*				
b Vertical pair, imperf. horizontally		*1,750.00*				
c Tagging omitted		11.00				
1609 Not assigned						
1610 $1 Rush Lamp and Candle	07/02/79	2.00	.20	8.50	(4)	3.00
a Brown omitted		*225.00*				
b Tan, orange and yellow omitted		*275.00*				
c Brown inverted		*20,000.00*				
d Tagging omitted		*15.00*				
1611 $2 Kerosene Table Lamp	11/16/78	3.75	.75	16.00	(4)	5.00
1612 $5 Railroad Conductor's Lantern	08/23/79	8.50	1.75	36.00	(4)	12.50

Issues of 1975-1981		Un	U	PB/LP	#	FDC
Coil Stamps, Perf. 10 Vertically						
1613 3.1¢ Six String Guitar	10/25/79	.20	.20	1.25	(2)	1.00
a Untagged (Bureau precanceled)		.35	.35	5.25	(2)	
b Imperf., pair		1,400.00		3,600.00	(2)	
1614 7.7¢ Saxhorns	11/20/76	.20	.20	.90	(2)	1.00
a Untagged (Bureau precanceled)		.40	.30	3.25	(2)	
b As "a," imperf., pair			1,600.00	4,250.00	(2)	
1615 7.9¢ Drum	04/23/76	.20	.20	.75	(2)	1.00
a Untagged (Bureau precanceled)		.40	.40			
b Imperf., pair		600.00				
1615C 8.4¢ Steinway Grand Piano	07/13/78	.20	.20	3.25	(2)	1.00
d Untagged (Bureau precanceled)		.50	.40			
e As "d," pair, imperf. between			60.00	125.00	(2)	
f As "d," imperf., pair			17.50	35.00	(2)	
Americana Issue, Perf. 10 Vertically (See also #1581-82, 1584-85, 1590-99, 1603-05, 1811, 1813, 1816)						
1616 9¢ slate green Capitol						
Dome (1591)	03/05/76	.20	.20	.90	(2)	1.00
a Imperf., pair		160.00		375.00	(2)	
b Untagged (Bureau precanceled)		1.15	.75	42.50	(2)	
c As "b," imperf., pair			700.00	—	(2)	
1617 10¢ purple Contemplation of						
Justice (1592)	11/04/77	.20	.20	1.00	(2)	1.00
Dull finish gum		.30		2.50	(2)	
a Untagged (Bureau precanceled)		42.50	1.35	1,150.00	(2)	
b Imperf., pair		60.00		125.00	(2)	
1618 13¢ brown Liberty Bell (1595)	11/25/75	.25	.20	.75	(2)	1.00
a Untagged (Bureau precanceled)		5.75	.75	90.00	(2)	
b Imperf., pair		25.00		65.00	(2)	
g Pair, imperf. between		—				
1618C 15¢ Ft. McHenry Flag (1597)	06/30/78	.50	.20			1.00
d Imperf., pair		25.00				
e Pair, imperf. between		150.00				
f Gray omitted		40.00				
i Tagging omitted		20.00				
1619 16¢ blue Head of Liberty						
(1599)	03/31/78	.35	.20	1.50	(2)	1.00
a Huck Press printing (white background with a bluish tinge, fraction of a millimeter smaller)		.50	.20			
1620-21 Not assigned						
Perf. 11 x 10.75						
1622 13¢ Flag over Independence						
Hall	11/15/75	.25	.20	5.75	(20)	1.00
a Horizontal pair, imperf. between		50.00				
b Imperf., pair		600.00				
e Horizontal pair, imperf. vertically		—				
f Tagging omitted		4.00				
Perf. 11.25						
1622C 13¢ Star Flag over Independence Hall		1.00	.25	20.00	(6)	
d Vertical pair, imperf.		150.00				
Booklet Stamps, Perf. 11						
1623 13¢ Flag over Capitol, single						
from booklet (1623a)		.25	.20			1.50
a Booklet pane of 8, (1 #1590						
and 7 #1623)	03/11/77	2.25	1.25			25.00
d Attached pair, #1590 and 1623		.70	1.00			

1613   **1614**   **1615**   **1615C**

1622

1623a

1629   1630   1631   1631a

1632

1633   1634   1635

1636   1637

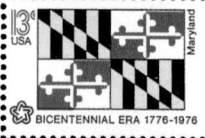

1638   1639   1640

1641   1642

1643   1644   1645

1646   1647

Issues of 1975-1977		Un	U	PB	#	FDC	Q(M)
Booklet Stamps, Perf. 10 x 9.75							
1623B 13¢ Single from booklet		.80	.80				
c Booklet pane of 8,							
(1 #1590a and 7 #1623b)		26.50	—			12.50	
e Attached pair, #1590a and 1623b		21.50	21.50				
#1623, 1623b issued only in booklets. All stamps are imperf. at one side or imperf. at one side and bottom.							
1624 Not assigned							
Coil Stamp, Perf. 10 Vertically							
1625 13¢ Flag over Independence							
Hall (1622)	11/15/75	.25	.20			1.00	
a Imperf. pair		25.00					
American Bicentennial Issue, Perf. 11							
1629 13¢ Drummer Boy	01/01/76	.25	.20			1.25	73
1630 13¢ Old Drummer	01/01/76	.25	.20			1.25	73
1631 13¢ Fifer	01/01/76	.25	.20			1.25	73
a Strip of 3, #1629-31		.75	.75	3.50	(12)	2.00	
b As "a," imperf.		1,050.00					
c Imperf., pair, #1631		800.00					
1632 13¢ *Interphil* 76	01/17/76	.20	.20	1.00	(4)	1.00	158
State Flags							
1633 13¢ Delaware	02/23/76	.25	.20			1.50	9
1634 13¢ Pennsylvania	02/23/76	.25	.20			1.50	9
1635 13¢ New Jersey	02/23/76	.25	.20			1.50	9
1636 13¢ Georgia	02/23/76	.25	.20			1.50	9
1637 13¢ Connecticut	02/23/76	.25	.20			1.50	9
1638 13¢ Massachusetts	02/23/76	.25	.20			1.50	9
1639 13¢ Maryland	02/23/76	.25	.20			1.50	9
1640 13¢ South Carolina	02/23/76	.25	.20			1.50	9
1641 13¢ New Hampshire	02/23/76	.25	.20			1.50	9
1642 13¢ Virginia	02/23/76	.25	.20			1.50	9
1643 13¢ New York	02/23/76	.25	.20			1.50	9
1644 13¢ North Carolina	02/23/76	.25	.20			1.50	9
1645 13¢ Rhode Island	02/23/76	.25	.20			1.50	9
1646 13¢ Vermont	02/23/76	.25	.20			1.50	9
1647 13¢ Kentucky	02/23/76	.25	.20			1.50	9

AMERICAN CLOCK

The second stamp issued in the American Design series features an artistic rendering of the dial, or face, of a banjo clock made circa 1805 by Simon Willard. The Willard brothers, and later their sons and grandsons, were well-known watch and clock-makers in the Boston, Massachusetts, area during the nineteenth century. The most noted of the Willard clock-makers, Simon, was known for his inventive designs. In 1802 he patented a new style of wall clock which he described as an "improved time-piece." This clock would become known as a banjo clock in part because it resembled the musical instrument. The clock's stylish shape, polished metal fittings, and decorative glass panels appealed to consumers who

made it one of the most famous designs in American clockmaking. The banjo clock depicted on the stamp is made of brass and steel and has a painted iron dial and a mahogany case crowned by a brass eagle. It is part of the collection of New England clocks at Old Sturbridge Village in Sturbridge, Massachusetts. ❏

1976

Issues of 1976		Un	U	FDC	Q(M)
American Bicentennial Issue (continued), State Flags					
1648 13¢ Tennessee	02/23/76	.25	.20	1.50	9
1649 13¢ Ohio	02/23/76	.25	.20	1.50	9
1650 13¢ Louisiana	02/23/76	.25	.20	1.50	9
1651 13¢ Indiana	02/23/76	.25	.20	1.50	9
1652 13¢ Mississippi	02/23/76	.25	.20	1.50	9
1653 13¢ Illinois	02/23/76	.25	.20	1.50	9
1654 13¢ Alabama	02/23/76	.25	.20	1.50	9
1655 13¢ Maine	02/23/76	.25	.20	1.50	9
1656 13¢ Missouri	02/23/76	.25	.20	1.50	9
1657 13¢ Arkansas	02/23/76	.25	.20	1.50	9
1658 13¢ Michigan	02/23/76	.25	.20	1.50	9
1659 13¢ Florida	02/23/76	.25	.20	1.50	9
1660 13¢ Texas	02/23/76	.25	.20	1.50	9
1661 13¢ Iowa	02/23/76	.25	.20	1.50	9
1662 13¢ Wisconsin	02/23/76	.25	.20	1.50	9
1663 13¢ California	02/23/76	.25	.20	1.50	9
1664 13¢ Minnesota	02/23/76	.25	.20	1.50	9
1665 13¢ Oregon	02/23/76	.25	.20	1.50	9
1666 13¢ Kansas	02/23/76	.25	.20	1.50	9
1667 13¢ West Virginia	02/23/76	.25	.20	1.50	9

AMERICAN ★ COMMEMORATIVE ★ **COLLECTIBLES**

American Commemorative Panels

Obtain photo or steel engravings, mint condition stamps and subject related text presented on a beautifully designed page. Only $6.00* each, depending on the value of the stamps.

For more information call
1-800-STAMP-24

Prices subject to change without notice.

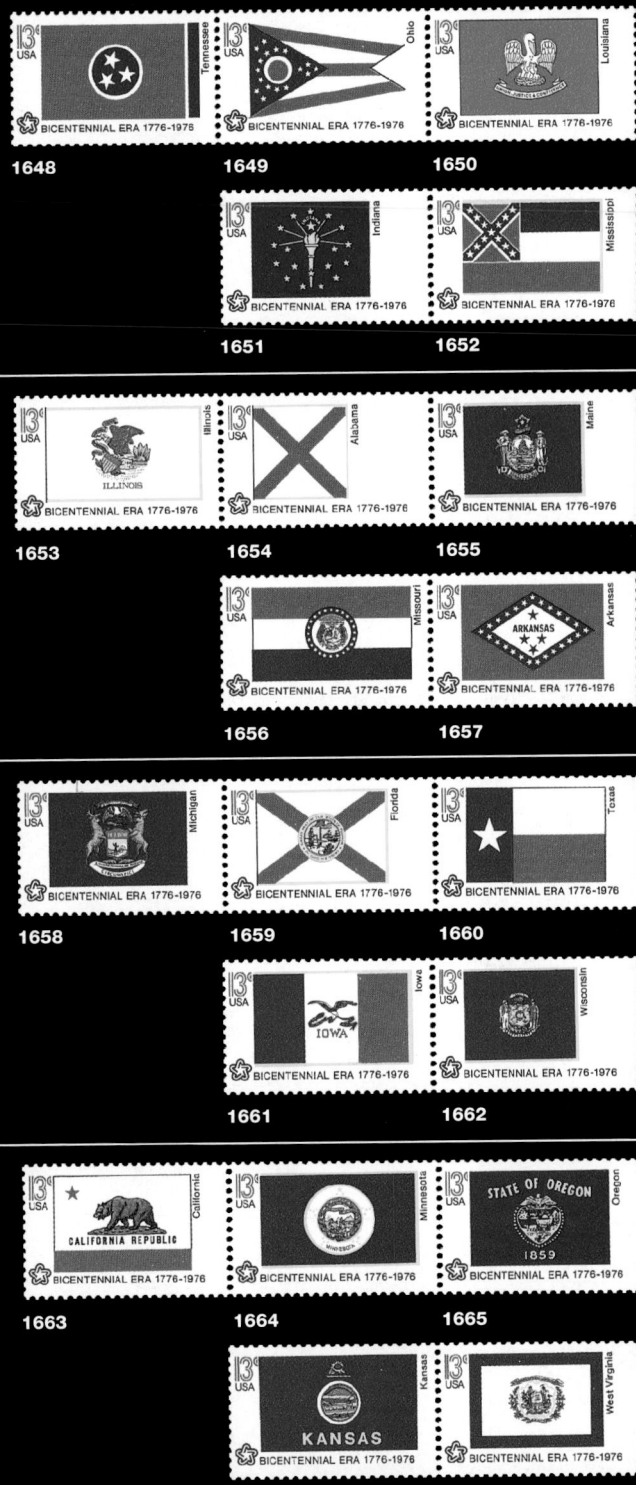

1648

1649

1650

1651

1652

1653

1654

1655

1656

1657

1658

1659

1660

1661

1662

1663

1664

1665

1666

1667

| 13¢ USA | Nevada | BICENTENNIAL ERA 1776-1976 | 13¢ USA | Nebraska | BICENTENNIAL ERA 1776-1976 | 13¢ USA | Colorado | BICENTENNIAL ERA 1776-1976 |

1668 **1669** **1670**

| 13¢ USA | North Dakota | BICENTENNIAL ERA 1776-1976 | 13¢ USA | South Dakota | BICENTENNIAL ERA 1776-1976 |

1671 **1672**

| 13¢ USA | Montana | BICENTENNIAL ERA 1776-1976 | 13¢ USA | Washington | BICENTENNIAL ERA 1776-1976 | 13¢ USA | Idaho | BICENTENNIAL ERA 1776-1976 |

1673 **1674** **1675**

| 13¢ USA | Wyoming | BICENTENNIAL ERA 1776-1976 | 13¢ USA | Utah | BICENTENNIAL ERA 1776-1976 |

1676 **1677**

| 13¢ USA | Oklahoma | OKLAHOMA | BICENTENNIAL ERA 1776-1976 | 13¢ USA | New Mexico | BICENTENNIAL ERA 1776-1976 | 13¢ USA | Arizona | BICENTENNIAL ERA 1776-1976 |

1678 **1679** **1680**

| 13¢ USA | Alaska | BICENTENNIAL ERA 1776-1976 | 13¢ USA | Hawaii | BICENTENNIAL ERA 1776-1976 |

1681 **1682**

Issues of 1976			Un	U	FDC	Q(M)
American Bicentennial Issue (continued), State Flags						
1668	13¢ Nevada	02/23/76	.25	.20	1.50	9
1669	13¢ Nebraska	02/23/76	.25	.20	1.50	9
1670	13¢ Colorado	02/23/76	.25	.20	1.50	9
1671	13¢ North Dakota	02/23/76	.25	.20	1.50	9
1672	13¢ South Dakota	02/23/76	.25	.20	1.50	9
1673	13¢ Montana	02/23/76	.25	.20	1.50	9
1674	13¢ Washington	02/23/76	.25	.20	1.50	9
1675	13¢ Idaho	02/23/76	.25	.20	1.50	9
1676	13¢ Wyoming	02/23/76	.25	.20	1.50	9
1677	13¢ Utah	02/23/76	.25	.20	1.50	9
1678	13¢ Oklahoma	02/23/76	.25	.20	1.50	9
1679	13¢ New Mexico	02/23/76	.25	.20	1.50	9
1680	13¢ Arizona	02/23/76	.25	.20	1.50	9
1681	13¢ Alaska	02/23/76	.25	.20	1.50	9
1682	13¢ Hawaii	02/23/76	.25	.20	1.50	9
a	Pane of 50, #1633-82		15.00	—	27.50	

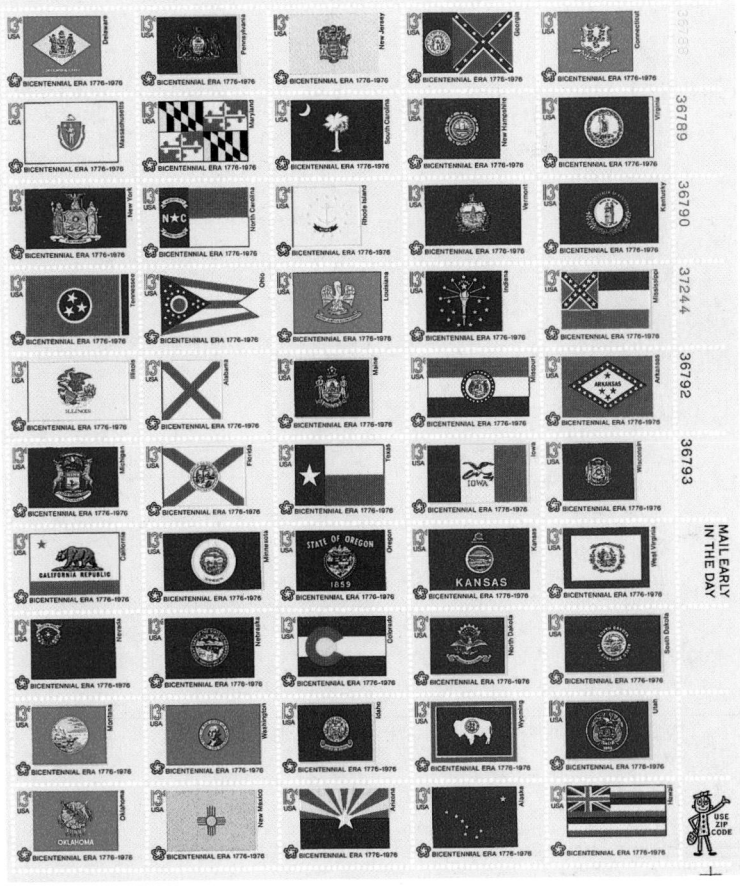

Example of 1682a

Issues of 1976		Un	U	PB	#	FDC	Q(M)
1683 13¢ Telephone Centennial	03/10/76	.25	.20	1.10	(4)	1.00	158
1684 13¢ Commercial Aviation	03/19/76	.25	.20	2.75	(10)	1.25	156
1685 13¢ Chemistry	04/06/76	.25	.20	3.25	(12)	1.50	158
Pair with full vertical gutter between		—					

American Bicentennial Issue Souvenir Sheets, 5 stamps each, Perf. 11

		Un	U	PB	#	FDC	Q(M)
1686 13¢ The Surrender of Lord Cornwallis at Yorktown, by John Trumbull	05/29/76	3.25	—			7.50	2
a 13¢ Two American Officers		.45	.40				2
b 13¢ Gen. Benjamin Lincoln		.45	.40				2
c 13¢ George Washington		.45	.40				2
d 13¢ John Trumbull, Col. David Cobb, General Friedrich von Steuben, Marquis de Lafayette and Thomas Nelson		.45	.40				2
e 13¢ Alexander Hamilton, John Laurens and Walter Stewart		.45	.40				2
f "USA/13¢" omitted on "b," "c" and "d," imperf.		—	2,250.00				
g "USA/13¢" omitted on "a" and "e"		450.00	—				
h Imperf. (untagged)			2,250.00				
i "USA/13¢" omitted on "b," "c" and "d"		450.00					
j "USA/13¢" double on "b"		—					
k "USA/13¢" omitted on "c" and "d"		750.00					
l "USA/13¢" omitted on "e"		500.00					
m "USA/13¢" omitted, imperf. (untagged)		—					
n As "g", imperf., untagged		—					
1687 18¢ The Declaration of Independence, 4 July 1776 at Philadelphia, by John Trumbull	05/29/76	4.25	—			7.50	2
a 18¢ John Adams, Roger Sherman and Robert R. Livingston		.55	.55				2
b 18¢ Thomas Jefferson and Benjamin Franklin		.55	.55				2
c 18¢ Thomas Nelson, Jr., Francis Lewis, John Witherspoon and Samuel Huntington		.55	.55				2
d 18¢ John Hancock and Charles Thomson		.55	.55				2
e 18¢ George Read, John Dickinson and Edward Rutledge		.55	.55				2
f Design and marginal inscriptions omitted		3,000.00					
g "USA/18¢" omitted on "a" and "c"		750.00					
h "USA/18¢" omitted on "b," "d" and "e"		450.00					
i "USA/18¢" omitted on "d"		500.00	500.00				
j Black omitted in design		2,000.00					
k "USA/18¢" omitted, imperf. (untagged)		2,750.00					
m "USA/18¢" omitted on "b" and "e"		500.00					

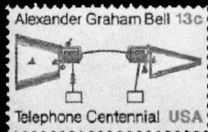

1683 **1684** **1685**

The Surrender of Lord Cornwallis at Yorktown
From a Painting by John Trumbull

1686

The Declaration of Independence, 4 July 1776 at Philadelphia
From a Painting by John Trumbull

1687

Washington Crossing the Delaware
From a Painting by Emanuel Leutze / Eastman Johnson

1688

Washington Reviewing His Ragged Army at Valley Forge
From a Painting by William T. Trego

1689

Issues of 1976		Un	U	FDC	Q(M)
American Bicentennial Issue Souvenir Sheets, 5 stamps each (continued)					
1688	24¢ Washington Crossing the Delaware, by Emanuel Leutze/ Eastman Johnson 05/29/76	5.25	—	7.50	2
a	24¢ Boatmen	.70	.70		2
b	24¢ George Washington	.70	.70		2
c	24¢ Flagbearer	.70	.70		2
d	24¢ Men in Boat	.70	.70		2
e	24¢ Steersman and Men on Shore	.70	.70		2
f	"USA/24¢" omitted, imperf.	3,500.00			
g	"USA/24¢" omitted on "d" and "e"	450.00	450.00		
h	Design and marginal inscriptions omitted	3,250.00			
i	"USA/24¢" omitted on "a," "b" and "c"	500.00	—		
j	Imperf. (untagged)	3,000.00			
k	"USA/24¢" inverted on "d" and "e"	—			
1689	31¢ Washington Reviewing His Ragged Army at Valley Forge, by William T. Trego 05/29/76	6.25	—	7.50	2
a	31¢ Two Officers	.85	.85		2
b	31¢ George Washington	.85	.85		2
c	31¢ Officer and Brown Horse	.85	.85		2
d	31¢ White Horse and Officer	.85	.85		2
e	31¢ Three Soldiers	.85	.85		2
f	"USA/31¢" omitted, imperf.	2,750.00			
g	"USA/31¢" omitted on "a" and "c"	400.00			
h	"USA/31¢" omitted on "b," "d" and "e"	450.00	—		
i	"USA/31¢" omitted on "e"	450.00			
j	Black omitted in design	2,000.00			
k	Imperf. (untagged)		2,250.00		
l	"USA/31¢" omitted on "b" and "d"	—			
m	"USA/31¢" omitted on "a," "c" and "e"	—			
n	As "m," imperf. (untagged)	—			
p	As "h," imperf. (untagged)		2,500.00		
q	As "g," imperf. (untagged)	2,750.00			
r	"USA/31¢" omitted on "d" & "e"	—			
s	As "f", untagged	2,250.00			

	Issues of 1976		Un	U	PB	#	FDC	Q(M)
	American Bicentennial Issue, Perf. 11							
1690	13¢ Bust of Benjamin Franklin, Map of North America, 1776	06/01/76	.25	.20	1.10	(4)	1.00	165
a	Light blue omitted		225.00					
b	Tagging omitted		7.50					
	Declaration of Independence, by John Trumbull							
1691	13¢ Delegates	07/04/76	.30	.20			1.00	41
1692	13¢ Delegates and John Adams	07/04/76	.30	.20			1.00	41
1693	13¢ Roger Sherman, Robert R. Livingston, Thomas Jefferson and Benjamin Franklin	07/04/76	.30	.20			1.00	41
1694	13¢ John Hancock, Charles Thomson, George Read, John Dickinson and Edward Rutledge	07/04/76	.30	.20			1.00	41
a	Strip of 4, #1691-94		1.20	1.10	7.75	(20)	2.00	
	Olympic Games Issue							
1695	13¢ Diver and Olympic Rings	07/16/76	.25	.20			1.00	46
1696	13¢ Skier and Olympic Rings	07/16/76	.25	.20			1.00	46
1697	13¢ Runner and Olympic Rings	07/16/76	.25	.20			1.00	46
1698	13¢ Skater and Olympic Rings	07/16/76	.25	.20			1.00	46
a	Block of 4, #1695-98		1.10	1.40	3.25	(12)	2.00	
b	As "a," imperf.		650.00					
1699	13¢ Clara Maass	08/18/76	.25	.20	3.25	(12)	1.25	131
a	Horizontal pair, imperf. vertically		450.00					
1700	13¢ Adolph S. Ochs	09/18/76	.25	.20	1.10	(4)	1.00	158
	Christmas Issue							
1701	13¢ Nativity, by John Singleton Copley	10/27/76	.25	.20	3.25	(12)	1.00	810
a	Imperf., pair		100.00					
1702	13¢ "Winter Pastime," by Nathaniel Currier	10/27/76	.25	.20	2.75	(10)	1.00	482*
a	Imperf., pair		100.00					
	*Includes #1703 printing							
1703	13¢ as #1702	10/27/76	.25	.20	6.00	(20)	1.00	
a	Imperf., pair		100.00					
b	Vertical pair, imperf. between		400.00					
c	Tagging omitted		12.50					

#1702 has overall tagging. Lettering at base is black and usually ½mm below design. As a rule, no "snowflaking" in sky or pond. Pane of 50 has margins on 4 sides with slogans. #1703 has block tagging the size of the printed area. Lettering at base is gray-black and usually ¾mm below design. "Snowflaking" generally in sky and pond. Pane of 50 has margin only at right or left and no slogans.

	Issues of 1977, American Bicentennial Issue		Un	U	PB	#	FDC	Q(M)
1704	13¢ Washington, Nassau Hall, Hessian Prisoners and 13-star Flag, by Charles Willson Peale	01/03/77	.25	.20	2.75	(10)	1.00	150
a	Horizontal pair, imperf. vertically		550.00					
1705	13¢ Sound Recording	03/23/77	.25	.20	1.10	(4)	1.25	177

1690

1691   **1692**   **1693**   **1694** **1694a**

1695   **1696**

1699   **1700**

  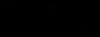

1697   **1698** **1698a**

1701   **1702**   **1703**

1705

1704

1706   1707

1710

1711

1708   1709   1709a

1712   1713

Lafayette

US Bicentennial 13c

1716

1714   1715   1715a

1717   1718

1721

1719   1720   1720a

Issues of 1977		Un	U	PB	#	FDC	Q(M)
American Folk Art Issue, Pueblo Pottery, Perf. 11							
1706	13¢ Zia Pot 04/13/77	.25	.20			1.00	49
1707	13¢ San Ildefonso Pot 04/13/77	.25	.20			1.00	49
1708	13¢ Hopi Pot 04/13/77	.25	.20			1.00	49
1709	13¢ Acoma Pot 04/13/77	.25	.20			1.00	49
a	Block of 4, #1706-09	1.00	1.00	2.75	(10)	2.00	
b	As "a," imperf. vertically	2,250.00					
1710	13¢ Solo Transatlantic Flight 05/20/77	.25	.20	3.25	(12)	2.00	209
a	Imperf. pair	1,000.00					
1711	13¢ Colorado Statehood 05/21/77	.25	.20	3.25	(12)	1.00	192
a	Horizontal pair, imperf. between	600.00					
b	Horizontal pair, imperf. vertically	900.00					
c	Perf. 11.2	.35	.25	20.00	(12)		
	Butterfly Issue						
1712	13¢ Swallowtail 06/06/77	.25	.20			2.00	55
1713	13¢ Checkerspot 06/06/77	.25	.20			2.00	55
1714	13¢ Dogface 06/06/77	.25	.20			2.00	55
1715	13¢ Orange-Tip 06/06/77	.25	.20			2.00	55
a	Block of 4, #1712-15	1.00	1.00	3.25	(12)	2.00	
b	As "a," imperf. horizontally	15,000.00					
	American Bicentennial Issue						
1716	13¢ Marquis de Lafayette 06/13/77	.25	.20	1.10	(4)	1.00	160
	Skilled Hands for Independence						
1717	13¢ Seamstress 07/04/77	.25	.20			1.00	47
1718	13¢ Blacksmith 07/04/77	.25	.20			1.00	47
1719	13¢ Wheelwright 07/04/77	.25	.20			1.00	47
1720	13¢ Leatherworker 07/04/77	.25	.20			1.00	47
a	Block of 4, #1717-20	1.00	1.00	3.25	(12)	2.00	
	Perf. 11 x 10.5						
1721	13¢ Peace Bridge 08/04/77	.25	.20	1.10	(4)	1.00	164

ETHEL MERMAN

(1908-1984)

ETHEL MERMAN—born Ethel Agnes Zimmerman in the borough of Queens in New York City—knew she wanted to be a singer, but her father insisted that she learn stenography in case she was not successful. After working two jobs—stenographer during the day and singer at night—for a short time, Merman quit her day job to concentrate on show business. She signed a contract with Warner Bros. in 1930, the same year she became a Broadway star in the George and Ira Gershwin musical *Girl Crazy*. She made a number of motion pictures with co-stars such as Eddie Cantor, Bing Crosby, and Donald O'Connor, but Broadway—where her voice carried to the farthest seats—was her kingdom. Merman had a leading role in Cole Porter's *Anything Goes* and in 1946, she starred in Irving Berlin's *Annie Get Your Gun* and found her personal theme song, "There's No Business Like Show Business." Starring roles in Broadway musicals such as *Call Me Madam*, *Gypsy*, and *Hello Dolly!* confirmed that "the little girl with the big voice" was indeed the "queen of show business." ❑

	Issues of 1977		Un	U	PB	#	FDC	Q(M)
	American Bicentennial Issue, Perf. 11							
1722	13¢ Herkimer at Oriskany,							
	by Frederick Yohn	08/06/77	.25	.20	2.75	(10)	1.00	156
	Energy Issue							
1723	13¢ Energy Conservation	10/20/77	.25	.20			1.25	79
1724	13¢ Energy Development	10/20/77	.25	.20			1.25	79
a	Attached pair, #1723-24		.50	.50	3.25	(12)		
1725	13¢ First Civil Settlement							
	Alta, California	09/09/77	.25	.20	1.10	(4)	1.00	154
	American Bicentennial Issue							
1726	13¢ Members of Continental							
	Congress in Conference	09/30/77	.25	.20	1.10	(4)	1.00	168
1727	13¢ Talking Pictures	10/06/77	.25	.20	1.10	(4)	1.50	157
	American Bicentennial Issue							
1728	13¢ Surrender of Burgoyne,							
	at Saratoga	10/07/77	.25	.20	2.75	(10)	1.00	154
	Christmas Issue							
1729	13¢ Washington at Valley							
	Forge, by J.C. Leyendecker	10/21/77	.25	.20	5.75	(20)	1.00	882
a	Imperf., pair		75.00					
1730	13¢ Rural Mailbox	10/21/77	.25	.20	2.75	(10)	1.00	922
a	Imperf., pair		300.00					
	Issues of 1978							
1731	13¢ Carl Sandburg	01/06/78	.25	.20	1.25	(4)	1.00	157
	Captain Cook Issue							
1732	13¢ Capt. James Cook							
	Alaska, by Nathaniel Dance	01/20/78	.25	.20			1.25	101
1733	13¢ *Resolution* and *Discovery*							
	Hawaii, by John Webber	01/20/78	.25	.20			1.25	101
a	Vertical pair, imperf. horizontally		—					
b	Attached pair, #1732-33		.50	.50	1.10	(4)		
c	As " b," imperf. between		4,500.00					
1734	13¢ Indian Head Penny	01/11/78	.25	.20	1.25	(4)	1.00	
	Pair with full horizontal gutter between		—					
a	Horizontal pair, imperf. vertically		300.00					
1735	(15¢) "A" Stamp	05/22/78	.25	.20	1.25	(4)	1.00	
a	Imperf., pair		90.00					
b	Vertical pair, imperf. horizontally		700.00					
c	Perf. 11.2		.25	.20	1.75	(4)		
	Booklet Stamp, Perf. 11 x 10.5							
1736	(15¢) "A" orange Eagle (1735),							
	single from booklet	05/22/78	.25	.20			1.00	
a	Booklet pane of 8	05/22/78	2.25	1.25			2.50	
	Roses Booklet Issue, Perf. 10							
1737	15¢ Roses, single from							
	booklet	07/11/78	.25	.20			1.00	
a	Booklet pane of 8	07/11/78	2.25	1.25			2.50	
b	As "a," imperf.		—					
c	As "a," tagging omitted		40.00	—				

#1736-37 issued only in booklets. All stamps are imperf. on one side or on one side and bottom.

1722

1723

1725

1724 **1724a**

1726

1727

1728

1729

1730

1732

1731

1733 **1733b**

1734

1735

1737

1738   1739   1740   1741   1742 1742a

1744

1745  1746

1747   1748

1748a

1749

1750

1752

1751   1752a

French Alliance 1778

US Bicentennial 13c

1753

1754   1755   1756

Issues of 1980		Un	U	PB/LP	#	FDC	Q(M)
Windmills Booklet Issue, Perf. 11							
1738 15¢ Virginia, 1720	02/07/80	.30	.20			1.00	
1739 15¢ Rhode Island, 1790	02/07/80	.30	.20			1.00	
1740 15¢ Massachusetts, 1793	02/07/80	.30	.20			1.00	
1741 15¢ Illinois, 1860	02/07/80	.30	.20			1.00	
1742 15¢ Texas, 1890	02/07/80	.30	.20			1.00	
a Booklet pane of 10, #1738-42		3.50	3.00			3.50	
b Strip of 5, #1730-1742		1.50	1.40				
#1737-42 issued only in booklets. All stamps are imperf. top or bottom, or top or bottom and right side.							
Issues of 1978, Coil Stamp, Perf. 10 Vertically							
1743 (15¢) "A" orange Eagle (1735)	05/22/78	.25	.20	.65	(2)	1.00	
a Imperf., pair		90.00		—	(2)		
Black Heritage Issue, Perf. 10.5 x 11							
1744 13¢ Harriet Tubman and Cart Carrying Slaves	02/01/78	.25	.20	3.25	(12)	1.75	157
American Folk Art Issue, Quilts, Perf. 11							
1745 13¢ Basket design, red and orange	03/08/78	.25	.20			1.00	41
1746 13¢ Basket design, red	03/08/78	.25	.20			1.00	41
1747 13¢ Basket design, orange	03/08/78	.25	.20			1.00	41
1748 13¢ Basket design, brown	03/08/78	.25	.20			1.00	41
a Block of 4, #1745-48		1.00	1.00	3.25	(12)	2.00	
American Dance Issue							
1749 13¢ Ballet	04/26/78	.25	.20			1.00	39
1750 13¢ Theater	04/26/78	.25	.20			1.00	39
1751 13¢ Folk	04/26/78	.25	.20			1.00	39
1752 13¢ Modern	04/26/78	.25	.20			1.00	39
a Block of 4, #1749-52		1.00	1.00	3.25	(12)	2.00	
American Bicentennial Issue, French Alliance							
1753 13¢ King Louis XVI and Benjamin Franklin, by Charles Gabriel Sauvage	05/04/78	.25	.20	1.10	(4)	1.00	103
Perf. 10.5 x 11							
1754 13¢ Early Cancer Detection	05/18/78	.25	.20	1.10	(4)	1.00	152
Performing Arts Issue, Perf. 11							
1755 13¢ Jimmie Rodgers with Guitar and Brakeman's Cap, Locomotive	05/24/78	.25	.20	3.25	(12)	1.00	95
1756 15¢ George M. Cohan, "Yankee Doodle Dandy" and Stars	07/03/78	.30	.20	4.00	(12)	1.25	152

Issues of 1978		Un	U	PB	#	FDC	Q(M)
CAPEX '78 Souvenir Sheet, Perf. 11							
1757 13¢ Souvenir sheet of 8	06/10/78	2.00	2.00	2.25	(8)	2.75	15
a 13¢ Cardinal		.25	.20				15
b 13¢ Mallard		.25	.20				15
c 13¢ Canada Goose		.25	.20				15
d 13¢ Blue Jay		.25	.20				15
e 13¢ Moose		.25	.20				15
f 13¢ Chipmunk		.25	.20				15
g 13¢ Red Fox		.25	.20				15
h 13¢ Raccoon		.25	.20	2.25	(8)		15
i Yellow, green, red, brown and black (litho.) omitted		7,000.00					
1758 15¢ Photography	06/26/78	.30	.20	4.00	(12)	1.00	163
1759 15¢ Viking Missions to Mars	07/20/78	.30	.20	1.35	(4)	1.00	159
Wildlife Conservation: American Owls Issue							
1760 15¢ Great Gray Owl	08/26/78	.30	.20			1.25	47
1761 15¢ Saw-Whet Owl	08/26/78	.30	.20			1.25	47
1762 15¢ Barred Owl	08/26/78	.30	.20			1.25	47
1763 15¢ Great Horned Owl	08/26/78	.30	.20			1.25	47
a Block of 4, #1760-63		1.25	1.25	1.40	(4)	2.00	
Wildlife Conservation: American Trees Issue							
1764 15¢ Giant Sequoia	10/09/78	.30	.20			1.25	42
1765 15¢ White Pine	10/09/78	.30	.20			1.25	42
1766 15¢ White Oak	10/09/78	.30	.20			1.25	42
1767 15¢ Gray Birch	10/09/78	.30	.20			1.25	42
a Block of 4, #1764-67		1.25	1.25	4.00	(12)	2.00	
b As "a," imperf. horizontally		15,000.00					

ZORA NEALE HURSTON

(1891-1960)

Novelist, folklorist, and anthropologist ZORA NEALE HURSTON was a central figure in the Harlem Renaissance, a flowering of African-American literature, music, and art that took place primarily in the 1920s and 1930s. She wrote four novels, two books of folklore, an autobiography, and more than 50 short stories and essays. Although her writing went out of fashion in the 1950s, it enjoyed a dramatic revival in the 1970s. Today Hurston is considered one of America's most original and accomplished writers. Born in Alabama, Hurston was raised in Eatonville, Florida, a self-governing, all-black town near Orlando. Her family and community imbued her with self-confidence and pride in her heritage. From an early age she was fascinated by African-American oral culture. In 1925 Hurston moved to New York where her wit, style, and storytelling made her a favorite in Harlem. She enrolled at Barnard College—the only African-American student at the time—and in 1928 received a bachelor's degree in anthropology. From the late 1920s through the early 1940s, Hurston made a series of trips to collect black folklore and wrote extensively. *Their Eyes Were Watching God*, considered Hurston's masterpiece, was published in 1937. ❑

a   b   c   d

1757   e   f   g   h

1759

1760   1761

1758

1762   1763   1763a

1764   1765

1766   1767   1767a

1768

1769

1770

1771

1772

1775   1776

1773

1774

1777   1778   1778a

1779   1780

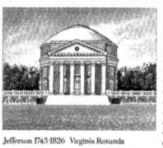

1781   1782   1782a

1783   1784

1785   1786   1786a

Issues of 1978		Un	U	PB	#	FDC	Q(M)
Christmas Issues, Perf. 11							
1768	15¢ Madonna and Child						
	with Cherubim,						
	by Andrea della Robbia 10/18/78	.30	.20	4.00	(12)	1.00	963
a	Imperf., pair	90.00					
1769	15¢ Child on Hobby Horse						
	and Christmas Trees 10/18/78	.30	.20	4.00	(12)	1.00	917
	Pair with full horizontal gutter between	—					
a	Imperf., pair	100.00					
b	Vertical pair, imperf. horizontally	2,000.00					
Issues of 1979, Perf. 11							
1770	15¢ Robert F. Kennedy 01/12/79	.35	.20	1.75	(4)	1.50	159
Black Heritage Issue							
1771	15¢ Martin Luther King, Jr.,						
	and Civil Rights Marchers 01/13/79	.30	.20	4.00	(12)	2.00	166
a	Imperf., pair	—					
1772	15¢ International Year						
	of the Child 02/15/79	.30	.20	1.40	(4)	1.00	163
Literary Arts Issue, Perf. 10.5 x 11							
1773	15¢ John Steinbeck,						
	by Philippe Halsman 02/27/79	.30	.20	1.40	(4)	1.00	155
1774	15¢ Albert Einstein 03/04/79	.35	.20	1.75	(4)	3.00	157
	Pair with full horizontal gutter between	—					
American Folk Art: Pennsylvania Toleware Issue, Perf. 11							
1775	15¢ Straight-Spout Coffeepot 04/19/79	.30	.20			1.00	44
1776	15¢ Tea Caddy 04/19/79	.30	.20			1.00	44
1777	15¢ Sugar Bowl 04/19/79	.30	.20			1.00	44
1778	15¢ Curved-Spout Coffeepot 04/19/79	.30	.20			1.00	44
a	Block of 4, #1775-78	1.25	1.25	3.25	(10)	2.00	
b	As "a," imperf. horizontally	4,250.00					
American Architecture Issue							
1779	15¢ Virginia Rotunda,						
	by Thomas Jefferson 06/04/79	.30	.20			1.00	41
1780	15¢ Baltimore Cathedral,						
	by Benjamin Latrobe 06/04/79	.30	.20			1.00	41
1781	15¢ Boston State House,						
	by Charles Bulfinch 06/04/79	.30	.20			1.00	41
1782	15¢ Philadelphia Exchange,						
	by William Strickland 06/04/79	.30	.20			1.00	41
a	Block of 4, #1779-82	1.25	1.50	1.45	(4)	2.00	
Endangered Flora Issue							
1783	15¢ Persistent Trillium 06/07/79	.30	.20			1.00	41
1784	15¢ Hawaiian Wild						
	Broadbean 06/07/79	.30	.20			1.00	41
1785	15¢ Contra Costa Wallflower 06/07/79	.30	.20			1.00	41
1786	15¢ Antioch Dunes						
	Evening Primrose 06/07/79	.30	.20			1.00	41
a	Block of 4, #1783-86	1.25	1.25	4.00	(12)	2.00	
	As "a," full vertical gutter between	—					
b	As "a," imperf.	600.00					

	Issues of 1979		Un	UPB	PB	#	FDC	Q(M)
1787	15¢ Seeing Eye Dogs	06/15/79	.30	.20	6.50	(20)	1.25	162
a	Imperf., pair		425.00					
b	Tagging omitted		10.00					
1788	15¢ Special Olympics	08/09/79	.30	.20	3.25	(10)	1.25	166
	American Bicentennial Issue, Perf. 11 x 12							
1789	15¢ John Paul Jones,							
	by Charles Willson Peale	09/23/79	.30	.20	3.25	(10)	1.50	160
c	Vertical pair, imperf. horizontally		175.00					
1789A	Perf. 11		.55	.20	4.00	(10)		
d	Vertical pair,							
	imperf. horizontally		150.00					
1789B	Perf. 12		3,500.00	3,500.00	40,000.00	(10)		
	Numerous varieties of printer's waste of #1789 exist							
	Olympic Summer Games Issue, Perf. 11 (See also #C97)							
1790	10¢ Javelin Thrower	09/05/79	.20	.20	3.00	(12)	1.00	67
1791	15¢ Runner	09/28/79	.30	.20			1.25	47
1792	15¢ Swimmer	09/28/79	.30	.20			1.25	47
1793	15¢ Rowers	09/28/79	.30	.20			1.25	47
1794	15¢ Equestrian Contestant	09/28/79	.30	.20			1.25	47
a	Block of 4, #1791-94		1.25	1.50	4.00	(12)	2.00	
b	As "a," imperf.		1,500.00					
	Issues of 1980, Olympic Winter Games Issue, Perf. 11 x 10.5							
1795	15¢ Speed Skater	02/01/80	.35	.20			1.25	52
1796	15¢ Downhill Skier	02/01/80	.35	.20			1.25	52
1797	15¢ Ski Jumper	02/01/80	.35	.20			1.25	52
1798	15¢ Ice Hockey	02/01/80	.35	.20			1.25	52
a	Perf. 11, #1795-98		1.05	.60				
b	Block of 4, #1795-98		1.50	1.40	4.50	(12)	2.00	
c	Block of 4, #1795a-98a		4.25	3.50	14.00	(12)		
	Issues of 1979, Christmas Issue, Perf. 11							
1799	15¢ Virgin and Child with							
	Cherubim, by Gerard David	10/18/79	.30	.20	4.00	(12)	1.25	874
a	Imperf., pair		90.00					
b	Vertical pair, imperf. horizontally		700.00					
c	pair, imperf. between		2,250.00					
1800	15¢ Santa Claus, Christmas							
	Tree Ornament	10/18/79	.30	.20	4.00	(12)	1.25	932
a	Green and yellow omitted		625.00					
b	Green, yellow and tan omitted		700.00					
	Performing Arts Issue							
1801	15¢ Will Rogers and Rogers as a							
	Cowboy Humorist	11/04/79	.30	.20	4.00	(12)	1.50	161
a	Imperf., pair		225.00					
1802	15¢ Vietnam Veterans	11/11/79	.30	.20	3.25	(10)	2.75	173
	Issues of 1980 (continued), Performing Arts Issue							
1803	15¢ W.C. Fields and							
	Fields as a Juggler	01/29/80	.30	.20	4.00	(12)	1.75	169
	Black Heritage Issue							
1804	15¢ Benjamin Banneker							
	and Banneker as Surveyor	02/15/80	.35	.20	4.50	(12)	2.00	160
a	Horizontal pair, imperf. vertically		800.00					

1787

1788

1789

1790

1791  **1792**

1793 **1794**

1794a

1795  **1796**

1797  **1798**

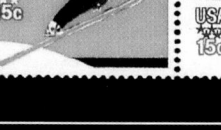

1798b

1799

1800

1801

1802

1803

1804

1805

1807

1809

1813

1806

1808

1810

1816

1818

1822

1821

1823

1824

1825

1826

1827   **1828**

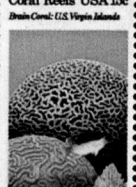

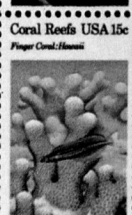

1829   **1830**   **1830a**

	Issues of 1980		Un	U	PB/LP	#	FDC	Q(M)
	Letter Writing Issue, Perf. 11							
1805	15¢ Letters Preserve Memories	02/25/80	.30	.20			1.00	39
1806	15¢ purple P.S. Write Soon	02/25/80	.30	.20			1.00	39
1807	15¢ Letters Lift Spirits	02/25/80	.30	.20			1.00	39
1808	15¢ green P.S. Write Soon	02/25/80	.30	.20			1.00	39
1809	15¢ Letters Shape Opinions	02/25/80	.30	.20			1.00	39
1810	15¢ red and blue P.S. Write Soon	02/25/80	.30	.20			1.00	39
a	Vertical Strip of 6, #1805-10		1.85	2.25	12.00	(36)	2.50	
	Issues of 1980-1981, Americana Issue, Coil Stamps, Perf. 10 Vertically							
	(See also #1581-82, 1584-85, 1590-99, 1603-06, 1608, 1610-19, 1622-23, 1625)							
1811	1¢ dark blue, greenish Inkwelll							
	and Quill (1581)	03/06/80	.20	.20	.40	(2)	1.00	
a	Imperf., pair		175.00		275.00	(2)		
1812	Not assigned							
1813	3.5¢ Weaver Violins	06/23/80	.20	.20	1.00	(2)	1.00	
a	Untagged (Bureau precanceled)		.20	.20	1.95	(2)		
b	Imperf., pair		225.00		450.00	(2)		
1814-15	Not assigned							
1816	12¢ red brown, *beige* Torch from							
	Statue of Liberty (1594)	04/08/81	.25	.20	1.50	(2)	1.00	
a	Untagged (Bureau precanceled)		1.15	1.15	47.50	(2)		
b	Imperf., pair		175.00		350.00	(2)		
1817	Not assigned							
	Issues of 1981, Perf. 11 x 10.5							
1818	(18¢) "B" Stamp	03/15/81	.35	.20	1.60	(4)	1.25	
	Booklet Stamp, Perf. 10							
1819	(18¢) "B" Stamp (1818),							
	single from booklet	03/15/81	.40	.20			1.00	
a	Booklet pane of 8	03/15/81	3.75	2.25			3.00	
	Coil Stamp, Perf. 10 Vertically							
1820	(18¢) "B" Stamp (1818)	03/15/81	.40	.20	1.60	(2)	1.00	
a	Imperf., pair		100.00		250.00	(2)		
	Issues of 1980, Perf. 10.5 x 11							
1821	15¢ Frances Perkins	04/10/80	.30	.20	1.30	(4)	1.00	164
	Perf. 11							
1822	15¢ Dolley Madison	05/20/80	.30	.20	1.40	(4)	1.00	257
1823	15¢ Emily Bissell	05/31/80	.35	.20	1.75	(4)	1.00	96
a	Vertical pair, imperf. horizontally		400.00					
1824	15¢ Helen Keller/Anne Sullivan	06/27/80	.30	.20	1.30	(4)	1.00	154
1825	15¢ Veterans Administration	07/21/80	.30	.20	1.30	(4)	1.50	160
a	Horizontal pair, imperf. vertically		450.00					
	American Bicentennial Issue							
1826	15¢ General Bernardo de Galvez,							
	Battle of Mobile	07/23/80	.30	.20	1.30	(4)	1.00	104
a	Red, brown and blue omitted		800.00					
b	Bl., brn., red and yel. omitted		1,400.00					
	Coral Reefs Issue							
1827	15¢ Brain Coral, Beaugregory							
	Fish	08/26/80	.30	.20			1.00	51
1828	15¢ Elkhorn Coral, Porkfish	08/26/80	.30	.20			1.00	51
1829	15¢ Chalice Coral, Moorish Idol	08/26/80	.30	.20			1.00	51
1830	15¢ Finger Coral, Sabertooth							
	Blenny	08/26/80	.30	.20			1.00	51
a	Block of 4, #1827-30		1.25	1.10	4.00	(12)	2.00	
b	As "a," imperf.		900.00					
c	As "a," imperf. between, vertically		—					
d	As "a," imperf. vertically		3,000.00					

1980

	Issues of 1980		Un	U	PB	#	FDC	Q(M)
1831	15¢ Organized Labor	09/01/80	.30	.20	3.50	(12)	1.00	167
a	Imperf., pair		375.00					
	Literary Arts Issue, Edith Wharton, Perf. 10.5 x 11							
1832	15¢ Edith Wharton Reading							
	Letter	09/05/80	.30	.20	1.30	(4)	1.00	163
	Perf. 11							
1833	15¢ Education	09/12/80	.30	.20	1.90	(6)	1.50	160
a	Horizontal pair, imperf. vertically		240.00					
	American Folk Art Issue, Pacific Northwest Indian Masks							
1834	15¢ Heiltsuk, Bella Bella Tribe	09/25/80	.30	.20			1.00	39
1835	15¢ Chilkat Tlingit Tribe	09/25/80	.30	.20			1.00	39
1836	15¢ Tlingit Tribe	09/25/80	.30	.20			1.00	39
1837	15¢ Bella Coola Tribe	09/25/80	.30	.20			1.00	39
a	Block of 4, #1834-37		1.25	1.25	4.50	(10)	2.00	
	American Architecture Issue							
1838	15¢ Smithsonian Institution,							
	by James Renwick	10/09/80	.30	.20			1.00	39
1839	15¢ Trinity Church, by Henry							
	Hobson Richardson	10/09/80	.30	.20			1.00	39
1840	15¢ Pennsylvania Academy							
	of Fine Arts, by Frank Furness	10/09/80	.30	.20			1.00	39
1841	15¢ Lyndhurst, by Alexander							
	Jefferson Davis	10/09/80	.30	.20			1.00	39
a	Block of 4, #1838-41		1.25	1.50	1.50	(4)	1.75	
b	As "a", red omitted on #1838,1839		400.00					
	Christmas Issue							
1842	15¢ Madonna and Child							
	from Epiphany Window,							
	Washington Cathedral	10/31/80	.30	.20	4.00	(12)	1.25	693
a	Imperf., pair		70.00					
	Pair with full vertical gutter between		—					
1843	15¢ Wreath and Toys	10/31/80	.30	.20	6.50	(20)	1.25	719
a	Imperf., pair		70.00					
b	Buff omitted		25.00					
c	Vertical pair, imperf. horizontally		—					
d	Horizontal pair, imperf. between		4,000.00					

AMERICAN ★ COMMEMORATIVE ★ COLLECTIBLES

First Day of Issue Ceremony Programs

Receive detailed information about each first day of issue ceremony held for all new stamps and stationery issuances.

Collect these valuable programs for only $4.95 each.*

For more information call
1-800-STAMP-24

*Unless the stamp value exceeds $4.95 then the price is determined by the actual value of the stamps.

Organized Labor
Proud and Free
USA 15c

1831

Edith Wharton
USA 15c

1832

1834   **1835**

Heiltsuk, Bella Bella
Indian Art USA 15c

Chilkat Tlingit
Indian Art USA 15c

Tlingit
Indian Art USA 15c

Bella Coola
Indian Art USA 15c

1836   **1837**   **1837a**

Edw by Josef Albers USA 15c
Learning
never ends

1833

1838   **1839**

Renwick 1818-1895 Smithsonian Washington
Architecture USA 15c

Richardson 1838-1886 Trinity Church Boston
Architecture USA 15c

Furness 1839-1912 Penn Academy Philadelphia
Architecture USA 15c

A J Davis 1803-1892 Lyndhurst Tarrytown NY
Architecture USA 15c

1840   **1841**   **1841a**

Christmas USA 15c

USA 15c
Season's Greetings

1842   **1843**

1844

1845

1846

1847

1848

1849

1850

1851

1852

1853

1854

1855

1856

1857

1858

1859

1860

1861

1862

1863

Issues of 1980-1985		Un	U	PB	#	FDC
Great Americans Issue, Perf. 11 (See also #2168-73, 2176-80, 2182-86, 2188, 2190-92, 2194-97)						
1844 1¢ Dorothea Dix	09/23/83	.20	.20	.35	(6)	1.00
a Imperf., pair		300.00				
b Vertical pair, imperf. between		3,000.00				
c Perf. 10.9, small block tagging		.20	.20	.35	(6)	
d Perf. 10.9, large block tagging		.20	.20	.35	(6)	
e Vertical pair, imperf. horizontally		—				
Perf. 11 x 10.5						
1845 2¢ Igor Stravinsky	11/18/82	.20	.20	.35	(4)	1.00
Vertical pair, full gutter between		—				
1846 3¢ Henry Clay	07/13/83	.20	.20	.55	(4)	1.00
a Tagging omitted		4.00				
1847 4¢ Carl Schurz	06/03/83	.20	.20	.65	(4)	1.00
a Tagging omitted		4.00				
1848 5¢ Pearl Buck	06/25/83	.20	.20	.70	(4)	1.00
Perf. 11						
1849 6¢ Walter Lippman	09/19/85	.20	.20	.85	(6)	1.00
a Vertical pair, imperf. between		2,000.00				
1850 7¢ Abraham Baldwin	01/25/85	.20	.20	.95	(6)	1.00
1851 8¢ Henry Knox	07/25/85	.20	.20	.85	(4)	1.00
1852 9¢ Sylvanus Thayer	06/07/85	.20	.20	1.30	(6)	1.25
1853 10¢ Richard Russell	05/31/84	.25	.20	2.00	(6)	1.00
a Large block tagging		.30	.20	2.25	(6)	
b Vertical pair, imperf. between						
and at bottom		850.00				
c Horizontal pair, imperf. between		2,000.00				
1854 11¢ Alden Partridge	02/12/85	.30	.20	1.60	(4)	1.25
a Tagging omitted		9.00				
Perf. 11 x 10.5						
1855 13¢ Crazy Horse	01/15/82	.30	.20	2.00	(4)	1.25
a Tagging omitted		7.50				
Perf. 11						
1856 14¢ Sinclair Lewis	03/21/85	.30	.20	2.25	(6)	1.00
a Large block tagging		.30	.20	2.25	(6)	
b Vertical pair, imperf. horizontally		120.00				
c Horizontal pair, imperf. between		9.00				
d Vertical pair, imperf. between		1,500.00				
Perf. 11 x 10.5						
1857 17¢ Rachel Carson	05/28/81	.35	.20	2.00	(4)	1.00
a Tagging omitted		10.00				
1858 18¢ George Mason	05/07/81	.35	.20	3.00	(4)	1.00
a Tagging omitted		7.50				
1859 19¢ Sequoyah	12/27/80	.40	.20	2.75	(4)	1.25
1860 20¢ Ralph Bunche	01/12/82	.40	.20	3.75	(4)	1.75
a Tagging omitted		7.50				
1861 20¢ Thomas H. Gallaudet	06/10/83	.50	.20	4.00	(4)	1.25
Perf. 11						
1862 20¢ Harry S. Truman	01/26/84	.40	.20	4.50	(6)	1.25
a Perf. 11.2, large block tagging, dull gum.40		.40	.20	3.00	(4)	
b Perf. 11.2, overall tagging, dull gum		.40	—	3.75	(4)	
c Perf. 11.2, tagging omitted		8.50				
1863 22¢ John J. Audubon	04/23/85	.75	.20	6.00	(6)	1.25
a Large block tagging		1.00	.20	8.00	(6)	
b Perf. 11.2, large block tagging		.55	.20	7.00	(4)	
c Tagging omitted		7.50				
d Vertical pair, imperf. horizontally		2,500.00				
e Vertical pair, imperf. between		—				
f Horizontal pair, imperf. between		2,000.00				

	Issues of 1981-1985		Un	U	PB/PNC	#	FDC	Q(M)
	Great Americans Issue (continued), Perf. 11							
1864	30¢ Frank C. Laubach	09/02/84	.60	.20	3.50	(6)	1.25	
a	Perf. 11.2, large block tagging		.55	.20	3.25	(4)		
b	Perf. 11.2, overall tagging		1.75	.20	22.50	(4)		
	Perf. 11 x 10.5							
1865	35¢ Charles R. Drew, MD	06/03/81	.75	.20	4.25	(4)	1.75	
1866	37¢ Robert Millikan	01/26/82	.80	.20	3.75	(4)	1.25	
a	Tagging omitted		10.00					
	Perf. 11							
1867	39¢ Grenville Clark	03/20/85	.90	.20	5.75	(6)	1.25	
a	Vertical pair, imperf. horizontally		500.00					
b	Vertical pair, imperf. between		2,000.00					
c	Perf. 10.9, large block tagging		.90	.20	5.75	(6)		
d	Perf. 11.2, large block tagging		.90	.20	5.75	(4)		
1868	40¢ Lillian M. Gilbreth	02/24/84	.90	.20	6.50	(6)	1.50	
a	Perf. 11.2, large block tagging		.90	.20	6.50	(4)		
1869	50¢ Chester W. Nimitz	02/22/85	.95	.20	7.50	(4)	2.00	
a	Perf. 11.2, large block tagging, dull gum		.95	.20	6.25	(4)		
b	Tagging omitted		11.00					
c	Perf. 11.2, tagging omitted, dull gum		8.00					
d	Perf. 11.2, overall tagging, dull gum		1.50	.20	8.50	(4)		
e	Perf. 11.2, prephosphored uncoated paper, shiny gum		.90	.20	5.00	(4)		
1870-73	Not assigned							
1874	15¢ Everett Dirksen	01/04/81	.30	.20	1.40	(4)	1.00	160
	Black Heritage Issue							
1875	15¢ Whitney Moore Young at Desk	01/30/81	.35	.20	1.75	(4)	1.75	160
	Flower Issue							
1876	18¢ Rose	04/23/81	.35	.20			1.00	53
1877	18¢ Camellia	04/23/81	.35	.20			1.00	53
1878	18¢ Dahlia	04/23/81	.35	.20			1.00	53
1879	18¢ Lily	04/23/81	.35	.20			1.00	53
a	Block of 4, #1876-79		1.40	1.25	1.75	(4)	2.50	
	Wildlife Booklet Issue							
1880	18¢ Bighorn Sheep	05/14/81	.55	.20			1.00	
1881	18¢ Puma	05/14/81	.55	.20			1.00	
1882	18¢ Harbor Seal	05/14/81	.55	.20			1.00	
1883	18¢ Buffalo	05/14/81	.55	.20			1.00	
1884	18¢ Brown Bear	05/14/81	.55	.20			1.00	
1885	18¢ Polar Bear	05/14/81	.55	.20			1.00	
1886	18¢ Elk (Wapiti)	05/14/81	.55	.20			1.00	
1887	18¢ Moose	05/14/81	.55	.20			1.00	
1888	18¢ White-Tailed Deer	05/14/81	.55	.20			1.00	
1889	18¢ Pronghorn Antelope	05/14/81	.55	.20			1.00	
a	Booklet pane of 10, #1880-89		8.50	7.00			5.00	
	#1880-89 issued only in booklets. All stamps are imperf. at one side or imperf. at one side and bottom.							
	Flag and Anthem Issue							
1890	18¢ "…for amber waves of grain"	04/24/81	.35	.20	2.25	(6)	1.00	
a	Imperf., pair		100.00					
b	Vertical pair, imperf. horizontally		850.00					
	Coil Stamp, Perf. 10 Vertically							
1891	18¢ "…from sea to shining sea"	04/24/81	.35	.20	4.00	(3)	1.50	
a	Imperf., pair		30.00	—				

Beginning with #1891, all coil stamps except 1947 feature a small plate number at the bottom of the design at varying intervals in a roll, depending on the press used. The basic "plate number coil" (PNC) collecting unit is a strip of three stamps, with the plate number appearing on the middle stamp. PNC values are for the most common plate number.

Frank C. Laubach
USA 30c
1864

Charles R Drew MD
USA 35c
1865

Robert Millikan
37c USA
1866

Grenville Clark
USA 39
1867

Lillian M.Gilbreth
USA 40c
1868

USA 50 ☆ ☆
Chester W. Nimitz
1869

USA 15c
Everett Dirksen
1874

Whitney Moore Young
Black Heritage USA 15c
1875

1876   **1877**

Rose USA 18c   Camellia USA 18c
Dahlia USA 18c   Lily USA 18c
1878   **1879** **1879a**

1880   **1881**
1882   **1883**
1884   **1885**
1886   **1887**
1888   **1889**

USA 18c
1889a

USA 18c
...for amber waves of grain
1890

USA 18c
...from sea to shining sea
1891

199

1892

1893

1894

1893a

1897

1897A

1898

1898A

1899

1900

1901

1902

1903

1904

Issues of 1981-1982		Un	U	PB/PNC/LP	#	FDC	Q(M)
Booklet Stamps, Perf. 11							
1892 6¢ USA Circle of Stars,							
single from booklet (1893a)	04/24/81	.50	.20			1.00	
1893 18¢ "...for purple mountain majesties,"							
single from booklet (1893a)	04/24/81	.30	.20			1.00	
a Booklet pane of 8 (2 #1892 & 6 #1893)		3.00	2.50			2.50	
b As "a," imperf. vertically between		75.00					
c Se-tenant pair, #1892 and #1893		.90	1.00				
#1892-93 issued only in booklets. All stamps are imperf. at one side or imperf. at one side and bottom.							
Flag Over Supreme Court Issue							
1894 20¢ Flag Over Supreme Court	12/17/81	.40	.20	2.75	(6)	1.00	
a Imperf., pair		35.00					
b Vertical pair, imperf. horizontally		525.00					
c Dark blue omitted		85.00					
d Black omitted		325.00					
e Perf. 11.2, shiny gum		.35	.20	2.50	(6)		
Coil Stamp, Perf. 10 Vertically							
1895 20¢ Flag Over Supreme							
Court (1894)	12/17/81	.40	.20	3.50	(3)	1.00	
a Narrow block tagging		.40	.20	3.25	(3)		
b Untagged (Bureau precanceled)		.50	.50	57.50	(3)		
c Tagging omitted		—					
d Imperf., pair		10.00					
e Pair, imperf. between		1,250.00					
f Black omitted		50.00					
g Blue omitted		1,500.00					
Booklet Stamp, Perf. 11 x 10.5							
1896 20¢ Flag over Supreme Court							
(1894), single from booklet	12/17/81	.40	.20			1.00	
a Booklet pane of 6	12/17/81	3.00	2.25			6.00	
b Booklet pane of 10	06/01/82	5.25	3.25			10.00	
Issues of 1981-1984, Transportation Issue, Coil Stamps, Perf. 10 Vertically							
(See also #2123-36, 2225-26, 2228, 2231, 2252-66, 2452-53A, 2457, 2464, 2468)							
1897 1¢ Omnibus 1880s	08/19/83	.20	.20	.30	(3)	1.00	
b Imperf., pair		675.00		—	(2)		
1897A 2¢ Locomotive 1870s	05/20/82	.20	.20	.45	(3)	1.50	
c Imperf., pair		52.50		—	(2)		
1898 3¢ Handcar 1880s	03/25/83	.20	.20	.65	(3)	1.00	
1898A 4¢ Stagecoach 1890s	08/19/82	.20	.20	.95	(3)	1.00	
b Untagged (Bureau precanceled)		.20	.20	4.75	(3)		
c As "b," imperf., pair		750.00					
d Imperf., pair		850.00	—				
1899 5¢ Motorcycle 1913	10/10/83	.20	.20	.85	(3)	1.50	
a Imperf., pair		2,750.00					
1900 5.2¢ Sleigh 1880s	03/21/83	.20	.20	6.00	(3)	1.00	
a Untagged (Bureau precanceled)		.20	.20	9.25	(3)		
1901 5.9¢ Bicycle 1870s	02/17/82	.25	.20	6.75	(3)	1.25	
a Untagged (Bureau precanceled)		.20	.20	24.00	(3)		
b As "a," imperf., pair		200.00		—	(2)		
1902 7.4¢ Baby Buggy 1880s	04/07/84	.20	.20	8.00	(3)	1.00	
a Untagged (Bureau precanceled)		.20	.20	5.00	(3)		
1903 9.3¢ Mail Wagon 1880s	12/15/81	.30	.20	7.50	(3)	1.00	
a Untagged (Bureau precanceled)		.25	.25	11.50	(3)		
b As "a," imperf., pair		120.00		200.00	(2)		
1904 10.9¢ Hansom Cab 1890s	03/26/82	.30	.20	15.00	(3)	1.00	
a Untagged (Bureau precanceled)		.30	.25	20.00	(3)		
b As "a," imperf., pair		150.00			(2)		

	Issues of 1981-1984		Un	U	PB	#	FDC	Q(M)
	Transportation Issue (continued)							
1905	11¢ RR Caboose 1890s	02/03/84	.30	.20	3.50	(3)	1.50	
a	Untagged (Bureau precanceled)		.25	.20	3.00	(3)		
1906	17¢ Electric Auto 1917	06/25/81	.35	.20	2.00	(3)	1.00	
a	Untagged (Bureau precanceled)		.35	.35	3.50	(3)		
b	Imperf., pair		165.00		—	(2)		
c	As "a," imperf., pair		650.00		—	(2)		
1907	18¢ Surrey 1890s	05/18/81	.35	.20	2.75	(3)	1.00	
a	Imperf., pair		140.00		—	(2)		
1908	20¢ Fire Pumper 1860s	12/10/81	.35	.20	2.00	(3)	2.00	
a	Imperf., pair		110.00		300.00	(2)		

Values for plate # coil strips of 3 stamps for #1897-1908 are for the most common plate numbers. Other plate #s and strips of 5 stamps may have higher values.

	Issue of 1983, Express Mail Booklet Issue, Perf. 10 Vertically							
1909	$9.35 Eagle and Moon,							
	single from booklet	08/12/83	22.50	15.00			45.00	
a	Booklet pane of 3		70.00	—			125.00	

#1909 issued only in booklets. All stamps are imperf. at top and bottom or imperf. at top, bottom and right side.

	Issues of 1981, Perf. 10.5 x 11							
1910	18¢ American Red Cross	05/01/81	.35	.20	1.50	(4)	1.25	165
	Perf. 11							
1911	18¢ Savings and Loans	05/08/81	.35	.20	1.50	(4)	1.00	107
	Space Achievement Issue, Perf. 11							
1912	18¢ Exploring the Moon — Moon Walk	05/21/81	.40	.20			1.00	42
1913	18¢ Benefiting Mankind (upper left) Columbia Space Shuttle	05/21/81	.40	.20			1.00	42
1914	18¢ Benefiting Mankind— Space Shuttle Deploying Satellite	05/21/81	.40	.20			1.00	42
1915	18¢ Understanding the Sun— Skylab	05/21/81	.40	.20			1.00	42
1916	18¢ Probing the Planets— Pioneer 11	05/21/81	.40	.20			1.00	42
1917	18¢ Benefiting Mankind— Columbia Space Shuttle Lifting Off	05/21/81	.40	.20			1.00	42
1918	18¢ Benefiting Mankind—Space Shuttle Preparing to Land	05/21/81	.40	.20			1.00	42
1919	18¢ Comprehending the Universe — Telescope	05/21/81	.40	.20			1.00	42
a	Block of 8, #1912-19		3.25	3.00	3.75	(8)	3.00	
b	As "a," imperf.		8,000.00					
1920	18¢ Professional Management	06/18/81	.35	.20	1.50	(4)	1.00	99
	Preservation of Wildlife Habitats Issue							
1921	18¢ Save Wetland Habitats— Great Blue Heron	06/26/81	.35	.20			1.00	45
1922	18¢ Save Grassland Habitats— Badger	06/26/81	.35	.20			1.00	45
1923	18¢ Save Mountain Habitats— Grizzly Bear	06/26/81	.35	.20			1.00	45
1924	18¢ Save Woodland Habitats— Ruffled Grouse	06/26/81	.35	.20			1.00	45
a	Block of 4, #1921-24		1.50	1.25	2.00	(4)	2.50	

1905

1906

1907

1908

1909

1910

1911

1912   **1913**   **1914**   **1915**

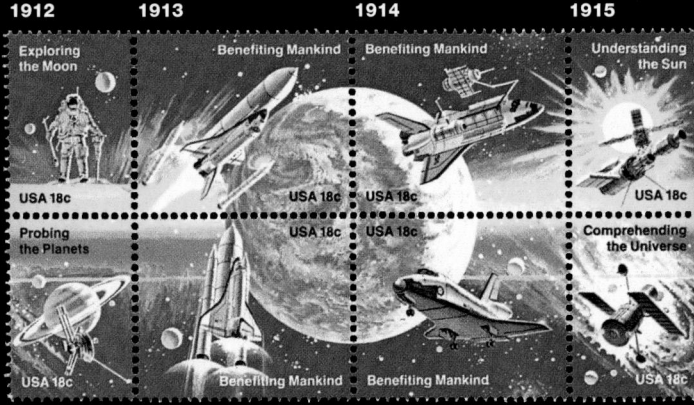

1916   **1917**   **1918**   **1919**   **1919a**

1920

1921

1922

1923

1924

1924a

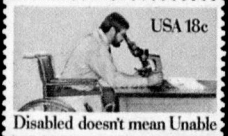

1925

1926

1927

1928  **1929**

1930 **1931**

1931a

1932

1933

1934

1935

1936

1937

1938 **1938a**

Issues of 1981		Un	U	PB	#	FDC	Q(M)
Perf. 11							
1925	18¢ International Year of the Disabled 06/29/81	.35	.20	1.50	(4)	1.00	100
a	Vertical pair, imperf. horizontally	2,600.00					
1926	18¢ Edna St. Vincent Millay 07/10/81	.35	.20	1.50	(4)	1.00	100
a	Black omitted	300.00	—				
1927	18¢ Alcoholism 08/19/81	.40	.20	10.00	(6)	2.00	98
a	Imperf., pair	400.00					
b	Vertical pair, imperf. horizontally	2,500.00					
American Architecture Issue							
1928	18¢ NYU Library, by Sanford White 08/28/81	.40	.20			1.00	42
1929	18¢ Biltmore House, by Richard Morris Hunt 08/28/81	.40	.20			1.00	42
1930	18¢ Palace of the Arts, by Bernard Maybeck 08/28/81	.40	.20			1.00	42
1931	18¢ National Farmer's Bank, by Louis Sullivan 08/28/81	.40	.20			1.00	42
a	Block of 4, #1928-31	1.65	1.75	2.10	(4)	2.50	
American Sports Issue, Perf. 10.5 x 11							
1932	18¢ Babe Zaharias Holding Trophy 09/22/81	.40	.20	3.00	(4)	6.50	102
1933	18¢ Bobby Jones Teeing off 09/22/81	.40	.20	3.00	(4)	10.00	99
Perf. 11							
1934	18¢ Frederic Remington 10/09/81	.35	.20	1.60	(4)	1.25	101
a	Vertical pair, imperf. between	275.00					
b	Brown omitted	425.00					
1935	18¢ James Hoban 10/13/81	.35	.20	1.60	(4)	1.00	101
1936	20¢ James Hoban 10/13/81	.35	.20	1.65	(4)	1.00	167
American Bicentennial Issue							
1937	18¢ Battle of Yorktown 1781 10/16/81	.35	.20			1.00	81
1938	18¢ Battle of the Virginia Capes 1781 10/16/81	.35	.20			1.00	81
a	Attached pair, #1937-38	.90	.75	2.00	(4)	1.50	
b	As "a," black omitted	400.00					

JOHN JAMES AUDUBON

(1785-1851)

JOHN JAMES AUDUBON was a self-taught artist and naturalist whose magnum opus, *Birds of America*, has been described as "the finest pictorial ornithological book ever produced." Born in Saint-Domingue (now Haiti), Audubon was raised in France. He moved to the United States in 1803 and became a citizen a few years later. By 1820, after a series of unsuccessful business enterprises, Audubon dedicated himself to the project that became his life's work and greatest passion—a comprehensive survey of American birds, beautifully and realistically illustrated and shown in their natural habitats. "My business went on profitably when I attended to it," wrote Audubon in 1828. "But birds were birds and my thoughts were ever and anon turning towards them as to my greatest delight." Audubon has been honored on U.S. postage stamps as a Famous American (1940), a Great American (1985), and an American Artist (1963); his art has appeared on an Air Mail stamp (1967), in Four Centuries of American Art (1998), and in 2002 was the American Treasures issuance. ❑

	Issues of 1981		Un	U	PB/LP	#	FDC	Q(M)
	Christmas Issue							
1939	20¢ Madonna and Child,							
	by Botticelli	10/28/81	.40	.20	1.75	(4)	1.00	598
a	Imperf., pair		125.00					
b	Vertical pair, imperf. horizontally		1,650.00					
1940	20¢ Felt Bear on Sleigh	10/28/81	.40	.20	1.75	(4)	1.00	793
a	Imperf., pair		260.00					
b	Vertical pair, imperf. horizontally		2,500.00					
1941	20¢ John Hanson	11/05/81	.40	.20	1.75	(4)	1.00	167
	Desert Plants Issue, Perf. 11							
1942	20¢ Barrel Cactus	12/11/81	.35	.20			1.00	48
1943	20¢ Agave	12/11/81	.35	.20			1.00	48
1944	20¢ Beavertail Cactus	12/11/81	.35	.20			1.00	48
1945	20¢ Saguaro	12/11/81	.35	.20			1.00	48
a	Block of 4, #1942-45		1.50	1.25	1.90	(4)	2.50	
b	As "a," deep brown omitted		3,500.00					
c	#1945 vertical pair, imperf.		5,250.00					
	Perf. 11 x 10.5							
1946	(20¢) "C" Stamp	10/11/81	.40	.20	2.00	(4)	1.00	
a	Tagging omitted		9.00					
	Coil Stamp, Perf. 10 Vertically							
1947	(20¢) "C" brown Eagle (1946)	10/11/81	.60	.20	1.50	(2)	1.00	
a	Imperf., pair		1,400.00		—	(2)		
	Booklet Stamp, Perf. 11 x 10.5							
1948	(20¢) "C" brown Eagle (1946),							
	single from booklet	10/11/81	.40	.20			1.00	
a	Booklet pane of 10	10/11/81	4.50	3.25			3.50	
	Issues of 1982, Perf. 11							
1949	20¢ Bighorn Sheep,							
	single from booklet	01/08/82	.55	.20			1.25	
a	Booklet pane of 10		5.50	2.50			6.00	
b	As "a," imperf. between		110.00					
c	Type II		.55	.20				
d	Type II, booklet pane of 10		11.00	—				
e	As #1949, tagging omitted		5.00	—				
f	As "e," booklet pane of 10		50.00	—				
	#1949 issued only in booklets. All stamps are imperf. at one side or imperf. at one side and bottom.							
1950	20¢ Franklin D. Roosevelt	01/30/82	.40	.20	1.75	(4)	1.00	164
	Perf. 11 x 10.5							
1951	20¢ Love	02/01/82	.40	.20	1.75	(4)	1.00	447
b	Imperf., pair		260.00					
c	Blue omitted		225.00					
d	Yellow omitted		1,000.00					
e	Purple omitted		—					
1951A	Perf. 11.25 x 10.5		.75	.25	3.50	(4)		
	Perf. 11							
1952	20¢ George Washington	02/22/82	.40	.20	1.75	(4)	1.25	181

1939

1940

1941

1942　　　**1943**　　　　　**1945**

1944　　　　　　　　**1945a**

1946

1949

1950

1951

1952

Alabama	Alaska	Arizona	Arkansas	California
USA 20c	USA 20c	USA 20c	USA 20c	USA 20c
Yellowhammer & Camellia	Willow Ptarmigan & Forget-Me-Not	Cactus Wren & Saguaro Cactus Blossom	Mockingbird & Apple Blossom	California Quail & California Poppy
1953	**1954**	**1955**	**1956**	**1957**

Colorado	Connecticut	Delaware	Florida	Georgia
USA 20c	USA 20c	USA 20c	USA 20c	USA 20c
Lark Bunting & Rocky Mountain Columbine	Robin & Mountain Laurel	Blue Hen Chicken & Peach Blossom	Mockingbird & Orange Blossom	Brown Thrasher & Cherokee Rose
1958	**1959**	**1960**	**1961**	**1962**

Hawaii	Idaho	Illinois	Indiana	Iowa
USA 20c	USA 20c	USA 20c	USA 20c	USA 20c
Hawaiian Goose & Hibiscus	Mountain Bluebird & Syringa	Cardinal & Violet	Cardinal & Peony	Eastern Goldfinch & Wild Rose
1963	**1964**	**1965**	**1966**	**1967**

Kansas	Kentucky	Louisiana	Maine	Maryland
USA 20c	USA 20c	USA 20c	USA 20c	USA 20c
Western Meadowlark & Sunflower	Cardinal & Goldenrod	Brown Pelican & Magnolia	Chickadee & White Pine Cone and Tassel	Baltimore Oriole & Black-Eyed Susan
1968	**1969**	**1970**	**1971**	**1972**

Massachusetts	Michigan	Minnesota	Mississippi	Missouri
USA 20c	USA 20c	USA 20c	USA 20c	USA 20c

Black-Capped Chickadee & Mayflower	Robin & Apple Blossom	Common Loon & Showy Lady Slipper	Mockingbird & Magnolia	Eastern Bluebird & Red Hawthorn
1973	**1974**	**1975**	**1976**	**1977**

Issues of 1982		Un	U	FDC	Q(M)
State Birds & Flowers Issue, Perf. 10.5 x 11					
1953 20¢ Alabama: Yellowhammer and Camellia	04/14/82	.50	.25	1.25	13
1954 20¢ Alaska: Willow Ptarmigan and Forget-Me-Not	04/14/82	.50	.25	1.25	13
1955 20¢ Arizona: Cactus Wren and Saguaro Cactus Blossom	04/14/82	.50	.25	1.25	13
1956 20¢ Arkansas: Mockingbird and Apple Blossom	04/14/82	.50	.25	1.25	13
1957 20¢ California: California Quail and California Poppy	04/14/82	.50	.25	1.25	13
1958 20¢ Colorado: Lark Bunting and Rocky Mountain Columbine	04/14/82	.50	.25	1.25	13
1959 20¢ Connecticut: Robin and Mountain Laurel	04/14/82	.50	.25	1.25	13
1960 20¢ Delaware: Blue Hen Chicken and Peach Blossom	04/14/82	.50	.25	1.25	13
1961 20¢ Florida: Mockingbird and Orange Blossom	04/14/82	.50	.25	1.25	13
1962 20¢ Georgia: Brown Thrasher and Cherokee Rose	04/14/82	.50	.25	1.25	13
1963 20¢ Hawaii: Hawaiian Goose and Hibiscus	04/14/82	.50	.25	1.25	13
1964 20¢ Idaho: Mountain Bluebird and Syringa	04/14/82	.50	.25	1.25	13
1965 20¢ Illinois: Cardinal and Violet	04/14/82	.50	.25	1.25	13
1966 20¢ Indiana: Cardinal and Peony	04/14/82	.50	.25	1.25	13
1967 20¢ Iowa: Eastern Goldfinch and Wild Rose	04/14/82	.50	.25	1.25	13
1968 20¢ Kansas: Western Meadowlark and Sunflower	04/14/82	.50	.25	1.25	13
1969 20¢ Kentucky: Cardinal and Goldenrod	04/14/82	.50	.25	1.25	13
1970 20¢ Louisiana: Brown Pelican and Magnolia	04/14/82	.50	.25	1.25	13
1971 20¢ Maine: Chickadee and White Pine Cone and Tassel	04/14/82	.50	.25	1.25	13
1972 20¢ Maryland: Baltimore Oriole and Black-Eyed Susan	04/14/82	.50	.25	1.25	13
1973 20¢ Massachusetts: Black-Capped Chickadee and Mayflower	04/14/82	.50	.25	1.25	13
1974 20¢ Michigan: Robin and Apple Blossom	04/14/82	.50	.25	1.25	13
1975 20¢ Minnesota: Common Loon and Showy Lady Slipper	04/14/82	.50	.25	1.25	13
1976 20¢ Mississippi: Mockingbird and Magnolia	04/14/82	.50	.25	1.25	13
1977 20¢ Missouri: Eastern Bluebird and Red Hawthorn	04/14/82	.50	.25	1.25	13

Issues of 1982			Un	U	FDC	Q(M)
State Birds & Flowers Issue (continued)						
1978	20¢ Montana: Western Meadowlark & Bitterroot	04/14/82	.50	.25	1.25	13
1979	20¢ Nebraska: Western Meadowlark & Goldenrod	04/14/82	.50	.25	1.25	13
1980	20¢ Nevada: Mountain Bluebird & Sagebrush	04/14/82	.50	.25	1.25	13
1981	20¢ New Hampshire: Purple Finch & Lilac	04/14/82	.50	.25	1.25	13
1982	20¢ New Jersey: American Goldfinch & Violet	04/14/82	.50	.25	1.25	13
1983	20¢ New Mexico: Roadrunner & Yucca Flower	04/14/82	.50	.25	1.25	13
1984	20¢ New York: Eastern Bluebird & Rose	04/14/82	.50	.25	1.25	13
1985	20¢ North Carolina: Cardinal & Flowering Dogwood	04/14/82	.50	.25	1.25	13
1986	20¢ North Dakota: Western Meadowlark & Wild Prairie Rose	04/14/82	.50	.25	1.25	13
1987	20¢ Ohio: Cardinal & Red Carnation	04/14/82	.50	.25	1.25	13
1988	20¢ Oklahoma: Scissor-tailed Flycatcher & Mistletoe	04/14/82	.50	.25	1.25	13
1989	20¢ Oregon: Western Meadowlark & Oregon Grape	04/14/82	.50	.25	1.25	13
1990	20¢ Pennsylvania: Ruffed Grouse & Mountain Laurel	04/14/82	.50	.25	1.25	13
1991	20¢ Rhode Island: Rhode Island Red & Violet	04/14/82	.50	.25	1.25	13
1992	20¢ South Carolina: Carolina Wren & Carolina Jessamine	04/14/82	.50	.25	1.25	13
1993	20¢ South Dakota: Ring-Necked Pheasant & Pasqueflower	04/14/82	.50	.25	1.25	13
1994	20¢ Tennessee: Mockingbird & Iris	04/14/82	.50	.25	1.25	13
1995	20¢ Texas: Mockingbird & Bluebonnet	04/14/82	.50	.25	1.25	13
1996	20¢ Utah: California Gull & Sego Lily	04/14/82	.50	.25	1.25	13
1997	20¢ Vermont: Hermit Thrush & Red Clover	04/14/82	.50	.25	1.25	13
1998	20¢ Virginia: Cardinal & Flowering Dogwood	04/14/82	.50	.25	1.25	13
1999	20¢ Washington: American Goldfinch & Rhododendron	04/14/82	.50	.25	1.25	13
2000	20¢ West Virginia: Cardinal & Rhododendron Maximum	04/14/82	.50	.25	1.25	13
2001	20¢ Wisconsin: Robin & Wood Violet	04/14/82	.50	.25	1.25	13
2002	20¢ Wyoming: Western Meadowlark & Indian Paintbrush	04/14/82	.50	.25	1.25	13
a	Any single, perf. 11.25 x 11		.55	.30		
b	Pane of 50 (with plate #)		25.00	—	30.00	
c	Pane of 50, perf. 11.25 x 11		27.50	—		
d	Pane of 50, imperf.		27,500.00			

AMISH QUILTS

In 2001 the U.S. Postal Service paid tribute to a uniquely American folk art form—the Amish quilt, the first issuance in the American Treasures series. Distinctive in its simplicity, symmetry, deft needlework, and broad fields of deep color, the Amish quilt is one of the most expressive traditions in American design. Amish quilting traditions vary from region to region, yet all are influenced by the religious and social values of Amish daily life: humility, simplicity, modesty, and serviceability. The four quilts—made by unknown Amish quilt makers—display the saturated colors, bold geometric patterns, and central design motifs characteristic of quilts made in Lancaster County, Pennsylvania, during the first half of the 20th century. From left to right, the quilts are: Diamond in the Square, circa 1920; Lone Star, circa 1920; Sunshine and Shadow, circa 1910; and Double Ninepatch (variation), circa 1940. □

Montana — USA 20c — *Western Meadowlark & Bitterroot* — 1978
Nebraska — USA 20c — *Western Meadowlark & Goldenrod* — 1979
Nevada — USA 20c — *Mountain Bluebird & Sagebrush* — 1980
New Hampshire — USA 20c — *Purple Finch & Lilac* — 1981
New Jersey — USA 20c — *American Goldfinch & Violet* — 1982

New Mexico — USA 20c — *Roadrunner & Yucca Flower* — 1983
New York — USA 20c — *Eastern Bluebird & Rose* — 1984
North Carolina — USA 20c — *Cardinal & Flowering Dogwood* — 1985
North Dakota — USA 20c — *Western Meadowlark & Wild Prairie Rose* — 1986
Ohio — USA 20c — *Cardinal & Red Carnation* — 1987

Oklahoma — USA 20c — *Scissor-tailed Flycatcher & Mistletoe* — 1988
Oregon — USA 20c — *Western Meadowlark & Oregon Grape* — 1989
Pennsylvania — USA 20c — *Ruffed Grouse & Mountain Laurel* — 1990
Rhode Island — USA 20c — *Rhode Island Red & Violet* — 1991
South Carolina — USA 20c — *Carolina Wren & Carolina Jessamine* — 1992

South Dakota — USA 20c — *Ring-Necked Pheasant & Pasqueflower* — 1993
Tennessee — USA 20c — *Mockingbird & Iris* — 1994
Texas — USA 20c — *Mockingbird & Bluebonnet* — 1995
Utah — USA 20c — *California Gull & Sego Lily* — 1996
Vermont — USA 20c — *Hermit Thrush & Red Clover* — 1997

Virginia — USA 20c — *Cardinal & Flowering Dogwood* — 1998
Washington — USA 20c — *American Goldfinch & Rhododendron* — 1999
West Virginia — USA 20c — *Cardinal & Rhododendron Maximum* — 2000
Wisconsin — USA 20c — *Robin & Wood Violet* — 2001
Wyoming — USA 20c — *Western Meadowlark & Indian Paintbrush* — 2002

2003

2004

2005

2006   2007

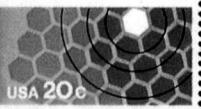

2008   2009   2009a

2010   2012

2011

2013

2014

2015

2016

2019   2020

2017

2018

2021   2022   2022a

Issues of 1982		Un	U	PB/PNC/LP	#	FDC	Q(M)
Perf. 11							
2003	20¢ USA/The Netherlands	04/20/82	.40	.20	3.50	(6)	1.00	109
a	Imperf., pair		325.00					
2004	20¢ Library of Congress	04/21/82	.40	.20	1.75	(4)	1.00	113
Coil Stamp, Perf. 10 Vertically							
2005	20¢ Consumer Education	04/27/82	.55	.20	22.50	(3)	1.00	
a	Imperf., pair		100.00		400.00	(2)		
b	Tagging omitted		7.50					

Value for plate no. coil strip of 3 stamps is for most common plate nos. Other plate nos. and strips of 5 stamps may have higher values.

	Knoxville World's Fair Issue, Perf. 11						
2006	20¢ Solar Energy	04/29/82	.40	.20			1.00	31
2007	20¢ Synthetic Fuels	04/29/82	.40	.20			1.00	31
2008	20¢ Breeder Reactor	04/29/82	.40	.20			1.00	31
2009	20¢ Fossil Fuels	04/29/82	.40	.20			1.00	31
a	Block of 4, #2006-09		1.65	1.50	2.25	(4)	2.50	
2010	20¢ Horatio Alger	04/30/82	.40	.20	1.75	(4)	1.00	108
2011	20¢ Aging Together	05/21/82	.40	.20	1.75	(4)	1.00	173
Performing Arts Issue							
2012	20¢ John, Ethel and Lionel Barrymore	06/08/82	.40	.20	1.75	(4)	1.00	107
2013	20¢ Dr. Mary Walker	06/10/82	.40	.20	1.75	(4)	1.00	109
2014	20¢ International Peace Garden	06/30/82	.40	.20	1.75	(4)	1.00	183
a	Black and green omitted		260.00					
2015	20¢ America's Libraries	07/13/82	.40	.20	1.75	(4)	1.00	169
a	Vertical pair, imperf. horizontally		300.00					
b	Tagging omitted		7.50					
Black Heritage Issue, Perf. 10.5 x 11							
2016	20¢ Jackie Robinson and Robinson Stealing Home Plate	08/02/82	1.10	.20	5.50	(4)	6.00	164
Perf. 11							
2017	20¢ Touro Synagogue	08/22/82	.40	.20	12.50	(20)	1.50	110
a	Imperf., pair		2,500.00					
2018	20¢ Wolf Trap Farm Park	09/01/82	.40	.20	1.75	(4)	1.00	111
American Architecture Issue							
2019	20¢ Fallingwater, by Frank Lloyd Wright	09/30/82	.45	.20			1.00	41
2020	20¢ Illinois Institute of Technology, by Ludwig Mies van der Rohe	09/30/82	.45	.20			1.00	41
2021	20¢ Gropius House, by Walter Gropius	09/30/82	.45	.20			1.00	41
2022	20¢ Dulles Airport by Eero Saarinen	09/30/82	.45	.20			1.00	41
a	Block of 4, #2019-22		2.00	1.75	2.50	(4)	2.50	

1982-1983

	Issues of 1982		Un	U	PB	#	FDC	Q(M)
2023	20¢ St. Francis of Assisi	10/07/82	.40	.20	1.75	(4)	1.00	174
2024	20¢ Ponce de Leon	10/12/82	.40	.20	3.25	(6)	1.00	110
a	Imperf., pair		500.00					
	Christmas Issue							
2025	13¢ Puppy and Kitten	11/03/82	.25	.20	1.40	(4)	1.25	234
a	Imperf., pair		650.00					
2026	20¢ Madonna and Child,							
	by Tiepolo	10/28/82	.40	.20	11.00	(20)	1.00	703
a	Imperf., pair		150.00					
b	Horizontal pair, imperf. vertically		—					
c	Vertical pair, imperf. horizontally		—					
	Seasons Greetings Issue							
2027	20¢ Children Sledding	10/28/82	.50	.20			1.00	197
2028	20¢ Children Building							
	a Snowman	10/28/82	.50	.20			1.00	197
2029	20¢ Children Skating	10/28/82	.50	.20			1.00	197
2030	20¢ Children Trimming a Tree	10/28/82	.50	.20			1.00	197
a	Block of 4, #2027-30		2.10	1.50	2.50	(4)	2.50	
b	As "a," imperf.		2,750.00					
c	As "a," imperf. horizontally		750.00					
	Issues of 1983							
2031	20¢ Science & Industry	01/19/83	.40	.20	1.75	(4)	1.00	119
a	Black omitted		1,400.00					
	Balloons Issue							
2032	20¢ Intrepid, 1861	03/31/83	.40	.20			1.00	57
2033	20¢ Hot Air Ballooning							
	(wording lower right)	03/31/83	.40	.20			1.00	57
2034	20¢ Hot Air Ballooning							
	(wording upper left)	03/31/83	.40	.20			1.00	57
2035	20¢ Explorer II, 1935	03/31/83	.40	.20			1.00	57
a	Block of 4, #2032-35		1.65	1.50	1.75	(4)	2.50	
b	As "a," imperf.		4,250.00					
c	As "a," right stamp perf.,							
	otherwise imperf.		4,500.00					
2036	20¢ U.S./Sweden Treaty	03/24/83	.40	.20	1.75	(4)	1.00	118
2037	20¢ Civilian Conservation							
	Corps	04/05/83	.40	.20	1.75	(4)	1.00	114
a	Imperf., pair		2,900.00					
2038	20¢ Joseph Priestley	04/13/83	.40	.20	1.75	(4)	1.00	165
2039	20¢ Voluntarism	04/20/83	.40	.20	3.00	(6)	1.00	120
a	Imperf., pair		750.00					
2040	20¢ Concord-German							
	Immigration, Apr. 29	04/29/83	.40	.20	1.75	(4)	1.00	117

2023

2024

2025

2027 **2028**

2026

2029 **2030** **2030a**

2032 **2033**

2031

2034 **2035** **2035a**

2036

2037

2038

2039

2040

215

2041

2042

2043

2044

2045

2046

2047

2048

2049

2050

2051

2051a

2052

2055

2056

2053

2057

2058

2058a

2054

	Issues of 1983		Un	U	PB	#	FDC	Q(M)
	Tagged, Perf. 11							
2041	20¢ Brooklyn Bridge	05/17/83	.40	.20	1.75	(4)	1.75	182
2042	20¢ Tennessee Valley Authority	05/18/83	.40	.20	10.00	(20)	1.00	114
2043	20¢ Physical Fitness	05/14/83	.40	.20	3.00	(6)	1.25	112
	Black Heritage Issue							
2044	20¢ Scott Joplin Portrait							
	and Joplin Playing the Piano	06/09/83	.40	.20	2.00	(4)	1.75	115
a	Imperf., pair		475.00					
2045	20¢ Medal of Honor	06/07/83	.40	.20	1.75	(4)	4.50	109
a	Red omitted		240.00					
	American Sports Issue, Perf. 10.5 x 11							
2046	20¢ Babe Ruth Hitting							
	a Home Run	07/06/83	1.40	.20	6.50	(4)	5.00	185
	Literary Arts Issue, Perf. 11							
2047	20¢ Nathaniel Hawthorne,							
	by Cephus Giovanni Thompson	07/08/83	.45	.20	2.10	(4)	1.00	111
	Olympic Summer Games Issue (See also #2082-85, C101-12)							
2048	13¢ Discus Thrower	07/28/83	.35	.20			1.25	99
2049	13¢ High Jumper	07/28/83	.35	.20			1.25	99
2050	13¢ Archer	07/28/83	.35	.20			1.25	99
2051	13¢ Boxers	07/28/83	.35	.20			1.25	99
a	Block of 4, #2048-51		1.50	1.25	1.75	(4)	2.50	
	American Bicentennial Issue							
2052	20¢ Signing of Treaty of Paris							
	(John Adams, Benjamin Franklin							
	and John Jay observing David							
	Hartley), by Benjamin West	09/02/83	.40	.20	1.75	(4)	1.00	104
2053	20¢ Civil Service	09/09/83	.40	.20	3.00	(6)	1.00	115
2054	20¢ Metropolitan Opera	09/14/83	.40	.20	1.75	(4)	1.50	113
	American Inventors Issue							
2055	20¢ Charles Steinmetz							
	and Curve on Graph	09/21/83	.45	.20			1.00	48
2056	20¢ Edwin Armstrong and							
	Frequency Modulator	09/21/83	.45	.20			1.00	48
2057	20¢ Nikola Tesla and							
	Induction Motor	09/21/83	.45	.20			1.00	48
2058	20¢ Philo T. Farnsworth and							
	First Television Camera	09/21/83	.45	.20			1.00	48
a	Block of 4, #2055-58		1.80	1.25	2.50	(4)	2.50	
b	As "a," black omitted		375.00					

	Issues of 1983		Un	U	PB	#	FDC	Q(M)
	Streetcars Issue, Perf. 11							
2059	20¢ First American Streetcar	10/08/83	.45	.20			1.00	52
2060	20¢ Early Electric Streetcar	10/08/83	.45	.20			1.00	52
2061	20¢ "Bobtail" Horsecar	10/08/83	.45	.20			1.00	52
2062	20¢ St. Charles Streetcar	10/08/83	.45	.20			1.00	52
a	Block of 4, #2059-62		1.80	1.40	2.50	(4)	2.50	
b	As "a," black omitted		375.00					
c	As "a," black omitted on #2059, 2061		—					
	Christmas Issue							
2063	20¢ Niccolini-Cowper Madonna, by Raphael	10/28/83	.40	.20	1.75	(4)	1.00	716
2064	20¢ Santa Claus	10/28/83	.40	.20	3.00	(6)	1.00	849
a	Imperf., pair		175.00					
2065	20¢ Martin Luther	11/11/83	.40	.20	1.75	(4)	1.50	165
	Issues of 1984							
2066	20¢ 25th Anniversary of Alaska Statehood	01/03/84	.40	.20	1.75	(4)	1.00	120
	Winter Olympic Games Issue, Perf. 10.5 x 11							
2067	20¢ Ice Dancing	01/06/84	.50	.20			1.00	80
2068	20¢ Downhill Skiing	01/06/84	.50	.20			1.00	80
2069	20¢ Cross-country Skiing	01/06/84	.50	.20			1.00	80
2070	20¢ Hockey	01/06/84	.50	.20			1.00	80
a	Block of 4, #2067-70		2.10	1.50	3.00	(4)	2.50	
	Perf. 11							
2071	20¢ Federal Deposit Insurance Corporation	01/12/84	.40	.20	1.75	(4)	1.00	103

GEORGIA O'KEEFFE

(1887-1986)

GEORGIA O'KEEFFE, one of the foremost American painters of the 20th century, spent her childhood on a farm in Wisconsin. She took art lessons as a child and, encouraged by her teachers, decided to become an artist. After studying at the Art Institute of Chicago and the Art Students League of New York, O'Keeffe became an art teacher and continued to study art at the University of Virginia and Columbia University. In 1916, noted American photographer Alfred Stieglitz—who married O'Keeffe in 1924—exhibited her work at his avant-garde gallery in New York City. He continued to promote O'Keeffe and her work through exhibitions he sponsored every year until his death in 1946. In the late 1940s, O'Keeffe moved to New Mexico where she continued to live and work the rest of her life. In 1996 the Postal Service honored O'Keeffe with a stamp featuring *Red Poppy, 1927*—one of more than 200 flower paintings produced by O'Keeffe between 1918-1932. The tiny masterpiece—it measures only 7 inches by 9 inches—is an excellent example of the monumental scale, intense color, and sensuality found in these works. ❑

2059   **2060**

2061   **2062**   **2062a**

2064

2063

2065

2067   **2068**

2066

2071

2069   **2070**   **2070a**

2072　　　**2073**　　　**2074**　　　**2075**

2076　　**2077**

2080

2081

2078　　**2079**　　**2079a**

2082　　**2083**

2086

2087

2084　　**2085**　　**2085a**

Issues of 1984		Un	U	PB	#	FDC	Q(M)
Perf. 11 x 10.5							
2072 20¢ Love	01/31/84	.40	.20	11.50	(20)	1.00	555
a	Horizontal pair, imperf. vertically	175.00					
b	Tagging omitted	5.00					
Black Heritage Issue, Carter G. Woodson, Perf. 11							
2073 20¢ Carter G. Woodson							
Holding History Book	02/01/84	.40	.20	2.00	(4)	1.75	120
a	Horizontal pair, imperf. vertically	1,600.00					
2074 20¢ Soil and Water							
Conservation	02/06/84	.40	.20	1.75	(4)	1.00	107
2075 20¢ 50th Anniversary							
of Credit Union Act	02/10/84	.40	.20	1.75	(4)	1.00	107
Orchids Issue							
2076 20¢ Wild Pink	03/05/84	.50	.20			1.00	77
2077 20¢ Yellow Lady's-Slipper	03/05/84	.50	.20			1.00	77
2078 20¢ Spreading Pogonia	03/05/84	.50	.20			1.00	77
2079 20¢ Pacific Calypso	03/05/84	.50	.20			1.00	77
a	Block of 4, #2076-79	2.00	1.50	2.50	(4)	2.50	
2080 20¢ 25th Anniversary							
of Hawaii Statehood	03/12/84	.40	.20	1.70	(4)	1.00	120
2081 20¢ National Archives	04/16/84	.40	.20	1.70	(4)	1.00	108
Olympic Summer Games Issue (See also #2048-52, C101-12)							
2082 20¢ Diving	05/04/84	.55	.20			1.25	78
2083 20¢ Long Jump	05/04/84	.55	.20			1.25	78
2084 20¢ Wrestling	05/04/84	.55	.20			1.25	78
2085 20¢ Kayak	05/04/84	.55	.20			1.25	78
a	Block of 4, #2082-85	2.40	1.90	3.50	(4)	2.50	
2086 20¢ Louisiana World							
Exposition	05/11/84	.40	.20	1.75	(4)	1.00	130
2087 20¢ Health Research	05/17/84	.40	.20	1.75	(4)	1.00	120

NATHANIEL HAWTHORNE

(1804-1864)

Novelist and short story writer NATHANIEL HAWTHORNE was born into a prominent New England family with ties to the 1692 Salem, Massachusetts, witchcraft trials. Hawthorne led a solitary life—his widowed mother was a recluse—before attending Bowdoin College. After graduating, he held a variety of government positions while writing short fictional stories that appeared in *The Token* and other periodicals. These stories were collected and published as *Twice-Told Tales* in 1837 and 1842. In a complimentary review of Hawthorne's stories, fellow author Edgar Allan Poe defined for the first time a new American literary genre—the short story—which Poe and Hawthorne would share credit for creating. Hawthorne married in 1842 and lived briefly in the midst of the transcendentalist movement. Needing to support his growing family, he returned to civil service and

began writing the novel that became his masterpiece. *The Scarlet Letter*—often considered the first American psychological novel—was published in 1850 to critical and financial success. Other novels include *The House of Seven Gables* (1851) and *The Blithedale Romance* (1852). In 1983, Hawthorne was honored by the Postal Service as a Literary Arts issue. ❏

Issues of 1984		Un	U	PB	#	FDC	Q(M)
Performing Arts Issue, Perf. 11							
2088	20¢ Douglas Fairbanks Portrait						
	and Fairbanks in Pirate Role 05/23/84	.40	.20	11.00	(20)	1.00	117
American Sports Issue							
2089	20¢ Jim Thorpe						
	on Football Field 05/24/84	.40	.20	2.00	(4)	3.00	116
Performing Arts Issue							
2090	20¢ John McCormack Portrait						
	and McCormack in Tenor Role 06/06/84	.40	.20	1.75	(4)	1.00	117
2091	20¢ 25th Anniversary						
	of St. Lawrence Seaway 06/26/84	.40	.20	1.75	(4)	1.00	120
2092	20¢ Migratory Bird Hunting						
	and Preservation Act 07/02/84	.50	.20	2.50	(4)	1.00	124
a	Horizontal pair, imperf. vertically	400.00					
2093	20¢ Roanoke Voyages 07/13/84	.40	.20	1.75	(4)	1.00	120
	Pair with full horizontal gutter between	—					
Literary Arts Issue							
2094	20¢ Herman Melville 08/01/84	.40	.20	1.75	(4)	1.50	117
2095	20¢ Horace Moses 08/06/84	.45	.20	3.50	(6)	1.00	117
2096	20¢ Smokey the Bear 08/13/84	.40	.20	2.00	(4)	3.00	96
a	Horizontal pair, imperf. between	300.00					
b	Vertical pair, imperf. between	225.00					
c	Block of 4, imperf. between						
	vertically and horizontally	5,500.00					
d	Horizontal pair, imperf. vertically	1,500.00					
American Sports Issue							
2097	20¢ Roberto Clemente in Pirates Cap, Puerto						
	Rican Flag in Background 08/17/84	1.60	.20	7.50	(4)	9.00	119
a	Horizontal pair, imperf. vertically	2,000.00					
American Dogs Issue							
2098	20¢ Beagle and Boston Terrier 09/07/84	.45	.20			1.50	54
2099	20¢ Chesapeake Bay Retriever						
	and Cocker Spaniel 09/07/84	.45	.20			1.50	54
2100	20¢ Alaskan Malamute						
	and Collie 09/07/84	.45	.20			1.50	54
2101	20¢ Black and Tan Coonhound						
	and American Foxhound 09/07/84	.45	.20			1.50	54
a	Block of 4, #2098-2101	1.90	1.90	3.00	(4)	3.00	

AMERICAN ★ COMMEMORATIVE ★ **COLLECTIBLES**

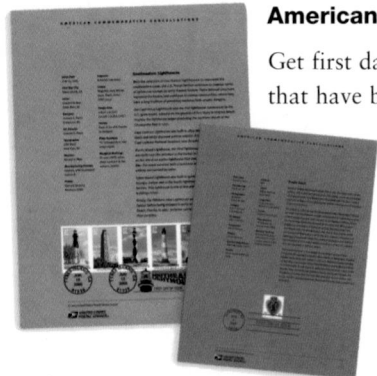

2088

2089

2090

2091

2092

2093

2094

2095

2096

2097

2098   2099

2100   2101   2101a

2102

2103

2104

2105

2106

2107

2108

2109

2110

2111

2114   **2115b**   **2116**

	Issues of 1984		Un	U	PB/PNC	#	FDC	Q(M)
2102	20¢ Crime Prevention	09/26/84	.40	.20	1.75	(4)	1.25	120
2103	20¢ Hispanic Americans	10/31/84	.40	.20	1.75	(4)	1.75	108
a	Vertical pair, imperf. horizontally		2,250.00					
2104	20¢ Family Unity	10/01/84	.40	.20	12.50	(20)	1.00	118
a	Horizontal pair, imperf. vertically		550.00					
b	Tagging omitted		7.50					
2105	20¢ Eleanor Roosevelt	10/11/84	.40	.20	2.00	(4)	1.00	113
2106	20¢ A Nation of Readers	10/16/84	.40	.20	1.90	(4)	1.00	117
	Christmas Issue							
2107	20¢ Madonna and Child,							
	by Fra Filippo Lippi	10/30/84	.40	.20	1.70	(4)	1.00	751
2108	20¢ Santa Claus	10/30/84	.40	.20	1.70	(4)	1.00	786
a	Horizontal pair, imperf. vertically		950.00					
2109	20¢ Vietnam Veterans'							
	Memorial	11/10/84	.40	.20	2.25	(4)	3.50	105
	Issues of 1985, Performing Arts Issue							
2110	22¢ Jerome Kern Portrait and							
	Kern Studying Sheet Music	01/23/85	.40	.20	1.75	(4)	1.00	125
a	Tagging omitted		7.50					
2111	(22¢)"D" Stamp	02/01/85	.55	.20	4.50	(6)	1.00	
a	Imperf., pair		35.00					
b	Vertical pair, imperf. horizontally		1,350.00					
	Coil Stamp, Perf. 10 Vertically							
2112	(22¢)"D" green Eagle (2111)	02/01/85	.60	.20	5.00	(3)	1.00	
a	Imperf., pair		45.00					
b	As "a," tagging omitted		125.00					
	Booklet Stamp, Perf. 11							
2113	(22¢)"D" green Eagle (2111),							
	single from booklet	02/01/85	.80	.20			1.00	
a	Booklet pane of 10	02/01/85	8.50	3.00			7.50	
b	As "a," imperf. between horizontally		—					
	Issues of 1985-1987, Flag Over Capitol Issue							
2114	22¢ Flag Over Capitol	03/29/85	.40	.20	1.90	(4)	1.00	
	Pair with full horizontal gutter between		—					
	Coil Stamp, Perf. 10 Vertically							
2115	22¢ Flag Over Capitol (2114)	03/29/85	.40	.20	3.00	(3)	1.00	
a	Narrow block tagging		.40	.20	3.00	(3)	1.00	
b	Inscribed "T" at bottom	05/23/87	.50	.40	3.00	(3)		
c	Black field of stars		—	—				
	#2115b issued for test on prephosphored paper. Paper is whiter and colors are brighter than on 2115.							
d	Tagging omitted		4.50					
e	Imperf., pair		12.50					
	Booklet Stamp, Perf. 10 Horizontally							
2116	22¢ Flag over Capitol,							
	single from booklet		.50	.20			1.00	
a	Booklet pane of 5	03/29/85	2.50	1.25			3.50	
	#2116 issued only in booklets. All stamps are imperf. at both sides or imperf. at both sides and bottom.							

	Issues of 1985		Un	U	PNC	#	FDC
	Seashells Booklet Issue, Perf. 10						
2117	22¢ Frilled Dogwinkle	04/04/85	.40	.20			1.00
2118	22¢ Reticulated Helmet	04/04/85	.40	.20			1.00
2119	22¢ New England Neptune	04/04/85	.40	.20			1.00
2120	22¢ Calico Scallop	04/04/85	.40	.20			1.00
2121	22¢ Lightning Whelk	04/04/85	.40	.20			1.00
a	Booklet pane of 10		4.00	*3.00*			*7.50*
b	As "a," violet omitted		*800.00*				
c	As "a," imperf. between vertically		*600.00*				
e	Strip of 5, #2117-21		2.00	—			
	Express Mail Booklet Issue, Perf. 10 Vertically						
2122	$10.75 Eagle and Moon,						
	booklet single	04/29/85	19.00	7.50			40.00
a	Booklet pane of 3		60.00	—			*95.00*
b	Type II		22.50	10.00			
c	As "b," booklet pane of 3		70.00	—			
	#2122 issued only in booklets. All stamps are imperf. at top and bottom or at top, bottom and one side.						
	Issues of 1985-1989, Coil Stamps, Transportation Issue (See also #1897-1908, 2225-31, 2252-66, 2451-68)						
2123	3.4¢ School Bus 1920s	06/08/85	.20	.20	.90	(5)	1.00
a	Untagged (Bureau precanceled)		.20	.20	4.25	(5)	
2124	4.9¢ Buckboard 1880s	06/21/85	.20	.20	.85	(5)	1.00
a	Untagged (Bureau precanceled)		.20	.20	1.40	(5)	
2125	5.5¢ Star Route Truck 1910s	11/01/86	.20	.20	1.50	(5)	1.00
a	Untagged (Bureau precanceled)		.20	.20	1.75	(5)	
2126	6¢ Tricycle 1880s	05/06/85	.20	.20	1.50	(5)	1.00
a	Untagged (Bureau precanceled)		.20	.20	1.75	(5)	
b	As "a," imperf., pair		*200.00*				
2127	7.1¢ Tractor 1920s	02/06/87	.20	.20	2.10	(5)	1.00
a	Untagged (Bureau precanceled "Nonprofit org.")		.20	.20	3.00	(5)	5.00
b	Untagged (Bureau precanceled "Nonprofit 5-Digit ZIP + 4")	05/26/89	.20	.20	1.75	(5)	
2128	8.3¢ Ambulance 1860s	06/21/85	.20	.20	1.50	(5)	1.00
a	Untagged (Bureau precanceled)		.20	.20	1.50	(5)	
2129	8.5¢ Tow Truck 1920s	01/24/87	.20	.20	3.00	(5)	1.25
a	Untagged (Bureau precanceled)		.20	.20	2.75	(5)	
2130	10.1¢ Oil Wagon 1890s	04/18/85	.25	.20	2.50	(5)	1.25
a	Untagged (Bureau precanceled, red)		.25	.25	2.25	(5)	1.25
	Untagged (Bureau precanceled, black)		.25	.25	2.50	(5)	
b	As "a," red precancel, imperf., pair		15.00		100.00	(6)	
	As "a," black precancel, imperf., pair		*95.00*				
2131	11¢ Stutz Bearcat 1933	06/11/85	.25	.20	1.40	(5)	1.25
2132	12¢ Stanley Steamer 1909	04/02/85	.25	.20	2.25	(5)	1.25
a	Untagged (Bureau precanceled)		.25	.25	2.40	(5)	
b	As "a," type II		.40	.30	19.00	(5)	
	Type II has "Stanley Steamer 1909" .5 mm shorter (17.5 mm) than #2132 (18mm).						
2133	12.5¢ Pushcart 1880s	04/18/85	.25	.20	3.00	(5)	1.25
a	Untagged (Bureau precanceled)		.25	.25	3.00	(5)	
b	As "a," imperf., pair		50.00				
2134	14¢ Iceboat 1880s	03/23/85	.30	.20	2.25	(5)	1.25
a	Imperf., pair		100.00				
b	Type II		.30	.20	3.25	(5)	
2135	17¢ Dog Sled 1920s	08/20/86	.35	.20	3.25	(5)	1.25
a	Imperf., pair		*450.00*				
2136	25¢ Bread Wagon 1880s	11/22/86	.45	.20	3.50	(5)	1.25
a	Imperf., pair		10.00				
b	Pair, imperf. between		*750.00*				
c	Tagging omitted		25.00				

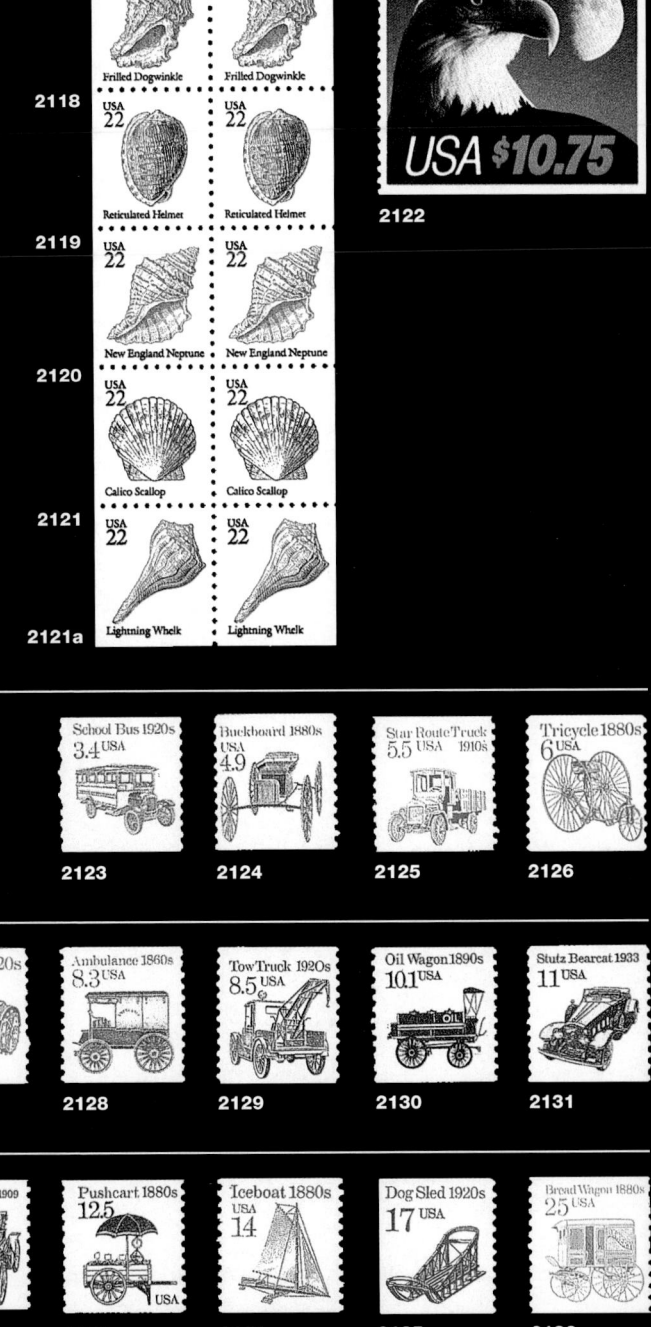

2117 USA 22 Frilled Dogwinkle / Frilled Dogwinkle

2118 USA 22 Reticulated Helmet / Reticulated Helmet

2119 USA 22 New England Neptune / New England Neptune

2120 USA 22 Calico Scallop / Calico Scallop

2121 USA 22 Lightning Whelk / Lightning Whelk

2121a

2122 USA $10.75

2123 School Bus 1920s 3.4 USA

2124 Buckboard 1880s USA 4.9

2125 Star Route Truck 5.5 USA 1910s

2126 Tricycle 1880s 6 USA

2127 Tractor 1920s 7.1 USA

2128 Ambulance 1860s 8.3 USA

2129 Tow Truck 1920s 8.5 USA

2130 Oil Wagon 1890s 10.1 USA

2131 Stutz Bearcat 1933 11 USA

2132 Stanley Steamer 1909 USA 12

2133 Pushcart 1880s 12.5 USA

2134 Iceboat 1880s USA 14

2135 Dog Sled 1920s 17 USA

2136 Bread Wagon 1880s 25 USA

2137

2138   **2139**

2140   **2141**   **2141a**

2142

2143

2144

2145

2146

2147

2149

2150

2152

2153

	Issues of 1985		Un	U	PB/PNC	#	FDC	Q(M)
	Black Heritage Issue, Perf. 11							
2137	22¢ Mary McLeod Bethune	03/05/85	.40	.20	2.60	(4)	1.50	120
	American Folk Art: Duck Decoys Issue							
2138	22¢ Broadbill Decoy	03/22/85	.65	.20			1.00	75
2139	22¢ Mallard Decoy	03/22/85	.65	.20			1.00	75
2140	22¢ Canvasback Decoy	03/22/85	.65	.20			1.00	75
2141	22¢ Redhead Decoy	03/22/85	.65	.20			1.00	75
a	Block of 4, #2138-41		4.00	2.75	4.75	(4)	2.50	
2142	22¢ Winter Special Olympics	03/25/85	.40	.20	1.75	(4)	1.00	121
a	Vertical pair, imperf. horizontally		525.00					
2143	22¢ Love	04/17/85	.40	.20	1.70	(4)	1.00	730
a	Imperf., pair		1,500.00					
2144	22¢ Rural Electrification Administration	05/11/85	.45	.20	17.50	(20)	1.00	125
2145	22¢ AMERIPEX '86	05/25/85	.40	.20	1.75	(4)	1.00	203
a	Red, black and blue omitted		200.00					
b	Red and black omitted		1,250.00					
2146	22¢ Abigail Adams	06/14/85	.40	.20	2.00	(4)	1.00	126
a	Imperf., pair		260.00					
2147	22¢ Frederic A. Bartholdi	07/18/85	.40	.20	1.90	(4)	1.00	130
2148	Not assigned							
	Coil Stamps, Perf. 10 Vertically							
2149	18¢ George Washington, Washington Monument	11/06/85	.35	.20	3.00	(5)	1.00	
a	Untagged (Bureau precanceled)		.35	.35	6.00	(5)		
b	Imperf., pair		950.00					
c	As "a," imperf. pair		800.00					
d	Tagging omitted		—	—				
e	As "a," tagged (error), dull gum		2.00	1.75	—			
2150	21.1¢ Sealed Envelopes	10/22/85	.40	.20	3.25	(5)	1.00	
a	Untagged (Bureau precanceled)		.40	.40	40.00	(5)		
b	As "a," tagged (error)		.40	.40	3.25	(5)		
2151	Not assigned							
	Perf. 11							
2152	22¢ Korean War Veterans	07/26/85	.40	.20	2.50	(4)	2.00	120
2153	22¢ Social Security Act, 50th Anniversary	08/14/85	.40	.20	1.90	(4)	1.00	120

Issues of 1985, Perf. 11		Un	U	PB	#	FDC	Q(M)
2154	22¢ World War I Veterans	08/26/85	.40	.20	2.25	(4)	1.50	120
American Horses Issue								
2155	22¢ Quarter Horse	09/25/85	1.00	.20			1.50	37
2156	22¢ Morgan	09/25/85	1.00	.20			1.50	37
2157	22¢ Saddlebred	09/25/85	1.00	.20			1.50	37
2158	22¢ Appaloosa	09/25/85	1.00	.20			1.50	37
a	Block of 4, #2155-58		6.00	5.00	7.50	(4)	2.50	
2159	22¢ Public Education	10/01/85	.45	.20	2.75	(4)	1.00	120
International Youth Year Issue								
2160	22¢ YMCA Youth Camping	10/07/85	.65	.20			1.00	33
2161	22¢ Boy Scouts	10/07/85	.65	.20			2.00	33
2162	22¢ Big Brothers/Big Sisters	10/07/85	.65	.20			1.00	33
2163	22¢ Camp Fire	10/07/85	.65	.20			1.00	33
a	Block of 4, #2160-63		3.00	2.25	4.00	(4)	2.50	
2164	22¢ Help End Hunger	10/15/85	.45	.20	2.00	(4)	1.00	120
Christmas Issue								
2165	22¢ Genoa Madonna, by Luca Della Robbia	10/30/85	.40	.20	1.75	(4)	1.00	759
a	Imperf., pair		100.00					
2166	22¢ Poinsettia Plants	10/30/85	.40	.20	1.70	(4)	1.00	758
a	Imperf., pair		130.00					

LOUISE NEVELSON

(1899-1988)

LOUISE NEVELSON arrived in the United States in 1905, a young immigrant from Kiev, Russia. After her marriage at age 20 to Charles Nevelson, the tall, flamboyant young woman moved from Maine to New York City, where she studied voice, drawing, and acting; and lived and worked most of the rest of her life. Considered one of the most gifted sculptors of the 20th century, she introduced a new form of sculpture that consisted of carved, recycled, and painted wood objects—such as discarded furniture, picture frames and balustrades—arranged in boxes that were stacked to form sculptural walls. She described this "found wood" in an interview: "Wood was the thing I could communicate with almost spontaneously and get what I was looking for...it's very alive." Nevelson also created clay and plaster sculptures, and large steel sculptures such as those installed in a square, now named in her honor, on Maiden Lane in the Wall Street area of Manhattan. Among the many tributes she received during her life was a National Medal of Arts from President Ronald Reagan in 1985. ❑

2154

2155 2156

2157 2158 2158a

2159

2160 2161

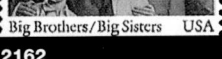

2162 2163 2163a

2164

2165

2166

1986-1994

Arkansas
Statehood
1836-1986

Old State House
Little Rock

USA 22

2167

Margaret Mitchell
USA 1

Mary Lyon
USA 2

Paul Dudley White MD
USA 3

Father Flanagan
USA 4

Hugo L. Black
5 USA

	Issues of 1986		Un	U	PB	#	FDC	Q(M)
2167	22¢ Arkansas Statehood	01/03/86	.50	.20	2.50	(4)	1.00	130
a	Vertical pair, imperf. horizontally		—					
	Issues of 1986-1991, Great Americans Issue (See also #1844-69)							
2168	1¢ Margaret Mitchell	06/30/86	.20	.20	.25	(4)	2.00	
a	Tagging omitted		5.00					
2169	2¢ Mary Lyon	02/28/87	.20	.20	.30	(4)	1.00	
a	Untagged		.20	.20	.35	(4)		
2170	3¢ Paul Dudley White, MD	09/15/86	.20	.20	.50	(4)	1.00	
a	Untagged, dull gum		.20	.20	.50	(4)		
2171	4¢ Father Flanagan	07/14/86	.20	.20	.60	(4)	1.00	
a	Grayish violet, untagged		.20	.20	.40	(4)		
b	Deep grayish blue, untagged		.20	.20	.50	(4)		
2172	5¢ Hugo L. Black	02/27/86	.20	.20	.65	(4)	1.00	
a	Tagging omitted		10.00					
2173	5¢ Luis Munoz Marin	02/18/90	.20	.20	.75	(4)	1.00	
a	Untagged		.20	.20	.60	(4)		
2174	Not assigned							
2175	10¢ Red Cloud	08/15/87	.20	.20	.85	(4)	1.50	
a	Overall tagging	1990	.30	.20	10.00	(4)		
b	Tagging omitted		12.50					
c	Prephosphored coated paper (solid tagging)		.30	.20	1.40	(4)		
d	Prephosphored uncoated paper (mottled tagging)		.20	.20	1.25	(4)		
e	Carmine, prephosphored uncoated paper (mottled tagging)		.25	.20	1.25	(4)		
2176	14¢ Julia Ward Howe	02/12/87	.25	.20	1.50	(4)	1.00	
2177	15¢ Buffalo Bill Cody	06/06/88	.35	.20	10.00	(4)	1.25	
a	Overall tagging	1990	.30	—	3.25	(4)		
b	Prephosphored coated paper (solid tagging)		.40	—	3.25	(4)		
c	Tagging omitted		15.00	—				
2178	17¢ Belva Ann Lockwood	06/18/86	.35	.20	2.00	(4)	1.00	
a	Tagging omitted		10.00					
	Perf. 11 x 11.1							
2179	20¢ Virginia Apgar	10/24/94	.40	.20	2.00	(4)	1.00	
a	Orange brown		.40	.20	2.25	(4)		
	Perf. 11							
2180	21¢ Chester Carlson	10/21/88	.40	.20	2.50	(4)	1.00	
2181	23¢ Mary Cassatt	11/04/88	.45	.20	2.50	(4)	1.00	
a	Overall tagging, dull gum		.45	—	5.00	(4)		
b	Prephosphored coated paper (solid tagging)		.60	—	3.25	(4)		
c	Prephosphored uncoated paper (mottled tagging)		.50	.20	3.25	(4)		
d	Tagging omitted		7.50					
2182	25¢ Jack London	01/11/86	.45	.20	2.75	(4)	1.25	
a	Booklet pane of 10	05/03/88	4.50	3.75			6.00	
b	Tagging omitted	1990	—	—				
2183	28¢ Sitting Bull	09/28/89	.50	.20	2.50	(4)	1.50	
2184	29¢ Earl Warren	03/09/92	.55	.20	2.50	(4)	1.25	
	Perf. 11.5 x 11							
2185	29¢ Thomas Jefferson	04/13/93	.50	.20	2.50	(4)	1.25	
2186	35¢ Dennis Chavez	04/03/91	.65	.20	3.25	(4)	1.25	
2187	40¢ Claire Lee Chennault	09/06/90	.70	.20	3.75	(4)	2.00	
a	Prephosphored coated paper (solid tagging)		.75	.35	4.25	(4)		
c	Prephosphored uncoated paper (mottled tagging)		.75	.20	7.50	(4)		
2188	45¢ Harvey Cushing, MD	06/17/88	.85	.20	3.75	(4)	1.25	
a	Overall tagging	1990	1.65	.20	11.00	(4)		
b	Tagging omitted		15.00					
2189	52¢ Hubert H. Humphrey	06/03/91	1.10	.20	7.50	(4)	1.40	
a	Prephosphored uncoated paper (mottled tagging)		1.10	—	5.50	(4)		
2190	56¢ John Harvard	09/03/86	1.10	.20	6.00	(4)	2.50	
2191	65¢ H.H. 'Hap' Arnold	11/05/88	1.20	.20	5.00	(4)	2.50	

Issues of 1986-1992		Un	U	PB	#	FDC	Q(M)
Perf. 11							
2192 75¢ Wendell Willkie	02/16/92	1.30	.20	5.50	(4)	2.50	
a Prephosphored uncoated paper (mottled tagging)		1.30	—	5.50	(4)		
2193 $1 Bernard Revel	09/23/86	2.50	.50	14.00	(4)	3.50	
2194 $1 Johns Hopkins	06/07/89	1.75	.50	7.00	(4)	3.00	
b Overall tagging	1990	1.75	.50	7.00	(4)		
c Tagging omitted		10.00					
d Dark blue, prephosphored coated paper (solid tagging)		1.75	.50	7.00	(4)		
e Blue, prephosphored uncoated paper (mottled tagging)		2.00	.60	8.00	(4)		
f Blue, prephosphored coated paper (grainy solid tagging)		1.75	.50	7.00	(4)		
2195 $2 William Jennings Bryan	03/19/86	4.00	.50	19.00	(4)	5.50	
a Tagging omitted		45.00					
2196 $5 Bret Harte	08/25/87	8.50	1.00	35.00	(4)	15.00	
a Tagging omitted		—					
b Prephosphored paper (solid tagging)		8.50	—	35.00	(4)		
Booklet Stamp, Perf. 10							
2197 25¢ Jack London (2182), single from booklet	.45	.45	.20			1.00	
a Booklet pane of 6	05/03/88	3.00	2.25			4.00	
b Tagging omitted		4.50					
c As "b," booklet pane of 6		60.00					
United States — Sweden Stamp Collecting Booklet Issue, Perf. 10 Vertically							
2198 22¢ Handstamped Cover	01/23/86	.45	.20			1.00	17
2199 22¢ Boy Examining Stamp Collection	01/23/86	.45	.20			1.00	17
2200 22¢ #836 Under Magnifying Glass	01/23/86	.45	.20			1.00	17
2201 22¢ 1986 Presidents Miniature Sheet	01/23/86	.45	.20			1.00	17
a Booklet pane of 4, #2198-2201		2.00	1.75			4.00	17
b As "a," black omitted on #2198, 2201		50.00	—				
c As "a," blue omitted on #2198-2200		2,500.00					
d As "a," buff omitted		—					
#2198-2201 issued only in booklets. All stamps are imperf. at top and bottom or imperf. at top, bottom and right side.							
Perf. 11							
2202 22¢ Love	01/30/86	.40	.20	1.75	(4)	1.00	949
Black Heritage Issue							
2203 22¢ Sojourner Truth and Truth Lecturing	02/04/86	.40	.20	2.00	(4)	1.75	130
2204 22¢ Republic of Texas, 150th Anniversary	03/02/86	.40	.20	1.90	(4)	1.75	137
a Horizontal pair, imperf. vertically		1,100.00					
b Dark red omitted		2,750.00					
c Dark blue omitted		8,500.00					
Fish Booklet Issue, Perf. 10 Horizontally							
2205 22¢ Muskellunge	03/21/86	.60	.20			1.25	44
2206 22¢ Atlantic Cod	03/21/86	.60	.20			1.25	44
2207 22¢ Largemouth Bass	03/21/86	.60	.20			1.25	44
2208 22¢ Bluefin Tuna	03/21/86	.60	.20			1.25	44
2209 22¢ Catfish	03/21/86	.60	.20			1.25	44
a Booklet pane of 5, #2205-09		5.50	2.75			3.50	44
#2205-09 issued only in booklets. All stamps are imperf. at sides or imperf. at sides and bottom.							

2192

2193

2194

2195

2196

2198

2199

2200

2201   2201a

2202

2203

2205

2206

2207

2208

San Jacinto 1836
Republic of Texas
2204

2209

2209a

2210

2211

2216a

2216b

2216c

2216d

2216e

2216f

2216g

2216h

2216i

2217a

2217b

2217c

2217d

2217e

2217f

2217g

2217h

2217i

Issues of 1986		Un	U	PB	#	FDC	Q(M)
Perf. 11							
2210 22¢ Public Hospitals	04/11/86	.40	.20	1.75	(4)	1.00	130
a	Vertical pair, imperf. horizontally	325.00					
b	Horizontal pair, imperf. vertically	1,300.00					
Performing Arts Issue							
2211 22¢ Duke Ellington							
and Piano Keys	04/29/86	.40	.20	1.90	(4)	2.25	130
a	Vertical pair, imperf. horizontally	1,000.00					
2212-15 Not assigned							
AMERIPEX '86 Issue, Presidents Miniature Sheets							
2216 Sheet of 9	05/22/86	4.25	—			4.00	6
a	22¢ George Washington	.45	.25			1.50	
b	22¢ John Adams	.45	.25			1.50	
c	22¢ Thomas Jefferson	.45	.25			1.50	
d	22¢ James Madison	.45	.25			1.50	
e	22¢ James Monroe	.45	.25			1.50	
f	22¢ John Quincy Adams	.45	.25			1.50	
g	22¢ Andrew Jackson	.45	.25			1.50	
h	22¢ Martin Van Buren	.45	.25			1.50	
i	22¢ William H. Harrison	.45	.25			1.50	
j	Blue omitted	3,250.00					
k	Black inscription omitted	2,000.00					
l	Imperf.	10,500.00					
2217 Sheet of 9	05/22/86	4.25	—			4.00	6
a	22¢ John Tyler	.45	.25			1.50	
b	22¢ James Polk	.45	.25			1.50	
c	22¢ Zachary Taylor	.45	.25			1.50	
d	22¢ Millard Fillmore	.45	.25			1.50	
e	22¢ Franklin Pierce	.45	.25			1.50	
f	22¢ James Buchanan	.45	.25			1.50	
g	22¢ Abraham Lincoln	.45	.25			1.50	
h	22¢ Andrew Johnson	.45	.25			1.50	
i	22¢ Ulysses S. Grant	.45	.25			1.50	

#2216

#2217

Issues of 1986		Un	U	FDC	Q(M)
AMERIPEX '86 Issue (continued), Presidents Miniature Sheets					
2218 Sheet of 9	05/22/86	4.25	—	4.00	6
a	22¢ Rutherford B. Hayes	.45	.25	1.50	
b	22¢ James A. Garfield	.45	.25	1.50	
c	22¢ Chester A. Arthur	.45	.25	1.50	
d	22¢ Grover Cleveland	.45	.25	1.50	
e	22¢ Benjamin Harrison	.45	.25	1.50	
f	22¢ William McKinley	.45	.25	1.50	
g	22¢ Theodore Roosevelt	.45	.25	1.50	
h	22¢ William H. Taft	.45	.25	1.50	
i	22¢ Woodrow Wilson	.45	.25	1.50	
j	Brown omitted	—			
k	Black inscription omitted	2,9000.00			
2219 Sheet of 9	05/22/86	4.25	—	4.00	6
a	22¢ Warren G. Harding	.45	.25	1.50	
b	22¢ Calvin Coolidge	.45	.25	1.50	
c	22¢ Herbert Hoover	.45	.25	1.50	
d	22¢ Franklin D. Roosevelt	.45	.25	1.50	
e	22¢ White House	.45	.25	1.50	
f	22¢ Harry S. Truman	.45	.25	1.50	
g	22¢ Dwight D. Eisenhower	.45	.25	1.50	
h	22¢ John F. Kennedy	.45	.25	2.50	
i	22¢ Lyndon B. Johnson	.45	.25	1.50	
j	Blackish blue inscription omitted	—			
k	Tagging omitted	—			

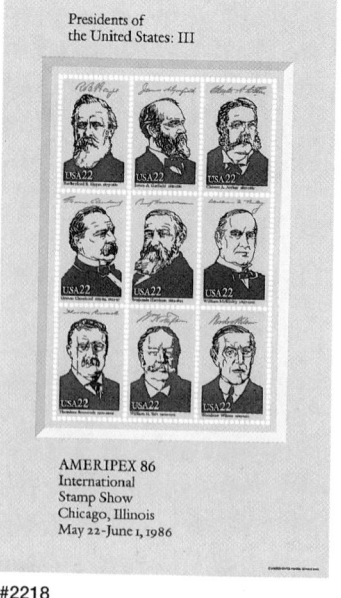

#2218

#2219

2218a **2218b** **2218c** **2218d** **2218e**

2218f **2218g** **2218h** **2218i**

2219a **2219b** **2219c** **2219d** **2219e**

2219f **2219g** **2219h** **2219i**

2220   2221

USA 22 — Elisha Kent Kane

USA 22 — Adolphus W. Greely

USA 22 — Vilhjalmur Stefansson

USA 22 — Robert E. Peary, Matthew Henson

2222   2223   2223a

Liberty 1886-1986 — USA 22

2224

Omnibus 1880s — 1 USA — MADISON

2225

Locomotive 1870s — 2 USA

2226

2235   2236

Museum of the American Indian — Navajo Art USA 22

Museum of the American Indian — Navajo Art USA 22

Love Art Museum — Navajo Art USA 22

Museum of the American Indian — Navajo Art USA 22

2237   2238   2238a

T.S. Eliot — 22 USA

2239

2240   2241

Wood Carving: Highlander Figure — Folk Art USA 22

Wood Carving: Ship Figurehead — Folk Art USA 22

Wood Carving: Nautical Figure — Folk Art USA 22

Wood Carving: Cigar Store Figure — Folk Art USA 22

2242   2243   2243a

CHRISTMAS 22 USA — Perugino, National Gallery

2244

USA 22 — GREETINGS

2245

USA 22 — 1837-1987 Michigan Statehood

2246

22 USA — Pan American Games Indianapolis 1987

2247

LOVE — USA 22

2248

Jean Baptiste Pointe Du Sable 22 — Black Heritage USA

2249

Issues of 1986		Un	U	PB/PNC	#	FDC	Q(M)
Arctic Explorers Issue, Perf. 11							
2220	22¢ Elisha Kent Kane	05/28/86	.65	.20			1.25	33
2221	22¢ Adolphus W. Greely	05/28/86	.65	.20			1.25	33
2222	22¢ Vilhjalmur Stefansson	05/28/86	.65	.20			1.25	33
2223	22¢ Robt. Peary, Matt. Henson	05/28/86	.65	.20			1.25	33
a	Block of 4, #2220-23		2.75	2.25	4.50	(4)	3.75	
b	As "a," black omitted		8,500.00					
2224	22¢ Statue of Liberty	07/04/86	.40	.20	2.25	(4)	1.25	221
Issues of 1986-1987, Reengraved Transportation Issue, Coil Stamps, Perf. 10 Vertically							
(See also #1897-1908, 2123-36, 2252-66, 2452-53A, 2457, 2464, 2468)							
2225	1¢ Omnibus	11/26/86	.20	.20	.60	(5)	1.00	
a	Prephosphored uncoated paper							
	(mottled tagging)		.20	.20	15.00	(5)		
b	Untagged, dull gum		.20	.20	.65	(5)		
c	Imperf., pair		2,000.00					
2226	2¢ Locomotive	03/06/87	.20	.20	.70	(5)	1.50	
a	Untagged, dull gum		.20	.20	.70	(5)		
2227, 2229-30, 2232-34 Not assigned							
2228	4¢ Stagecoach (1898A)	08/86	.20	.20	1.25	(5)		
a	Overall tagging		.70	.20	11.00	(5)		
b	Imperf., pair		300.00					
2231	8.3¢ Ambulance (2128)							
	(Bureau precanceled)	08/29/86	.20	.20	5.25	(5)		
On #2228, "Stagecoach 1890s" is 17mm long; on #1898A, it is 19.5mm long. On #2231,							
"Ambulance 1860s" is 18mm long; on #2128, it is 18.5mm long.							
American Folk Art: Navajo Art Issue, Perf. 11							
2235	22¢ Navajo Art, four "+" marks							
	horizontally through middle	09/04/86	.50	.20			1.00	60
2236	22¢ Navajo Art, vertical							
	diamond pattern	09/04/86	.50	.20			1.00	60
2237	22¢ Navajo Art, horizontal							
	diamond pattern	09/04/86	.50	.20			1.00	60
2238	22¢ Navajo Art, jagged line							
	horizontally through middle	09/04/86	.50	.20			1.00	60
a	Block of 4, #2235-38		2.50	2.25	4.00	(4)	2.00	
b	As "a," black omitted		350.00					
Literary Arts Issue							
2239	22¢ T.S. Eliot	09/26/86	.40	.20	1.90	(4)	1.00	132
American Folk Art: Wood Carved Figurines Issue							
2240	22¢ Highlander Figure	10/01/86	.40	.20			1.00	60
2241	22¢ Ship Figurehead	10/01/86	.40	.20			1.00	60
2242	22¢ Nautical Figure	10/01/86	.40	.20			1.00	60
2243	22¢ Cigar Store Figure	10/01/86	.40	.20			1.00	60
a	Block of 4, #2240-43		1.75	2.00	3.00	(4)	2.00	
b	As "a," imperf. vertically		1,250.00					
Christmas Issue							
2244	22¢ Madonna and Child	10/24/86	.40	.20	2.00	(4)	1.00	690
2245	22¢ Village Scene	10/24/86	.40	.20	1.90	(4)	1.00	882
Issues of 1987							
2246	22¢ Michigan Statehood	01/26/87	.40	.20	1.90	(4)	1.00	167
	Pair with full vertical gutter between							
2247	22¢ Pan American Games	01/29/87	.40	.20	1.90	(4)	1.00	167
a	Silver omitted		1,500.00					
Perf. 11.5 x 11							
2248	22¢ Love	01/30/87	.40	.20	1.90	(4)	1.00	842
Black Heritage Issue, Perf. 11							
2249	22¢ Jean Baptiste Point Du Sable							
	and Chicago Settlement	02/20/87	.40	.20	1.90	(4)	1.50	143
a	Tagging omitted		10.00					

1987-1988

	Issues of 1987-1988		Un	U	PNC	#	FDC	Q(M)
	Performing Arts Issue							
2250	22¢ Enrico Caruso as the Duke							
	of Mantua in Rigoletti	02/27/87	.40	.20	1.90	(4)	1.00	130
a	Black (engr.) omitted		5,000.00					
2251	22¢ Girl Scouts	03/12/87	.40	.20	1.90	(4)	2.50	150
a	All litho colors omitted		2,500.00					
	Coil Stamps, Transportation Issue, Perf. 10 Vertically							
	(See also #1897-1908, 2123-36, 2225-31, 2451-68)							
2252	3¢ Conestoga Wagon 1800s	02/29/88	.20	.20	.90	(5)	1.00	
a	Untagged, dull gum		.20	.20	1.25	(5)		
2253	5¢ Milk Wagon 1900s	09/25/87	.20	.20	.90	(5)	1.00	
2254	5.3¢ Elevator 1900s,							
	Bureau precanceled	09/16/88	.20	.20	1.10	(5)	1.00	
2255	7.6¢ Carreta 1770s,							
	Bureau precanceled	08/30/88	.20	.20	2.25	(5)	1.00	
2256	8.4¢ Wheel Chair 1920s,							
	Bureau precanceled	08/12/88	.20	.20	1.90	(5)	1.00	
a	Imperf., pair		700.00					
2257	10¢ Canal Boat 1880s	04/11/87	.20	.20	2.50	(5)	1.00	
a	Overall tagging, dull gum		.20	.20	4.00	(5)		
b	Prephosphored uncoated paper		.20	.20	3.25	(5)		
d	Tagging omitted		20.00					
2258	13¢ Patrol Wagon 1880s,							
	Bureau precanceled	10/29/88	.30	.25	3.25	(5)	1.50	
2259	13.2¢ Coal Car 1870s,							
	Bureau precanceled	07/19/88	.25	.25	2.75	(5)	1.00	
a	Imperf., pair		100.00					
2260	15¢ Tugboat 1900s	07/12/88	.25	.20	2.00	(5)	1.00	
a	Overall tagging		.25	.20	3.25	(5)		
b	Tagging omitted		3.75		150.00	(5)		
c	Imperf., pair		800.00					
2261	16.7¢ Popcorn Wagon 1902,							
	Bureau precanceled	07/07/88	.30	.30	2.75	(5)	1.00	
a	Imperf., pair		225.00					
2262	17.5¢ Racing Car 1911	09/25/87	.30	.20	3.00	(5)	1.00	
a	Untagged (Bureau precanceled)		.35	.30	3.50	(5)		
b	Imperf., pair		1,750.00					
2263	20¢ Cable Car 1880s	10/28/88	.35	.20	3.50	(5)	1.00	
a	Imperf., pair		65.00					
b	Overall tagging		.35	.20	8.00	(5)		
2264	20.5¢ Fire Engine 1920s,							
	Bureau precanceled	09/28/88	.40	.40	4.75	(5)	1.50	
2265	21¢ Railroad Mail Car 1920s,							
	Bureau precanceled	08/16/88	.40	.40	3.50	(5)	1.00	
a	Imperf., pair		55.00					
2266	24.1¢ Tandem Bicycle 1890s,							
	Bureau precanceled	10/26/88	.45	.45	4.00	(5)	1.00	
	Issues of 1987, Special Occasions Booklet Issue, Perf. 10							
2267	22¢ Congratulations!	04/20/87	.65	.20			1.00	1,222
2268	22¢ Get Well!	04/20/87	.80	.20			1.00	611
2269	22¢ Thank you!	04/20/87	.80	.20			1.00	611
2270	22¢ Love You, Dad!	04/20/87	.80	.20			1.00	611
2271	22¢ Best Wishes!	04/20/87	.80	.20			1.00	611
2272	22¢ Happy Birthday!	04/20/87	.65	.20			1.00	1,222
2273	22¢ Love You, Mother!	04/20/87	1.25	.20			1.00	611
2274	22¢ Keep In Touch!	04/20/87	.80	.20			1.00	611
a	Booklet pane of 10, #2268-71, 2273-74							
	and 2 each of #2267, 2272		10.00	5.00			5.00	611

#2267-74 issued only in booklets. All stamps are imperf. at one or two sides or imperf. at sides and bottom.

Enrico Caruso 22 USA

2250

GIRL SCOUTS USA 22

2251

Conestoga Wagon 1800s USA 3

2252

Milk Wagon 1900s 5

2253

Elevator 1900s 5.3 USA Nonprofit Carrier Route Sort

2254

Carreta 1770s 7.6 USA Nonprofit

2255

Wheel Chair 1920s 8.4 USA Nonprofit

2256

Canal Boat 1880s 10 USA

2257

Patrol Wagon 1880s USA 13 Presorted First-Class

2258

Coal Car 1870s 13.2 Bulk Rate USA

2259

Tugboat 1900s USA 15

2260

Popcorn Wagon 16.7 USA 1902 Bulk Rate

2261

Racing Car 1911 USA 17.5

2262

USA 20 Cable Car 1880s

2263

Fire Engine 1900s 20.5 USA ZIP+4 Presort

2264

Railroad Mail Car 1920s Presorted First-Class 21 USA

2265

Tandem Bicycle 1890s 24.1 USA ZIP+4

2266

2267

Congratulations! USA 22

2268

2269

Get Well! USA 22 / Thank You! USA 22

2270

Love You, Dad! USA 22

2271 **2272**

Best Wishes! USA 22 / Happy Birthday! USA 22

2273

Love You, Mother! USA 22

2274 **2272**

Keep In Touch! USA 22 / Happy Birthday! USA 22

2267

Congratulations! USA 22

2274a

2275

2276

2277

2278

2279

2280

2281

2282a

2283

2283c

2285b

2284

2285

	Issues of 1987		Un	U	PB/PNC	#	FDC	Q(M)
2275	22¢ United Way	04/28/87	.40	.20	1.90	(4)	1.00	157
2276	22¢ Flag with Fireworks	05/09/87	.40	.20	1.90	(4)	1.00	
a	Booklet pane of 20	11/30/87	8.50	—			8.00	
	Issues of 1988-1989 (All issued in 1988 except #2280 on prephosphored paper)							
2277	(25¢) "E" Stamp	03/22/88	.45	.20	2.00	(4)	1.25	
2278	25¢ Flag with Clouds	05/06/88	.45	.20	1.90	(4)	1.25	
	Pair with full vertical gutter between		—					
	Coil Stamps, Perf. 10 Vertically							
2279	(25¢) "E" Earth	03/22/88	.45	.20	2.75	(5)	1.25	
a	Imperf., pair		85.00	—				
2280	25¢ Flag over Yosemite	05/20/88	.45	.20	3.50	(5)	1.25	
a	Prephosphored paper	02/14/89	.45	.20	3.50	(5)	1.25	
b	Imperf., pair, large block tagging		32.50					
c	Imperf., pair, prephosphored paper		14.00					
d	Tagging omitted		5.00					
e	Black trees		100.00	—				
f	Pair, imperf. between		750.00					
2281	25¢ Honeybee	09/02/88	.45	.20	3.75	(3)	1.25	
a	Imperf., pair		50.00					
b	Black (engr.) omitted		60.00					
c	Black (litho) omitted		400.00					
d	Pair, imperf. between		1,000.00					
e	Yellow (litho) omitted		1,200.00					
	Booklet Stamp, Perf. 10							
2282	(25¢) "E" Earth (#2277), single from booklet		.50	.20			1.25	
a	Booklet pane of 10	03/22/88	6.50	3.50			6.00	
	Pheasant Booklet Issue, Perf. 11							
2283	25¢ Pheasant, single from booklet		.50	.20			1.25	
a	Booklet pane of 10	04/29/88	6.00	3.50			6.00	
b	Single, red removed from sky		6.25	.20				
c	As "b," booklet pane of 10		67.50	—				
d	As "a," imperf. horizontally between		2,000.00					
	#2283 issued only in booklets. All stamps have one or two imperf. edges. Imperf. and part perf. pairs and panes exist from printer's waste.							
	Owl and Grosbeak Booklet Issue, Perf. 10							
2284	25¢ Grosbeak, single from booklet		.50	.20			1.25	
2285	25¢ Owl, single from booklet		.50	.20			1.25	
b	Booklet pane of 10, 5 each of #2284, 2285	05/28/88	5.00	3.50			6.00	
d	Pair, #2284, 2285		1.10	.25				
e	As "d," tagging omitted		12.50					
	#2284 and 2285 issued only in booklets. All stamps are imperf. at one side or imperf. at one side and bottom.							
2285A	25¢ Flag with Clouds (#2278), single from booklet		.50	.20			1.00	
c	Booklet pane of 6	07/05/88	3.00	2.00			4.00	

Issues of 1987			Un	U	FDC	Q(M)
American Wildlife Issue, Perf. 11						
2286	22¢ Barn Swallow	06/13/87	.85	.20	1.50	13
2287	22¢ Monarch Butterfly	06/13/87	.85	.20	1.50	13
2288	22¢ Bighorn Sheep	06/13/87	.85	.20	1.50	13
2289	22¢ Broad-tailed Hummingbird	06/13/87	.85	.20	1.50	13
2290	22¢ Cottontail	06/13/87	.85	.20	1.50	13
2291	22¢ Osprey	06/13/87	.85	.20	1.50	13
2292	22¢ Mountain Lion	06/13/87	.85	.20	1.50	13
2293	22¢ Luna Moth	06/13/87	.85	.20	1.50	12
2294	22¢ Mule Deer	06/13/87	.85	.20	1.50	13
2295	22¢ Gray Squirrel	06/13/87	.85	.20	1.50	13
2296	22¢ Armadillo	06/13/87	.85	.20	1.50	13
2297	22¢ Eastern Chipmunk	06/13/87	.85	.20	1.50	13
2298	22¢ Moose	06/13/87	.85	.20	1.50	13
2299	22¢ Black Bear	06/13/87	.85	.20	1.50	13
2300	22¢ Tiger Swallowtail	06/13/87	.85	.20	1.50	13
2301	22¢ Bobwhite	06/13/87	.85	.20	1.50	13
2302	22¢ Ringtail	06/13/87	.85	.20	1.50	13
2303	22¢ Red-winged Blackbird	06/13/87	.85	.20	1.50	13
2304	22¢ American Lobster	06/13/87	.85	.20	1.50	13
2305	22¢ Black-tailed Jack Rabbit	06/13/87	.85	.20	1.50	13
2306	22¢ Scarlet Tanager	06/13/87	.85	.20	1.50	13
2307	22¢ Woodchuck	06/13/87	.85	.20	1.50	13
2308	22¢ Roseate Spoonbill	06/13/87	.85	.20	1.50	13
2309	22¢ Bald Eagle	06/13/87	.85	.20	1.50	13
2310	22¢ Alaskan Brown Bear	06/13/87	.85	.20	1.50	13

BILLIE HOLIDAY

(1915-1959)

The woman considered by many to be the greatest singer of them all, BILLIE HOLIDAY, approached her art as if she were a jazz instrumentalist, altering rhythm, melody, and harmony as she saw fit. She detached the melody from the beat, stretching or compressing notes, and is noted for the depth of emotion she conveyed even in seemingly simple songs. Holiday was born in Baltimore as Eleanor Fagan. She moved at a young age to New York, where she began singing for $10 a week, and is said to have taken the name Billie after one of her idols, screen star Billie Dove. One of her early fans was the impresario John Hammond, who arranged for Holiday to make her recording debut. Her sessions with a small studio band between 1935 and 1942 produced an extremely influential body of jazz music, often featuring tenor saxophonist Lester Young, with whom Holiday worked particularly well. She became known as "Lady Day" and eventually won international fame; the white gardenias worn in her hair became one of her trademarks, along with such signature songs as "God Bless the Child" and "Strange Fruit." ❑

2286 2287 2288 2289 2290

2291 2292 2293 2294 2295

2296 2297 2298 2299 2300

2301 2302 2303 2304 2305

2306 2307 2308 2309 2310

22 USA Iiwi	22 USA Badger	22 USA Pronghorn	22 USA River Otter	22 USA Ladybug
2311	2312	2313	2314	2315

22 USA Beaver	22 USA White-tailed Deer	22 USA Blue Jay	22 USA Pika	22 USA Bison
2316	2317	2318	2319	2320

22 USA Snowy Egret	22 USA Gray Wolf	22 USA Mountain Goat	22 USA Deer Mouse	22 USA Black-tailed Prairie Dog
2321	2322	2323	2324	2325

22 USA Box Turtle	22 USA Wolverine	22 USA American Elk	22 USA California Sea Lion	22 USA Mockingbird
2326	2327	2328	2329	2330

22 USA Raccoon	22 USA Bobcat	22 USA Black-footed Ferret	22 USA Canada Goose	22 USA Red Fox
2331	2332	2333	2334	2335

Issues of 1987		Un	U	FDC	Q(M)
American Wildlife Issue (continued), Perf. 11					
2311	22¢ Iiwi	06/13/87	.85	.20	1.50	13
2312	22¢ Badger	06/13/87	.85	.20	1.50	13
2313	22¢ Pronghorn	06/13/87	.85	.20	1.50	13
2314	22¢ River Otter	06/13/87	.85	.20	1.50	13
2315	22¢ Ladybug	06/13/87	.85	.20	1.50	13
2316	22¢ Beaver	06/13/87	.85	.20	1.50	13
2317	22¢ White-tailed Deer	06/13/87	.85	.20	1.50	13
2318	22¢ Blue Jay	06/13/87	.85	.20	1.50	13
2319	22¢ Pika	06/13/87	.85	.20	1.50	13
2320	22¢ Bison	06/13/87	.85	.20	1.50	13
2321	22¢ Snowy Egret	06/13/87	.85	.20	1.50	13
2322	22¢ Gray Wolf	06/13/87	.85	.20	1.50	13
2323	22¢ Mountain Goat	06/13/87	.85	.20	1.50	13
2324	22¢ Deer Mouse	06/13/87	.85	.20	1.50	13
2325	22¢ Black-tailed Prairie Dog	06/13/87	.85	.20	1.50	13
2326	22¢ Box Turtle	06/13/87	.85	.20	1.50	13
2327	22¢ Wolverine	06/13/87	.85	.20	1.50	13
2328	22¢ American Elk	06/13/87	.85	.20	1.50	13
2329	22¢ California Sea Lion	06/13/87	.85	.20	1.50	13
2330	22¢ Mockingbird	06/13/87	.85	.20	1.50	13
2331	22¢ Raccoon	06/13/87	.85	.20	1.50	13
2332	22¢ Bobcat	06/13/87	.85	.20	1.50	13
2333	22¢ Black-footed Ferret	06/13/87	.85	.20	1.50	13
2334	22¢ Canada Goose	06/13/87	.85	.20	1.50	13
2335	22¢ Red Fox	06/13/87	.85	.20	1.50	13
a	Pane of 50, #2286-2335		47.50		50.00	

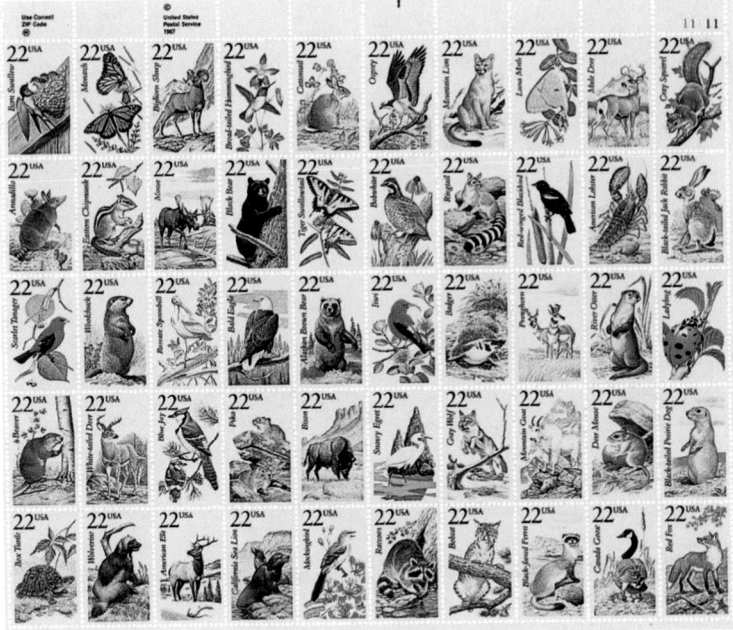

Example of 2335a

Issues of 1987-1990			Un	U	PB	#	FDC	Q(M)
Ratification of the Constitution Issue, Perf. 11								
2336	22¢ Delaware	07/04/87	.60	.20	2.75	(4)	1.50	168
2337	22¢ Pennsylvania	08/26/87	.60	.20	2.75	(4)	1.50	187
2338	22¢ New Jersey	09/11/87	.60	.20	2.75	(4)	1.50	184
a	Black omitted		5,500.00					
2339	22¢ Georgia	01/06/88	.60	.20	2.75	(4)	1.50	169
2340	22¢ Connecticut	01/09/88	.60	.20	2.75	(4)	1.50	155
2341	22¢ Massachusetts	02/06/88	.60	.20	2.75	(4)	1.50	102
2342	22¢ Maryland	02/15/88	.60	.20	2.75	(4)	1.50	103
2343	25¢ South Carolina	05/23/88	.60	.20	2.75	(4)	1.50	162
2344	25¢ New Hampshire	06/21/88	.60	.20	2.75	(4)	1.50	153
2345	25¢ Virginia	06/25/88	.60	.20	2.75	(4)	1.50	160
2346	25¢ New York	07/26/88	.60	.20	2.75	(4)	1.50	183
2347	25¢ North Carolina	08/22/89	.60	.20	2.75	(4)	1.50	
2348	25¢ Rhode Island	05/29/90	.60	.20	2.75	(4)	1.50	164
2349	22¢ Friendship with Morocco	07/18/87	.40	.20	1.75	(4)	1.00	157
a	Black omitted		275.00					
Literary Arts Issue								
2350	22¢ William Faulkner	08/03/87	.40	.20	2.50	(4)	1.00	156
American Folk Art: Lace Making Issue								
2351	22¢ Squash Blossoms	08/14/87	.45	.20			1.00	41
2352	22¢ Floral Piece	08/14/87	.45	.20			1.00	41
2353	22¢ Floral Piece	08/14/87	.45	.20			1.00	41
2354	22¢ Dogwood Blossoms	08/14/87	.45	.20			1.00	41
a	Block of 4, #2351-54		1.90	1.90	3.25	(4)	2.50	
b	As "a," white omitted		950.00					

DUKE ELLINGTON

(1899-1974)

EDWARD KENNEDY ELLINGTON, who would be known as Duke Ellington for most of his life, was born in Washington, D.C., at the turn of the century. By the time of his death, he was considered one of the world's greatest composers and musicians. Early piano lessons made little impression on Ellington but in his late teens he decided that music would be his life. In 1923 Ellington moved to New York and made his first recording. Ellington and his band, the Washingtonians, played the exclusive New York clubs of the day—Ciro's, the Plantation Club, and Harlem's Cotton Club. Radio broadcasts of their performances, particularly those from the Cotton Club, enhanced the band's popularity and reputation. Ultimately, the Ellington band played worldwide—Los Angeles, London, Chicago, Cairo—for audiences that included royalty (Queen Elizabeth II) and presidents (Nixon).

Among Ellington's greatest musical works are "Sophisticated Lady," "Mood Indigo," and "Satin Doll." Another composition, "Take The 'A' Train," became the band's theme song. Ellington won numerous Grammy awards for his jazz and pop music and in 1969 was presented the Presidential Medal of Freedom. The U.S. Postal Service honored Ellington in 1986 in its Performing Arts series. ❑

Dec 7,1787 USA
Delaware 22

2336

Dec 12,1787
Pennsylvania

2337

Dec 18,1787 USA
New Jersey 22

2338

January 2, 1788
Georgia

2339

January 9,1788
Connecticut

2340

Feb 6,1788 USA
Massachusetts

2341

April 28,1788 USA
Maryland 22

2342

May 23,1788
South Carolina

2343

June 21,1788
New Hampshire

2344

June 25, 1788 USA
Virginia 25

2345

July 26, 1788 USA
New York 25

2346

November 21,1789
North Carolina

2347

May 29,1790
Rhode Island

2348

2351   **2352**

Friendship
with Morocco
1787-1987

USA 22

2349

William Faulkner

USA 22

2350

Lacemaking USA 22 : Lacemaking USA 22

Lacemaking USA 22 : Lacemaking USA 22

2353   **2354**   **2354a**

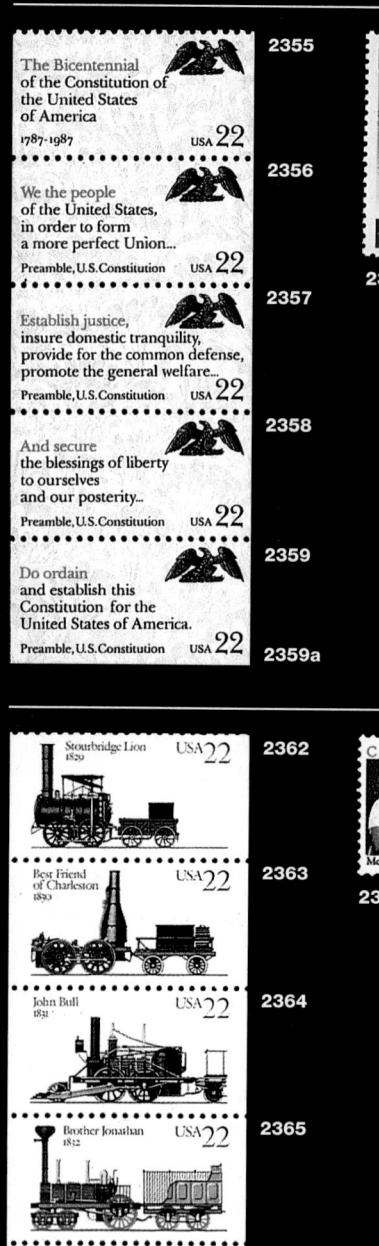

The Bicentennial
of the Constitution of
the United States
of America
1787-1987 USA **22**

2355

We the people
of the United States,
in order to form
a more perfect Union...
Preamble, U.S. Constitution USA **22**

2356

Establish justice,
insure domestic tranquility,
provide for the common defense,
promote the general welfare...
Preamble, U.S. Constitution USA **22**

2357

And secure
the blessings of liberty
to ourselves
and our posterity...
Preamble, U.S. Constitution USA **22**

2358

Do ordain
and establish this
Constitution for the
United States of America.
Preamble, U.S. Constitution USA **22**

2359

2359a

2360

2361

Stourbridge Lion
1829 USA **22**

2362

Best Friend
of Charleston
1830 USA **22**

2363

John Bull
1831 USA **22**

2364

Brother Jonathan
1832 USA **22**

2365

Gowan & Marx
1839 USA **22**

2366

2366a

CHRISTMAS **22** USA
Moroni, National Gallery

2367

USA **22** GREETINGS

2368

Issues of 1987		Un	U	PB	#	FDC	Q(M)
Drafting of the Constitution Booklet Issue, Perf. 10 Horizontally							
2355	22¢ "The Bicentennial..." 08/28/87	.55	.20			1.25	122
2356	22¢ "We the people..." 08/28/87	.55	.20			1.25	122
2357	22¢ "Establish justice..." 08/28/87	.55	.20			1.25	122
2358	22¢ "And secure..." 08/28/87	.55	.20			1.25	122
2359	22¢ "Do ordain..." 08/28/87	.55	.20			1.25	122
a	Booklet pane of 5, #2355-59	2.75	2.25			4.00	122
	#2355-59 issued only in booklets. All stamps are imperf. at sides or imperf. at sides and bottom.						
Signing of the Constitution Issue, Perf. 11							
2360	22¢ Constitution and Signer's Hand-Holding Quill Pen 09/17/87	.45	.20	2.25	(4)	1.25	169
2361	22¢ Certified Public Accountants 09/21/87	1.50	.20	7.00	(4)	7.50	163
a	Black omitted	725.00					
Locomotives Booklet Issue, Perf. 10 Horizontally							
2362	22¢ Stourbridge Lion, 1829 10/01/87	.55	.20			1.25	143
2363	22¢ Best Friend of Charleston, 1830 10/01/87	.55	.20			1.25	143
2364	22¢ John Bull, 1831 10/01/87	.55	.20			1.25	143
2365	22¢ Brother Jonathan, 1832 10/01/87	.55	.20			1.25	143
a	Red omitted	—					
2366	22¢ Gowan & Marx, 1839 10/01/87	.55	.20			1.25	143
a	Booklet pane of 5, #2362-66	2.75	2.50			3.00	143
	#2362-66 issued only in booklets. All stamps are imperf. at sides or imperf. at sides and bottom.						
Christmas Issue, Perf. 11							
2367	22¢ Madonna and Child, by Moroni 10/23/87	.40	.20	2.00	(4)	1.25	529
2368	22¢ Christmas Ornaments 10/23/87	.40	.20	1.75	(4)	1.25	978
	Pair with full vertical gutter between	—					

AMERICAN TOLEWARE

In 2002 the AMERICAN TOLEWARE stamp launched the American Design series of definitive stamps that would feature examples of the rich diversity of American design and showcase objects from various regions, eras, and ethnic cultures that combine utility with beauty and function with form. The stamp features a painted detail of a toleware coffeepot from the Winterthur Museum in Delaware. An inscription—"James H. Robbins Philadelphia"—is scratched into the base of the coffeepot. Although curators at Winterthur believe the pot was manufactured in Philadelphia between 1850 and 1875 they acknowledge that addi-

tional information about the inscription might refute this. Produced primarily in New England and Pennsylvania, American toleware was especially popular during the 19th century. Toleware is japanned (varnished) or painted tinware fashioned into a variety of household objects—teapots, coffeepots, cups, trays, and candlesticks—which are decorated with motifs such as fruits and flowers. Typically these designs, in colors such as deep red, green, and pumpkin yellow, are either hand-painted or stenciled onto a black background. ❑

1988

Issues of 1988		Un	U	PB	#	FDC	Q(M)
Winter Olympic Games Issue, Perf. 11							
2369	22¢ Skier and Olympic Rings 01/10/88	.40	.20	1.75	(4)	1.00	159
2370	22¢ Australia Bicentennial 01/10/88	.40	.20	1.75	(4)	1.75	146
Black Heritage Issue							
2371	22¢ James Weldon Johnson and Music from "Lift Ev'ry Voice and Sing" 02/02/88	.40	.20	2.00	(4)	1.75	97
American Cats Issue							
2372	22¢ Siamese and Exotic Shorthair 02/05/88	.45	.20			2.00	40
2373	22¢ Abyssinian and Himalayan 02/05/88	.45	.20			2.00	40
2374	22¢ Maine Coon and Burmese 02/05/88	.45	.20			2.00	40
2375	22¢ American Shorthair and Persian 02/05/88	.45	.20			2.00	40
a	Block of 4, #2372-75	1.90	1.90	4.00	(4)	4.50	
American Sports Issue							
2376	22¢ Knute Rockne Holding Football on Field 03/09/88	.40	.20	2.50	(4)	3.50	97
2377	25¢ Francis Ouimet and Ouimet Hitting Fairway Shot 06/13/88	.45	.20	2.50	(4)	4.50	153
2378	25¢ Love 07/04/88	.45	.20	1.90	(4)	1.00	841
a	Imperf., pair	3,250.00					
2379	45¢ Love 08/08/88	.65	.20	3.25	(4)	1.25	180
Summer Olympic Games Issue							
2380	25¢ Gymnast on Rings 08/19/88	.45	.20	1.90	(4)	1.25	157

ANDY WARHOL

(1928-1987)

Andy Warhol USA 37

ANDY WARHOL, a leading figure in the pop art movement, was one of the most influential artists of his time. Warhol's serial images of celebrities such as Marilyn Monroe and everyday objects such as Campbell's soup cans are perhaps his best known works. His career also included ventures in design, photography, film, television, writing, and publishing. Born in Pittsburgh, Pennsylvania, to immigrant parents, he graduated in 1949 from Carnegie Institute of Technology (now Carnegie Mellon University) with a fine arts degree and moved to New York City to work as a commercial illustrator. By the mid-1950s Warhol had made a name for himself in the advertising world with his whimsical and award-winning illustrations. In 1962 his paintings achieved instant notoriety with his solo exhibition in Los Angeles of the now famous Campbell's Soup Can paintings. That same year, his Coca-Cola bottles and portraits of Marilyn Monroe and Elvis Presley were exhibited in New York City. A shy man, who nevertheless sought publicity and fame, Warhol attracted many followers. His studio, known as the Factory, became a popular New York haunt for an eclectic group of artists, socialites, and musicians. Warhol has remained world-famous far longer than the transitory fifteen minutes he once predicted for everyone. The stamp art, *Self-Portrait, 1964*, is based on a photo-booth photograph. ❑

2369

2370

2371

2372   **2373**

2374   **2375**   **2375a**

2376

2377

2378

2379

2380

2381

1928 Locomobile

2382

1929 Pierce-Arrow

2383

1931 Cord

2384

1932 Packard

2385

1935 Duesenberg

2385a

2390   2391

2392   2393   2393a

2386   2387

Nathaniel Palmer   Lt. Charles Wilkes

Richard E. Byrd   Lincoln Ellsworth

2388   2389   2389a

Issues of 1988		Un	U	PB	#	FDC	Q(M)
Classic Cars Booklet Issue, Perf. 10 Horizontally							
2381 25¢ 1928 Locomobile	08/25/88	.60	.20			1.25	127
2382 25¢ 1929 Pierce-Arrow	08/25/88	.60	.20			1.25	127
2383 25¢ 1931 Cord	08/25/88	.60	.20			1.25	127
2384 25¢ 1932 Packard	08/25/88	.60	.20			1.25	127
2385 25¢ 1935 Duesenberg	08/25/88	.60	.20			1.25	127
a Booklet pane of 5, #2381-85		6.00	2.25			3.00	127
#2381-85 issued only in booklets. All stamps are imperf. at sides or imperf. at sides and bottom.							
Antarctic Explorers Issue, Perf. 11							
2386 25¢ Nathaniel Palmer	09/14/88	.65	.20			1.25	41
2387 25¢ Lt. Charles Wilkes	09/14/88	.65	.20			1.25	41
2388 25¢ Richard E. Byrd	09/14/88	.65	.20			1.25	41
2389 25¢ Lincoln Ellsworth	09/14/88	.65	.20			1.25	41
a Block of 4, #2386-89		2.75	2.00	4.50	(4)	3.00	
b As "a," black omitted		1,400.00					
c As "a," imperf. horizontally		3,000.00					
American Folk Art Issue, Carousel Animals							
2390 25¢ Deer	10/01/88	.65	.20			1.25	76
2391 25¢ Horse	10/01/88	.65	.20			1.25	76
2392 25¢ Camel	10/01/88	.65	.20			1.25	76
2393 25¢ Goat	10/01/88	.65	.20			1.25	76
a Block of 4, #2390-93		3.00	2.00	4.00	(4)	3.00	

FOLK ART: DUCK DECOYS

American folk art celebrates many objects that served utilitarian purposes before they were recognized as works of art. In 1985 the U.S. Postal Service acknowledged this evolution when it issued a block of stamps featuring decoys of four ducks: the Broadbill, Redhead, Canvasback, and Mallard. Originally created for hunters who depended on ducks for food or income, decoys have become highly collectible and acknowledged works of art. Although it is not possible to pinpoint precisely when duck decoys stopped being hunting paraphernalia and became art, in the 1930s a number of whittlers and carvers in the Carolinas, near the Chesapeake Bay, in New York, and in the Mississippi Valley began to see decoys as sculpture. The tradition that began with these decoy makers has passed down to today's carvers who continue to create specimens that amaze the viewers who flock to decoy exhibitions and vie for the few that are for sale. Collectors treasure, and museums collect, the decoys carved by the old craftsmen who created an art form from a utilitarian object. ❑

1988

	Issues of 1988		Un	U	PB	#	FDC	Q(M)
2394	$8.75 Express Mail	10/04/88	13.50	8.00	54.00	(4)	27.50	
	Special Occasions Booklet Issue, Perf. 11							
2395	25¢ Happy Birthday	10/22/88	.50	.20			1.25	120
2396	25¢ Best Wishes	10/22/88	.50	.20			1.25	120
a	Booklet pane of 6, 3 #2395 and							
	3 #2396 with gutter between		3.50	3.25			4.00	
2397	25¢ Thinking of You	10/22/88	.50	.20			1.25	120
2398	25¢ Love You	10/22/88	.50	.20			1.25	120
a	Booklet pane of 6, 3 #2397 and							
	3 #2398 with gutter between		3.50	3.25			4.00	
b	As "a," imperf. horizontally		—					
	#2395-98a issued only in booklets. All stamps are imperf. on one side or on one side and							
	top or bottom.							
	Christmas Issue, Perf. 11.5							
2399	25¢ Madonna and Child,							
	by Botticelli	10/20/88	.45	.20	1.90	(4)	1.25	844
a	Gold omitted		30.00					
2400	25¢ One-Horse Open							
	Sleigh and Village Scene	10/20/88	.45	.20	1.90	(4)	1.25	1,038
	Pair with full vertical gutter between		—					

OGDEN NASH

(1902-1971)

A gentle satirist, OGDEN NASH poked fun at human foibles without cynicism in poems that expressed his wry wit and demonstrated his playfulness with language. "I'm very fond of the English language. I tease it, and you tease only the things you love," Nash reportedly said. He invented words and used puns, creative misspellings, irregular line lengths, and unexpected rhymes to make his verse humorous and memorable. Because of his unique style, many consider Nash as one of the most accomplished American writers of light verse in the 20th century. Born in Rye, New York, he attended Harvard University for a year, then worked in publishing before beginning to write full-time. He first found fame in 1930 when his poem "Invocation" appeared in *The New Yorker*. His first book of poetry, *Hard Lines* (1931), was a best-seller; some 20 other volumes of verse followed, including *The Bad Parents' Garden of Verse* (1936), *I'm a Stranger Here Myself* (1938), and *Everyone But Thee and Me* (1962). He wrote children's books, lyrics for several musical comedies, and regularly appeared on radio and television programs. In 1950 the National Institute of Arts and Letters elected Nash to its select membership of 250 artists, writers, and musicians; and, in 1965, he was elected to the American Academy of Arts and Sciences. ❑

1988

2394

2395   2396   2396a

2397   2398   2398a

2399

2400

2401

2402

2403

2404

2405

2406

2407

2408

2409

2409a

2410   **2411**

2412   **2413**

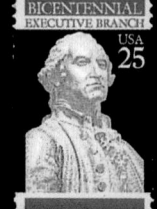

2414   **2415**

2416

2417

2418

	Issues of 1989		Un	U	PB	#	FDC	Q(M)
2401	25¢ Montana Statehood	01/15/89	.45	.20	2.00	(4)	1.25	165
	Black Heritage Issue, Perf. 11							
2402	25¢ A. Philip Randolph, Pullman							
	Porters and Railroad Cars	02/03/89	.45	.20	2.00	(4)	1.75	152
2403	25¢ North Dakota Statehood	02/21/89	.45	.20	2.00	(4)	1.00	163
2404	25¢ Washington Statehood	02/22/89	.45	.20	2.00	(4)	1.00	265
	Steamboats Booklet Issue, Perf. 10 Horizontally							
2405	25¢ Experiment 1788-90	03/03/89	.45	.20			1.25	159
2406	25¢ Phoenix 1809	03/03/89	.45	.20			1.25	159
2407	25¢ New Orleans 1812	03/03/89	.45	.20			1.25	159
2408	25¢ Washington 1816	03/03/89	.45	.20			1.25	159
2409	25¢ Walk in the Water 1818	03/03/89	.45	.20			1.25	159
a	Booklet pane of 5, #2405-09		2.25	1.75			3.00	159
	#2405-09 issued only in booklets. All stamps are imperf. at sides or imperf. at sides and bottom.							
	Perf. 11							
2410	25¢ World Stamp Expo '89	03/16/89	.45	.20	1.90	(4)	1.00	164
	Performing Arts Issue, Perf. 11							
2411	25¢ Arturo Toscanini							
	Conducting with Baton	03/25/89	.45	.20	2.00	(4)	1.00	152
	Issues of 1989-1990, Constitution Bicentennial Issue, Perf. 11							
2412	25¢ U.S. House of							
	Representatives	04/04/89	.50	.20	2.25	(4)	1.25	139
2413	25¢ U.S. Senate	04/06/89	.50	.20	2.50	(4)	1.25	138
2414	25¢ Executive Branch, George							
	Washington	04/16/89	.50	.20	2.25	(4)	1.25	139
2415	25¢ Supreme Court, Chief Justice							
	John Marshall	02/02/90	.50	.20	2.25	(4)	1.25	151
	Issues of 1989							
2416	25¢ South Dakota							
	Statehood	05/03/89	.45	.20	1.90	(4)	1.00	165
	American Sports Issue							
2417	25¢ Lou Gehrig,							
	Gehrig Swinging Bat	06/10/89	.50	.20	3.00	(4)	4.00	263
	Literary Arts Issue							
2418	25¢ Ernest Hemingway, African							
	Landscape in Background	07/17/89	.45	.20	2.00	(4)	1.25	192

USPS Binder and Pages

The home your collection deserves. This elegant binder comes with a matching slipcase to keep your stamps safe. With 10 different pocket combinations, the pages let you display your stamps any number of ways.

To order call **1-800-STAMP-24** or visit us online at **www.usps.com**

USPS Binder and Pages $42.00–Item #014002

1989

	Issues of 1989		Un	U	PB	#	FDC	Q(M)
	Priority Mail Issue, Perf. 11 x 11.5							
2419	$2.40 Moon Landing	07/20/89	4.00	2.00	17.50	(4)	7.50	
a	Black (engr.) omitted		2,500.00					
b	Imperf., pair		750.00					
c	Black (litho.) omitted		3,250.00					
	Perf. 11							
2420	25¢ Letter Carriers	08/30/89	.45	.20	1.90	(4)	1.25	188
	Constitution Bicentennial Issue							
2421	25¢ Bill of Rights	09/25/89	.45	.20	3.00	(4)	1.00	192
a	Black omitted		325.00					
	Prehistoric Animals Issue, Perf. 11							
2422	25¢ Tyrannosaurus	10/01/89	.65	.20			1.50	102
2423	25¢ Pteranodon	10/01/89	.65	.20			1.50	102
2424	25¢ Stegosaurus	10/01/89	.65	.20			1.50	102
2425	25¢ Brontosaurus	10/01/89	.65	.20			1.50	102
a	Block of 4, #2422-25		3.00	2.00	3.50	(4)	3.00	
b	As "a," black omitted		750.00					
	America/PUAS Issue (See also #C121)							
2426	25¢ Southwest Carved Figure (A.D. 1150-1350), Emblem of the Postal Union of the Americas	10/12/89	.45	.20	2.00	(4)	1.00	137
	Christmas Issue, Perf. 11.5							
2427	25¢ Madonna and Child, by Caracci	10/19/89	.45	.20	2.00	(4)	1.00	913
a	Booklet pane of 10		4.75	3.50			6.00	
b	Red (litho.) omitted		750.00					
	Perf. 11							
2428	25¢ Sleigh Full of Presents	10/19/89	.45	.20	1.90	(4)	1.00	900
a	Vertical pair, imperf. horizontally		2,000.00					
	Booklet Stamp Issue, Perf. 11.5 on 2 or 3 sides							
2429	25¢ Single from booklet pane (#2428)	10/19/89	.45	.20			1.00	399
a	Booklet pane of 10		4.75	3.50			6.00	40
b	As "a," imperf. horiz. between		—					
c	Vertical pair, imperf. horizontally		—					
d	As "a," red omitted		—					
e	Imperf., pair		—					
	In #2429, runners on sleigh are twice as thick as in 2428; bow on package at rear of sleigh is same color as package; board running underneath sleigh is pink.							
2430	Not assigned							
	Self-Adhesive, Die-Cut							
2431	25¢ Eagle and Shield	11/10/89	.50	.20			1.25	75
a	Booklet pane of 18		11.00					
b	Vertical pair, no die-cutting between		500.00					
2432	Not assigned							

2420

2421

2419

2422

2423

2426

2424

2425

2425a

2427

2428

2431

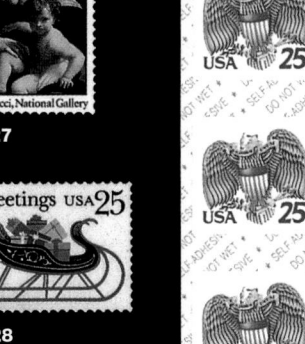

2431 coil

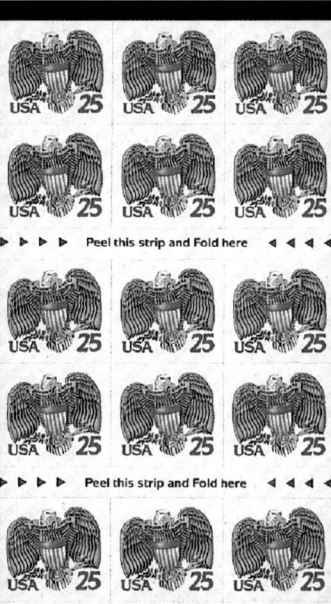

2431a

WORLD STAMP EXPO '89

The classic 1869 U.S. Abraham Lincoln stamp is reborn in these four larger versions commemorating World Stamp Expo'89, held in Washington, D.C. during the 20th Universal Postal Congress of the UPU. These stamps show the issued colors and three of the trial proof color combinations.

2433

2439

2434

2435

2440

2436

2437

2437a

2442

20th Universal Postal Congress

A review of historical methods of delivering the mail in the United States is the theme of these four stamps issued in commemoration of the convening of the 20th Universal Postal Congress in Washington, D.C. from November 13 through December 15, 1989. The United States, as host nation to the Congress for the first time in ninety-two years, welcomed more than 1,000 delegates from most of the member nations of the Universal Postal Union to the major international event.

2443

2438

Issues of 1989		Un	U	PB	#	FDC	Q(M)
World Stamp Expo '89 Issue Souvenir Sheet, Imperf.							
2433	Reproduction of #122, 90¢ Lincoln,						
	and three essays of #122	11/17/89	14.00	9.00			7.00	2
a-d	Single stamp from sheet		2.00	1.75				
20th UPU Congress Issues, Classic Mail Transportation, Perf. 11							
(See also #C122-25)							
2434	25¢ Stagecoach	11/19/89	.45	.20			1.25	41
2435	25¢ Paddlewheel Steamer	11/19/89	.45	.20			1.25	41
2436	25¢ Biplane	11/19/89	.45	.20			1.25	41
2437	25¢ Depot-Hack Type						
	Automobile	11/19/89	.45	.20			1.25	41
a	Block of 4, #2434-37		2.00	1.75	3.75	(4)	2.50	
b	As "a," dark blue omitted		600.00					
Souvenir Sheet, Imperf. (See also #C126)							
2438	Designs of #2434-37	11/28/89	4.00	1.75			3.00	2
a-d	Single stamp from sheet		.65	.25				
Issues of 1990, Perf. 11							
2439	25¢ Idaho Statehood	01/06/90	.45	.20	2.00	(4)	1.25	173
Perf. 12.5 x 13							
2440	25¢ Love	01/18/90	.45	.20	2.00	(4)	1.25	886
a	Imperf., pair		800.00					
Booklet Stamp, Perf. 11.5							
2441	25¢ Love, single from booklet	01/18/90	.45	.20			1.00	995
a	Booklet pane of 10	01/18/90	4.75	3.50			6.00	
b	As "a," bright pink omitted		1,700.00					
c	As "b," single stamp		160.00					
Black Heritage Issue, Perf. 11							
2442	25¢ Ida B. Wells,						
	Marchers in Background	02/01/90	.45	.20	2.25	(4)	2.00	153
Beach Umbrella Booklet Issue, Perf. 11							
2443	15¢ Beach Umbrella,						
	single from booklet	02/03/90	.30	.20			1.25	
a	Booklet pane of 10	02/03/90	3.00	2.00			4.25	
b	As "a," blue omitted		1,400.00					
c	As #2443, blue omitted		140.00					

#2443 issued only in booklets. All stamps are imperf. at one side or imperf. at one side and bottom.

TIFFANY LAMP

The third stamp in the American Design series features an artistic rendering by Lou Nolan of a Tiffany lamp. Louis Comfort Tiffany (1848–1933) was a designer of glass, ceramics, jewelry, enamelware, and metalwork who transformed everyday objects into works of art. Born in New York, he was the son of the founder and owner of Tiffany & Company, Jewelers. He studied art in the United States and in Europe where he was inspired by the stained glass windows in France. He returned home to experiment and ultimately create an American art form. Tiffany's stained-glass lampshades glow with soft, colorful light. Considered one of the greatest designers of glass in his era, Tiffany is also remembered as a leader in the art nouveau movement, a style in the visual arts that transformed design in the United States and Europe from the 1890s to World War I. ❑

	Issues of 1990		Un	U	PB	#	FDC	Q(M)
	Perf 11							
2444	25¢ Wyoming Statehood	02/23/90	.45	.20	2.00	(4)	1.00	169
a	Black (engr.) omitted		1,900.00	—				
	Classic Films Issue							
2445	25¢ The Wizard of Oz	03/23/90	1.00	.20			2.50	44
2446	25¢ Gone With the Wind	03/23/90	1.00	.20			2.50	44
2447	25¢ Beau Geste	03/23/90	1.00	.20			2.50	44
2448	25¢ Stagecoach	03/23/90	1.00	.20			2.50	44
a	Block of 4, #2445-48		4.50	3.50	6.00	(4)	5.00	
	Literary Arts Issue							
2449	25¢ Marianne Moore	04/18/90	.45	.20	2.00	(4)	1.25	150
2450	Not assigned							
	Issues of 1990-1995, Transportation Issue, Coil Stamps, Perf. 9.8 Vertically							
2451	4¢ Steam Carriage 1866	01/25/91	.20	.20	1.10	(5)	1.25	
a	Imperf., pair		700.00					
b	Untagged		.20	.20	1.10	(5)		
2452	5¢ Circus Wagon 1900s,							
	intaglio printing	08/31/91	.20	.20	1.25	(5)	1.50	
a	Untagged, dull gum		.20	.20	1.25	(5)		
c	Imperf., pair		700.00					
2452B	5¢ Circus Wagon							
	(2452), gravure printing	12/08/92	.20	.20	1.50	(5)	1.50	
f	Printed with luminescent ink		.20	.20	2.10	(5)		
2452D	5¢ Circus Wagon							
	(2452), gravure printing	03/20/95	.20	.20	1.60	(5)	2.00	
e	Imperf., pair		—					
g	Printed with luminescent ink		.20	.20	1.90	(5)		
2453	5¢ Canoe 1800s, precanceled,							
	intaglio printing	05/25/91	.20	.20	1.50	(5)	1.25	
a	Imperf., pair		300.00					
2454	5¢ Canoe 1800s,							
	precanceled, gravure printing	10/22/91	.20	.20	1.40	(5)	1.25	
2455-56	Not assigned							
2457	10¢ Tractor Trailer, Bureau							
	precanceled, intaglio printing	05/25/91	.20	.20	2.10	(5)	1.25	
a	Imperf., pair		250.00					
2458	10¢ Tractor Trailer, Bureau							
	precanceled, gravure printing	05/25/94	.30	.20	2.50	(5)	1.25	
2459-62	Not assigned							
2463	20¢ Cog Railway Car 1870s	06/09/95	.40	.20	4.00	(5)	1.25	
a	Imperf., pair		125.00					
2464	23¢ Lunch Wagon 1890s	04/12/91	.45	.20	3.75	(5)	1.25	
a	Prephosphored uncoated paper		.45	.20	4.50	(5)		
b	Imperf., pair		150.00					
2465	Not assigned							
2466	32¢ Ferryboat 1900s	06/02/95	.60	.20	5.50	(5)	1.25	
a	Imperf., pair		600.00					
b	Bright blue, prephosphored							
	uncoated paper		6.00	4.50	140.00	(5)		
2467	Not assigned							
2468	$1 Seaplane 1914	04/20/90	1.75	.50	9.25	(5)	2.50	
a	Imperf., pair		2,750.00	—				
b	Prephosphored uncoated paper		1.75	.50	9.25	(5)		
c	Prephosphored coated paper		1.75	.50	9.00	(5)		
2469	Not assigned							

2444

2445   **2446**

2447  **2448**

2448a

2449

2451

2452

2452D

2453

2454

2457

2463

2464

2466

2468

2474a

2470   2471   2472   2473   2474

2475

2476   2477   2478

2479   2480   2481   2482

2483   2484   2485

Issues of 1990-1995		Un	U	PB	#	FDC	Q(M)
Lighthouses Booklet Issue, Tagged, Perf. 10 Vertically on 1 or 2 sides							
2470	25¢ Admiralty Head, WA 04/26/90	1.00	.20			1.50	147
2471	25¢ Cape Hatteras, NC 04/26/90	1.00	.20			1.50	147
2472	25¢ West Quoddy Head, ME 04/26/90	1.00	.20			1.50	147
2473	25¢ American Shoals, FL 04/26/90	1.00	.20			1.50	147
2474	25¢ Sandy Hook, NJ 04/26/90	1.00	.20			1.50	147
a	Booklet pane of 5, #2470-74	5.50	2.00			3.00	147
b	As "a," white (USA 25) omitted	80.00	—				
Self-Adhesive, Untagged, Die-Cut							
2475	25¢ Flag, single from pane 05/18/90	.50	.25			1.00	36
a	Pane of 12 05/18/90	6.00					
Flora and Fauna Issues, Untagged, Perf. 11, Perf. 11.2 (#2477)							
2476	1¢ American Kestrel 06/22/91	.20	.20	.20	(4)	1.00	
2477	1¢ American Kestrel 05/10/95	.20	.20	.20	(4)	1.00	
2478	3¢ Eastern Bluebird 06/22/91	.20	.20	.30	(4)	1.00	
Tagged, Perf. 11.5 x 11							
2479	19¢ Fawn 03/11/91	.35	.20	1.75	(4)	1.00	
a	Tagging omitted	10.00					
b	Red omitted	850.00					
2480	30¢ Cardinal 06/22/91	.50	.20	2.25	(4)	1.25	
Perf. 11							
2481	45¢ Pumpkinseed Sunfish 12/02/92	.80	.20	3.90	(4)	1.75	
a	Black omitted	450.00	—				
2482	$2 Bobcat 06/01/90	3.00	1.25	12.00	(4)	5.00	
a	Black omitted	300.00					
b	Tagging omitted	15.00					
Perf. 10.9 x 9.8							
2483	20¢ Blue Jay 06/15/95	.50	.20			1.25	
a	Booklet pane of 10	5.25	2.25				
Wood Duck Booklet Issue, Tagged, Perf. 10 on 2 or 3 sides							
2484	29¢ Black and multicolored 04/12/91	.50	.20			1.00	
a	Booklet pane of 10	5.50	3.75			4.00	
b	Vertical pair, imperf. between	200.00					
c	As "b," booklet pane of 10	1,000.00					
d	Prephosphored coated paper	.40	.20				
Perf. 11 on 2 or 3 sides							
2485	29¢ Red and multicolored 04/12/91	.50	.20			1.00	
a	Booklet pane of 10	5.50	4.00			4.00	
b	Vertical pair, imperf. between	3,000.00					
c	Imperf, pair	—					
#2484-85a issued only in bklts. All stamps are imperf. top or bottom, or top or bottom and right edge.							

VISIT US ONLINE AT **THE POSTAL STORE**

AT **WWW.USPS.COM**

OR CALL **1-800-STAMP-24**

Issues of 1993-1995			Un	U	PB	#	FDC	Q(M)
Perf. 10 x 11 on 2 or 3 sides								
2486	29¢ African Violet	10/08/93	.50	.20			1.00	
a	Booklet pane of 10		5.50	*4.00*			4.00	
2487	32¢ Peach	07/08/95	.60	.20			1.50	
2488	32¢ Pear	07/08/95	.60	.20			1.50	
a	Booklet pane, 5 each #2487-88		6.00	*4.25*			7.50	
b	Pair, #2487-88		1.25	.30				
Issues of 1993, Self-Adhesive, Die-Cut								
2489	29¢ Red Squirrel	06/25/93	.50	.20			1.25	
a	Booklet pane of 18		10.00					
2490	29¢ Red Rose	08/19/93	.50	.20			1.25	
a	Booklet pane of 18		10.00					
2491	29¢ Pine Cone	11/05/93	.50	.20			1.25	
a	Booklet pane of 18		11.00					
b	Horizontal pair, no die cutting between		*250.00*					
c	Coil with plate #B1		—	5.00	6.75	(5)		
Serpentine Die-Cut 11.3 x 11.7 on 2, 3 or 4 sides								
2492	32¢ Pink Rose	06/02/95	.60	.20			1.25	
a	Booklet pane of 20 plus label		12.00					
b	Booklet pane of 15 plus label		8.75					
c	Horizontal pair, no die cutting between		—					
d	As "a," 2 stamps and parts of 7 others printed on backing liner		—					
e	Booklet pane of 14		21.00					
f	Booklet pane of 16		21.00					
g	Coil with plate #S111		—	3.00	6.00	(5)		
h	Vertical pair, no die cutting between		—					
2493	32¢ Peach	07/08/95	.60	.20			1.25	
2494	32¢ Pear	07/08/95	.60	.20			1.25	
a	Booklet pane, 10 each #2493-2494		12.50					
b	Pair, #2493-2494		1.20					
Coil Stamps, Serpentine Die-Cut 8.8 Vertically								
2495	32¢ Peach	07/08/95	.60	.20			1.25	
2495A	32¢ Pear	07/08/95	.60	.20			1.25	
b	Pair #2495-2495A		1.20		6.25	(5)		
Issues of 1990, Olympians Issue, Perf. 11								
2496	25¢ Jesse Owens	07/06/90	.60	.20			1.25	36
2497	25¢ Ray Ewry	07/06/90	.60	.20			1.25	36
2498	25¢ Hazel Wightman	07/06/90	.60	.20			1.25	36
2499	25¢ Eddie Eagan	07/06/90	.60	.20			1.25	36
2500	25¢ Helene Madison	07/06/90	.60	.20			1.25	36
a	Strip of 5, #2496-2500		3.25	2.50	8.00	(10)	4.00	7
Indian Headdresses Booklet Issue, Perf. 11 on 2 or 3 sides								
2501	25¢ Assiniboine Headdress	08/17/90	.80	.20			1.25	124
2502	25¢ Cheyenne Headdress	08/17/90	.80	.20			1.25	124
2503	25¢ Comanche Headdress	08/17/90	.80	.20			1.25	124
2504	25¢ Flathead Headdress	08/17/90	.80	.20			1.25	124
2505	25¢ Shoshone Headdress	08/17/90	.80	.20			1.25	124
a	Booklet pane of 10, 2 each of #2501-05		8.50	3.50			6.00	62
b	As "a," black omitted		*3,250.00*					
c	Strip of 5		2.75	1.00				
d	As "a," horizontal imperf. between		—					

#2501-05 issued only in booklets. All stamps imperf. top or bottom, or top or bottom and right edge.

2486

2487   **2488**

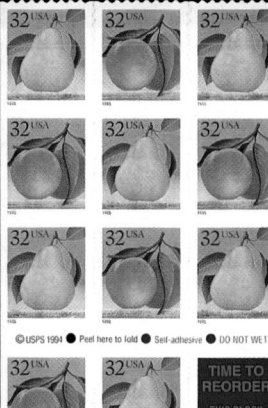
2487-2488a

2489   **2490**   **2491**   **2492**

2496   **2497**   **2498**   **2499**   **2500** **2500a**

2501   **2502**   **2503**   **2504**   **2505** **2505a**

2506   2507   2507a

2508   2509

2510   2511   2511a

2512

2513

2514   2515

         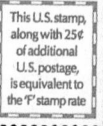

2517   2519   2520   2521

2522   2523   2523A

	Issues of 1990		Un	U	PB	#	FDC	Q(M)
	Micronesia/Marshall Islands Issue, Perf. 11							
2506	25¢ Canoe and Flag of the							
	Federated States of Micronesia	09/28/90	.45	.20			1.25	76
2507	25¢ Stick Chart, Canoe and							
	Flag of the Marshall Islands	09/28/90	.45	.20			1.25	76
a	Pair, #2506-07		.90	.60	2.25	(4)	2.00	61
b	As "a," black omitted		2,750.00					
	Creatures of the Sea Issue, Perf. 11							
2508	25¢ Killer Whales	10/03/90	.45	.20			1.25	70
2509	25¢ Northern Sea Lions	10/03/90	.45	.20			1.25	70
2510	25¢ Sea Otter	10/03/90	.45	.20			1.25	70
2511	25¢ Common Dolphin	10/03/90	.45	.20			1.25	70
a	Block of 4, #2508-11		1.90	1.90	2.50	(4)	3.00	70
b	As "a," black omitted		700.00					
	America/PUAS Issue, (See also #C127) 1990-1991, Perf. 11							
2512	25¢ Grand Canyon	10/12/90	.45	.20	2.00	(4)	1.25	151
2513	25¢ Dwight D. Eisenhower	10/13/90	.60	.20	3.00	(4)	1.25	143
a	Imperf., pair		2,250.00					
	Christmas Issue, Perf. 11.5							
2514	25¢ Madonna and							
	Child, by Antonello	10/18/90	.45	.20	2.00	(4)	1.25	500
b	Booklet pane of 10		5.00	3.25			6.00	23
	Perf. 11							
2515	25¢ Christmas Tree	10/18/90	.45	.20	2.00	(4)	1.25	599
a	Vertical pair, imperf. horizontally		1,100.00					
	Booklet Stamp, Perf. 11.5 x 11 on 2 or 3 sides							
2516	Single (2515) from booklet pane	10/18/90	.45	.20			1.00	
a	Booklet pane of 10	10/18/90	5.00	3.25			6.00	32
	Issues of 1991, Perf. 13							
2517	(29¢) "F" Stamp	01/22/91	.55	.20	2.60	(4)	1.25	
a	Imperf., pair		700.00					
b	Horizontal pair, imperf. vertically		1,250.00					
	Coil Stamp, Perf. 10 Vertically							
2518	(29¢) "F" Tulip (2517)	01/22/91	.55	.20	3.50	(5)	1.25	
a	Imperf., pair		37.50					
	Booklet Stamps, Perf. 11 on 2 or 3 sides							
2519	(29¢) "F", single from booklet		.55	.20			1.00	
a	Booklet pane of 10	01/22/91	6.50	4.50			7.25	
2520	(29¢) "F", single from booklet		.55	.20			1.25	
a	Booklet pane of 10	01/22/91	18.00	4.50			8.00	
	#2519 has bull's-eye perforations that measure approximately 11.2. #2520 has less-pronounced black lines in the leaf, which is a much brighter green than on #2519.							
	Perf. 11							
2521	(4¢) Makeup Rate	01/22/91	.20	.20	.40	(4)	1.25	
a	Vertical pair, imperf. horizontally		100.00					
	Self-Adhesive, Die-Cut, Imperf.							
2522	(29¢) F Flag, single from pane		.55	.25			1.25	
a	Pane of 12	01/22/91	7.00					
	Coil Stamps, Perf. 10 Vertically							
2523	29¢ Flag Over Mt. Rushmore,							
	intaglio printing	03/29/91	.55	.20	4.25	(5)	1.25	
b	Imperf., pair		25.00					
c	Blue, red and brown		5.00	—	175.00	(5)		
d	Prephosphored coated paper		5.00	—	850.00	(5)		
2523A	29¢ Flag Over Mt. Rushmore,							
	gravure printing	07/04/91	.55	.20	4.00	(5)	1.25	

	Issues of 1991		Un	U	PB	#	FDC	Q(M)
	Perf. 11							
2524	29¢ Tulip	04/05/91	.55	.20	2.50	(4)	1.00	
2524A	Perf. 13		.75	.20	9.00	(4)		
	Coil Stamps, Roulette 10 Vertically							
2525	29¢ Tulip	08/16/91	.55	.20	4.50	(5)	1.00	
	Issues of 1992, Perf. 10 Vertically							
2526	29¢ Tulip	03/03/92	.55	.20	4.50	(5)	1.00	
	Issues of 1991, Booklet Stamp, Perf. 11 on 2 or 3 sides							
2527	29¢ Tulip (2524), single from bklt.		.55	.20			1.00	
a	Booklet pane of 10	04/05/91	5.50	3.50			4.00	
b	As "a," vertically imperf. between		1,500.00					
c	Horizontal pair, imperf. vertically		225.00					
d	As "a," imperf. horizontal		2,500.00					
	Flag With Olympic Rings Booklet Issue, Perf. 11							
2528	29¢ U.S. Flag, Olympic Rings, single from booklet	04/21/91	.55	.20			1.25	
a	Booklet pane of 10	04/21/91	5.50	3.50			5.00	
	Issues of 1991-94, Perf. 9.8 Vertically							
2529	19¢ Fishing Boat	08/08/91	.35	.20	3.25	(5)	1.50	
a	New printing, Type II	1993	.35	.20	3.75	(5)		
b	As "a," untagged		1.00	.40	7.50	(5)		
	Perf. 9.8							
2529C	19¢ Fishing Boat	06/25/94	.50	.20	5.25	(5)	1.50	
	Type II stamps have finer dot pattern, smoother edges along type. #2529C has only one loop of rope tying up the boat.							
	Issue of 1991, Ballooning Booklet Issue, Perf. 10							
2530	19¢ Overhead View of Balloon, single from booklet	05/17/91	.35	.20			1.25	
a	Booklet pane of 10	05/17/91	3.50	2.75			5.00	
	#2530 was issued only in booklets. All stamps are imperf. on one side or on one side and bottom.							
	Perf. 11							
2531	29¢ Flags on Parade	05/30/91	.55	.20	2.50	(4)	1.00	
	Self-Adhesive, Die-Cut, Imperf.							
2531A	29¢ Liberty Torch, single stamp from pane	06/25/91	.55	.25			1.25	
b	Pane of 18	06/25/91	10.50					
	Perf. 11							
2532	50¢ Founding of Switzerland	02/22/91	1.00	.25	5.00	(4)	1.40	100
a	Vertical pair, imperf. horizontally		2,250.00					
2533	29¢ Vermont Statehood	03/01/91	.60	.20	4.00	(4)	1.50	0.1
2534	29¢ Savings Bonds	04/30/91	.55	.20	2.50	(4)	1.25	151
	Perf. 12.5 x 13							
2535	29¢ Love	05/09/91	.55	.20	2.50	(4)	1.25	631
2535A	Perf. 11		.75	.20	4.00	(4)		
	Booklet Stamp, Perf. 11 on 2 or 3 sides							
2536	29¢ (2535), single from booklet		.55	.20			1.25	
a	Booklet pane of 10	05/09/91	5.50	3.50			5.00	
	Perf. 11							
2537	52¢ Love	05/09/91	.90	.20	4.50	(4)	1.25	200

2524   **2525**   **2526**

2528

2529   **2529C**

2530

2531

2531A

2532

2533   **2534**

2535

2537

2538

2539

2540

2541

2542

2543

2544

2544A

2545

2546

2547

2548

2549

2549a

	Issues of 1991		Un	U	PB	#	FDC	Q(M)
	Literary Arts Issue, Perf. 11							
2538	29¢ William Saroyan	05/22/91	.55	.20	2.50	(4)	1.50	161
	Issues of 1991–93, Perf. 11							
2539	$1 USPS Logo/Olympic Rings	09/29/91	1.75	.50	8.00	(4)	2.25	
2540	$2.90 Priority Mail	07/07/91	6.00	2.50	24.00	(4)	5.50	
2541	$9.95 Domestic Express Mail	06/16/91	20.00	7.50	80.00	(4)	15.00	
2542	$14 International Express Mail	08/31/91	25.00	10.00	100.00	(4)	19.00	
a	Red omitted		1,500.00					
	Perf 11 x 10.5							
2543	$2.90 Space Vehicle	06/03/93	5.00	2.25	22.50	(4)	6.00	
	Perf. 11.2							
2544	$3 Space Shuttle *Challenger*	06/22/95	5.25	2.25	21.00	(4)	6.00	
	Express Mail Rate, Perf. 11							
2544A	$10.75 Space Shuttle *Endeavour*	08/04/95	19.00	7.50	77.50	(4)	15.00	
	Issues of 1991, Fishing Flies Booklet Issue, Perf. 11 Horizontally							
2545	29¢ Royal Wulff	05/31/91	1.00	.20			1.25	149
2546	29¢ Jock Scott	05/31/91	1.00	.20			1.25	149
2547	29¢ Apte Tarpon Fly	05/31/91	1.00	.20			1.25	149
2548	29¢ Lefty's Deceiver	05/31/91	1.00	.20			1.25	149
2549	29¢ Muddler Minnow	05/31/91	1.00	.20			1.25	149
a	Booklet pane of 5, #2545-49		5.50	2.50			3.00	149

#2545-49 were issued only in booklets. All stamps are imperf. at sides or imperf. at sides and bottom.

LEONARD BERNSTEIN

(1918-1990)

LEONARD BERNSTEIN—conductor, composer, pianist, teacher, and author—brought worldwide recognition to American composers and musicians. He made hundreds of recordings and wrote many books on music. His educational television programs made music accessible to, and understandable by, general audiences. Bernstein studied piano as a boy, later earning degrees in music (Harvard University) and in conducting (Curtis Institute of Music in Philadelphia). In August 1943, at age 25, he was named assistant conductor of the New York Philharmonic. Three months later, he was a last-minute substitute for guest conductor Bruno Walter in a nationally broadcast concert which received rave reviews. Soon orchestras worldwide were inviting him to serve as guest conductor. In 1958, Bernstein was appointed music director of the New York Philharmonic, the first U.S.-born and trained con-

ductor to hold that position. On December 15, 1971, he conducted his 1,000th concert with the Philharmonic—an unprecedented achievement in that orchestra's history. Bernstein composed symphonies, chamber music, and works for ballet, opera, and film. His many contributions to musical theater include scores for *On the Town*, the comic operetta *Candide*, and *West Side Story*, which was made into an Academy Award-winning film. ❑

Issues of 1991		Un	U	PB	#	FDC	Q(M)
Performing Arts Issue, Perf. 11							
2550	29¢ Cole Porter at Piano,						
	Sheet Music 06/08/91	.55	.20	2.50	(4)	1.25	150
a	Vertical pair, imperf. horizontally	650.00					
2551	29¢ Operations Desert Shield/						
	Desert Storm 07/02/91	.55	.20	2.50	(4)	2.50	200
a	Vertical pair, imperf. horizontally	1,500.00					
Booklet Stamp, Perf. 11 on 1 or 2 sides							
2552	29¢ Operations Desert Shield/Desert						
	Storm (2551), single from booklet 07/02/91	.55	.20			2.50	200
a	Booklet pane of 5 07/02/91	2.75	2.25			4.75	40
Summer Olympic Games Issue, Perf. 11							
2553	29¢ Pole Vaulter 07/12/91	.55	.20			1.25	34
2554	29¢ Discus Thrower 07/12/91	.55	.20			1.25	34
2555	29¢ Women Sprinters 07/12/91	.55	.20			1.25	34
2556	29¢ Javelin Thrower 07/12/91	.55	.20			1.25	34
2557	29¢ Women Hurdlers 07/12/91	.55	.20			1.25	34
a	Strip of 5, #2553-57	2.75	2.25	7.50	(10)	3.00	34
2558	29¢ Numismatics 08/13/91	.55	.20	2.50	(4)	1.25	150
World War II Issue, 1941: A World at War, Miniature Sheet, Perf. 11							
2559	Sheet of 10 and central label 09/03/91	5.50	5.00			7.00	15
a	29¢ Burma Road	.55	.30			1.50	15
b	29¢ America's First Peacetime Draft	.55	.30			1.50	15
c	29¢ Lend-Lease Act	.55	.30			1.50	15
d	29¢ Atlantic Charter	.55	.30			1.50	15
e	29¢ Arsenal of Democracy	.55	.30			1.50	15
f	29¢ Destroyer *Reuben James*	.55	.30			1.50	15
g	29¢ Civil Defense	.55	.30			1.50	15
h	29¢ Liberty Ship	.55	.30			1.50	15
i	29¢ Pearl Harbor	.55	.30			1.50	15
j	29¢ U.S. Declaration of War	.55	.30			1.50	15
k	29¢ Black omitted	10,000.00					

CLARA WARD

(1924-1973)

Gospel singer CLARA WARD, who was born in Philadelphia, began playing the piano when she was six. By 1934 she was the accompanist for the Ward Trio, a family group consisting of Ward, her mother, and her sister. In 1943 the trio gained national fame when they sang for the National Baptist Convention and toured the East and South. When Marion Williams and Henrietta Waddy joined in 1947, the group became known as the Ward Singers. Their recording in 1949 of "Surely, God is Able" made them one of the most popular female gospel groups in the 1950s. They performed at the Newport Jazz Festival in 1957 and at New York's Carnegie Hall. Ward's powerful contralto voice and talent as an arranger, composer, and pianist made her one of the first commercially successful gospel singers. Three other celebrated female gospel singers—Mahalia Jackson, Sister Rosetta Tharpe, and Roberta Martin—were honored with Ward in the 1998 Legends of American Music series. ❑

2550

2551

2553

2554

2555

2556

2557   2557a

2558

a

b

c

d

e

f

g

h

i

j

2559

2560

2561

2562

2563

2564

2565

2566   **2566a**

2567

2568   **2569**   **2570**   **2571**   **2572**

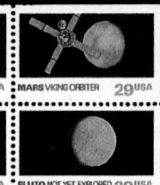

2573   **2574**   **2575**   **2576**   **2577**   **2577a**

	Issues of 1991		Un	U	PB	#	FDC	Q(M)
2560	29¢ Basketball	08/28/91	.50	.20	2.50	(4)	2.25	150
2561	29¢ District of Columbia	09/07/91	.55	.20	2.50	(4)	1.25	149
a	Black omitted		110.00					
	Comedians Booklet Issue, Perf. 11 on 2 or 3 sides							
2562	29¢ Stan Laurel and Oliver Hardy	08/29/91	.65	.20			1.25	140
2563	29¢ Edgar Bergen and							
	Dummy Charlie McCarthy	08/29/91	.65	.20			1.25	140
2564	29¢ Jack Benny	08/29/91	.65	.20			1.25	140
2565	29¢ Fanny Brice	08/29/91	.65	.20			1.25	140
2566	29¢ Bud Abbott and Lou Costello	08/29/91	.65	.20			1.25	140
a	Booklet pane of 10,							
	2 each of #2562-66		9.00	3.50			3.00	70
b	As "a," scarlet and bright violet omitted		700.00					
c	Strip of 5		3.00	—				
	#2562-66 issued only in booklets. All stamps are imperf. at top or bottom, or at top or bottom and right side.							
	Black Heritage Issue, Perf. 11							
2567	29¢ Jan Matzeliger and							
	Shoe-Lasting Machine Diagram	09/15/91	.55	.20	2.50	(4)	1.75	149
a	Horizontal pair, imperf. vertically		1,250.00					
b	Vertical pair, imperf. horizontally		1,250.00					
c	Imperf., pair		750.00					
	Space Exploration Booklet Issue, Perf. 11 on 2 or 3 sides							
2568	29¢ Mercury, Mariner 10	10/01/91	.85	.20			1.25	33
2569	29¢ Venus, Mariner 2	10/01/91	.85	.20			1.25	33
2570	29¢ Earth, Landsat	10/01/91	.85	.20			1.25	33
2571	29¢ Moon, Lunar Orbiter	10/01/91	.85	.20			1.25	33
2572	29¢ Mars, Viking Orbiter	10/01/91	.85	.20			1.25	33
2573	29¢ Jupiter, Pioneer 11	10/01/91	.85	.20			1.25	33
2574	29¢ Saturn, Voyager 2	10/01/91	.85	.20			1.25	33
2575	29¢ Uranus, Voyager 2	10/01/91	.85	.20			1.25	33
2576	29¢ Neptune, Voyager 2	10/01/91	.85	.20			1.25	33
2577	29¢ Pluto	10/01/91	.85	.20			1.25	33
a	Booklet pane of 10, #2568-77		9.00	3.50			5.00	33
	#2568-77 issued only in booklets. All stamps are imperf. at top or bottom, or at top or bottom and right side.							

1991-1995

Issues of 1991-1995			Un	U	PB	#	FDC	Q(M)
	Christmas Issue, Perf. 11							
2578	29¢ Madonna and Child,							
	by Antoniazzo Romano	10/17/91	.55	.20	2.50	(4)	1.25	401
a	Booklet pane of 10		5.50	3.25				30
b	As "a," single, red and black omitted		3,500.00					
2579	29¢ Santa Claus in Chimney	10/17/91	.55	.20	2.50	(4)	1.25	900
a	Horizontal pair, imperf. vertically		300.00					
b	Vertical pair, imperf. horizontally		500.00					
	Booklet Stamps, Perf. 11 on 2 or 3 sides							
2580	29¢ Santa Claus (2579),							
	Type I, single from booklet	10/17/91	2.00	.20			1.25	
2581	29¢ Santa Claus (2579),							
	Type II, single from booklet	10/17/91	2.00	.20			1.25	
a	Pair, #2580, 2581	10/17/91	4.00	.50				28
b	Booklet pane, 2 each		9.00	1.25			2.50	
	The extreme left brick in top row of chimney is missing from Type II, #2581.							
2582	29¢ Santa Claus Checking							
	List, single from booklet	10/17/91	.55	.20			1.25	
a	Booklet pane of 4	10/17/91	2.00	1.25			2.50	28
2583	29¢ Santa Claus with Present							
	Under Tree, single from booklet	10/17/91	.55	.20			1.25	
a	Booklet pane of 4	10/17/91	2.00	1.25			2.50	28
2584	29¢ Santa Claus at Fireplace,							
	single from booklet	10/17/91	.55	.20			1.25	
a	Booklet pane of 4	10/17/91	2.25	1.25			2.50	28
2585	29¢ Santa Claus and Sleigh,							
	single from booklet	10/17/91	.55	.20			1.25	
a	Booklet pane of 4	10/17/91	2.25	1.25			2.50	28
	#2582-85 issued only in booklets. All stamps are imperf. at top or bottom, or at top or bottom and right side.							
	Perf. 11.2							
2587	32¢ James K. Polk	11/02/95	.60	.20	3.00	(4)	1.25	
	Issues of 1994, Perf. 11.5							
2590	$1 Victory at Saratoga	05/05/94	1.90	.50	7.60	(4)	2.50	
2592	$5 Washington and Jackson	08/19/94	8.00	2.50	40.00	(4)	12.50	

2578

2579

2580   **2581**   **2581a**

2582

2583

2584

2585

2587

2590

2592

2593

2594

2595

2596

2597

2598

2599

2602

2603

2604

2605

2606

2607

2608

2609

	Issues of 1991-1994		Un	U	PB	#	FDC	Q(M)
	Perf. 10 on 2 or 3 sides							
2593	29¢ Pledge of Allegiance	09/08/92	.55	.20			1.25	
a	Booklet of 10		5.50	4.25			5.00	
	Perf. 11 x 10 on 2 or 3 sides							
2593B	Pledge of Allegiance, shiny gum		1.40	.50				
c	Booklet pane of 10, shiny gum		14.00	7.50				
2594	29¢ Pledge of Allegiance	04/08/93	.55	.20				
a	Booklet of 10		5.50	4.25				
b	Imperf., pair		900.00					
	Self-Adhesive Booklet and Coil Stamps							
2595	29¢ Eagle and Shield							
	(brown lettering)	09/25/92	.55	.25			1.50	
a	Pane of 17 + label		13.00					
b	Pair, no die-cutting		175.00					
c	Brown omitted		450.00					
d	As "a," no die-cutting		1,500.00					
2596	29¢ Eagle and Shield							
	(green lettering)	09/25/92	.55	.25			1.50	
a	Pane of 17 + label		12.00					
2597	29¢ Eagle and Shield							
	(red lettering)	09/25/92	.55	.25			1.50	
a	Pane of 17 + label		10.00					
	Self-Adhesive, Die-Cut							
2598	29¢ Eagle	02/04/94	.55	.20			1.25	
a	Booklet pane of 18		10.00					
b	Coil		—	3.75	6.75	(5)		
2599	29¢ Statue of Liberty	06/24/94	.55	.20			1.25	
a	Booklet pane of 18		10.00					
b	Coil		—	4.00	6.75	(5)		
	Perf. 10 Vertically							
2602	10¢ Eagle and Shield							
	(inscribed "Bulk Rate USA")	12/13/91	.20	.20	2.50	(5)	1.25	
2603	10¢ Eagle and Shield							
	(inscribed "USA Bulk Rate")	05/29/93	.20	.20	3.00	(5)	1.25	
a	Imperf., pair		30.00					
b	Tagged (error), shiny gum		2.00	1.50	13.00	(5)		
2604	10¢ Eagle and Shield (metallic,							
	inscribed "USA Bulk Rate")	05/29/93	.20	.20	3.25	(5)	1.25	
2605	23¢ Flag, Presorted First-Class	09/27/91	.40	.40	3.50	(5)	1.25	
	Perf. 11							
2606	23¢ USA	07/21/92	.40	.40	4.00	(5)	1.25	
2607	23¢ USA (Bureau)							
	(In #2607, "23" is 7mm long)	10/09/92	.40	.40	4.00	(5)	1.25	
a	Tagged (error), shiny gum		5.00	4.50	140.00	(5)		
c	Imperf., pair		90.00					
2608	23¢ USA (violet)	05/14/93	.40	.40	4.25	(5)	1.25	
2609	29¢ Flag Over White House	04/23/92	.55	.20	4.50	(5)	1.25	
a	Imperf., pair		20.00					
b	Pair, imperf. between		90.00					

	Issues of 1992		Un	U	PB	#	FDC	Q(M)
	Winter Olympic Games Issue, Perf. 11							
2611	29¢ Hockey	01/11/92	.55	.20			1.25	32
2612	29¢ Figure Skating	01/11/92	.55	.20			1.25	32
2613	29¢ Speed Skating	01/11/92	.55	.20			1.25	32
2614	29¢ Skiing	01/11/92	.55	.20			1.25	32
2615	29¢ Bobsledding	01/11/92	.55	.20			1.25	32
a	Strip of 5, #2611-15		2.75	2.50	6.50	(10)	3.50	
2616	29¢ World Columbian							
	Stamp Expo	01/24/92	.55	.20	2.50	(4)	1.25	149
a	Tagging omitted		8.50					
	Black Heritage Issue, Perf. 11							
2617	29¢ W.E.B. DuBois	01/31/92	.55	.20	2.50	(4)	1.75	150
2618	29¢ Love	02/06/92	.55	.20	2.50	(4)	1.25	835
a	Horizontal pair, imperf. vertically		700.00					
2619	29¢ Olympic Baseball	04/03/92	.55	.20	2.75	(4)	2.00	160
	First Voyage of Christopher Columbus Issue, Perf. 11							
2620	29¢ Seeking Queen Isabella's							
	Support	04/24/92	.55	.20			1.25	40
2621	29¢ Crossing The Atlantic	04/24/92	.55	.20			1.25	40
2622	29¢ Approaching Land	04/24/92	.55	.20			1.25	40
2623	29¢ Coming Ashore	04/24/92	.55	.20			1.25	40
a	Block of 4, #2620-23		2.20	2.00	2.50	(4)	2.75	

ALEXANDER CALDER

(1898-1976)

Sculptor ALEXANDER CALDER, inventor of the mobile and the similar but stationary stabile, created an array of dazzling artworks during an illustrious career that spanned most of the 20th century. Born into an artistic family in Philadelphia, Calder studied mechanical engineering in college and painting at the Art Students League of New York. In 1926 in Paris he created a miniature animated circus, Cirque Calder, which held "performances" wherever Calder went. Encouraged by several influential Parisian artists, Calder expanded his art form to create a variety of kinetic abstract objects. His mobiles, so named by artist Marcel Duchamp, incorporated types of motion reminiscent of planets in motion. In his later years he concentrated on creating monumental sculptures for public spaces, including mobiles hanging at New York's John F. Kennedy International Airport and the National Gallery of Art in Washington and a mobile/stabile in the atrium of the Hart Senate Office Building. In 1998 the U.S. Postal Service honored Calder on the centenary of his birth. ❏

2611   **2612**   **2613**   **2614**   **2615**   **2615a**

2616

2617   **2618**   **2619**

2620   **2621**

2622   **2623**   **2623a**

2624

2625

2626

2627

2628

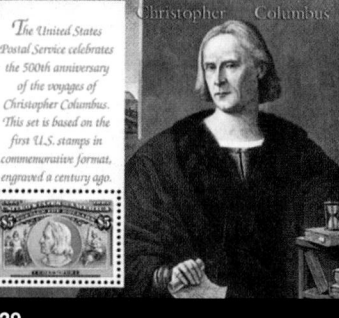

2629

Issues of 1992		Un	U	PB	#	FDC	Q(M)
The Voyages of Columbus Souvenir Sheets, Perf. 10.5							
2624	First Sighting of Land,						
	sheet of 3 05/22/92	1.90	—			2.10	2
a	1¢ deep blue	.20	.20			1.50	
b	4¢ ultramarine	.20	.20			1.50	
c	$1 salmon	1.75	1.00			2.00	
2625	Claiming a New World,						
	sheet of 3 05/22/92	7.25	—			8.00	2
a	2¢ brown violet	.20	.20			1.50	
b	3¢ green	.20	.20			1.50	
c	$4 crimson lake	7.00	4.00			8.00	
2626	Seeking Royal Support,						
	sheet of 3 05/22/92	1.50	—			1.75	2
a	5¢ chocolate	.20	.20			1.50	
b	30¢ orange brown	.55	.30			1.50	
c	50¢ slate blue	.85	.50			1.50	
2627	Royal Favor Restored,						
	sheet of 3 05/22/92	5.25	—			6.25	2
a	6¢ purple	.20	.20			1.50	
b	8¢ magenta	.20	.20			1.50	
c	$3 yellow green	5.00	3.00			6.00	
2628	Reporting Discoveries,						
	sheet of 3 05/22/92	4.00	—			4.50	2
a	10¢ black brown	.20	.20			1.50	
b	15¢ dark green	.30	.20			1.50	
c	$2 brown red	3.50	2.00			4.00	
2629	$5 Christopher Columbus,						
	sheet of 1 05/22/92	8.75	—			10.00	2
a	$5 black	8.50	5.00				

AMERICAN INDIAN DANCES

When we dance, we enter a totally Indian world, and we shake the earth and touch the sky as we continue our culture.

—George Horse Capture, Áani (Gros Ventre Tribe) Traditional Dancer

In 1996 the Postal Service issued five se-tenant stamps featuring AMERICAN INDIAN DANCES. Illustrated by Keith Birdsong of Muskogee, Oklahoma, the stamps depict five traditional tribal or regional dances: Fancy, Butterfly, Traditional, Raven, and Hoop. Performed at powwows, social functions, special ceremonies, and in theaters, each dance requires a special costume, often made by the dancer, and props such as hoops, decorated clubs, and in the case of the Butterfly dance, a bouquet of flowers. In the difficult Hoop dance, the dancer creates designs by manipulating as many as 36 hoops while keeping time with the music. The dances symbolize the richness of American Indian culture and, as the selvage reminds, are performed "to assure the continuation of ancient life ways, to honor deities and each other, and to affirm their Indian identities." ❑

Issues of 1992		Un	U	PB	#	FDC	Q(M)
Perf. 11							
2630	29¢ New York Stock Exchange						
	Bicentennial	05/17/92	.55	.20	2.50	(4)	2.50	148
	Space Adventures Issue							
2631	29¢ Cosmonaut, US Space							
	Shuttle	05/29/92	.55	.20			1.50	37
2632	29¢ Astronaut, Russian							
	Space Station	05/29/92	.55	.20			1.50	37
2633	29¢ Sputnik, Vostok, Apollo							
	Command and Lunar Modules	05/29/92	.55	.20			1.50	37
2634	29¢ Soyuz, Mercury and							
	Gemini Spacecraft	05/29/92	.55	.20			1.50	37
a	Block of 4, #2631-34		2.20	1.90	2.50	(4)	2.75	
2635	29¢ Alaska Highway, 50th							
	Anniversary	05/30/92	.55	.20	2.50	(4)	1.25	147
a	Black (engr.) omitted		500.00					
2636	29¢ Kentucky Statehood							
	Bicentennial	06/01/92	.55	.20	2.50	(4)	1.25	160
	Summer Olympic Games Issue							
2637	29¢ Soccer	06/11/92	.55	.20			1.25	32
2638	29¢ Gymnastics	06/11/92	.55	.20			1.25	32
2639	29¢ Volleyball	06/11/92	.55	.20			1.25	32
2640	29¢ Boxing	06/11/92	.55	.20			1.25	32
2641	29¢ Swimming	06/11/92	.55	.20			1.25	32
a	Strip of 5, #2637-41		2.75	2.50	6.00	(10)	3.00	
	Hummingbirds Issue, Perf. 11 Vertically on 1 or 2 sides							
2642	29¢ Ruby-Throated	06/15/92	.55	.20			1.25	88
2643	29¢ Broad-Billed	06/15/92	.55	.20			1.25	88
2644	29¢ Costa's	06/15/92	.55	.20			1.25	88
2645	29¢ Rufous	06/15/92	.55	.20			1.25	88
2646	29¢ Calliope	06/15/92	.55	.20			1.25	88
a	Booklet pane of 5, #2642-46		2.75	2.50			3.00	

AMERICAN ★ COMMEMORATIVE ★ **COLLECTIBLES**

American Commemorative Collection

An easy and uniform way to collect and learn about commemorative issues.

Just mount the stamps on the specially designed sheet and place them in a three ring binder. Just $3.25* each, depending on the value of the stamps.

For more information call **1-800-STAMP-24**

*Prices subject to change without notice.

2630

2631 **2632**

2633 **2634**

2634a

2635

2636

2637 **2638** **2639** **2640** **2641** **2641a**

2642 **2643** **2644** **2645** **2646** **2646a**

Indian Paintbrush
2647

Fragrant Water Lily
2648

Meadow Beauty
2649

Jack-in-the-Pulpit
2650

California Poppy
2651

Large-flowered Trillium
2652

Tickseed
2653

Shooting Star
2654

Stream Violet
2655

Bluets
2656

Herb Robert
2657

Marsh Marigold
2658

Sweet White Violet
2659

Claret Cup Cactus
2660

White Mountain Avens
2661

Sessile Bellwort
2662

Blue Flag
2663

Harlequin Lupine
2664

Twinflower
2665

Common Sunflower
2666

Sego Lily
2667

Virginia Bluebells
2668

Ohi'a Lehua
2669

Rosebud Orchid
2670

Showy Evening Primrose
2671

Issues of 1992			Un	U	FDC	Q(M)
Wildflowers Issue, Perf. 11						
2647	29¢ Indian Paintbrush	07/24/92	.55	.20	1.25	11
2648	29¢ Fragrant Water Lily	07/24/92	.55	.20	1.25	11
2649	29¢ Meadow Beauty	07/24/92	.55	.20	1.25	11
2650	29¢ Jack-in-the-Pulpit	07/24/92	.55	.20	1.25	11
2651	29¢ California Poppy	07/24/92	.55	.20	1.25	11
2652	29¢ Large-Flowered Trillium	07/24/92	.55	.20	1.25	11
2653	29¢ Tickseed	07/24/92	.55	.20	1.25	11
2654	29¢ Shooting Star	07/24/92	.55	.20	1.25	11
2655	29¢ Stream Violet	07/24/92	.55	.20	1.25	11
2656	29¢ Bluets	07/24/92	.55	.20	1.25	11
2657	29¢ Herb Robert	07/24/92	.55	.20	1.25	11
2658	29¢ Marsh Marigold	07/24/92	.55	.20	1.25	11
2659	29¢ Sweet White Violet	07/24/92	.55	.20	1.25	11
2660	29¢ Claret Cup Cactus	07/24/92	.55	.20	1.25	11
2661	29¢ White Mountain Avens	07/24/92	.55	.20	1.25	11
2662	29¢ Sessile Bellwort	07/24/92	.55	.20	1.25	11
2663	29¢ Blue Flag	07/24/92	.55	.20	1.25	11
2664	29¢ Harlequin Lupine	07/24/92	.55	.20	1.25	11
2665	29¢ Twinflower	07/24/92	.55	.20	1.25	11
2666	29¢ Common Sunflower	07/24/92	.55	.20	1.25	11
2667	29¢ Sego Lily	07/24/92	.55	.20	1.25	11
2668	29¢ Virginia Bluebells	07/24/92	.55	.20	1.25	11
2669	29¢ Ohi'a Lehua	07/24/92	.55	.20	1.25	11
2670	29¢ Rosebud Orchid	07/24/92	.55	.20	1.25	11
2671	29¢ Showy Evening Primrose	07/24/92	.55	.20	1.25	11

JOSH WHITE

(1915-1969)

JOSHUA DANIEL WHITE grew up in South Carolina in a religious family. As a child, he learned songs from an assortment of street evangelists and blind gospel singers and picked up an astonishing guitar technique. In 1928, when he was only 13, he sang falsetto and played the guitar on a recording with Blind Joe Taggart. White played primarily in the southeastern blues tradition, drawing from both sacred and secular black music. An active performer for more than 40 years, White fostered a deep sense of social protest during much of his career. One of his most powerful ballads, "Free and Equal Blues," reflected these themes. By 1940 White was performing in New York with his own group, the Carolinians. He sang with Paul Robeson and performed at the White House. A versatile performer of blues, gospel, and folk songs, White was honored in 1998 along with Leadbelly, Woody Guthrie, and Sonny Terry as Folk Musicians in the Legends of American Music series. ❏

	Issues of 1992		Un	U	FDC	Q(M)
	Wildflowers Issue (continued)					
2672	29¢ Fringed Gentian	07/24/92	.55	.20	1.25	11
2673	29¢ Yellow Lady's Slipper	07/24/92	.55	.20	1.25	11
2674	29¢ Passionflower	07/24/92	.55	.20	1.25	11
2675	29¢ Bunchberry	07/24/92	.55	.20	1.25	11
2676	29¢ Pasqueflower	07/24/92	.55	.20	1.25	11
2677	29¢ Round-Lobed Hepatica	07/24/92	.55	.20	1.25	11
2678	29¢ Wild Columbine	07/24/92	.55	.20	1.25	11
2679	29¢ Fireweed	07/24/92	.55	.20	1.25	11
2680	29¢ Indian Pond Lily	07/24/92	.55	.20	1.25	11
2681	29¢ Turk's Cap Lily	07/24/92	.55	.20	1.25	11
2682	29¢ Dutchman's Breeches	07/24/92	.55	.20	1.25	11
2683	29¢ Trumpet Honeysuckle	07/24/92	.55	.20	1.25	11
2684	29¢ Jacob's Ladder	07/24/92	.55	.20	1.25	11
2685	29¢ Plains Prickly Pear	07/24/92	.55	.20	1.25	11
2686	29¢ Moss Campion	07/24/92	.55	.20	1.25	11
2687	29¢ Bearberry	07/24/92	.55	.20	1.25	11
2688	29¢ Mexican Hat	07/24/92	.55	.20	1.25	11
2689	29¢ Harebell	07/24/92	.55	.20	1.25	11
2690	29¢ Desert Five Spot	07/24/92	.55	.20	1.25	11
2691	29¢ Smooth Solomon's Seal	07/24/92	.55	.20	1.25	11
2692	29¢ Red Maids	07/24/92	.55	.20	1.25	11
2693	29¢ Yellow Skunk Cabbage	07/24/92	.55	.20	1.25	11
2694	29¢ Rue Anemone	07/24/92	.55	.20	1.25	11
2695	29¢ Standing Cypress	07/24/92	.55	.20	1.25	11
2696	29¢ Wild Flax	07/24/92	.55	.20	1.25	11
a	Pane of 50, #2647-96		27.50	—	30.00	11

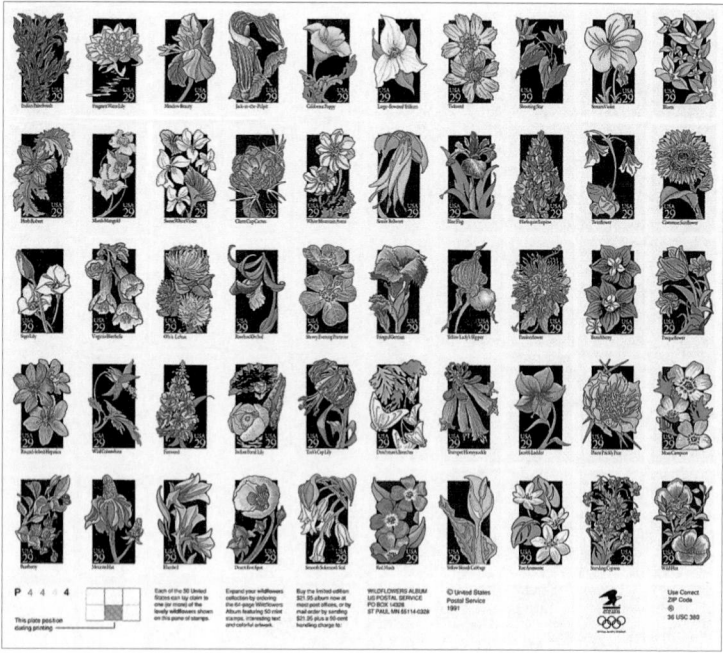

Example of #2696a

Fringed Gentian

2672

Yellow Lady's Slipper

2673

Passionflower

2674

Bunchberry

2675

Pasqueflower

2676

Round-lobed Hepatica

2677

Wild Columbine

2678

Fireweed

2679

Indian Pond Lily

2680

Turk's Cap Lily

2681

Dutchman's Breeches

2682

Trumpet Honeysuckle

2683

Jacob's Ladder

2684

Plains Prickly Pear

2685

Moss Campion

2686

Bearberry

2687

Mexican Hat

2688

Harebell

2689

Desert Five Spot

2690

Smooth Solomon's Seal

2691

Red Maids

2692

Yellow Skunk Cabbage

2693

Rue Anemone

2694

Standing Cypress

2695

Wild Flax

2696

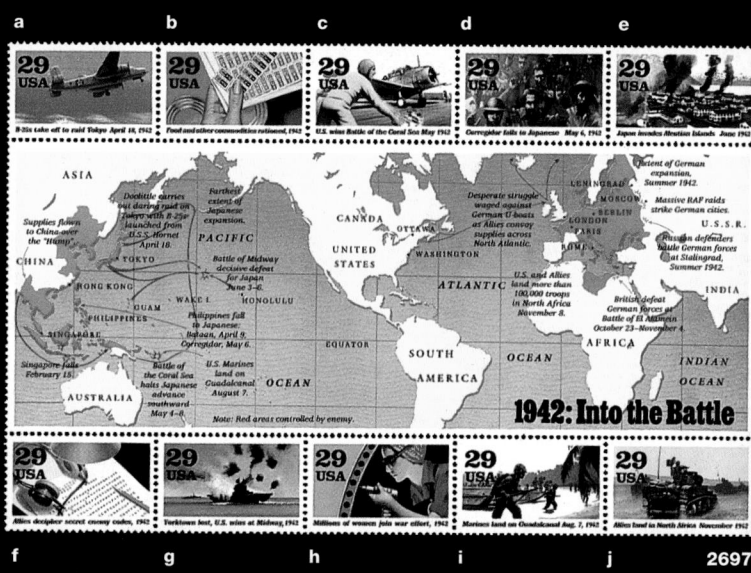

a — B-25s take off to raid Tokyo April 18, 1942
b — Food and other commodities rationed, 1942
c — U.S. wins Battle of the Coral Sea May 1942
d — Corregidor falls to Japanese May 6, 1942
e — Japan invades Aleutian Islands June 1942

1942: Into the Battle

f — Allies decipher secret enemy codes, 1942
g — Yorktown lost, U.S. wins at Midway, 1942
h — Millions of women join war effort, 1942
i — Marines land on Guadalcanal Aug. 7, 1942
j — Allies land in North Africa November 1942

2697

2698

Theodore von Kármán
Aerospace Scientist

USA 29

2699

Minerals USA 29 — Azurite — 2700
Minerals USA 29 — Copper — 2701

Minerals USA 29 — Variscite — 2702
Minerals USA 29 — Wulfenite — 2703

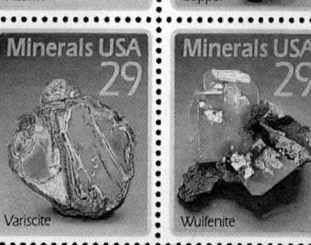

2702   2703   2703a

Explorer of California 1542
USA 29
Juan Rodríguez CABRILLO

2704

Issues of 1992		Un	U	PB	#	FDC	Q(M)
World War II Issue, 1942: Into the Battle, Miniature Sheet, Perf. 11							
2697	Sheet of 10 and central label 08/17/92	5.50	5.00			7.00	12
a	29¢ B-25s Take Off to Raid Tokyo	.55	.30			1.55	12
b	29¢ Food and Other Commodities Rationed	.55	.30			1.50	12
c	29¢ U.S. Wins Battle of the Coral Sea	.55	.30			1.50	12
d	29¢ Corregidor Falls to Japanese	.55	.30			1.50	12
e	29¢ Japan Invades Aleutian Islands	.55	.30			1.50	12
f	29¢ Allies Decipher Secret Enemy Codes	.55	.30			1.50	12
g	29¢ *Yorktown Lost*	.55	.30			1.50	12
h	29¢ Millions of Women Join War Effort	.55	.30			1.50	12
i	29¢ Marines Land on Guadalcanal	.55	.30			1.50	12
j	29¢ Allies Land in North Africa	.55	.30			1.50	12
k	Red (litho.) omitted	8,000.00					
Literary Arts Issue, Perf. 11							
2698	29¢ Dorothy Parker 08/22/92	.55	.20	2.50	(4)	1.50	105
2699	29¢ Dr. Theodore von Karman 08/31/92	.55	.20	2.50	(4)	1.50	143
Minerals Issue, Perf. 11							
2700	29¢ Azurite 09/17/92	.55	.20			1.25	37
2701	29¢ Copper 09/17/92	.55	.20			1.25	37
2702	29¢ Variscite 09/17/92	.55	.20			1.25	37
2703	29¢ Wulfenite 09/17/92	.55	.20			1.25	37
a	Block of 4, #2700-03	2.20	2.00	2.50	(4)	2.75	
b	As "a," silver (litho.) omitted	8,500.00					
2704	29¢ Juan Rodriguez Cabrillo 09/28/92	.55	.20	2.50	(4)	1.25	85
a	Black (engr.) omitted	3,000.00					

EDNA FERBER

(1885-1968)

Pulitzer Prize-winning author EDNA FERBER, one of the most popular authors of her time, published 13 novels, dozens of short stories, and two autobiographies during her lifetime. Her first story, "The Homely Heroine," appeared in 1910; her first novel a year later. By 1915 her short stories about saleswoman Emma McChesney were so popular they were adapted into a Broadway production starring Ethel Barrymore. *So Big,* her inspiring novel about a widow struggling to make a life for her son, won the Pulitzer Prize in 1925 and became Ferber's first best-seller. From the Texas oil fields of *Giant* (1952) to the wilds of Alaska in *Ice Palace* (1958), Ferber's works painted a vivid portrait of American life in the early 20th century. "What a country it is!" she exclaimed in her 1939 autobiography, *A Peculiar Treasure.* The musical version of *Show Boat,* Ferber's romantic 1926 novel of life on the Mississippi River aboard a floating theater, enjoyed a record-breaking 572 performances during its first run on Broadway. The 1931 screen adaptation of *Cimarron,* her novel about the Oklahoma land rush, won an Academy Award for best picture. Broadway successes included *Stage Door* (1926), co-written with playwright George S. Kaufman. ❑

Issues of 1992		Un	U	PB	#	FDC	Q(M)
Wild Animals Issue, Perf. 11 Horizontally							
2705	29¢ Giraffe 10/01/92	.55	.20			1.25	80
2706	29¢ Giant Panda 10/01/92	.55	.20			1.25	80
2707	29¢ Flamingo 10/01/92	.55	.20			1.25	80
2708	29¢ King Penguins 10/01/92	.55	.20			1.25	80
2709	29¢ White Bengal Tiger 10/01/92	.55	.20			1.25	80
a	Booklet pane of 5, #2705-09	2.75	2.25			3.25	
b	As "a," imperf.	3,000.00					
Christmas Issue, Perf. 11.5 x 11							
2710	29¢ Madonna and Child by Giovanni Bellini 10/22/92	.55	.20	2.50	(4)	1.25	300
a	Booklet pane of 10	5.50	3.50			7.25	349
2711	29¢ Horse and Rider 10/22/92	.55	.20			1.25	125
2712	29¢ Toy Train 10/22/92	.55	.20			1.25	125
2713	29¢ Toy Steamer 10/22/92	.55	.20			1.25	125
2714	29¢ Toy Ship 10/22/92	.55	.20			1.25	125
a	Block of 4, #2711-14	2.20	1.10	2.75	(4)	2.75	
Perf. 11							
2715	29¢ Horse and Rider 10/22/92	.85	.20			1.25	102
2716	29¢ Toy Train 10/22/92	.85	.20			1.25	102
2717	29¢ Toy Steamer 10/22/92	.85	.20			1.25	102
2718	29¢ Toy Ship 10/22/92	.85	.20			1.25	102
a	Booklet pane of 4, #2715-18	3.50	1.25			2.75	
2719	29¢ Toy Train (self-adhesive) 10/22/92	.60	.20			1.25	22
a	Booklet pane of 18	11.00					
Lunar New Year Issue							
2720	29¢ Year of the Rooster 12/30/92	.55	.20	2.20	(4)	2.25	

IRVING BERLIN

(1888-1989)

IRVING BERLIN, who had an ear for songs that would be universally appealing, helped change the direction of American popular music. During his long career he wrote more than 1,000 songs, many becoming standards that are still favorites today. In 1893 Berlin emigrated with his family from Russia to the United States. As a teenager, he earned a living singing for coins. Initially a lyricist, Berlin began to compose music for his lyrics and in 1911, "Alexander's Ragtime Band" sold one million copies. Many of his most popular songs originated on

Broadway: "A Pretty Girl Is Like a Melody," "Easter Parade," and "There's No Business Like Show Business." Berlin's songs also found their way to the silver screen— "White Christmas" earned him an Academy Award in 1942. When Kate Smith performed "God Bless America" on her 1938 Armistice Day radio broadcast, the song—written by Berlin in 1918 shortly after he became an American citizen—was an immediate hit. His classic songs—still performed on Broadway, in movies, and by vocal artists from opera to country, cabaret, and jazz—will be with us "Always." ❑

2705
Giraffe

2706
Giant Panda

2707
Flamingo

2708
King Penguins

2709
White Bengal Tiger

2709a

CHRISTMAS
29
USA

Bellini c.1490 National Gallery

2710

2711   **2712**
GREETINGS   GREETINGS
2713   **2714**   **2714a**
GREETINGS   GREETINGS

2715   **2716**
GREETINGS   GREETINGS
A 11111
2717   **2718**   **2718a**
GREETINGS   GREETINGS

29
USA
GREETINGS

2719

HAPPY
NEW
YEAR!
29 USA

2720

2721

2722

2723

2724   **2725**   **2726**   **2727**   **2728**

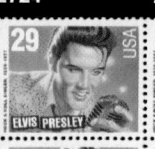    

 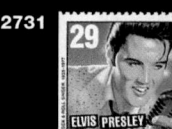

2729   **2730**

2731

2732

2733

2734

2735

2736

2737

2731

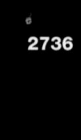

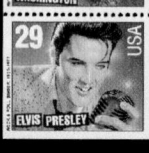

2737b   **2737a**

Issues of 1993		Un	U	PB	#	FDC	Q(M)
Legends of American Music Series, Perf. 11							
2721	29¢ Elvis Presley	01/08/93	.55	.20	2.50	(4)	1.75	517
Perf. 10							
2722	29¢ *Oklahoma!*	03/30/93	.55	.20	4.00	(4)	1.25	150
2723	29¢ Hank Williams	06/09/93	.55	.20	4.00	(4)	1.25	152
Perf. 11.2 x 11.5							
2723A	29¢ Hank Williams		22.50	10.00	140.00	(4)	—	
Legends of American Music Series, Rock & Roll/Rhythm & Blues Issue, Perf. 10							
2724	29¢ Elvis Presley	06/16/93	.60	.20			1.25	14
2725	29¢ Bill Haley	06/16/93	.60	.20			1.25	14
2726	29¢ Clyde McPhatter	06/16/93	.60	.20			1.25	14
2727	29¢ Ritchie Valens	06/16/93	.60	.20			1.25	14
2728	29¢ Otis Redding	06/16/93	.60	.20			1.25	14
2729	29¢ Buddy Holly	06/16/93	.60	.20			1.25	14
2730	29¢ Dinah Washington	06/16/93	.60	.20			1.25	14
a	Vertical strip of 7, #2724-30		4.25		8.00	(10)	5.00	
Perf. 11 Horizontally							
2731	29¢ Elvis Presley	06/16/93	.55	.20			1.25	99
2732	29¢ Bill Haley (2725)	06/16/93	.55	.20			1.25	33
2733	29¢ Clyde McPhatter (2726)	06/16/93	.55	.20			1.25	33
2734	29¢ Ritchie Valens (2727)	06/16/93	.55	.20			1.25	33
2735	29¢ Otis Redding	06/16/93	.55	.20			1.25	66
2736	29¢ Buddy Holly	06/16/93	.55	.20			1.25	66
2737	29¢ Dinah Washington	06/16/93	.55	.20			1.25	66
a	Booklet pane, 2 #2731, 1 each #2732-37		5.00	2.25			5.25	
b	Booklet pane of 4, #2731, 2735-37		2.25	*1.50*			2.75	
2738-40	Not assigned							

THORNTON WILDER

(1897-1975)

THORNTON WILDER, the only American author to receive three Pulitzer Prizes in fiction and drama, was born in Wisconsin but traveled the world as his father, a member of the diplomatic corps, was assigned to places such as Hong Kong and Shanghai. A 1920 graduate of Yale, Wilder taught at a boys' boarding school where he wrote his first novel. His second novel—*The Bridge of San Luis Rey* (1927)—was a best-seller and won for Wilder his first Pulitzer Prize. He wrote more fiction before beginning to write for the stage. In 1938, *Our Town*—his first full-length Broadway play—became an instant American classic and brought Wilder a second Pulitzer Prize. After

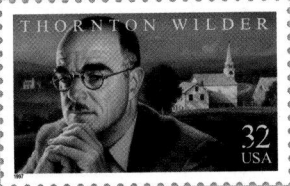

a brief interlude in Hollywood, Wilder returned to New York and dazzled audiences in 1942 with *The Skin of Our Teeth*, winning his third Pulitzer Prize. A revised and renamed play, *The Matchmaker*, became the inspiration for the 1964 Broadway musical, *Hello, Dolly!* In 1965 Wilder received the National Book Committee's first National Medal for Literature. He was honored by the Postal Service in 1997 in the Literary Arts series. ❑

Issues of 1993			Un	U	PB	#	FDC	Q(M)
Space Fantasy Issue, Perf. 11 Vertically on 1 or 2 sides								
2741	29¢ multicolored	01/25/93	.55	.20			1.25	140
2742	29¢ multicolored	01/25/93	.55	.20			1.25	140
2743	29¢ multicolored	01/25/93	.55	.20			1.25	140
2744	29¢ multicolored	01/25/93	.55	.20			1.25	140
2745	29¢ multicolored	01/25/93	.55	.20			1.25	140
a	Booklet pane of 5, #2741-45		2.75	2.25			3.25	
Black Heritage Issue, Perf. 11								
2746	29¢ Percy Lavon Julian	01/29/93	.55	.20	2.50	(4)	1.75	105
2747	29¢ Oregon Trail	02/12/93	.55	.20	2.50	(4)	1.25	110
a	Tagging omitted		20.00					
2748	29¢ World University Games	02/25/93	.55	.20	2.50	(4)	1.50	110
2749	29¢ Grace Kelly	03/25/93	.55	.20	2.50	(4)	2.50	173
Circus Issue, Perf. 11								
2750	29¢ Clown	04/06/93	.55	.20			1.50	66
2751	29¢ Ringmaster	04/06/93	.55	.20			1.50	66
2752	29¢ Trapeze Artist	04/06/93	.55	.20			1.50	66
2753	29¢ Elephant	04/06/93	.55	.20			1.50	66
a	Block of 4, #2750-53		2.20	1.75	5.00	(6)	3.00	
2754	29¢ Cherokee Strip	04/17/93	.55	.20	2.20	(4)	1.25	110
2755	29¢ Dean Acheson	04/21/93	.55	.20	2.50	(4)	1.25	116
Sporting Horses Issue, Perf. 11 x 11.5								
2756	29¢ Steeplechase	05/01/93	.55	.20			1.75	40
2757	29¢ Thoroughbred Racing	05/01/93	.55	.20			1.75	40
2758	29¢ Harness Racing	05/01/93	.55	.20			1.75	40
2759	29¢ Polo	05/01/93	.55	.20			1.75	40
a	Block of 4, #2756-59		2.20	2.00	2.50	(4)	3.50	

JAMES DEAN

(1931-1955)

The second stamp in the Legends of Hollywood series honored JAMES DEAN, whose untimely death at age 24 ended his short but exciting movie career. Born and raised in Indiana, Dean first acted in high school plays and later studied drama in California. In 1951, on the advice of his acting coach James Whitmore, he headed for New York where he studied at the Actors' Guild and found work on Broadway. In 1954 motion picture director Elia Kazan signed him for the film adaptation of John Steinbeck's *East of Eden*. Dean's performance mesmerized critics and audiences alike. Two films—*Rebel Without a Cause* and *Giant*—quickly followed. Both were released after Dean's death in an automobile accident in September 1955. Dean, who played a lonely, misunderstood outsider in each of his film roles, helped define a new style of American film acting in which heightened physical

dimension suggests feelings that couldn't be put into words. Nearly 50 years after his death, fans are still paying tribute to Dean. ❑

2741   2742   2743   2744   2745   2745a

2747   2748   2749

2746

2750   2751

2752   2753

2754

2753a   2755

2756  2757

2758   2759

2759a

2760   2761   2762   2763   2764   2764a

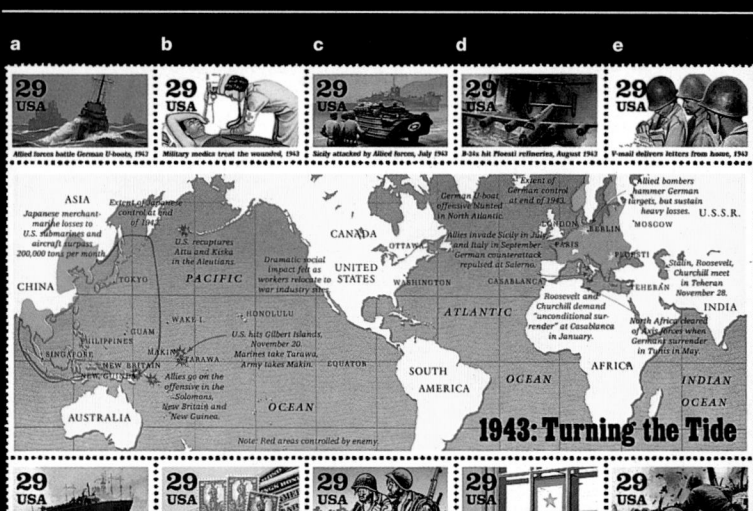

a   b   c   d   e

1943: Turning the Tide

f   g   h   i   j   2765

2766

2767

2768

2769

2770

2770a

Issues of 1993			Un	U	PB	#	FDC	Q(M)
Garden Flowers Issue, Perf. 11 Vertically								
2760	29¢ Hyacinth	05/15/93	.55	.20			1.50	200
2761	29¢ Daffodil	05/15/93	.55	.20			1.50	200
2762	29¢ Tulip	05/15/93	.55	.20			1.50	200
2763	29¢ Iris	05/15/93	.55	.20			1.50	200
2764	29¢ Lilac	05/15/93	.55	.20			1.50	200
a	Booklet pane of 5, #2760-64		2.75	2.25			3.00	
b	As "a," black omitted		200.00					
c	As "a," imperf.		2,250.00					
World War II Issue, 1943: Turning The Tide, Miniature Sheet, Perf. 11								
2765	Sheet of 10 and central label	05/31/93	5.50	5.00			7.00	
a	29¢ Allied Forces Battle German U-boats		.55	.30			1.50	12
b	29¢ Military Medics Treat the Wounded.		.55	.30			1.50	12
c	29¢ Sicily Attacked by Allied Forces		.55	.30			1.50	12
d	29¢ B-24s Hit Ploesti Refineries		.55	.30			1.50	12
e	29¢ V-Mail Delivers Letters from Home.		.55	.30			1.55	12
f	29¢ Italy Invaded by Allies		.55	.30			1.50	12
g	29¢ Bonds and Stamps Help War Effort		.55	.30			1.50	12
h	29¢ "Willie and Joe" Keep Spirits High.		.55	.30			1.50	12
i	29¢ Gold Stars Mark World War II Losses		.55	.30			1.50	12
j	29¢ Marines Assault Tarawa		.55	.30			1.50	12
2766	29¢ Joe Louis	06/22/93	.55	.20	2.50	(4)	2.50	160
Legends of American Music Series, Broadway Musicals Issue, Perf. 11 Horizontally								
2767	29¢ Show Boat	07/14/93	.55	.20			1.25	129
2768	29¢ Porgy & Bess	07/14/93	.55	.20			1.25	129
2769	29¢ Oklahoma!	07/14/93	.55	.20			1.25	129
2770	29¢ My Fair Lady	07/14/93	.55	.20			1.25	129
a	Booklet pane of 4, #2767-70		2.75	2.25			3.50	

DIMITRI TIOMKIN

(1894-1979)

DIMITRI TIOMKIN, composer of the famous ballad, "Do Not Forsake Me, Oh My Darlin'," from the Academy-Award winning film *High Noon*, was born in Russia and studied music at the St. Petersburg Conservatory. A concert pianist, Tiomkin made his debut with the Berlin Philharmonic; he then went to Paris where he was hired to play the American vaudeville circuit. Tiomkin settled in New York City but soon moved to Hollywood to seek his fortune in the film industry. His successful musical score for the 1937 film, *Lost Horizon*, launched his second career as a film score composer. Best remembered for his work on westerns, Tiomkin—who became a naturalized citizen in 1937—also wrote superb and award-winning scores for a variety of Hollywood films including *Friendly Persuasion*, *Dial M for Murder*, and *The Guns of Navarone*. His music won five Academy Awards and many international awards. Tiomkin was honored with fellow Hollywood composers Max Steiner, Bernard Herrmann, Alfred Newman, Franz Waxman, and Erich Wolfgang Korngold in 1999 in the Legends of American Music series. ❑

Issues of 1993		Un	U	PB	#	FDC	Q(M)
Legends of American Music Series, Country & Western Issue, Perf. 10							
2771	29¢ Hank Williams (2775) 09/25/93	.55	.20			1.25	25
2772	29¢ Patsy Cline (2777) 09/25/93	.55	.20			1.25	25
2773	29¢ The Carter Family (2776) 09/25/93	.55	.20			1.25	25
2774	29¢ Bob Wills (2778) 09/25/93	.55	.20			1.25	25
a	Block or horiz. strip of 4, #2771-74	2.20	1.75	3.00	(4)	3.00	
Booklet Stamps, Perf. 11 Horizontally							
2775	29¢ Hank Williams 09/25/93	.55	.20			1.25	170
2776	29¢ The Carter Family 09/25/93	.55	.20			1.25	170
2777	29¢ Patsy Cline 09/25/93	.55	.20			1.25	170
2778	29¢ Bob Wills 09/25/93	.55	.20			1.25	170
a	Booklet pane of 4, #2775-78	2.50	2.00			3.00	
National Postal Museum Issue, Perf. 11							
2779	Independence Hall, Benjamin Franklin, Printing Press, Colonial Post Rider 07/30/93	.55	.20			1.25	38
2780	Pony Express Rider, Civil War Soldier, Concord Stagecoach 07/30/93	.55	.20			1.25	38
2781	Biplane, Charles Lindbergh, Railway Mail Car, 1931 Model A Ford Mail Truck 07/30/93	.55	.20			1.25	38
2782	California Gold Rush Miner's Letter, Barcode and Circular Date Stamp 07/30/93	.55	.20			1.25	38
a	Block or strip of 4, #2779-82	2.20	2.00	2.25	(4)	2.75	
c	As "a," imperf.	3,500.00					
American Sign Language Issue, Perf. 11.5							
2783	29¢ Recognizing Deafness 09/20/93	.55	.20			1.25	42
2784	29¢ American Sign Language 09/20/93	.55	.20			1.25	42
a	Pair, #2783-84	1.10	.75	2.25	(4)	2.25	
Classic Books Issues, Perf. 11							
2785	29¢ Rebecca of Sunnybrook Farm 10/23/93	.55	.20			1.25	38
2786	29¢ Little House on the Prairie 10/23/93	.55	.20			1.25	38
2787	29¢ The Adventures of Huckleberry Finn 10/23/93	.55	.20			1.25	38
2788	29¢ Little Women 10/23/93	.55	.20			1.25	38
a	Block or horiz. strip of 4, #2785-88	2.20	2.00	5.00	(4)	2.75	
b	As "a," imperf.	3,000.00					

2771 2772

2773 2774 2774a

2775

2776

2777

2778

2778a

2779 2780

2781 2782 2782a

2783 2784 2784a

2785 2786

2787 2788 2788a

2791 **2792**

2795 **2796**

2789

2790

2793 **2794** **2794a**

2797 **2798** **2798c**

 2799   **2800**

2801 **2802** **2802a**

2803

2804

2805

2806

2806a

	Issues of 1993		Un	U	PB	#	FDC	Q(M)
	Christmas Issue, Perf. 11							
2789	29¢ Madonna and Child	10/21/93	.55	.20	2.50	(4)	1.25	500
	Booklet Stamps, Perf. 11.5 x 11 on 2 or 3 sides							
2790	29¢ Madonna and Child (2789)	10/21/93	.55	.20			1.25	500
a	Booklet pane of 4		2.25	1.75			2.50	
	Perf. 11.5							
2791	29¢ Jack-in-the-Box	10/21/93	.55	.20			1.25	250
2792	29¢ Red-Nosed Reindeer	10/21/93	.55	.20			1.25	250
2793	29¢ Snowman	10/21/93	.55	.20			1.25	250
2794	29¢ Toy Soldier	10/21/93	.55	.20			1.25	250
a	Block or strip of 4, #2791-94		2.20	2.00	3.75	(4)	2.75	
	Booklet Stamps, Perf. 11 x 10 on 2 or 3 sides							
2795	29¢ Toy Soldier (2794)	10/21/93	.85	.20			1.25	200
2796	29¢ Snowman (2793)	10/21/93	.85	.20			1.25	200
2797	29¢ Red-Nosed Reindeer (2792)	10/21/93	.85	.20			1.25	200
2798	29¢ Jack-in-the-Box (2791)	10/21/93	.85	.20			1.25	200
a	Booklet pane, 3 each #2795-96, 2 each #2797-98		8.50	4.00			6.50	
b	Booklet pane, 3 each #2797-98, 2 each #2795-96		8.50	4.00			6.50	
c	Block of 4		3.40	1.75				
	Self-Adhesive, Die-Cut							
2799	29¢ Snowman	10/28/93	.55	.20			1.25	120
a	Coil with plate		—	3.50	6.00	(5)		
2800	29¢ Toy Soldier	10/28/93	.55	.20			1.25	120
2801	29¢ Jack-in-the-Box	10/28/93	.55	.20			1.25	120
2802	29¢ Red-Nosed Reindeer	10/28/93	.55	.20			1.25	120
a	Booklet pane, 3 each #2799-2802		7.00					
b	Block of 4		2.20					
2803	29¢ Snowman	10/28/93	.55	.20			1.25	18
a	Booklet pane of 18		10.00					
	Perf. 11							
2804	29¢ Northern Mariana Islands	11/04/93	.55	.20	2.25	(4)	1.25	88
	Perf. 11.2							
2805	29¢ Columbus Landing in Puerto Rico	11/19/93	.55	.20	2.50	(4)	1.25	105
2806	29¢ AIDS Awareness	12/01/93	.55	.20	2.50	(4)	1.75	100
a	Booklet version		.55	.20			1.75	250
b	Booklet pane of 5		2.75	2.00			3.75	

VISIT US ONLINE AT **THE POSTAL STORE**

AT **WWW.USPS.COM**

OR CALL **1-800-STAMP-24**

	Issues of 1994		Un	U	PB	#	FDC	Q(M)
	Winter Olympic Games Issue, Perf. 11.2							
2807	29¢ Slalom	01/06/94	.55	.20			1.25	36
2808	29¢ Luge	01/06/94	.55	.20			1.25	36
2809	29¢ Ice Dancing	01/06/94	.55	.20			1.25	36
2810	29¢ Cross-Country Skiing	01/06/94	.55	.20			1.25	36
2811	29¢ Ice Hockey	01/06/94	.55	.20			1.25	36
a	Strip of 5, #2807-11		2.75	2.50	5.50	(10)	3.00	36
2812	29¢ Edward R. Murrow	01/21/94	.55	.20	2.50	(4)	1.25	151
	Self-Adhesive, Die-Cut							
2813	29¢ Love Sunrise	01/27/94	.55	.20			1.25	358
a	Booklet of 18 (self-adhesive)		11.00					
b	Coil with plate		—	3.75	6.75	(5)		
	Perf. 10.9 x 11.1							
2814	29¢ Love Stamp	02/14/94	.55	.20			1.25	830
a	Booklet pane of 10		5.50	3.50			6.50	
	Perf. 11.1							
2814C	29¢ Love Stamp	06/11/94	.55	.20	2.50	(4)	1.25	300
	Perf. 11.2							
2815	52¢ Love Birds	02/14/94	1.00	.20	5.00	(4)	1.50	175
	Black Heritage Issue							
2816	29¢ Dr. Allison Davis	02/01/94	.55	.20	2.25	(4)	2.00	156
	Lunar New Year Issue							
2817	29¢ Year of the Dog	02/05/94	.55	.20	2.25	(4)	1.75	105
	Perf. 11.5 x 11.2							
2818	29¢ Buffalo Soldiers	04/22/94	.55	.20	2.25	(4)	2.50	186
	Stars of the Silent Screen Issue, Perf. 11.2							
2819	29¢ Rudolph Valentino	04/27/94	.55	.20			1.50	19
2820	29¢ Clara Bow	04/27/94	.55	.20			1.50	19
2821	29¢ Charlie Chaplin	04/27/94	.55	.20			1.50	19
2822	29¢ Lon Chaney	04/27/94	.55	.20			1.50	19
2823	29¢ John Gilbert	04/27/94	.55	.20			1.50	19
2824	29¢ Zasu Pitts	04/27/94	.55	.20			1.50	19
2825	29¢ Harold Lloyd	04/27/94	.55	.20			1.50	19
2826	29¢ Keystone Cops	04/27/94	.55	.20			1.50	19
2827	29¢ Theda Bara	04/27/94	.55	.20			1.50	19
2828	29¢ Buster Keaton	04/27/94	.55	.20			1.50	19
a	Block of 10 #2819-2828		5.50	4.00	6.50	(10)	6.50	19
b	As "a," black (litho.) omitted		—					
c	As "a," black, red & bright violet (litho.) omitted		—					

2807 2808 2809 2810 2811 2811a

2812 2813 2814 2814C

2815

2816 2817 2818

2819 2820 2821 2822 2823

2824 2825 2826 2827 2828 2828a

| 2829 | 2830 | 2831 | 2832 | 2833 | 2833a |

| 2834 | 2835 | 2836 |

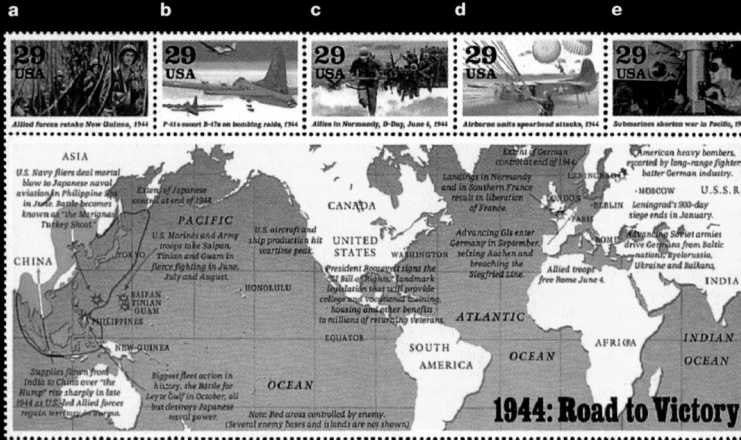

2838

	Issues of 1994		Un	U	PB	#	FDC	Q(M)
	Garden Flowers Booklet Issue, Perf. 10.9 Vertically							
2829	29¢ Lily	04/28/94	.55	.20			1.25	166
2830	29¢ Zinnia	04/28/94	.55	.20			1.25	166
2831	29¢ Gladiola	04/28/94	.55	.20			1.25	166
2832	29¢ Marigold	04/28/94	.55	.20			1.25	166
2833	29¢ Rose	04/28/94	.55	.20			1.25	166
a	Booklet pane of 5, #2829-2833		2.75				3.25	
b	As "a," imperf.		2,000.00					
c	As "a," black (engr.) omitted		200.00					
	1994 World Cup Soccer Championships Issue, Perf. 11.1							
2834	29¢ Soccer Player	05/26/94	.55	.20	2.25	(4)	1.25	201
2835	40¢ Soccer Player	05/26/94	.80	.20	3.20	(4)	1.40	300
2836	50¢ Soccer Player	05/26/94	1.00	.20	4.00	(4)	1.50	269
2837	Souvenir Sheet of 3,							
	#2834-2836	05/26/94	2.50	2.00			3.00	60
a	29¢ Soccer Player							
b	40¢ Soccer Player							
c	50¢ Soccer Player							
	World War II Issue, 1944: Road to Victory Miniature, Sheet, Perf. 10.9							
2838	Sheet of 10 and central label	06/06/94	6.00	5.50			7.00	12
a	29¢ Allies Retake New Guinea		.60	.30			1.50	12
b	29¢ Bombing Raids		.60	.30			1.50	12
c	29¢ Allies in Normandy, D-Day		.60	.30			1.50	12
d	29¢ Airborne Units		.60	.30			1.50	12
e	29¢ Submarines Shorten War		.60	.30			1.50	12
f	29¢ Allies Free Rome, Paris		.60	.30			1.50	12
g	29¢ Troops Clear Siapan Bunkers		.60	.30			1.50	12
h	29¢ Red Ball Express		.60	.30			1.50	12
i	29¢ Battle for Leyte Gulf		.60	.30			1.50	12
j	29¢ Battle of the Bulge		.60	.30			1.50	12

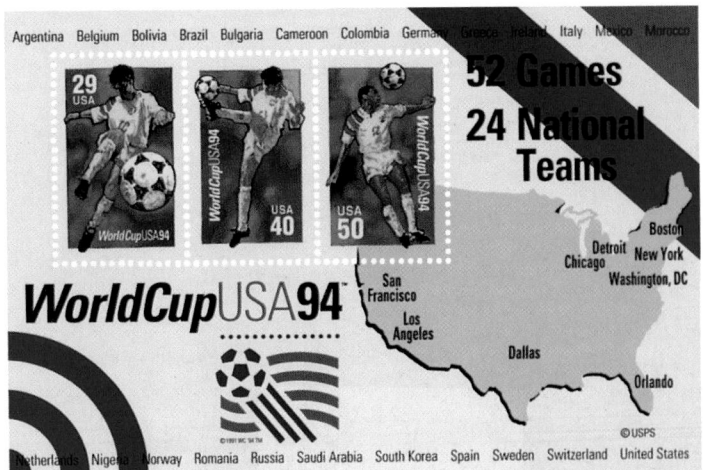

Example of #2837

Issues of 1994			Un	U	PB	#	FDC	Q(M)
Norman Rockwell Issue, Perf. 10.9 x 11.1								
2839	29¢ Rockwell Self-Portrait	07/01/94	.55	.20	2.50	(4)	1.25	209
2840	Four Freedoms souvenir sheet	07/01/94	4.00	2.75			3.50	20
a	50¢ Freedom from Want		1.00	.65			1.50	20
b	50¢ Freedom from Fear		1.00	.65			1.50	20
c	50¢ Freedom of Speech		1.00	.65			1.50	20
d	50¢ Freedom of Worship		1.00	.65			1.50	20
First Moon Landing Issue, Perf. 11.2 x 11.1								
2841	29¢ sheet of 12	07/20/94	7.50	—			6.50	13
a	Single stamp		.60	.60			1.50	155
Perf. 10.7 x 11.1								
2842	$9.95 Moon Landing	07/20/94	17.50	7.50	70.00	(4)	17.50	101
Locomotives Issue, Perf. 11 Horizontally								
2843	29¢ Hudson's General	07/28/94	.55	.20			1.50	159
2844	29¢ McQueen's Jupiter	07/28/94	.55	.20			1.50	159
2845	29¢ Eddy's No. 242	07/28/94	.55	.20			1.50	159
2846	29¢ Ely's No. 10	07/28/94	.55	.20			1.50	159
2847	29¢ Buchanan's No. 999	07/28/94	.55	.20			1.50	159
a	Booklet pane of 5, #2843-2847		2.75	2.00			3.25	159
Perf. 11.1 x 11								
2848	29¢ George Meany	08/16/94	.55	.20	2.50	(4)	1.25	151
Legends of American Music Series, Popular Singers Issue, Perf. 10.1 x 10.2								
2849	29¢ Al Jolson	09/01/94	.60	.20			1.50	35
2850	29¢ Bing Crosby	09/01/94	.60	.20			1.50	35
2851	29¢ Ethel Waters	09/01/94	.60	.20			1.50	35
2852	29¢ Nat "King" Cole	09/01/94	.60	.20			1.50	35
2853	29¢ Ethel Merman	09/01/94	.60	.20			1.50	35
a	Vert. strip of 5, #2849-2853		3.00	2.00	6.50	(6)	4.50	

RICHARD TUCKER

(1913-1975)

Tenor RICHARD TUCKER, born Reuben Ticker in Brooklyn, New York, began his singing career in synagogues and on the radio. In 1945 Tucker debuted in *La gioconda* at the Metropolitan Opera. Two years later in his European operatic debut in Verona, Italy, Tucker sang Enzo to Maria Callas's Gioconda. For three decades Tucker sang leading roles at the "Met" and enjoyed the frequent comparisons of his singing to that of Italian tenor Enrico Caruso. Tucker sang with all of the major American opera companies and most of the leading orchestras. In his last performance at the Met, just weeks before he died, Tucker sang the lead role in *Pagliacci*. His funeral was the first ever held at the Metropolitan Opera House. In 1997 Tucker was honored by the Postal Service in the Legends of American Music series along with three other opera singers: sopranos Rosa Ponselle and Lily Pons and baritone Lawrence Tibbett. ❑

2839

a   b

Norman Rockwell

From our doughboys in WWI to our astronauts striding across the moon, Norman Rockwell's artwork has captured America's traditional values along with the characteristic optimism of its people. Rockwell loved people, and people loved him. He was an enormously skilled technician and, according to several new reassessments, a true artist. He had a genius for capturing the emotional content of the commonplace. © USPS 1993

1894 1894

c   d

2840

2841a

2842

2843

2844

2845

2846

2847

2847a

2848

2849

2850

2851

2852

2853

2853a

2854   2855   2856   2857   2858

2859   2860   2861

2862

2863   2864

2865   2866

2866a

2867   2868   2868a

Issues of 1994		Un	U	PB	#	FDC	Q(M)
Legends of American Music Series, Jazz and Blues Singers Issue, Perf. 11 x 10.8							
2854	29¢ Bessie Smith	09/17/94	.60	.20			1.25	25
2855	29¢ Muddy Waters	09/17/94	.60	.20			1.25	25
2856	29¢ Billie Holiday	09/17/94	.60	.20			1.25	25
2857	29¢ Robert Johnson	09/17/94	.60	.20			1.25	20
2858	29¢ Jimmy Rushing	09/17/94	.60	.20			1.25	20
2859	29¢ "Ma" Rainey	09/17/94	.60	.20			1.25	20
2860	29¢ Mildred Bailey	09/17/94	.60	.20			1.25	20
2861	29¢ Howlin' Wolf	09/17/94	.60	.20			1.25	20
a	Block of 9, #2854-2861							
	+ 1 additional stamp		5.50	4.50	8.50	(10)	6.00	
Literary Arts Issue, Perf. 11							
2862	29¢ James Thurber	09/10/94	.55	.20	2.50	(4)	1.25	151
Wonders of the Sea Issue, Perf. 11 x 10.9							
2863	29¢ Diver, Motorboat	10/03/94	.55	.20			1.25	56
2864	29¢ Diver, Ship	10/03/94	.55	.20			1.25	56
2865	29¢ Diver, Ship's Wheel	10/03/94	.55	.20			1.25	56
2866	29¢ Diver, Coral	10/03/94	.55	.20			1.25	56
a	Block of 4, #2963-2966		2.20	1.50	2.25	(4)	2.75	56
b	As "a" imperf.		1,750.00					
Cranes Issue, Perf. 10.8 x 11							
2867	29¢ Black-Necked Crane	10/09/94	.55	.20			1.25	78
2868	29¢ Whooping Crane	10/09/94	.55	.20			1.25	78
a	Pair, #2867-2868		1.10	.75	2.25	(4)	2.50	78
b	Black and magenta (engr.) omitted		2,000.00					

NAVAJO ART

Long before the founding of the United States, Native Americans in the Navajo nation in the southwest were developing a unique art form: weaving. The rugs, blankets, and serapes we see today represent a centuries-old weaving tradition passed down from generation to generation. Using simple upright looms, the weavers transform single strands of brightly colored yarn into beautiful blankets, rugs, and sashes featuring abstract and geometric designs. Some designs depict natural phenomena such as the sun, rain, lightning, or clouds. Though a few Navajo men continue to weave rugs featuring reproductions of sand paintings, most of the items are created by the women of the tribe, who learn at an early age how to spin, card, and weave. In 1986 the Postal Service issued four stamps featuring Navajo weavings as part of the American Folk Art series. ❑

Issues of 1994		Un	U	PB	#	FDC	Q(M)
Legends of the West Issue, Perf. 10.1 x 10							
2869	Sheet of 20	10/18/94	12.00	—			14.00	20
a	29¢ Home on the Range		.60	.20			1.75	20
b	29¢ Buffalo Bill Cody		.60	.20			1.75	20
c	29¢ Jim Bridger		.60	.20			1.75	20
d	29¢ Annie Oakley		.60	.20			1.75	20
e	29¢ Native American Culture		.60	.20			1.75	20
f	29¢ Chief Joseph		.60	.20			1.75	20
g	29¢ Bill Pickett		.60	.20			1.75	20
h	29¢ Bat Masterson		.60	.20			1.75	20
i	29¢ John C. Fremont		.60	.20			1.75	20
j	29¢ Wyatt Earp		.60	.20			1.75	20
k	29¢ Nellie Cashman		.60	.20			1.75	20
l	29¢ Charles Goodnight		.60	.20			1.75	20
m	29¢ Geronimo		.60	.20			1.75	20
n	29¢ Kit Carson		.60	.20			1.75	20
o	29¢ Wild Bill Hickok		.60	.20			1.75	20
p	29¢ Western Wildlife		.60	.20			1.75	20
q	29¢ Jim Beckwourth		.60	.20			1.75	20
r	29¢ Bill Tilghman		.60	.20			1.75	20
s	29¢ Sacagawea		.60	.20			1.75	20
t	29¢ Overland Mail		.60	.20			1.75	20
2870	29¢ Sheet of 20 (recalled)	10/18/94	200.00	—				0.1

THOMAS WOLFE

(1900-1938)

In 2000 the U.S. Postal Service honored writer THOMAS WOLFE—on the centenary of his birth in Asheville, North Carolina—in the Literary Arts series. Considered one of the great writers of the 20th century, Wolfe is best known for his novel *Look Homeward, Angel*, published in 1929. The book, based on Wolfe's early life in Asheville, created a stir in the mountain community as residents sought to identify the townspeople who appeared as thinly disguised characters in the novel. An excellent student, Wolfe attended the University of North Carolina in Chapel Hill, where he edited the student newspaper and graduated in 1920 with a bachelor of arts degree. He continued his formal education at Harvard University, earning a master of arts degree in 1922. Wolfe taught at New York University while trying to find a publisher for his plays and stories. He ultimately worked with Maxwell E. Perkins, an editor at Scribner's, to organize thousands of pages of raw material into his first novel. Wolfe also wrote other literary works including *Of Time and the River* (1935), *The Web and the Rock* (1939), and *You Can't Go Home Again* (1940). The last two books were published posthumously. ❑

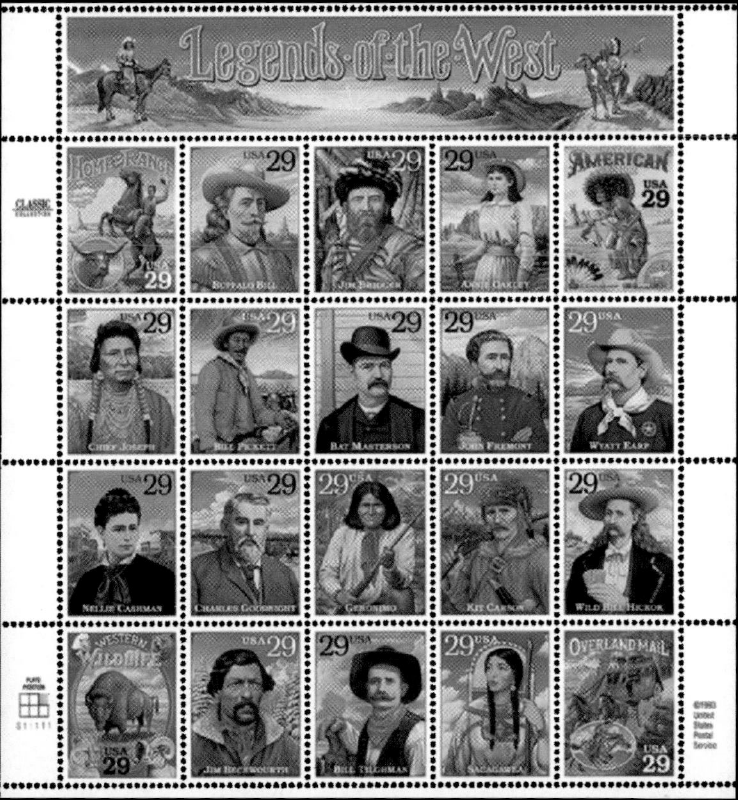

Legends of the West

CLASSIC COLLECTION

HOME on the RANGE | BUFFALO BILL | JIM BRIDGER | ANNIE OAKLEY | AMERICAN

CHIEF JOSEPH | BILL PICKETT | BAT MASTERSON | JOHN FREMONT | WYATT EARP

NELLIE CASHMAN | CHARLES GOODNIGHT | GERONIMO | KIT CARSON | WILD BILL HICKOK

PLATE POSITION | JIM BECKWOURTH | BILL TILGHMAN | SACAGAWEA | OVERLAND MAIL

©1993 United States Postal Service

2869	a	b	c	d	e
	f	g	h	i	j
	k	l	m	n	o
	p	q	r	s	t

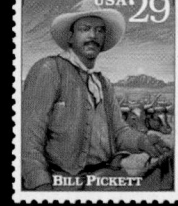

2870g

2871   **2872**

2873   **2874**

2875

2876

2877   **2878**

Issues of 1994			Un	U	PB	#	FDC	Q(M)
Christmas Issue, Perf. 11.25								
2871	29¢ Madonna and Child	10/20/94	.55	.20	2.50	(4)	1.25	
2871A	Perf. 9.8 x 10.8		.60	.20			1.25	
b	As "a," booklet pane of 10		6.25	3.50				50
c	As "b," Imperf.		2,250.00					
2872	29¢ Stocking	10/20/94	.55	.20	2.50	(4)	1.25	603
a	Booklet pane of 20		11.00	3.00				30
Self-Adhesive								
2873	29¢ Santa Claus	10/20/94	.55	.20	6.75	(5)	1.25	240
a	Booklet pane of 12		6.75					20
2874	29¢ Cardinal in Snow	10/20/94	.55	.20			1.25	36
a	Booklet pane of 18		10.00					2
Bureau of Engraving and Printing Issue, Perf.11								
2875	$2.00 Sheet of 4	11/03/94	15.00	—			17.50	5
a	Single stamp		3.00	1.25				20
Lunar New Year Issue, Perf. 11.2 x 11.1								
2876	29¢ Year of the Boar	12/30/94	.55	.20	2.25	(4)	1.50	80
Untagged, Perf. 11 x 10.8								
2877	(3¢) Dove Make-Up Rate	12/13/94	.20	.20	.30	(4)	1.25	
a	Imperf., pair		200.00					
Perf. 10.8 x 10.9								
2878	(3¢) Dove Make-Up Rate	12/13/94	.20	.20	.30	(4)	1.25	

COUNT BASIE

(1904-1984)

Noted jazz pianist, composer, and Big Band leader WILLIAM "COUNT" BASIE was born in Red Bank, New Jersey. Taught piano by his mother, he spent much of his youth in New York City listening to ragtime pianists such as Fats Waller and James P. Johnson. When the musical group he traveled with folded in Kansas City, Basie formed his own band and played the local jazz clubs. In 1936, Basie's band came to New York where it played the Famous Door Club and made the first of many successful recordings. Radio broadcasts, record sales, and film appearances brought fame to Basie and his musicians. The first all-black band to play at New York's Waldorf-Astoria Hotel, the group toured Europe and Japan. When rock music became popular in the 1960s, the Basie band recorded big-band arrangements of the tunes. In addition to its theme song, "One O'Clock Jump," other hits include "Jumpin' at the Woodside" and "Swingin' the Blues." In 1996 Basie was honored with Benny Goodman, Glenn Miller, and Tommy and Jimmy Dorsey in the Big Band Leaders issuance in the Legends of American Music series. ❑

	Issues of 1994-1997		Un	U	PB	#	FDC	Q(M)
	Tagged, Perf. 11.2 x 11.1							
2879	(20¢) Old Glory Postcard Rate	12/13/94	.40	.20	5.00	(4)	1.25	
	Perf. 11 x 10.9							
2880	(20¢) Old Glory Postcard Rate	12/13/94	.50	.20	9.00	(4)	1.25	
	Perf. 11.2 x 11.1							
2881	(32¢) "G" Old Glory	12/13/94	.75	.20	70.00	(4)	1.25	
a	Booklet pane of 10		6.00	3.75			6.75	
	Perf. 11 x 10.9							
2882	(32¢) "G" Old Glory	12/13/94	.60	.20	3.00	(4)	1.25	
	Booklet Stamps, Perf. 10 x 9.9 on 2 or 3 sides							
2883	(32¢) "G" Old Glory	12/13/94	.60	.20			1.25	
a	Booklet pane of 10		6.25	3.75			6.75	
	Perf. 10.9 on 2 or 3 sides							
2884	(32¢) "G" Old Glory	12/13/94	.60	.20			1.25	
a	Booklet pane of 10		6.00	3.75			6.75	
	Perf. 11 x 10.9 on 2 or 3 sides							
2885	(32¢) "G" Old Glory	12/13/94	.85	.20			1.25	
a	Booklet pane of 10		8.50	4.50			6.75	
	Self-Adhesive, Die-Cut							
2886	(32¢) "G" Old Glory	12/13/94	.75	.20	5.50	(5)	1.25	
a	Booklet pane of 18		14.00					
b	Coil with plate		—	3.25				
2887	(32¢) "G" Old Glory	12/13/94	.75	.20			1.25	
a	Booklet pane of 18		14.00					
	Coil Stamps, Perf. 9.8 Vertically							
2888	(25¢) Old Glory First-Class Presort	12/13/94	.50	.50	4.50	(5)	1.25	
2889	(32¢) Black "G"	12/13/94	.90	.20	11.50	(5)	1.25	
a	Imperf., pair		325.00					
2890	(32¢) Blue "G"	12/13/94	.60	.20	5.00	(5)	1.25	
2891	(32¢) Red "G"	12/13/94	.75	.20	6.00	(5)	1.25	
	Rouletted 9.8 Vertically							
2892	(32¢) Red "G"	12/13/94	.60	.20	6.00	(5)	1.25	
	Coil Stamps, Untagged, Perf. 9.8 Vertically							
2893	(5¢) Green	01/12/95	.30	.20	2.50	(5)		
	Tagged, Perf. 10.4							
2897	32¢ Flag Over Porch	05/19/95	.60	.20	3.00	(4)	1.25	
	Coil Stamps, Untagged, Perf. 9.8 Vertically							
2902	(5¢) Butte	03/10/95	.20	.20	1.50	(5)	1.25	
a	Imperf., pair		750.00					
	Self-Adhesive, Serpentine Die-Cut 11.5 Vertically							
2902B	(5¢) Butte	06/15/96	.20	.20	1.50	(5)	1.25	550
	Perf. 9.8 Vertically							
2903	(5¢) Mountain, purple and multi	03/16/96	.20	.20	1.50	(5)	1.25	150
a	Tagged (error)		4.00	3.50	85.00	(5)		
2904	(5¢) Mountain, blue and multi	03/16/96	.20	.20	1.50	(5)	1.25	150
c	Imperf., pair		500.00					
	Self-Adhesive, Serpentine Die-Cut 11.2 Vertically							
2904A	(5¢) Mountain, purple and multi	06/15/96	.20	.20	1.75	(5)	1.25	
	Self-Adhesive, Serpentine Die-Cut 9.8 Vertically							
2904B	(5¢) Mountain, purple and multi	01/24/97	.20	.20	1.50	(5)	1.25	148
c	Tagged (error)		4.00	3.50	85.00	(5)		
	Perf. 9.8 Vertically							
2905	(10¢) Automobile	03/10/95	.20	.20	2.40	(5)	1.25	
	Self-Adhesive, Serpentine Die-Cut 11.5 Vertically							
2906	(10¢) Automobile	06/15/96	.20	.20	2.50	(5)	1.25	450
2907	(10¢) Eagle and Shield	05/21/96	.20	.20	2.75	(5)	1.25	450

2879

2880

2881

2882

2883

2884

2885

2886

2887

2888

2889

2890

2891

2892

2893

2897

2902

2903

2904

2905

2906

2907

VISIT US ONLINE AT **THE POSTAL STORE**

AT **WWW.USPS.COM**

OR CALL **1-800-STAMP-24**

2908

2909

2910

2911

2912

2913

2914

2915

2916

2919

2920

2921

2933

2934

2935

2936

2938

2940

2941

Issues of 1995-1999		Un	U	PB	#	FDC	Q(M)
Perf. 9.8 Vertically							
2908	(15¢) Auto Tail Fin, bureau printing 03/17/95	.30	.30	3.00	(5)	1.25	
2909	(15¢) Auto Tail Fin, private printing 03/17/95	.30	.30	2.75	(5)	1.25	
Self-Adhesive, Serpentine Die-Cut 11.5 Vertically							
2910	(15¢) Auto Tail Fin 06/15/96	.30	.30	2.90	(5)	1.25	
Perf. 9.8 Vertically							
2911	(25¢) Juke Box, bureau printing 03/17/95	.50	.50	4.25	(5)	1.25	
2912	(25¢) Juke Box, private printing 03/17/95	.50	.50	3.75	(5)	1.25	
Self-Adhesive, Serpentine Die-Cut 11.5 Vertically							
2912A	(25¢) Juke Box 06/15/96	.50	.50	5.00	(5)	1.25	550
Self-Adhesive, Serpentine Die-Cut 9.8 Vertically							
2912B	(25¢) Juke Box 01/24/97	.50	.50	3.75	(5)	1.25	20
Tagged, Perf. 9.8 Vertically							
2913	32¢ Flag Over Porch 05/19/95	.60	.20	5.25	(5)	1.25	
a	Imperf., pair		45.00				
2914	32¢ Flag Over Porch 05/19/95	.60	.20	4.50	(3)	1.25	
Self-Adhesive, Serpentine Die-Cut 8.7 Vertically							
2915	32¢ Flag Over Porch 04/18/95	.75	.30	7.50	(5)	1.25	
Self-Adhesive, Serpentine Die-Cut Perf. 9.8 Vertically							
2915A	32¢ Flag Over Porch 05/21/96	.60	.20	5.00	(5)	1.25	
Self-Adhesive, Serpentine Die-Cut 11.5 Vertically							
2915B	32¢ Flag Over Porch 06/15/96	.75	.90	7.00	(5)	1.25	
Self-Adhesive, Serpentine Die-Cut 10.9 Vertically							
2915C	32¢ Flag Over Porch 06/21/96	1.00	.40	17.50	(5)	2.00	
Self-Adhesive, Serpentine Die-Cut 9.8 Vertically							
2915D	32¢ Flag Over Porch 01/24/97	.75	.90	7.50	(5)	1.25	300
Booklet Stamps, Perf. 10.8 x 9.8 on 2 or 3 adjacent sides							
2916	32¢ Flag Over Porch 05/19/95	.65	.20			1.25	
a	Booklet pane of 10	6.50	3.25			7.50	
b	As "a," imperf.	—					
Self-Adhesive, Die-Cut							
2919	32¢ Flag Over Field 03/17/95	.60	.20			1.25	
a	Booklet pane of 18	11.00					
Self-Adhesive, Serpentine Die-Cut 8.7 on 2, 3 or 4 adjacent sides							
2920	32¢ Flag Over Porch 04/18/95	.60	.20			1.25	
a	Booklet pane of 20 + label	12.00					
b	Small date	4.50	.35				
c	As "b," booklet pane of 20 + label	110.00					
f	As #2920, pane of 15 + label	9.00					
h	As #2920, booklet pane of 15	35.00					
Self-Adhesive, Serpentine Die-Cut 11.3 on 3 sides							
2920D	32¢ Flag Over Porch 01/20/96	.70	.25				789
e	Booklet pane of 10	7.50					
Self-Adhesive, Serpentine Die-Cut Perf. 9.8 on 2 or 3 adjacent sides							
2921	32¢ Flag Over Porch 05/21/96	.75	.20			1.25	7,344
a	Booklet pane of 10	7.50					
b	As #2921, dated red "1997"	.75	.20				
c	As "a," dated red "1997"	7.50					
d	Booklet pane of 5 + label	3.75					
Great Americans Issue, Perf. 11.2							
2933	32¢ Milton S. Hershey 09/13/95	.60	.20	3.00	(4)	1.25	
2934	32¢ Cal Farley 04/26/96	.60	.20	3.00	(4)	1.25	150
2935	32¢ Henry R. Luce 04/03/98	.60	.20	2.60	(4)	1.25	
2936	32¢ Lila and DeWitt Wallace 07/16/98	.60	.20	2.60	(4)	1.25	
2938	46¢ Ruth Benedict 10/20/95	.90	.20	4.50	(4)	1.40	
2940	55¢ Alice Hamilton, MD 07/11/95	1.10	.20	5.50	(4)	1.40	
Tagged, Self-Adhesive, Serpentine Die-Cut 11.7 x 11.5							
2941	55¢ Justin S. Morrill 07/17/99	1.10	.20	4.40	(4)	1.40	

Issues of 1995-1998		Un	U	PB	#	FDC
Tagged, Self-Adhesive, Serpentine Die-Cut 11.7 x 11.5						
2942	77¢ Mary Breckinridge	11/09/98	1.50	.20	6.00	(4)	1.75
Tagged, Perf. 11.2						
2943	78¢ Alice Paul	08/18/95	1.60	.20	7.50	(4)	1.75
a	78¢ dull violet		1.60	.20	7.50	(4)	
b	78¢ pale violet		1.75	.30	12.00	(4)	
Love Issue, Tagged, Perf. 11.2						
2948	(32¢) Love, Cherub from Sistine Madonna, by Raphael	02/01/95	.60	.20	3.00	(4)	1.50
Self-Adhesive, Die-Cut						
2949	(32¢) Love, Cherub from Sistine Madonna, by Raphael	02/01/95	.60	.20			1.50
a	Booklet pane of 20 + label		12.00				
b	Red (engr.) omitted		450.00				
c	As "a," red (engr.) omitted		9,000.00				
Tagged, Perf. 11.1						
2950	32¢ Florida Statehood, 150th Anniversary	03/03/95	.60	.20	2.40	(4)	1.25
Kids Care Earth Day Issue, Tagged, Perf. 11.1 x 11						
2951	32¢ Earth Clean-Up	04/20/95	.60	.20			1.25
2952	32¢ Solar Energy	04/20/95	.60	.20			1.25
2953	32¢ Tree Planting	04/20/95	.60	.20			1.25
2954	32¢ Beach Clean-Up	04/20/95	.60	.20			1.25
a	Block of 4, #2951-54		2.40	1.75	2.40	(4)	2.75
Tagged, Perf. 11.2						
2955	32¢ Richard Nixon	04/26/95	.60	.20	3.00	(4)	1.25
a	Red (engr.) omitted		1,250.00				
Black Heritage Series, Tagged, Perf. 11.2						
2956	32¢ Bessie Coleman	04/27/95	.60	.20	3.00	(4)	1.75
Love Issue, Tagged, Perf. 11.2						
2957	32¢ Love, Cherub from Sistine Madonna, by Raphael	05/12/95	.60	.20	3.00	(4)	1.25
2958	55¢ Love, Cherub from Sistine Madonna, by Raphael	05/12/95	1.10	.20	5.50	(4)	1.25
Booklet Stamps, Perf. 9.8 x 10.8						
2959	32¢ Love, Cherub from Sistine Madonna, by Raphael	05/12/95	.60	.20			1.25
a	Booklet pane of 10		6.00	3.25			7.50
Self-Adhesive, Die-Cut						
2960	55¢ Love, Cherub from Sistine Madonna, by Raphael	05/12/95	1.10	.20			1.40
a	Booklet pane of 20 + label		22.50				
Recreational Sports Issue, Tagged, Perf. 11.2						
2961	32¢ Volleyball	05/20/95	.60	.20			1.50
2962	32¢ Softball	05/20/95	.60	.20			1.50
2963	32¢ Bowling	05/20/95	.60	.20			1.50
2964	32¢ Tennis	05/20/95	.60	.20			1.50
2965	32¢ Golf	05/20/95	.60	.20			1.50
a	Vertical strip of 5, #2961-65		3.00	2.00	6.00	(10)	3.25
b	As "a," imperf.						
c	As "a," yellow omitted		2,250.00				
d	As "a," yellow, blue and magenta omitted		2,250.00				
Tagged, Perf. 11.2						
2966	32¢ Prisoners of War and Missing in Action	05/29/95	.60	.20	2.40	(4)	2.00
	Pane of 20		12.00	—			

2942

2943

2948

2950

2951

2952

2953

2954

2955

2954a

2956

2958

2961

2962

2963

2965

2964

2965a

2966

2967

2968

2969 **2970** **2971** **2972** **2973** **2973a**

Issues of 1995		Un	U	PB	#	FDC
Legends of Hollywood Issue, Perf. 11.1						
2967	32¢ Marilyn Monroe	06/01/95	.60	.20	5.00	(4)	2.50
a	Imperf., pair		500.00				
Perf. 11.2						
2968	32¢ Texas Statehood	06/16/95	.60	.20	2.40	(4)	1.75
Great Lakes Lighthouses Issue, Perf. 11.2 Vertically						
2969	32¢ Split Rock, Lake Superior	06/17/95	.60	.20			2.00
2970	32¢ St. Joseph, Lake Michigan	06/17/95	.60	.20			2.00
2971	32¢ Spectacle Reef, Lake Huron	06/17/95	.60	.20			2.00
2972	32¢ Marblehead, Lake Erie	06/17/95	.60	.20			2.00
2973	32¢ Thirty Mile Point, Lake Ontario	06/17/95	.60	.20			2.00
a	Booklet pane of 5, #2969-73		3.00	2.75			5.00

AMERICAN GLASS

Considered by many as America's first industry, glassmaking combines beauty, form, and function. In 1999 the Postal Service recognized this American art by issuing four se-tenant stamps honoring different aspects—free-blown, mold-blown, pressed, and art—of the tradition of glassmaking. In colonial America, the most common items made in glass factories were free-blown windows and bottles. Leftover glass was used to make gifts for family and friends. Mold-blown glass— liquid glass blown into metal molds—was introduced in the early 19th century. This method often was used to make bottles and flasks. Pressed glass was perfected in the United States in the 1820s and represents America's greatest contribution to glassmaking. Molten glass was poured into a metal mold and assumed the shape and the decorative pattern of the mold. Glass made primarily for decorative use is known as art glass. Artists such as Louis Comfort Tiffany convinced America that a carefully crafted piece of glass could be valued simply for its beauty and design. ❑

Issues of 1995		Un	U	PB	#	FDC
Perf. 11.2						
2974	32¢ United Nations, 50th Anniversary 06/26/95	.60	.20	2.40	(4)	1.50
	Civil War Issue, Perf. 10.1					
2975	Sheet of 20 06/29/95	17.50	—			16.00
a	32¢ *Monitor and Virginia*	.80	.20			1.50
b	32¢ Robert E. Lee	.80	.20			1.50
c	32¢ Clara Barton	.80	.20			1.50
d	32¢ Ulysses S. Grant	.80	.20			1.50
e	32¢ Battle of Shiloh	.80	.20			1.50
f	32¢ Jefferson Davis	.80	.20			1.50
g	32¢ David Farragut	.80	.20			1.50
h	32¢ Frederick Douglass	.80	.20			1.50
i	32¢ Raphael Semmes	.80	.20			1.50
j	32¢ Abraham Lincoln	.80	.20			1.50
k	32¢ Harriet Tubman	.80	.20			1.50
l	32¢ Stand Watie	.80	.20			1.50
m	32¢ Joseph E. Johnston	.80	.20			1.50
n	32¢ Winfield Hancock	.80	.20			1.50
o	32¢ Mary Chesnut	.80	.20			1.50
p	32¢ Battle of Chancellorsville	.80	.20			1.50
q	32¢ William T. Sherman	.80	.20			1.50
r	32¢ Phoebe Pember	.80	.20			1.50
s	32¢ "Stonewall" Jackson	.80	.20			1.50
t	32¢ Battle of Gettysburg	.80	.20			1.50

UNITED NATIONS
1945-1995
USA 32

2974

CIVIL WAR
1861   THE WAR BETWEEN THE STATES   1865

CLASSIC
COLLECTION

MONITOR·VIRGINIA 32 USA	32 USA Robert E. Lee	32 USA Clara Barton	32 USA Ulysses S. Grant	SHILOH 32 USA
32 USA Jefferson Davis	32 USA David Farragut	32 USA Frederick Douglass	32 USA Raphael Semmes	32 USA Abraham Lincoln
32 USA Harriet Tubman	32 USA Stand Watie	32 USA Joseph E. Johnston	USA 32 Winfield Hancock	32 USA Mary Chesnut
CHANCELLORSVILLE 32 USA	32 USA William T. Sherman	32 USA Phoebe Pember	32 USA "Stonewall" Jackson	GETTYSBURG 32 USA

PLATE POSITION
S 111

©1994 United States Postal Service

2975   a   b   c   d   e

2976 2977

2980

2978 2979 2979a

a b c d e

f g h i j 2981

Issues of 1995	Un	U	PB	#	FDC
Carousel Horse Issue, Perf. 11					
2976 32¢ Golden Horse with Roses 07/21/95	.60	.20			1.25
2977 32¢ Black Horse with Gold Bridle 07/21/95	.60	.20			1.25
2978 32¢ Horse with Armor 07/21/95	.60	.20			1.25
2979 32¢ Brown Horse with Green Bridle 07/21/95	.60	.20			1.25
a Block of 4, #2976-79	2.40	2.00	2.40	(4)	3.25
Perf. 11.1 x 11					
2980 32¢ Women's Suffrage 08/26/95	.60	.20	3.00	(4)	1.25
a Black (engr.) omitted	425.00				
World War II Issue, 1945: Victory at Last, Miniature Sheet, Perf. 11.1					
2981 Block of 10 and central label 09/02/95	6.00	5.50			7.00
a 32¢ Marines Raise Flag on Iwo Jima	.60	.30			1.50
b 32¢ Fierce Fighting Frees Manila by March 3, 1945	.60	.30			1.50
c 32¢ Soldiers Advancing: Okinawa, the Last Big Battle	.60	.30			1.50
d 32¢ Destroyed Bridge: U.S. and Soviets Link Up at Elbe River	.60	.30			1.50
e 32¢ Allies Liberate Holocaust Survivors	.60	.30			1.50
f 32¢ Germany Surrenders at Reims	.60	.30			1.50
g 32¢ Refugees: By 1945, World War II Has Uprooted Millions	.60	.30			1.50
h 32¢ Truman Announces Japan's Surrender	.60	.30			1.50
i 32¢ Sailor Kissing Nurse: News of Victory Hits Home	.60	.30			1.50
j 32¢ Hometowns Honor Their Returning Veterans	.60	.30			1.50

JEROME KERN

(1885-1945)

JEROME DAVID KERN was still a teenager in 1902 when his first tune was published. He went on to write more than 1000 unforgettable songs and 100 theatrical scores in the next 43 years. His innovative combination of the European operetta form with American themes earned him the name, "Father of American Musical Theater." In 1927 Kern and Oscar Hammerstein II collaborated on the music for *Show Boat*, creating songs such as "Ol' Man River" and "Why Do I Love You" that have remained popular into the 21st century. After 1935 Kern wrote principally for film, winning Academy Awards for "The Last Time I Saw Paris" (written for *Swing Time*, 1936) and "The Way You Look Tonight" (from *Lady Be Good*, 1941). In 1945 Kern's life was the subject of a film, *Till the Clouds Roll By*. The U.S. Postal Service honored the popular songwriter in 1985 with a stamp in the Performing Arts series. ❑

Issues of 1995		Un	U	PB	#	FDC	Q(M)
Legends of American Music Series, Jazz Musicians Issue, Perf. 11.1 x 11							
2982	32¢ Louis Armstrong, white denomination 09/01/95	.80	.20	3.20	(4)	1.75	
2983	32¢ Coleman Hawkins 09/16/95	1.00	.20			1.50	
2984	32¢ Louis Armstrong, black denomination 09/16/95	1.00	.20			1.50	
2985	32¢ James P. Johnson 09/16/95	1.00	.20			1.50	
2986	32¢ Jelly Roll Morton 09/16/95	1.00	.20			1.50	
2987	32¢ Charlie Parker 09/16/95	1.00	.20			1.50	
2988	32¢ Eubie Blake 09/16/95	1.00	.20			1.50	
2989	32¢ Charles Mingus 09/16/95	1.00	.20			1.50	
2990	32¢ Thelonious Monk 09/16/95	1.00	.20			1.50	
2991	32¢ John Coltrane 09/16/95	1.00	.20			1.50	
2992	32¢ Erroll Garner 09/16/95	1.00	.20			1.50	
a	Vertical block of 10, #2983-92	10.00	—	10.00	(10)	6.50	
	Pane of 20	20.00	—				
Garden Flowers Issue, Perf. 10.9 Vertically							
2993	32¢ Aster 09/19/95	.60	.20			1.25	800
2994	32¢ Chrysanthemum 09/19/95	.60	.20			1.25	800
2995	32¢ Dahlia 09/19/95	.60	.20			1.25	800
2996	32¢ Hydrangea 09/19/95	.60	.20			1.25	800
2997	32¢ Rudbeckia 09/19/95	.60	.20			1.25	800
a	Booklet pane of 5, #2993-97	3.00	2.25			4.00	
Perf. 11.25							
2998	60¢ Eddie Rickenbacker, Aviator 09/25/95	1.40	.30	9.00	(4)	1.75	
a	Large date, 2000	1.40	.30	9.00	(4)		
Perf. 11.1							
2999	32¢ Republic of Palau 09/29/95	.60	.20	3.00	(4)	1.25	

JACK BENNY

(1894-1974)

Comedian JACK BENNY (born Benjamin Kublesky) almost began in show business with the Marx Brothers who asked the teenaged pianist and violinist to tour with them. Benny's mother said no, and he turned to comedy. A successful vaudeville performer, Benny was intrigued by radio. His appearance on a show hosted by Ed Sullivan led to his first radio program and first corporate sponsor. Named the most popular comedian on radio, he acquired new sponsors and a cast that included Don Wilson, Eddie "Rochester" Anderson, Phil Harris, Dennis Day, and his real-life wife, Mary Livingston. In addition to his phenomenal success in radio, Benny also starred in films, among them *Charley's Aunt* (1941) and *To Be or Not To Be* (1942). His first television show in October 1950 was quickly followed by specials and a weekly show. In 1957 he won an Emmy; the following year the show won as Best Comedy series. Although his last regular television program aired in April 1965, Benny continued to host specials, make guest appearances, and perform as a violinist at symphony orchestra benefits. He died shortly before his third "farewell" special planned for early 1975. ❏

2982

2983

2984

2985

2986

2987

2988

2989

2990

2991

2992

2992a

2993   2994   2995   2996   2997   2997a

2998   2999

COMIC STRIP CLASSICS

 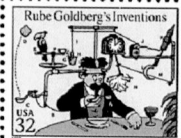  

3000	a	b	c	d
	e	f	g	h
	i	j	k	l
	m	n	o	p
	q	r	s	t

3001

3002

Issues of 1995		Un	U	PB	#	FDC
Comic Strip Classics Issue, Perf. 10.1						
3000 Pane of 20	10/01/95	12.00	—			13.00
a 32¢ The Yellow Kid		.60	.20			1.75
b 32¢ Katzenjammer Kids		.60	.20			1.75
c 32¢ Little Nemo in Slumberland		.60	.20			1.75
d 32¢ Bringing Up Father		.60	.20			1.75
e 32¢ Krazy Kat		.60	.20			1.75
f 32¢ Rube Goldberg's Inventions		.60	.20			1.75
g 32¢ Toonerville Folks		.60	.20			1.75
h 32¢ Gasoline Alley		.60	.20			1.75
i 32¢ Barney Google		.60	.20			1.75
j 32¢ Little Orphan Annie		.60	.20			1.75
k 32¢ Popeye		.60	.20			1.75
l 32¢ Blondie		.60	.20			1.75
m 32¢ Dick Tracy		.60	.20			1.75
n 32¢ Alley Oop		.60	.20			1.75
o 32¢ Nancy		.60	.20			1.75
p 32¢ Flash Gordon		.60	.20			1.75
q 32¢ Li'l Abner		.60	.20			1.75
r 32¢ Terry and the Pirates		.60	.20			1.75
s 32¢ Prince Valiant		.60	.20			1.75
t 32¢ Brenda Starr, Reporter		.60	.20			1.75
Perf 10.9						
3001 32¢ U.S. Naval Academy, 150th Anniversary	10/10/95	.60	.20	2.40	(4)	1.75
Literary Arts Issue, Perf 11.1						
3002 32¢ Tennessee Williams	10/13/95	.60	.20	2.40	(4)	1.25

LANGSTON HUGHES

(1902-1967)

Although JAMES LANGSTON HUGHES wrote in many literary genres, from short stories to drama, he considered himself a poet first. His innovative poetry combined jazz, blues, and the black vernacular with the traditions of poetry in English. Admired in his own time, Hughes is now considered one of the most important American writers of the 20th century. Having decided in high school to be a writer, at age 19 he published a poem in *The Crisis*, the journal of the National Association for the Advancement of Colored People. His first book of poetry was published in 1926; that same year he enrolled at Lincoln University where he earned a bachelor's degree in 1929. Hughes played a leading role in the Harlem Renaissance. His essay "The Negro Artist and the Racial Mountain," which proclaimed the importance of both creative freedom and racial pride, served as a manifesto for Harlem Renaissance writers. Hughes wrote about social and political issues, Africa, the Caribbean, famous African Americans, and jazz. He edited anthologies of black poetry and prose bringing the richness of black cultures to all readers. His last book of poetry, *The Panther and the Lash: Poems of Our Times*, about racial inequality and the struggle for civil rights was published posthumously. ❑

	Issues of 1995		Un	U	PB	#	FDC
	Christmas Issue, Perf. 11.2						
3003	32¢ Madonna and Child,						
	by Giotto di Bondone	10/19/95	.60	.20	3.00	(4)	1.25
c	Black (engr., denom.) omitted		250.00				
	Booklet Stamp, Perf. 9.8 x 10.9						
3003A	32¢ Madonna and Child	10/19/95	.65	.20			1.25
b	Booklet pane of 10		6.50	4.00			7.25
3004	32¢ Santa Claus Entering Chimney	09/30/95	.60	.20			1.25
3005	32¢ Child Holding Jumping Jack	09/30/95	.60	.20			1.25
3006	32¢ Child Holding Tree	09/30/95	.60	.20			1.25
3007	32¢ Santa Claus Working on Sled	09/30/95	.60	.20			1.25
a	Block of 4, #3004-07		2.40	1.25	3.00	(4)	3.25
b	Booklet pane of 10, 3 each #3004-05,						
	2 each 3006-07		6.00	4.00			7.25
c	Booklet pane of 10, 2 each #3004-05,						
	3 each 3006-07		6.00	4.00			7.25
d	As "a," imperf.		600.00				
	Self-Adhesive, Serpentine Die-Cut 11.25 on 2, 3 or 4 sides						
3008	32¢ Santa Claus Working on Sled	09/30/95	.75	.20			1.25
3009	32¢ Child Holding Jumping Jack	09/30/95	.75	.20			1.25
3010	32¢ Santa Claus Entering Chimney	09/30/95	.75	.20			1.25
3011	32¢ Child Holding Tree	09/30/95	.75	.20			1.25
a	Booklet pane of 20, 5 each						
	#3008-11 + label		15.00				3.25
	Serpentine Die-Cut 11.3 x 11.6 on 2, 3 or 4 sides						
3012	32¢ Midnight Angel	10/19/95	.60	.20			1.25
a	Booklet pane of 20 + label		12.00				
	Self-Adhesive, Die-Cut						
3013	32¢ Children Sledding	10/19/95	.60	.20			1.25
a	Booklet pane of 18		11.00				
	Self-Adhesive Coil Stamps, Serpentine Die-Cut 11.2 Vertically						
3014	32¢ Santa Claus Working on Sled	09/30/95	.60	.30			1.25
3015	32¢ Child Holding Jumping Jack	09/30/95	.60	.30			1.25
3016	32¢ Santa Claus Entering Chimney	09/30/95	.60	.30			1.25
3017	32¢ Child Holding Tree	09/30/95	.60	.30			1.25
a	Strip of 4, #3014-17		2.40		11.00	(8)	2.50
	Serpentine Die-Cut 11.6 Vertically						
3018	32¢ Midnight Angel	10/19/95	.60	.30	6.25	(5)	1.25

3003

3004 **3005**

3006 **3007**

3007a

3008 **3009** **3010** **3011** **3011a**

3012 **3013**

3019

3020

3021

3022

3023

3023a

3024

3025　　3026　　3027　　3028　　3029　3029a

3030　　3032　　3033　　3036　　3044

3048　　3049　　3050

	Issues of 1995-1999		Un	U	PB	#	FDC	Q(M)
	Antique Automobiles Issue, Perf. 10.1 x 11.1							
3019	32¢ 1893 Duryea	11/03/95	.90	.20			1.25	
3020	32¢ 1894 Haynes	11/03/95	.90	.20			1.25	
3021	32¢ 1898 Columbia	11/03/95	.90	.20			1.25	
3022	32¢ 1899 Winton	11/03/95	.90	.20			1.25	
3023	32¢ 1901 White	11/03/95	.90	.20			1.25	
a	Vertical or horizontal strip of 5, #3019-23		4.50	2.00			3.00	
	Perf. 11.1							
3024	32¢ Utah Statehood	01/04/96	.60	.20	3.00	(4)	1.25	
	Issues of 1996, Garden Flowers Issue, Perf 10.9 Vertically							
3025	32¢ Crocus	01/19/96	.60	.20			1.25	
3026	32¢ Winter Aconite	01/19/96	.60	.20			1.25	
3027	32¢ Pansy	01/19/96	.60	.20			1.25	
3028	32¢ Snowdrop	01/19/96	.60	.20			1.25	
3029	32¢ Anemone	01/19/96	.60	.20			1.25	
a	Booklet pane of 5, #3025-3029		3.00	2.50			3.50	
	Love Issue, Serpentine Die-Cut Perf. 11.3 x 11.7							
3030	32¢ Love Cherub from Sistine Madonna, by Raphael	01/20/96	.60	.20			1.25	
a	Booklet pane of 20 + label		12.00					
b	Booklet pane of 15 + label		9.00					
	Flora and Fauna Issue, Self-Adhesive, Serpentine Die-Cut 10.75							
3031	1¢ American Kestrel	11/19/99	.20	.20	.25	(4)	1.50	120
	Perf. 11							
3032	2¢ Red-Headed Woodpecker	02/02/96	.20	.20	.25	(4)	1.25	311
3033	3¢ Eastern Bluebird	04/03/96	.20	.20	.25	(4)	1.25	317
	Self-Adhesive, Serpentine Die-Cut 11.5 x 11.25							
3036	$1 Red Fox	08/14/98	2.00	.50	8.00	(4)	3.50	
	Self-Adhesive, Serpentine Die-Cut 11.75 x 11							
3036a	$1 Red Fox	2002	2.00	.50	8.00	(4)		
	Coil Stamps, Perf. 9.75 Vertically							
3044	1¢ American Kestrel	01/20/96	.20	.20	.60	(5)	1.25	
a	Large date		.20	.20	.85	(5)		
3045	2¢ Red-Headed Woodpecker	06/22/99	.20	.20	.80	(5)	1.25	100
	Booklet Stamps, Self-Adhesive, Serpentine Die-Cut 10.4 x 10.8 on 3 sides							
3048	20¢ Blue Jay	08/02/96	.40	.20			1.25	491
a	Booklet pane of 10		4.00					
b	Booklet pane of 4		1.60					
c	Booklet pane of 6		2.40					
	Serpentine Die-Cut 11.3 x 11.7 on 2, 3 or 4 sides							
3049	32¢ Yellow Rose	10/24/96	.60	.20			1.25	2,900
a	Booklet pane of 20 and label		12.00					
b	Booklet pane of 4	12/96	2.75					
c	Booklet pane of 5	12/96	3.20					
d	Booklet pane of 6	12/96	3.60					
	Serpentine Die-Cut 11.2 on 2 or 3 sides							
3050	20¢ Ring-neck Pheasant	07/31/98	.40	.20			1.25	
a	Booklet pane of 10		4.00					
	Serpentine Die-Cut 10.5 x 11 on 3 sides							
3051	20¢ Ring-neck Pheasant	07/99	.60	.20				634
a	Serpentine Die-Cut 10.5 on 3 Sides		3.75	.50				
b	Booklet pane of 5, 4 #3051, 1 #3051a turned sideways at top		6.00					
c	Booklet pane of 5, 4 #3051, 1 #3051a turned sideways at bottom		6.00					

	Issues of 1996-2000		Un	U	PB	#	FDC	Q(M)
	Serpentine Die-Cut 11.5 x 11.25 on 2, 3 or 4 sides							
3052	33¢ Coral Pink Rose	08/13/99	.80	.20			1.25	1,000
a	Booklet pane of 4		3.20					
b	Booklet pane of 5 + label		4.00					
c	Booklet pane of 6		4.80					
d	Booklet pane of 20		13.00					
	Serpentine Die Cut 10.75 x 10.5 on 2 or 3 Sides							
3052E	33¢ Coral Pink Rose	04/07/00	.65	.20			1.25	
f	Booklet pane of 20		13.00					
	Coil Stamps, Serpentine Die-Cut 11.5 Vertically							
3053	20¢ Blue Jay	08/02/96	.40	.20	3.25	(5)	1.25	330
	Coil Stamps, Self-Adhesive, Serpentine Die-Cut 9.75 Vertically							
3054	32¢ Yellow Rose	08/01/97	.60	.20	5.25	(5)	1.25	
a	Imperf., pair		90.00					
3055	20¢ Ring-necked Pheasant	07/31/98	.40	.20	3.50	(5)	1.25	
a	Imperf., pair		200.00					
	Black Heritage Issue, Perf. 11.1							
3058	32¢ Ernest E. Just	02/01/96	.60	.20	2.40	(4)	1.75	92
	Perf. 11.1							
3059	32¢ Smithsonian Institution	02/07/96	.60	.20	2.40	(4)	1.25	115
	Lunar New Year Issue							
3060	32¢ Year of the Rat	02/08/96	.60	.20	3.00	(4)	1.50	93
	Pioneers of Communication Issue, Perf. 11.1 x 11							
3061	32¢ Eadweard Muybridge	02/22/96	.60	.20			1.25	96
3062	32¢ Ottmar Mergenthaler	02/22/96	.60	.20			1.25	96
3063	32¢ Frederic E. Ives	02/22/96	.60	.20			1.25	96
3064	32¢ William Dickson	02/22/96	.60	.20			1.25	96
a	Block or strip of 4, #3061-3064		2.40	2.00	2.40	(4)	2.50	
	Perf. 11.1							
3065	32¢ Fulbright Scholarships	02/28/96	.60	.20	3.00	(4)	1.25	130
	Pioneers of Aviation Issue, Perf. 11.1							
3066	50¢ Jacqueline Cochran	03/09/96	1.00	.20	5.00	(4)	1.40	314
a	Black omitted		60.00					
3067	32¢ Marathon	04/11/96	.60	.20	2.40	(4)	1.75	209

3052

3058

3059

3060

3063

3064

3061

3062

3064a

3065

3066

3067

Atlanta 1996
CENTENNIAL OLYMPIC GAMES

CLASSIC
COLLECTIONS

32
x 20
$6.40

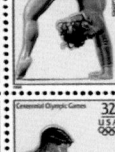

PLATE
POSITION

© 1996
United
States
Postal
Service

3068	a	b	c	d	e
	f	g	h	i	j
	k	l	m	n	o
	p	q	r	s	t

3069

3070

3072	3073	3074	3075	3076	3076a

Issues of 1996		Un	U	PB	#	FDC	Q(M)
Summer Olympic Games Issue, Perf. 10.1							
3068 Pane of 20	05/02/96	12.00	—			13.00	324
a	32¢ Decathlon	.60	.20			1.25	
b	32¢ Canoeing	.60	.20			1.25	
c	32¢ Women's running	.60	.20			1.25	
d	32¢ Women's diving	.60	.20			1.25	
e	32¢ Cycling	.60	.20			1.25	
f	32¢ Freestyle wrestling	.60	.20			1.25	
g	32¢ Women's gymnastic	.60	.20			1.25	
h	32¢ Women's sailboarding	.60	.20			1.25	
i	32¢ Shot put	.60	.20			1.25	
j	32¢ Women's soccer	.60	.20			1.25	
k	32¢ Beach volleyball	.60	.20			1.25	
l	32¢ Rowing	.60	.20			1.25	
m	32¢ Sprinting	.60	.20			1.25	
n	32¢ Women's swimming	.60	.20			1.25	
o	32¢ Women's softball	.60	.20			1.25	
p	32¢ Hurdles	.60	.20			1.25	
q	32¢ Swimming	.60	.20			1.25	
r	32¢ Gymnastics	.60	.20			1.25	
s	32¢ Equestrian	.60	.20			1.25	
t	32¢ Basketball	.60	.20			1.25	
Perf. 11.6 x 11.4							
3069 32¢ Georgia O'Keeffe	05/23/96	.65	.20	3.00	(4)	1.25	156
a	Imperf., pair	*175.00*					
Perf. 11.1							
3070 32¢ Tennessee Statehood	05/31/96	.60	.20	3.00	(4)	1.25	100
Self-Adhesive, Serpentine Die-Cut 9.9 x 10.8							
3071 32¢ Tennessee Statehood	05/31/96	.7 0	.30			1.25	60
a	Booklet pane of 20	14.00					
American Indian Dances Issue, Perf. 11.1							
3072 32¢ Fancy Dance	06/07/96	.60	.20			1.25	139
3073 32¢ Butterfly Dance	06/07/96	.60	.20			1.25	139
3074 32¢ Traditional Dance	06/07/96	.60	.20			1.25	139
3075 32¢ Raven Dance	06/07/96	.60	.20			1.25	139
3076 32¢ Hoop Dance	06/07/96	.60	.20			1.25	139
a	Strip of 5, #3072-3076	3.00	2.00	6.00	(10)	2.75	139

1996

	Issues of 1996		Un	U	PB	#	FDC	Q(M)
	Prehistoric Animals Issue, Perf. 11.1 x 11							
3077	32¢ Eohippus	06/08/96	.60	.20			1.50	150
3078	32¢ Woolly Mammoth	06/08/96	.60	.20			1.50	150
3079	32¢ Mastodon	06/08/96	.60	.20			1.50	150
3080	32¢ Saber-tooth Cat	06/08/96	.60	.20			1.50	150
a	Block or strip of 4, #3077-3080		2.40	1.50	2.40	(4)	2.75	150
	Pane of 20		12.00	—				
	Perf. 11.1							
3081	32¢ Breast Cancer Awareness	06/15/96	.60	.20	2.40	(4)	1.25	96
	Pane of 20		12.00	—				
	Legends of Hollywood Issue, Perf. 11.1							
3082	32¢ James Dean	06/24/96	.60	.20	3.00	(4)	1.75	300
	Pane of 20		15.00	—				
a	Imperf., pair		325.00					
	Folks Heroes Issue, Perf. 11.1 x 11							
3083	32¢ Mighty Casey	07/11/96	.60	.20			1.25	113
3084	32¢ Paul Bunyan	07/11/96	.60	.20			1.25	113
3085	32¢ John Henry	07/11/96	.60	.20			1.25	113
3086	32¢ Pecos Bill	07/11/96	.60	.20			1.25	113
a	Block or strip of 4, #3083-3086		2.40	2.00	2.40	(4)	2.75	
	Pane of 20		12.00	—				
	Centennial Olympic Games Issue, Perf. 11.1							
3087	32¢ Centennial Olympic Games	07/11/96	.65	.20	4.00	(4)	1.25	134
	Pane of 20		18.50	—				
3088	32¢ Iowa Statehood	08/01/96	.60	.20	3.00	(4)	1.25	103
	Booklet Stamp, Self-Adhesive, Serpentine Die-Cut 11.6 x 11.4							
3089	32¢ Iowa Statehood	08/01/96	.70	.30			1.25	60
a	Booklet pane of 20		14.00					
	Perf. 11.2 x 11							
3090	32¢ Rural Free Delivery	08/07/96	.60	.20	2.40	(4)	1.25	134

AMERICAN ★ COMMEMORATIVE ★ **COLLECTIBLES**

American Commemorative Collection

An easy and uniform way to collect and learn about commemorative issues.

Just mount the stamps on the specially designed sheet and place them in a three ring binder. Just $3.25* each, depending on the value of the stamps.

For more information call **1-800-STAMP-24**

*Prices subject to change without notice.

3077 Eohippus 32 USA

3078 Woolly mammoth 32 USA

3079 Mastodon 32 USA

3080 Saber-tooth cat 32 USA

3080a

Breast Cancer Awareness 32 USA

3081

JAMES DEAN USA 32

3082

3083

3086

MIGHTY CASEY 32 USA

PECOS BILL 32 USA

3085

3084

JOHN HENRY 32 USA

PAUL BUNYAN 32 USA

3086a

3087

1846 IOWA USA 32

3088

RURAL FREE DELIVERY RFD USA 32

3090

32 USA

3091

ROBT. E. LEE
1866 1876

32 USA

3092

SYLVAN DELL
1872 1919

32 USA

3093

FAR WEST
1870 1883

32 USA

3094

REBECCA EVERINGHAM
1880 1884

32 USA

3095

BAILEY GATZERT
1890 1923

3095a

3096   3097

32 USA
COUNT BASIE

32 USA
TOMMY & JIMMY DORSEY

32 USA
GLENN MILLER

32 USA
BENNY GOODMAN

3098   3099   3099a

3100

3101

3102

32 USA
HAROLD ARLEN

32 USA
JOHNNY MERCER

32 USA
DOROTHY FIELDS

32 USA
HOAGY CARMICHAEL

3103

3103a

F. SCOTT FITZGERALD
23 USA

3104

Issues of 1996		Un	U	PB	#	FDC	Q(M)
Riverboats Issue, Serpentine Die-Cut 11 x 11.1							
3091	32¢ Robert E. Lee 08/22/96	.60	.20			1.25	160
3092	32¢ Sylvan Dell 08/22/96	.60	.20			1.25	160
3093	32¢ Far West 08/22/96	.60	.20			1.25	160
3094	32¢ Rebecca Everingham 08/22/96	.60	.20			1.25	160
3095	32¢ Bailey Gatzert 08/22/96	.60	.20			1.25	160
a	Vertical strip of 5, #3091-3095	3.00		6.00	(10)	3.50	
b	Strip of 5, #3091-3095 with special die-cutting	75.00	50.00	140.00	(10)		
Legends of American Music Series, Big Band Leaders Issue, Perf. 11.1 x 11							
3096	32¢ Count Basie 09/11/96	.60	.20			1.25	92
3097	32¢ Tommy and Jimmy Dorsey 09/11/96	.60	.20			1.25	92
3098	32¢ Glenn Miller 09/11/96	.60	.20			1.25	92
3099	32¢ Benny Goodman 09/11/96	.60	.20			1.25	92
a	Block or strip of 4, #3096-3099	2.40	1.75	3.00	(4)	3.25	
Legends of American Music Series, Songwriters Issue							
3100	32¢ Harold Arlen 09/11/96	.70	.20			1.25	92
3101	32¢ Johnny Mercer 09/11/96	.70	.20			1.25	92
3102	32¢ Dorothy Fields 09/11/96	.70	.20			1.25	92
3103	32¢ Hoagy Carmichael 09/11/96	.70	.20			1.25	92
a	Block or strip of 4, #3100-3103	2.80	1.75	3.00	(4)	3.25	
Literary Arts Issue, Perf. 11.1							
3104	23¢ F. Scott Fitzgerald 09/11/96	.45	.20	2.25	(4)	1.25	300

ALFRED LUNT
(1892-1977)
LYNN FONTANNE
(1887-1983)

ALFRED LUNT and LYNN FONTANNE are considered by many to be the greatest husband-and-wife team in the history of the American stage. Remembered for their sophisticated humor, perfect timing, and remarkable versatility, they reigned on Broadway for nearly 40 years. Lunt, who was born in Milwaukee, Wisconsin, met the young English actress in 1919 in New York. The story goes that he was standing on an iron staircase, stepped forward to shake her hand, and fell on his face. Their incredible relationship began and in 1922 they were married.

In 1928, the couple made it a condition of their employment with the Theatre Guild that they act together in every production. They also required summers off so they could retreat to their Wisconsin estate, where they hosted the country's leading artists. Lunt and Fontanne won many honors and awards for their appearances together in 26 plays, 3 films, and 4 television programs. Their best known roles include the leads in *The Guardsman*, 1924; *Design for Living*, 1933; *The Taming of the Shrew*, 1935; and their final Broadway play, *The Visit*, 1958. ❑

1996

Issues of 1996			Un	U	PB	#	FDC	Q(M)
	Endangered Species Issue, Perf. 11.1 x 11							
3105	Pane of 15	10/02/96	9.00	—			7.50	224
a	32¢ Black-footed ferret		.60	.20			1.25	
b	32¢ Thick-billed parrot		.60	.20			1.25	
c	32¢ Hawaiian monk seal		.60	.20			1.25	
d	32¢ American crocodile		.60	.20			1.25	
e	32¢ Ocelot		.60	.20			1.25	
f	32¢ Schaus swallowtail butterfly		.60	.20			1.25	
g	32¢ Wyoming toad		.60	.20			1.25	
h	32¢ Brown pelican		.60	.20			1.25	
i	32¢ California condor		.60	.20			1.25	
j	32¢ Gilatrout		.60	.20			1.25	
k	32¢ San Francisco garter snake		.60	.20			1.25	
l	32¢ Woodland caribou		.60	.20			1.25	
m	32¢ Florida panther		.60	.20			1.25	
n	32¢ Piping plover		.60	.20			1.25	
o	32¢ Florida manatee		.60	.20			1.25	
	Perf. 10.9 x 11.1							
3106	32¢ Computer Technology	10/08/96	.60	.20	3.00	(4)	1.75	94
	Christmas Issue, Perf. 11.1 x 11.2							
3107	32¢ Madonna and Child							
	by Paolo de Matteis	10/08/96	.60	.20	3.00	(4)	1.25	848
	Perf. 11.3							
3108	32¢ Family at Fireplace	10/08/96	.60	.20			1.25	226
3109	32¢ Decorating Tree	10/08/96	.60	.20			1.25	226
3110	32¢ Dreaming of Santa Claus	10/08/96	.60	.20			1.25	226
3111	32¢ Holiday Shopping	10/08/96	.60	.20			1.25	226
a	Block or strip of 4, #3108-3111		2.40	1.75	3.00	(4)	2.75	
	Self-Adhesive Booklet Stamps, Serpentine Die-Cut 10 on 2, 3 or 4 sides							
3112	32¢ Madonna and Child							
	by Paolo de Matteis	10/08/96	.60	.20			1.25	244
a	Booklet pane of 20 + label		12.00					
b	No die-cutting, pair		70.00					
	Serpentine Die-Cut 11.8 x 11.5 on 2, 3 or 4 sides							
3113	32¢ Family at Fireplace	10/08/96	.60	.20			1.25	1,805
3114	32¢ Decorating Tree	10/08/96	.60	.20			1.25	1,805
3115	32¢ Dreaming of Santa Claus	10/08/96	.60	.20			1.25	1,805
3116	32¢ Holiday Shopping	10/08/96	.60	.20			1.25	1,805
a	Booklet pane, 5 ea #3113-3116		12.00				3.25	
	Die-Cut							
3117	32¢ Skaters	10/08/96	.60	.20			1.25	495
a	Booklet pane of 18		11.00					
	Self-Adhesive, Serpentine Die-Cut 11.1							
3118	32¢ Hanukkah	10/22/96	.60	.20	2.40	(4)	1.75	104
	Cycling Issue, Perf. 11 x 11.1							
3119	32¢ Souvenir sheet of 2	11/01/96	2.00	2.00			3.25	
a	50¢ orange		1.00	1.00			1.75	
b	50¢ blue and green		1.00	1.00			1.75	

Endangered Species

National Stamp Collecting Month 1996 highlights these 15 species to promote awareness of endangered wildlife. Each generation must work to protect the delicate balance of nature, so that future generations may share a sound and healthy planet.

a b c

d e f

g h i

j k l

m n o

3106

3107

3108   3111

3109   3110 3111a

3117

3118

3119a   3119b

3120

3121

3122

3123

3124

3125

3126

3127

3130

3131

3132

3133

3134

3135

	Issues of 1997		Un	U	PB	#	FDC	Q(M)
	Lunar New Year Issue, Perf. 11.2							
3120	32¢ Year of the Ox	01/05/97	.60	.20	2.40	(4)	1.50	106
	Black Heritage Issue, Serpentine Die-Cut 11.4							
3121	32¢ Brig. Gen. Benjamin							
	O. Davis Sr.	01/28/97	.60	.20	2.40	(4)	1.75	112
	Self-Adhesive Booklet Stamps, Serpentine Die-Cut 11 on 2, 3 or 4 sides							
3122	32¢ Statue of Liberty,							
	Type of 1994	02/01/97	.60	.20			1.25	2,855
a	Booklet panel of 20 + label		12.00					
b	Booklet pane of 4		2.50					
c	Booklet pane of 5 + label		3.20					
d	Booklet pane of 6		3.60					
	Self-Adhesive, Serpentine Die-Cut 11.5 x 11.8 on 2, 3 or 4 sides							
3122E	32¢ Statue of Liberty		1.10	.20				
f	Booklet pane of 20 + label		35.00					
g	Booklet pane of 6		7.00					
	Self-Adhesive, Serpentine Die-Cut 11.8 x 11.6 on 2, 3 or 4 sides							
3123	32¢ Love Swans	02/04/97	.60	.20			1.25	1,660
a	Booklet pane of 20 + label		12.00					
b	No die-cutting, pair		*175.00*					
	Serpentine Die-Cut 11.6 x 11.8 on 2, 3 or 4 sides							
3124	55¢ Love Swans	02/04/97	1.00	.20			1.50	814
a	Booklet pane of 20 + label		21.00					
	Self-Adhesive, Serpentine Die-Cut 11.6 x 11.7							
3125	32¢ Helping Children Learn	02/18/97	.60	.20	2.40	(4)	1.25	122
	Merian Botanical Print Issues, Self-Adhesive,							
	Serpentine Die-Cut 10.9 x 10.2 on 2, 3 or 4 sides							
3126	32¢ Citron, Roth, Larvae,							
	Pupa, Beetle	03/03/97	.60	.20			1.25	2,048
3127	32¢ Flowering Pineapple,							
	Cockroaches	03/03/97	.60	.20			1.25	2,048
a	Booklet pane, 10 each #3126-3127 + label		12.00					
b	Pair, #3126-3127		1.20					
	Serpentine Die-Cut 11.2 x 10.8 on 2 or 3 sides							
3128	32¢ Citron, Roth, Larvae,							
	Pupa, Beetle	03/03/97	1.25	.20			1.25	30
b	Booklet pane, 2 each #3128-3129		7.50					
3129	32¢ Flowering Pineapple,							
	Cockroaches	03/03/97	1.00	.20			1.25	30
b	Booklet pane of 5,							
	2 each #3128-29, 1 #3129a		6.00					
c	Pair, #3128-3129		2.25					
	Pacific 97 Issues, Perf. 11.2							
3130	32¢ Sailing Ship	03/13/97	.60	.20			1.25	130
3131	32¢ Stagecoach	03/13/97	.60	.20			1.25	130
a	Pair #3130-31		1.25	.60	2.50	(4)	1.75	
	Coil Stamps, Self-Adhesive, Imperf.							
3132	25¢ Juke Box	03/14/97	.60	.50	5.00	(5)	1.25	24
	Coil Stamps, Serpentine Die-Cut 9.9 Vertically							
3133	32¢ Flag Over Porch	03/14/97	.60	.20	6.50	(5)	1.25	1
	Literary Arts Issue, Perf. 11.1							
3134	32¢ Thornton Wilder	04/17/97	.60	.20	2.40	(4)	1.25	98
3135	32¢ Raoul Wallenberg	04/24/97	.60	.20	2.40	(4)	2.00	96

Issues of 1997		Un	U	FDC	Q(M)
The World of Dinosaurs Issue, Perf. 11 x 11.1					
3136	Sheet of 15 05/01/97	9.00	—	7.50	219
a	32¢ Ceratosaurus	.60	.20	1.25	
b	32¢ Camptosaurus	.60	.20	1.25	
c	32¢ Camarasaurus	.60	.20	1.25	
d	32¢ Brachiosaurus	.60	.20	1.25	
e	32¢ Goniopholis	.60	.20	1.25	
f	32¢ Stegosaurus	.60	.20	1.25	
g	32¢ Allosaurus	.60	.20	1.25	
h	32¢ Opisthias	.60	.20	1.25	
i	32¢ Edmontonia	.60	.20	1.25	
j	32¢ Einiosaurus	.60	.20	1.25	
k	32¢ Daspletosaurus	.60	.20	1.25	
l	32¢ Palaeosaniwa	.60	.20	1.25	
m	32¢ Corythosaurus	.60	.20	1.25	
n	32¢ Ornithominus	.60	.20	1.25	
o	32¢ Parasaurolophus	.60	.20	1.25	
Looney Tunes Issue, Self-Adhesive, Serpentine Die-Cut 11					
3137	Bugs Bunny Pane of 10 05/22/97	6.00			265
a	32¢ single	.60	.20	1.75	
b	Booklet pane of 9	5.40			
c	Booklet pane of 1	.60			
	Die-cutting on #3137b does not extend through the backing paper.				
3138	Pane of 10 05/22/97	*125.00*			
a	32¢ single	*2.00*			
b	Booklet pane of 9	—			
c	Booklet pane of 1, imperf.	—			
	Die-cutting on #3138b extends through the backing paper.				

GEORGE M. COHAN

(1878-1942)

Give my regards to old Broadway
And say that I'll be there 'ere long.
Lyrics such as these were just one of the brilliant components that made GEORGE M. COHAN America's first superstar and the best-known theater man in the nation. A successful songwriter, playwright, dancer, actor, stage director, and producer, he began his show business career as the youngest member of his family's song-and-dance vaudeville act, The Four Cohans. He "managed" the family act to great success while simultaneously acting and writing plays and songs. In 1904 Cohan and Samuel Henry Harris formed a partnership that produced countless successful Broadway musicals, including *Little Johnny Jones* with

its hit song, "Give My Regards To Broadway." Ambitious and talented, Cohan continued to act and play starring roles on Broadway. In 1917 he wrote the most popular World War I song, "Over There." The life of this dynamo of stage and screen was memorialized in 1942 in the smash hit, *Yankee Doodle Dandy*, in which James Cagney portrayed Cohan and won the Academy Award for Best Actor. The Postal Service honored Cohan in 1978 in the Performing Arts series. ❑

3136 a b c d f g

e h

i j k m n o

l

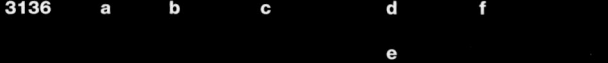

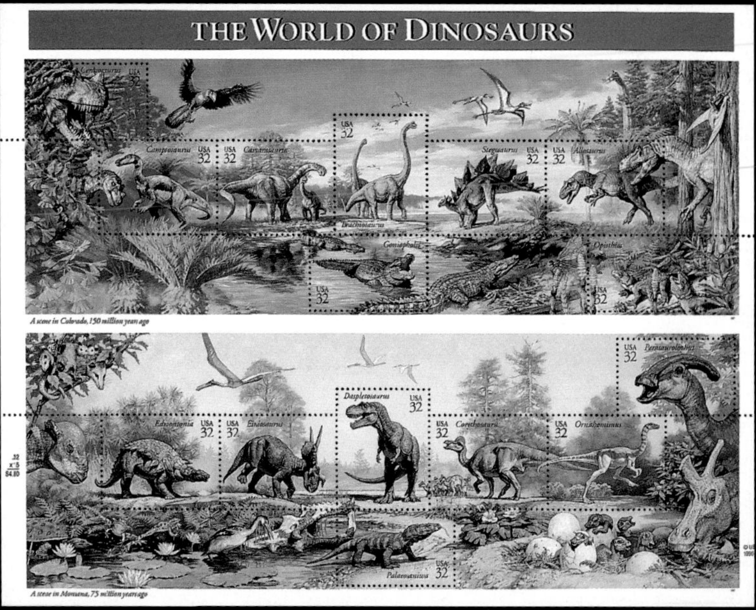

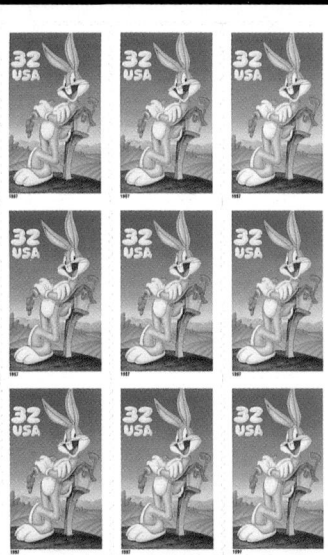

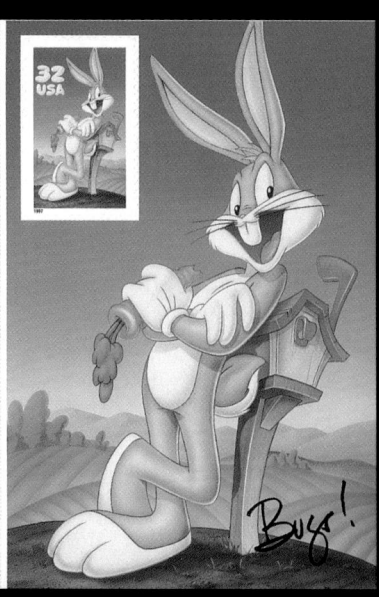

3137

3139

3140

3141

Issues of 1997		Un	U	PB	#	FDC	Q(M)
Pacific 97 Issues, Perf. 10.5 x 10.4							
3139 Benjamin Franklin Pane of 12	05/29/97	12.00	—			12.00	56
a 50¢ single		1.00	.50			2.00	
3140 George Washington Pane of 12	05/30/97	14.50	—			12.00	56
a 60¢ single		1.20	.60			2.00	
The Marshall Plan, 50th Anniversary Issue, Perf. 11.1							
3141 32¢ The Marshall Plan	06/04/97	.60	.20	2.40	(4)	1.25	45

AMERICAN ★ COMMEMORATIVE ★ **COLLECTIBLES**

Acquire all of your stamp collectibles! It's easy and affordable.

Choose any or all of the official U.S. Postal Service American Commemorative Collectibles to enhance your collection.

American Commemorative Collection

An easy and uniform way to collect and learn about commemorative issues. Just mount the stamps on the specially designed sheet and place them in a three ring binder. Just $3.25* each, depending on the value of the stamps.

American Commemorative Cancellations

Get first day cancellations and stamp(s) that have been affixed to colorful, specially tinted sheets to enhance your display. About $2.00* each, depending on the value of the stamps.

First Day of Issue Ceremony Programs

Receive detailed information about each first day of issue ceremony held for all new stamps and stationery issuances. Collect these valuable programs for only $4.95 each.

American Commemorative Panels

Obtain photo or steel engravings, mint condition stamps and subject related text presented on a beautifully designed page. Only $6.00* each, depending on the value of the stamps.

For information call **1-800-STAMP-24**

*Prices subject to change without notice.

Issues of 1997			Un	U	PB	#	FDC	Q(M)
Classic American Aircraft Issue, Perf. 10.1								
3142	Pane of 20	07/19/97	12.00	—			10.00	161
a	32¢ Mustang		.60	.20			1.25	
b	32¢ Model B		.60	.20			1.25	
c	32¢ Cub		.60	.20			1.25	
d	32¢ Vega		.60	.20			1.25	
e	32¢ Alpha		.60	.20			1.25	
f	32¢ B-10		.60	.20			1.25	
g	32¢ Corsair		.60	.20			1.25	
h	32¢ Stratojet		.60	.20			1.25	
i	32¢ Gee Bee		.60	.20			1.25	
j	32¢ Staggerwing		.60	.20			1.25	
k	32¢ Flying Fortress		.60	.20			1.25	
l	32¢ Stearman		.60	.20			1.25	
m	32¢ Constellation		.60	.20			1.25	
n	32¢ Lightning		.60	.20			1.25	
o	32¢ Peashooter		.60	.20			1.25	
p	32¢ Tri-Motor		.60	.20			1.25	
q	32¢ DC-3		.60	.20			1.25	
r	32¢ 314 Clipper		.60	.20			1.25	
s	32¢ Jenny		.60	.20			1.25	
t	32¢ Wildcat		.60	.20			1.25	
Legendary Football Coaches Issue, Perf. 11.2								
3143	32¢ Bear Bryant	07/25/97	.60	.20			1.50	90
3144	32¢ Pop Warner	07/25/97	.60	.20			1.50	90
3145	32¢ Vince Lombardi	07/25/97	.60	.20			1.50	90
3146	32¢ George Halas	07/25/97	.60	.20			1.50	90
a	Block or strip of 4, #3143-3146		2.40	—	2.40	(4)	2.50	

LYNDHURST

AJ Davis 1803-1892 Lyndhurst Tarrytown NY
Architecture USA 15c

LYNDHURST—one of America's finest Gothic Revival mansions—overlooks the Hudson River at Tarrytown, New York. Architect Alexander Jackson Davis designed the grand home in 1838 for former New York mayor William Paulding. Completed in 1842, the design was criticized because the turrets and asymmetrical shape were a departure from most buildings in the post-colonial period. In 1865 Davis doubled the size of the mansion for its new owner, George Merritt, who called the estate "Lyndenhurst" for the property's many linden trees.

In 1880, railroad magnate Jay Gould bought the estate for his country retreat. He died in 1892 but Lyndhurst, as it was now called, remained in his family until 1961 when his daughter, Anna, Duchess of Talleyrand-Perigord, died and passed the estate to the National Trust for Historic Preservation. The 19th-century landscape design features wide, curved lawns, accent trees and shrubs, evergreens planted to repeat the angular Gothic roofline, and a curving driveway with views that surprise visitors approaching the house. ❑

CLASSIC
AMERICAN AIRCRAFT

CLASSIC
COLLECTION

| Mustang | Model B | Cub | Vega |
| 32 USA | 32 USA | 32 USA | 32 USA |

32
x 20
$6.40

| Alpha | B-10 | Corsair | Stratojet |
| 32 USA | 32 USA | 32 USA | 32 USA |

| Gee Bee | Staggerwing | Flying Fortress | Stearman |
| 32 USA | 32 USA | 32 USA | 32 USA |

| Constellation | Lightning | Peashooter | Tri-Motor |
| 32 USA | 32 USA | 32 USA | 32 USA |

PLATE POSITION
S 1 1 1 1

| DC-3 | 314 Clipper | Jenny | Wildcat |
| 32 USA | 32 USA | 32 USA | 32 USA |

© 1996
United
States
Postal
Service

3142   a   b   c   d

e   f   g   h

i   j   k   l

m   n   o   p

q   r   s   t

LEGENDARY
Football Coaches

3145   3146   3143   3144   3146a

1997

3147

3148

3149

3150

CLASSIC

American Dolls

32
x15
$4.80

© 1996 U

PLATE
POSITION

P 11111

"Alabama Baby" and Martha Chase   "The Columbian Doll"   Johnny Gruelle's "Raggedy Ann"   Martha Chase   "American Child"
"Baby Coos"   Plains Indian   Izannah Walker   "Babyland Flag"   "Scootles"
Ludwig Greiner   "Betsy McCall"   Percy Crosby's "Skippy"   "Maggie Mix-up"   Albert Schoenhut

The above names include doll makers, designers, trade names and common names.

3151   **a**   **b**   **c**   **d**   **e**

Issues of 1997			Un	U	PB	#	FDC	Q(M)
Legendary Football Coaches Issue, Perf. 11								
3147	32¢ Vince Lombardi	08/05/97	.60	.30	3.00	(4)	1.50	20
3148	32¢ Bear Bryant	08/07/97	.60	.30	3.00	(4)	1.50	20
3149	32¢ Pop Warner	08/08/97	.60	.30	3.00	(4)	1.50	10
3150	32¢ George Halas	08/16/97	.60	.30	3.00	(4)	1.50	10
Classic American Dolls Issue, Perf. 10.9 x 11.1								
3151	Pane of 15	07/28/97	12.50	—			8.00	105
a	32¢ "Alabama Baby," and doll by Martha Chase		.80	.20			1.25	
b	32¢ "Columbian Doll"		.80	.20			1.25	
c	32¢ Johnny Gruelle's "Raggedy Ann"		.80	.20			1.25	
d	32¢ Doll by Martha Chase		.80	.20			1.25	
e	32¢ "American Child"		.80	.20			1.25	
f	32¢ "Baby Coos"		.80	.20			1.25	
g	32¢ Plains Indian		.80	.20			1.25	
h	32¢ Doll by Izannah Walker		.80	.20			1.25	
i	32¢ "Babyland Rag"		.80	.20			1.25	
j	32¢ "Scootles"		.80	.20			1.25	
k	32¢ Doll by Ludwig Greiner		.80	.20			1.25	
l	32¢ "Betsy McCall"		.80	.20			1.25	
m	32¢ Percy Crosby's "Skippy"		.80	.20			1.25	
n	32¢ "Maggie Mix-up"		.80	.20			1.25	
o	32¢ Dolls by Albert Schoenhut		.80	.20			1.25	

MARY CASSATT

(1844-1926)

American artist MARY STEVENSON CASSATT was born in Pittsburgh, Pennsylvania. She attended the Pennsylvania Academy of Fine Arts in Philadelphia and continued her studies in Europe, settling permanently in Paris in the mid-1870s. At the invitation of her friend and mentor Edgar Degas, Cassatt exhibited her works with those of the revolutionary French painters known as the Impressionists. She was the only American artist ever invited to exhibit with this group. Her first major solo exhibition in the United States—a critical and commercial success—was held in New York City in 1895. By the end of the 19th century she was recognized in both France and the United States as a preeminent artist. Cassatt's brilliant paintings, pastels, prints, and etchings portray children engaging in various pastimes and

contemporary women pursuing everyday activities such as entertaining visitors, reading, and caring for children. Four of her works are featured in the third issuance in the American Treasures series, which showcases beautiful works of American fine art and crafts. ❑

Issues of 1997		Un	U	PB	#	FDC	Q(M)
Legends of Hollywood Issue, Perf. 11.1							
3152	32¢ Humphrey Bogart	07/31/97	.60	.20	2.50	(4)	1.50	195
3153	32¢ "The Stars and Stripes Forever"	08/21/97	.60	.20	3.00	(4)	1.25	323
Legends of American Music Series, Opera Singers Issue, Perf. 11							
3154	32¢ Lily Pons	09/10/97	.65	.20			1.25	86
3155	32¢ Richard Tucker	09/10/97	.65	.20			1.25	86
3156	32¢ Lawrence Tibbett	09/10/97	.65	.20			1.25	86
3157	32¢ Rosa Ponselle	09/10/97	.65	.20			1.25	86
a	Block or strip of 4, #3154-3157		2.60	1.75	2.60	(4)	2.75	

THE BARRYMORES

Three members of the theatrical Barrymore family were honored by the Postal Service in 1982 with a stamp in the Performing Arts series. Lionel, Ethel, and John Barrymore were the children of actors Herbert Blythe—whose stage name was Maurice Barrymore—and Georgianna Drew, who herself came from a family of actors. LIONEL BARRYMORE (1878-1954)—the oldest of the three siblings—worked principally in movies, winning an Academy Award in 1931 for his role in *A Free Soul*. He wrote a book about the family, *We Barrymores*, and annually recreated the role of Scrooge in radio broadcasts of Dickens's *A Christmas Carol*. Often called the "First Lady of the American Theater," ETHEL BARRYMORE (1879-1959) preferred the stage to movies. Nevertheless, in 1944, she won an Academy Award for Best Actress for her role in *None but the Lonely Heart*. JOHN BARRYMORE (1882-1942), a film and stage actor, is perhaps best known for his acclaimed portrayal of the title character in Shakespeare's *Hamlet*. A silent film star, he made a successful transition to "talking pictures." Major films include *Dr. Jekyll and Mr. Hyde* and *Dinner at Eight*. The family tradition continues into the 21st century with his granddaughter, actress Drew Barrymore. ❏

3153

3152

3154

3155

3156

3157

3157a

LILY PONS

RICHARD TUCKER

LAWRENCE TIBBETT

ROSA PONSELLE

AMERICAN ★ COMMEMORATIVE ★ **COLLECTIBLES**

First Day of Issue Ceremony Programs

Receive detailed information about each first day of issue ceremony held for all new stamps and stationery issuances.

Collect these valuable programs
for only $4.95* each.

For more information
call **1-800-STAMP-24**

*Unless the stamp value
exceeds $4.95 then the price
is determined by the actual
value of the stamps.

3158 3159 3160 3161

LEOPOLD STOKOWSKI | ARTHUR FIEDLER | GEORGE SZELL | EUGENE ORMANDY

SAMUEL BARBER | FERDE GROFE | CHARLES IVES | LOUIS MOREAU GOTTSCHALK

3162 3163 3164 3165 3165a

3166 3167

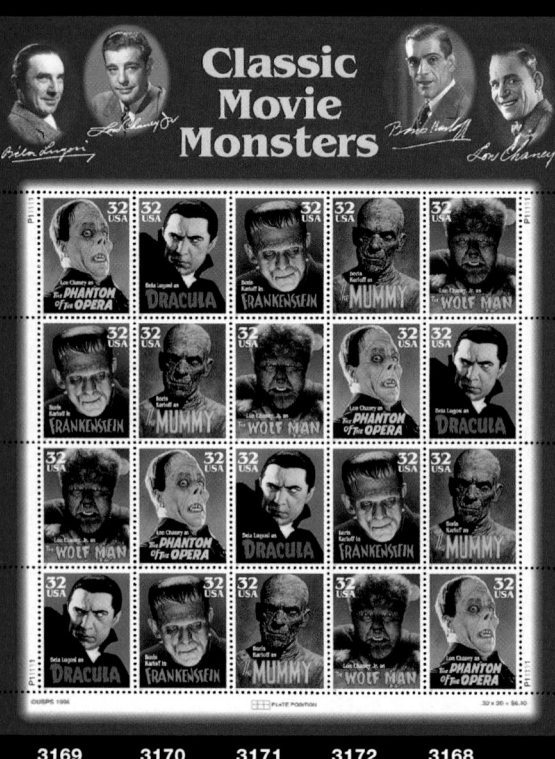

3169 3170 3171 3172 3168

Issues of 1997		Un	U	PB	#	FDC	Q(M)
Legends of American Music Series, Classical Composers & Conductors Issue, Perf. 11							
3158	32¢ Leopold Stokowski	09/12/97	.65	.20			1.25	86
3159	32¢ Arthur Fiedler	09/12/97	.65	.20			1.25	86
3160	32¢ George Szell	09/12/97	.65	.20			1.25	86
3161	32¢ Eugene Ormandy	09/12/97	.65	.20			1.25	86
3162	32¢ Samuel Barber	09/12/97	.65	.20			1.25	86
3163	32¢ Ferde Grofé	09/12/97	.65	.20			1.25	86
3164	32¢ Charles Ives	09/12/97	.65	.20			1.25	86
3165	32¢ Louis Moreau Gottschalk	09/12/97	.65	.20			1.25	86
a	Block of 8, #3158-3165		5.25	4.00	8.00	(8)	5.25	
	Perf. 11.2							
3166	32¢ Padre Félix Varela	09/15/97	.60	.20	2.40	(4)	1.25	2,855
Department of the Air Force, 50th Anniversary Issue, Perf. 11.2 x 11.1							
3167	32¢ Thunderbirds Aerial Demonstration Squadron	09/18/97	.60	.20	2.40	(4)	1.50	45
Classic Movie Monsters Issue, Perf. 10.2							
3168	32¢ Lon Chaney as the Phantom of the Opera	09/30/97	.60	.20			1.50	145
3169	32¢ Bela Lugosi as Dracula	09/30/97	.60	.20			1.50	145
3170	32¢ Boris Karloff as Frankenstein's Monster	09/30/97	.60	.20			1.50	145
3171	32¢ Boris Karloff as the Mummy	09/30/97	.60	.20			1.50	145
3172	32¢ Lon Chaney, Jr. as the Wolf Man	09/30/97	.60	.20			1.50	145
a	Strip of 5, #3168-3172		3.00	2.25	6.00	(10)	3.75	

Beginning with No. 3167, a hidden 3-D design can be seen on some stamps when they are viewed with a special viewer sold by the post office.

THE PALACE OF FINE ARTS

Bernard Maybeck 1862-1957 Palace of Arts San Francisco
Architecture USA 18c

In 1915, San Francisco hosted the Panama-Pacific International Exposition to celebrate the discovery of the Pacific Ocean and the building of the Panama Canal. One of many exhibition halls built expressly for the exposition, the PALACE OF FINE ARTS was designed and built to display the work of living artists, principally Impressionists. Architect Bernard R. Maybeck planned a romantic overgrown Roman ruin with a colonnade and a rotunda, reflected in a nearby lagoon. Although built as a temporary building, when the exposition closed the Palace continued to be used for art exhibits. In 1934, there began a series of odd uses—indoor tennis courts, a storage garage for Army vehicles during World War II, a phone book distribution center, and a temporary Fire Department headquarters—that turned the "Roman ruin" into a genuine ruin. Rebuilt as a permanent structure, since September 1969 the Palace of Fine Arts continues to be a popular venue for concerts, lectures, film festivals, dance events, and weddings; it also houses a hands-on science museum known as The Exploratorium. ❑

Issues of 1997-1998		Un	U	PB	#	FDC	Q(M)
Self-Adhesive, Serpentine Die-Cut 11.4							
3173	32¢ First Supersonic Flight, 50th Anniversary 10/14/97	.60	.20	2.40	(4)	1.50	173
Perf. 11.1							
3174	32¢ Women in Military Service 10/18/97	.60	.20	2.40	(4)	1.50	
Self-Adhesive, Serpentine Die-Cut 11							
3175	32¢ Kwanzaa 10/22/97	.60	.20	3.00	(4)	1.75	133
Holiday Traditional Issue, Self-Adhesive Booklet Stamps, Serpentine Die-Cut 9.9 on 2, 3 or 4 sides							
3176	32¢ Madonna and Child by Sano di Pietro 10/09/97	.60	.20			1.25	883
a	Booklet pane of 20 + label	12.00					
Holiday Contemporary Issue, Self-Adhesive Booklet Stamps, Serpentine Die-Cut 11.2 x 11.8 on 2, 3 or 4 sides							
3177	32¢ American Holly 10/30/97	.60	.20			1.25	180
a	Booklet pane of 20 + label	12.00					
b	Booklet pane of 4	2.50					
c	Booklet pane of 5 + label	3.00					
d	Booklet pane of 6	3.75					
Mars Pathfinder, Perf. 11 x 11.1							
3178	$3 Mars Rover Sojourner 12/10/97	6.00	3.00			7.50	15
a	$3, single stamp	5.50	2.75				
Lunar New Year Issue, Perf. 11.2							
3179	32¢ Year of the Tiger 01/05/98	.60	.20	3.00	(4)	1.50	
Winter Sports Issue, Perf. 11.2							
3180	32¢ Winter Sports-Skiing 1/2/98	.60	.20	2.40	(4)	1.25	80
Black Heritage Issue, Self-Adhesive, Serpentine Die-Cut 11.6 x 11.3							
3181	32¢ Madam C. J. Walker 1/28/98	.60	.20	2.40	(4)	1.75	45

AMERICAN ★ COMMEMORATIVE ★ COLLECTIBLES

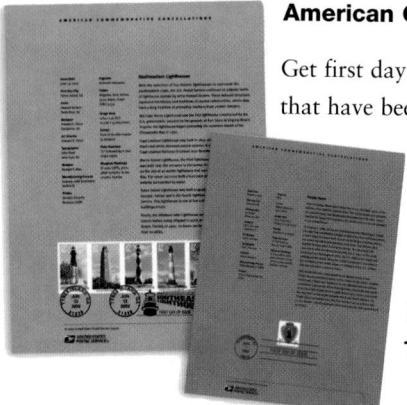

American Commemorative Cancellations

Get first day cancellations and stamp(s) that have been affixed to colorful sheets featuring technical and historical information about the stamps. About $2.50* each, depending on the value of the stamps.

For information call
1-800-STAMP-24

*Prices subject to change without notice.

3173

3174

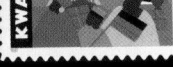

3175

3176

3177

3178

3179

3180

3181

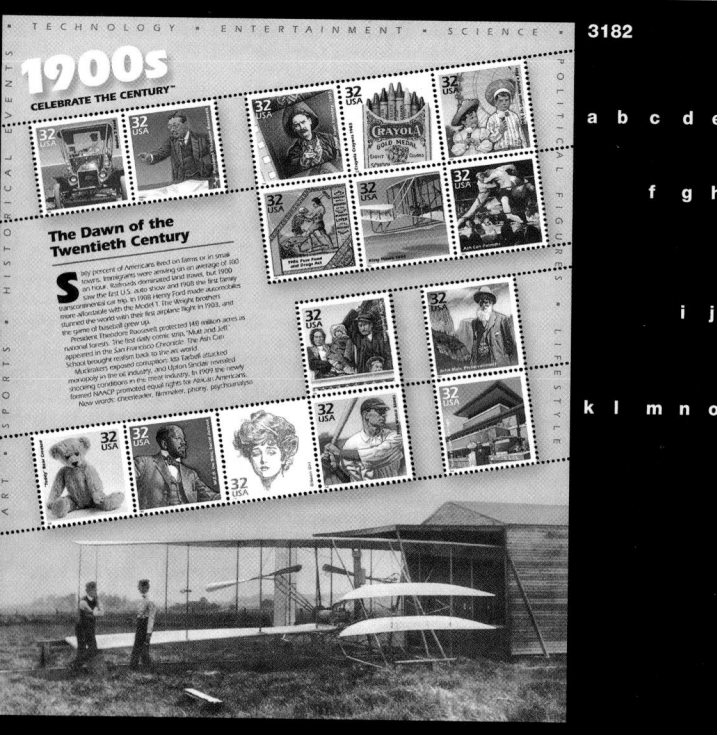

3182

a b c d e

f g h

i j

k l m n o

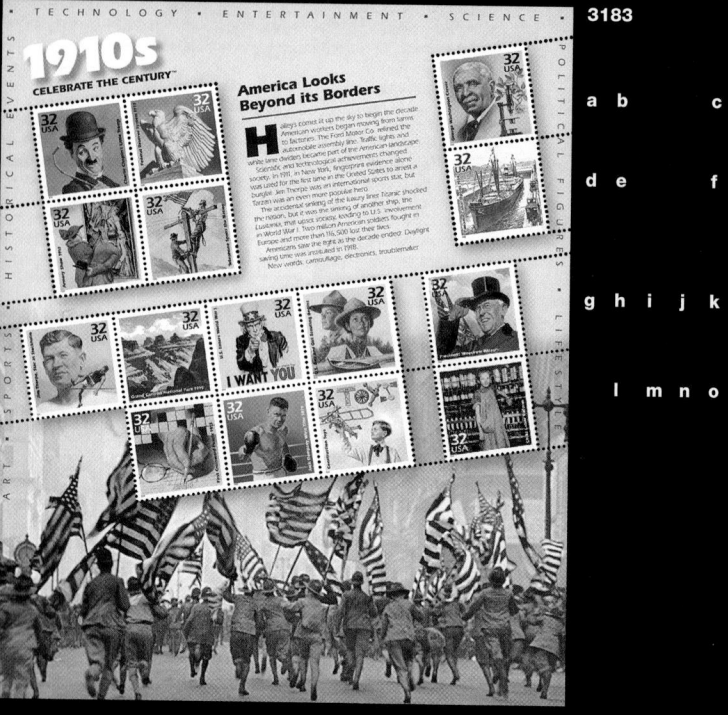

3183

a b c

d e f

g h i j k

l m n o

Issues of 1998			Un	U	PB	#	FDC	Q(M)
Celebrate The Century® Issue, Perf. 11.5								
3182	Pane of 15, 1900-1909	2/3/98	9.00	—			8.50	188
a	32¢ Model T Ford		.60	.30			1.50	
b	32¢ Theodore Roosevelt		.60	.30			1.50	
c	32¢ Motion picture, "The Great Train Robbery"		.60	.30			1.50	
d	32¢ Crayola Crayons introduced, 1903		.60	.30			1.50	
e	32¢ St. Louis World's Fair, 1904		.60	.30			1.50	
f	32¢ Design used on Hunt's Remedy stamp (#RS56), Pure Food & Drug Act, 1906		.60	.30			1.50	
g	32¢ Wright Brothers first flight, Kitty Hawk, 1903		.60	.30			1.50	
h	32¢ Boxing match shown in painting "Stag at Sharkey's," by George Bellows of the Ash Can School		.60	.30			1.50	
i	32¢ Immigrants arrive		.60	.30			1.50	
j	32¢ John Muir, preservationist		.60	.30			1.50	
k	32¢ "Teddy" Bear created		.60	.30			1.50	
l	32¢ W.E.B. Du Bois, social activist		.60	.30			1.50	
m	32¢ Gibson Girl		.60	.30			1.50	
n	32¢ First baseball World Series, 1903		.60	.30			1.50	
o	32¢ Robie House, Chicago, designed by Frank Lloyd Wright		.60	.30			1.50	
Celebrate The Century® Issue, Perf. 11.5								
3183	Pane of 15, 1910-1919	02/03/98	9.00	—			8.50	188
a	32¢ Charlie Chaplin as the Little Tramp		.60	.30			1.50	
b	32¢ Federal Reserve System created, 1913		.60	.30			1.50	
c	32¢ George Washington Carver		.60	.30			1.50	
d	32¢ Avant-garde art introduced at Armory Show, 1913		.60	.30			1.50	
e	32¢ First transcontinental telephone line, 1914		.60	.30			1.50	
f	32¢ Panama Canal opens, 1914		.60	.30			1.50	
g	32¢ Jim Thorpe wins decathlon at Stockholm Olympics, 1912		.60	.30			1.50	
h	32¢ Grand Canyon National Park, 1919		.60	.30			1.50	
i	32¢ U.S. enters World War I		.60	.30			1.50	
j	32¢ Boy Scouts started in 1910, Girl Scouts formed in 1912		.60	.30			1.50	
k	32¢ Woodrow Wilson		.60	.30			1.50	
l	32¢ First crossword puzzle published, 1913		.60	.30			1.50	
m	32¢ Jack Dempsey wins heavyweight title, 1919		.60	.30			1.50	
n	32¢ Construction toys		.60	.30			1.50	
o	32¢ Child labor reform		.60	.30			1.50	

Issues of 1998		Un	U	FDC	Q(M)
Celebrate The Century® Issue, Perf. 11.5					
3184 Pane of 15, 1920-1929	05/28/98	9.00	—	8.50	188
a	32¢ Babe Ruth	.60	.30	1.50	
b	32¢ The Gatsby style	.60	.30	1.50	
c	32¢ Prohibition enforced	.60	.30	1.50	
d	32¢ Electric toy trains	.60	.30	1.50	
e	32¢ Nineteenth Amendment (woman voting)	.60	.30	1.50	
f	32¢ Emily Post's Etiquette	.60	.30	1.50	
g	32¢ Margaret Mead, anthropologist	.60	.30	1.50	
h	32¢ Flappers do the Charleston	.60	.30	1.50	
i	32¢ Radio entertains America	.60	.30	1.50	
j	32¢ Art Deco style (Chrysler Building)	.60	.30	1.50	
k	32¢ Jazz flourishes	.60	.30	1.50	
l	32¢ Four Horsemen of Notre Dame	.60	.30	1.50	
m	32¢ Lindbergh flies the Atlantic	.60	.30	1.50	
n	32¢ American realism (The Automat, by Edward Hopper)	.60	.30	1.50	
o	32¢ Stock Market crash, 1929	.60	.30	1.50	
Celebrate The Century Issue®, Perf. 11.5					
3185 Pane of 15, 1930-1939	09/10/98	9.00	—	8.50	188
a	32¢ Franklin D. Roosevelt	.60	.30	1.50	
b	32¢ The Empire State Building	.60	.30	1.50	
c	32¢ First Issue of Life Magazine, 1936	.60	.30	1.50	
d	32¢ Eleanor Roosevelt	.60	.30	1.50	
e	32¢ FDR's New Deal	.60	.30	1.50	
f	32¢ Superman arrives, 1938	.60	.30	1.50	
g	32¢ Household conveniences	.60	.30	1.50	
h	32¢ "Snow White and the Seven Dwarfs," 1937	.60	.30	1.50	
i	32¢ "Gone with the Wind," 1936	.60	.30	1.50	
j	32¢ Jesse Owens	.60	.30	1.50	
k	32¢ Streamline design	.60	.30	1.50	
l	32¢ Golden Gate Bridge	.60	.30	1.50	
m	32¢ America survives the Depression	.60	.30	1.50	
n	32¢ Bobby Jones wins golf Grand Slam, 1938	.60	.30	1.50	
o	32¢ The Monopoly Game	.60	.30	1.50	

VISIT US ONLINE AT **THE POSTAL STORE**

AT **WWW.USPS.COM**

OR CALL **1-800-STAMP-24**

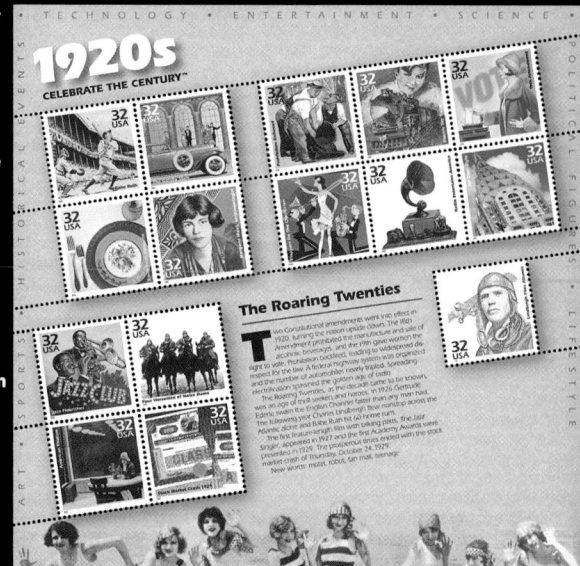

3184

TECHNOLOGY • ENTERTAINMENT • SCIENCE
POLITICAL FIGURES • LIFESTYLE
ART • SPORTS • HISTORICAL EVENTS
1920s
CELEBRATE THE CENTURY™
The Roaring Twenties
Two Constitutional amendments went into effect in 1920, turning the nation upside down. The 18th Amendment prohibited the manufacture and sale of alcoholic beverages, and the 19th gave women the right to vote. Prohibition backfired, leading to widespread disrespect for the law. A federal highway system was organized and the number of automobiles nearly tripled. Spreading electrification spawned the golden age of radio.
The Roaring Twenties, as the decade came to be known, was an age of thrill seekers and heroes. In 1926 Gertrude Ederle swam the English Channel faster than any man had. The following year Charles Lindbergh flew nonstop across the Atlantic alone and Babe Ruth hit 60 home runs.
The first feature-length film with talking parts, The Jazz Singer, appeared in 1927 and the first Academy Awards were presented in 1929. The prosperous times ended with the stock market crash of Thursday, October 24, 1929.
New words: motel, robot, fan mail, teenage
JAZZ CLUB
Stock Market Crash 1929

b c d e

g h i j

l m

o

3185

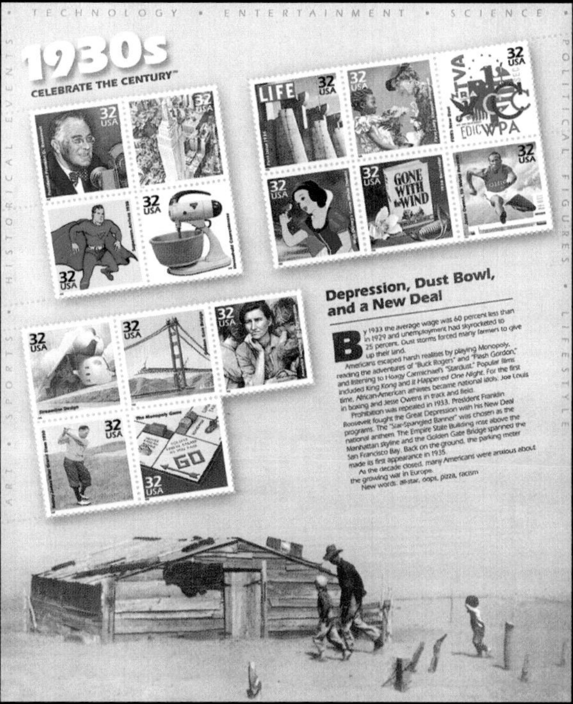
TECHNOLOGY • ENTERTAINMENT • SCIENCE
POLITICAL FIGURES • LIFESTYLE
ART • SPORTS • HISTORICAL EVENTS
1930s
CELEBRATE THE CENTURY™
LIFE
GONE WITH the WIND
WPA
Depression, Dust Bowl, and a New Deal
By 1933 the average wage was 60 percent less than in 1929 and unemployment had skyrocketed to 25 percent. Dust storms forced many farmers to give up their land.
Americans escaped harsh realities by playing Monopoly, reading the adventures of "Buck Rogers" and "Flash Gordon," and listening to Hoagy Carmichael's "Stardust." Popular films included King Kong and It Happened One Night. For the first time, African-American athletes became national idols: Joe Louis in boxing and Jesse Owens in track and field.
Prohibition was repealed in 1933. President Franklin Roosevelt fought the Great Depression with his New Deal programs. The "Star-Spangled Banner" was chosen as the national anthem. The Empire State Building rose above the Manhattan skyline and the Golden Gate Bridge spanned the San Francisco Bay. Back on the ground, the parking meter made its first appearance in 1935.
As the decade closed, many Americans were anxious about the growing war in Europe.
New words: all-star, oops, pizza, racism
GO

b c d e

g h i j

l m

o

3186

a b c

d e f

g h i j k

l m n o

3187

a b c d e

f g h

i j

k l m n o

Issues of 1999		Un	U	FDC	Q(M)
Celebrate The Century®, Perf. 11.5					
3186	Pane of 15, 1940-1949 02/18/99	9.75	—	8.50	12.5
a	33¢ World War II	.65	.30	1.50	
b	33¢ Antibiotics save lives	.65	.30	1.50	
c	33¢ Jackie Robinson	.65	.30	1.50	
d	33¢ Harry S. Truman	.65	.30	1.50	
e	33¢ Women support war effort	.65	.30	1.50	
f	33¢ TV entertains America	.65	.30	1.50	
g	33¢ Jitterbug sweeps nation	.65	.30	1.50	
h	33¢ Jackson Pollock, Abstract Expressionism	.65	.30	1.50	
i	33¢ GI Bill, 1944	.65	.30	1.50	
j	33¢ The Big Band Sound	.65	.30	1.50	
k	33¢ International style of architecture	.65	.30	1.50	
l	33¢ Postwar baby boom	.65	.30	1.50	
m	33¢ Slinky, 1945	.65	.30	1.50	
n	33¢ "A Streetcar Named Desire", 1947	.65	.30	1.50	
o	33¢ Orson Welles' "Citizen Kane"	.65	.30	1.50	
Celebrate The Century®, Perf. 11.5					
3187	Pane of 15, 1950-1959 05/26/99	9.75	—	8.50	12.5
a	33¢ Polio vaccine developed	.65	.30	1.50	
b	33¢ Teen fashions	.65	.30	1.50	
c	33¢ The "Shot Heard 'Round the World"	.65	.30	1.50	
d	33¢ U.S. launches satellites	.65	.30	1.50	
e	33¢ Korean War	.65	.30	1.50	
f	33¢ Desegregating public schools	.65	.30	1.50	
g	33¢ Tail fins, chrome	.65	.30	1.50	
h	33¢ Dr. Seuss' "The Cat in the Hat"	.65	.30	1.50	
i	33¢ Drive-in movies	.65	.30	1.50	
j	33¢ World Series rivals	.65	.30	1.50	
k	33¢ Rocky Marciano, undefeated boxer	.65	.30	1.50	
l	33¢ "I Love Lucy"	.65	.30	1.50	
m	33¢ Rock 'n Roll	.65	.30	1.50	
n	33¢ Stock car racing	.65	.30	1.50	
o	33¢ Movies go 3-D	.65	.30	1.50	

AMERICAN ★ COMMEMORATIVE ★ COLLECTIBLES

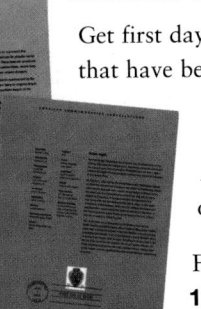

American Commemorative Cancellations

Get first day cancellations and stamp(s) that have been affixed to colorful sheets featuring technical and historical information about the stamps. About $2.50* each, depending on the value of the stamps.

For information call
1-800-STAMP-24

*Prices subject to change without notice.

1999

Issues of 1999			Un	U	FDC	Q(M)
Celebrate The Century®, Perf. 11.5						
3188	Pane of 15, 1960-1969	09/17/99	9.75	—	8.50	8
a	33¢ "I have a dream"		.65	.30	1.50	
b	33¢ Woodstock		.65	.30	1.50	
c	33¢ Man walks on the moon		.65	.30	1.50	
d	33¢ Green Bay Packers		.65	.30	1.50	
e	33¢ Star Trek		.65	.30	1.50	
f	33¢ The Peace Corps		.65	.30	1.50	
g	33¢ The Vietnam War		.65	.30	1.50	
h	33¢ Ford Mustang		.65	.30	1.50	
i	33¢ Barbie Doll		.65	.30	1.50	
j	33¢ The integrated circuit		.65	.30	1.50	
k	33¢ Lasers		.65	.30	1.50	
l	33¢ Super Bowl I		.65	.30	1.50	
m	33¢ Peace Symbol		.65	.30	1.50	
n	33¢ Roger Maris, 61 in '61		.65	.30	1.50	
o	33¢ The Beatles					
Celebrate The Century®, Perf. 11.5						
3189	Pane of 15, 1970-1979	11/18/99	9.75	—	8.50	6
a	33¢ Earth Day celebrated		.65	.30	1.50	
b	33¢ TV series "All in the Family"		.65	.30	1.50	
c	33¢ "Sesame Street"		.65	.30	1.50	
d	33¢ Disco music		.65	.30	1.50	
e	33¢ Steelers win four Super Bowls		.65	.30	1.50	
f	33¢ U.S. celebrates 200th birthday		.65	.30	1.50	
g	33¢ Secretariat wins the Triple Crown		.65	.30	1.50	
h	33¢ VCRs transform entertainment		.65	.30	1.50	
i	33¢ Pioneer 10		.65	.30	1.50	
j	33¢ Women's Rights Movement		.65	.30	1.50	
k	33¢ 1970s fashions		.65	.30	1.50	
l	33¢ "Monday Night Football"		.65	.30	1.50	
m	33¢ America smiles		.65	.30	1.50	
n	33¢ Jumbo jet		.65	.30	1.50	
o	33¢ Medical imaging		.65	.30	1.50	

American Commemorative Collections Binder

You'll find this binder is a great way to keep your panels and sheets in mint condition.

Item #880600–$21.95

USPS Binder and Pages

This elegant binder comes with a matching slipcase to keep your stamps safe.

Item #014002–$42.00

To order call **1-800-STAMP-24** or visit us online at **www.usps.com**

3188

a b c d e

f g h i j

k l m

n o

3189

a b c

d e f

g h i j k

l m n o

3190

a b c d e

f g h i j

k l m

n o

To order these new stamps and other related philatelic products call 1-800-STAMP-24 or visit us online at www.usps.com

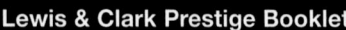

Lewis & Clark Prestige Booklet

This 32-page booklet commemorating the 200th anniversary of the Lewis and Clark expedition includes two stamp designs: individual portraits of Meriwether Lewis and William Clark.

Lewis & Clark Bicentennial Stamp

This stamp depicts expedition leaders Meriwether Lewis and William Clark surveying the countryside.

CTC Issues of 2000		Un	U	FDC	Q(M)
Celebrate The Century®, Perf. 11.6					
3190 Pane of 15, 1980-1989	01/12/00	9.75	—	8.50	6
a	33¢ Space Shuttle Program	.65	.30	1.50	
b	33¢ "Cats", Broadway show	.65	.30	1.50	
c	33¢ San Francisco 49ers	.65	.30	1.50	
d	33¢ Hostages Come Home	.65	.30	1.50	
e	33¢ Figure Skating	.65	.30	1.50	
f	33¢ Cable TV	.65	.30	1.50	
g	33¢ Vietnam Veterans Memorial	.65	.30	1.50	
h	33¢ Compact Discs	.65	.30	1.50	
i	33¢ Cabbage Patch Kids	.65	.30	1.50	
j	33¢ "The Cosby Show"	.65	.30	1.50	
k	33¢ Fall of the Berlin Wall	.65	.30	1.50	
l	33¢ Video Games	.65	.30	1.50	
m	33¢ "E.T. The Extra-Terrestrial"	.65	.30	1.50	
n	33¢ Personal Computers	.65	.30	1.50	
o	33¢ Hip-Hop Culture	.65	.30	1.50	

ELVIS PRESLEY

(1935-1977)

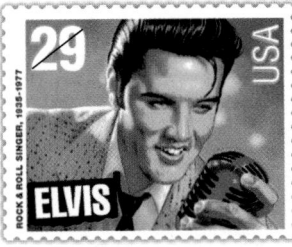

In 1993 the U.S. Postal Service launched the Legends of American Music series with the issuance of a stamp honoring ELVIS PRESLEY and featuring an image of the "King of Rock 'n' Roll" that had been chosen by the American public. The majority of more than a million voters, given a choice between portraying the charismatic singer early or later in his career, chose the "younger" Elvis. In 1955 Presley, who was born in Mississippi and raised in Memphis, Tennessee, released his first record, "Heartbreak Hotel" and became a star. During the next 22 years, Presley released hit after hit, among them "Don't Be Cruel," "Love Me Tender," "All Shook Up," and "It's Now Or Never." With each new recording, he set or broke another sales record. Presley interrupted a successful singing and movie career to serve a tour with the U.S. Army in Germany. He returned to the U.S. in 1960 and recorded several more hits before the music of the Beatles and other British groups pushed him from his top spot. Presley made a comeback with a 1968 TV special and resumed touring and recording. His many fans continue to pay homage to him on visits to Graceland, his Memphis home. ❏

CTC Issues of 2000			Un	U	FDC	Q(M)
Celebrate The Century®, Perf. 11.6						
3191	Pane of 15, 1990-1999	05/02/00	9.75	—	8.50	5.5
a	33¢	New Baseball Records	.65	.30	1.50	
b	33¢	Gulf War	.65	.30	1.50	
c	33¢	"Seinfeld", television series	.65	.30	1.50	
d	33¢	Extreme Sports	.65	.30	1.50	
e	33¢	Improving Education	.65	.30	1.50	
f	33¢	Computer Art and Graphics	.65	.30	1.50	
g	33¢	Recovering Species	.65	.30	1.50	
h	33¢	Return to Space	.65	.30	1.50	
i	33¢	Special Olympics	.65	.30	1.50	
j	33¢	Virtual Reality	.65	.30	1.50	
k	33¢	"Jurassic Park"	.65	.30	1.50	
l	33¢	"Titanic"	.65	.30	1.50	
m	33¢	Sports Utility Vehicle	.65	.30	1.50	
n	33¢	World Wide Web	.65	.30	1.50	
o	33¢	Cellular Phones	.65	.30	1.50	

3191

a b c

d e f

g h i j k

l m n o

To order these new stamps and other related philatelic products
*call **1-800-STAMP-24** or visit us online at **www.usps.com***

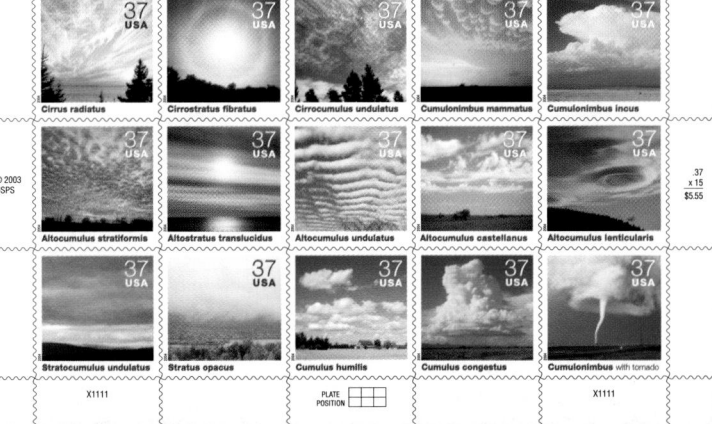

C L O U D S C A P E S

© 2003
USPS

Cirrus radiatus

Cirrostratus fibratus

Cirrocumulus undulatus

Cumulonimbus mammatus

Cumulonimbus incus

Altocumulus stratiformis

Altostratus translucidus

Altocumulus undulatus

Altocumulus castellanus

Altocumulus lenticularis

.37
x 15
$5.55

Stratocumulus undulatus

Stratus opacus

Cumulus humilis

Cumulus congestus

Cumulonimbus with tornado

X1111

PLATE
POSITION

X1111

3192

3193   3194   3195   3196   3197   3197a

 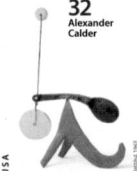 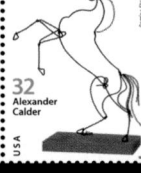 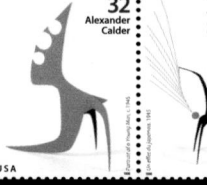

3198   3199   3200   3201   3202   3202a

3203

	Issues of 1998		Un	U	PB	#	FDC	Q(M)
	Perf. 11.2 x 11							
3192	32¢ "Remember the Maine"							
	Spanish-American War	02/15/98	.60	.20	2.40	(4)	1.75	30
	Flowering Trees Issue, Die-Cut, Perf. 11.3							
3193	32¢ Southern Magnolia	03/19/98	.60	.20			1.50	
3194	32¢ Blue Paloverde	03/19/98	.60	.20			1.50	
3195	32¢ Yellow Poplar	03/19/98	.60	.20			1.50	
3196	32¢ Prairie Crab Apple	03/19/98	.60	.20			1.50	
3197	32¢ Pacific Dogwood	03/19/98	.60	.20			1.50	
a	Strip of 5, #3193-3197	03/19/98	3.00		6.00	(10)	3.75	250
	Alexander Calder Issue, Perf. 10.2							
3198	32¢ Black Cascade	03/25/98	.60	.20			1.50	
3199	32¢ Untitled	03/25/98	.60	.20			1.50	
3200	32¢ Rearing Stallion	03/25/98	.60	.20			1.50	
3201	32¢ Portrait of a Young Man	03/25/98	.60	.20			1.50	
3202	32¢ Un Effet du Japonais	03/25/98	.60	.20			1.50	
a	Strip of 5, #3198-3202	03/25/98	3.00	2.25	6.00	(10)	3.75	80
	Holiday Celebrations Issue, Self-Adhesive, Serpentine Die-Cut 11.7 x 10.9							
3203	32¢ Cinco de Mayo	04/16/98	.60	.20	2.40	(4)	1.25	85
	Looney Tunes Issue, Self-Adhesive, Serpentine Die-Cut 11.1							
3204	Sylvester & Tweety Pane of 10	04/27/98	6.00					300
a	32¢ single		.60	.20			1.25	
b	Booklet pane of 9, #3204a		5.40					
c	Booklet pane of 1, #3204a		.60					

LOUIS ARMSTRONG

(1901-1971)

LOUIS ARMSTRONG, who became America's most popular jazz cornet and trumpet soloist, was born into poverty in New Orleans, Louisiana. As a child he learned to play an assortment of musical instruments. He joined a Chicago jazz band where his playing caught the attention of New York bandleader Fletcher Henderson, at the time acknowledged as having the best jazz band in the nation. Henderson hired Armstrong but it wasn't long before Armstrong, frustrated with a big band and short solos, returned to Chicago to form his own group, The Hot Five (sometimes The Hot Seven). In the early 1930s Armstrong made the first of many successful European tours with his band. His unique improvisational singing led to roles in films, on radio, and later on television. His raspy voice and ready smile, and his skill with the trumpet, helped "Satchmo" create classics such as "What A Wonderful World," "Mack the Knife," and "Hello, Dolly!" One of America's most famous jazz musicians, Armstrong and fellow jazz notables Coleman Hawkins, James P. Johnson, Jelly Roll Morton, Charlie Parker, Eubie Blake, Charles Mingus, Thelonious Monk, John Coltrane, and Erroll Garner were honored by the Postal Service in 1995 in the Legends of American Music series. ❏

	Issues of 1998		Un	U	PB	#	FDC	Q(M)
	Self-Adhesive, Serpentine Die-Cut 10.8 x 10.9							
3206	32¢ Wisconsin Statehood	05/29/98	.60	.30	2.40	(4)	1.25	16
	American Scenes Issue, Coil Stamps, Perf. 10 Vertically							
3207	5¢ Wetlands (Nonprofit)	06/05/98	.20	.20	1.50	(5)	1.25	
	Coil Stamps, Self-Adhesive, Serpentine Die-Cut 9.7 Vertically							
3207A	5¢ Wetlands (Nonprofit)	12/04/98	.20	.20	1.50	(5)	1.25	650
	American Culture Issue, Coil Stamps, Perf. 10 Vertically							
3208	25¢ Diner	06/05/98	.50	.50	3.75	(5)	1.25	400
	Coil Stamps, Self-Adhesive, Serpentine Die-Cut 9.8 Vertically							
3208A	25¢ Diner	09/30/98	.50	.50	4.00	(5)	1.25	
	1898 Trans-Mississippi Reissue, Perf. 12 x 12.4							
3209	Pane of 9	06/18/98	7.75	5.00			6.50	19.8
a	1¢ Marquette on the Mississippi		.20	.20			1.50	
b	2¢ Mississippi River Bridge		.20	.20			1.50	
c	4¢ Indian Hunting Buffalo		.20	.20			1.50	
d	5¢ Fremont on the Rocky Mountains		.20	.20			1.50	
e	8¢ Troops Guarding Train		.20	.20			1.50	
f	10¢ Hardships of Emigration		.20	.20			1.50	
g	50¢ Western Mining Prospector		1.00	.60			2.00	
h	$1 Western Cattle in Storm		2.00	1.25			2.50	
i	$2 Farm in the West		4.00	2.50			4.50	
3210	Pane of 9 #3209h, single	06/18/98	18.00	—			15.00	
	Perf. 11.2							
3211	32¢ Berlin Airlift	06/26/98	.60	.20	2.40	(4)	1.25	30

TRINITY CHURCH, BOSTON

Richardson 1838-1886 Trinity Church Boston
Architecture USA 15c

In June 1872 renowned American architect Henry Hobson Richardson (1838-1886) won a competition to design Trinity Church, Boston. The Louisiana-born Richardson had studied architecture at Harvard and at the Ecole des Beaux-Arts in Paris where he was only the second American to study. When he returned to the United States to work, Richardson initiated a revival of French Romanesque design that would be known as Richardsonian-Romanesque. The architect's personal interpretation of this style in Trinity's design combined weighty Romanesque forms with colorful building materials and a variety of surface textures. Considered by many architects as one of the ten greatest buildings in the nation, Trinity is noteworthy as well for its many art treasures such as stained-glass windows designed by American landscape painter John LaFarge—whose murals adorn the church's interior—and by English artists William Morris and Edward Burne-Jones. Serving as an apprentice on LaFarge's mural project was Augustus Saint-Gaudens, who would become one of the foremost American sculptors of the 19th century. Saint-Gaudens later carved the statue of Bishop Philips Brooks that stands outside Trinity's north transcept. ☐

3207A

3208A

3206

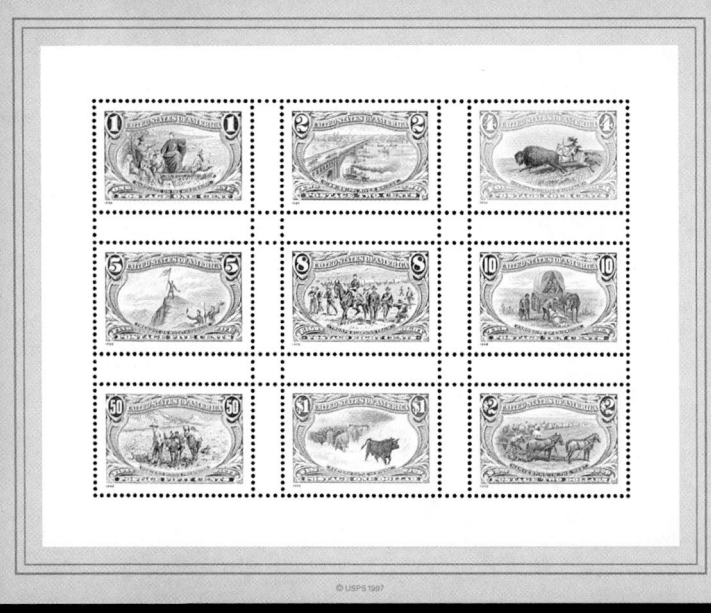

1998 Bi-Color Re-Issue of the 1898 Trans-Mississippi Stamp Designs

© USPS 1997

3209 a b c

d e f

g h i

3210

3211

3212 **3213**

3214 **3215** 3215a

3219 **3218**

3216 **3217** 3219a

3220 **3221**

3222 **3223**

3224 **3225** 3225a

Issues of 1998		Un	U	PB	#	FDC	Q(M)
Legends of American Music Series, Folk Musicians, Perf. 10.1 x 10.2							
3212	32¢ Huddle "Leadbelly"						
	Ledbetter	06/26/98	.60	.20			1.25	
3213	32¢ Woody Guthrie	06/26/98	.60	.20			1.25	
3214	32¢ Sonny Terry	06/26/98	.60	.20			1.25	
3215	32¢ Josh White	6/26/98	.60	.20			1.25	
a	Block or strip of 4, #3212-3215	06/26/98	2.50	2.00	2.50	(4)	3.25	45
Legends of American Music Series, Gospel Singers Issue, Perf. 10.1 x 10.3							
3216	32¢ Mahalia Jackson	07/15/98	.60	.20			1.25	
3217	32¢ Roberta Martin	07/15/98	.60	.20			1.25	
3218	32¢ Clara Ward	07/15/98	.60	.20			1.25	
3219	32¢ Sister Rosetta Tharpe	07/15/98	.60	.20			1.25	
a	Block or strip of 4, #3216-3219	07/15/98	2.40	2.00	3.00	(4)	3.25	45
Perf. 11.2							
3220	32¢ Spanish Settlement of						
	the Southwest	07/11/98	.60	.20	2.40	(4)	1.25	46
Literary Arts Series							
3221	32¢ Stephen Vincent Benét	07/22/98	.60	.20	2.40	(4)	1.25	
Tropical Birds Issue							
3222	32¢ Antillean Euphonia	07/29/98	.60	.20			1.25	
3223	32¢ Green-throated Carib	07/29/98	.60	.20			1.25	
3224	32¢ Crested Honeycreeper	07/29/98	.60	.20			1.25	
3225	32¢ Cardinal Honeyeater	07/29/98	.60	.20			1.25	
a	Block of 4, #3222-3225		2.40	2.00	2.40	(4)	3.00	70

GERTRUDE KÄSEBIER

(1852-1934)

Eminent portrait photographer GERTRUDE KÄSEBIER began taking pictures of her family in the late 1880s. In her late thirties and the mother of three children, she enrolled in art classes at the Pratt Institute. Turning from painting to photography, in 1897 she opened a highly successful portrait studio in New York. She pioneered an evocative soft-focus style that established her as a guiding force in the pictorialist movement. Käsebier's successful exhibits at the Philadelphia Salons, turn-of-the-century's prestigious juried shows, brought her worldwide fame. Among her best-known works are those depicting motherhood. In 1907 she wrote, "…I have longed unceasingly to make pictures of people and to make likenesses that are biographies, to bring out in each photograph the essential personality." In 2002 Käsebier was honored along with 19 other important and influential American photographers in the Postal Service issuance, Masters of American Photography. *Blessed Art Thou Among Women*—a sensitive and artistic portrayal of author Agnes Rand Lee and her daughter Peggy made in 1899—is featured on Käsebier's stamp. ❑

Gertrude Käsebier 1852-1934

	Issues of 1998		Un	U	PB	#	FDC	Q(M)
	Legends of Hollywood Issue, Perf. 11.1							
3226	32¢ Alfred Hitchcock	08/03/98	.60	.20	3.00	(4)	1.50	65
	Self-Adhesive, Serpentine Die-Cut 11.7							
3227	32¢ Organ & Tissue Donation	08/05/98	.60	.20	2.40	(4)	1.25	25
	Coil Stamp, Self-Adhesive, Serpentine Die-Cut 9.8 Vertically							
3228	(10¢) Green Bicycle	08/14/98	.20	.20	2.75	(5)	1.25	
	Coil Stamp, Perf. 9.9 Vertically							
3229	(10¢) Green Bicycle	08/14/98	.20	.20	2.50	(5)	1.25	
	Bright Eyes Issue, Self-Adhesive, Serpentine Die-Cut 9.9							
3230	32¢ Dog	08/20/98	.60	.20			1.50	
3231	32¢ Goldfish	08/20/98	.60	.20			1.50	
3232	32¢ Cat	08/20/98	.60	.20			1.50	
3233	32¢ Parakeet	08/20/98	.60	.20			1.50	
3234	32¢ Hamster	08/20/98	.60	.20			1.50	
a	Strip of 5, #3230-3234	08/20/98	3.00		6.00	(8)	3.25	180
	Perf. 11.1							
3235	32¢ Klondike Gold Rush	08/21/98	.60	.20	2.40	(4)	1.50	28

Gift Collection for Kids

Give a youngster the thrill of stamp collecting with this fun, educational *Gift Collection for Kids!* This gift provides a child with colorful collectibles specially chosen to bring joy to all young collectors.

Prices subject to change without notice.

In your collection you will receive:

★ interesting and exciting stamps and stamp products

★ exclusive commemorative binder and acetate pages to keep your collection safe for years to come

★ official personalized membership certificate

★ stamp decoder to reveal hidden images on certain stamps

And throughout the year, kids have the excitement of receiving something in the mail just for them.

Your young friend will receive four shipments, each with stamps and stamp products in a variety of formats and the Cool-lecting newsletter.

Item #20122A–Gift Collection for Kids: Annual subscription $49.95

To order, call **1-800-STAMP-24**

3226

3227

3228

3230

3235

3231

3232

3233

3234

3234a

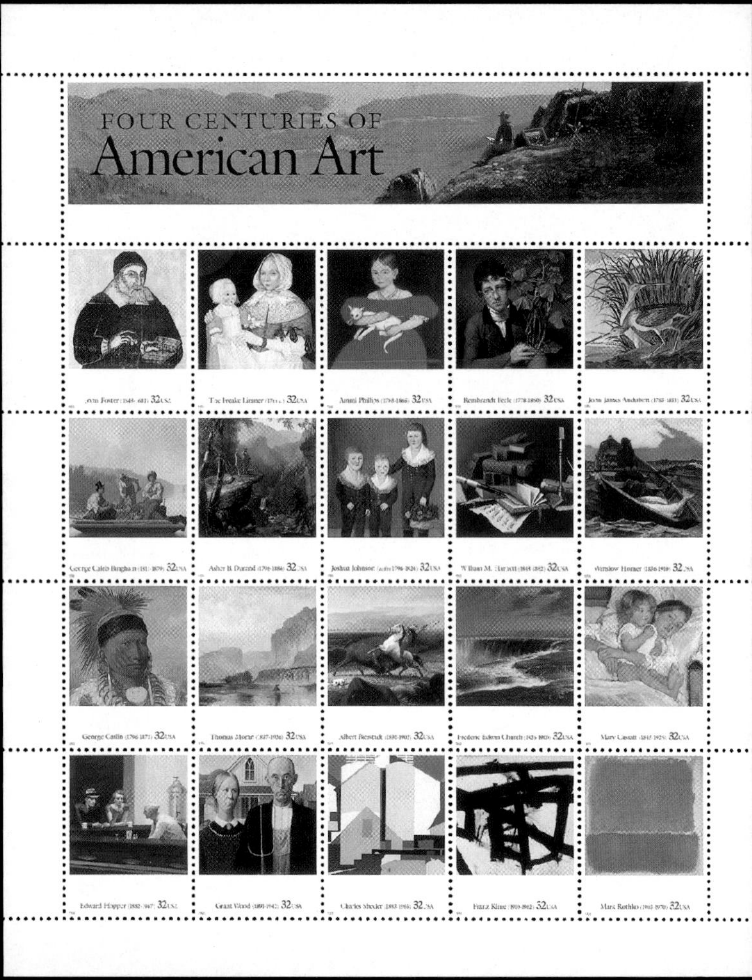
FOUR CENTURIES OF
American Art

3236 a b c d e

f g h i j

k l m n o

p q r s t

32
USA
BALLET

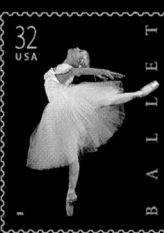

3237

Issues of 1998		Un	U	PB	#	FDC	Q(M)
Four Centuries of American Art Issue, Perf. 10.2							
3236	Pane of 20 08/27/98	12.00	—			9.00	80
a	32¢ "Portrait of Richard Mather," by John Foster	.60	.20			1.25	
b	32¢ "Mrs. Elizabeth Freake and Baby Mary," by The Freake Limner	.60	.20			1.25	
c	32¢ "Girl in Red Dress with Cat and Dog," by Ammi Phillips	.60	.20			1.25	
d	32¢ "Rubens Peale with a Geranium," by Rembrandt Peale	.60	.20			1.25	
e	32¢ "Long-billed Curlew, Numenius Longrostris," by John James Audubon	.60	.20			1.25	
f	32¢ "Boatmen on the Missouri," by George Caleb Bingham	.60	.20			1.25	
g	32¢ "Kindred Spirits," by Asher B. Durand	.60	.20			1.25	
h	32¢ "The Westwood Children," by Joshua Johnson	.60	.20			1.25	
i	32¢ "Music and Literature," by William Harnett	.60	.20			1.25	
j	32¢ "The Fog Warning," by Winslow Homer	.60	.20			1.25	
k	32¢ "The White Cloud, Head Chief of the Iowas," by George Catlin	.60	.20			1.25	
l	32¢ "Cliffs of Green River," by Thomas Moran	.60	.20			1.25	
m	32¢ "The Last of the Buffalo," by Alfred Bierstadt	.60	.20			1.25	
n	32¢ "Niagara," by Frederic Edwin Church	.60	.20			1.25	
o	32¢ "Breakfast in Bed," by Mary Cassatt	.60	.20			1.25	
p	32¢ "Nighthawks," by Edward Hopper	.60	.20			1.25	
q	32¢ "American Gothic," by Grant Wood	.60	.20			1.25	
r	32¢ "Two Against the White," by Charles Sheeler	.60	.20			1.25	
s	32¢ "Mahoning," by Franz Kline	.60	.20			1.25	
t	32¢ "No. 12" by Mark Rothko	.60	.20			1.25	
	Perf. 10.9 x 11.1						
3237	32¢ Ballet 09/16/98	.60	.20	2.40	(4)	1.25	130

Issues of 1998		Un	U	PB	#	FDC	Q(M)
Space Discovery Issue, Perf. 11.1							
3238 32¢ Multicolored	10/01/98	.60	.20			1.25	
3239 32¢ Multicolored	10/01/98	.60	.20			1.25	
3240 32¢ Multicolored	10/01/98	.60	.20			1.25	
3241 32¢ Multicolored	10/01/98	.60	.20			1.25	
3242 32¢ Multicolored	10/01/98	.60	.20			1.25	
a Strip of 5, #3238-3242		3.00	2.25	6.00	(10)	3.75	
Self-Adhesive, Serpentine Die-Cut 11.1							
3243 32¢ Philanthropy,							
Giving and Sharing	10/07/98	.60	.20	2.40	(4)	1.25	50
Holiday Traditional, Booklet Stamps, Self-Adhesive, Serpentine Die-Cut 10.1 x 9.9 on 2, 3 or 4 sides							
3244 32¢ The Madonna and Child							
by Hans Memling	10/15/98	.60	.20			1.25	925.2
a Booklet pane of 20 + label		12.00					
Holiday Contemporary, Booklet Stamps, Self-Adhesive, Serpentine Die-Cut 11.3 x 11.6 on 2 or 3 sides							
3245 32¢ Evergreen Wreath	10/15/98	2.25	.20			1.25	
3246 32¢ Victorian Wreath	10/15/98	2.25	.20			1.25	
3247 32¢ Chili Pepper Wreath	10/15/98	2.25	.20			1.25	
3248 32¢ Tropical Wreath	10/15/98	2.25	.20			1.25	
a Booklet pane of 4, #3245-3248		22.50				3.25	
b Booklet pane of 5, #3245, #3246,							
3248, 2 #3247 and label		27.50					
c Booklet pane of 6, #3247-3248,							
2 each #3245-3246		32.50					
Serpentine Die-Cut 11.4 x 11.6 on 2, 3 or 4 sides							
3249 32¢ Evergreen Wreath	10/15/98	.60	.20			1.25	
3250 32¢ Victorian Wreath	10/15/98	.60	.20			1.25	
3251 32¢ Chili Pepper Wreath	10/15/98	.60	.20			1.25	
3252 32¢ Tropical Wreath	10/15/98	.60	.20			1.25	
a Block of 4, #3249-3252		2.40		3.00	(4)	3.00	
b Booklet pane, 5 each #3249-3252		12.00					
Perf. 11.2							
3257 (1¢) Make-Up Rate Weathervane	11/09/98	.20	.20	.25	(4)	1.25	
3258 (1¢) Make-Up Rate Weathervane	11/09/98	.20	.20	.25	(4)	1.25	
#3257 is 18mm high, has thin letters, white USA, and black 1998.							
#3258 is 17mm high, has thick letters, pale blue USA, and blue 1998.							
Self-Adhesive, Serpentine Die-Cut 10.8							
3259 22¢ Uncle Sam	11/09/98	.45	.20	2.50	(4)	1.25	
Perf. 11.2							
3260 (33¢) H-Series	11/09/98	.65	.20	2.60	(4)	1.25	

3238   3239   3240   3241   3242 3242a

3243

3245

3246

3244   3247

3248

3248a

3258   3259   3260

VISIT US ONLINE AT **THE POSTAL STORE**

AT **WWW.USPS.COM**

OR CALL **1-800-STAMP-24**

3261

3262

B1

Issues of 1998		Un	U	PB	#	FDC	Q(M)
Self-Adhesive, Serpentine Die-Cut 11.5							
3261 $3.20 Space Shuttle Landing	11/09/98	6.00	3.00	24.00	(4)	5.00	245
Self-Adhesive, Serpentine Die-Cut 11.5							
3262 $11.75 Express Mail	11/19/98	22.50	11.50	90.00	(4)	25.00	21
Coil Stamps, Self-Adhesive, Serpentine Die-Cut 9.9 Vertically							
3263 22¢ Uncle Sam	11/09/98	.45	.20	3.50	(5)	1.25	
Perf. 9.8 Vertically							
3264 33¢ Unce Sam's Hat	11/09/98	.65	.20	5.00	(5)	1.25	
Self-Adhesive, Serpentine Die-Cut 9.9 Vertically							
3265 33¢ H-Series	11/09/98	.65	.20	5.50	(5)	1.25	
Serpentine Die-Cut 9.9 Vertically							
3266 33¢ Uncle Sam's Hat	11/09/98	.65	.20	5.00	(5)	1.50	
Booklet Stamps, Self-Adhesive, Serpentine Die-Cut 9.9 on 2 or 3 sides							
3267 33¢ H-Series	11/09/98	.65	.20			1.25	
a	Booklet pane of 10	6.50					
Serpentine Die-Cut 11.2 x 11.1 on 2, 3 or 4 sides							
3268 33¢ Uncle Sam's Hat	11/09/98	.65	.20			1.25	
a	Booklet pane of 10	6.50					
b	Serpentine die-cut II	.65	.20				
c	As "b", booklet pane of 20 + label	13.00					
Die-Cut 8 on 2, 3 or 4 sides							
3269 33¢ Uncle Sam's Hat	11/09/98	.65	.20			1.25	
a	Booklet pane of 18	12.00					
Coil Stamps, Perf. 9.8 Vertically							
3270 10¢ Eagle with Shield	12/14/98	.20	.20	2.75	(5)	1.25	
Self-Adhesive, Serpentine Die-Cut 9.9 Vertically							
3271 10¢ Eagle with Shield	12/14/98	.20	.20	2.75	(5)	1.25	
a	Large date	.20	.20	3.25	(5)		
b	Tagged (error)	1.25	1.10	10.50	(5)		
Semi-postal Stamp, Self-Adhesive, Serpentine Die-Cut 11							
B1 (32¢ + 8¢) Breast Cancer							
Research	07/29/98	.80	.25	3.25	(4)		618

Issues of 1999			Un	U	PB	#	FDC	Q(M)
	Lunar New Year Issue, Perf. 11.2							
3272	33¢ Year of the Rabbit	01/05/99	.65	.20	2.60	(4)	1.50	51
	Black Heritage Issue, Self-Adhesive, Serpentine Die-Cut 11.4							
3273	33¢ Malcolm X	01/20/99	.65	.20	2.60	(4)	1.75	100
	Booklet Stamp, Self-Adhesive, Die-Cut							
3274	33¢ Love	01/28/99	.65	.20			1.25	1,500
a	Booklet pane of 20		13.00					
3275	55¢ Love	01/20/99	1.10	.20	4.40	(4)	1.50	300
	Serpentine Die-Cut 11.4							
3276	33¢ Hospice Care	02/09/99	.65	.20	2.80	(4)	1.25	100
	Perf. 11.2							
3277	33¢ City Flag	02/25/99	.65	.20	25.00	(4)	1.25	200
	Self-Adhesive, Serpentine Die-Cut 11 on 2, 3 or 4 sides							
3278	33¢ City Flag	02/25/99	.65	.20	4.00	(4)	1.25	
a	Booklet pane of 4		2.60					
b	Booklet pane of 5 + label		3.25					
c	Booklet pane of 6		3.90					
d	Booklet pane of 10		6.50					
e	Booklet pane of 20 + label		13.00					
	Booklet Stamps, Serpentine Die-Cut 11.5 x 11.75 on 2, 3 or 4 sides							
3278F	33¢ City Flag		.65	.20				
g	Booklet pane of 20 + label		13.00					
	Self-Adhesive, Serpentine Die-Cut 9.8 on 2 or 3 sides							
3279	33¢ City Flag	02/25/99	.65	.20			1.25	
a	Booklet pane of 10		6.50					
	Coil Stamps, Perf. 9.9 Vertically							
3280	33¢ City Flag	02/25/99	.65	.20	5.00	(5)	1.25	
	Self-Adhesive, Serpentine Die-Cut 9.8 Vertically							
3281	33¢ City Flag	02/25/99	.65	.20	5.00	(5)	1.25	
3282	33¢ City Flag	02/25/99	.65	.20	5.00	(5)	1.25	
	Rounded corners.							
	Booklet Stamp, Self-Adhesive, Serpentine Die-Cut 7.9 on 2, 3 or 4 sides							
3283	33¢ Flag and Chalkboard	03/13/99	.65	.20			1.25	306
a	Booklet pane of 18		12.00					
	Perf. 11.2							
3286	33¢ Irish Immigration	02/26/99	.65	.20	2.60	(4)	1.50	40.4
3287	33¢ Alfred Lunt & Lynn Fontanne	03/02/99	.65	.20	2.60	(4)	1.25	42.5

3272

3273

3274

3275

3276

3277

3278

3279

3280

3286

3287

3288 3289 3290 3291 3292 3292a

Issues of 1999		Un	U	PB	#	FDC	Q(M)
Arctic Animals Issue, Perf. 11							
3288	33¢ Arctic Hare	03/12/99	.65	.20			1.25	15.3
3289	33¢ Arctic Fox	03/12/99	.65	.20			1.25	15.3
3290	33¢ Snowy Owl	03/12/99	.65	.20			1.25	15.3
3291	33¢ Polar Bear	03/12/99	.65	.20			1.25	15.3
3292	33¢ Gray Wolf	03/12/99	.65	.20			1.25	15.3
a	Strip of 5, #3288-3292		3.25				3.25	

Gift Collection for Kids

Give a youngster the thrill of stamp collecting with this fun, educational **Gift Collection for Kids!**

*Prices subject to change without notice.

This gift provides a child with colorful collectibles specially chosen to bring joy to all young collectors.

In your collection you will receive:

★ interesting and exciting stamps and stamp products

★ exclusive commemorative binder and acetate pages to keep your collection safe for years to come

★ official personalized membership certificate

★ stamp decoder to reveal hidden images on certain stamps

And throughout the year, kids have the excitement of receiving something in the mail just for them.

Your young friend will receive four shipments, each with stamps and stamp products in a variety of formats and the Cool-lecting newsletter.

Item #20122A–Gift Collection for Kids: Annual subscription $49.95

To order, call **1-800-STAMP-24**

1999-2000

	Issues of 1999-2000		Un	U	PB	#	FDC	Q(M
Sonoran Desert Issue, Self-Adhesive, Serpentine Die-Cut Perf. 11.2								
3293	Pane of 10	04/06/99	6.50				6.75	10.3
a	33¢ Cactus Wren, brittlebush,							
	teddy bear cholla		.65	.20			1.25	
b	33¢ Desert tortoise		.65	.20			1.25	
c	33¢ White-winged dove		.65	.20			1.25	
d	33¢ Gambel quail		.65	.20			1.25	
e	33¢ Saguaro cactus		.65	.20			1.25	
f	33¢ Desert mule deer		.65	.20			1.25	
g	33¢ Desert cottontail, hedgehog cactus		.65	.20			1.25	
h	33¢ Gila monster		.65	.20			1.25	
i	33¢ Western diamondback rattlesnake,							
	cactus mouse		.65	.20			1.25	
j	33¢ Gila woodpecker		.65	.20			1.25	
Fruit Berries Issue, Self-Adhesive, Serpentine Die-Cut 11.25 x 11.75 on 2,3 or 4 sides, Serpentine Die-Cut 11.5 x 11.75 on 2 or 3 sides (3294a-3297a)								
3294	33¢ Blueberries	04/10/99	.65	.20			1.25	
a	Dated "2000"	03/15/00	.65	.20			1.25	
3295	33¢ Raspberries	04/10/99	.65	.20			1.25	
a	Dated "2000"	03/15/00	.65	.20			1.25	
3296	33¢ Strawberries	04/10/99	.65	.20			1.25	
a	Dated "2000"	03/15/00	.65	.20			1.25	
3297	33¢ Blackberries	04/10/99	.65	.20			1.25	
a	Dated "2000"	03/15/00	.65	.20			1.25	
b	Booklet pane, 5 each #3294-3297 + label		13.00				3.25	
c	Block of 4, #3294-3297		2.60					
d	Booklet pane, 5 #3297e		13.00					
e	Block of 4, #3294a-3297a		2.60					
Serpentine Die-Cut 9.5 x 10 on 2 or 3 sides								
3298	33¢ Blueberries	04/10/99	.65	.20			1.25	
3299	33¢ Raspberries	04/10/99	.65	.20			1.25	
3300	33¢ Strawberries	04/10/99	.65	.20			1.25	
3301	33¢ Blackberries	04/10/99	.65	.20			1.25	
a	Booklet pane of 4							
	#3298-#3301		2.60				3.25	
b	Booklet pane of 5							
	#3298, #3299, #3301							
	2 #3300 + label		3.25					
c	Booklet pane of 6							
	#3300, #3301,							
	2 #3298, #3299		4.00					
d	Block of 4, #3298-#3301		2.60					
Coil Stamps, Serpentine Die-Cut 8.5 Vertically								
3302	33¢ Blueberries	04/10/99	.75	.20			1.25	
3303	33¢ Raspberries	04/10/99	.75	.20			1.25	
3304	33¢ Strawberries	04/10/99	.75	.20			1.25	
3305	33¢ Blackberries	04/10/99	.75	.20			1.25	
a	Strip of 4		3.00				3.25	

3293

e

c   f   j

a   b   d   g   h

i

3294   **3296**

3295   **3297**

3297c

3305a

1999

3309

3306a

3308

3310   **3311**

3314

3312   **3313**   **3313a**

3316

3315

3317   **3318**   **3319**   **3320**   **3320a**

Issues of 1999			Un	U	PB	#	FDC	Q(M)
Looney Tunes Issue, Self-Adhesive, Serpentine Die-Cut 11.1								
3306	Pane of 10	04/16/99	6.50					
a	33¢ Daffy Duck		.65	.20			1.50	427
b	Booklet pane of 9 #3306a		5.85					
c	Booklet pane of 1 #3306a		.65					
3307	Pane of 10		6.50					
a	33¢ Single		.65					
Literary Arts Issue, Perf. 11.2								
3308	33¢ Ayn Rand	04/22/99	.65	.20	2.60	(4)	1.25	42.5
Self-Adhesive, Serpentine Die-Cut 11.6 x 11.3								
3309	33¢ Cinco De Mayo	04/27/99	.65	.20	2.60	(4)	1.25	113
Tropical Flowers Issue, Self-Adhesive, Serpentine Die-Cut 10.9 on 2 or 3 sides								
3310	33¢ Bird of Paradise	05/01/99	.65	.20			1.25	
3311	33¢ Royal Poinciana	05/01/99	.65	.20			1.25	
3312	33¢ Gloriosa Lily	05/01/99	.65	.20			1.25	
3313	33¢ Chinese Hibiscus	05/01/99	.65	.20			1.25	
a	Block of 4 #3310-3313		2.60				3.25	
b	Booklet pane of 5 #3313a		13.00					
Self-Adhesive, Perf. 11.5								
3314	33¢ John & William Bartram	05/18/99	.65	.20	2.60	(4)	1.25	145
Self-Adhesive, Perf. 11								
3315	33¢ Prostate Cancer Awareness	05/28/99	.65	.20	2.60	(4)	1.25	78
Perf. 11.25								
3316	33¢ California Gold Rush 1849	06/18/99	.65	.20	2.60	(4)	1.25	89
Aquarium Fish Issue, Self-Adhesive, Serpentine Die-Cut 11.5								
3317	33¢ Yellow fish, red fish, cleaner shrimp	06/24/99	.65	.20			1.25	39
3318	33¢ Fish, thermometer	06/24/99	.65	.20			1.25	39
3319	33¢ Red fish, blue & yellow fish	06/24/99	.65	.20			1.25	39
3320	33¢ Fish, heater/aerator	06/24/99	.65	.20			1.25	39
b	Strip of 4, #3317-3320		2.60		5.20	(8)	3.25	

COVERLET EAGLE

Woven coverlets were among the most popular textiles during the first half of the 19th century. Often made of the owner's homespun wool or cotton, they were prized by middle-class American households for their beauty and warmth. A short-lived folk art form—mechanization would take over the weaving industry after the Civil War—coverlets were never plentiful and today are highly collectible. In 2002 an artistic rendering of a detail from a mid-nineteenth century coverlet appeared on a stamp. The coverlet was woven for Calista C. James by Harry Tyler (1801-1858), a well-known weaver who lived in Jefferson County, New York. It was Tyler's practice to weave into the two bottom corners of his coverlets his signature—in this instance an eagle—and where he wove the textile, as well as the identity of the owner and the date of the coverlet. This detail, artistically rendered in watercolor and graphite on paper by Arthur Merkley circa 1941, is part of the Index of American Design, a visual record of American material culture that is housed at the National Gallery of Art in Washington, D.C. ❑

Issues of 1999			Un	U	PB	#	FDC	Q(M)
Extreme Sports Issue, Self-Adhesive, Serpentine Die-Cut 11								
3321	33¢ Skateboarding	06/25/99	.65	.20			1.25	38
3322	33¢ BMX Biking	06/25/99	.65	.20			1.25	38
3323	33¢ Snowboarding	06/25/99	.65	.20			1.25	38
3324	33¢ Inline Skating	06/15/99	.65	.20			1.25	38
a	Block of 4, #3321-3324		2.60		2.60	(4)	3.00	
American Glass Issue, Perf. 11								
3325	33¢ Free-Blown Glass	06/29/99	.65	.20			1.25	29
3326	33¢ Mold-Blown Glass	06/29/99	.65	.20			1.25	29
3327	33¢ Pressed Glass	06/29/99	.65	.20			1.25	29
3328	33¢ Art Glass	06/29/99	.65	.20			1.25	29
a	Strip or block of 4, #3325-3328		2.60	—			3.00	
Legends of Hollywood Issue, Perf. 11								
3329	33¢ James Cagney	07/22/99	.65	.20	2.60	(4)	1.50	75.5
Pioneers of Aviation Issue, Self-Adhesive, Serpentine Die-Cut 9.75 x 10								
3330	55¢ Gen. William "Billy" L. Mitchell	07/30/99	1.10	.20	4.40	(4)	1.50	101
Self-Adhesive, Serpentine Die-Cut 11								
3331	33¢ Honoring Those Who Served	08/16/99	.65	.20	2.60	(4)	1.50	102
Perf. 11								
3332	45¢ Universal Postal Union	08/25/99	.90	.20	3.60	(4)	1.25	43
ALL ABOARD! Twentieth Century Trains Issue, Perf. 11								
3333	33¢ Daylight	08/26/99	.65	.20			1.50	24
3334	33¢ Congressional	08/26/99	.65	.20			1.50	24
3335	33¢ 20th Century Limited	08/26/99	.65	.20			1.50	24
3336	33¢ Hiawatha	08/26/99	.65	.20			1.50	24
3337	33¢ Super Chief	08/26/99	.65	.20			1.50	24
a	Strip of 5, #3333-3337		3.25	—	5.25	(8)	3.75	

D.W. GRIFFITH

(1875-1948)

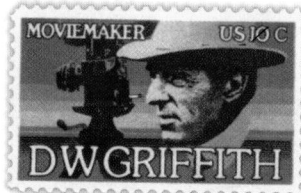

Early in his career as a motion picture director, D.W. GRIFFITH produced the nation's first full-length film, considered by many to be the first "epic" film with its large cast and big budget. *The Birth of a Nation* (1915), a controversial film about the Civil War and Reconstruction told from a southern point of view, was the target of protests by African Americans and others who were offended by the attitudes of the film's characters and its director. Despite the outcry, the film was a financial success. Undaunted by the criticism, Griffith would go on to direct some 500 films—mostly silent—among them *Intolerance* (1916), *Broken Blossoms* (1919), and *America* (1924). In his films Griffith introduced an array of innovative film-making techniques—such as the close-up, panning in and out, and backlighting—that transformed the movie-making industry. In 1919 Griffith and actors Charlie Chaplin, Douglas Fairbanks, and Mary Pickford established United Artists Corporation. Today a specialty films unit of MGM, United Artists is one of the oldest and most successful film companies. In the early 1930s when talking movies became the rage, Griffith sold his interest in United Artists and retired from the industry. ❑

3321   3322

3325   3326

3323   3324   3324a

3327   3328   3328a

3329   3330

3333

3334

3335

3336

3337

3331

3332

3337a

3338

3339

3340

3341

3342

3343

3344

3344a

3345

3346

3347

3348

3349

3350

3350a

	Issues of 1999		Un	U	PB	#	FDC	Q(M)
	Perf. 11							
3338	33¢ Frederick Law Olmstead	09/13/99	.65	.20	2.60	(4)	1.25	42.5
	Legends of American Music Series, Hollywood Composers Issue							
3339	33¢ Max Steiner	09/16/99	.65	.20			1.25	
3340	33¢ Dimitri Tiomkin	09/16/99	.65	.20			1.25	
3341	33¢ Bernard Herrmann	09/16/99	.65	.20			1.25	
3342	33¢ Franz Waxman	09/16/99	.65	.20			1.25	
3343	33¢ Alfred Newman	09/16/99	.65	.20			1.25	
3344	33¢ Erich Wolfgang Korngold	09/16/99	.65	.20			1.25	
a	Block of 6, #3339-3344		3.90	—	3.90	(6)	3.75	
	Legends of American Music Series, Broadway Songwriters Issue							
3345	33¢ Ira & George Gershwin	09/21/99	.65	.20			1.25	
3346	33¢ Lerner & Loewe	09/21/99	.65	.20			1.25	
3347	33¢ Lorenz Hart	09/21/99	.65	.20			1.25	
3348	33¢ Rodgers & Hammerstein	09/21/99	.65	.20			1.25	
3349	33¢ Meredith Willson	09/21/99	.65	.20			1.25	
3350	33¢ Frank Loesser	09/21/99	.65	.20			1.25	
a	Block of 6, #3345-3350		3.90	—	3.90	(6)	3.75	

AMERICAN ★ COMMEMORATIVE ★ COLLECTIBLES

American Commemorative Collection

An easy and uniform way to collect and learn about commemorative issues.

Just mount the stamps on the specially designed sheet and place them in a three ring binder. Just $3.25* each, depending on the value of the stamps.

For more information call **1-800-STAMP-24**

*Prices subject to change without notice.

Issues of 1999		Un	U	PB	#	FDC	Q(M
Insects & Spiders Issue, Perf. 11							
3351 Pane of 20	10/01/99	13.00	—			10.00	4.23
a	Black widow	.65	.20			1.25	
b	Elderberry longhorn	.65	.20			1.25	
c	Lady beetle	.65	.20			1.25	
d	Yellow garden spider	.65	.20			1.25	
e	Dogbane beetle	.65	.20			1.25	
f	Flower Fly	.65	.20			1.25	
g	Assassin bug	.65	.20			1.25	
h	Ebony jewelwing	.65	.20			1.25	
i	Velvet ant	.65	.20			1.25	
j	Monarch caterpillar	.65	.20			1.25	
k	Monarch butterfly	.65	.20			1.25	
l	Eastern Hercules beetle	.65	.20			1.25	
m	Bombardier beetle	.65	.20			1.25	
n	Dung beetle	.65	.20			1.25	
o	Spotted water beetle	.65	.20			1.25	
p	True katydid	.65	.20			1.25	
q	Spinybacked spider	.65	.20			1.25	
r	Periodical cicada	.65	.20			1.25	
s	Scorpionfly	.65	.20			1.25	
t	Jumping spider	.65	.20			1.25	

MOSS HART

(1904-1961)

In 2004 the Postal Service honored award-winning dramatist and director MOSS HART. A gifted playwright, Hart wrote a series of sparkling comedies in the 1930s with George S. Kaufman. A brilliant director, he staged one of the most dazzling musicals of his era, *My Fair Lady*. A witty and charming personality who embodied the glamour of Broadway, Hart penned what many consider the best theatrical memoir ever written, *Act One*. Born in New York City, Hart dreamed of making his mark in the theater. In 1930 he succeeded with the long-running and popular comedy *Once in a Lifetime*, which he wrote with the noted playwright and director George S. Kaufman. From 1930 through 1940 Hart and Kaufman collaborated on eight plays, including *The Man Who Came to Dinner* (1939) and *You Can't Take It with You* (1936), which won the Pulitzer Prize for drama in 1937. Hart also collaborated on musicals with some of the top songwriters of the era, among them Irving Berlin and Cole Porter. As a director, his triumphs were on the musical stage. He won a Tony Award for his direction of *My Fair Lady* (1956), one of the longest-running Broadway musicals in history. A successful Hollywood screenwriter, he wrote *A Star Is Born* (1954), one of Judy Garland's greatest screen triumphs. In 1959 Hart published his autobiography, *Act One*. The book is dedicated to his wife, the actress and singer Kitty Carlisle, who urged him to record his memories of a golden age in the American theater. ❑

INSECTS & SPIDERS

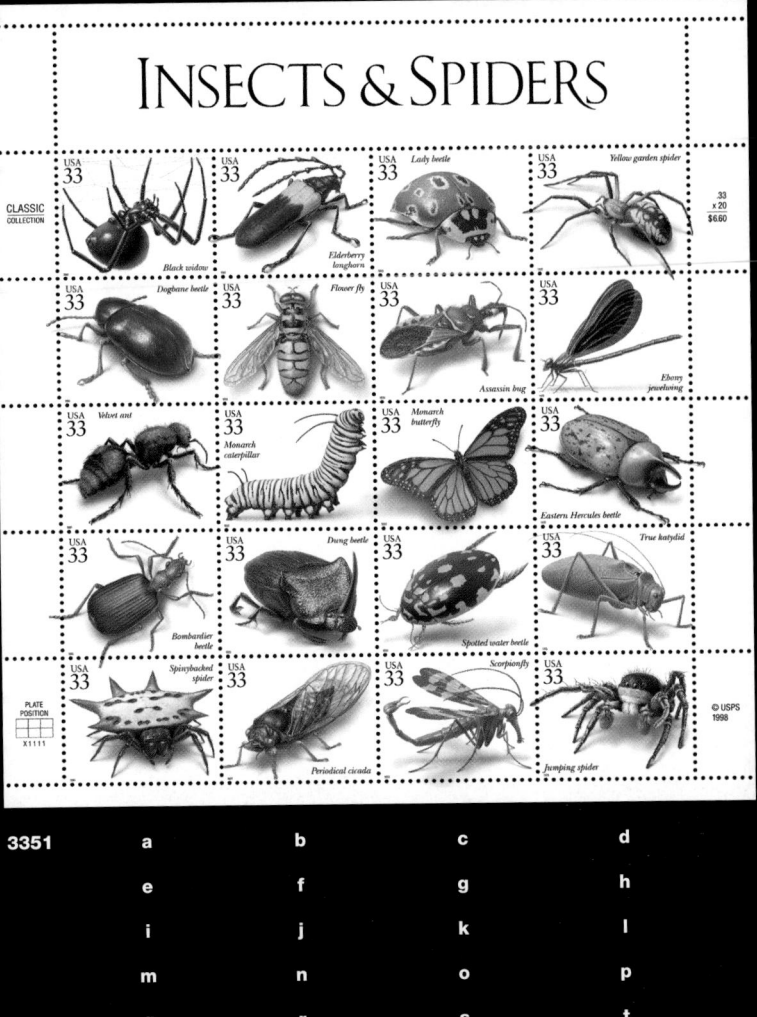

3351   a   b   c   d

        e   f   g   h

        i   j   k   l

        m   n   o   p

        q   r   s   t

1999

3352

3353

3354

3355

3356

3357

3359

3358

3359a

3368

	Issues of 1999		Un	U	PB	#	FDC	Q(M)
	Self-Adhesive, Serpentine Die-Cut 11							
3352	33¢ Hanukkah	10/08/99	.65	.20	2.60	(4)	1.50	65
	Coil Stamp, Perf. 9.75							
3353	22¢ Uncle Sam	10/08/99	.45	.20	3.50	(5)	1.25	150
	Perf. 11.25							
3354	33¢ NATO 50th Anniversary	10/13/99	.65	.20	2.60	(4)	1.25	44.6
	Holiday Traditional, Issue, Self-Adhesive Booklet Stamps, Serpentine Die-Cut 11.25 on 2 or 3 sides							
3355	33¢ Madonna and child by Bartolomeo Vivarini	10/20/99	.65	.15			1.25	1,556
a	Booklet pane of 20		13.00					
	Holiday Contemporary Issue, Self-Adhesive, Serpentine Die-Cut 11.25							
3356	33¢ Red Deer	10/20/99	.65	.20			1.25	
3357	33¢ Blue Deer	10/20/99	.65	.20			1.25	
3358	33¢ Purple Deer	10/20/99	.65	.20			1.25	
3359	33¢ Green Deer	10/20/99	.65	.20			1.25	
a	Block or strip, #3356-3359		2.60		2.60	(4)	3.00	
	Booklet Stamps, Serpentine Die-Cut 11.25 on 2, 3 or 4 sides							
3360	33¢ Red Deer	10/20/99	.65	.20			1.25	
3361	33¢ Blue Deer	10/20/99	.65	.20			1.25	
3362	33¢ Purple Deer	10/20/99	.65	.20			1.25	
3363	33¢ Green Deer	10/20/99	.65	.20			1.25	
a	Booklet pane of 20		13.00				3.00	
	Booklet Stamps, Serpentine Die-Cut 11.5 x 11.25 on 2 or 3 sides							
3364	33¢ Red Deer	10/20/99	1.00	.20			1.25	
3365	33¢ Blue Deer	10/20/99	1.00	.20			1.25	
3366	33¢ Purple Deer	10/20/99	1.00	.20			1.25	
3367	33¢ Green Deer	10/20/99	1.00	.20			1.25	
a	Booklet pane of 4		4.25				3.00	
b	Block pane of 5, #3364, #3366, #3367, 2 #3365 + label		5.25					
c	Block pane of 6, #3365, #3367, 2 #3364, #3366		6.50					
	Self-Adhesive, Serpentine Die-Cut 11							
3368	33¢ Kwanzaa	10/29/99	.65	.20	2.60	(4)	1.75	95

VISIT US ONLINE AT **THE POSTAL STORE**

AT **WWW.USPS.COM**

OR CALL **1-800-STAMP-24**

Issues of 1999-2000		Un	U	PB	#	FDC	Q(M)
Self-Adhesive, Serpentine Die-Cut 11.25							
3369	33¢ Year 2000 — 12/27/99	.65	.20	3.00	(4)	1.25	124
Lunar New Year Issue, Perf. 11.25							
3370	33¢ Year of the Dragon — 01/06/00	.65	.20	2.60	(4)	1.50	106
Black Heritage Issue, Serpentine Die-Cut 11.5 x 11.25							
3371	33¢ Patricia Harris — 01/27/00	.65	.20	2.60	(4)	1.75	150
U.S. Navy Submarines Issue, Perf. 11							
3372	33¢ *Los Angeles* Class — 03/27/00	.75	.20	3.00	(4)	1.50	65.15
3373	22¢ *S* Class — 03/27/00	.75	.20			1.50	3
3374	33¢ *Los Angeles* Class — 03/27/00	1.00	.30			1.50	3
3375	55¢ *Ohio* Class — 03/27/00	1.60	.50			1.75	3
3376	60¢ USS *Holland* — 03/27/00	2.00	.55			1.75	3
3377	$3.20 *Gato* Class — 03/27/00	10.00	3.00			6.00	3
a	Booklet Pane of 5, #3373-3377	17.50	—			8.00	

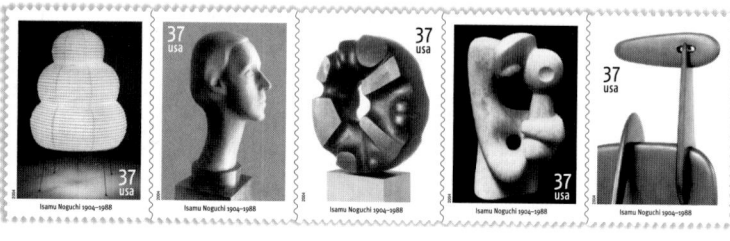

ISAMU NOGUCHI

(1904-1988)

Honored by the Postal Service on the 100th anniversary of his birth, sculptor ISAMU NOGUCHI is noted for merging Western and Eastern influence in creations that include portraiture, abstract sculpture, graceful meditation gardens, and sprawling landscapes. Noguchi also created furniture, theater sets, and other functional objects that demonstrated his desire to make sculpture useful to society. Noguchi—whose father was a famous Japanese poet and mother, an American writer—was born in Los Angeles, California, but lived in Japan until 1918. After high school in Indiana, he enrolled in pre-med studies at Columbia University, while also studying sculpture at New York's Leonardo da Vinci Art School. From 1927 until 1929, Noguchi studied in Paris under renowned sculptor Constantin Brancusi. On returning to New York, he supported himself by creating portrait sculptures while further developing his bold, abstract style. Throughout his career, Noguchi strove to expand the role of the sculptor. In addition to working with a variety of materials—wood, stone, marble, steel, bamboo, paper, and even water—he also created works on an ever-increasing scale, including gardens inspired by Japanese tradition but marked by Western influence. Seeing art and design as different facets of sculpture, Noguchi designed building interiors and courtyards as well as furniture and other functional objects, including a modern glass-top coffee table (in the 1940s) and his famous Akari lamps (still commercially available). Fascinated by the theater, Noguchi designed stage sets for renowned choreographers Martha Graham and George Balanchine. His many honors include the National Medal of Arts awarded by President Ronald Reagan in 1987. ❑

3369

3370

3371

3372

3376   **3373**

3377

3374   **3375**

3377a

PACIFIC COAST RAIN FOREST

SECOND IN A SERIES

USA 33

USA 33

USA 33

USA 33

USA 33

USA 33

USA 33

USA 33

USA 33

USA 33

N A T U R E   O F   A M E R I C A

3378

a   b   c   d

e   f   g   h   i   j

3379   3380   3381   3382   3383   3383a

Issues of 2000		Un	U	PB	#	FDC	Q(M)
Pacific Coast Rain Forest Issue, Self-Adhesive, Serpentine Die-Cut 11.25 x 11.5							
3378 Pane of 10	03/29/00	6.50				6.75	10
a 33¢ Harlequin duck		.65	.20			1.25	10
b 33¢ Dwarf oregongrape, snail eating ground beetle		.65	.20			1.25	10
c 33¢ American dipper, horizontal		.65	.20			1.25	10
d 33¢ Cutthroat trout, horizontal		.65	.20			1.25	10
e 33¢ Roosevelt elk		.65	.20			1.25	10
f 33¢ Winter wren		.65	.20			1.25	10
g 33¢ Pacific giant salamander, Rough-skinned newt		.65	.20			1.25	10
h 33¢ Western tiger swallowtail, horizontal		.65	.20			1.25	10
i 33¢ Douglass squirrel, foliose lichen		.65	.20			1.25	10
j 33¢ Foliose lichen, banana slug		.65	.20			1.25	10
Louise Nevelson Issue, Perf. 11 x 11.25							
3379 33¢ Silent Music I	04/06/00	.65	.20	6.50	(10)	1.25	11
3380 33¢ Royal Tide I	04/06/00	.65	.20	6.50	(10)	1.25	11
3381 33¢ Black Chord	04/06/00	.65	.20	6.50	(10)	1.25	11
3382 33¢ Nightsphere-Light	04/06/00	.65	.20	6.50	(10)	1.25	11
3383 33¢ Dawn's Wedding Chapel I	04/06/00	.65	.20	6.50	(10)	1.25	11
a Strip of 5, #3379-3383		3.25	—	6.50	(10)		3.25

THEODOR SEUSS GEISEL

(1904-1991)

Pulitzer Prize-winning author and illustrator, THEODOR SEUSS GEISEL introduced countless children to the joys of reading. He graduated from Dartmouth College and studied at Oxford University in England, but returned home to Springfield, Massachusetts, to be an artist and writer. In 1927 Geisel made his first sale—a cartoon—to *The Saturday Evening Post.* The next year he created the catchphrase, "Quick, Henry, the Flit!" for an ad campaign for the insect repellant Flit. In 1937 the first of his 44 books for children, *And to Think That I Saw It on Mulberry Street,* was published. Subsequent books introduced characters—among them Horton the elephant in *Horton Hatches the Egg* (1940) and the Grinch in *How the Grinch Stole Christmas!* (1957)—that became part of American popular culture. Many consider *The Cat in the Hat* (1957) his most innovative book. Challenged by an editor to write a book for beginning readers, Geisel—who wrote as Dr. Seuss—worked from a vocabulary list of only 225 words to create this bestseller. A filmmaker, he won three Academy Awards, including best cartoon for *Gerald McBoing-Boing* (1951). Television productions include Peabody Award-winning adaptations of *How the Grinch Stole Christmas!* (1966) and *Horton Hears a Who!* (1970)—with animator Chuck Jones—and four Emmy Award-winning specials. In 1984 Geisel was honored with a Pulitzer Prize "for his special contribution over nearly half a century to the education and enjoyment of America's children and their parents." ❑

Issues of 2000		Un	U	PB	#	FDC	Q(M)
Edwin Powell Hubble/Telescope, Perf. 11							
3384	33¢ Eagle Nebula	04/10/00	.65	.20	6.50	(10)	1.25	21.07
3385	33¢ Ring Nebula	04/10/00	.65	.20	6.50	(10)	1.25	21.07
3386	33¢ Lagoon Nebula	04/10/00	.65	.20	6.50	(10)	1.25	21.07
3387	33¢ Egg Nebula	04/10/00	.65	.20	6.50	(10)	1.25	21.07
3388	33¢ Galaxy NGC 1316	04/10/00	.65	.20	6.50	(10)	1.25	21.07
a	Strip of 5, #3384-3388		3.25	—	6.50	(10)	3.25	
3389	33¢ American Samoa	04/17/00	.65	.20	2.60	(4)	1.25	16
3390	33¢ Library of Congress	04/24/00	.65	.20	2.60	(4)	1.25	55
Looney Tunes Issue, Self-Adhesive, Serpentine Die-Cut 11							
3391	Pane of 10	04/26/00	6.50					
a	33¢ Road Runner & Wile E. Coyote		.65	.20			1.25	300
3392	Pane of 10		6.50					
Distinguished Soldiers Issue, Perf. 11							
3393	33¢ Maj. Gen. John L. Hines	08/16/00	.65	.20	2.60	(4)	1.25	13.75
3394	33¢ Gen. Omar N. Bradley	08/16/00	.65	.20	2.60	(4)	1.25	13.75
3395	33¢ Sgt. Alvin C. York	08/16/00	.65	.20	2.60	(4)	1.25	13.75
3396	33¢ Second Lt. Audie L. Murphy	08/16/00	.65	.20	2.60	(4)	1.25	13.75
a	Block Strip of 4, #3393-3396		2.60	—	2.60	(4)	3.25	
Perf. 11							
3397	33¢ Summer Sports	05/05/00	.65	.20	2.60	(4)	1.25	90.6

Ready to Mail Stamped Cards

Southeastern Lighthouses 23¢
Twenty Stamped Cards
Five Designs
Item #454466–$9.75

Old Glory 23¢
Twenty Stamped Cards
Five Designs
Item #882066–$9.75

Holiday Music Makers 23¢
Twenty Stamped Cards
Four Designs
Item #564066–$9.75

*Prices subject to change without notice

To order call **1-800-STAMP-24** or visit us online at **www.usps.com**

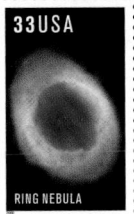
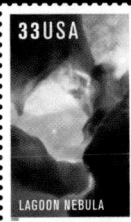

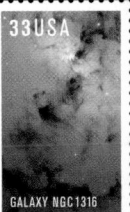

3384　　**3385**　　**3386**　　**3387**　　**3388** **3388a**

3389

3390

3391a

3393
3394
3395
3396

3396a

3397

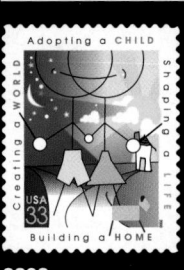

Adopting a CHILD
Creating a WORLD
Shaping a LIFE
Building a HOME
USA 33

3398

3399

3400

USA 33
USA 33
33 USA
33 USA

3401

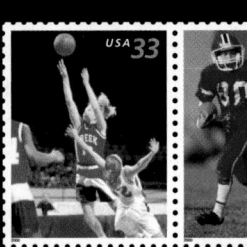

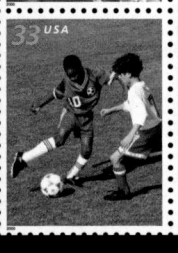

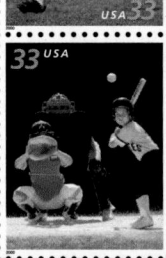

3402

3402a

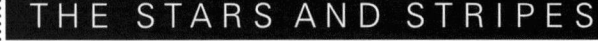

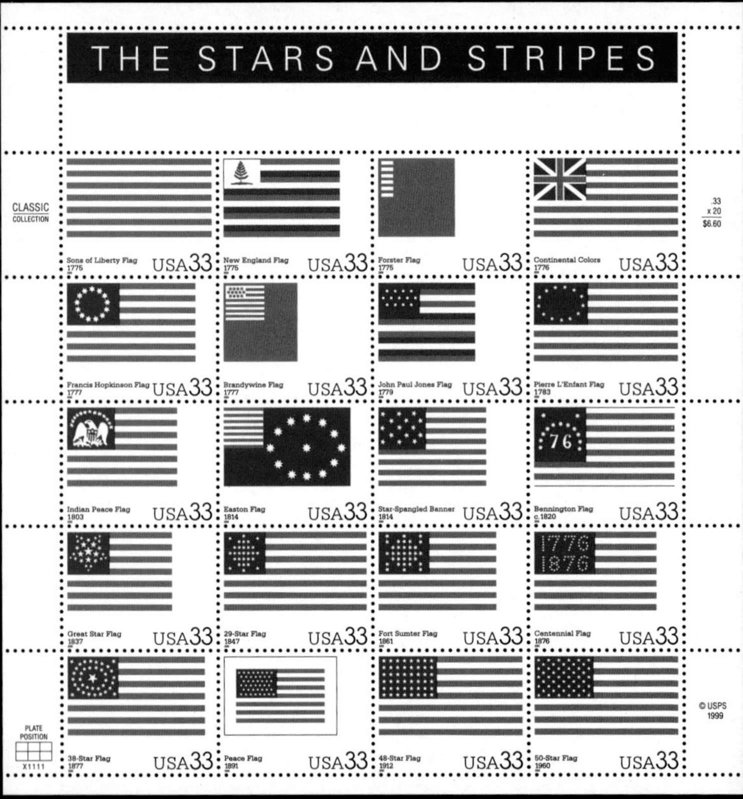
THE STARS AND STRIPES
CLASSIC COLLECTION
.33 x 20 $6.60
Sons of Liberty Flag 1775 USA33
New England Flag 1775 USA33
Forster Flag 1775 USA33
Continental Colors 1776 USA33
Francis Hopkinson Flag 1777 USA33
Brandywine Flag 1777 USA33
John Paul Jones Flag 1779 USA33
Pierre L'Enfant Flag 1783 USA33
Indian Peace Flag 1803 USA33
Easton Flag 1814 USA33
Star-Spangled Banner 1814 USA33
Bennington Flag c.1820 USA33
Great Star Flag 1837 USA33
29-Star Flag 1847 USA33
Fort Sumter Flag 1861 USA33
Centennial Flag 1876 USA33
38-Star Flag 1877 USA33
Peace Flag 1891 USA33
48-Star Flag 1912 USA33
50-Star Flag 1960 USA33
PLATE POSITION
X1111
© USPS 1999

3403 a b c d

Issues of 2000		Un	U	PB	#	FDC	Q(M)
Self-Adhesive, Serpentine Die-Cut 11.5							
3398	33¢ Adoption 05/10/00	.65	.20	2.60	(4)	1.25	200
Youth Team Sports Issue, Tagged, Perf. 11							
3399	33¢ Basketball 05/27/00	.65	.20	2.60	(4)	1.25	22
3400	33¢ Football 05/27/00	.65	.20	2.60	(4)	1.25	22
3401	33¢ Soccer 05/27/00	.65	.20	2.60	(4)	1.25	22
3402	33¢ Baseball 05/27/00	.65	.20	2.60	(4)	1.25	22
a	Block strip of 4, #3399-3402	2.60	—	2.60	(4)	3.25	
The Stars and Stripes Issue, Perf. 10.5 x 11							
3403	Pane of 20 06/14/00	13.00				10.00	
a	33¢ Sons of Liberty Flag, 1775	.65	.30			1.25	80
b	33¢ New England Flag, 1775	.65	.30			1.25	80
c	33¢ Forster Flag, 1775	.65	.30			1.25	80
d	33¢ Continental Colors, 1776	.65	.30			1.25	80
e	33¢ Francis Hopkinson Flag, 1777	.65	.30			1.25	80
f	33¢ Brandywine Flag, 1777	.65	.30			1.25	80
g	33¢ John Paul Jones Flag, 1779	.65	.30			1.25	80
h	33¢ Pierre L'Enfant Flag, 1783	.65	.30			1.25	80
i	33¢ Indian Peace Flag, 1803	.65	.30			1.25	80
j	33¢ Easton Flag, 1814	.65	.30			1.25	80
k	33¢ Star-Spangled Banner, 1814	.65	.30			1.25	80
l	33¢ Bennington Flag, c. 1820	.65	.30			1.25	80
m	33¢ Great Star Flag, 1837	.65	.30			1.25	80
n	33¢ 29-Star Flag, 1847	.65	.30			1.25	80
o	33¢ Fort Sumter Flag, 1861	.65	.30			1.25	80
p	33¢ Centennial Flag, 1876	.65	.30			1.25	80
q	33¢ 38-Star Flag, 1877	.65	.30			1.25	80
r	33¢ Peace Flag, 1891	.65	.30			1.25	80
s	33¢ 48-Star Flag, 1912	.65	.30			1.25	80
t	33¢ 50-Star Flag, 1960	.65	.30			1.25	80

JACKSON POLLOCK

(1912-1956)

One of the greatest 20th-century American painters, JACKSON POLLOCK was the acknowledged leader of the Abstract Expressionist movement in the 1940s. Born in Cody, Wyoming, Pollock grew up in southern California where he was introduced to art. In 1930, despite having doubts about his artistic ability, Pollock moved to New York to study with Thomas Hart Benton at the Art Students League. By the late 1940s he had developed a style in which he dripped and poured paint onto can-vas laid on the floor of his studio in East Hampton, Long Island. Sarcastically dubbed "Jack the Dripper" by *Time* magazine, Pollock was constantly in motion, walking around the canvas, dripping, flinging, and pouring paint on it. Pollock died at the age of 44 when the car he was driving sped off the road. In 1994 his home and studio—where the floor is still covered in paint— were designated a National Historic Landmark. The Postal Service honored Pollock in its 1940s Celebrate The Century® issue in 1999. ❑

	Issues of 2000		Un	U	PB	#	FDC	Q(M)
	Fruit Berries Issue, Self-Adhesive, Serpentine Die-Cut 8.5 Horizontally							
3404	33¢ Blueberries	06/16/00	.75	.20			1.25	82.5
3405	33¢ Strawberries	06/16/00	.75	.20			1.25	82.5
3406	33¢ Blackberries	06/16/00	.75	.20			1.25	82.5
3407	33¢ Raspberries	06/16/00	.75	.20			1.25	82.5
a	Strip of 4, #3404-3407		3.00				3.25	
	Legends of Baseball Issue, Self-Adhesive, Serpentine Die-Cut 11.25							
3408	Pane of 20	07/06/00	13.00				10.00	
a	33¢ Jackie Robinson		.65	.20			1.50	11.25
b	33¢ Eddie Collins		.65	.20			1.50	11.25
c	33¢ Christy Mathewson		.65	.20			1.50	11.25
d	33¢ Ty Cobb		.65	.20			1.50	11.25
e	33¢ George Sisler		.65	.20			1.50	11.25
f	33¢ Rogers Hornsby		.65	.20			1.50	11.25
g	33¢ Mickey Cochrane		.65	.20			1.50	11.25
h	33¢ Babe Ruth		.65	.20			1.50	11.25
i	33¢ Walter Johnson		.65	.20			1.50	11.25
j	33¢ Roberto Clemente		.65	.20			1.50	11.25
k	33¢ Lefty Grove		.65	.20			1.50	11.25
l	33¢ Tris Speaker		.65	.20			1.50	11.25
m	33¢ Cy Young		.65	.20			1.50	11.25
n	33¢ Jimmie Foxx		.65	.20			1.50	11.25
o	33¢ Pie Traynor		.65	.20			1.50	11.25
p	33¢ Satchel Paige		.65	.20			1.50	11.25
q	33¢ Honus Wagner		.65	.20			1.50	11.25
r	33¢ Josh Gibson		.65	.20			1.50	11.25
s	33¢ Dizzy Dean		.65	.20			1.50	11.25
t	33¢ Lou Gehrig		.65	.20			1.50	11.25

HENRY OSSAWA TANNER

(1859-1937)

HENRY OSSAWA TANNER—the first African-American artist to win international acclaim—was born in Pittsburgh, the oldest of nine children. His father, a minister in the African Methodist Episcopal Church, and his mother, a teacher who had been a slave, moved the family to Philadelphia where Tanner attended a school that encouraged artistic talent. By age thirteen, he knew he wanted to be an artist. Tanner began his formal training at the Pennsylvania Academy of Fine Arts, where he studied with the famous American painter Thomas Eakins. He continued his studies in Paris where he remained for much of his life. In 1897 when the French government bought his *Raising of Lazarus* for the Louvre, Tanner's career soared. He was not yet 50 at the time of his first solo exhibit in New York. The recipient of the French Legion of Honor in 1923, Tanner was the first African American named to full membership in the National Academy of Art and Design. He was honored by the Postal Service in the American Arts issue of 1973. ❏

3404   3405   3406   3407   3407a

Legends of Baseball

ALL
CENTURY
TEAM

CLASSIC
COLLECTION

.33
x 20
$6.60

USA 33 JACKIE ROBINSON	USA 33 EDDIE COLLINS	USA 33 CHRISTY MATHEWSON	USA 33 TY COBB	USA 33 GEORGE SISLER
USA 33 ROGERS HORNSBY	USA 33 MICKEY COCHRANE	USA 33 BABE RUTH	USA 33 WALTER JOHNSON	USA 33 ROBERTO CLEMENTE
USA 33 LEFTY GROVE	USA 33 TRIS SPEAKER	USA 33 CY YOUNG	USA 33 JIMMIE FOXX	USA 33 PIE TRAYNOR
USA 33 SATCHEL PAIGE	USA 33 HONUS WAGNER	USA 33 JOSH GIBSON	USA 33 DIZZY DEAN	USA 33 LOU GEHRIG

© USPS
2000

PLATE
POSITION
X1111

3408   a   b   c   d   e

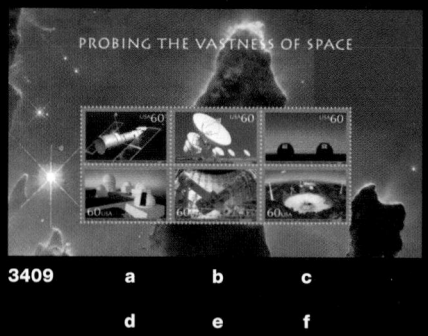

3409   a   b   c

           d   e   f

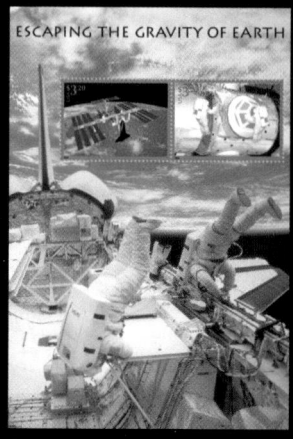

3410   a   3411   a   b

      e   b

      d   c

3412

3413

Issues of 2000		Un	U	PB	#	FDC	Q(M)
Space Issue, Perf. 10.5 x 11							
3409 Probing the Vastness of Space	07/10/00	7.50	—			6.00	1.695
a	60¢ Hubble Space Telescope	1.25	.60			1.50	
b	60¢ Radio interferometer very large array,						
	New Mexico	1.25	.60			1.50	
c	60¢ Optical and infrared telescopes,						
	Keck Observatory, Hawaii	1.25	.60			1.50	
d	60¢ Optical telescopes Cerro Tololo						
	Observatory, Chile	1.25	.60			1.50	
e	60¢ Optical telescope, Mount Wilson						
	Observatory, California	1.25	.60			1.50	
f	60¢ Radio telescope, Arecibo Observatory,						
	Puerto Rico	1.25	.60			1.50	
Perf. 10.75							
3410 Exploring the Solar System	07/11/00	10.00	—			9.00	1.695
a	$1 Sun and corona	2.00	1.00			2.00	
b	$1 Cross-section of sun	2.00	1.00			2.00	
c	$1 Sun and earth	2.00	1.00			2.00	
d	$1 Sun and solar flare	2.00	1.00			2.00	
e	$1 Sun and clouds	2.00	1.00			2.00	
Hologram, Perf. 10.5, 10.75 (#3412)							
3411 Escaping the Gravity of Earth	07/09/00	12.50	—			9.50	1.695
a	$3.20 Space Shuttle and Space Station	6.25	3.00			3.75	
b	$3.20 Astronauts working in space	6.25	3.00			3.75	
3412 $11.75 Space Achievement and							
Exploration	07/07/00	22.50	11.50			17.50	1.695
3413 $11.75 Landing on the Moon	07/08/00	22.50	11.50			17.50	1.695
Uncut sheet of 5 panes #3409-3412							
(not shown)		75.00					

ERNEST HEMINGWAY

(1899-1961)

One of the most influential writers of the 20th century, ERNEST HEMINGWAY was born in Chicago, Illinois. The second of six children, he was taught to love and cope with nature by his father; he learned about music and the arts from his mother. When Hemingway graduated from high school, he went to work as a newspaper reporter in Kansas City, Missouri. A few months later he enlisted in the American Field Service and went to Europe where he drove an ambulance during World War I. A life of adventure and challenges— he was a foreign correspondent in France, a big game hunter, and bullfighter, for example— served as the basis for many of his stories. Among the best known are *The Sun Also Rises* (1926), *A Farewell to Arms* (1929), and *For Whom The Bell Tolls* (1940). A war correspondent during World War II, Hemingway wrote about heroism and courage in a world of violence. In 1953 he won a Pulitzer Prize for *The Old Man and the Sea*; in 1954, he won the Nobel Prize for literature. Hemingway was honored by the Postal Service in 1989 in the Literary Arts series. ☐

Issues of 2000-2002		Un	U	PB	#	FDC	Q(M)
Stampin' The Future™ Issue, Self-Adhesive, Serpentine Die-Cut 11.25							
3414	33¢ By Zachary Canter	07/13/00	.65	.20	5.25	(8)	1.25	25
3415	33¢ By Sarah Lipsey	07/13/00	.65	.20	5.25	(8)	1.25	25
3416	33¢ By Morgan Hill	07/13/00	.65	.20	5.25	(8)	1.25	25
3417	33¢ By Ashley Young	07/13/00	.65	.20	5.25	(8)	1.25	25
a	Horizontal Strip of 4, #3414-3417		2.60		5.25	(8)	3.25	
Distinguished Americans Perf. 11							
3420	10¢ Joseph W. Stilwell	08/24/00	.20	.20	.80	(4)	1.50	100
3426	33¢ Claude Pepper	09/07/00	.65	.20	2.60	(4)	1.25	56
Self-Adhesive, Serpentine Die-Cut 11							
3431	76¢ Hattie Caraway	02/21/01	1.50	.20	6.00	(4)	1.75	108
Self-Adhesive, Serpentine Die-Cut 11.5 x 11							
3432	76¢ Hattie Caraway	02/21/01	3.25	3.00	14.00	(4)	1.75	108
Self-Adhesive, Serpentine Die-Cut 11 x 11.75							
3433	83¢ Edna Ferber	07/29/02	1.60	.30	6.50	(4)	1.75	108
Self-Adhesive, Serpentine Die-Cut 11.25							
3434	83¢ Edna Ferber	08/03	1.60	.30	6.50	(4)	1.75	108
Self-Adhesive, Serpentine Die-Cut 11							
3438	33¢ California Statehood	09/08/00	.65	.20	2.60	(4)	1.25	53
Deep Sea Creatures Issue, Perf. 10 x 10.25							
3439	33¢ Fanfin Angelfish	10/02/00	.65	.20			1.25	17
3440	33¢ Sea Cucumber	10/02/00	.65	.20			1.25	17
3441	33¢ Fangtooth	10/02/00	.65	.20			1.25	17
3442	33¢ Amphipod	10/02/00	.65	.20			1.25	17
3443	33¢ Medusa	10/02/00	.65	.20			1.25	17
a	Vertical Strip 5, #3439-3443		3.25	—			3.75	

EDITH WHARTON

(1862-1937)

EDITH WHARTON was born into aristocratic New York society during the Victorian era. An intelligent girl, she was educated privately and eventually married a man of her social class. With a friend, the architect Ogden Codman, she wrote her first book, *The Decoration of Houses*, published in 1897. It was an immediate success. Wharton was unhappy playing the role that was expected of her; her marriage dissolved and she took up permanent residence in France. In her long career, she published more than 40 books including novels, short stories, essays, poems, travel books, and an autobiography, *A Backward Glance*. Her novel *The House of Mirth*, published in 1905, concerns Lily Bart, a young woman in New York who attempts to marry above her station and is ostracized. A novelette, *Ethan Frome*, is about impoverished people in rural New England. *The Age of Innocence*, a novel about old New York published in 1920, won the Pulitzer Prize. Whether set in high society or among the less wealthy, a central theme of Wharton's fiction was the way public convention thwarts private happiness. ◻

3414

3415

3416

3417

3417a

3420

3426

3431

3433

3438

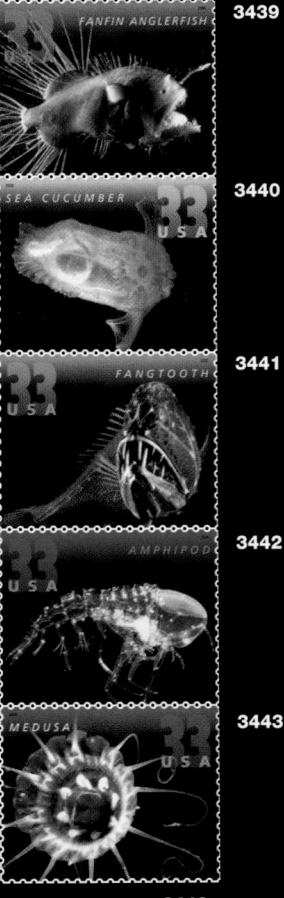

3439

3440

3441

3442

3443

3443a

2000

3444

3445

3446

3447

3448

3451

3454   3455

3456   3457   3457a

Issues of 2000		Un	U	PB	#	FDC	Q(M)
Literary Arts Issue, Perf. 11							
3444 33¢ Thomas Wolfe	10/03/00	.65	.20	2.60	(4)	1.25	53
Serpentine Die-Cut 11.25							
3445 33¢ White House	10/18/00	.65	.20	2.60	(4)	1.25	125
Legends of Hollywood Issue, Perf. 11							
3446 33¢ Edward G. Robinson	10/24/00	.65	.20	2.60	(4)	1.50	52
Serpentine Die-Cut 11.5 Vertically							
3447 (10¢) The New York Public Library	11/09/00	.20	.20	3.00	(5)	1.25	100
Perf. 11.25							
3448 (34¢) Flag Over Farm	12/15/00	.65	.20	2.60	(4)	1.25	25
Self-Adhesive, Serpentine Die-Cut 11.25							
3449 (34¢) Flag Over Farm	12/15/00	.65	.20	2.60	(4)	1.25	200
Booklet Stamps, Self-Adhesive, Serpentine Die-Cut 8 on 2, 3 or 4 sides							
3450 (34¢) Flag Over Farm	12/15/00	.75	.20			1.25	
a Booklet Pane of 18		14.00					300
Booklet Stamps, Self-Adhesive, Serpentine Die-Cut 11 on 2, 3 or 4 sides							
3451 34¢ Statue of Liberty	12/15/00	.65	.20	2.60	(4)	1.25	1.5
Coil Stamps, Perf. 9.75 Vertically							
3452 34¢ Statue of Liberty	12/15/00	.65	.20	5.00	(5)	1.25	200
Serpentine Die-Cut 10 Vertically							
3453 34¢ Statue of Liberty	12/15/00	.65	.20	5.00	(5)	1.25	
Booklet Stamps, Self-Adhesive, Serpentine Die-Cut 10.25 x 10.75 on 2 or 3 sides							
3454 (34¢) Purple Flower	12/15/00	.65	.20			1.25	375
3455 (34¢) Tan Flower	12/15/00	.65	.20			1.25	375
3456 (34¢) Green Flower	12/15/00	.65	.20			1.25	375
3457 (34¢) Red Flower	12/15/00	.65	.20			1.25	375
a Block of 4		2.60				3.25	
b Booklet pane of 4		2.60					
c Booklet pane of 6		3.90					
d Booklet pane of 6		3.90					
e Booklet pane of 20		13.00					
Booklet Stamps, Self-Adhesive, Serpentine Die-Cut 11.5 x 11.75 on 2 or 3 sides							
3458 34¢ Purple Flower	12/15/00	.65	.20			1.25	125
3459 34¢ Tan Flower	12/15/00	.65	.20			1.25	125
3460 34¢ Green Flower	12/15/00	.65	.20			1.25	125
3461 34¢ Red Flower	12/15/00	.65	.20			1.25	125
a Block of 4		2.60				3.25	
b Booklet pane of 20, 2 each #3461a		25.00					
c Booklet pane of 20, 3 each #3461a		30.00					
Coil Stamps, Serpentine Die-Cut 8.5 Vertically							
3462 34¢ Green Flower	12/15/00	.75	.20			1.25	125
3463 34¢ Red Flower	12/15/00	.75	.20			1.25	125
3464 34¢ Tan Flower	12/15/00	.75	.20			1.25	125
3465 34¢ Purple Flower	12/15/00	.75	.20			1.25	125
a Strip of 4		3.00		6.00	(5)	3.25	

	Issues of 2001		Un	U	PB	#	FDC	Q(M)
	Coil Stamp, Self-Adhesive, Serpentine Die-Cut 9.75							
3466	34¢ Statue of Liberty	01/07/01	.65	.20	5.00	(5)	1.25	240
	Tagged, Self-Adhesive, Serpentine Die-Cut 11							
3468	21¢ Buffalo	02/22/01	.40	.20	1.60	(4)	1.25	25
	Tagged, Serpentine Die-Cut, Perf. 11.25							
3469	34¢ Flag Over Farm	02/07/01	.65	.20	9.00	(4)	1.25	200
	Self-Adhesive, Serpentine Die-Cut 11.25							
3470	34¢ Flag Over Farm	03/06/01	.65	.20	2.60	(4)	1.25	204
	Self-Adhesive, Serpentine Die-Cut 10.75							
3471	55¢ Art Deco Eagle	02/22/01	1.10	.20	4.40	(4)	1.50	100
	Self-Adhesive, Serpentine Die-Cut 11.25 x 11.5							
3472	$3.50 U. S. Capitol	01/29/01	7.00	3.50	28.00	(4)	6.25	125
	Self-Adhesive, Serpentine Die-Cut 11.25 x 11.5							
3473	$12.25 Washington Monument	01/29/01	22.50	10.00	90.00	(4)	15.00	35
	Coil Stamp, Self-Adhesive, Serpentine Die-Cut 8.5 Vertically							
3475	21¢ Buffalo	02/22/01	.40	.20	3.50	(5)	1.25	680
	Self-Adhesive, Perf. 9.75 Vertically							
3476	34¢ Statue of Liberty	02/07/01	.65	.20	5.00	(5)	1.25	379.8
	Self-Adhesive, Serpentine Die-Cut 9.75 Vertically							
3477	34¢ Statue of Liberty	02/07/01	.65	.20	5.00	(5)	1.25	281

ARTHUR FIEDLER

(1894-1979)

Violinist, conductor and musical innovator, Maestro Fiedler has bridged the gap between popular and classical music and given millions around the world a greater appreciation of America's rich cultural heritage.

So reads the citation accompanying the Presidential Medal of Freedom awarded in 1977 to ARTHUR FIEDLER, conductor of the Boston Pops Orchestra for nearly 50 years. Born in Boston into a musical family, Fiedler studied music in Europe, returning to the U.S. at the outbreak of World War I. In 1915 he joined the Boston Symphony. An accomplished violinist, Fiedler also played viola, piano, organ, and percussion; but his ambition was to conduct. In 1924 he

formed a chamber orchestra, the Boston Sinfoniatta; several years later, he organized free open-air symphony concerts in a wooden concert shell built beside Boston's Charles River. In 1930 Fiedler became the first American conductor of the Boston Pops. During his long tenure, "Mr. Pops" became one of the best-known musicians in the country.

He combined popular tunes—including rock 'n' roll—with new music by American composers and classical pieces and audiences loved it. Highly successful recordings and worldwide tours guaranteed the international reputation and incredible popularity of the Boston Pops and its conductor. Fiedler and seven other classical composers and conductors were honored in the 1997 Legends of American Music series. ❑

3466

3468

3470

3471

3472

3473

3478  3479

3480 3481

3481a

3482

  3492a

3491 3492

3499

3497

3500

3501

	Issues of 2001		Un	U	PB	#	FDC	Q(M)
	Coil Stamps, Self-Adhesive, Serpentine Die-Cut 8.5 Vertically							
3478	34¢ Green Flower	02/07/01	.65	.20			1.25	200
3479	34¢ Red Flower	02/07/01	.65	.20			1.25	200
3480	34¢ Tan Flower	02/07/01	.65	.20			1.25	200
3481	34¢ Purple Flower	02/07/01	.65	.20			1.25	200
a	Strip of 4, #3478-3481		2.60		4.50	(5)	3.25	
	Booklet Stamps, Self-Adhesive, Serpentine Die-Cut 11.25 on 3 sides							
3482	20¢ George Washington	02/22/01	.40	.20			1.25	20.5
a	Booklet pane of 10		4.00					
b	Booklet pane of 4		1.60					
c	Booklet pane of 6		2.40					
	Self-Adhesive, Serpentine Die-Cut 10.5 x 11.25 on 3 sides							
3483	20¢ George Washington	02/22/01	1.75	1.50			1.25	
a	Booklet pane of 4		9.00					
b	Booklet pane of 6		15.00					
c	Booklet pane of 10		16.00					
d	Booklet pane of 4		9.00					
e	Booklet pane of 6		15.00					
f	Booklet pane of 10		16.00					
	Self-Adhesive, Serpentine Die-Cut 11 on 2, 3 or 4 sides							
3485	34¢ Statue of Liberty	02/07/01	.65	.20			1.25	
a	Booklet pane of 10		6.50					
b	Booklet pane of 20		13.00					
c	Booklet pane of 4		2.60					
d	Booklet pane of 6		3.90					
	Self-Adhesive, Serpentine Die-Cut 10.25 x 10.75 on 2 or 3 sides							
3487	34¢ Purple Flower	02/07/01	.65	.20			1.25	
3488	34¢ Tan Flower	02/07/01	.65	.20			1.25	
3489	34¢ Green Flower	02/07/01	.65	.20			1.25	
3490	34¢ Red Flower	02/07/01	.65	.20			1.25	
	Block of 4, #3487-3490		2.60				3.25	
	Self-Adhesive, Serpentine Die-Cut 11.25 on 2, 3 or 4 sides							
3491	34¢ Apple	03/06/01	.65	.20			1.25	3
3492	34¢ Orange	03/06/01	.65	.20			1.25	3
a	Pair, #3491-3492		1.30				2.25	
b	Booklet pane of 20, #3491-3492		13.00					
	Booklet Stamps, Self-Adhesive, Serpentine Die-Cut 11.5 x 10.75 on 2 or 3 sides							
3493	34¢ Apple	05/01	.65	.20				101
3494	34¢ Orange	05/01	.65	.20				101
a	Pair, #3493-3494		1.30		2.60	(4)		
b	Booklet pane of 2, #3493-3494		2.60					
	Self-Adhesive, Serpentine Die-Cut 11.75, on 2, 3 or 4 sides							
3496	34¢ Rose and Love Letter	01/19/01	.65	.20			1.25	
a	Booklet pane of 20		13.00					
	Self-Adhesive, Serpentine Die-Cut 11.25							
3497	34¢ Rose and Love Letter	02/14/01	.65	.20			1.25	1.50
a	Booklet pane of 20		13.00					
	Self-Adhesive, Serpentine Die-Cut 11.5 x 10.75 on 2 or 3 sides							
3498	34¢ Rose and Love Letter	02/14/01	.65	.20			1.25	81
a	Booklet pane of 4		2.60					
b	Booklet pane of 6		3.90					
3499	55¢ Rose and Love Letter	02/14/01	1.10	.20	4.50	(4)	1.50	
	Lunar New Year Issue, Self-Adhesive, Serpentine Die-Cut, Perf. 11.25							
3500	34¢ Year of the Snake	01/20/01	.65	.20	2.60	(4)	1.50	55
	Black Heritage Issue, Self-Adhesive, Serpentine Die-Cut 11.5 x 11.25							
3501	34¢ Roy Wilkins	01/24/01	.65	.20	2.60	(4)	1.25	200

Issues of 2001		Un	U	PB	#	FDC	Q(M)
American Illustrators Issue, Self-Adhesive, Serpentine Die-Cut 11.25							
3502	Pane of 20 02/01/01	16.00				9.50	
a	34¢ James Montgomery Flagg	1.00	.35			1.25	144.8
b	34¢ Maxfield Parrish	1.00	.35			1.25	144.8
c	34¢ J. C. Leyendecker	1.00	.35			1.25	144.8
d	34¢ Robert Fawcett	1.00	.35			1.25	144.8
e	34¢ Coles Phillips	1.00	.35			1.25	144.8
f	34¢ Al Parker	1.00	.35			1.25	144.8
g	34¢ A. B. Frost	1.00	.35			1.25	144.8
h	34¢ Howard Pyle	1.00	.35			1.25	144.8
i	34¢ Rose O'Neill	1.00	.35			1.25	144.8
j	34¢ Dean Cornwell	1.00	.35			1.25	144.8
k	34¢ Edwin Austin Abbey	1.00	.35			1.25	144.8
l	34¢ Jessie Willcox Smith	1.00	.35			1.25	144.8
m	34¢ Neysa McMein	1.00	.35			1.25	144.8
n	34¢ Jon Whitcomb	1.00	.35			1.25	144.8
o	34¢ Harvey Dunn	1.00	.35			1.25	144.8
p	34¢ Frederic Remington	1.00	.35			1.25	144.8
q	34¢ Rockwell Kent	1.00	.35			1.25	144.8
r	34¢ N. C. Wyeth	1.00	.35			1.25	144.8
s	34¢ Norman Rockwell	1.00	.35			1.25	144.8
t	34¢ John Held, Jr.	1.00	.35			1.25	144.8
	Self-Adhesive, Serpentine Die-Cut 11.25						
3503	34¢ Diabetes Awareness 03/16/01	.65	.20	2.60	(4)	1.25	100
	Tagged, Perf. 11						
3504	34¢ The Nobel Prize 03/22/01	.65	.20	2.60	(4)	1.50	35

JOHN McCORMACK

(1884-1945)

One of the greatest singers of the 20th century, Irish-born tenor JOHN FRANCIS McCORMACK began his singing career in a Catholic church in Dublin. In 1903, with little formal training, he won a medal at the Irish National Music Festival. Four years later, after studying and performing in Italy, he made his operatic debut at London's Covent Garden. McCormack—whose repertoire included opera, oratorio, Irish folk songs, and ballads—enjoyed a long and successful career in the United States and abroad. Although best known as a concert performer, McCormack was also a successful recording star, reputedly earning royalties exceeding those of his contemporary, the famous Italian tenor Enrico Caruso. McCormack, who regularly performed to sold-out houses, attributed his popularity to the songs he presented. He explained that his programs included songs he loved, songs he thought the audience should like or would learn to like, and songs they wanted to hear "for such songs they have every right to expect." A naturalized American citizen, McCormack was honored by the Postal Service in 1984. ❑

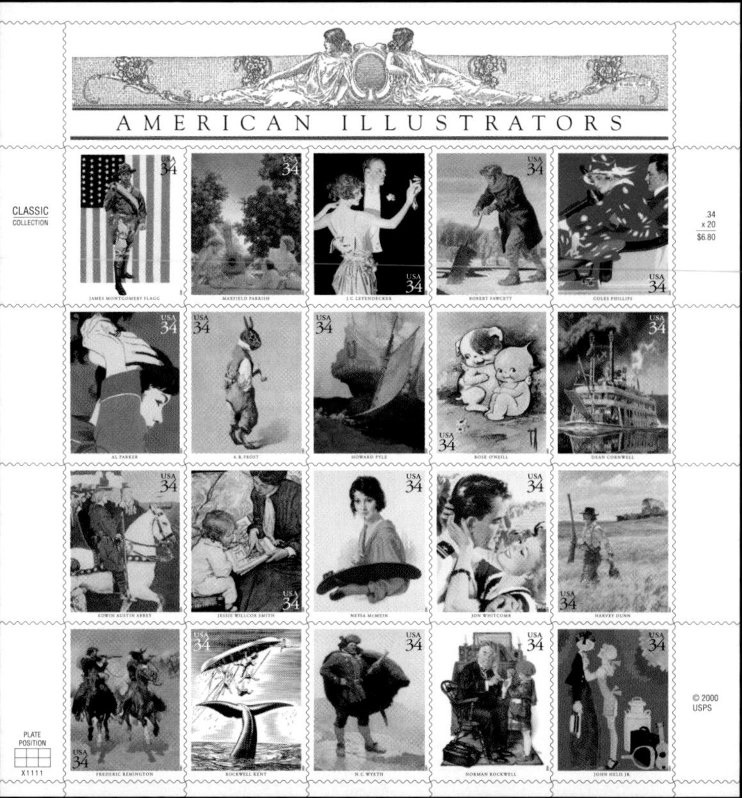
AMERICAN ILLUSTRATORS
CLASSIC COLLECTION
.34 x 20 $6.80
JAMES MONTGOMERY FLAGG
MAXFIELD PARRISH
J.C. LEYENDECKER
ROBERT FAWCETT
COLES PHILLIPS
AL PARKER
A.B. FROST
HOWARD PYLE
ROSE O'NEILL
DEAN CORNWELL
EDWIN AUSTIN ABBEY
JESSIE WILLCOX SMITH
NEYSA McMEIN
JON WHITCOMB
HARVEY DUNN
FREDERIC REMINGTON
ROCKWELL KENT
N.C. WYETH
NORMAN ROCKWELL
JOHN HELD, JR.
© 2000 USPS
PLATE POSITION
X1111

3502 a b c d e

f g h i j

k l m n o

p q r s t

KNOW MORE ABOUT
DIABETES
34 USA

3503

The Nobel Prize
1901-2001
USA 34
ALFRED NOBEL

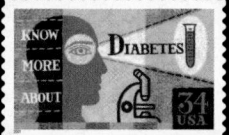

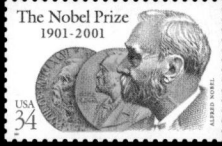

3504

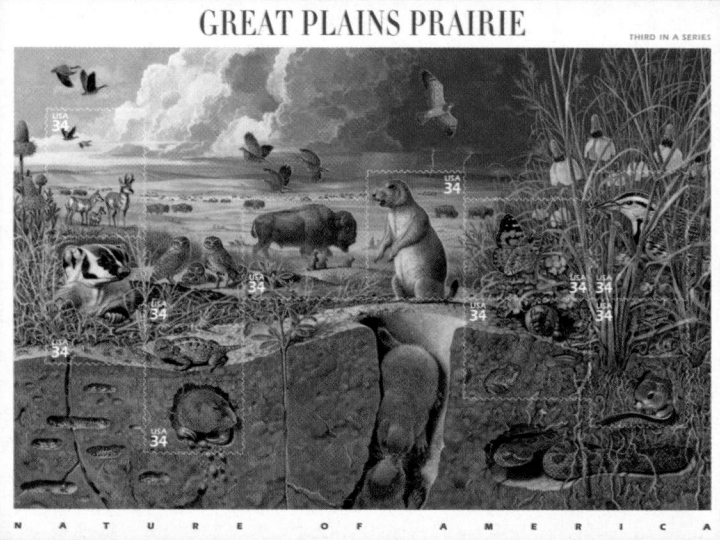

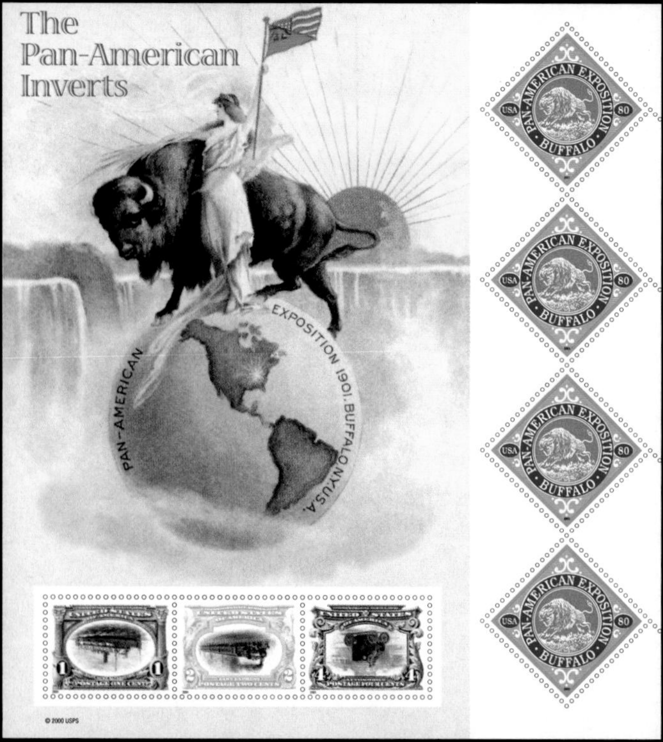
The
Pan-American
Inverts
PAN-AMERICAN
EXPOSITION 1901. BUFFALO.N.Y.U.S.A.
PAN-AMERICAN EXPOSITION
BUFFALO
USA
80
© 2000 USPS

3505 a b c d

GREAT PLAINS PRAIRIE
THIRD IN A SERIES
USA
34
N A T U R E O F A M E R I C A

3506 a b c d e f

g h i j

Issues of 2001		Un	U	PB	#	FDC	Q(M)
The Pan-American Inverts Issue, Tagged, Perf. 12							
3505	34¢ Pane of 7 03/29/01	6.75	—			6.00	11.18
a	1¢ green	.20	.20			1.25	
b	2¢ carmine	.20	.20			1.25	
c	4¢ deep red brown	.20	.20			1.25	
d	80¢ red & blue	1.60	.35			1.75	
Great Plains Prairie Issue, Self-Adhesive, Serpentine Die-Cut 10							
3506	Pane of 10 04/19/01	7.00				7.00	89.6
a	34¢ Pronghorns, Canada geese	.65	.20				
b	34¢ Burrowing owls, American buffalo	.65	.20				
c	34¢ American buffalo, Black-tailed prairie dogs, wild alfalfa	.65	.20				
d	34¢ Black-tailed prairie dog, American buffalo	.65	.20				
e	34¢ Painted lady butterfly, American buffalo, prairie coneflowers, prairie wild roses	.65	.20				
f	34¢ Western meadowlark, camel cricket, prairie coneflowers, prairie wild roses	.65	.20				
g	34¢ Badger, harvester ants	.65	.20				
h	34¢ Eastern short-horned lizard, plains pocket gopher	.65	.20				
i	34¢ Plains spadefoot, dung beetle, prairie wild roses	.65	.20				
j	34¢ Two-stripped grasshopper, Ord's kangaroo rat	.65	.20				

An American Postal Portrait

The rich history of the U.S. Postal Service from 1860 until the present day comes to life in more than 200 dazzling photographs—from behind-the-scenes stories of individual postal workers, to a visual record of the growth of technology. The book also includes color reproductions of every U.S. stamp that commemorates the Post Office and its employees. Sixty-one stamp images and four stationery selections make this book a fascinating tribute to America's leading communications institution.

To order call **1-800-STAMP-24** or visit us online at **www.usps.com**

Item #989100–2001 Portrait Book: An American Postal Portrait $31.50

Issues of 2001		Un	U	PB	#	FDC	Q(M)
Peanuts Comic Strip Issue, Self-Adhesive, Serpentine Die-Cut 11.25 x 11.5							
3507	34¢ Snoopy 05/17/01	.65	.20	2.60	(4)	1.25	125
Self-Adhesive, Serpentine Die-Cut 11.25 x 11.5							
3508	34¢ Honoring Veterans 05/23/01	.65	.20	2.60	(4)	1.50	200
Self-Adhesive, Serpentine Die-Cut, Perf. 11.25							
3509	34¢ Frida Kahlo 06/21/01	.65	.20	2.60	(4)	1.25	55
Baseball's Legendary Playing Fields, Self-Adhesive, Serpentine Die-Cut, Perf. 11.25 x 11.5							
3510	34¢ Ebbets Field, Brooklyn 06/27/01	.65	.20			1.50	125
3511	34¢ Tiger Stadium, Detroit 06/27/01	.65	.20			1.50	125
3512	34¢ Crosley Field, Cincinnati 06/27/01	.65	.20			1.50	125
3513	34¢ Yankee Stadium, New York City 06/27/01	.65	.20			1.50	125
3514	34¢ Polo Grounds, New York City 06/27/01	.65	.20			1.50	125
3515	34¢ Forbes Field, Pittsburgh 06/27/01	.65	.20			1.50	125
3516	34¢ Fenway Park, Boston 06/27/01	.65	.20			1.50	125
3517	34¢ Comiskey Park, Chicago 06/27/01	.65	.20			1.50	125
3518	34¢ Shibe Park, Philadelphia 06/27/01	.65	.20			1.50	125
3519	34¢ Wrigley Field, Chicago 06/27/01	.65	.20			1.50	125
a	Block of 10, #3510-3519	6.50		6.50	(10)	6.50	
Self-Adhesive, Serpentine Die-Cut 8.5 Vertically							
3520	10¢ *Atlas* Statue 06/29/01	.20	.20	2.75	(5)	1.25	400
Self-Adhesive, Serpentine Die-Cut, Perf. 11.25							
3521	34¢ Leonard Bernstein 07/10/01	.65	.20	2.60	(4)	1.25	55
Coil Stamp, Self-Adhesive, Serpentine Die-Cut 11.5 Vertically							
3522	15¢ Woody Wagon 08/03/01	.30	.20	3.00	(5)	1.25	160
Legends of Hollywood Issue, Self-Adhesive Serpentine Die-Cut 11							
3523	34¢ Lucille Ball 08/06/01	.65	.20	2.60	(4)	1.50	110

MARTIN JOHNSON HEADE

(1819-1904)

MARTIN JOHNSON HEADE, today considered one of the finest 19th-century painters of landscapes and still lifes, started painting in his late teens. Initially taught by the folk artist Edward Hicks, he traveled in the United States and Europe, copying works by the masters and painting portraits and genre scenes. In the late 1850s, influenced by Hudson River School artists such as Frederic Edwin Church, he began painting landscapes and still lifes. From the early 1860s—when he began to develop his own very individual style—to the early 1880s, Heade painted coastal and inland views, floral still lifes, and tropical landscapes with hummingbirds and flowers. In 1883 he married and settled in St. Augustine, Florida. He painted Florida's rivers and marshes, but his primary subjects were the state's native flowers, especially the Cherokee rose and the giant magnolia. A prolific artist who exhibited widely, Heade was only moderately successful during his lifetime and was forgotten for decades after his death. Rediscovered in the 1940s, Heade is now respected and admired as a remarkably talented and innovative painter. *Giant Magnolias on a Blue Velvet Cloth*, a circa 1890 oil-on-canvas, is featured on this stamp in the American Treasures series. ❑

3507

3508

3509

3510

3511

3512

3513

3514

3515

3516

3517

3518

3519

3519a

3520

3521

3522

3523

3524 3525

3526 3527

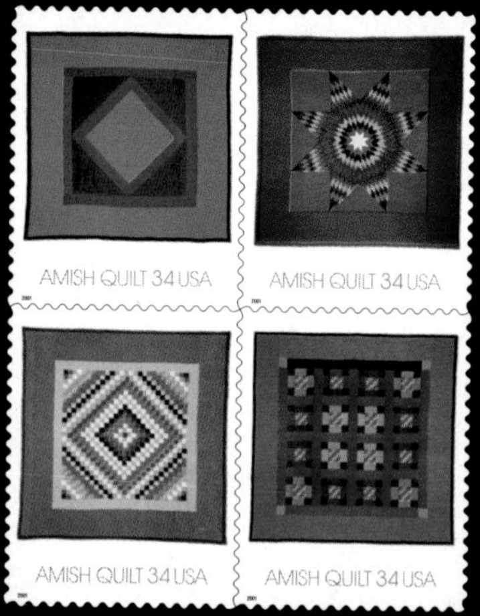
AMISH QUILT 34 USA
AMISH QUILT 34 USA
AMISH QUILT 34 USA
AMISH QUILT 34 USA

3527a

3528 3529

3530 3531

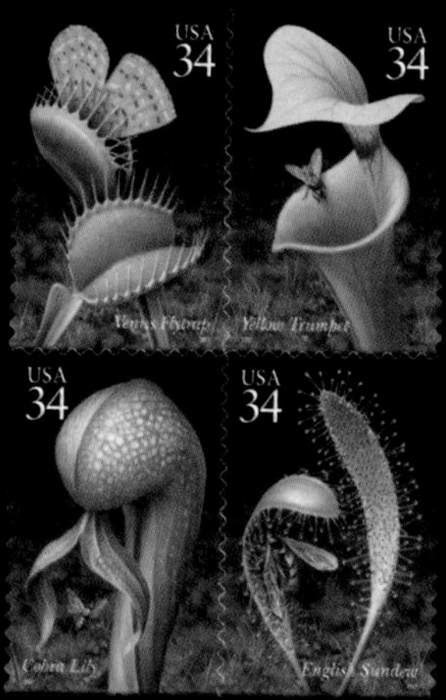
USA 34
Venus Flytrap
USA 34
Yellow Trumpet
USA 34
Cobra Lily
USA 34
English Sundew

3531a

EID
34 USA
GREETINGS

3532

USA Enrico
34 Fermi

3533

That's all Folks!
USA
34

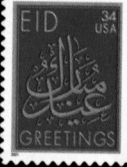

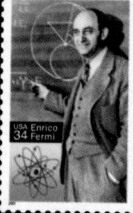

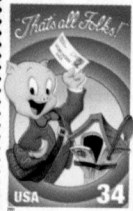

3534a

	Issues of 2001		Un	U	PB	#	FDC	Q(M)
	American Treasures Issue: Amish Quilts, Self-Adhesive, Serpentine Die-Cut 11.25 x 11.5							
3524	34¢ Diamond in the Square	08/09/01	.65	.20			1.25	96
3525	34¢ Lone Star	08/09/01	.65	.20			1.25	96
3526	34¢ Sunshine and Shadow	08/09/01	.65	.20			1.25	96
3527	34¢ Double Ninepatch	08/09/01	.65	.20			1.25	96
a	Block or strip of 4 #3524-3527		2.60		2.60	(4)	3.25	
	Carnivorous Plants Issue, Self-Adhesive, Serpentine Die-Cut 11.5							
3528	34¢ Venus Flytrap	08/23/01	.65	.20				98.6
3529	34¢ Yellow Trumpet	08/23/01	.65	.20				98.6
3530	34¢ Cobra Lily	08/23/01	.65	.20				98.6
3531	34¢ English Sundew	08/23/01	.65	.20				98.6
a	Block or strip of 4 #3528-3531		2.60		2.60	(4)		
	Holiday Celebrations, Self-Adhesive, Serpentine Die-Cut 11.25							
3532	34¢ Eid	09/01/01	.65	.20	2.60	(4)		75
	Perf. 11							
3533	34¢ Enrico Fermi	09/29/01	.65	.20	2.60	(4)	1.25	30
	Looney Tunes Issue, Self-Adhesive, Serpentine Die-Cut 11							
3534	Pane of 10	10/01/01	6.50					
a	34¢ Porky Pig "That's all Folks!"		.65	.20			1.25	275

PAUL ROBESON

(1898-1976)

The 27th stamp in the Black Heritage series honors PAUL ROBESON, who is remembered as an actor, singer, and athlete and for his uncompromising commitment to civil rights and social justice. Paul Leroy Robeson, a Princeton, New Jersey, native, graduated from Rutgers University in 1919 as valedictorian, a member of Phi Beta Kappa, and an All-American football player. Trained as a lawyer at New York's Columbia Law School, he chose to devote himself to a career as a performer. Acclaimed for his definitive portrayal on stage of the title character in Shakespeare's *Othello*, Robeson also starred in films including *The Emperor Jones* and *The Proud Valley*. Concerts, which regularly included his signature song, "Ol' Man River," helped establish African-American spirituals as an American art form. In 1945 the NAACP awarded him the prestigious Spingarn Medal. Controversy about his advocacy of civil rights and support of the Soviet Union in the late 1940s and 1950s temporarily interrupted his career. As public opinion became more favorable in the 1960s, Robeson received many honors, including a Carnegie Hall celebration of his 75th birthday. Posthumous honors include his induction into the College Football Hall of Fame and his Grammy Award for Lifetime Achievement. ❑

Issues of 2001			Un	U	PB	#	FDC	Q(M)
Holiday Celebrations: Christmas Issue, Self-Adhesive Booklet Stamps, Serpentine Die-Cut 11.5 on 2 or 3 sides								
3536	34¢ Madonna and Child by Lorenzo Costa	10/10/01	.65	.20			1.25	800
a	Pane of 20		13.00					
Holiday Celebrations: Holiday Issue, Self-Adhesive, Serpentine Die-Cut 10.75 x 11								
3537	34¢ Santa wearing tan hood	10/10/01	.65	.20			1.25	81
3538	34¢ Santa wearing blue hat	10/10/01	.65	.20			1.25	81
3539	34¢ Santa wearing red hat	10/10/01	.65	.20			1.25	81
3540	34¢ Santa wearing gold hood	10/10/01	.65	.20			1.25	81
b	Block of 4 #3537-3540		2.60		2.60	(4)	3.25	
Self-Adhesive, Serpentine Die-Cut 11 x 11.25								
3545	34¢ James Madison	10/18/01	.65	.20	2.60	(4)	1.25	70
Holiday Celebrations, Self-Adhesive, Serpentine Die-Cut 11.25								
3546	34¢ We Give Thanks	10/19/01	.65	.20	2.60	(4)	1.25	
Self-Adhesive, Serpentine Die-Cut 11								
3547	34¢ Hanukkah	10/21/01	.65	.20	2.60	(4)	1.25	40
3548	34¢ Kwanzaa	10/21/01	.65	.20	2.60	(4)	1.25	40
Serpentine Die-Cut 11.25 on 2, 3 or 4 sides								
3549	34¢ United We Stand	10/24/01	.65	.20			1.50	70
Coil Stamp, Serpentine Die-Cut 9.75 Vertically								
3550	34¢ United We Stand	10/24/01	.65	.20	5.00	(5)	1.50	
Self-Adhesive, Serpentine Die-Cut 11.25								
3551	57¢ Rose and Love Letter	11/19/01	1.10	.20	4.40	(4)	1.50	

JAMES BALDWIN

(1924-1987)

JAMES BALDWIN, one of the foremost American writers of the 20th century, is honored by the Postal Service on the 20th stamp in the Literary Arts series. Baldwin's essays, plays, novels, short stories, and poems explore various subjects, including race relations, the arts, love, and sexuality, and always show their author's strong moral conscience. Born in New York City, Baldwin planned a career as a minister. However, by the time he graduated from high school, he knew he wanted to be a writer. Baldwin's first novel, *Go Tell It on the Mountain*, was published in 1953. Partly autobiographical, this account of a young boy's struggle with personal and spiritual issues elicited praise for Baldwin's exceptional talent. His first essay collection, *Notes of a Native Son*, followed in 1955. Baldwin's second and third novels, *Giovanni's Room* (1956) and *Another Country* (1962), surprised readers with their matter-of-fact portrayals of homosexual relationships. An acknowledged master of American prose, Baldwin was known for eloquently articulating the complexities of race relations during the years of the civil rights movement. In 1963 *The Fire Next Time* solidified his status and landed him on the cover of *Time*. ☐

3536

3537

3538

3539

3540

3540a

3545

3546

3547

3548

3549

3552

3553

3554

3555

3555a

3556

3557

3558

3559

3560

	Issues of 2002		Un	U	PB	#	FDC	Q(M)
	Winter Olympics, Tagged, Self-Adhesive, Serpentine Die-Cut 11.5 x 10.75							
3552	34¢ Ski Jumping	01/08/02	.65	.20	2.60	(4)	1.25	79.64
3553	34¢ Snowboarding	01/08/02	.65	.20	2.60	(4)	1.25	79.64
3554	34¢ Ice Hockey	01/08/02	.65	.20	2.60	(4)	1.25	79.64
3555	34¢ Figure Skating	01/08/02	.65	.20	2.60	(4)	1.25	79.64
a	Block or strip of 4, #3552-3555	01/08/02	2.60		2.60	(4)	3.25	
	Tagged, Self-Adhesive, Serpentine Die-Cut 11 x 10.75							
3556	34¢ Mentoring a Child	01/10/02	.65	.20	2.60	(4)	1.25	132.6
	Black Heritage Series, Tagged, Self-Adhesive, Serpentine Die-Cut 10.25 x 10.5							
3557	34¢ Langston Hughes	02/01/02	.65	.20	2.60	(4)	1.25	120
	Tagged, Self-Adhesive, Serpentine Die-Cut 11							
3558	34¢ Happy Birthday	02/08/02	.65	.20	2.60	(4)	1.25	79.6
	Lunar New Year Issue, Tagged, Self-Adhesive, Serpentine Die-Cut 10.5 x 10.25							
3559	34¢ Year of the Horse	02/11/02	.65	.20	2.60	(4)	1.25	70
	Tagged, Self-Adhesive, Serpentine Die-Cut 10.5 x 11							
3560	34¢ U.S. Military Academy	03/16/02	.65	.20	2.60	(4)	1.25	55

Ready to Mail Stamped Cards

Southeastern Lighthouses 23¢
Twenty Stamped Cards
Five Designs
Item #454466–$9.75

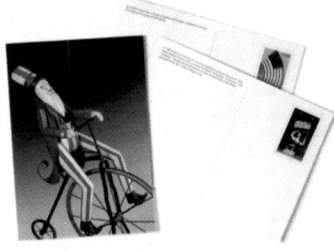

Old Glory 23¢
Twenty Stamped Cards
Five Designs
Item #882066–$9.75

Holiday Music Makers 23¢
Twenty Stamped Cards
Four Designs
Item #564066–$9.75

*Prices subject to change without notice

To order call **1-800-STAMP-24** or visit us online at **www.usps.com**

2002

	Issues of 2002		Un	U	PB	#	FDC	Q(M)
	Greetings From America, Tagged, Self-Adhesive, Serpentine Die-Cut 10.75							
3561	34¢ Alabama	04/04/02	.65	.20			1.25	190
3562	34¢ Alaska	04/04/02	.65	.20			1.25	190
3563	34¢ Arizona	04/04/02	.65	.20			1.25	190
3564	34¢ Arkansas	04/04/02	.65	.20			1.25	190
3565	34¢ California	04/04/02	.65	.20			1.25	190
3566	34¢ Colorado	04/04/02	.65	.20			1.25	190
3567	34¢ Connecticut	04/04/02	.65	.20			1.25	190
3568	34¢ Delaware	04/04/02	.65	.20			1.25	190
3569	34¢ Florida	04/04/02	.65	.20			1.25	190
3570	34¢ Georgia	04/04/02	.65	.20			1.25	190
3571	34¢ Hawaii	04/04/02	.65	.20			1.25	190
3572	34¢ Idaho	04/04/02	.65	.20			1.25	190
3573	34¢ Illinois	04/04/02	.65	.20			1.25	190
3574	34¢ Indiana	04/04/02	.65	.20			1.25	190
3575	34¢ Iowa	04/04/02	.65	.20			1.25	190
3576	34¢ Kansas	04/04/02	.65	.20			1.25	190
3577	34¢ Kentucky	04/04/02	.65	.20			1.25	190
3578	34¢ Louisiana	04/04/02	.65	.20			1.25	190
3579	34¢ Maine	04/04/02	.65	.20			1.25	190
3580	34¢ Maryland	04/04/02	.65	.20			1.25	190
3581	34¢ Massachusetts	04/04/02	.65	.20			1.25	190
3582	34¢ Michigan	04/04/02	.65	.20			1.25	190
3583	34¢ Minnesota	04/04/02	.65	.20			1.25	190
3584	34¢ Mississippi	04/04/02	.65	.20			1.25	190
3585	34¢ Missouri	04/04/02	.65	.20			1.25	190
3586	34¢ Montana	04/04/02	.65	.20			1.25	190
3587	34¢ Nebraska	04/04/02	.65	.20			1.25	190
3588	34¢ Nevada	04/04/02	.65	.20			1.25	190
3589	34¢ New Hampshire	04/04/02	.65	.20			1.25	190
3590	34¢ New Jersey	04/04/02	.65	.20			1.25	190
3591	34¢ New Mexico	04/04/02	.65	.20			1.25	190
3592	34¢ New York	04/04/02	.65	.20			1.25	190
3593	34¢ North Carolina	04/04/02	.65	.20			1.25	190
3594	34¢ North Dakota	04/04/02	.65	.20			1.25	190
3595	34¢ Ohio	04/04/02	.65	.20			1.25	190
3596	34¢ Oklahoma	04/04/02	.65	.20			1.25	190
3597	34¢ Oregon	04/04/02	.65	.20			1.25	190
3598	34¢ Vermont	04/04/02	.65	.20			1.25	190
3599	34¢ Rhode Island	04/04/02	.65	.20			1.25	190
3600	34¢ South Carolina	04/04/02	.65	.20			1.25	190
3601	34¢ South Dakota	04/04/02	.65	.20			1.25	190
3602	34¢ Tennessee	04/04/02	.65	.20			1.25	190
3603	34¢ Texas	04/04/02	.65	.20			1.25	190
3604	34¢ Utah	04/04/02	.65	.20			1.25	190
3605	34¢ Vermont	04/04/02	.65	.20			1.25	190
3606	34¢ Virginia	04/04/02	.65	.20			1.25	190
3607	34¢ Washington	04/04/02	.65	.20			1.25	190
3608	34¢ West Virginia	04/04/02	.65	.20			1.25	190
3609	34¢ Wisconsin	04/04/02	.65	.20			1.25	190
3610	34¢ Wyoming	04/04/02	.65	.20			1.25	190
a	Pane of 50, #3561-3610		32.50					

3610a	3561	3562	3563	3564	3565
	3566	3567	3568	3569	3570
	3571	3572	3573	3574	3575
	3576	3577	3578	3579	3580
	3581	3582	3583	3584	3585
	3586	3587	3588	3589	3590
	3591	3592	3593	3594	3595
	3596	3597	3598	3599	3600
	3601	3602	3603	3604	3605

LONGLEAF PINE FOREST

FOURTH IN A SERIES

N A T U R E   O F   A M E R I C A

3611   a   b   c   d
           e   f   g   h
               i   j

3612

3613

3616

3620

Purple Heart
Matted Keepsake

12" x 16"

This collectible honors the
sacrifices of the men and
women who defend our nation.

*To order this philatelic product
call 1-800-STAMP-24 or
visit us online at www.usps.com*
Item #108982–$21.95

	Issues of 2002		Un	U	PB	#	FDC	Q(M)
	Longleaf Pine Forest, Tagged, Self-Adhesive, Serpentine Die-Cut 10.5 x 10.75, 10.75 x 10.5							
3611	34¢ Wildlife and Flowers, Pane of 10	04/26/02	7.00				7.00	70
a	Bachman's sparrow		.65	.20			1.25	
b	Northern bobwhite,							
	yellow pitcher plants		.65	.20			1.25	
c	Fox squirrel,							
	red-bellied woodpecker		.65	.20			1.25	
d	Brown-headed nuthatch		.65	.20			1.25	
e	Broadhead skink,							
	yellow pitcher plants, pipeworts		.65	.20			1.25	
f	Eastern towhee, yellow pitcher							
	plants, Savannah meadow beauties,							
	toothache grass		.65	.20			1.25	
g	Gray fox, gopher tortoise, horiz.		.65	.20			1.25	
h	Blind click beetle, sweetbay,							
	pine woods treefrog		.65	.20			1.25	
i	Rosebud orchid, pipeworts,							
	southern toad, yellow pitcher plants		.65	.20			1.25	
j	Grass-pink orchid, yellow-sided							
	skimmer, pipeworts, yellow pitcher							
	plants, horiz.		.65	.20			1.25	70
	American Design Series, Coil, Perf. 10 Vertically							
3612	5¢ American Toleware	05/31/02	.20	.20	1.60	(5)	1.25	300
	Coil, Self-Adhesive, Serpentine Die-Cut 11							
3613	3¢ Star (year at lower left)	06/07/02	.20	.20	.25	(4)	1.25	
	Coil, Self-Adhesive, Serpentine Die-Cut 10							
3614	3¢ Star (year at lower right)	06/07/02	.20	.20	.25	(4)	1.25	
3615	3¢ Star (year at lower left)	06/07/02	.20	.20	1.00	(5)	1.25	
	Tagged, Perf. 11.25							
3616	23¢ George Washington (green)	06/07/02	.45	.20	1.80	(4)	1.00	25
	Coil, Self-Adhesive, Serpentine Die-Cut 8.5 Vertically							
3617	23¢ George Washington (gray green)	06/07/02	.45	.20	3.00	(5)	1.00	
	Booklet Stamps, Self-Adhesive Serpentine Die-Cut 11.25 on 3 sides							
3618	23¢ George Washington (green)	06/07/02	.45	.20			1.00	495.5
a	Booklet pane of 4		1.80					
b	Booklet pane of 6		2.70					
	Self-Adhesive, Serpentine Die-Cut 10. 5 x 11.25 on 3 sides							
3619	23¢ George Washington (green)	06/07/02	1.75	1.25				40.7
a	Booklet pane of 4		*6.00*					
b	Booklet pane of 6		*9.50*					
	Tagged, Perf. 11.25 x 11							
3620	(37¢) U.S. Flag (First Class)	06/07/02	.70	.20	2.80	(4)	1.25	
	Self-Adhesive, Serpentine Die-Cut 11.25 x 11							
3621	(37¢) U.S. Flag (First Class)	06/07/02	.70	.20	2.80	(4)	1.25	
	Coil, Self-Adhesive, Serpentine Die-Cut 10 Vertically							
3622	(37¢) U.S. Flag (First Class)	06/07/02	.70	.20	5.25	(5)	1.25	
	Booklet, Self-Adhesive, Serpentine Die-Cut 11.25 on 2, 3 or 4 sides							
3623	(37¢) U.S. Flag (First Class)	06/07/02	.70	.20			1.25	
a	Booklet pane of 20		14.00					
	Booklet, Self-Adhesive, Serpentine Die-Cut 10.5 x 10.75 on 2 or 3 sides							
3624	(37¢) U.S. Flag (First Class)	06/07/02	.70	.20			1.25	
a	Booklet pane of 4		2.80					
b	Booklet pane of 6		4.20					
	Booklet, Self-Adhesive, Serpentine Die-Cut 8 on 2, 3 or 4 sides							
3625	(37¢) U.S. Flag (First Class)	06/07/02	.70	.20			1.25	
a	Booklet pane of 18		13.00					

	Issues of 2002-2003		Un	U	PB	#	FDC	Q(M)
	Antique Toys, Booklet, Self-Adhesive, Serpentine Die-Cut 11 on 2, 3 or 4 sides							
3626	(37¢) Toy Mail Wagon	06/07/02	.70	.20			1.25	120
3627	(37¢) Toy Locomotive	06/07/02	.70	.20			1.25	120
3628	(37¢) Toy Taxicab	06/07/02	.70	.20			1.25	120
3629	(37¢) Toy Fire Pumper	06/07/02	.70	.20			1.25	120
a	Block of 4, #3626-3629		2.80				3.25	
	Self-Adhesive, Serpentine Die-Cut 11.25 x 11							
3630	37¢ U.S. Flag	06/07/02	.70	.20	2.80	(4)	1.25	300
	Coil, Perf 10 Vertically							
3631	37¢ U.S. Flag	06/07/02	.70	.20	5.25	(5)	1.25	
	Self-Adhesive, Serpentine Die-Cut 9.75 Vertically							
3632	37¢ U.S. Flag	06/07/02	.70	.20	4.75	(5)	1.25	
	Self-Adhesive, Serpentine Die-Cut 8.5 Vertically							
3633	37¢ U.S. Flag	06/07/02	.70	.20	5.25	(5)	1.25	
	Booklet, Self-Adhesive, Serpentine Die-Cut 11 on 3 sides							
3634	37¢ U.S. Flag	06/07/02	.70	.20			1.25	
	Booklet, Self-Adhesive, Serpentine Die-Cut 11.25 on 2, 3 or 4 sides							
3635	37¢ U.S. Flag	06/07/02	.70	.20			1.25	
	Booklet, Serpentine Die-Cut 10.5 x 10.75 on 2 or 3 sides							
3636	37¢ U.S. Flag	06/07/02	.70	.20			1.25	
	Booklet, Self-Adhesive, Serpentine Die-Cut 8 on 2, 3 or 4 sides							
3637	37¢ U.S. Flag	02/04/03	.70	.20			1.25	
	Antique Toys, Coil, Self-Adhesive, Serpentine Die-Cut 8.5 Horizontally							
3638	37¢ Toy Locomotive	07/26/02	.70	.20			1.25	
3639	37¢ Toy Mail Wagon	07/26/02	.70	.20			1.25	
3640	37¢ Toy Fire Pumper	07/26/02	.70	.20			1.25	
3641	37¢ Toy Taxicab	07/26/02	.70	.20			1.25	
	Antique Toys, Booklet, Self-Adhesive, Serpentine Die-Cut 11 on 2, 3 or 4 sides							
3642	37¢ Toy Mail Wagon	07/26/02	.70	.20			1.25	
3643	37¢ Toy Locomotive	07/26/02	.70	.20			1.25	
3644	37¢ Toy Taxicab	07/26/02	.70	.20			1.25	
3645	37¢ Toy Fire Pumper	07/26/02	.70	.20			1.25	
	Self-Adhesive, Serpentine Die-Cut 11 x 11.25							
3646	60¢ Coverlet Eagle	07/12/02	1.25	.25	5.00	(4)		100.3
3647	$3.85 Jefferson Memorial	07/30/02	7.50	3.75	30.00	(4)		68.4
3648	$13.65 Capitol Dome	07/30/02	27.50	12.50	110.00	(4)		22.64
	Masters of American Photography, Tagged, Self-Adhesive Serpentine Die-Cut 10.5 x 10.75							
3649	37¢ Pane of 20	06/13/02	14.00				10.00	62.68
a	Southworth & Hawes		.70	.30			1.25	
b	Timothy H. O'Sullivan		.70	.30			1.25	
c	Carleton E. Watkins		.70	.30			1.25	
d	Gertrude Käsebier		.70	.30			1.25	
e	Lewis W. Hine		.70	.30			1.25	
f	Alvin Langdon Coburn		.70	.30			1.25	
g	Edward Steichen		.70	.30			1.25	
h	Alfred Stieglitz		.70	.30			1.25	
i	Man Ray		.70	.30			1.25	
j	Edward Weston		.70	.30			1.25	
k	James VanDerZee		.70	.30			1.25	
l	Dorothea Lange		.70	.30			1.25	
m	Walker Evans		.70	.30			1.25	
n	W. Eugene Smith		.70	.30			1.25	
o	Paul Strand		.70	.30			1.25	
p	Ansel Adams		.70	.30			1.25	
q	Imogen Cunningham		.70	.30			1.25	
r	André Kertész		.70	.30			1.25	
s	Garry Winogrand		.70	.30			1.25	
t	Minor White		.70	.30			1.25	
	Sheet of 120		85.00					

3626  **3627**

3630

3646

3628  **3629**

3629a

3647

3648

MASTERS OF
American
Photography

 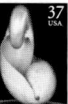

© 2001 USPS   20 x 37 = $7.40

3649   a   b   c   d

3650

3651

Andy Warhol

3652

3653 Teddy Bears USA 37   Teddy Bears USA 37 3654

3655 Teddy Bears USA 37   Teddy Bears USA 37 3656

3656a

3657

3658

3659

3660

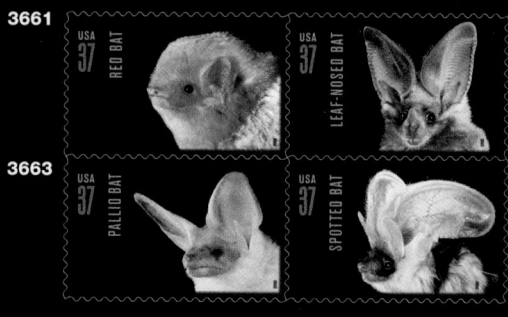

3661 RED BAT   LEAF-NOSED BAT 3662

3663 PALLID BAT   SPOTTED BAT 3664

3664a

	Issues of 2002		Un	U	PB	#	FDC	Q(M)
	American Treasures, Self-Adhesive, Serpentine Die-Cut 10.75							
3650	37¢ John James Audubon	06/27/02	.70	.20	2.80	(4)	1.25	69.5
	Pane of 20			14.00				
	Tagged, Self-Adhesive, Serpentine Die-Cut 11.25							
3651	37¢ Harry Houdini	07/03/02	.70	.20	2.80	(4)	1.25	61
	Pane of 20		14.00		—			
	Tagged, Self-Adhesive, Serpentine Die-Cut 10.5 x 10.75							
3652	37¢ Andy Warhol	08/09/02	.70	.20	2.80	(4)	1.25	61
	Tagged, Self-Adhesive, Serpentine Die-Cut 10.5							
3653	37¢ Bruin Teddy Bear	08/15/02	.70	.20			1.25	210.8
3654	37¢ "Stick" Teddy Bear	08/15/02	.70	.20			1.25	210.8
3655	37¢ Gund Teddy Bear	08/15/02	.70	.20			1.25	210.8
3656	37¢ Ideal Teddy Bear	08/15/02	.70	.20			1.25	210.8
a	Block or vertical strip of 4							
	#3653-3656		2.80		2.80	(4)	3.25	
	Tagged, Booklet, Self-Adhesive, Serpentine Die-Cut 11 on 2, 3 or 4 sides							
3657	37¢ Love	08/16/02	.70	.20			1.25	805
a	Booklet pane of 20			14.00				
	Self-Adhesive, Serpentine Die-Cut 11							
3658	60¢ Love	08/16/02	1.25	.25	5.00	(4)	1.50	75
3659	37¢ Ogden Nash	08/19/02	.70	.20	2.80	(4)	1.25	60
	Tagged, Self-Adhesive, Serpentine Die-Cut 11.5 x 11.75							
3660	37¢ Duke Kahanamoku	08/24/02	.70	.20	2.80	(4)	1.25	62.8
	American Bats Issue, Tagged, Self-Adhesive, Serpentine Die-Cut 10.75							
3661	37¢ Red Bat	09/13/02	.70	.20			1.25	111
3662	37¢ Leaf-nosed Bat	09/13/02	.70	.20			1.25	111
3663	37¢ Pallid Bat	09/13/02	.70	.20			1.25	111
3664	37¢ Spotted Bat	09/13/02	.70	.20			1.25	111
a	Block or horizontal strip of 4							
	#3661-3664		2.80		2.80	(4)	3.25	

JAMES CAGNEY

(1904-1986)

JAMES CAGNEY was not simply the quintessential "tough guy;" he was also a talented song-and-dance actor. Born and raised in New York City, he attended Columbia University but left before graduating due to family problems. Although he had no formal training as an actor, he tried out for a part in a play and got it—on his first try. He worked as a vaudeville performer and stage actor before being signed to a movie contract by Warner Bros. In 1930 he played the lead opposite Joan Blondell in his first movie, *Sinner's Holiday*. A year later, his outstanding performance as a gangster in *The Public Enemy* launched a successful film career that included films such as *G-Men* (1935), *Angels with Dirty Faces* (1938), and *The Roaring Twenties* (1939). In 1942 Cagney won an Academy Award for his performance as song-and-dance man George M. Cohan in the hit movie *Yankee Doodle Dandy*. The citation accompanying his 1984 Presidential Medal of Freedom acknowledged that the film and Cagney's role in it had "inspired a nation at war when it sorely needed a lift in spirit." ❑

Issues of 2002		Un	U	PB	#	FDC	Q(M)
Women in Journalism Issue, Self-Adhesive, Serpentine Die-Cut 11 x 10.5							
3665	37¢ Nellie Bly	09/14/02	.70	.20			1.25	60.99
3666	37¢ Ida M. Tarbell	09/14/02	.70	.20			1.25	60.99
3667	37¢ Ethel L. Payne	09/14/02	.70	.20			1.25	60.99
3668	37¢ Marguerite Higgins	09/14/02	.70	.20			1.25	60.99
a	Block or horizontal strip of 4							
	#3665-3668		2.80		2.80	(4)	3.25	
3669	37¢ Irving Berlin	09/15/02	.70	.20	2.80	(4)	1.25	61
Serpentine Die-Cut 10.75 x 10.5							
3670	37¢ Neuter & Spay (Kitten)	09/20/02	.70	.20			1.25	84.9
3671	37¢ Neuter & Spay (Puppy)	09/20/02	.70	.20			1.25	84.9
Holiday Celebrations, Self-Adhesive, Serpentine Die-Cut 11							
3672	37¢ Hanukkah	10/10/02	.70	.20	2.80	(4)	1.25	35
3673	37¢ Kwanzaa	10/10/02	.70	.20	2.80	(4)	1.25	
3674	37¢ Eid	10/10/02	.70	.20	2.80	(4)	1.25	35
Holiday Celebrations: Christmas Issue, Self-Adhesive, Serpentine Die-Cut 11 x 11.25 on 2, 3 or 4 sides							
3675	37¢ Madonna and Child							
	by Gossaert	10/10/02	.70	.20			1.25	536.2
a	Booklet pane of 20		14.00					
Holiday Celebrations: Holiday Issue, Self-Adhesive, Serpentine Die-Cut 11							
3676	37¢ Snowman w/red & green							
	plaid scarf	10/28/02	.70	.20			1.25	125
3677	37¢ Snowman w/blue plaid scarf	10/28/02	.70	.20			1.25	125
3678	37¢ Snowman w/pipe	10/28/02	.70	.20			1.25	125
3679	37¢ Snowman w/top hat	10/28/02	.70	.20			1.25	125
a	Block or vertical strip of 4, #3676-3679		2.80		2.80	(4)	3.25	
Coil, Self-Adhesive, Serpentine Die-Cut 8.5 Vertically							
3680	37¢ Snowman w/blue plaid scarf	10/28/02	.70	.20			1.25	
3681	37¢ Snowman w/pipe	10/28/02	.70	.20			1.25	
3682	37¢ Snowman w/top hat	10/28/02	.70	.20			1.25	
3683	37¢ Snowman w/red & green							
	plaid scarf	10/28/02	.70	.20			1.25	
a	Strip of 4, #3680-3683		2.80		5.50	(5)	3.25	
Booklet, Self-Adhesive, Serpentine Die-Cut 10.75 x 11 on 2 or 3 sides							
3684	37¢ Snowman w/red & green							
	plaid scarf	10/28/02	.70	.20			1.25	4
3685	37¢ Snowman w/blue plaid scarf	10/28/02	.70	.20			1.25	4
3686	37¢ Snowman w/pipe	10/28/02	.70	.20			1.25	4
3687	37¢ Snowman w/top hat	10/28/02	.70	.20			1.25	4
a	Block of 4, #3684-3687		2.80				3.25	
Booklet, Self-Adhesive, Serpentine Die-Cut 11 on 2 or 3 sides							
3688	37¢ Snowman w/red & green							
	plaid scarf	10/28/02	.70	.20			1.25	
3689	37¢ Snowman w/blue plaid scarf	10/28/02	.70	.20			1.25	
3690	37¢ Snowman w/pipe	10/28/02	.70	.20			1.25	
3691	37¢ Snowman w/top hat	10/28/02	.70	.20			1.25	
a	Block of 4 #3688-3691		2.80				3.25	
Legends of Hollywood Issue, Self-Adhesive, Serpentine Die-Cut 10.75							
3692	37¢ Cary Grant	10/15/02	.70	.20	2.80	(4)	1.25	80
Coil, Self-Adhesive, Serpentine Die-Cut 8.5 Vertically							
3693	(5¢) Sea Coast	10/21/02	.20	.20	1.50	(5)	1.25	1,000

3665  **3666**

3669

3667  **3668**

3668a

3670 **3671**
3672

3673 **3674** **3675**

3676  **3677**

3678 **3679**

3692 **3693**

3679a

The "Hawaiian Missionary" Stamps of 1851-1853

The first official Hawaiian post office was established in December 1850. Postmaster Henry M. Whitney had stamps printed locally in three denominations. Philatelists call these rare stamps "Hawaiian Missionaries" because virtually all were used by Christian missionaries on outbound mail. Only 28 covers with Missionary stamps are known to exist; only the Dawson cover (right) bears the 2¢ stamp. The two 13¢ stamps were unusual as they prepaid postage in two countries–Hawaii and the U.S.

© 2001 USPS

3694

a   b   c   d

3695

3696

B2

	Issues of 2002		Un	U	PB	#	FDC	Q(M)
3694	37¢ Hawaiian Missionary	10/24/02	2.80	.80			3.25	6.44
a	37¢-2¢ of 1851 (Hawaii Scott 1)		.70	.20			1.25	
b	37¢-5¢ of 1851 (Hawaii Scott 2)		.70	.20			1.25	
c	37¢-13¢ of 1851 (Hawaii Scott 3)		.70	.20			1.25	
d	37¢-13¢ of 1852 (Hawaii Scott 4)		.70	.20			1.25	
	Tagged, Self-Adhesive, Serpentine Die-Cut 11							
3695	37¢ Happy Birthday	10/25/02	.70	.20	2.80	(4)	1.25	50
	Greetings From America, Tagged, Self-Adhesive, Serpentine Die-Cut 10.75							
3696	37¢ Alabama	10/25/02	.70	.20			1.25	200
3697	37¢ Alaska	10/25/02	.70	.20			1.25	200
3698	37¢ Arizona	10/25/02	.70	.20			1.25	200
3699	37¢ Arkansas	10/25/02	.70	.20			1.25	200
3700	37¢ California	10/25/02	.70	.20			1.25	200
3701	37¢ Colorado	10/25/02	.70	.20			1.25	200
3702	37¢ Connecticut	10/25/02	.70	.20			1.25	200
3703	37¢ Delaware	10/25/02	.70	.20			1.25	200
3704	37¢ Florida	10/25/02	.70	.20			1.25	200
3705	37¢ Georgia	10/25/02	.70	.20			1.25	200
3706	37¢ Hawaii	10/25/02	.70	.20			1.25	200
3707	37¢ Idaho	10/25/02	.70	.20			1.25	200
3708	37¢ Illinois	10/25/02	.70	.20			1.25	200
3709	37¢ Indiana	10/25/02	.70	.20			1.25	200
3710	37¢ Iowa	10/25/02	.70	.20			1.25	200
3711	37¢ Kansas	10/25/02	.70	.20			1.25	200
3712	37¢ Kentucky	10/25/02	.70	.20			1.25	200
3713	37¢ Louisiana	10/25/02	.70	.20			1.25	200
3714	37¢ Maine	10/25/02	.70	.20			1.25	200
3715	37¢ Maryland	10/25/02	.70	.20			1.25	200
3716	37¢ Massachusetts	10/25/02	.70	.20			1.25	200
3717	37¢ Michigan	10/25/02	.70	.20			1.25	200
3718	37¢ Minnesota	10/25/02	.70	.20			1.25	200
3719	37¢ Mississippi	10/25/02	.70	.20			1.25	200
3720	37¢ Missouri	10/25/02	.70	.20			1.25	200
3721	37¢ Montana	10/25/02	.70	.20			1.25	200
3722	37¢ Nebraska	10/25/02	.70	.20			1.25	200
3723	37¢ Nevada	10/25/02	.70	.20			1.25	200
3724	37¢ New Hampshire	10/25/02	.70	.20			1.25	200
3725	37¢ New Jersey	10/25/02	.70	.20			1.25	200
3726	37¢ New Mexico	10/25/02	.70	.20			1.25	200
3727	37¢ New York	10/25/02	.70	.20			1.25	200
3728	37¢ North Carolina	10/25/02	.70	.20			1.25	200
3729	37¢ North Dakota	10/25/02	.70	.20			1.25	200
3730	37¢ Ohio	10/25/02	.70	.20			1.25	200
3731	37¢ Oklahoma	10/25/02	.70	.20			1.25	200
3732	37¢ Oregon	10/25/02	.70	.20			1.25	200
3733	37¢ Pennsylvania	10/25/02	.70	.20			1.25	200
3734	37¢ Rhode Island	10/25/02	.70	.20			1.25	200
3735	37¢ South Carolina	10/25/02	.70	.20			1.25	200
3736	37¢ South Dakota	10/25/02	.70	.20			1.25	200
3737	37¢ Tennessee	10/25/02	.70	.20			1.25	200
3738	37¢ Texas	10/25/02	.70	.20			1.25	200
3739	37¢ Utah	10/25/02	.70	.20			1.25	200
3740	37¢ Vermont	10/25/02	.70	.20			1.25	200
3741	37¢ Virginia	10/25/02	.70	.20			1.25	200
3742	37¢ Washington	10/25/02	.70	.20			1.25	200
3743	37¢ West Virginia	10/25/02	.70	.20			1.25	200
3744	37¢ Wisconsin	10/25/02	.70	.20			1.25	200
3745	37¢ Wyoming	10/25/02	.70	.20			1.25	200
a	Pane of 50, #3696-3745		35.00					
	Tagged, Self-Adhesive, Serpentine Die-Cut 11.25							
B2	(34¢+11¢) Heroes of 2001	06/07/02	.90	.65	3.60	(4)	2.00	255

2003

Issues of 2003			Un	U	PB	#	FDC	Q(M)
Black Heritage Series, Tagged, Self-Adhesive, Serpentine Die-Cut 11.5								
3746	37¢ Thurgood Marshall	01/07/03	.70	.20	2.80	(4)	1.25	150
Lunar New Year Series, Tagged, Self-Adhesive, Serpentine Die-Cut 11.5								
3747	37¢ Year of the Ram	01/15/03	.70	.20	2.80	(4)	1.25	70
Literary Arts, Tagged, Self-Adhesive, Serpentine Die-Cut 10.75								
3748	37¢ Zora Neale Hurston	01/24/03	.70	.20	2.80	(4)	1.25	70
American Design Series, Tagged, Self-Adhesive, Serpentine Die-Cut 11.25 x 11								
3751	37¢ American Clock	01/24/03	.20	.20	.80	(4)	1.25	150
Coil, Perf. 10 Vertically								
3757	37¢ Tiffany Lamp	03/01/03	.20	.20			1.25	210
American Culture Series, Tagged, Self-Adhesive, Serpentine Die-Cut 11.25 x 11								
3766	$1 Wisdom	02/28/03	2.00	.50	8.00	(4)	2.50	100
Coil, Untagged, Perf. 10 Vertically								
3769	(10¢) New York Public Library Lion	02/04/03	.20	.20			1.25	170
Coil, Untagged, Self-Adhesive, Serpentine Die-Cut 11, Vertically								
3770	(10¢) Atlas Statue dated "2003"	11/03	.20	.20	2.75	(5)		400
Tagged, Self-Adhesive, Serpentine Die-Cut 11								
3771	80¢ Special Olympics	02/13/03	1.60	.35	6.40	(4)	1.75	60
American Filmmaking: Behind the Scenes								
Tagged, Self-Adhesive, Serpentine Die-Cut 11, Horizontally								
3772	37¢ Pane of 10	02/25/03	7.00				7.25	70
a	Screenwriting (script from *Gone With the Wind*)		.70	.20			1.25	
b	Directing (John Cassavetes)		.70	.20			1.25	
c	Costume Design (Edith Head)		.70	.20			1.25	
d	Music (Max Steiner working on score)		.70	.20			1.25	
e	Makeup (Jack Pierce-Boris Karloff for *Frankenstein*)		.70	.20			1.25	
f	Art Direction (Perry Ferguson for *Citizen Kane*)		.70	.20			1.25	
g	Cinematography (Paul Hill for *Nagana*)		.70	.20			1.25	
h	Film Editing (J. Watson Webb for *The Razor's Edge*)		.70	.20			1.25	
i	Special Effects (Mark Siegel for *E.T. Extra-Terrestrial*)		.70	.20			1.25	
j	Sound (Gary Summers)		.70	.20			1.25	

BRET HARTE
(1836-1902)

FRANCIS BRETT HARTE was born in Albany, New York, and went as a young man to California, where he tried his luck at various occupations, including mining. Signing himself as Bret Harte, he became a prominent literary figure and was appointed editor of the *Overland Monthly*, in which he published stories of California life such as "The Luck of Roaring Camp," about an infant raised in an all-male mining camp after his mother dies in childbirth, and "The Outcasts of Poker Flat." Those and other stories were collected in *The Luck of Roaring Camp and Other Sketches*, published in 1870, which brought Harte international fame. In addition to stories, he wrote novels, poetry, and plays; in collaboration with Mark Twain, he produced *Ah Sin*, a dramatic adaptation of one of his stories. His earlier writing was his most successful. In 1878, Harte began work as U.S. consul in Prussia, and later accepted a similar post in Scotland; he lived the latter part of his life in London. Harte's stories balance comic and sentimental elements; his characters often conceal integrity and even nobility beneath a rough exterior. ❏

3746

3747

3748

3751

3757

3766

3771

3772

a   f

b   g

c   h

d   i

e   j

3773

3774

3776

3777

3778

3779

3780   3780a

3781

3782

3783

3784

3786

Issues of 2003		Un	U	PB	#	FDC	Q(M)
	Tagged, Self-Adhesive, Serpentine Die-Cut 11.75 x 11.5						
3773	37¢ Ohio Statehood	03/01/03	.70	.20	2.80	(4)	1.25	50
	Tagged, Self-Adhesive, Serpentine Die-Cut 12 x 11.5						
3774	37¢ Pelican Island Natural						
	Wildlife Refuge	03/14/03	.70	.20	2.80	(4)	1.25	55
	Coil, Untagged, Perf. 9.75 Vertically						
3775	(5¢) Sea Coast	03/19/03	.20	.20	1.50	(5)	1.25	200
	Old Glory, Booklet, Tagged, Self-Adhesive, Serpentine Die-Cut 10 x 9.75						
3776	37¢ Uncle Sam on Bicycle						
	with Liberty Flag	04/03/03	.70	.20			1.25	
3777	37¢ 1888 Presidential Campaign	04/03/03	.70	.20			1.25	
3778	37¢ 1893 Silk Bookmark	04/03/03	.70	.20			1.25	
3779	37¢ Modern Hand Fan	04/03/03	.70	.20			1.25	
3780	37¢ Carving of Woman with Flag & Sword						
	19th Century	04/03/03	.70	.20			1.25	
a	Horizontal strip of 5 #3776-3780		3.50				4.00	60
b	Booklet pane, 2 #3780a		7.00					
	Tagged, Self-Adhesive, Serpentine Die-Cut 11.75 x 11.5						
3781	37¢ Cesar E. Chavez	04/23/03	.70	.20	2.80	(4)	1.25	75
	Tagged, Self-Adhesive, Serpentine Die-Cut 10.75						
3782	37¢ Louisiana Purchase	04/30/03	.70	.20	2.80	(4)	1.25	54
	Booklet, Tagged, Self-Adhesive, Serpentine Die-Cut 11						
3783	37¢ First Flight	05/22/03	.70	.20			1.25	85
a	Booklet pane of 9		6.30					
b	Booklet pane of 1		.70					
	Tagged, Self-Adhesive, Serpentine Die-Cut 11.25 x 10.75						
3784	37¢ Purple Heart	05/30/03	.70	.20	2.80	(4)	1.25	120
	Tagged, Self-Adhesive, Serpentine Die-Cut 10.75 x 10.25						
3784A	37¢ Purple Heart	05/30/03	.70	.20	2.80	(4)		
	Coil, Untagged, Self-Adhesive, Serpentine Die-Cut 9.5 x 10						
3785	(5¢) Sea Coast	06/03	.20	.20	1.50	(5)		50
	Legends of Hollywood Issue, Tagged, Self-Adhesive, Serpentine Die-Cut 10.75						
3786	37¢ Audrey Hepburn	06/11/03	.70	.20	2.80	(4)	1.25	80

JACK LONDON

(1876-1916)

JOHN GRIFFITH LONDON, one of the most popular and prolific writers of his time, packed a variety of experiences into his short life. He was born in San Francisco but traveled widely and did many types of work before selling his first story. As a young man, he traveled to the Yukon during the Alaska gold rush; joined a sealing cruise that took him to Japan; worked in a laundry and a cannery; and had several other adventures. His first collection of stories, *The Son of the Wolf*, published in 1900,

brought him fame. Another collection, *Lost Face* (1910), contained his popular work, "To Build a Fire," about a freezing man's desperate attempts to stay warm in the Arctic. London's novels include two complementary tales: *The Call of the Wild* (1903) is about a dog who escapes from civilization, while *White Fang* (1906) tells the story of a wild dog who is tamed. His many other novels include *The Sea-Wolf* (1904), about the powerful captain of a sealing ship, and *The Iron Heel* (1908), an account of class struggle reflecting London's interest in socialism. ❑

	Issues of 2003		Un	U	PB	#	FDC	Q(M)
	Southeastern Lighthouses, Tagged, Self-Adhesive, Serpentine Die-Cut 10.75							
3787	37¢ Old Cape Henry, Virginia	06/13/03	.70	.20			1.25	
3788	37¢ Cape Lookout, North Carolina	06/13/03	.70	.20			1.25	
3789	37¢ Morris Island, South Carolina	06/13/03	.70	.20			1.25	
3790	37¢ Tybee Island, Georgia	06/13/03	.70	.20			1.25	
3791	37¢ Hillsboro Inlet, Florida	06/13/03	.70	.20			1.25	
a	Strip of 5, #3587-3791		3.50				4.00	125
	American Eagle Issue, Untagged, Coil, Serpentine Die-Cut 11.75 Vertically							
3792	(25¢) gray background & gold eagle	06/26/03	.50	.20			1.25	
3793	(25¢) gold background & red eagle	06/26/03	.50	.20			1.25	
3794	(25¢) dull blue background & gold eagle	06/26/03	.50	.20			1.25	
3795	(25¢) gold background & Prussian blue eagle	06/26/03	.50	.20			1.25	
3796	(25¢) green background & gold eagle	06/26/03	.50	.20			1.25	
3797	(25¢) gold background & grey eagle	06/26/03	.50	.20			1.25	
3798	(25¢) Prussian blue background & gold eagle	06/26/03	.50	.20			1.25	
3799	(25¢) gold background & dull blue eagle	06/26/03	.50	.20			1.25	
3800	(25¢) red background & gold eagle	06/26/03	.50	.20			1.25	
3801	(25¢) gold background & green eagle	06/26/03	.50	.20			1.25	
a	Strip of 10, #3792-3801		5.00				6.00	310
	Arctic Tundra Issue, Tagged, Self-Adhesive, Serpentine Die-Cut 10.75 x 10.5, 10.5 x 10.75							
3802	Wildlife & Vegetation pane of 10	07/02/03	.70	.20			7.50	60
a	37¢ Gyrfalcon		.70	.20			1.25	
b	37¢ Gray wolf		.70	.20			1.25	
c	37¢ Common raven		.70	.20			1.25	
d	37¢ Musk oxen & caribou		.70	.20			1.25	
e	37¢ Grizzly beatytrs, caribou		.70	.20			1.25	
f	37¢ Caribou, willow ptarmigans		.70	.20			1.25	
g	37¢ Arctic ground squirrel		.70	.20			1.25	
h	37¢ Willow ptarmigan, bearberry		.70	.20			1.25	
i	37¢ Arctic grayling		.70	.20			1.25	
j	37¢ Singing vole, thin-legged wolf spider, lingonberry, Labrador tea		.70	.20			1.25	

NAT "KING" COLE

(1919-1965)

NAT "KING" COLE was already an acclaimed jazz pianist when his warm, relaxed vocal style brought him even greater success as a balladeer. His many hits include "Straighten Up and Fly Right," "Mona Lisa," "The Christmas Song," and "Unforgettable." He was born in Alabama but grew up in Chicago, where his father was a minister and his mother a church organist. Taught by his mother, Cole learned how to play piano as a child; he could play pop songs at the age of four. To indulge his love for music, he would sneak out of the house and hang around outside the jazz clubs, listening to the likes of Louis Armstrong and Earl "Fatha" Hines. He made his first recording in 1936 with his brother Eddie's band, and formed his own trio in 1939. Cole's jazz arrangements emphasized the piano as a solo instrument. He was handsome, suave, and elegant; he performed internationally and in 1960 gave a command performance for Queen Elizabeth II in the London Palladium Theatre. ❑

3787   3788   3789   3790   3791   3791a

3801a

3797   3798   3799   3800   3801   3792   3793   3794   3795   3796

3802   a

b

c   d   f   e

g

j   h   i

3804

3805

3803

3806

3807

3807a

3808

3809

3810

3811

3811a

3812

3813

Issues of 2003		Un	U	PB	#	FDC	Q(M)
Self-Adhesive, Serpentine Die-Cut 11.5 x 11.75							
3803	37¢ Korean War Veterans Memorial	07/27/03	.70	.20	2.80	(4)	1.25	86.8
American Treasures Issue, Self-Adhesive, Serpentine Die-Cut 10.75 on 2 or 3 sides							
3804	37¢ Mary Cassatt—Young Mother	08/07/03	.70	.20			1.25	
3805	37¢ Mary Cassatt—Children Playing on the Beach	08/07/03	.70	.20			1.25	
3806	37¢ Mary Cassatt—On a Balcony	08/07/03	.70	.20			1.25	
3807	37¢ Mary Cassatt—Child in a Straw Hat	08/07/03	.70	.20			1.25	
a	Block of 4, #3804-3807		2.80				3.25	778.8
Early Football Heroes, Self-Adhesive, Serpentine Die-Cut 11.5 x 11.75							
3808	37¢ Bronko Nagurski	08/08/03	.70	.20			1.25	
3809	37¢ Ernie Nevers	08/08/03	.70	.20			1.25	
3810	37¢ Walter Camp	08/08/03	.70	.20			1.25	
3811	37¢ Red Grange	08/08/03	.70	.20			1.25	
a	Block of 4, #3808-3811		2.80		2.80	(4)	3.25	70
Self-Adhesive, Serpentine Die-Cut 11							
3812	37¢ Roy Acuff	09/13/03	.70	.20	2.80	(4)	1.25	52
3813	37¢ District of Columbia	09/23/03	.70	.20	2.80	(4)	1.25	72

WOODCARVED FIGURINES

In 1986 the Postal Service issued four stamps in the American Folk Art series featuring familiar examples of the art of woodcarving. Some of America's earliest artists were average citizens—farmers, blacksmiths, and storekeepers—who expressed themselves in wood, the most abundant medium available. These early woodcarvers combined symbolism with practicality to create objects that were beautiful as well as useful. Eighteenth-century ships featured hand-carved wooden figureheads and stern pieces in the form of mermaids, eagles, or sometimes the captain's wife. Nineteenth-century merchants attracted customers by displaying life-size figures of Indians, well-dressed gentlemen, or Scottish Highlanders outside their shops. Hunters carved life-like wooden decoys to attract ducks and geese and homeowners set out small whirligigs—figures with bladed arms that twirled in the breeze—as decoration. Throughout the 18th and 19th centuries, these popular figurines expressed the ingenuity and imagination of the growing nation. ❑

#	Issues of 2003		Un	U	PB	#	FDC	Q(M)
	Reptiles and Amphibians, Self-Adhesive, Serpentine Die-Cut 11							
3814	37¢ Scarlet Kingsnake	10/07/03	.70	.20			1.25	
3815	37¢ Blue-Spotted Salamander	10/07/03	.70	.20			1.25	
3816	37¢ Reticulate Collared Lizard	10/07/03	.70	.20			1.25	
3817	37¢ Ornate Chorus Frog	10/07/03	.70	.20			1.25	
3818	37¢ Ornate Box Turtle	10/07/03	.70	.20			1.25	
a	Vert. strip of 5, #3814-3818		3.50		7.00	(10)	4.00	100
	Self-Adhesive, Serpentine Die-Cut 11							
3819	23¢ George Washington Type of 2002	10//03	.45	.20	1.80	(4)	1.25	200
	Holiday Celebrations: Christmas Issue, Booklet, Self-Adhesive, Serpentine Die-Cut 11 x 11.25 on 2 or 3 sides							
3820	37¢ Madonna and Child by Gossaert	10/23/03	.70	.20			1.25	
a	Booklet pane of 20		14.00					700
	Holiday Celebrations: Holiday Issue, Music Makers, Self-Adhesive, Serpentine Die-Cut 11.75 x 11							
3821	37¢ Reindeer with Pan Pipes	10/23/03	.70	.20			1.25	
3822	37¢ Santa Claus with Drum	10/23/03	.70	.20			1.25	
3823	37¢ Santa Claus with Trumpet	10/23/03	.70	.20			1.25	
3824	37¢ Reindeer with Horn	10/23/03	.70	.20			1.25	
a	Block of 4, #3821-3824		2.80		2.80	(4)	3.25	125
	Booklet, Self-Adhesive, Serpentine Die-Cut 10.5 x 10.75 on 2 or 3 sides							
3825	37¢ Reindeer with Pan Pipes	10/23/03	.70	.20			1.25	
3826	37¢ Santa Claus with Drum	10/23/03	.70	.20			1.25	
3827	37¢ Santa Claus with Trumpet	10/23/03	.70	.20			1.25	
3828	37¢ Reindeer with Horn	10/23/03	.70	.20			1.25	
a	Block of 4, #3825-3828		2.80				3.25	200
	Coil, Self-Adhesive, Serpentine Die-Cut 8.5 Vertically							
3829	37¢ Snowy Egret	10/24/03	.70	.20	5.25	(5)	1.25	2,000
	Semi-Postal Stamp, Self-Adhesive, Serpentine Die-Cut 11							
B3	(37¢+8¢) Stop Family Violence	10/08/03	.90	.65	3.60	(4)	1.60	125

ALFRED HITCHCOCK

(1899-1980)

ALFRED JOSEPH HITCHCOCK was born in London, England, and attended the University of London before working as a card illustrator for silent movies. He volunteered to direct his first film when the director became ill and followed that experience by directing a string of successful films. Although reluctant to leave his homeland, Hitchcock knew that there was only one place to make films: Hollywood. His first American film, *Rebecca*—an adaptation of the Daphne du Maurier novel—won the 1940 Academy Award for best picture. During his long career, he directed more than 50 films including *Rear Window* (1954), *Dial M for Murder* (1954),

Vertigo (1958), *Psycho* (1960), and *The Birds* (1963). From 1955-1965 his television series *Alfred Hitchcock Presents* introduced Hitchcock to millions of viewers who loved his witty and suspenseful preludes and closings. The fourth honoree in the Legends of Hollywood series, he became a naturalized U.S. citizen in 1955. Shortly before his death in 1980, Hitchcock—the inveterate Englishman—was knighted by Queen Elizabeth II. ◻

3814

Scarlet Kingsnake

USA 37
2003

3815

Blue-spotted Salamander

USA 37
2003

3816

Reticulate Collared Lizard

USA 37
2003

3817

Ornate Chorus Frog

USA 37
2003

3818

Ornate Box Turtle

USA 37
2003

3818a

CHRISTMAS

37 USA

J. Gossaert   Art Institute of Chicago

3820

3821   3822

37 USA 2003

37 USA 2003

37 USA 2003

37 USA 2003

3823   3824   3824a

USA 37
2003

3829

FIRST-CLASS + USA

STOP FAMILY VIOLENCE

2003

B3

C1

C2

C3

C3a

C4

C5

C6

C7

C10

C11

C12

C13

C14

C15

C18

C20

C21

C23

Issues of 1918-1938		Un	U	PB	#	FDC	Q(M)
	Perf. 11						
	For prepayment of postage on all mailable matter sent by airmail. All unwatermarked.						
C1	6¢ Curtiss Jenny 12/10/18	65.00	30.00	725.00	(6)	*32,500.00*	3
	Double transfer	90.00	45.00				
C2	16¢ Curtiss Jenny 07/11/18	85.00	35.00	1,000.00	(6)	*32,500.00*	4
C3	24¢ Curtiss Jenny 05/13/18	80.00	35.00	400.00	(4)	*27,500.00*	2
a	Center Inverted	*170,000.00*		*1,200,000.00*	(4)		0.0001
C4	8¢ Airplane Radiator and						
	Wooden Propeller 08/15/23	22.50	14.00	225.00	(6)	450.00	6
C5	16¢ Air Service Emblem 08/17/23	80.00	30.00	1,550.00	(6)	650.00	5
C6	24¢ De Havilland Biplane 08/21/23	90.00	30.00	2,050.00	(6)	850.00	5
C7	10¢ Map of U.S. and						
	Two Mail Planes 02/13/26	2.60	.35	35.00	(6)	60.00	42
	Double transfer	5.75	1.10				
C8	15¢ olive brown (C7) 09/18/26	3.00	2.50	35.00	(6)	75.00	16
C9	20¢ yellow green (C7) 01/25/27	7.50	2.00	75.00	(6)	100.00	18
C10	10¢ Lindbergh's						
	"Spirit of St. Louis" 06/18/27	7.25	2.50	90.00	(6)	25.00	20
a	Booklet pane of 3 05/26/28	80.00	*65.00*			875.00	
C11	5¢ Beacon on Rocky						
	Mountains 07/25/28	5.00	.75	175.00	(8)	50.00	107
	Recut frame line at left	6.50	1.25				
a	Vertical pair, imperf. between	*5,500.00*					
C12	5¢ Winged Globe 02/10/30	10.00	.50	135.00	(6)	12.00	98
a	Horizontal pair, imperf. between	*4,500.00*					
	Graf Zeppelin Issue						
C13	65¢ Zeppelin over						
	Atlantic Ocean 04/19/30	250.00	160.00	2,250.00	(6)	1,250.00	0.09
C14	$1.30 Zeppelin						
	Between Continents 04/19/30	475.00	375.00	5,600.00	(6)	1,100.00	0.07
C15	$2.60 Zeppelin						
	Passing Globe 04/19/30	700.00	575.00	8,000.00	(6)	1,250.00	0.06
	Perf. 10.5 x 11						
C16	5¢ violet (C12) 08/19/31	5.25	.60	75.00	(4)	175.00	57
C17	8¢ olive bister (C12) 09/26/32	2.25	.40	27.50	(4)	15.00	77
	Century of Progress Issue, Perf. 11						
C18	50¢ Zeppelin, Federal Building						
	at Chicago Exposition and						
	Hangar at Friedrichshafen 10/02/33	65.00	65.00	525.00	(6)	200.00	0.3
	Beginning with #C19, unused values are for never-hinged stamps.						
	Perf. 10.5 x 11						
C19	6¢ dull orange (C12) 06/30/34	3.50	.25	21.00	(4)	*190.00*	302
	Trans-Pacific Issue, Perf. 11						
C20	25¢ "China Clipper"						
	over the Pacific 11/22/35	1.40	1.00	20.00	(6)	40.00	10
C21	20¢ "China Clipper"						
	over the Pacific 02/15/37	11.00	1.75	100.00	(6)	45.00	13
C22	50¢ carmine (C21) 02/15/37	10.00	5.00	100.00	(6)	50.00	9
C23	6¢ Eagle Holding Shield,						
	Olive Branch and Arrows 05/14/38	.50	.20	7.00	(4)	15.00	350
	6¢ ultramarine and carmine	*150.00*	*1,500.00*	1,500.00	(4)		
a	Vertical pair, imperf. horizontally	*325.00*		1,250	(4)		
b	Horizontal pair, imperf. vertically	*12,500.00*		37,500.00	(4)		

	Issue of 1939		Un	U	PB/LP	#	FDC	Q(M)
	Transatlantic Issue, Perf. 11							
C24	30¢ Winged Globe	05/16/39	10.50	1.50	130.00	(6)	47.50	20
	Perf. 11 x 10.5							
C25	6¢ Twin-Motor Transport Plane	06/25/41	.20	.20	.60	(4)	3.75	4,477
a	Booklet pane of 3	03/18/43	5.00	1.50			25.00	
	Singles of #C25a are imperf. at sides or imperf. at sides and bottom.							
b	Horizontal pair, imperf. between		2,250.00					
C26	8¢ olive green (C25)	03/21/44	.20	.20	1.10	(4)	3.75	1,745
C27	10¢ violet (C25)	08/15/41	1.25	.20	5.75	(4)	8.00	67
C28	15¢ brn. carmine (C25)	08/19/41	2.25	.35	10.50	(4)	10.00	78
C29	20¢ bright green (C25)	08/27/41	2.25	.30	10.00	(4)	12.50	42
C30	30¢ blue (C25)	09/25/41	2.25	.35	10.50	(4)	20.00	60
C31	50¢ orange (C25)	10/29/41	11.00	3.25	52.50	(4)	40.00	11
C32	5¢ DC-4 Skymaster	09/25/46	.20	.20	.45	(4)	2.00	865
	Perf. 10.5 x 11							
C33	5¢ DC-4 Skymaster	03/26/47	.20	.20	.55	(4)	2.00	972
	Perf. 11 x 10.5							
C34	10¢ Pan American Union Bldg., Washington, D.C. and Martin 2-0-2	08/30/47	.25	.20	1.10	(4)	2.00	208
a	Dry printing		.40	.20	1.75	(4)		
C35	15¢ Statue of Liberty, N.Y. Skyline and Lockheed Constellation	08/20/47	.35	.20	1.50	(4)	1.75	756
a	Horizontal pair, imperf. between		2,400.00					
b	Dry printing		.55	.20	2.50	(4)		
C36	25¢ San Francisco-Oakland Bay Bridge and Boeing Stratocruiser	07/30/47	.90	.20	3.75	(4)	2.25	133
a	Dry printing		1.10	.20	4.75	(4)		
	Perf. 10 Horizontally							
C37	5¢ carmine (C33)	01/15/48	1.00	.80	10.00	(2)	1.75	33
	Perf. 11 x 10.5							
C38	5¢ New York City	07/31/48	.20	.20	3.50	(4)	1.75	38
	Perf. 10.5 x 11							
C39	6¢ carmine (C33)	01/18/49	.20	.20	.50	(4)	1.50	5,070
a	Booklet pane of 6	11/18/49	10.00	5.00			10.00	
b	Dry printing		.50	.20	2.25	(4)		
c	As "a," dry printing		20.00	—				
	Perf. 11 x 10.5							
C40	6¢ Alexandria, Virginia	05/11/49	.20	.20	.50	(4)	1.50	75
	Coil Stamp, Perf. 10 Horizontally							
C41	6¢ carmine (C33)	08/25/49	3.00	.20	14.00	(2)	1.25	260
	Universal Postal Union Issue, Perf. 11 x 10.5							
C42	10¢ Post Office Dept. Bldg.	11/18/49	.20	.20	1.40	(4)	1.75	21
C43	15¢ Globe and Doves Carrying Messages	10/07/49	.30	.25	1.25	(4)	2.75	37
C44	25¢ Boeing Stratocruiser and Globe	11/30/49	.60	.40	5.25	(4)	3.75	16
C45	6¢ Wright Brothers	12/17/49	.20	.20	.65	(4)	2.75	80
C46	80¢ Diamond Head, Honolulu, Hawaii	03/26/52	5.00	1.25	22.50	(4)	17.50	19
C47	6¢ Powered Flight	05/29/53	.20	.20	.55	(4)	1.50	78
C48	4¢ Eagle in Flight	09/03/54	.20	.20	1.25	(4)	1.00	50

C24

C25

C32

C33

C34

C35

C36

C38

C40

C42

C43

C44

C45

C46

C47

C48

C49

C51

C53

C54

C55

C56

C57

C58

C59

C61

C62

C63

C64

C66

C67

C68

C69

C70

C71

Issue of 1957		Un	U	PB/LP	#	FDC	Q(M)
Perf. 11 x 10.5							
C49 6¢ Air Force	08/01/57	.20	.20	.65	(4)	1.25	63
C50 5¢ rose red (C48)	07/31/58	.20	.20	1.25	(4)	1.00	72
Perf. 10.5 x 11							
C51 7¢ Jet Airliner	07/31/58	.20	.20	.60	(4)	1.00	1,327
a Booklet pane of 6		12.50	7.00			9.00	221
Coil Stamp, Perf. 10 Horizontally							
C52 7¢ blue (C51)	07/31/58	2.00	.20	14.00	(2)	1.00	157
Perf. 11 x 10.5							
C53 7¢ Alaska Statehood	01/03/59	.20	.20	.60	(4)	1.25	90
Perf. 11							
C54 7¢ Balloon Jupiter	08/17/59	.20	.20	.60	(4)	1.75	79
Perf. 11 x 10.5							
C55 7¢ Hawaii Statehood	08/21/59	.20	.20	.60	(4)	1.00	85
Perf. 11							
C56 10¢ Pan American Games	08/27/59	.25	.25	1.25	(4)	1.00	39
C57 10¢ Liberty Bell	06/10/60	1.10	.70	4.75	(4)	1.25	40
C58 15¢ Statue of Liberty	11/20/59	.35	.20	1.50	(4)	1.25	98
C59 25¢ Abraham Lincoln	04/22/60	.50	.20	2.00	(4)	1.25	
a Tagged	12/29/66	.60	.30	2.50	(4)	50.00	
Perf. 10.5 x 11							
C60 7¢ carmine (C61)	08/12/60	.20	.20	.60	(4)	1.00	1,289
Pair with full horizontal gutter between							
a Booklet pane of 6	08/19/60	14.00	8.00			8.00	
b Vertical pair, imperf. between		5,500.00					
Coil Stamp, Perf. 10 Horizontally							
C61 7¢ Jet Airliner	10//22/60	4.00	.25	35.00	(2)	1.00	87
Perf. 11							
C62 13¢ Liberty Bell	06/28/61	.40	.20	1.65	(4)	1.00	
a Tagged	02/15/67	.75	.50	5.00	(4)	50.00	
C63 15¢ Statue of Liberty	01/13/61	.30	.20	1.25	(4)	1.00	
a Tagged	01/11/67	.35	.20	1.50	(4)	50.00	
b As "a," horiz. pair, imperf. vertically		15,000.00					
#C63 has a gutter between the two parts of the design; C58 does not.							
Perf. 10.5 x 11							
C64 8¢ Jetliner over Capitol	12/05/62	.20	.20	.65	(4)	1.00	
a Tagged	08/01/63	.20	.20	.65	(4)	1.25	
b Bklt. pane of 5 + label		7.00	3.00			3.50	
c As "b," tagged	1964	2.00	.75				
Coil Stamp, Perf. 10 Horizontally							
C65 8¢ carmine (C64)	12/05/62	.40	.20	3.75	(2)	1.00	
a Tagged	01/14/65	.35	.20	1.50	(2)	50.00	
Perf. 11							
C66 15¢ Montgomery Blair	05/03/63	.60	.55	2.60	(4)	1.10	42
Perf. 11 x 10.5							
C67 6¢ Bald Eagle	07/12/63	.20	.20	1.60	(4)	1.00	
a Tagged	02/15/67	4.00	3.00	55.00	(4)	50.00	
Perf. 11							
C68 8¢ Amelia Earhart	07/24/63	.20	.20	1.00	(4)	3.00	64
C69 8¢ Robert H. Goddard	10/05/64	.40	.20	1.75	(4)	3.00	62
C70 8¢ Alaska Purchase	03/30/67	.25	.20	1.25	(4)	1.25	56
C71 20¢ "Columbia Jays," by Audubon, (See also #1241)	04/26/67	.80	.20	3.50	(4)	2.00	165
a Tagging omitted		10.00					

Issues of 1968		Un		PB/LP	#	FDC	Q(M)
Unwmk., Perf. 11 x 10.5							
C72	10¢ 50-Star Runway	01/05/68	.20	.20	.90	(4)	1.00	
b	Booklet pane of 8		2.00	.75			3.75	
c	Booklet pane of 5 + label	01/06/68	3.75	.75			125.00	
Coil Stamp, Perf. 10 Vertically							
C73	10¢ carmine (C72)	01/05/68	.30	.20	1.75	(2)	1.00	
a	Imperf., pair		600.00		900.00	(2)		
Perf. 11							
C74	10¢ U.S. Air Mail Service	05/15/68	.25	.20	2.00	(4)	1.50	
b	Tagging omitted		7.50					
C75	20¢ USA and Jet	11/22/68	.35	.20	1.75	(4)	1.25	
a	Tagging omitted		10.00					
C76	10¢ Moon Landing	09/09/69	.25	.20	1.10	(4)	5.00	152
a	Rose red omitted		500.00		—			
Perf. 10.5 x 11							
C77	9¢ Delta Wing Plane	05/15/71	.20	.20	.90	(4)	1.00	
Perf. 11 x 10.5							
C78	11¢ Silhouette of Jet	05/07/71	.20	.20	.90	(4)	1.00	
a	Booklet pane of 4 + 2 labels		1.25	.75			2.25	
b	Untagged (Bureau precanceled)		.85	.85				
c	Tagging omitted (not Bureau precanceled)		7.50					
C79	13¢ Winged Airmail Envelope	11/16/73	.25	.20	1.10	(4)	1.00	
a	Booklet pane of 5 + label	12/27/73	1.50	.75			2.25	
b	Untagged (Bureau precanceled)		.85	.85				
Perf. 11							
C80	17¢ Statue of Liberty	07/13/71	.35	.20	1.60	(4)	1.25	
a	Tagging omitted		10.00	—				
C81	21¢ USA and Jet	05/21/71	.40	.20	2.00	(4)	1.00	
a	Tagging omitted		10.00					
Coil Stamps, Perf. 10 Vertically							
C82	11¢ carmine (C78)	05/07/71	.25	.20	.80	(2)	1.00	
a	Imperf., pair		275.00		425.00	(2)		
C83	13¢ carmine (C79)	12/27/73	.30	.20	1.10	(2)	1.00	
a	Imperf., pair		75.00		150.00	(2)		
National Parks Centennial Issue, Perf. 11 (See also #1448-54)							
C84	11¢ Kii Statue and Temple at City of Refuge Historical National Park, Honaunau, Hawaii	05/03/72	.20	.20	.90	(4)	1.00	78
a	Blue and green omitted		800.00					
Olympic Games Issue, Perf. 11 x 10.5 (See also #1460-62)							
C85	11¢ Skiers and Olympic Rings	08/17/72	.20	.20	2.50	(10)	1.00	96
Progress in Electronics Issue, Perf. 11 (See also #1500-02)							
C86	11¢ DeForest Audions	07/10/73	.20	.20	.95	(4)	1.00	59
a	Vermilion and green omitted		1,100.00					
b	Tagging omitted		20.00					
C87	18¢ Statue of Liberty	01/11/74	.35	.30	1.50	(4)	1.00	
a	Tagging omitted		17.50					
C88	26¢ Mount Rushmore National Memorial	01/02/74	.50	.20	2.25	(4)	1.50	
a	Tagging omitted		17.50					
C89	25¢ Plane and Globes	01/02/76	.50	.20	2.25	(4)	1.00	
C90	31¢ Plane, Globes and Flag	01/02/76	.60	.20	2.60	(4)	1.25	
a	Tagging omitted		10.00					

C72 **C74**

C75

FIRST MAN ON THE MOON

C76

C77

C78 **C79** **C80** **C81**

C84

C85

C86

C87

C88

C89

C90

1978-1983

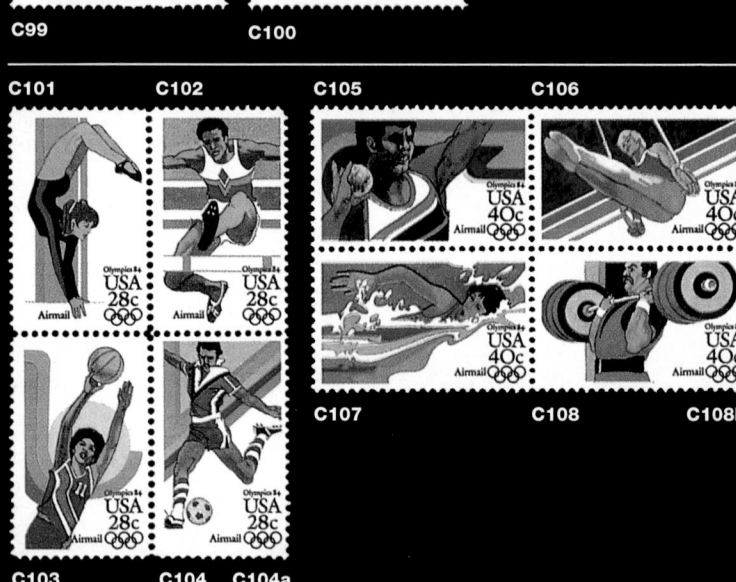

C91 **C93** **C95**

C92 **C92a** **C94** **C94a** **C96** **C96a**

C97

C98

C99

C100

C101 **C102**

C103 **C104** **C104a**

C105 **C106**

C107 **C108** **C108b**

C109 **C110**

C111 **C112** **C112a**

Issues of 1978			Un	U	PB	#	FDC	Q(M)
Aviation Pioneers Issue, Perf. 11								
C91	31¢ Wright Brothers, Flyer A	09/23/78	.65	.30			3.00	157
C92	31¢ Wright Brothers, Flyer A and Shed	09/23/78	.65	.30			3.00	157
a	Vert. pair, #C91-92		1.30	1.20	3.00	(4)	4.00	
b	As "a," ultramarine and black omitted		750.00					
c	As "a," black omitted		—					
d	As "a," black, yellow, magenta, blue and brown omitted		2,250.00					
Aviation Pioneers Issue, Tagged, Perf. 11 (See also #C99-100)								
C93	21¢ Octave Chanute and Biplane Hang-Glider	03/29/79	.70	.35			3.00	29
C94	21¢ Biplane Hang-Glider and Chanute	03/29/79	.70	.35			3.00	29
a	Attached pair, #C93-94		1.40	1.20	3.25	(4)	4.00	
b	As "a," ultramarine and black omitted		4,500.00					
C95	25¢ Wiley Post and "Winnie Mae"	11/20/79	1.10	.45			3.00	32
C96	25¢ NR-105-W, Post in Pressurized Suit and Portrait	11/20/79	1.10	.45			3.00	32
a	Vert. pair, #C95-96		2.25	1.50	5.00	(4)	4.00	
Olympic Summer Games Issue, Tagged, Perf. 11								
C97	31¢ High Jumper	11/01/79	.70	.30	9.50	(12)	1.50	47
C98	40¢ Philip Mazzei	10/13/80	.80	.20	10.00	(12)	1.50	81
b	Imperf., pair		2,750.00					
d	Tagging omitted		10.00					
Tagged, Perf. 10.5 x 11.25								
C98A	40¢ Philip Mazzei	1982	7.50	1.50	125.00	(12)		
Aviation Pioneers Issue, Tagged, Perf. 11								
C99	28¢ Blanche Stuart Scott and Biplane	12/30/80	.60	.20	8.50	(12)	1.50	20
C100	35¢ Glen Curtiss and "Pusher" Biplane	12/30/80	.65	.20	9.00	(12)	1.50	23
Olympic Summer Games Issue, Tagged, Perf. 11								
C101	28¢ Gymnast	06/17/83	1.00	.30			1.75	43
C102	28¢ Hurdler	06/17/83	1.00	.30			1.75	43
C103	28¢ Basketball Player	06/17/83	1.00	.30			1.75	43
C104	28¢ Soccer Player	06/17/83	1.00	.30			1.75	43
a	Block of 4, #C101-04		4.25	2.50	5.50	(4)	3.75	
Olympic Summer Games Issue, Perf. 11.2 Bullseye								
C105	40¢ Shotputter	04/08/83	.90	.40			1.75	67
a	Perf. 11 line		1.00	.45				
C106	40¢ Gymnast	04/08/83	.90	.40			1.75	67
a	Perf. 11 line		1.00	.45				
C107	40¢ Swimmer	04/08/83	.90	.40			1.75	67
a	Perf. 11 line		1.00	.45				
C108	40¢ Weightlifter	04/08/83	.90	.40			1.75	67
a	Perf. 11 line		1.00	.45			5.00	
b	Block of 4, #C105-#C108		4.25	3.00	5.00	(4)		
c	Block of 4, #C105a-#C108a		5.00	4.00	7.50	(4)		
d	Block of 4, imperf.		1,250.00					
Olympic Summer Games Issue, Tagged, Perf. 11								
C109	35¢ Fencer	11/04/83	.90	.55			1.75	43
C110	35¢ Bicyclist	11/04/83	.90	.55			1.75	43
C111	35¢ Volleyball Players	11/04/83	.90	.55			1.75	43
C112	35¢ Pole Vaulter	11/04/83	.90	.55			1.75	43
a	Block of 4, #C109-12		4.00	3.25	7.00	(4)	4.50	

	Issues of 1985		Un	U	PB	#	FDC	Q(M)
	Aviation Pioneers Issues, Tagged, Perf. 11(See also #C128-29)							
C113	33¢ Alfred Verville							
	and Airplane Diagram	02/13/85	.65	.20	3.25	(4)	1.50	168
a	Imperf., pair		850.00					
C114	39¢ Lawrence and							
	Elmer Sperry	02/13/85	.80	.25	3.75	(4)	1.50	168
a	Imperf., pair		1,500.00					
C115	44¢ Transpacific Airmail	02/15/85	.85	.25	4.00	(4)	1.75	209
a	Imperf., pair		850.00					
C116	44¢ Junipero Serra	08/22/85	1.00	.35	8.50	(4)	2.00	164
a	Imperf., pair		1,500.00					
C117	44¢ New Sweden	03/29/88	1.00	.25	6.75	(4)	1.50	137
C118	45¢ Samuel P. Langley	05/14/88	.90	.20	4.25	(4)	1.50	406
a	Overall tagging		3.00	.50	30.00	(4)		
C119	36¢ Igor Sikorsky	06/23/88	.70	.25	3.25	(4)	1.75	179
	Tagged, Perf. 11.5 x 11							
C120	45¢ French Revolution	07/14/89	.95	.20	4.75	(4)	1.50	38
	America/PUAS Issue, Perf. 11 (See also #2426)							
C121	45¢ Southeast Carved Wood Figure,							
	Key Marco Cat (A.D. 700-1450),							
	Emblem of the Postal Union of the							
	Americas and Spain	10/12/89	.90	.20	5.25	(4)	1.50	39
	20th UPU Congress Issue, Perf. 11 (See also #2434-38)							
C122	45¢ Hypersonic Airliner	11/27/89	1.00	.50			1.75	27
C123	45¢ Air-Cushion Vehicle	11/27/89	1.00	.50			1.75	27
C124	45¢ Surface Rover	11/27/89	1.00	.50			1.75	27
C125	45¢ Shuttle	11/27/89	1.00	.50			1.75	27
a	Block of 4, #C122-25		4.25	3.25	5.50	(4)	6.50	
b	As "a," light blue omitted		800.00					

AMERICAN ★ COMMEMORATIVE ★ COLLECTIBLES

American Commemorative Panels

Obtain photo or steel engravings, mint condition stamps and subject related text presented on a beautifully designed page. Only $6.00* each, depending on the value of the stamps.

For more information call
1-800-STAMP-24

Prices subject to change without notice.

C113

C114

C115

C116

C117

C118

C119

C120

C121

C122   **C123**

C124   **C125**

C125a

20th Universal Postal Congress

A glimpse at several potential mail delivery methods of the future is the theme of these four stamps issued by the U.S. in commemoration of the convening of the 20th Universal Postal Congress in Washington, D.C. from November 13 through December 14, 1989. The United States, as host nation to the Congress for the first time in ninety-two years, welcomed more than 1,000 delegates from most of the member nations of the Universal Postal Union to the major international event.

©USPS 1988

C126

C127

C128

C129

C130

C131

C133

C134

C135

C136

C137

C138

CE1

CE2

	Issues of 1989		Un	U	PB	#	FDC	Q(M)
	20th UPU Congress Issue Souvenir Sheet, Tagged, Imperf.							
C126	Designs of #C122-25	11/24/89	4.75	3.75			6.50	2
a-d	Single stamp from sheet		1.00	.50				
	America/PUAS Issue, Tagged, Perf. 11 (See also #2512)							
C127	45¢ Tropical Coast	10/12/90	.90	.20	6.75	(4)	1.50	39
	Aviation Pioneers Issues, Tagged, Perf. 11							
C128	50¢ Harriet Quimby							
	and Early Plane	04/27/91	1.00	.25	5.50	(4)	1.50	
a	Vertical pair, imperf. horizontally		1,900.00					
b	Perf. 11.2	04/27/91	1.10	.25	6.00	(4)		
C129	40¢ William T. Piper							
	and Piper Cub Airplane	05/17/91	.80	.20	4.00	(4)	1.50	
	Tagged, Perf. 11							
C130	50¢ Antarctic Treaty	06/21/91	1.00	.35	5.00	(4)	1.50	113
	America/PUAS Issue, Tagged, Perf. 11							
C131	50¢ Eskimo and Bering							
	Land Bridge	10/12/91	1.00	.35	5.25	(4)	1.50	15
	Tagged, Perf. 11							
C132	40¢ William T. Piper, Type of 1991	1993	1.40	.35	35.00	(4)		
	Self-Adhesive, Tagged, Perf. 11							
C133	48¢ Niagara Falls	05/12/99	.95	.20	4.00	(4)	1.40	
	Self-Adhesive, Tagged, Serpentine Die-Cut 11							
C134	40¢ RioGrande	07/30/99	.80	.60	3.20	(4)	1.25	
	Self-Adhesive, Tagged, Serpentine Die-Cut 11.25 x 11.5							
C135	60¢ Grand Canyon	01/20/2000	1.25	.25	5.00	(4)	1.50	100
C136	70¢ Nine-Mile Prairie	03/06/01	1.40	.30	5.60	(4)	1.50	
	Self-Adhesive, Tagged, Serpentine Die-Cut 11							
C137	80¢ Mount McKinley	04/17/01	1.60	.35	6.40	(4)	1.75	
	Self-Adhesive, Tagged, Serpentine Die-Cut 11.25 x 11.5							
C138	60¢ Acadia National Park	05/30/01	1.25	.25	5.00	(4)	1.50	
	Airmail Special Delivery Stamps							
	Unwmk. Perf. 11							
CE1	16¢ Great Seal of the							
	United States	08/30/34	.60	.70	15.00	(6)	25.00	
	For imperforate variety see #771							
CE2	16¢ red and blue	02/10/36	.40	.25	6.50	(4)	17.50	
a	Horizontal pair, imperf. vertically		4,250.00					

Official and Penalty Mail Stamps

1873-2002

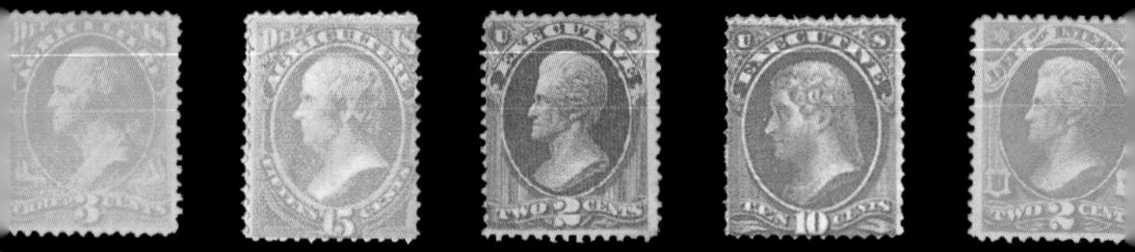

O3 O7 O11 O14 O16

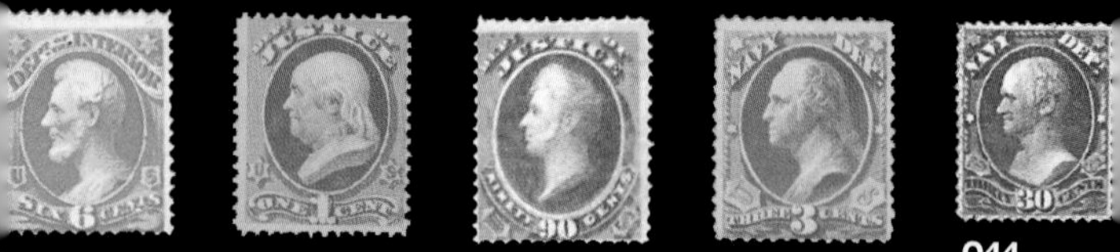

O18 O25 O34 O37 O44

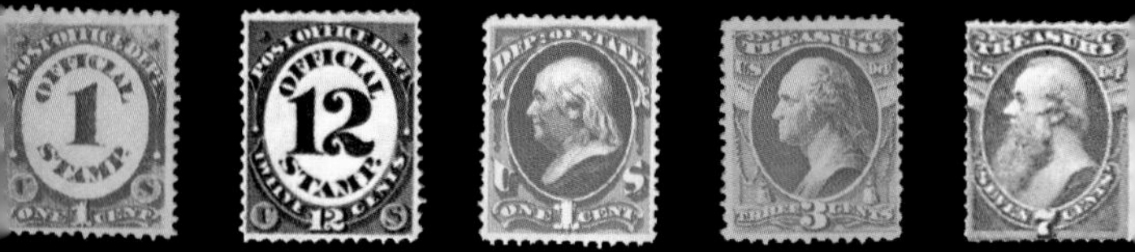

O47 O52 O57 O74 O76

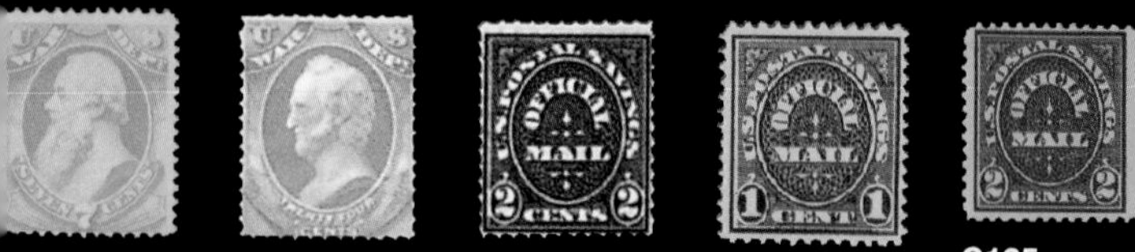

O87 O91 O121 O124 O125

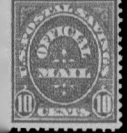

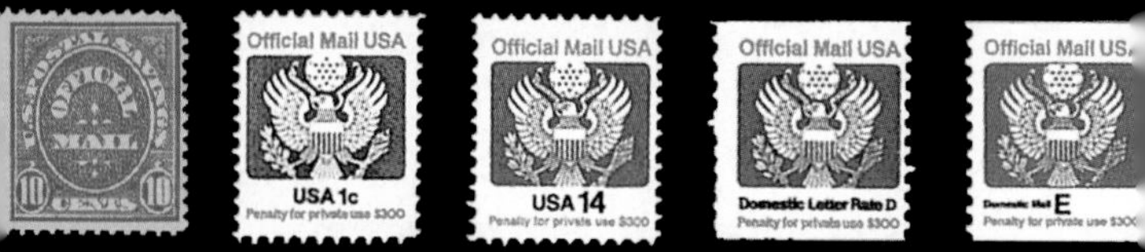

O126 O127 O129A O139 O140

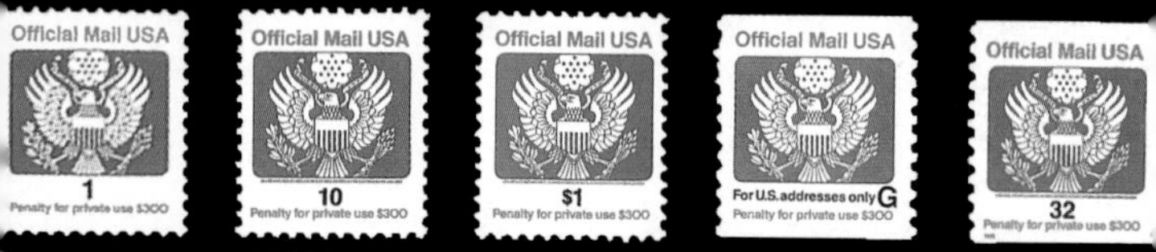

O143 O146A O151 O152 O153

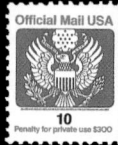

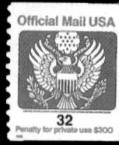

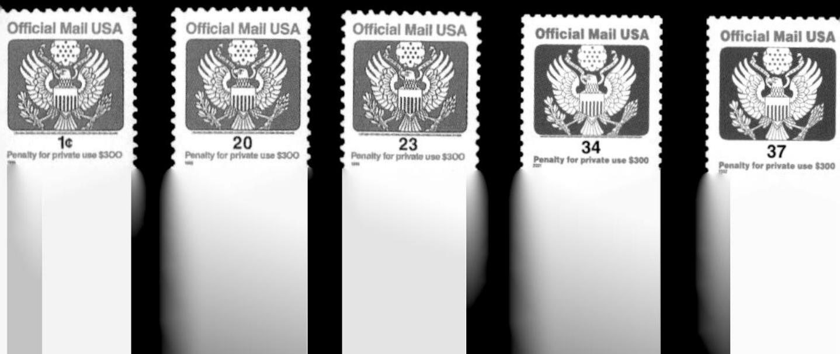

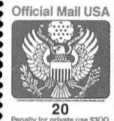

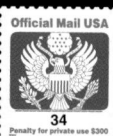

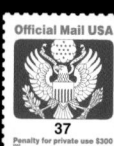

Issues of 1873	Un	U
Thin, Hard Paper, Perf. 12, Unwmkd.		

Official Stamps

The franking privilege having been abolished as of July 1, 1873, these stamps were provided for each of the departments of government for the prepayment on official matter. These stamps were supplanted on May 1, 1879, by penalty envelopes and on July 5, 1884, were declared obsolete.

	Department of Agriculture Issue: Yellow		
O1	1¢ Franklin	175.00	160.00
	Ribbed paper	185.00	160.00
O2	2¢ Jackson	140.00	70.00
O3	3¢ Washington	125.00	13.00
	Double transfer	—	—
O4	6¢ Lincoln	140.00	52.50
O5	10¢ Jefferson	290.00	180.00
	10¢ golden yellow	300.00	185.00
	10¢ olive yellow	310.00	190.00
O6	12¢ Clay	380.00	240.00
	12¢ golden yellow	400.00	250.00
O7	15¢ Webster	325.00	210.00
	15¢ olive yellow	375.00	230.00
O8	24¢ Scott	325.00	200.00
	24¢ golden yellow	350.00	210.00
O9	30¢ Hamilton	400.00	250.00
	30¢ olive yellow	450.00	275.00
	Executive Dept. Issue: Carmine		
O10	1¢ Franklin	675.00	425.00
O11	2¢ Jackson	450.00	210.00
O12	3¢ Washington	500.00	175.00
O13	6¢ Lincoln	750.00	500.00
O14	10¢ Jefferson	725.00	575.00
	Dept. of the Interior Issue: Vermilion		
O15	1¢ Franklin	42.50	8.50
	Ribbed paper	47.50	9.50
O16	2¢ Jackson	35.00	10.00
O17	3¢ Washington	55.00	5.25
O18	6¢ Lincoln	42.50	7.50
O19	10¢ Jefferson	42.50	16.00
O20	12¢ Clay	55.00	9.00
O21	15¢ Webster	100.00	18.00
	Double transfer		
	of left side	160.00	26.00
O22	24¢ Scott	75.00	15.00
O23	30¢ Hamilton	100.00	15.00
O24	90¢ Perry	210.00	40.00
	Dept. of Justice Issue: Purple		
O25	1¢ Franklin	130.00	90.00
O26	2¢ Jackson	220.00	90.00
O27	3¢ Washington	220.00	25.00
O28	6¢ Lincoln	200.00	35.00

Issues of 1873	Un	U
Dept. of Justice Issue: Purple (continued)		
O29	10¢ Jefferson	225.00	75.00
	Double transfer	—	—
O30	12¢ Clay	180.00	60.00
O31	15¢ Webster	350.00	160.00
O32	24¢ Scott	900.00	350.00
O33	30¢ Hamilton	900.00	275.00
	Double transfer at top	975.00	300.00
O34	90¢ Perry	1,350.00	525.00
	Navy Dept. Issue: Ultramarine		
O35	1¢ Franklin	85.00	42.50
a	1¢ dull blue	90.00	45.00
O36	2¢ Jackson	70.00	20.00
a	2¢ dull blue	75.00	18.00
	2¢ gray blue	75.00	18.00
O37	3¢ Washington	125.00	11.50
a	3¢ dull blue	120.00	12.50
O38	6¢ Lincoln	65.00	17.50
a	6¢ dull blue	70.00	17.50
	Vertical line through		
	"N" of "NAVY"	130.00	25.00
O39	7¢ Stanton	450.00	200.00
a	7¢ dull blue	450.00	200.00
O40	10¢ Jefferson	90.00	35.00
a	10¢ dull blue	90.00	35.00
	Plate scratch	*180.00*	—
O41	12¢ Clay	110.00	35.00
	Double transfer		
	of left side	275.00	180.00
O42	15¢ Webster	190.00	60.00
O43	24¢ Scott	220.00	70.00
a	24¢ dull blue	210.00	—
O44	30¢ Hamilton	160.00	40.00
O45	90¢ Perry	750.00	250.00
a	Double impression		*4,000.00*
	Post Office Dept. Issue: Black		
O47	1¢ Figure of Value	15.00	10.00
O48	2¢ Figure of Value	20.00	7.50
a	Double impression	500.00	400.00
O49	3¢ Figure of Value	6.50	1.25
	Cracked plate	—	—
O50	6¢ Figure of Value	20.00	6.50
	Vertical ribbed paper	—	11.00
O51	10¢ Figure of Value	80.00	45.00
O52	12¢ Figure of Value	40.00	9.00
O53	15¢ Figure of Value	55.00	15.00
	Double transfer	—	—
O54	24¢ Figure of Value	70.00	18.50
O55	30¢ Figure of Value	75.00	18.00
O56	90¢ Figure of Value	100.00	17.50

Issues of 1873	Un	U
Dept. of State Issue: Green, Perf. 12		
O57 1¢ Franklin	140.00	60.00
O58 2¢ Jackson	225.00	85.00
O59 3¢ Washington	110.00	20.00
Double paper	—	—
O60 6¢ Lincoln	100.00	25.00
O61 7¢ Stanton	180.00	55.00
Ribbed paper	200.00	60.00
O62 10¢ Jefferson	140.00	45.00
Short transfer	180.00	57.50
O63 12¢ Clay	220.00	110.00
O64 15¢ Webster	230.00	75.00
O65 24¢ Scott	450.00	200.00
O66 30¢ Hamilton	425.00	150.00
O67 90¢ Perry	850.00	300.00
O68 $2 Seward	1,250.00	800.00
O69 $5 Seward	6,000.00	4,250.00
O70 $10 Seward	4,500.00	3,500.00
O71 $20 Seward	3,500.00	2,500.00
Treasury Dept. Issue: Brown		
O72 1¢ Franklin	40.00	5.50
Double transfer	47.50	6.75
O73 2¢ Jackson	50.00	5.50
Double transfer	—	9.00
Cracked plate	67.50	—
O74 3¢ Washington	50.00	1.50
Shaded circle outside		
right frame line	—	—
O75 6¢ Lincoln	50.00	3.00
Dirty plate	50.00	4.50
O76 7¢ Stanton	100.00	27.50
O77 10¢ Jefferson	100.00	9.00
O78 12¢ Clay	100.00	6.50
O79 15¢ Webster	95.00	9.00
O80 24¢ Scott	500.00	75.00
O81 30¢ Hamilton	200.00	10.00
Short transfer top right	250.00	20.00
O82 90¢ Perry	200.00	11.00
War Dept. Issue: Rose		
O83 1¢ Franklin	150.00	12.00
O84 2¢ Jackson	135.00	12.00
Ribbed paper	145.00	14.00
O85 3¢ Washington	140.00	4.00
O86 6¢ Lincoln	475.00	7.50
O87 7¢ Stanton	130.00	77.50
O88 10¢ Jefferson	50.00	17.50

Issues of 1873	Un	U
War Dept. Issue: Rose (continued)		
O89 12¢ Clay	180.00	10.00
Ribbed paper	200.00	11.00
O90 15¢ Webster	45.00	12.00
Ribbed paper	50.00	15.00
O91 24¢ Scott	45.00	10.00
O92 30¢ Hamilton	47.50	9.00
O93 90¢ Perry	100.00	42.50
Issues of 1879, Soft, Porous Paper		
Dept. of Agriculture: Yellow		
O94 1¢ Franklin, issued		
without gum	*4,250.00*	
O95 3¢ Washington	400.00	75.00
Dept. of the Interior Issue: Vermilion		
O96 1¢ Franklin	250.00	230.00
O97 2¢ Jackson	6.00	2.50
O98 3¢ Washington	5.50	1.10
O99 6¢ Lincoln	10.00	6.50
O100 10¢ Jefferson	90.00	65.00
O101 12¢ Clay	180.00	100.00
O102 15¢ Webster	350.00	240.00
Double transfer	400.00	—
O103 24¢ Scott	*4,000.00*	—
O104-05 Not assigned		
Dept. of Justice Issue: Bluish Purple		
O106 3¢ Washington	110.00	75.00
O107 6¢ Lincoln	275.00	190.00
Post Office Dept. Issue: Black		
O108 3¢ Figure of Value	20.00	6.50
Treasury Dept. Issue: Brown		
O109 3¢ Washington	65.00	7.50
O110 6¢ Lincoln	100.00	40.00
O111 10¢ Jefferson	180.00	65.00
O112 30¢ Hamilton	1,600.00	325.00
O113 90¢ Perry	2,500.00	325.00
War Dept. Issue: Rose Red		
O114 1¢ Franklin	4.50	4.00
O115 2¢ Jackson	7.00	3.50
O116 3¢ Washington	7.00	1.50
b Double impression	*900.00*	
Double transfer	11.00	5.00
O117 6¢ Lincoln	7.00	2.50
O118 10¢ Jefferson	45.00	40.00
O119 12¢ Clay	35.00	11.00
O120 30¢ Hamilton	120.00	75.00

Issues of 1910-1985	Un	U
Perf. 12		
Official Postal Savings Mail		

These stamps were used to prepay postage on official correspondence of the Postal Savings Division of the Post Office Department. Discontinued Sept. 23, 1914.

		Un	U
O121	2¢ Postal Savings	15.00	1.75
	Double transfer	20.00	3.50
O122	50¢ dark green	145.00	50.00
O123	$1 ultramarine	135.00	12.50
	Wmkd. 190		
O124	1¢ dark violet	8.00	1.50
O125	2¢ Postal Savings (O121)	47.50	5.50
O126	10¢ carmine	18.00	6.50
	Penalty Mail Stamps		

Stamps for use by government departments were reinstituted in 1983. Now known as Penalty Mail stamps, they help provide a better accounting of actual mail costs for official departments and agencies, etc.

Beginning with #O127, unused values are for never-hinged stamps.

Issues of 1983-1985, Unwmkd., Perf. 11 x 10.5, Perf. 11 (O129A)		Un	U
O127	1¢, Jan. 12, 1983	.20	.20
O128	4¢, Jan. 12, 1983	.20	.25
O129	13¢, Jan. 12, 1983	.45	.75
O129A	14¢, May 15, 1985	.45	.50
O130	17¢, Jan. 12, 1983	.60	.40
	Perf. 11 x 10.5		
O131, O134, O137, O142 Not assigned			
O132	$1, Jan. 12, 1983	2.00	1.00
O133	$5, Jan. 12, 1983	9.00	9.00
	Coil Stamp, Perf. 10 Vertically		
O135	20¢, Jan. 12, 1983	1.75	2.00
a	Imperf. pair	2,000.00	
O136	22¢, May 15, 1985	.80	2.00

Issues of 1983-2002	Un	U
Perf. 11		
O138 "D" postcard rate (14¢) Feb. 04, 1985	5.25	5.00
Coil Stamp, Perf. 10 Vertically		
O138A 15¢, June 11, 1988	.45	.50
O138B 20¢, May 19, 1988	.45	.30
O139 "D" (22¢), Feb. 04, 1985	5.25	3.00
O140 "E" (25¢), Mar. 22, 1988	.75	2.00
O141 25¢, June 11, 1988	.65	.50
Perf. 11		
O143 1¢, July 05, 1989	.20	.20
Coil Stamp, Perf. 10 Vertically		
O144 "F" (29¢), Jan. 22, 1991	.75	.50
O145 29¢, May 24, 1991	.65	.30
Perf. 11		
O146 4¢, Apr. 06, 1991	.20	.30
O146A 10¢, Oct. 19, 1993	.25	.30
O147 19¢, May 24, 1991	.40	.50
O148 23¢, May 24, 1991	.45	.30
a Imperf. pair	100.00	
O151 $1, Sept., 1993	2.00	.75
Coil Stamp, Perf. 9.8 Vertically		
O152 (32¢), Dec. 13, 1994	.65	—
O153 32¢, May 09, 1995	.65	.30
Coil Stamp, Perf. 11.2		
O154 1¢, May 09, 1995	.20	.20
O155 20¢, May 09, 1995	.45	.30
O156 23¢, May 09, 1995	.50	.30
Coil Stamp, Perf. 9.75 Vertically		
O157 33¢, Oct. 08, 1999	.65	—
Coil Stamp, Tagged, Perf. 9.75 Vertically		
O158 34¢, Feb. 27, 2001	.65	.30
Coil Stamp, Tagged, Perf. 10 Vertically		
O159 37¢, Aug. 02, 2002	.70	.35

Variable Rate Coil Stamps

These are coil postage stamps printed without denominations. The denomination is imprinted by the dispensing equipment called a Postage and Mailing Center (PMC). Denominations can be set between 1¢ and $99.99. In 1993, the minimum denomination was adjusted to 19¢ (the postcard rate at the time).

Date of Issue:
August 20, 1992
Printing: Intaglio

Date of Issue:
February 19, 1994
Printing: Gravure

Date of Issue:
January 26, 1996
Printing: Gravure

Migratory Bird Hunting & Conservation Stamps

934-1979

RW1

RW3

RW10

RW13

RW15

RW16

RW23

RW26

RW33

RW36

RW38

RW39

DUCK STAMP DOLLARS
BUY WETLANDS
FOR WATERFOWL.

IT IS UNLAWFUL TO HUNT
WATERFOWL UNLESS YOU
SIGN YOUR NAME IN INK
ON THE FACE OF THIS STAMP.

BUY DUCK STAMPS
SAVE WETLANDS

SEND IN ALL BIRD BANDS

SIGN YOUR DUCK STAMP

IT IS UNLAWFUL TO HUNT WATERFOWL UNLESS YOU
SIGN YOUR NAME IN INK ON THE FACE OF THIS STAMP

	Issues of 1934-1979		Un	U	PB	#	Q(M)
	Department of Agriculture Duck Stamps, Perf 11						
RW1	$1 Mallards Alighting	1934	800.00	130.00	16,500.00	(6)	0.6
a	Imperf. pair		—				
b	Vert. pair, imperf. horiz.		—				
RW2	$1 Canvasbacks	1935	700.00	150.00	11,500.00	(6)	0.4
RW3	$1 Canada Geese	1936	350.00	75.00	3,500.00	(6)	0.6
RW4	$1 Scaup Ducks	1937	300.00	60.00	2,750.00	(6)	0.8
RW5	$1 Pintail Drake						
	and Hen Alighting	1938	425.00	57.50	3,500.00	(6)	1
	Department of the Interior Duck Stamps						
RW6	$1 Green-winged Teal	1939	250.00	45.00	2,000.00	(6)	1
RW7	$1 Black Mallards	1940	225.00	45.00	2,000.00	(6)	1
RW8	$1 Ruddy Ducks	1941	225.00	45.00	2,000.00	(6)	1
RW9	$1 Baldpates	1942	225.00	45.00	2,000.00	(6)	1
RW10	$1 Wood Ducks	1943	90.00	32.50	625.00	(6)	1
RW11	$1 White-fronted Geese	1944	95.00	25.00	650.00	(6)	1
RW12	$1 Shoveller Ducks	1945	60.00	25.00	450.00	(6)	2
RW13	$1 Redhead Ducks	1946	45.00	16.00	300.00	(6)	2
RW14	$1 Snow Geese	1947	45.00	16.00	300.00	(6)	2
RW15	$1 Buffleheads in Flight	1948	50.00	15.00	350.00	(6)	2
RW16	$2 Goldeneye Ducks	1949	65.00	14.00	400.00	(6)	2
RW17	$2 Trumpeter Swans	1950	80.00	12.00	575.00	(6)	2
RW18	$2 Gadwall Ducks	1951	80.00	12.00	575.00	(6)	2
RW19	$2 Harlequin Ducks	1952	80.00	12.00	575.00	(6)	2
RW20	$2 Blue-winged Teal	1953	80.00	12.00	575.00	(6)	2
RW21	$2 Ring-necked Ducks	1954	80.00	10.50	575.00	(6)	2
RW22	$2 Blue Geese	1955	80.00	10.50	575.00	(6)	2
RW23	$2 American Merganser	1956	80.00	10.50	575.00	(6)	2
RW24	$2 American Eider	1957	80.00	10.50	575.00	(6)	2
RW25	$2 Canada Geese	1958	80.00	10.50	575.00	(6)	2
RW26	$3 Labrador Retriever						
	Carrying Mallard Drake	1959	110.00	11.00	550.00	(4)	2
RW27	$3 Redhead Ducks	1960	85.00	10.50	425.00	(4)	2
RW28	$3 Mallard Hen and Ducklings	1961	85.00	10.50	425.00	(4)	1
RW29	$3 Pintail Drakes	1962	110.00	10.50	575.00	(4)	1
RW30	$3 Pair of Brant Landing	1963	105.00	10.50	500.00	(4)	1
RW31	$3 Hawaiian Nene Geese	1964	100.00	10.50	2,100.00	(6)	2
RW32	$3 Three Canvasback Drakes	1965	100.00	10.50	500.00	(4)	2
RW33	$3 Whistling Swans	1966	100.00	10.50	500.00	(4)	2
RW34	$3 Old Squaw Ducks	1967	125.00	10.00	525.00	(4)	2
RW35	$3 Hooded Mergansers	1968	65.00	10.00	300.00	(4)	2
RW36	$3 White-winged Scoters	1969	65.00	7.00	300.00	(4)	2
RW37	$3 Ross's Geese	1970	65.00	7.00	300.00	(4)	2
RW38	$3 Three Cinnamon Teal	1971	42.50	7.75	200.00	(4)	2
RW39	$5 Emperor Geese	1972	25.00	7.00	110.00	(4)	2
	Department of the Interior Duck Stamps (continued)						
RW40	$5 Steller's Eiders	1973	18.00	7.00	90.00	(4)	2
RW41	$5 Wood Ducks	1974	18.00	6.00	75.00	(4)	2
RW42	$5 Canvasbacks Decoy,						
	3 Flying Canvasbacks	1975	15.00	6.00	60.00	(4)	2
RW43	$5 Canada Geese	1976	15.00	6.00	55.00	(4)	2
RW44	$5 Pair of Ross's Geese	1977	15.00	6.00	55.00	(4)	2
RW45	$5 Hooded Merganser Drake	1978	12.50	6.00	55.00	(4)	2
RW46	$7.50 Green-winged Teal	1979	14.00	7.00	55.00	(4)	2

	Issues of 1973-2003		Un	U	PB	#	Q(M)
	Department of the Interior Duck Stamps (continued)						
RW47	$7.50 Mallards	1980	14.00	7.00	55.00	(4)	2
RW48	$7.50 Ruddy Ducks	1981	14.00	7.00	55.00	(4)	2
RW49	$7.50 Canvasbacks	1982	15.00	7.00	55.00	(4)	2
RW50	$7.50 Pintails	1983	15.00	7.00	60.00	(4)	2
RW51	$7.50 Widgeons	1984	15.00	7.00	62.50	(4)	2
RW52	$7.50 Cinnamon Teal	1985	15.00	7.00	60.00	(4)	
RW53	$7.50 Fulvous Whistling Duck	1986	15.00	7.00	60.00	(4)	2
a	Black omitted		3,750.00				
	Perf 11.5 x 11						
RW54	$10 Redheads	1987	17.50	9.50	65.00	(4)	2
RW55	$10 Snow Goose	1988	17.00	10.00	75.00	(4)	1
RW56	$12.50 Lesser Scaup	1989	19.00	10.00	82.50	(4)	1
RW57	$12.50 Black Bellied						
	Whistling Duck	1990	19.00	10.00	82.50	(4)	1
RW58	$15 King Eiders	1991	24.00	11.00	110.00	(4)	1
RW59	$15 Spectacled Eider	1992	24.00	12.50	110.00	(4)	1
RW60	$15 Canvasbacks	1993	24.00	11.00	110.00	(4)	1
	Perf 11.25 x 11						
RW61	$15 Red-breasted Merganser	1994	24.00	11.00	110.00	(4)	1
RW62	$15 Mallards	1995	24.00	11.00	110.00	(4)	1
RW63	$15 Surf Scoters	1996	24.00	11.00	110.00	(4)	1
RW64	$15 Canada Goose	1997	22.50	11.00	110.00	(4)	1
	Perf 11.25						
RW65	$15 Barrow's Goldeneye	1998	24.00	11.00	110.00	(4)	1
RW66	$15 Greater Scaup	1999	22.50	11.00	100.00	(4)	1
RW67	$15 Mottled Duck	2000	22.50	11.00	100.00	(4)	1
RW68	$15 Northern Pintail	2001	22.50	11.00	100.00	(4)	1
RW69	$15 Black Scoters	2002	22.50	11.00	100.00	(4)	1
	Perf 11						
RW70	$15 Snow Geese	2003	22.50	11.00	100.00	(4)	1

TAKE PRIDE IN AMERICA
BUY DUCK STAMPS
SAVE WETLANDS
•
SEND IN ALL BIRD BANDS
•
SIGN YOUR DUCK STAMPS
IT IS UNLAWFUL TO HUNT WATERFOWL OR USE THIS STAMP
AS A NATIONAL WILDLIFE ENTRANCE PASS UNLESS YOU
SIGN YOUR NAME IN INK ON THE FACE OF THIS STAMP

RW57

TAKE PRIDE IN AMERICA
BUY DUCK STAMPS
SAVE WETLANDS
•
SEND IN ALL BIRD BANDS
•
IT IS UNLAWFUL TO HUNT WATERFOWL OR USE THIS STAMP
AS A NATIONAL WILDLIFE REFUGE ENTRANCE PASS UNLESS
YOU SIGN YOUR NAME IN INK ON THE FACE OF THIS STAMP.

RW58-present

Migratory Bird hunting and Conservation Stamps (popularity known as "Duck Stamps") are sold as hunting permits. While they are sold through many post offices, they are not usable for postage.

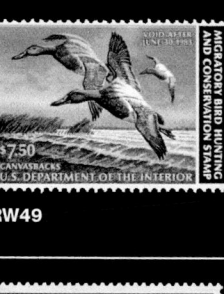

RW49

RW54

RW57

RW58

RW59

RW60

RW61

RW62

RW63

RW65

RW66

RW67

RW68

RW69

RW70

U9

U14

U19

U36

U45

U46

U62

U64

U84

U85

U97

U103

U113

U142

Issues of 1853-1865		Un	U
U1	3¢ red Washington (top		
	label 13mm wide), *buff*	350.00	35.00
U4	3¢ red Washington (top		
	label 15mm wide) *buff*	350.00	40.00
U5	3¢ red (label has		
	octagonal ends)	6,250.00	500.00
U7	3¢ red (label 20mm wide)	5,000.00	125.00
U9	3¢ red (label 14½mm)	40.00	4.00
U12	6¢ red Washington, *buff*	160.00	80.00
U14	6¢ green Washington, *buff*	225.00	100.00
U15	10¢ green Washington		
	(label 15½mm wide)	525.00	100.00
U17	10¢ green (label 20mm)	400.00	140.00
a	10¢ pale green	400.00	125.00
U19	1¢ blue Franklin (period		
	after "POSTAGE"), *buff*	40.00	15.00
U23	1¢ blue (bust touches		
	inner frame line), *orange*	750.00	350.00
U24	1¢ blue (no period		
	after "POSTAGE"), *buff*	375.00	125.00
U27	3¢ red, no label, *buff*	26.00	13.00
U28	3¢ + 1¢ (U12 and U9)	375.00	240.00
U30	6¢ red Wash., no label	3,500.00	1,500.00
U33	10¢ green, no label, *buff*	1,650.00	275.00
U34	3¢ pink Washington		
	(outline lettering)	30.00	5.75
U36	3¢ pink, blue (letter sheet)	80.00	50.00
U39	6¢ pink Washington, *buff*	80.00	62.50
U40	10¢ yellow green Wash.	45.00	30.00
U42	12¢ red, brn. Wash., *buff*	250.00	160.00
U44	24¢ Washington, *buff*	240.00	200.00
U45	40¢ blk., red Wash., *buff*	375.00	350.00
U46	2¢ black Jackson ("U.S.		
	POSTAGE" downstroke,		
	tail of "2" unite near point)	50.00	20.00
U49	2¢ black ("POSTAGE"		
	downstroke and tail of		
	"2" touch but do not		
	merge), *orange*	1,600.00	
U50	2¢ blk. Jack. ("U.S. POST."		
	stamp 24-25mm wide), *buff*	17.00	9.00
W51	2¢ blk. Jack. ("U.S. POST." stamp		
	24-25mm wide), *buff*	375.00	160.00
U54	2¢ blk. Jack. ("U.S. POST."		
	stp. 25½-26½mm), *buff*	17.50	9.00
W55	2¢ blk. Jack. ("U.S. POST."		
	stp. 25½-26½mm), *buff*	90.00	57.50
U58	3¢ pink Washington		
	(solid lettering)	10.00	1.60
U60	3¢ brown Washington	60.00	30.00
U62	6¢ pink Washington	87.50	29.00

Issues of 1863-1886		Un	U
U64	6¢ purple Washington	55.00	26.00
U66	9¢ lemon Washington, *buff*	450.00	250.00
U67	9¢ orange Washington, *buff*	150.00	90.00
U68	12¢ brn. Wash., *buff*	325.00	250.00
U69	12¢ red brown Wash., *buff*	150.00	55.00
U70	18¢ red Washington, *buff*	95.00	95.00
U71	24¢ bl. Washington, *buff*	100.00	95.00
U72	30¢ green Washington, *buff*	125.00	80.00
U73	40¢ rose Washington, *buff*	125.00	*250.00*
U75	1¢ blue Franklin (bust points		
	to end of "N" of "ONE"),		
	amber	37.50	27.50
U78	2¢ brown Jackson (bust		
	narrow at back; small,		
	thick numerals)	40.00	16.00
U84	3¢ grn. Washington		
	("ponytail" projects below		
	bust), *cream*	10.00	4.25
U85	6¢ dark red Lincoln		
	(neck very long at back)	30.00	16.00
a	6¢ vermilion	30.00	16.00
U88	7¢ verm. Stanton		
	(figures 7 normal), *amber*	50.00	*190.00*
U89	10¢ olive blk. Jefferson	925.00	850.00
U92	10¢ brown Jefferson,		
	amber	100.00	50.00
U93	12¢ plum Clay		
	(chin prominent)	110.00	82.50
U97	15¢ red orange Webster		
	(has side whiskers), *amber*	210.00	*300.00*
U99	24¢ purple Scott (locks of		
	hair project, top of head)	140.00	*140.00*
U103	30¢ black Hamilton (back of		
	bust very narrow), *amber*	250.00	*500.00*
U105	90¢ carmine Perry (front of		
	bust very narrow, pointed)	175.00	*350.00*
U113	1¢ lt. blue Frank. (lower part		
	of bust points to end of		
	"E" in "ONE")	1.75	1.00
a	1¢ dark blue	8.50	7.50
U114	1¢ lt. blue (lower part of bust		
	points to end of "E" in		
	"Postage"), *amber*	4.25	4.00
U122	2¢ brown Jackson		
	(bust narrow at back;		
	numerals thin)	125.00	40.00
U128	2¢ brown Jackson		
	(numerals in long ovals)	55.00	32.50
U132	2¢ brown, die 3		
	(left numeral touches oval)	80.00	27.50
U134	2¢ brown Jackson (similar		
	to U128-31 but "O" of		
	"TWO" has center netted		
	instead of plain)	1,400.00	150.00
U139	2¢ brown (bust broad;		
	numerals short, thick)	60.00	35.00
U142	2¢ verm. Jackson (U139)	8.50	3.00

Represented below is only a partial listing of stamped envelopes. At least one example is listed for most die types; most die types exist on several colors of envelope paper. Values are for cut squares; prices for entire envelopes are higher. Color in italic is the color of the envelope paper; when no color is specified, envelope paper is white. "W" with catalog number indicates wrapper instead of envelope.

1874-1893

Issues of 1874-1886	Un	U
U149 2¢ verm. Jackson (similar to U139-48 but circles around ovals much heavier)	60.00	30.00
W155 2¢ verm. Jackson (like U149 but middle stroke of "N" as thin as verticals), *manila*	22.50	9.50
U156 2¢ verm. Jackson (bottom of bust cut almost semi-circularly)	1,600.00	150.00
U159 3¢ grn. Wash. (thin letters, long numerals)	35.00	6.75
U163 3¢ grn. Wash. (thick letters, "ponytail" does not project below bust)	1.40	.30
U169 3¢ grn. (top of head egg-shaped; "ponytail" knot projects as point), *amber*	300.00	110.00
U172 5¢ Taylor, die 1 (numerals have thick, curved tops)	14.00	8.00
U177 5¢ blue, die 2 (numerals have long, thin tops)	11.00	6.75
U183 6¢ red Lincoln (neck short at back), *cream*	50.00	13.00
U186 7¢ verm. Stanton (figures turned up at ends), *amber*	140.00	62.50
U187 10¢ brown Jefferson (very large head)	42.50	20.00
U190 10¢ choc. Jeff. (knot of "ponytail" stands out) *amb.*	8.00	7.00
U195 12¢ plum Clay (chin receding)	475.00	100.00
U198 15¢ orange Webster (no side whiskers)	52.50	37.50
U201 24¢ purple Scott (hair does not project)	175.00	150.00
U204 30¢ blk. Hamilton (back of bust rather broad)	62.50	27.50
U212 90¢ carm. Perry (front of bust broad, sloping), *amber*	225.00	300.00
U218 3¢ red Post Rider, Train (1 line under "POSTAGE")	50.00	25.00
U225 5¢ brown Garfield, *blue*	80.00	35.00
U228 2¢ red Washington, *amber*	5.25	2.75
U234 2¢ red, four wavy lines in oval (wavy lines fine, clear), *fawn*	6.50	4.75
U236 2¢ red (wavy lines thick, blurred)	12.50	4.00
U240 2¢ red Washington (3½ links over left "2")	95.00	42.50
U244 2¢ red Wash. (2 links below right "2"), *amber*	325.00	75.00
U249 2¢ red Washington (round "O" in "TWO"), *fawn*	1,150.00	425.00
U250 4¢ green Jackson, die 1 (left numeral 2¾mm wide)	3.75	3.50

Issues of 1883-1893	Un	U
U256 4¢ green, die 2 (left numeral 3¼mm wide)	10.00	5.00
U259 4¢, die 2, amber *manila*	14.50	7.50
U262 2¢ brn. Wash. (U234), *blue*	20.00	10.00
U267 2¢ brn. Wash. (U236)	22.50	6.25
U270 2¢ brown Washington (2 links below right "2")	110.00	45.00
U274 2¢ brown Wash. (round "O" in "TWO"), *amber*	300.00	85.00
U277 2¢ brn. Washington (extremity of bust below "ponytail" forms point)	.50	.20
U288 2¢ brn. Wash. (extremity of bust is rounded)	375.00	42.50
U294 1¢ blue Franklin, no wavy lines	.55	.20
U302 1¢ dark blue, *manila*	27.50	11.00
U307 2¢ grn. Washington ("G" of "POSTAGE" has no bar), *oriental buff*	90.00	30.00
U314 2¢ green ("G" has bar, ear indicated by 1 heavy line), *blue*	.65	.30
U320 2¢ green (like U314 but ear indicated by 2 curved lines), *oriental buff*	175.00	40.00
U327 4¢ carmine Jackson, *blue*	6.00	4.00
U331 5¢ blue Grant (space between beard and collar), *amber*	5.25	2.25
U335 5¢ blue (collar touches beard), *amber*	14.00	7.50
U340 30¢ red brown Hamilton (U204), *manila*	55.00	47.50
U344 90¢ pur. Perry (U212), *oriental buff*	92.50	85.00
U348 1¢ Columbus and Liberty	2.25	1.25
U351 10¢ slate brown	35.00	30.00
U355 1¢ grn. Frank. (U294), bl.	14.00	7.50
U358 2¢ carm. Washington bust points to first notch of inner oval)	3.00	1.75
U362 2¢ carmine (bust points to middle of second notch of inner oval, "ponytail")	.35	.20
U368 2¢ carm. (same as U362 but hair flowing; no ribbon "ponytail"), *amber*	9.00	6.75
U371 4¢ brown Lincoln (bust pointed, undraped)	19.00	11.00
U374 4¢ brown (head larger; inner oval has no notches)	14.00	8.00
U377 5¢ blue Grant (like U331, U335 but smaller)	12.50	9.50

W155

U159

U172

U190

U204

U218

U250

U294

U314

U348

U351

U358

U368

U374

U377

U379

U386

U390

U393

U398

U400

U406

U416

U429

U447

U468

W485

U523

U524

	Issues of 1899-1906	Un	U
U379	1¢ green Franklin, horizontal oval	.70	.20
U386	2¢ carm. Wash. (1 short, 2 long vertical lines at right of "CENTS"), *amber*	1.90	.20
U390	4¢ chocolate Grant	22.50	11.00
U393	5¢ blue Lincoln	20.00	12.50
U398	2¢ carm. Washington, recut die (lines at end of "TWO CENTS" all short), *blue*	3.50	.90
U400	1¢ grn. Frank., oval, die 1 (wide "D" in "UNITED")	.30	.20
U401a	1¢ grn. Frank., die 2 (narrow "D"), *amber*	1.90	.70
U402b	1¢, grn. die 3 (wide "S" in "STATES"), *oriental buff*	12.00	1.50
U403c	1¢, die 4 (sharp angle at back of bust, "N," "E" of "ONE" are parallel), *blue*	8.00	1.25
U406	2¢ brn. red Wash., die 1 (oval "O" in "TWO" and "C" in "CENTS")	.80	.20
U407a	2¢, die 2 (like die 1, but hair recut in 2 distinct locks, top of head), *amb.*	250.00	45.00
U408b	2¢, die 3 (round "O" in "TWO" and "C" in "CENTS," coarse letters), *or. buff*	6.75	2.50
U411c	2¢ carmine, die 4 (like die 3 but lettering, hair lines fine, clear)	.40	.20
U412d	2¢ carmine Wash., die 5 (all S's wide), *amber*	.70	.35
U413e	2¢ carm., die 6 (like die 1 but front of bust narrow), *oriental buff*	.55	.35
U414f	2¢ carm., die 7 (like die 6 but upper corner of front of bust cut away), *blue*	32.50	19.00
g	2¢ carm., die 8 (like die 7 but lower stroke of "S" in "CENTS" straight line; hair as in die 2), *blue*	32.50	19.00
U416	4¢ blk. Wash., die 2 ("F" is 1¾mm from left "4")	4.75	3.00
a	4¢, die 1 ("F" is 1mm from left "4")	4.75	3.00
U420	1¢ grn. Frank., round, die 1 ("UNITED" nearer inner circle than outer circle)	.20	.20
U421a	1¢, die 2 (large "U"; "NT" closely spaced), *amber*	475.00	175.00
U423a	1¢ grn. die 3 (knob of hair at back of neck; large "NT" widely spaced), *blue*	.75	.45
b	1¢, die 4 ("UNITED" nearer outer circle than inner)	1.25	.65
c	1¢, die 5 (narrow, oval "C")	.80	.35

	Issues of 1907-1932	Un	U
U429	2¢ carmine Washington, die 1 (letters broad, numerals vertical, "E" closer than "N" to inner circle)	.20	.20
a	2¢, die 2 (like die 1 but "U" far from left circle), *amber*	14.00	6.00
b	2¢, die 3 (like die 2 but inner circles very thin)	45.00	25.00
U430b	2¢, die 4 (like die 1 but "C" very close to left circle), *amber*	50.00	20.00
c	2¢, die 5 (small head, 8¾mm from tip of nose to back of neck; "TS" of "CENTS" close at bottom)	1.10	.35
U431d	2¢, die 6 (like die 6 but "TS" of "CENTS" far apart at bottom; left numeral slopes right), *oriental buff*	3.00	2.00
e	2¢, die 7 (large head, both numerals slope right, T's have short top strokes)	2.75	1.75
U432h	2¢, die 8 (like die 7 but all T's have long top strokes), *blue*	.60	.25
i	2¢, die 9 (narrow, oval "C")	.90	.30
U436	3¢ dk. violet Washington, die 1 (as 2¢)	.30	.20
U440	4¢ black Washington	1.50	.60
U447	2¢ on 3¢ dark violet, rose surcharge	7.75	6.50
U458	Same as U447, black surcharge, bars 2mm apart	.50	.35
U468	Same as U458, bars 1½mm apart	.70	.45
U481	1½¢ brown Washington, die 1 (as U429)	.20	.20
W485	1½¢ brown, *manila*	.80	.20
U490	1½¢ on 1¢ grn. Franklin, black surcharge	6.00	3.50
U499	1½¢ on 1¢, *manila*	12.50	6.00
U510	1½¢ on 1¢ grn., outline numeral in surcharge	2.75	1.25
U522	2¢ carmine Liberty Bell	1.10	.50
a	2¢, center bar of "E" of "Postage" same length as top bar	7.00	3.75
U523	1¢ ol. grn. Mount Vernon	1.00	.80
U524	1½¢ choc. Mount Vernon	2.00	1.50

	Issues of 1916-1962	Un	U
U525	2¢ carmine Mount Vernon	.40	.20
a	2¢, die 2 "S" of		
	"POSTAGE" raised	70.00	16.00
U526	3¢ violet Mount Vernon	2.00	.35
U527	4¢ black Mount Vernon	18.00	16.00
U528	5¢ dark blue Mount Vernon	4.00	3.50
U529	6¢ orange Washington	5.50	4.00
U530	6¢ orange Wash., amber	11.00	10.00
U531	6¢ or. Washington, blue	11.00	10.00
U532	1¢ green Franklin	5.50	1.75
U533	2¢ carmine Wash. (oval)	.75	.25
U534	3¢ dk. violet Washington, die 4		
	(short N in UNITED, thin		
	crossbar in A of STATES)	.40	.20
U535	1½¢ brown Washington	5.50	3.50
U536	4¢ red violet Franklin	.80	.20
U537	2¢ + 2¢ Wash. (U429)	3.50	1.50
U538	2¢ + 2¢ Washington (U533)	.75	1.25
U539	3¢ + 1¢ purple, die 1		
	(4½mm tall, thick "3")	15.00	11.00
U540	3¢ + 1¢ purple, die 3		
	(4mm tall, thin "3")	.50	1.00
a	Die 2 (4½mm tall,		
	thin "3" in medium		
	circle), entire	—	—
U541	1¼¢ turquoise Franklin	.75	.50
a	Die 2 ("4" 3½mm		
	high), precanceled		1.50
U542	2½¢ dull blue Washington	.85	.50
U543	4¢ brn. Pony Express Rider	.60	.30
U544	5¢ dark blue Lincoln	.85	.20
c	With albino impression		
	of 4¢ U536)	85.00	—
U545	4¢ + 1¢, type 1 (U536)	1.40	1.25
U546	5¢ New York World's Fair	.60	.40
U547	1¼¢ brown Liberty Bell		.20
U548	1⁴⁄₁₀¢ brown Liberty Bell		.20
U548A	1⁶⁄₁₀¢ orange Liberty Bell		.20
U549	4¢ blue Old Ironsides	.75	.20
U550	5¢ purple Eagle	.75	.20
a	Tagged	2.00	.50
U551	6¢ green Statue of Liberty	.70	.20
U552	4¢ + 2¢ brt. bl. (U549)	3.75	2.00
U553	5¢ + 1¢ brt. pur. (U550)	3.50	2.75
U554	6¢ lt. blue Herman Melville	.50	.20
U555	6¢ Youth Conference	.75	.20
U556	1⁷⁄₁₀¢ lilac Liberty Bell		.20
U557	8¢ ultramarine Eagle	.40	.20
U561	6¢ + (2¢) lt. grn.	1.00	1.25
U562	6¢ + (2¢) lt. blue	2.00	2.50
U563	8¢ rose red Bowling	.70	.20
U564	8¢ Aging Conference	.50	.20
U565	8¢ Transpo '72	.50	.20
U566	8¢ + 2¢ brt. ultra.	.40	1.25
U567	10¢ emerald Liberty Bell	.40	.20
U568	1⁹⁄₁₀¢ Volunteer Yourself		.20

	Issues of 1962-1978	Un	U
U569	10¢ Tennis Centenary	.65	.20
U571	10¢ Compass Rose	.30	.20
a	Brown "10¢/USA"		
	omitted, entire	150.00	
U572	13¢ Quilt Pattern	.35	.20
U573	13¢ Sheaf of Wheat	.35	.20
U574	13¢ Mortar and Pestle	.35	.20
U575	13¢ Tools	.35	.20
U576	13¢ Liberty Tree	.30	.20
U577	2¢ red Nonprofit		.20
U578	2.1¢ yel. green Nonprofit		.20
U579	2.7¢ green Nonprofit		.20
U580	15¢ orange Eagle, A	.40	.20
U581	15¢ red Uncle Sam	.40	.20
U582	13¢ emerald Centennial	.35	.20
U583	13¢ Golf	.65	.20
U584	13¢ Energy Conservation	.40	.20
d	Blk, red omitted, ent.	425.00	
U585	13¢ Energy Development	.40	.20
U586	15¢ on 16¢ blue USA	.35	.20
U587	15¢ Auto Racing	.35	.20
a	Black omitted, entire	120.00	
U588	15¢ on 13¢ (U576)	.35	.20
U589	3.1¢ ultramarine nonprofit		.20
U590	3.5¢ purple Violins		.20
U591	5.9¢ Auth Nonprofit Org		.20
U592	18¢ violet Eagle, B	.45	.20
U593	18¢ dark blue Star	.45	.20
U594	20¢ brown Eagle, C	.45	.20
U595	15¢ Veterinary Medicine	.50	.20
U596	15¢ Summer Oly. Games	.60	.20
a	Red, grn. omitted, ent.	225.00	
U597	15¢ Highwheeler Bicycle	.40	.20
a	Blue "15¢ USA"		
	omitted, entire	100.00	
U598	15¢ America's Cup	.40	.20
U599	Brown 15¢ Honeybee	.35	.20
a	Brown "15¢ USA"		
	omitted, entire	125.00	
U600	18¢ Blind Veterans	.45	.20
U601	20¢ Capitol Dome	.45	.20
U602	20¢ Great Seal of U.S.	.45	.20
U603	20¢ Purple Heart	.65	.20
U604	5.2¢ Auth Nonprofit Org		.20
U605	20¢ Paralyzed Veterans	.45	.20
U606	20¢ Small Business	.50	.20
U607	22¢ Eagle, D	.55	.20
U608	22¢ Bison	.55	.20
U609	6¢ USS Constitution		.20
U610	8.5¢ Mayflower		.20
U611	25¢ Stars	.60	.20
U612	8.4¢ US Frigate Constellation		.20
U613	25¢ Snowflake	1.00	5.00
U614	25¢ USA, Stars (Philatelic Mail)	.50	.25

U530 **U531** **U541**

  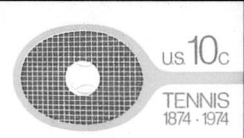

U542

U543 **U569**

U576 **U581** **U587**

U601 **U609** **U610**

U611 **U614**

U616

U617

U631

U632

U634

U635

U636

U637

Issues of 1989-1992	Un	U		Issues of 1992-1995	Un	U
U615 25¢ Stars (lined paper)	.50	.25	U627 29¢ Protect the Environment	.60	.30
U616 25¢ Love	.50	.25	U628 19.8¢ Bulk Rate precanceled		.40
U617 25¢ Space hologram	.90	.60	U629 29¢ Disabled Americans	.60	.30
U618 25¢ Football hologram	.90	.60	U630 29¢ Kitten	.90	.50
U619 29¢ Star	.60	.30	**U631** 29¢ Football	.60	.30
U620 11.1¢ Birds		.20	**U632** 32¢ Liberty Bell	.65	.30
U621 29¢ Love	.60	.30	U633 32¢ Old Glory	.65	.30
U622 29¢ Magazine Industry	.60	.30	**U634** 32¢ Old Glory	.65	.30
U623 29¢ Star and Bars	.60	.30	**U635** 5¢ Nonprofit		.20
U624 29¢ Country Geese	.60	.60	**U636** 10¢ Graphic Eagle		.20
U625 29¢ Space Shuttle	.90	.50	**U637** 32¢ Spiral Heart	.65	.30
U626 29¢ Western Americana	.60	.30			

AMERICAN ★ COMMEMORATIVE ★ **COLLECTIBLES**

Acquire all of your stamp collectibles! It's easy and affordable.

Choose any or all of the official U.S. Postal Service American Commemorative Collectibles to enhance your collection.

American Commemorative Collection

An easy and uniform way to collect and learn about commemorative issues. Just mount the stamps on the specially designed sheet and place them in a three ring binder. Just $3.25* each, depending on the value of the stamps.

American Commemorative Cancellations

Get first day cancellations and stamp(s) that have been affixed to colorful, specially tinted sheets to enhance your display. About $2.00* each, depending on the value of the stamps.

First Day of Issue Ceremony Programs

Receive detailed information about each first day of issue ceremony held for all new stamps and stationery issuances. Collect these valuable programs for only $4.95 each.

American Commemorative Panels

Obtain photo or steel engravings, mint condition stamps and subject related text presented on a beautifully designed page. Only $6.00* each, depending on the value of the stamps.

For information call **1-800-STAMP-24**

*Prices subject to change without notice.

Issues of 1995-1999		Un	U
U639	32¢ Space Shuttle	.65	.35
U640	32¢ Save Our Environment	.60	.30
U641	32¢ 1996 Paralympic Games	.60	.30
U642	33¢ Flag (yellow, red, blue)	.65	.30
U643	33¢ Flag (blue & red)	.65	.30
U644	33¢ Victorian Love	.65	.30
U645	33¢ Lincoln	.65	.30

Issues of 2001-2003			Un	U
U646	34¢ Federal Eagle	01/07/01	.65	.30
U647	34¢ Lovebirds	01/14/01	.65	.30
U648	34¢ Federal Eagle	02/20/01	.65	.30
U649	37¢ Ribbon Star	06/07/02	.75	.35
U650	(10¢) Presorted			
	Standard Eagle	08/08/02		.20
U651	37¢ Nuturing love	01/25/03	.75	.35

'Alabama Baby' and Martha Chase · 'Baby Coos' · Ludwig Greiner

"The Columbian Doll" · Plains Indian · "Betsy McCall"

Johnny Gruelle's "Raggedy Ann" · Izannah Walker · Percy Crosby's "Skippy"

Martha Chase · "Babyland Flag" · "Maggie Mix-up"

"American Child" · "Scootles" · Albert Schoenhut

The above names include doll makers, designers, trade names and common names.

CLASSIC AMERICAN DOLLS
In 1997 the Postal Service issued 15 stamps featuring CLASSIC AMERICAN DOLLS that reflected "the tradition, heritage, culture, and artistic style of various geographical regions" of the country. One of the dolls, Raggedy Ann, was created and patented in 1915 by John B. Gruelle—an artist, cartoonist, writer, and toy designer—who wrote and published books about the kindly rag doll and her companion, Raggedy Andy. The stamp features a Raggedy Ann doll manufactured in the 1940s. Another stamp features a doll manufactured in Philadelphia by Louis Griener, a German immigrant who received America's first doll patent—for a doll with a papier-mache head—in 1858. Izannah Walker—one of America's earliest known female doll makers—did not obtain a patent for her dolls until 1873 although it is believed she may have been making dolls in Massachusetts as early as 1828. Often resembling primitive folk-art portraits of children in the 1800s, a doll made by Walker appears on another of the stamps. ❑

U639

U640

U641

U642

U643

U644

U645

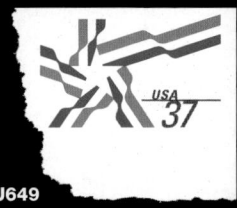

U646

U647

U648

U649

U650

U651

Airmail Envelopes and Aerogrammes

1929-1973

UC1

UC3

UC7

UC8

UC14

UC21

UC25

UC26

UC30

UC39

UC46

Issues of 1929-1945	Un	U
UC1 5¢ blue Airplane, die 1		
(vertical rudder is not		
semicircular)	3.50	2.00
1933 wmk., entire	*750.00*	*750.00*
1937 wmk., entire	—	*2,500.00*
Bicolored border		
omitted, entire	1,300.00	
UC2 5¢ blue, die 2 (vertical		
rudder is semicircular)	11.00	5.00
1929 wmk., entire	—	*1,500.00*
a 1933 wmk., entire	*650.00*	—
UC3 6¢ orange Airplane, die 2a		
("6" is 6½mm wide)	1.50	.40
a With #U436a added		
impression	*4,000.00*	
UC4 6¢ orange, die 2b		
("6" is 6mm wide)	2.75	2.00
UC5 6¢ orange, die 2c		
("6" is 5mm wide)	.75	.30
UC6 6¢ orange, die 3 (vertical≤		
rudder leans forward)	1.00	.35
a 6¢ orange, *blue*,		
entire	*3,500.00*	*2,400.00*
UC7 8¢ olive green Airplane	13.00	3.50
UC8 6¢ on 2¢ carm.		
Washington (U429)	1.25	.65
d 6¢ on 1¢ green		
(U420)	*1,750.00*	
f 6¢ on 3¢ purple		
(U437a)	*3,000.00*	
UC9 6¢ on 2¢ Wash. (U525)	70.00	35.00
Issues of 1946-1956		
UC10 5¢ on 6¢ orange (UC3)	2.75	1.50
a Double surcharge	60.00	
UC11 5¢ on 6¢ orange (UC4)	9.00	5.50
UC13 5¢ on 6¢ orange (UC6)	.80	.60
a Double surcharge	60.00	
UC14 5¢ carm. DC-4, die 1		
(end of wing on right		
is smooth curve)	.75	.20
UC16 10¢ red, DC-4		
2-line back inscription,		
entire, *pale blue*	8.50	6.00
a "Air Letter" on face,		
4-line back inscription	17.50	14.00
Die-cutting reversed	275.00	
b 10¢ chocolate	450.00	
c "Air Letter" and		
"Aerogramme" on face	45.00	12.50
d 3-line back inscription	9.00	8.00

Issues of 1946-1956	Un	U
UC17 5¢ Postage Centenary	.40	.25
UC18 6¢ carm. Airplane (UC14),		
type I (6's lean right)	.35	.20
a Type II (6's upright)	.75	.25
UC20 6¢ on 5¢ (UC15)	.85	.50
a 6¢ on 6¢ carmine,		
entire	*1,500.00*	
b Double surcharge	*500.00*	—
UC21 6¢ on 5¢ (UC14)	27.50	17.50
UC22 6¢ on 5¢ (UC14)	4.00	2.50
a Double surcharge	200.00	
UC23 6¢ on 5¢ (UC17)	1,250.00	
UC25 6¢ red Eagle	.75	.50
Issues of 1958-1973		
UC26 7¢ blue (UC14)	.65	.50
UC27 6¢ + 1¢ orange (UC3)	325.00	225.00
UC28 6¢ + 1¢ orange (UC4)	75.00	75.00
UC29 6¢ + 1¢ orange (UC5)	45.00	50.00
UC30 6¢ + 1¢ (UC5)	1.00	.50
UC32 10¢ Jet Airliner, back		
inscription in 2 lines	6.00	5.00
a Type 1, entire	10.00	5.00
UC33 7¢ blue Jet Silhouette	.60	.25
UC34 7¢ carmine (UC33)	.60	.25
UC35 11¢ Jet, Globe, entire	2.75	2.25
a Red omitted	*1,000.00*	
Die-cutting reversed	35.00	
UC36 8¢ red Jet Airliner	.55	.20
UC37 8¢ red Jet in Triangle	.35	.20
a Tagged	3.50	.30
UC39 13¢ John Kennedy, entire	3.00	2.75
a Red omitted	*900.00*	
UC40 10¢ Jet in Triangle	.50	.20
UC41 8¢ + 2¢ (UC37)	.65	.20
UC42 13¢ Human Rights, entire	8.00	4.00
Die-cutting reversed	75.00	
UC43 11¢ Jet in Circle	.50	.20
UC44 15¢ gray, red, white		
and blue Birds in Flight	1.50	1.10
UC45 10¢ + (1¢) (UC40)	1.50	.20
UC46 15¢ red, white, bl.	.75	.40

	Issues of 1973-1983	Un	U
UC47	13¢ red Bird in Flight	.30	.20
UC48	18¢ USA, entire	.90	.30
UC50	22¢ red and bl. USA, entire	.90	.40
UC51	22¢ blue USA, entire	.70	.25
	Die-cutting reversed	25.00	
UC52	22¢ Summer Olympic Games	1.50	.25
UC53	30¢ blue, red, brn. Tour the United States, entire	.65	1.00
a	Red "30" omitted	70.00	
UC54	30¢ yellow, magenta, blue and black (UC53), entire	.65	1.00
	Die-cutting reversed	20.00	
UC55	30¢ Made in USA, entire	.65	1.00
UC56	30¢ World Communications Year, entire	.65	1.00
	Die-cutting reversed	25.00	

	Issues of 1983-1999	Un	U
UC57	30¢ Olympic Games, entire	.65	1.50
UC58	36¢ Landsat, entire	.70	1.00
UC59	36¢ Tourism Week, entire	.70	1.00
UC60	36¢ Mark Twain/ Halley's Comet, entire	1.00	1.50
UC61	39¢ Envelope	.80	1.00
UC62	39¢ Montgomery Blair	.80	1.00
UC63	45¢ Eagle, entire, blue	.90	1.00
a	White paper	.90	1.00
UC64	50¢ Thaddeus Lowe, Balloonist	1.00	1.00
UC65	60¢ Voyageurs Nat'l Park, Minnesota	1.25	1.00

HENRY MANCINI
(1924-1994)

HENRY MANCINI, one of the most successful music composers in the history of television and film as well as a popular pianist and concert conductor, left a rich legacy of catchy TV themes, hit songs, and unforgettable film scores. Awards include 20 Grammys and 4 Oscars, with albums selling more than 30 million copies. In 1941 Mancini, an accomplished pianist, flutist, piccolo player, and composer, entered New York's Juilliard School of Music on scholarship. Within months he was drafted into the Army Air Corps and assigned to a military band. After the war, Mancini returned to New York and became pianist for the Glenn Miller Band. In 1947 he married Ginny O'Connor, a singer with the band, and moved to Burbank, California. His music for *Lost in Alaska (1952)* and arrangements for *The Glenn*

Miller Story (1954) were followed by the music for *Peter Gunn*, a TV drama. His first record album, *The Music from* Peter Gunn, sold more than a million copies, a first for a jazz album, and won two Grammys—Best Arrangement and Album of the Year—making Mancini a recording star. Mancini wrote scores for more than 70 films, notably *Breakfast at Tiffany's* (1961), *Days of Wine and Roses* (1962), *The Pink Panther* (1964), and *Charade* (1963) and wrote themes for *Mr. Lucky, Newhart,* and other TV shows. Mancini had a gift for weaving memorable melodies into inventive scores. It's impossible to think of *The Pink Panther* without recalling its theme. And who can forget Audrey Hepburn singing "Moon River" in *Breakfast at Tiffany's*? The music for that movie won five Grammys and two Academy Awards. ❏

UC48

UC52

UC53

UC56

UC57

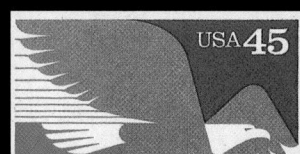

UC59

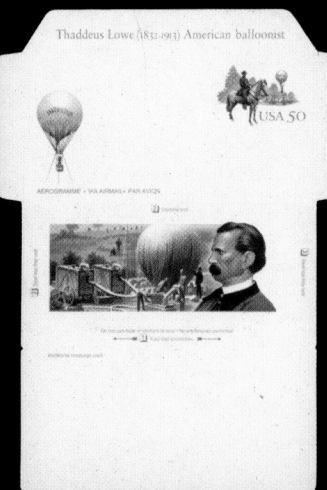

UC63

UC64

UC65

1873-2002

UO1

UO16

UO20

UO73

UO84

UO88

UO89

UO90

UO91

Issues of 1873-1875	Un	U
Official Envelopes		
Post Office Department		
Numeral 9½mm high		
UO1 2¢ black, *lemon*	22.50	9.00
Numeral 10½mm high		
UO5 2¢ black, *lemon*	10.00	4.00
UO9 3¢ black, *amber*	110.00	35.00
Postal Service		
UO16 blue, *amber*	200.00	30.00
War Department		
UO20 3¢ dk. red Washington	70.00	40.00
UO26 12¢ dark red Clay	175.00	50.00
UO39 10¢ vermilion Jefferson	350.00	
UO48 2¢ red Jackson, *amber*	35.00	14.00
UO55 3¢ red Washington, *fawn*	6.00	2.75

Issues of 1983-2002	Un	U
Penalty Mail Envelopes		
UO73 20¢ blue Great Seal	1.25	30.00
UO74 22¢ (seal embossed)	.90	15.00
UO75 22¢ (seal typographed)	1.00	20.00
UO76 "E" (25¢) Great Seal	1.10	20.00
UO77 25¢ black, blue Great Seal (seal embossed)	.80	15.00
UO78 25¢ (seal typographed)	.90	25.00
UO79 45¢ (stars illegible)	1.25	85.00
UO80 65¢ (stars illegible)	1.75	150.00
UO81 45¢ (stars clear)	1.25	75.00
UO82 65¢ (stars clear)	1.60	125.00
UO83 "F" (29¢) Great Seal	1.10	20.00
UO84 29¢ black, blue, entire	.75	10.00
UO88 32¢ Official Mail	.80	10.00
UO89 33¢ Official Mail	.70	10.00
UO90 34¢ Official Mail	.85	—
UO91 37¢ Official Mail	—	—

BOSTON STATE HOUSE: CHARLES BULFINCH

(1763-1844)

The BOSTON STATE HOUSE, the oldest building on Beacon Hill and for many years the tallest building in Boston, was designed by Charles Bulfinch, America's first native-born architect. Completed in 1798, the structure, which is still in use today by the Massachusetts legislature, is considered one of the most architecturally distinguished state government buildings in the nation. The neoclassical design features a gold-leaf dome—originally wood shingles—topped with a lantern and a pinecone, a symbol of the state's forests. Inside, the marble-floored corridors are lined with portraits and statues of many of the nation's early leaders.

A Boston native, Bulfinch pursued a classical studies program at Harvard College. After graduating, he traveled extensively in Europe to study architecture. On his return, Bulfinch worked as a "gentleman amateur" architect designing homes, churches, and other buildings, including the state house in Hartford, Connecticut. He earned his first commission—in the amount of $600.91—for his design for the Boston State House. Although he was a prolific designer, Bulfinch struggled financially. When President James Monroe visited Boston in 1817, he was so impressed by Bulfinch and the town's architecture that he named Bulfinch architect of the U.S. Capitol with an annual salary of $2,500. Bulfinch and his family lived in the nation's capital for the next 12 years, then returned to Boston to live among the buildings he knew so well. ☐

Postal Cards and Stamped Cards

1873-1968

UX5

UX6

UX11

UX14

UX16

UX18

UX25

UX27

UX28

UX37

UX43

UX44

UX45

UX46

UX48

UX49

UX50

UX56

Issues of 1873-1917	Un	U
Represented below is only a partial listing of postal cards. Values are for entire cards. Color in italic is color of card. Cards preprinted with written address or message usually sell for much less.		
UX1 1¢ brown Liberty, wmkd. (90 x 60mm)	350.00	20.00
UX3 1¢ brown Liberty, wmkd. (53 x 36mm)	75.00	2.50
UX4 1¢ blk. Liberty, wmkd., USPOD in monogram	2,500.00	350.00
UX5 1¢ blk. Liberty, unwmkd.	75.00	.45
UX6 2¢ blue Liberty, *buff*	32.50	25.00
a 2¢ dark blue, *buff*	30.00	25.00
UX7 1¢ (UX5), inscribed "Nothing But The Address"	65.00	.40
a 23 teeth below "One Cent"	1,250.00	50.00
b Printed on both sides	800.00	400.00
UX8 1¢ brown Jefferson, large "one-cent" wreath	50.00	1.25
c 1¢ chocolate	175.00	40.00
UX9 1¢ blk. Jefferson, *buff*	22.50	.55
a 1¢ blk., *dark buff*	45.00	5.00
UX10 1¢ black Grant	40.00	1.50
UX11 1¢ blue Grant	20.00	3.00
UX12 1¢ black Jefferson, wreath smaller than UX14	40.00	.65
UX13 2¢ blue Liberty, *cream*	190.00	85.00
UX14 1¢ Jefferson	35.00	.45
UX15 1¢ black John Adams	42.50	15.00
UX16 2¢ black Liberty	14.00	*17.00*
UX17 1¢ black McKinley	7,000.00	
UX18 1¢ black McKinley, facing left	14.00	.35
UX19 1¢ black McKinley, triangles in top corners	40.00	.50
UX20 1¢ (UX19), correspondence space at left	52.50	4.25
UX21 1¢ blue McKinley, shaded background	95.00	13.00
a 1¢ bronze blue, *bluish*	200.00	30.00
UX22 1¢ blue McKinley, white background	17.00	.35
UX23 1¢ red Lincoln, solid background	10.00	5.50
UX24 1¢ red McKinley	10.00	.35
UX25 2¢ red Grant	1.50	16.00
UX26 1¢ green Lincoln, solid background	13.00	7.50
UX27 1¢ Jefferson, *buff*	.25	.25
a 1¢ green, *cream*	3.50	.65
UX27C 1¢ green Jefferson, *gray*, die I	4,000.00	190.00
UX28 1¢ green Lincoln, *cream*	.60	.30
a 1¢ green, *buff*	1.50	.60
UX29 2¢ red Jefferson, *buff*	42.50	2.10
a 2¢ lake, *cream*	50.00	4.00
c 2¢ vermilion, *buff*	925.00	75.00

Issues of 1918-1968	Un	U
UX30 2¢ red Jefferson, *cream*	30.00	1.60
Surcharged in one line by canceling machine.		
UX31 1¢ on 2¢ red Jefferson	5,000.00	4,500.00
Surcharged in two lines by canceling machine.		
UX32 1¢ on 2¢ red Jeff., *buff*	52.50	12.50
a 1¢ on 2¢ vermilion	*150.00*	60.00
b Double surcharge	150.00	100.00
UX33 1¢ on 2¢ red Jefferson, *cream*	12.00	1.90
a Inverted surcharge	100.00	100.00
b Double surcharge	55.00	35.00
d Triple surcharge	350.00	
Surcharged in two lines by press printing.		
UX34 1¢ on 2¢ red (UX29)	550.00	52.50
UX35 1¢ on 2¢ red Jefferson, *cream*	225.00	37.50
UX36 1¢ on 2¢ red (UX25)		50,000.00
UX37 3¢ red McKinley, *buff*	4.50	*15.00*
UX38 2¢ carmine rose Franklin	.35	.25
a Double impression	500.00	
Surcharged by canceling machine in light green.		
UX39 2¢ on 1¢ green Jefferson, *buff*	.50	.35
b Double surcharge	20.00	*25.00*
UX40 2¢ on 1¢ green (UX28)	.65	.45
Surcharged typographically in dark green.		
UX41 2¢ on 1¢ green Jefferson, *buff*	4.50	2.00
a Inverted surcharge lower left	77.50	125.00
UX42 2¢ on 1¢ green (UX29)	5.00	2.50
b Surcharged on back	160.00	
UX43 2¢ carmine Lincoln	.30	*1.00*
UX44 2¢ FIPEX	.25	*1.00*
b Dk. vio. blue omitted	625.00	600.00
UX45 4¢ Statue of Liberty	1.50	*75.00*
UX46 3¢ purple Statue of Liberty	.50	.20
a "N GOD WE TRUST"	13.50	*25.00*
UX47 2¢ + 1¢ carmine rose Franklin	225.00	600.00
UX48 4¢ red violet Lincoln	.50	.20
UX49 7¢ World Vacationland	4.00	*45.00*
UX50 4¢ U.S. Customs	.50	*1.00*
a Blue omitted	625.00	
UX51 4¢ Social Security	.40	*1.00*
b Blue omitted	700.00	650.00
UX52 4¢ blue & red Coast Guard	.30	*1.00*
UX53 4¢ Bureau of the Census	.30	*1.00*
UX54 8¢ blue & red (UX49)	4.00	*45.00*
UX55 5¢ emerald Lincoln	.30	*.60*
UX56 5¢ Women Marines	.35	*1.00*

	Issues of 1970-1983	Un	U
UX57	5¢ Weather Services	.30	1.00
a	Yellow, black omitted	1,400.00	850.00
b	Blue omitted	1,400.00	
c	Black omitted	1,400.00	850.00
UX58	6¢ brown Paul Revere	.30	1.00
a	Double impression	300.00	
UX59	10¢ blue & red (UX49)	4.50	45.00
UX60	6¢ America's Hospitals	.30	1.00
a	Blue, yellow omitted	1,150.00	
UX61	6¢ USF *Constellation*	.85	10.00
a	Address side blank	300.00	
UX62	6¢ black Monument Valley	.40	10.00
UX63	6¢ Gloucester, MA	.40	6.00
UX64	6¢ blue John Hanson	.50	1.00
UX65	6¢ magenta Liberty	.25	1.00
UX66	8¢ orange Samuel Adams	.50	1.00
UX67	12¢ Visit USA/ Ship's Figurehead	.35	45.00
UX68	7¢ Charles Thomson	.30	9.00
UX69	9¢ John Witherspoon	.30	1.00
UX70	9¢ blue Caesar Rodney	.30	1.00
UX71	9¢ Federal Court House	.25	1.00
UX72	9¢ green Nathan Hale	.25	1.00
UX73	10¢ Cincinnati Music Hall	.30	1.00
UX74	10¢ John Hancock	.30	1.00
UX75	10¢ John Hancock	.30	1.00
UX76	14¢ Coast Guard Eagle	.40	30.00
UX77	10¢ Molly Pitcher	.30	1.60
UX78	10¢ George Rogers Clark	.30	1.50
UX79	10¢ Casimir Pulaski	.30	1.50
UX80	10¢ Olympic Sprinter	.60	1.50
UX81	10¢ Iolani Palace	.30	1.50
UX82	14¢ Olympic Games	.60	20.00
UX83	10¢ Salt Lake Temple	.25	1.50
UX84	10¢ Landing of Rochambeau	.25	1.50
UX85	10¢ Battle of Kings Mtn.	.25	1.50
UX86	19¢ Drake's Golden Hinde	.70	35.00
UX87	10¢ Battle of Cowpens	.25	16.00
UX88	12¢ violet Eagle, nondenominated	.30	.65
UX89	12¢ lt. bl. Isaiah Thomas	.30	.60
UX90	12¢ Nathanael Greene	.30	10.00
UX91	12¢ Lewis and Clark	.30	20.00
UX92	13¢ buff Robert Morris	.30	.60
UX93	13¢ buff Robert Morris	.30	.60
UX94	13¢ "Swamp Fox" Francis Marion	.30	1.00
UX95	13¢ LaSalle Claims Louisiana	.30	1.00
UX96	13¢ Academy of Music	.30	1.00
UX97	13¢ Old Post Office, St. Louis, Missouri	.30	1.00
UX98	13¢ Landing of Ogelthorpe	.30	1.00
UX100	13¢ Olympic Yachting	.30	1.00

	Issues of 1984-1990	Un	U
UX101	13¢ *Ark* and *Dove*, Maryland	.30	1.00
UX102	13¢ Olympic Torch	.30	1.00
UX103	13¢ Frederic Baraga	.30	1.00
UX104	13¢ Dominguez Adobe	.30	1.00
UX105	14¢ Charles Carroll	.45	.50
UX106	14¢ green Charles Carroll	.45	.50
UX107	25¢ Clipper *Flying Cloud*	.70	20.00
UX108	14¢ brt. grn. George Wythe	.30	.75
UX109	14¢ Settlement of Connecticut	.30	1.25
UX110	14¢ Stamp Collecting	.30	1.25
UX111	14¢ Francis Vigo	.30	1.25
UX112	14¢ Settling of Rhode Island	.30	1.25
UX113	14¢ Wisconsin Territory	.30	.85
UX114	14¢ National Guard	.30	1.25
UX115	14¢ Self-Scouring Plow	.30	1.25
UX116	14¢ Constitutional Convention	.30	.60
UX117	14¢ Stars and Stripes	.30	.60
UX118	14¢ Take Pride in America	.30	1.25
UX119	14¢ Timberline Lodge	.30	1.25
UX120	15¢ Bison and Prairie	.30	.60
UX121	15¢ Blair House	.30	.75
UX122	28¢ *Yorkshire*	.60	15.00
UX123	15¢ Iowa Territory	.30	.75
UX124	15¢ Ohio, Northwest Terr.	.30	.75
UX125	15¢ Hearst Castle	.30	.60
UX126	15¢ The Federalist Papers	.30	.75
UX127	15¢ Hawk and Desert	.30	.75
UX128	15¢ Healy Hall	.40	.75
UX129	15¢ Blue Heron and Marsh	.30	.75
UX130	15¢ Settling of Oklahoma	.30	.75
UX131	21¢ Geese and Mountains	.40	10.00
UX132	15¢ Seagull and Seashore	.30	.75
UX133	15¢ Deer and Waterfall	.30	.75
UX134	15¢ Hull House, Chicago	.30	.75
UX135	15¢ Ind. Hall, Philadelphia	.30	.75
UX136	15¢ Inner Harbor, Baltimore	.30	.75
UX137	15¢ Bridge, New York	.30	.75
UX138	15¢ Capitol, Washington	.30	.75
	#UX139-42 issued in sheets of 4 plus 2 inscribed labels, rouletted 9½ on 2 or 3 sides		
UX139	15¢ (UX135)	3.25	4.00
UX140	15¢ The White House	3.25	4.00
UX141	15¢ (UX137)	3.25	4.00
UX142	15¢ (UX138)	3.25	4.00
a	Sheet of 4, #UX139-42	13.00	
UX143	15¢ The White House	1.50	2.50
UX144	15¢ Jefferson Memorial	1.50	2.00
UX145	15¢ Papermaking	.30	.40
UX146	15¢ World Literacy Year	.30	.75

UX70

UX79

UX81

UX83

UX94

UX109

UX112

UX113

UX115

UX116

UX118

UX119

UX131

UX143

UX144

UX143 (picture side)

UX144 (picture side)

UX174

UX175

UX176

UX177

UX198

UX199

UX219A

UX220

UX241

UX262

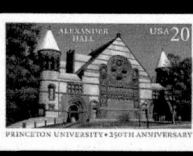

UX263

UX280

UX282

UX283

UX290

UX292

UX298

UX299

Issues of 1990-1993	Un	U
UX147 15¢ George Caleb Bingham	1.50	2.50
UX148 15¢ Isaac Royall House	.30	.75
UX150 15¢ Stanford University	.30	.60
UX151 15¢ Constitution Hall	1.50	2.00
UX152 15¢ Chicago Orchestra Hall	.30	.75
UX153 19¢ Flag	.40	.60
UX154 19¢ Carnegie Hall	.40	.60
UX155 19¢ Old Red, UT-Galveston	.50	.60
UX156 19¢ Bill of Rights	.40	.60
UX157 19¢ Notre Dame	.50	.60
UX158 30¢ Niagara Falls	.75	7.50
UX159 19¢ The Old Mill	.50	.75
UX160 19¢ Wadsworth Atheneum	.40	.75
UX161 19¢ Cobb Hall	.50	.75
UX162 19¢ Waller Hall	.50	.75
UX163 19¢ America's Cup	1.00	3.00
UX164 19¢ Columbia River Gorge	.40	.75
UX165 19¢ Ellis Island	.40	.75
UX166 19¢ National Cathedral	.40	.75
UX167 19¢ Wren Building	.50	.75
UX168 19¢ Holocaust Memorial	1.00	3.00
UX169 19¢ Fort Recovery	.40	.75
UX170 19¢ Playmakers Theatre	.50	.75
UX171 19¢ O'Kane Hall	.50	.75
UX172 19¢ Beecher Hall	.50	.75

Issues of 1993-1998	Un	U
UX173 19¢ Massachusetts Hall	.50	.75
UX174 19¢ Lincoln's Home	.40	.75
UX175 19¢ Wittenberg University	.50	.75
UX176 19¢ Canyon de Chelly	.40	.75
UX177 19¢ St. Louis Union Station	.40	.75
UX198 20¢ Red Barn	.40	.60
UX199 20¢ Old Glory	3.00	2.50
UX219A 50¢ Soaring Eagle	1.00	7.50
UX220 20¢ American Clipper Ships	.40	.75
UX241 20¢ Winter Scene	.40	.40
UX262 20¢ St. John's College	.50	.75
UX263 20¢ Princeton University	.50	.75
UX280 20¢ City College of New York	.50	.50
UX281 20¢ Bugs Bunny	1.25	2.00
UX282 20¢ Pacific 97 Golden Gate Bridge in Daylight	.40	.65
UX283 50¢ Pacific 97 Golden Gate Bridge at Sunset	1.00	2.50
UX284 20¢ Fort McHenry	.40	.50
UX290 20¢ University of Mississippi	.50	.50
UX291 20¢ Sylvester & Tweety	1.25	2.00
UX292 20¢ Girard College	.50	.50
UX298 20¢ Northeastern University	.50	.50
UX299 20¢ Brandeis University	.50	.50

HERMAN MELVILLE

(1819-1891)

While still a fairly young man, HERMAN MELVILLE wrote *Moby-Dick*, published in 1851 and now considered one of the greatest American novels. Melville was at that time already a noted author, but his creative blend of a realistic depiction of the whaling industry with a symbolic account of man's struggle with fate failed to impress the public. His earlier books, including *Typee* (1846), *Omoo* (1847), and others, were fairly straightforward tales based on Melville's experiences. He had worked on whaling ships, lived among natives in the South Pacific,

and spent more than a year as an ordinary seaman on a frigate. After his adventures at sea, which he regarded as the only university that was open to him, he began writing novels, short stories, and poems. As his works became more ambitious, Melville fell further out of popular favor; he worked for decades as a customs inspector on the docks of his native New York City and died unknown. Some thirty years after his death, Melville was rescued from obscurity by scholars, and is now regarded as a master stylist and a shrewd social critic. His novella *Billy Budd*, published posthumously in 1924, is also considered a classic. ❑

	Issues of 1999-2001	Un	U
UX301	20¢ University of Wisconsin-Madison	.50	.50
UX302	20¢ Washington and Lee University	.50	.50
UX303	20¢ Redwood Library & Athenæum	.50	.50
UX305	20¢ Mount Vernon	.40	.40
UX306	20¢ Block Island Lighthouse	.40	.45
UX312	20¢ University of Utah	.40	.45
UX313	20¢ Ryman Auditorium	.40	.45
UX316	20¢ Middlebury College	.40	.45
UX361	20¢ Yale University Stamped Card	.40	.60
UX362	20¢ University of South Carolina Stamped Card	.40	.60

	Issues of 1949-2003	Un	U
UX363	20¢ Northwestern University Stamped Card	.40	.60
UX364	20¢ University of Portland Stamped Card	.40	.50
UX375	21¢ White Barn Stamped Card	.45	.45
UX381	23¢ Carlsbad Caverns National Park Stamped Card	.50	.50
UX400	23¢ Ohio University	1.00	1.00
	Airmail Postal Cards		
UXC1	4¢ Orange Eagle	.50	.75
UXC2	5¢ Red Eagle (C48)	1.75	.75
UXC3	5¢ UXC2 redrawn "Air Mail-Postal Card" omitted	6.50	2.00
UXC4	6¢ Red Eagle	1.10	2.50

Ready to Mail Stamped Cards

Southeastern Lighthouses 23¢
Twenty Stamped Cards
Five Designs
Item #454466–$9.75

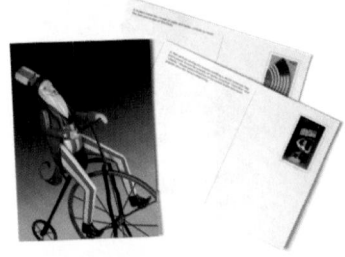

Old Glory 23¢
Twenty Stamped Cards
Five Designs
Item #882066–$9.75

Holiday Music Makers 23¢
Twenty Stamped Cards
Four Designs
Item #564066–$9.75

*Prices subject to change without notice

To order call **1-800-STAMP-24** or visit us online at **www.usps.com**

UX301 **UX302** **UX303**

UX305 **UX306** **UX312**

UX313 **UX316** **UX361**

UX362 **UX363** **UX364**

UX375 **UX381** **UX400**

UXC1 **UXC2** **UXC4**

UXC5

UXC6

UXC7

UXC8

UXC9

UXC10

UXC11

UXC12

UXC13

UXC19

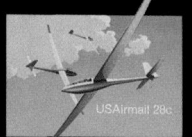

UXC20

UXC23

UXC25

UXC27

UXC28

UY12

UY41

UY43

UY44

UZ6

Issues of 1967-2001	Un	U
UXC5 11¢ Visit The USA	.65	20.00
UXC6 6¢ Virgin Islands	.75	10.00
a Red, yellow omitted	1,700.00	
UXC7 6¢ Boy Scout World Jamboree	.75	10.00
UXC8 13¢ blue & red (UXC5)	1.50	25.00
UXC9 8¢ Stylized Eagle	.75	2.50
UXC10 9¢ red & blue (UXC5)	.50	1.25
UXC11 15¢ Travel Service	1.75	45.00
UXC12 9¢ black Grand Canyon	.75	—
UXC13 15¢ black Niagara Falls	.75	75.00
UXC14 11¢ Stylized Eagle	1.10	20.00
UXC15 18¢ Eagle Weather Vane	1.10	20.00
UXC16 21¢ Angel Weather Vane	.85	20.00
UXC17 21¢ Curtiss Jenny	1.00	20.00
UXC18 21¢ Olympic Gymnast	1.25	20.00
UXC19 28¢ First Transpacific Flight	1.00	20.00
UXC20 28¢ Gliders	1.00	20.00
UXC21 28¢ Olympic Speed Skater	1.00	20.00
UXC22 33¢ China Clipper	1.00	20.00
UXC23 33¢ AMERIPEX '86	1.00	20.00
UXC24 36¢ DC-3	.85	20.00
UXC25 40¢ Yankee Clipper	.90	20.00
UXC27 55¢ Mt. Rainier	1.25	20.00
UXC28 70¢ Badlands	1.40	10.00

Issues of 1892-2002	Un	U
Paid Reply Postal Cards		
Prices are: Un=unsevered,		
U=severed card.		
UY1 1¢ + 1¢ black Grant	37.50	9.00
UY6 1¢ + 1¢ green G. and M. Washington, double frame line around instructions	160.00	25.00
UY7 1¢ + 1¢ green G. and M. Washington, single frame line	1.25	.50
UY12 3¢ + 3¢ red McKinley	10.00	25.00
UY18 4¢ + 4¢ Lincoln	3.00	2.50
UY23 6¢ + 6¢ John Adams	1.00	2.00
UY31 "A" (12¢ + 12¢) Eagle	1.00	2.00
UY39 15¢ + 15¢ Bison and Prairie	.75	1.00
UY40 19¢ + 19¢ Flag	.80	1.00
UY41 20¢ Red Barn	.80	1.25
UY43 21¢ White Barn	.90	1.25
UY44 23¢ Carlsbad Caverns	1.00	1.25
Issues of 1913-1995		
Official Mail Postal Cards		
UZ1 1¢ black Numeral	550.00	350.00
UZ2 13¢ blue Great Seal	.75	80.00
UZ3 14¢ blue Great Seal	.75	70.00
UZ4 15¢ blue Great Seal	.75	80.00
UZ5 19¢ blue Great Seal	.70	80.00
UZ6 20¢ Official Mail	.60	80.00

LUCILLE BALL

(1911-1989)

Everyone called her Lucy. A regular fixture on television for nearly three decades, LUCILLE BALL endeared herself to viewers in her role as Lucy Ricardo on *I Love Lucy* (1951-1957). The enormously popular show, which teamed Ball with her real-life husband Desi Arnaz, chronicled the unlikely adventures of a wacky, redheaded housewife and her husband, Cuban bandleader Ricky Ricardo. Audiences never knew what sort of fix she would get herself into each week, but they couldn't wait to find out. Other television series included *The Lucille Ball-Desi Arnaz Show*, *The Lucy Show*, *Here's Lucy*, and *Life with Lucy*. A versatile performer, Ball acted in radio comedy

and appeared in more than 70 movies opposite leading men such as Bob Hope and Henry Fonda. She became the first woman president of a major Hollywood production company. One of the first inductees into the Academy of Television Arts & Sciences Hall of Fame (1984), Ball won four Emmy Awards. In 1989 she was posthumously awarded the Presidential Medal of Freedom. The Postal Service honored her in 2001 in the Legends of Hollywood series. ❑

American Commemorative Cancellations

The Postal Service offers American Commemorative Cancellations (formerly known as Souvenir Pages) for new stamps. The series began with a page for the Yellowstone Park Centennial stamp issued March 1, 1972. The pages feature one or more stamps tied by the first day cancel, along with technical data and information on the subject of the issue. More than just collectors' items, American Commemorative Cancellations make wonderful show and conversation pieces. These pages are issued in limited editions. Number in parentheses ( ) indicates the number of stamps on page if there are more than one.

The identifying numbers used below are based on the Postal Service's numbering system for American Commemorative Cancellations; therefore, they do not follow the Scott numbering system.

1972

72-00	Family Planning	400.00
72-01	Yellowstone Park	80.00
72-01a	Yellowstone Park with DC cancel	—
72-02	2¢ Cape Hatteras	65.00
72-03	14¢ Fiorello LaGuardia	65.00
72-04	11¢ City of Refuge Park	70.00
72-05	6¢ Wolf Trap Farm Park	22.50
72-06	Colonial Craftsmen (4)	12.50
72-07	15¢ Mount McKinley	17.50
72-08	6¢-15¢ Olympic Games (4)	9.00
72-08E	Olympic Games with broken red circle on 6¢ stamp	—
72-09	PTA	4.50
72-10	Wildlife Conservation (4)	6.00
72-11	Mail Order	4.50
72-12	Osteopathic Medicine	4.50
72-13	Tom Sawyer	6.00
72-14	7¢ Benjamin Franklin	4.75
72-15	Christmas (2)	5.50
72-16	Pharmacy	6.00
72-17	Stamp Collecting	4.50

1973

73-01	$1 Eugene O'Neill	55.00
73-01E	$1 Eugene O'Neill picture perf. error	—
73-02	Love	5.50
73-03	Pamphleteer Printing	3.50
73-04	George Gershwin	4.50
73-05	Broadside	4.50
73-06	Copernicus	4.25
73-07	Postal Employees	4.75
73-08	Harry S. Truman	3.75
73-09	Post Rider	4.50
73-10	21¢ Amadeo Gianninni	3.50
73-11	Boston Tea Party (4)	4.75
73-12	6¢-15¢ Electronics (4)	5.75
73-13	Robinson Jeffers	3.50
73-14	Lyndon B. Johnson	2.75
73-15	Henry O. Tanner	4.00
73-16	Willa Cather	3.25
73-17	Colonial Drummer	3.25
73-18	Angus Cattle	2.75
73-19	Christmas (2)	5.00
73-20	13¢ Winged Envelope airmail	2.00
73-21	10¢ Crossed Flags	2.25
73-22	10¢ Jefferson Memorial	2.25
73-23	13¢ Winged Envelope airmail coil (2)	2.50

1974

74-01	26¢ Mount Rushmore airmail	4.00
74-02	ZIP Code	3.25
74-02E	ZIP Code with date error 4/4/74	—
74-03	18¢ Statue of Liberty airmail	4.50
74-04	18¢ Elizabeth Blackwell	2.00
74-05	VFW	2.50
74-06	Robert Frost	3.50
74-07	Expo '74	4.00
74-08	Horse Racing	4.00
74-09	Skylab	4.50
74-10	UPU (8)	4.75
74-11	Mineral Heritage (4)	4.75
74-12	Fort Harrod	2.25
74-13	Continental Congress (4)	3.50
74-14	Chautauqua	2.50
74-15	Kansas Wheat	1.90
74-16	Energy Conservation	2.00
74-17	6.3¢ Liberty Bell coil (2)	2.25
74-18	Sleepy Hollow	3.00
74-19	Retarded Children	2.00
74-20	Christmas (3)	4.25

1975

75-01	Benjamin West	2.25
75-02	Pioneer/Jupiter	5.00
75-03	Collective Bargaining	2.25
75-04	8¢ Sybil Ludington	2.25
75-05	Salem Poor	3.00
75-06	Haym Salomon	2.25
75-07	18¢ Peter Francisco	2.25
75-08	Mariner 10	4.25
75-09	Lexington & Concord	2.50
75-10	Paul Dunbar	3.00
75-11	D.W. Griffith	2.50
75-12	Bunker Hill	2.50
75-13	Military Uniforms (4)	5.00
75-14	Apollo Soyuz (2)	5.00
75-15	International Women's Year	2.00
75-16	Postal Service Bicentennial (4)	3.00
75-17	World Peace Through Law	2.00
75-18	Banking & Commerce (2)	3.00
75-19	Christmas (2)	3.00
75-20	3¢ Francis Parkman	2.50
75-21	11¢ Printing Press	1.75
75-22	24¢ Old North Church	1.90

75-23	Flag over Independence Hall (2)	2.00
75-24	9¢ Freedom to Assemble (2)	2.25
75-25	Liberty Bell coil (2)	2.00
75-26	Eagle & Shield	2.50

1976

76-01	Spirit of '76 (3)	3.25
76-01E	Spirit of '76 with cancellation error Jan. 2, 1976 (3)	—
76-02	25¢ and 31¢ Plane and Globes airmails (2)	2.25
76-03	Interphil '76	2.50
76-04	State Flags, DE to VA (10)	5.50
76-05	State Flags, NY to MS (10)	5.50
76-06	State Flags, IL to WI (10)	5.50
76-07	State Flags, CA to SD (10)	5.50
76-08	State Flags, MT to HI (10)	5.50
76-09	9¢ Freedom to Assemble coil (2)	1.75
76-10	Telephone Centennial	1.75
76-11	Commercial Aviation	1.75
76-12	Chemistry	1.75
76-13	7.9¢ Drum coil (2)	1.90
76-14	Benjamin Franklin	1.75
76-15	Bicentennial souvenir sheet	7.00
76-15E	13¢ Bicentennial souvenir sheet with perforation and numerical errors	7.00
76-16	18¢ Bicentennial souvenir sheet	7.00
76-17	24¢ Bicentennial souvenir sheet	7.00
76-18	31¢ Bicentennial souvenir sheet	7.00
76-19	Declaration of Independence (4)	3.50
76-20	Olympics (4)	3.50
76-21	Clara Maass	2.75
76-22	Adolph S. Ochs	2.25
76-23	Christmas (3)	2.25
76-24	7.7¢ Saxhorns coil (2)	1.75

1977

77-01	Washington at Princeton	1.75
77-02	Flag over Capitol booklet pane (9¢ and 13¢) Perf. 10 (8)	14.00
77-03	Sound Recording	2.00
77-04	Pueblo Pottery (4)	3.00
77-05	Lindbergh Flight	2.25
77-06	Colorado Centennial	1.90
77-07	Butterflies (4)	2.25
77-08	Lafayette	1.50
77-09	Skilled Hands (4)	2.25
77-10	Peace Bridge	1.60
77-11	Battle of Oriskany	1.60
77-12	Alta, CA, First Civil Settlement	1.60
77-13	Articles of Confederation	1.60
77-14	Talking Pictures	2.00
77-15	Surrender at Saratoga	2.25
77-16	Energy (2)	1.60
77-17	Christmas, Mailbox and Christmas, Valley Forge, Omaha cancel (2)	1.60
77-18	Same, Valley Forge cancel	—
77-19	10¢ Petition for Redress coil (2)	2.25
77-20	10¢ Petition for Redress sheet (2)	2.25
77-21	1¢-4¢ Americana (5)	2.00

1978

78-01	Carl Sandburg	2.00
78-02	Indian Head Penny	2.00
78-03	Captain Cook, Anchorage cancel (2)	2.00
78-04	Captain Cook, Honolulu cancel (2)	2.00
78-05	Harriet Tubman	3.00
78-06	American Quilts (4)	2.50
78-07	16¢ Statue of Liberty sheet and coil (2)	1.90
78-08	29¢ Sandy Hook Lighthouse	1.90
78-09	American Dance (4)	2.75
78-10	French Alliance	1.90
78-11	Early Cancer Detection	2.25
78-12	"A" (15¢) sheet and coil (2)	3.25
78-13	Jimmie Rodgers	3.00
78-14	CAPEX '78 (8)	5.50
78-15	Oliver Wendell Holmes coil	3.50
78-16	Photography	1.90
78-17	Fort McHenry Flag sheet and coil (2)	2.00
78-18	George M. Cohan	1.60
78-19	Rose booklet single	2.00
78-20	8.4¢ Piano coil (2)	2.00
78-21	Viking Missions	3.75
78-22	28¢ Ft. Nisqually	2.00
78-23	American Owls (4)	2.50
78-24	31¢ Wright Brothers airmails (2)	2.50
78-25	American Trees (4)	2.75
78-26	Christmas, Madonna	2.00
78-27	Christmas, Hobby Horse	2.00
78-28	$2 Kerosene Lamp	4.50

1979

79-01	Robert F. Kennedy	2.00
79-02	Martin Luther King, Jr.	3.50
79-03	International Year of the Child	2.00
79-04	John Steinbeck	2.50
79-05	Albert Einstein	3.00
79-06	21¢ Octave Chanute airmails (2)	2.50
79-07	Pennsylvania Toleware (4)	2.50
79-08	American Architecture (4)	2.25
79-09	Endangered Flora (4)	2.50
79-10	Seeing Eye Dogs	1.90
79-11	Candle & Holder	3.50
79-12	Special Olympics	1.90
79-13	$5 Lantern	9.00
79-14	30¢ Schoolhouse	2.50
79-15	10¢ Summer Olympics (2)	2.25
79-16	50¢ Whale Oil Lamp	3.00
79-17	John Paul Jones	2.00
79-18	Summer Olympics (4)	3.75
79-19	Christmas, Madonna	2.25
79-20	Christmas, Santa Claus	2.25
79-21	3.1¢ Guitar coil (2)	3.50
79-22	31¢ Summer Olympics airmail	3.00
79-23	Will Rogers	2.25
79-24	Vietnam Veterans	2.75
79-25	25¢ Wiley Post airmails (2)	3.00

1980

80-01	W.C. Fields	2.75
80-02	Winter Olympics (4)	3.50
80-03	Windmills booklet pane (10)	4.00

80-04	Benjamin Banneker	2.75	
80-05	Letter Writing (6)	2.00	
80-06	1¢ Ability to Write (2)	1.75	
80-07	Frances Perkins	1.50	
80-08	Dolley Madison	2.25	
80-09	Emily Bissell	1.90	
80-10	3.5¢ Violins coil (2)	2.50	
80-11	Helen Keller/ Anne Sullivan	1.75	
80-12	Veterans Administration	1.50	
80-13	General Bernardo de Galvez	1.75	
80-14	Coral Reefs (4)	2.75	
80-15	Organized Labor	2.25	
80-16	Edith Wharton	2.25	
80-17	Education	2.25	
80-18	Indian Masks (4)	2.50	
80-19	American Architecture (4)	2.00	
80-20	40¢ Philip Mazzei airmail	2.00	
80-21	Christmas, Madonna	2.25	
80-22	Christmas, Antique Toys	2.25	
80-23	Sequoyah	1.50	
80-24	28¢ Blanche Scott airmail	1.60	
80-25	35¢ Glenn Curtiss airmail	1.60	

1981

81-01	Everett Dirksen	1.50
81-02	Whitney M. Young	2.75
81-03	"B" (18¢) sheet and coil (3)	2.00
81-04	"B" (18¢) booklet pane (8)	2.00
81-05	12¢ Torch Sheet and coil (3)	2.25
81-06	Flowers block (4)	2.00
81-07	Flag and Anthem sheet and coil (3)	2.00
81-08	Flag and Anthem booklet pane (8 - 6¢ and 18¢)	2.00
81-09	American Red Cross	1.50
81-10	George Mason	1.50
81-11	Savings & Loans	1.50
81-12	Wildlife booklet pane (10)	3.50
81-13	Surrey coil (2)	1.75
81-14	Space Achievement (8)	6.75
81-15	17¢ Rachel Carson (2)	1.50
81-16	35¢ Charles Drew, MD	1.75
81-17	Professional Management	1.50

81-18	17¢ Electric Auto coil (2)	1.75
81-19	Wildlife Habitat (4)	2.00
81-20	Disabled	1.50
81-21	Edna St. Vincent Millay	1.75
81-22	Alcoholism	2.25
81-23	American Architecture (4)	2.50
81-24	Babe Zaharias	7.00
81-25	Bobby Jones	8.00
81-26	Frederic Remington	2.25
81-27	"C" (20¢) sheet and coil (3)	2.50
81-28	"C" (18¢) booklet pane (10)	2.50
81-29	18¢ and 20¢ Hoban (2)	1.50
81-30	Yorktown/ Virginia Capes (2)	2.00
81-31	Christmas, Madonna	2.00
81-32	Christmas, Bear on Sleigh	2.25
81-33	John Hanson	1.50
81-34	Fire Pumper coil (2)	3.25
81-35	Desert Plants (4)	2.00
81-36	9.3¢ Mail Wagon coil (3)	2.50
81-37	Flag over Supreme Court sheet and coil	3.00
81-38	Flag over Supreme Court booklet pane (6)	2.50

1982

82-01	Sheep booklet pane (10)	3.00
82-02	Ralph Bunche	4.00
82-03	13¢ Crazy Horse (2)	1.75
82-04	37¢ Robert Millikan	1.50
82-05	Franklin D. Roosevelt	1.50
82-06	Love	1.50
82-07	5.9¢ Bicycle coil (4)	4.75
82-08	George Washington	2.25
82-09	10.9¢ Hansom Cab coil (2)	2.75
82-10	Birds & Flowers, AL-GE (10)	7.00
82-11	Birds & Flowers, HI-MD (10)	7.00
82-12	Birds & Flowers, MA-NJ (10)	7.00
82-13	Birds & Flowers, NM-SC (10)	7.00
82-14	Birds & Flowers, SD-WY (10)	7.00

82-15	USA/Netherlands	1.50
82-16	Library of Congress	1.50
82-17	Consumer Education coil (2)	2.25
82-18	Knoxville World's Fair (4)	1.50
82-19	Horatio Alger	1.25
82-20	2¢ Locomotive coil (2)	2.25
82-21	Aging Together	1.25
82-22	The Barrymores	2.50
82-23	Mary Walker	1.50
82-24	Peace Garden	1.50
82-25	America's Libraries	1.50
82-26	Jackie Robinson	12.50
82-27	4¢ Stagecoach coil (3)	2.50
82-28	Touro Synagogue	1.75
82-29	Wolf Trap Farm Park	1.50
82-30	American Architecture (4)	1.75
82-31	Francis of Assisi	1.40
82-32	Ponce de Leon	1.40
82-33	13¢ Kitten & Puppy (2)	2.00
82-34	Christmas, Madonna	2.25
82-35	Christmas, Seasons Greetings (4)	2.25
82-36	2¢ Igor Stravinsky (2)	2.00

1983

83-01	1¢, 4¢, 13¢ Penalty Mail (5)	2.50
83-02	17¢ Penalty Mail (4)	2.25
83-03	Penalty Mail coil (2)	3.25
83-04	$1 Penalty Mail	4.00
83-05	$5 Penalty Mail	9.50
83-06	Science & Industry	1.50
83-07	5.2¢ Antique Sleigh coil (4)	2.75
83-08	Sweden/USA Treaty	1.50
83-09	3¢ Handcar coil (3)	2.00
83-10	Balloons (4)	1.75
83-11	Civilian Conservation Corps	1.25
83-12	40¢ Olympics airmails (4)	2.75
83-13	Joseph Priestley	1.50
83-14	Volunteerism	1.25
83-15	Concord/German Immigration	1.50
83-16	Physical Fitness	1.50
83-17	Brooklyn Bridge	2.00
83-18	TVA	1.50

83-19 4¢ Carl Schurz (5) 1.50
83-20 Medal of Honor 3.25
83-21 Scott Joplin 2.50
83-22 Thomas H. Gallaudet 1.75
83-23 28¢ Olympics (4) 3.00
83-24 5¢ Pearl S. Buck (4) 1.50
83-25 Babe Ruth 10.00
83-26 Nathaniel Hawthorne 1.50
83-27 3¢ Henry Clay (7) 1.50
83-28 13¢ Olympics (4) 3.00
83-29 $9.35 Eagle booklet single 75.00
83-30 $9.35 Eagle booklet pane (3) 125.00
83-31 1¢ Omnibus coil (3) 1.75
83-32 Treaty of Paris 1.25
83-33 Civil Service 1.25
83-34 Metropolitan Opera 1.75
83-35 Inventors (4) 1.75
83-36 1¢ Dorothea Dix (3) 2.25
83-37 Streetcars (4) 2.25
83-38 5¢ Motorcycle coil (4) 3.75
83-39 Christmas, Madonna 1.50
83-40 Christmas, Santa Claus 1.50
83-41 35¢ Olympics airmails (4) 2.75
83-42 Martin Luther 2.25
83-43 Flag over Supreme Court booklet pane (10) 2.50

1984

84-01 Alaska Statehood 1.50
84-02 Winter Olympics (4) 2.25
84-03 FDIC 1.50
84-04 Harry S. Truman 1.50
84-05 Love 1.50
84-06 Carter G. Woodson 2.25
84-07 11¢ RR Caboose coil (2) 2.25
84-08 Soil & Water Conservation 1.25
84-09 Credit Union Act 1.50
84-10 40¢ Lillian M. Gilbreth 1.50
84-11 Orchids (4) 2.25
84-12 Hawaii Statehood 2.00
84-13 7.4¢ Baby Buggy coil (3) 2.50
84-14 National Archives 1.25
84-15 20¢ Summer Olympics (4) 2.75
84-16 New Orleans World's Fair 1.25

84-17 Health Research 1.25
84-18 Douglas Fairbanks 3.00
84-19 Jim Thorpe 7.00
84-20 10¢ Richard Russell (2) 1.50
84-21 John McCormack 3.00
84-22 St. Lawrence Seaway 1.25
84-23 Migratory Bird Hunting and Pre-Conservation Stamp Act 3.00
84-24 Roanoke Voyages 1.25
84-25 Herman Melville 1.50
84-26 Horace Moses 1.25
84-27 Smokey Bear 7.00
84-28 Roberto Clemente 11.00
84-29 30¢ Frank C. Laubach 1.50
84-30 Dogs (4) 3.00
84-31 Crime Prevention 1.50
84-32 Family Unity 2.25
84-33 Eleanor Roosevelt 2.50
84-34 Nation of Readers 2.00
84-35 Christmas, Madonna 2.00
84-36 Christmas, Santa Claus 2.00
84-37 Hispanic Americans 1.25
84-38 Vietnam Veterans Memorial 3.25

1985

85-01 Jerome Kern 2.00
85-02 7¢ Abraham Baldwin (3) 1.75
85-03 "D" (22¢) sheet and coil (3) 1.50
85-04 "D" (22¢) booklet pane (10) 3.00
85-05 "D" (22¢) Penalty Mail sheet and coil (3) 1.50
85-06 11¢ Alden Partridge (2) 1.50
85-07 33¢ Alfred Verville airmail 1.25
85-08 39¢ Lawrence & Elmer Sperry airmail 1.75
85-09 44¢ Transpacific airmail 1.50
85-10 50¢ Chester Nimitz 1.75
85-11 Mary McLeod Bethune 2.75
85-12 39¢ Grenville Clark 1.50
85-13 14¢ Sinclair Lewis (2) 1.50

85-14 Duck Decoys (4) 3.25
85-15 14¢ Iceboat coil (2) 3.25
85-16 Winter Special Olympics 1.25
85-17 Flag over Capitol sheet and coil (3) 2.00
85-18 Flag over Capitol booklet pane (5) 2.50
85-19 12¢ Stanley Steamer coil (2) 2.75
85-20 Seashells booklet pane (10) 3.50
85-21 Love 2.25
85-22 10.1¢ Oil Wagon coil (3) 2.25
85-23 12.5¢ Pushcart coil (2) 2.50
85-24 John J. Audubon 1.75
85-25 $10.75 Eagle booklet single 30.00
85-26 $10.75 Eagle booklet pane (3) 65.00
85-27 6¢ Tricycle coil (4) 2.50
85-28 Rural Electrification Administration 1.25
85-29 14¢ and 22¢ Penalty Mail sheet and coil (4) 2.00
85-30 AMERIPEX '86 1.25
85-31 9¢ Sylvanus Thayer (3) 1.75
85-32 3.4¢ School Bus coil (7) 3.00
85-33 11¢ Stutz Bearcat coil (2) 2.50
85-34 Abigail Adams 1.25
85-35 4.9¢ Buckboard coil (5) 2.75
85-36 8.3¢ Ambulance coil (3) 2.75
85-37 Frederic Bartholdi 2.25
85-38 8¢ Henry Knox (3) 1.50
85-39 Korean War Veterans 2.00
85-40 Social Security Act 1.50
85-41 44¢ Father Junipero Serra airmail 1.50
85-42 World War I Veterans 1.75
85-43 6¢ Walter Lippmann (4) 1.50
85-44 Horses (4) 3.25
85-45 Public Education 1.50
85-46 International Youth Year (4) 2.50
85-47 Help End Hunger 1.60
85-48 21.1¢ Letters coil (2) 2.25
85-49 Christmas, Madonna 1.50

85-50 Christmas,
Poinsettias 2.50
85-51 18¢ Washington/
Washington
Monument
coil (2) 2.25

1986

86-01 Arkansas
Statehood 1.50
86-02 25¢ Jack London 1.50
86-03 Stamp Collecting
booklet pane (4) 3.00
86-04 Love 2.00
86-05 Sojourner Truth 2.50
86-06 5¢ Hugo L.
Black (5) 2.25
86-07 Republic of
Texas (2) 1.75
86-08 $2 William
Jennings Bryan 3.25
86-09 Fish booklet
pane (5) 3.00
86-10 Public Hospitals 1.50
86-11 Duke Ellington 3.25
86-12 Presidents,
Washington-
Harrison (9) 3.75
86-13 Presidents,
Tyler-Grant (9) 3.75
86-14 Presidents,
Hayes-Wilson (9) 3.75
86-15 Presidents,
Harding-
Johnson (9) 3.75
86-16 Polar
Explorers (4) 2.75
86-17 17¢ Belva Ann
Lockwood (2) 1.50
86-18 1¢ Margaret
Mitchell (3) 2.50
86-19 Statue of Liberty 2.25
86-20 4¢ Father
Flanagan (3) 1.60
86-21 17¢ Dog Sled
coil (2) 2.25
86-22 56¢ John
Harvard 2.00
86-23 Navajo
Blankets (4) 2.75
86-24 3¢ Paul Dudley
White, MD (8) 1.50
86-25 $1 Bernard Revel 1.75
86-26 T.S. Eliot 2.50
86-27 Wood-Carved
Figurines (4) 2.75
86-28 Christmas,
Madonna 1.75
86-29 Christmas,
Village Scene 1.75
86-30 5.5¢ Star Route
Truck coil (4) 3.00
86-31 25¢ Bread Wagon
coil 3.00

1987

87-01 8.5¢ Tow Truck
coil (5) 1.50
87-02 Michigan
Statehood 2.50
87-03 Pan American
Games 2.50
87-04 Love 2.00
87-05 7.1¢ Tractor
coil (5) 2.50
87-06 14¢ Julia Ward
Howe (2) 1.50
87-07 Jean Baptiste
Pointe Du Sable 4.00
87-08 Enrico Caruso 2.25
87-09 2¢ Mary Lyon (3) 1.50
87-10 Reengraved 2¢
Locomotive
coil (6) 2.25
87-11 Girl Scouts 3.50
87-12 10¢ Canal Boat
coil (5) 1.75
87-13 Special
Occasions
booklet pane (10) 3.75
87-14 United Way 1.50
87-15 Flag with
Fireworks 1.50
87-16 Flag over
Capitol coil,
prephosphored
paper (2) 2.25
87-17 Wildlife,
Swallow-
Squirrel (10) 4.00
87-18 Wildlife,
Armadillo-
Rabbit (10) 4.00
87-19 Wildlife,
Tanager-
Ladybug (10) 4.00
87-20 Wildlife,
Beaver-
Prairie Dog (10) 4.00
87-21 Wildlife,
Turtle-Fox (10) 4.00
87-22 Delaware
Statehood 2.00
87-23 U.S./Morocco
Friendship 1.50
87-24 William Faulkner 1.50
87-25 Lacemaking (4) 3.50
87-26 10¢ Red
Cloud (3) 1.75
87-27 $5 Bret Harte 8.00
87-28 Pennsylvania
Statehood 1.50
87-29 Drafting of the
Constitution
booklet pane (5) 2.50
87-30 New Jersey
Statehood 1.75
87-31 Signing of
Constitution 1.50

87-32 Certified Public
Accountants 3.25
87-33 5¢ Milk Wagon
and 17.5¢ Racing
Car coils (4) 2.75
87-34 Locomotives
booklet pane (5) 6.75
87-35 Christmas,
Madonna 1.50
87-36 Christmas,
Ornaments 1.50
87-37 Flag with
Fireworks
booklet-pair 2.25

1988

88-01 Georgia
Statehood 1.75
88-02 Connecticut
Statehood 1.75
88-03 Winter Olympics 1.50
88-04 Australia
Bicentennial 1.75
88-05 James Weldon
Johnson 2.75
88-06 Cats (4) 3.75
88-07 Massachusetts
Statehood 2.25
88-08 Maryland
Statehood 2.25
88-09 3¢ Conestoga
Wagon coil (8) 2.50
88-10 Knute Rockne 5.00
88-11 "E" (25¢) Earth
sheet and
coil (3) 2.75
88-12 "E" (25¢) Earth
booklet pane (10) 3.25
88-13 "E" (25¢) Penalty
Mail coil (2) 2.25
88-14 44¢ New Sweden
airmail 1.75
88-15 Pheasant
booklet pane (10) 3.25
88-16 Jack London
booklet pane (6) 2.25
88-17 Jack London
booklet pane (10) 4.25
88-18 Flag with Clouds 1.50
88-19 45¢ Samuel
Langley airmail 1.75
88-19A 20¢ Penalty Mail
coil (2) 1.75
88-20 Flag over
Yosemite coil (2) 1.75
88-21 South Carolina
Statehood 1.50
88-22 Owl & Grosbeak
booklet pane (10) 3.00
88-23 15¢ Buffalo Bill
Cody (2) 1.75
88-24 15¢ and 25¢
Penalty Mail
coils (4) 2.25
88-25 Francis Ouimet 4.00
88-26 45¢ Harvey
Cushing, MD 1.50

88-27	New Hampshire Statehood	1.75
88-28	36¢ Igor Sikorsky airmail	2.00
88-29	Virginia Statehood	2.00
88-30	10.1¢ Oil Wagon coil, precancel (3)	2.25
88-31	Love	2.00
88-32	Flag with Clouds booklet pane (6)	3.00
88-33	16.7¢ Popcorn Wagon coil (2)	2.50
88-34	15¢ Tugboat coil (2)	2.50
88-35	13.2¢ Coal Car coil (2)	2.75
88-36	New York Statehood	2.00
88-37	45¢ Love	1.75
88-38	8.4¢ Wheelchair coil (3)	2.50
88-39	21¢ Railroad Mail Car coil (2)	3.00
88-40	Summer Olympics	1.75
88-41	Classic Cars booklet pane (5)	3.75
88-42	7.6¢ Carreta coil (4)	2.25
88-43	Honeybee coil (2)	3.00
88-44	Antarctic Explorers (4)	2.75
88-45	5.3¢ Elevator coil (5)	2.25
88-46	20.5¢ Fire Engine coil (2)	3.00
88-47	Carousel Animals (4)	3.00
88-48	$8.75 Eagle	15.00
88-49	Christmas, Madonna	1.50
88-50	Christmas, Snow Scene	1.50
88-51	21¢ Chester Carlson	1.50
88-52	Special Occasions booklet pane (6), Love You, Thinking of You	9.25
88-53	Special Occasions booklet pane (6), Happy Birthday, Best Wishes	14.00
88-54	24.1¢ Tandem Bicycle coil (2)	2.50
88-55	20¢ Cable Car coil (2)	2.50
88-56	13¢ Patrol Wagon coil (2)	2.75
88-57	23¢ Mary Cassatt	1.50
88-58	65¢ H.H. "Hap" Arnold	2.25

1989

89-01	Montana Statehood	2.00
89-02	A. Philip Randolph	3.00
89-03	Flag over Yosemite coil, prephosphored paper (2)	1.75
89-04	North Dakota Statehood	1.50
89-05	Washington Statehood	1.50
89-06	Steamboats booklet pane (5)	3.50
89-07	World Stamp Expo '89	1.50
89-08	Arturo Toscanini	2.00
89-09	U.S. House of Representatives	1.50
89-10	U.S. Senate	1.50
89-11	Executive Branch	1.50
89-12	South Dakota Statehood	1.50
89-13	7.1¢ Tractor coil, precancel (4)	2.50
89-14	$1 Johns Hopkins	2.25
89-15	Lou Gehrig	10.00
89-16	1¢ Penalty Mail	2.25
89-17	45¢ French Revolution airmail	2.25
89-18	Ernest Hemingway	2.50
89-19	$2.40 Moon Landing	11.00
89-20	North Carolina Statehood	2.00
89-21	Letter Carriers	1.50
89-22	28¢ Sitting Bull	1.75
89-23	Drafting of the Bill of Rights	1.50
89-24	Prehistoric Animals (4)	5.50
89-25	25¢ and 45¢ PUAS/ America (2)	2.00
89-26	Christmas, Madonna	4.25
89-27	Christmas, Antique Sleigh	4.25
89-28	Eagle and Shield, self-adhesive	1.75
89-29	World Stamp Expo '89 souvenir sheet	7.00
89-30	Classic Mail Transportation (4)	2.75
89-31	Future Mail Transportation souvenir sheet	3.25

89-32	45¢ Future Mail Transportation airmails (4)	3.25
89-33	Classic Mail Transportation souvenir sheet	3.50

1990

90-01	Idaho Statehood	1.50
90-02	Love sheet and booklet pane (10)	3.00
90-03	Ida B. Wells	3.00
90-04	U.S. Supreme Court	1.50
90-05	15¢ Beach Umbrella booklet pane (10)	3.00
90-06	5¢ Luis Muñoz Marín (5)	2.00
90-07	Wyoming Statehood	2.25
90-08	Classic Films (4)	4.25
90-09	Marianne Moore	1.50
90-10	$1 Seaplane coil (2)	5.00
90-11	Lighthouses booklet pane (5)	5.00
90-12	Plastic Flag stamp	2.75
90-13	Rhode Island Statehood	2.00
90-14	$2 Bobcat	4.00
90-15	Olympians (5)	4.75
90-16	Indian Headdresses booklet pane (10)	5.50
90-17	5¢ Circus Wagon coil (5)	3.25
90-18	40¢ Claire Lee Chennault	2.50
90-19	Federated States of Micronesia/ Marshall Islands (2)	2.25
90-20	Creatures of the Sea (4)	4.75
90-21	25¢ and 45¢ PUAS/America (2)	2.25
90-22	Dwight D. Eisenhower	2.50
90-23	Christmas, Madonna, sheet and booklet pane (10)	5.00
90-24	Christmas, Yule Tree, sheet and booklet pane (10)	5.00

1991

91-01	"F" (29¢) Flower sheet and coil (3)	2.50
91-02	"F" (29¢) Flower booklet panes (20)	8.00
91-03	4¢ Makeup	2.00
91-04	"F" (29¢) Flag ATM booklet single	2.25
91-05	"F" (29¢) Penalty Mail coil (2)	2.50
91-06	4¢ Steam Carriage coil (7)	2.25
91-07	50¢ Switzerland	2.25
91-08	Vermont Statehood	2.50
91-09	19¢ Fawn (2)	2.25
91-10	Flag over Mount Rushmore coil (2)	2.50
91-11	35¢ Dennis Chavez	2.75
91-12	Flower sheet and booklet pane (10)	5.00
91-13	4¢ Penalty Mail (8)	2.00
91-14	Wood Duck booklet panes (10)	9.50
91-15	23¢ Lunch Wagon coil (2)	2.25
91-16	Flag with Olympic Rings booklet pane (10)	5.00
91-17	50¢ Harriet Quimby	2.25
91-18	Savings Bond	2.00
91-19	Love sheet and booklet pane, 52¢ Love (12)	6.00
91-20	19¢ Balloon booklet pane (10)	4.00
91-21	40¢ William Piper airmail	2.25
91-22	William Saroyan	2.75
91-23	Penalty Mail coil and 19¢ and 23¢ sheet (4)	2.50
91-24	5¢ Canoe and 10¢ Tractor Trailer coils (4)	2.25
91-25	Flags on Parade	2.50
91-26	Fishing Flies booklet pane (5)	5.25
91-27	52¢ Hubert H. Humphrey	2.00
91-28	Cole Porter	2.25
91-29	50¢ Antarctic Treaty airmail	2.75
91-30	1¢ Kestrel, 3¢ Bluebird and 30¢ Cardinal (3)	2.25
91-31	Torch ATM booklet single	2.50
91-32	Desert Shield/ Desert Storm sheet and booklet pane (11)	5.00
91-33	Flag over Mount Rushmore coil, gravure printing (darker, 3)	2.25
91-34	Summer Olympics (5)	4.00
91-35	Flower coil, slit perforations (3)	2.25
91-36	Numismatics	2.50
91-37	Basketball	5.25
91-38	through 91-47 are unassigned	
91-48	19¢ Fishing Boat coil (3)	2.50
91-49	Comedians booklet pane (10)	5.00
91-50	World War II miniature sheet (10)	6.50
91-51	District of Columbia	2.25
91-52	Jan Matzeliger	4.00
91-53	$1 USPS/ Olympic Logo	3.00
91-54	Space Exploration booklet pane (10)	6.75
91-55	50¢ PUASP/America airmail	2.25
91-56	Christmas, Madonna sheet and booklet pane (10)	7.50
91-57	Christmas, Santa Claus sheet and booklet pane (11)	11.00
91-58	5¢ Canoe coil, gravure printing (red, 6)	3.00
91-59	29¢ Eagle and Shield, self-adhesive (3)	4.00
91-60	23¢ Flag presort	2.50
91-61	$9.95 Express Mail	22.50
91-62	$2.90 Priority Mail	7.50
91-63	$14.00 Express Mail International	30.00

1992

92-01	Winter Olympic Games (5)	3.75
92-02	World Columbian Stamp Expo '92	2.50
92-03	W.E.B. DuBois	3.75
92-04	Love	2.50
92-05	75¢ Wendell Willkie	2.25
92-06	29¢ Flower coil, round perforations (2)	2.25
92-07	Earl Warren	3.00
92-08	Olympic Baseball	10.00
92-09	Flag over White House, coil (2)	2.50
92-10	First Voyage of Christopher Columbus (4)	3.75
92-11	New York Stock Exchange	2.50
92-12	Christopher Columbus	7.50
92-13	Columbus-Seeking Royal Support (3)	7.50
92-14	Columbus-First Sighting of Land (3)	7.50
92-15	Columbus-Claiming New World (3)	7.50
92-16	Columbus-Reporting Discoveries (3)	7.50
92-17	Columbus-Royal Favor Restored (3)	7.50
92-18	Space Adventures (4)	4.00
92-19	Alaska Highway	2.50
92-20	Kentucky Statehood	2.50
92-21	Summer Olympic Games (5)	3.75
92-22	Hummingbirds booklet pane (5)	5.00
92-22A	23¢ Presort USA (3)	2.50
92-23	Wildflowers (10)	6.50
92-24	Wildflowers (10)	6.50
92-25	Wildflowers (10)	6.50
92-26	Wildflowers (10)	6.50
92-27	Wildflowers (10)	6.50
92-28	World War II miniature sheet (10)	6.00
92-29	29¢ Variable Rate	2.75
92-30	Dorothy Parker	2.75
92-31	Theodore von Karman	3.50
92-32	Pledge of Allegiance (10)	7.00
92-33	Minerals (4)	4.00
92-34	Eagle and Shield (3)	3.75
92-35	Juan Rodriguez Cabrillo	2.50
92-36	Wild Animals booklet pane (5)	5.00
92-37	23¢ Presort (3)	2.75

92-38	Christmas Contemporary, sheet and booklet pane (8)	7.50
92-39	Christmas Traditional, sheet and booklet pane (11)	5.50
92-40	Pumpkinseed Sunfish	2.75
92-41	Circus Wagon	2.75
92-42	Year of the Rooster	7.75

1993

93-01	Elvis	10.00
93-02	Space Fantasy (5)	6.00
93-03	Percy Lavon Julian	3.50
93-04	Oregon Trail	2.75
93-05	World University Games	2.75
93-06	Grace Kelly	6.00
93-07	Oklahoma!	2.25
93-08	Circus	4.50
93-09	Thomas Jefferson	2.75
93-10	Cherokee Strip	3.50
93-11	Dean Acheson	3.00
93-12	Sporting Horses	5.50
93-13	USA Coil	2.75
93-14	Garden Flowers, booklet pane (5)	6.00
93-15	Eagle and Shield, coil	3.75
93-16	World War II miniature sheet (10)	5.50
93-17	Futuristic Space Shuttle	8.00
93-18	Hank Williams, sheet	5.00
93-19	Rock & Roll/ Rhythm & Blues, sheet single, booklet pane (8)	10.00
93-20	Joe Louis	7.50
93-21	Red Squirrel	2.75
93-22	Broadway Musicals, booklet pane (4)	4.50
93-23	National Postal Museum, strip (4)	3.25
93-24	Red Rose	2.50
93-25	American Sign Language, pair	2.75
93-26	Country & Western Music, sheet and booklet pane (4)	9.25
93-27	African Violets, booklet pane (10)	4.25
93-28	10¢ Official Mail	2.75
93-29	Contemporary Christmas, booklet pane (10), sheet and self-adhesive stamps	8.50

93-30	Traditional Christmas, sheet, booklet pane (4)	4.75
93-31	Classic Books, strip (4)	3.25
93-32	Mariana Islands	2.75
93-33	Pine Cone	2.50
93-34	Columbus' Landing in Puerto Rico	3.25
93-35	AIDS Awareness	4.75

1994

94-01	Winter Olympics	5.00
94-02	Edward R. Murrow	3.25
94-03	Love, self-adhesive	3.25
94-04	Dr. Allison Davis	4.50
94-05	29¢ Eagle, self-adhesive	3.50
94-06	Year of the Dog	4.00
94-07	Love, booklet pane (10), single sheet stamp	6.50
94-08	Postage and Mailing Center	5.50
94-09	Buffalo Soldiers	5.00
94-10	Silent Screen Stars	6.00
94-11	Garden Flowers, booklet pane (5)	6.00
94-12	Victory at Saratoga	4.75
94-13	10¢ Tractor Trailer gravure printing	5.00
94-14	World Cup Soccer	6.00
94-15	World Cup Soccer souvenir sheet	6.00
94-16	World War II miniature sheet (10)	5.50
94-17	Love, sheet stamp	3.25
94-18	Statue of Liberty	3.50
94-19	Fishing Boat, reissue	3.75
94-20	Norman Rockwell	9.00
94-21	$9.95 and 29¢ Moon Landing	15.00
94-22	Locomotives (5)	6.50
94-23	George Meany	3.25
94-24	$5.00 Washington/ Jackson	10.00
94-25	Popular Singers (5)	6.00
94-26	James Thurber	4.00
94-27	Jazz Singers/ Blues Singers (10)	9.00
94-28	Wonders of the Sea (4)	5.00

94-29	Chinese/Joint Issue (2)	4.00
94-30	Holiday Traditional (10)	8.50
94-31	Holiday Contemporary (4)	6.50
94-32	Holiday, self-adhesive	7.00
94-33	20¢ Virginia Apgar	4.50
94-34	BEP Centennial	15.00
94-35	Year of the Boar	5.50
94-G1	G1 (4) Rate Change	4.00
94-G2	G2 (6) Rate Change	4.00
94-G3	G3 (5) Rate Change	4.00
94-G4	G4 (2) Rate Change	8.00
94-36	Legends of West	12.00

1995

95-01	Love (2)	3.50
95-02	Florida Statehood	2.75
95-03	Butte (7)	5.50
95-04	Automobile (4)	4.50
95-05	Flag Over Field, self-adhesive	2.75
95-06	Juke Box (2+2)	3.00
95-07	Tail Fin (2+2)	4.50
95-08	Circus Wagon (7)	5.00
95-09	Kids Care (4)	3.50
95-10	Richard Nixon	3.50
95-11	Bessie Coleman	4.50
95-12	Official Mail	3.00
95-13	Kestrel with cent sign	16.00
95-14	Love 1 oz. and 2 oz.	3.50
95-15	Flag Over Porch	5.50
95-16	Recreational Sports (5)	9.00
95-17	POW & MIA	4.50
95-18	Marilyn Monroe	12.00
95-19	Pink Rose	5.00
95-20	Ferry Boat (3)	4.00
95-21	Cog Railway Car (3)	4.00
95-22	Blue Jay (10)	5.00
95-23	Texas Statehood	4.00
95-24	Great Lake Lighthouses (5)	9.00
95-25	Challenger Shuttle	10.00
95-26	United Nations	2.75
95-27	Civil War (front and back)	14.50
95-28	Peach & Pear	4.50
95-29	Alice Hamilton	2.75
95-30	Carousel Horses	5.25
95-31	Endeavor Shuttle	22.50
95-32	Alice Paul	2.75
95-33	Women's Suffrage	2.75

95-34	Louis Armstrong	4.50
95-35	World War II	6.00
95-36	Milton Hershey	2.75
95-37	Jazz Musicians	7.00
95-38	Fall Garden Flowers (5)	6.00
95-39	Eddie Rickenbacker (airmail)	4.50
95-40	Republic of Palau	3.50
95-41	Holiday Contemporary/ Santa (4)	5.00
95-42	American Comic Strips	15.00
95-43	Naval Academy	4.50
95-44	Tennessee Williams	4.50
95-45	Holiday Children Sledding	4.75
95-46	Holiday Traditional sheet and booklet pane (10)	5.50
95-47	Holiday Midnight Angel	4.75
95-48	Ruth Bendict	3.25
95-49	James K. Polk	7.00
95-50	Antique Automobiles, strip (5)	6.00

1996

96-01	Utah Statehood	3.50
96-02	Garden Flowers	6.00
96-03	Love/Kestrel	16.00
96-04	Postage and Mailing Center (3)	6.00
96-05	Ernest E. Just	5.00
96-06	Woodpecker	3.75
96-07	Smithsonian Institution	3.75
96-08	Year of the Rat	6.00
96-09	Pioneers of Communication	7.00
96-10	Fulbright Scholarships	3.75
96-11	Jacqueline Cochran	3.75
96-12	Mountain	10.00
96-13	Bluebird	3.75
96-14	Marathon	3.75
96-15	Flag over Porch/ Eagle & Shield	4.50
96-16	Cal Farley	3.25
96-17	Classic Olympic Collection	8.00
96-18	Georgia O'Keefe Art	4.75
96-19	Tennessee	3.75
96-20	American Indian Dances	4.75
96-21	Prehistoric Animals	4.75
96-22	Breast Cancer Awareness	4.75

96-23	Flag over Porch/ Juke Box/Butte/ Tail Fin Automobile/ Mountain	5.50
96-24	James Dean	6.00
96-25	Folk Heroes	5.00
96-26	Olympic/Discus	5.00
96-27	Iowa	5.00
96-28	Blue Jay	5.00
96-29	Rural Free Delivery	4.00
96-30	Riverboats	5.50
96-31	Big Band Leaders	6.00
96-32	Songwriters	6.00
96-33	F. Scott Fitzgerald	4.00
96-34	Endangered Species	15.00
96-35	Computer Technology	4.00
96-36	Holiday Family Scenes	6.00
96-37	Skaters	6.00
96-38	Hanukkah	5.00
96-39	Madonna and Child	6.00
96-40	Yellow Rose	6.00
96-41	Cycling	6.00

1997

97-01	Year of the Ox	6.00
97-02	Flag Over Porch/ Juke Box/ Mountain	5.50
97-03	Benjamin O. Davis Sr.	6.00
97-04	Statue of Liberty	5.50
97-05	Love Swans	5.50
97-06	Helping Children Learn	5.00
97-07	Merian Botanical Plants	5.50
97-08	Pacific 97 - Stagecoach and Ship	6.00
97-09	Linerless Flag Over Porch/ Juke Box	5.50
97-10	Thornton Wilder	5.00
97-11	Raoul Wallenberg	5.00
97-12	Dinosaurs	12.50
97-13	Pacific '97 - Franklin	10.00
97-14	Pacific '97 - Washington	10.00
97-15	Bugs Bunny	10.00
97-16	The Marshall Plan	5.00
97-17	Humphrey Bogart	6.00
97-18	Classic Aircraft	12.50
97-19	Classic American Dolls	10.00
97-20	Football Coaches	10.00
97-20A	George Halas	8.00
97-20B	Vince Lombardi	8.00
97-20C	Pop Warner	8.00
97-20D	Bear Bryant	8.00

97-21	Yellow Rose	7.00
97-22	"Stars and Stripes Forever"	6.00
97-23	Padre Félix Varela	6.00
97-24	Composers and Conducters	9.00
97-25	Opera Singers	8.00
97-26	Air Force	8.00
97-27	Movie Monsters	10.00
97-28	Supersonic Flight	8.00
97-29	Women in Military	6.00
97-30	Kwanzaa	7.50
97-31	Holiday Traditional, Madonna and Child	7.50
97-32	Holly	7.50
97-33	Mars Pathfinder	12.00

1998

98-01	Year of the Tiger	6.00
98-02	Winter Sports	6.00
98-03	Madam C. J. Walker	6.00
98-03A	Celebrate The Century® 1900s	10.00
98-03B	Celebrate The Century® 1910s	10.00
98-04	"Remember the Maine"	6.00
98-05	Flowering Trees	8.00
98-06	Alexander Calder	8.00
98-07	Henry R. Luce	5.50
98-08	Cinco De Mayo	6.00
98-09	Sylvester & Tweety	6.00
98-09A	Celebrate The Century® 1920s	10.00
98-10	Wisconsin	6.00
98-11	Trans-Mississippi Reissue of 1898	10.00
98-12	Trans-Mississippi (single stamp)	6.00
98-13	Folk Musicians	8.00
98-14	Berlin Airlift	5.50
98-15	Diner/Wetlands coil	5.50
98-16	Spanish Settlement of the Southwest	6.00
98-17	Gospel Singers	7.50
98-18	The Wallaces	5.50
98-19	Stephen Vincent Benet	6.00
98-20	Tropical Birds	8.00
98-21	Breast Cancer Research (semi-postal)	6.00
98-22	Ring-Neck Pheasant	7.00
98-23	Alfred Hitchcock	6.00

98-24	Organ Donations	6.00
98-24A	Red Fox	7.00
98-24B	Green Bicycle coil	6.00
98-25	Bright Eyes	7.50
98-26	Klondike Gold Rush	6.00
98-26A	Celebrate The Century® 1930s	10.00
98-27	American Art	10.00
98-28	Ballet	6.00
98-28A	Diner coil	5.50
98-29	Space Discovery	7.50
98-30	Philanthropy	6.00
98-31	Holiday Traditional	6.00
98-32	Holiday Contemporary	7.50
98-33	Hat Rate Change "H" Series/ Makeup Rate	7.00
98-34	Uncle Sam — Rate Change	7.50
98-35	Hat Rate Change "H" Series	7.00
98-36	Hat Rate Change "H" Series	7.00
98-37	Mary Breckinridge	4.50
98-38	Space Shuttle Landing	9.00
98-39	Shuttle Piggyback	17.50
98-40	Wetlands non-denominated nonprofit coil and Eagle & Shield non-denominated presort coil	6.50

1999

99-01	Year of the Hare	6.00
99-02	Malcolm X	6.00
99-03	33¢ Victorian — Love	7.50
99-04	55¢ Victorian — Love	6.50
99-05	Hospice Care	6.00
99-06	Celebrate The Century® 1940s	10.00
99-07	City Flag	6.50
99-08	Irish Immigration	6.00
99-09	Alfred Lunt and Lynn Fontanne	6.00
99-10	Arctic Animals	7.50
99-10A	Classroom Flag	6.00
99-11	Nature of America Sonoran Desert	10.00
99-11A	Fruit Berries	7.50
99-12	Daffy Duck	8.00
99-13	Ayn Rand	6.50
99-14	Cinco de Mayo	6.00

99-15	Tropical Flowers	7.50
99-16	Niagara Falls	6.50
99-17	John and William Bartram	6.00
99-18	Celebrate The Century® 1950s	10.00
99-19	Prostate Cancer	6.00
99-20	California Gold Rush	6.00
99-20A	Woodpecker Stamp	6.00
99-21	Aquarium Fish	7.50
99-22	Xtreme Sports	7.50
99-23	American Glass	7.50
99-24	Justin Morrill	5.50
99-25	James Cagney	7.50
99-26	Billy Mitchell	7.50
99-27	Rio Grande	6.00
99-28	Pink Coral Rose	7.00
99-29	Honoring Those Who Served	6.00
99-29A	UPU	6.00
99-30	All Aboard!	7.50
99-31	Frederick Law Olmsted	6.00
99-32	Hollywood Composers	7.50
99-33	Celebrate The Century® 1960s	10.00
99-34	Broadway Songwriters	7.50
99-35	Insects and Spiders	10.00
99-36	Hanukkah	6.00
99-37	Official Mail	6.00
99-38	Uncle Sam	6.00
99-39	Nato	6.00
99-40	Holiday Traditional, Madonna & Child	6.00
99-41	Holiday Contemporary, Deer	7.50
99-42	Kwanzaa	6.00
99-43	Celebrate The Century® 1970s	10.00
99-44	Kestrel	6.50
99-45 through 99-49	**are unassigned**	
99-50	Year 2000	6.00

2000

00-01	Year of the Dragon	6.00
00-02	Celebrate The Century® 1980s	10.00
00-03	Grand Canyon	6.00
00-04	Patricia Roberts Harris	6.00
00-05	Fruit Berries	6.00
00-06	U.S. Navy Submarine – Los Angeles Class	6.00

00-07	Pacific Coast Rain Forest	10.00
00-08	Louise Nevelson	7.50
00-09	Coral Pink Rose	7.00
00-10	Edwin Powell Hubble	7.50
00-11	American Somoa	6.00
00-12	Library of Congress	6.00
00-13	Wile E. Coyote/ Road Runner	7.50
00-14	Celebrate The Century® 1990s	10.00
00-15	Summer Sports	6.00
00-16	Adoption	6.00
00-17	Youth Team Sports	6.50
00-18	Distinguished Soldiers	8.00
00-19	The Stars and Stripes	10.00
00-20	Legends of Baseball	10.00
00-21	Stampin' The Future™	6.50
00-22	Joseph Stilwell	6.00
00-23	Claude Pepper	6.00
00-24	California Statehood	6.00
00-25	Edward G. Robinson	6.00
00-26	Deep Sea Creatures	7.50
00-27	Thomas Wolfe	6.00
00-28	White House	6.00
00-29	New York Public Library Lion Presort	6.00

2001

01-01	Farm Flag (1 oz.)	6.00
01-02	Statue of Liberty	6.00
01-03	Flowers	7.50
01-04	Statute of Liberty	6.00
01-05	Love Letters (1 oz.)	6.00
01-06	Year of the Snake	6.00
01-07	Roy Wilkins	6.00
01-08	Washington Monument	20.00
01-09	U.S. Capitol	10.00
01-10	American Illustrators (front & back)	10.00
01-11	Farm Flag (1 oz.)	6.00
01-12	Statute of Liberty	7.50
01-13	Flowers	7.50
01-14	Love Letters (1 oz. & 2 oz.)	7.50
01-15	Hattie Caraway (3 oz.)	6.00
01-16	Buffalo (2 oz.)	6.00
01-17	George Washington	6.00
01-18	Art Deco Eagle (2 oz.)	6.00

01-19	Official Mail	6.00
01-20	Apple and Orange	6.00
01-21	Nine-Mile Prairie	6.00
01-22	Farm Flag (1 oz.)	6.00
01-23	Diabetes Awareness	6.00
01-24	The Nobel Prize	6.00
01-25	The Pan-American Inverts (front and back)	10.00
01-26	Mt. McKinley (Int'l PC)	7.50
01-27	Great Plains Prairie (front and back)	10.00
01-28	Peanuts	6.00
01-29	Honoring Veterans	6.00
01-30	Acadia National Park	7.50
01-31	Frida Kahlo	6.00
01-32	Baseball's Legendary Playing Fields (front and back)	12.50
01-33	Atlas Statue	6.00
01-34	Leonard Bernstein	6.00
01-35	Woody Wagon	6.00
01-36	Lucille Ball	6.00
01-37	The Amish Quilts	7.50
01-38	Carnivorous Plants	7.50
01-39	Holiday Celebration–Eid	6.00
01-40	Dr. Enrico Fermi	6.00
01-41	Bison (2 oz.)	6.00
01-42	George Washington	6.00
01-43	Art Deco Eagle (2 oz.)	6.00
01-44	"That's All Folks!"	6.00
01-45	Holiday Traditional: Lorenza Costa–Virgin and Child	6.00
01-46	Holiday Contemporary: Santas	7.50
01-47	Holiday Celebration: Thanksgiving	6.00
01-48	James Madison	6.00
01-49	Kwanzaa	6.00
01-50	Hanukkah	6.00
01-51	Farm Flag (1 oz.)	6.00
01-52	Love Letters (2 oz.)	6.00
01-53	United We Stand	7.50

2002

02-01	Winter Sports	7.50
02-02	Mentoring a Child	6.00
02-03	Langston Hughes	6.00
02-04	Happy Birthday	6.00
02-05	Year of the Horse	6.00
02-06	U.S. Military Academy	6.00
02-07	Greetings From America	37.50
02-08	Longleaf Pine Forest	10.00
02-09	American Toleware	6.00
02-10	U.S. Flag	7.50
02-11	Antique Toys	7.50
02-12	Star	6.00
02-13	U.S. Flag	7.50
02-14	George Washington	7.50
02-15	Heroes 2001	6.00
02-16	Masters of American Photography	10.00
02-17	John James Audubon	6.00
02-18	Harry Houdini	6.00
02-19	Eagle Coverlet	6.00
02-20	Antique Toys	7.50
02-21	Edna Ferber	7.50
02-22	Jefferson Memorial	10.00
02-23	Capitol at Dusk	21.00
02-24	Official Mail	6.00
02-25	Andy Warhol	6.00
02-26	Teddy Bears	7.50
02-27	Love (1 oz. & 2 oz.)	7.50
02-28	Ogden Nash	6.00
02-29	Duke Kahanamoku	6.00
02-30	American Bats	7.50
02-31	Women in Journalism	7.50
02-32	Irving Berlin	6.00
02-33	Neuter or Spay	7.50
02-34	Christmas: Gossaert	6.00
02-35	Eid	6.00
02-36	Kwanzaa	6.00
02-37	Hanukkah	6.00
02-38	Cary Grant	6.00
02-39	Sea Coast Nonprofit	6.00
02-40	Hawaiian Missionaries	7.50
02-41	Happy Birthday	6.00
02-42	Greetings From America	37.50
02-43	Holiday: Snowmen	7.50

2003

03-01	Thurgood Marshall	—
03-02	Year of the Ram	—
03-03	Zora Neale Hurston	—
03-04	American Clock	—
03-05	U.S. Flag	—
03-06	The New York Public Library Lion	—
03-07	Special Oylmpics	—
03-08	American Filmmaking: Behind the Scenes	—
03-09	Wisdom	—
03-10	Tiffany Lamp	—
03-11	Ohio Statehood	—
03-12	Pelican Island National Wildlife Refuge	—
03-13	Sea Coast	—
03-14	Old Glory	—
03-15	Cesar E. Chavez	—
03-16	Louisiana Purchase	—
03-17	First Flight	—
03-18	Purple Heart	—
03-19	Audrey Hepburn	—
03-20	Southeastern Lighthouses	—
03-21	American Eagle	—
03-22	Arctic Tundra	—
03-23	Korean War Veterans Memorial	—
03-24	Purple Heart	—
03-25	Mary Cassatt	—
03-26	Early Football Heroes	—
03-27	Antique Toys	—
03-28	Roy Acuff	—
03-29	District of Columbia	—
03-30	Reptiles and Amphibians	—
03-31	Stop Family Violence	—
03-32	Holiday Music Makers	—
03-33	Christmas : Gossaert	—
03-34	Snowy Egret	—
02-31A	American Eagle	—

Note: Numbers and prices may be changed without notice due to additional USPS stamp issues and/or different information that may become available on older issues.

American Commemorative Panels

The Postal Service offers American Commemorative Panels for each new commemorative stamp and special Holiday and Love stamp issued. The series began in 1972 with the Wildlife Commemorative Panel. The panels feature mint stamps complemented by fine reproductions of steel line engravings and the stories behind the commemorated subjects.

The identifying numbers used below are based on the Postal Service's numbering system for American Commemorative Panels; therefore, they do not follow the Scott numbering system.

1972

1	Wildlife	4.75
2	Mail Order	4.75
3	Osteopathic Medicine	6.50
4	Tom Sawyer	5.00
5	Pharmacy	6.00
6	Christmas, Angels	8.00
7	Santa Claus	8.00
7E	Same with error date (1882)	—
8	Stamp Collecting	5.50

1973

9	Love	6.75
10	Pamphleteers	5.50
11	George Gershwin	6.00
12	Posting a Broadside	5.50
13	Copernicus	5.50
14	Postal Employees	5.25
15	Harry S. Truman	6.50
16	Postrider	6.00
17	Boston Tea Party	15.00
18	Electronics	5.50
19	Robinson Jeffers	4.75
20	Lyndon B. Johnson	6.50
21	Henry O. Tanner	5.50
22	Willa Cather	5.00
23	Drummer	8.25
24	Angus Cattle	5.50
25	Christmas, Madonna	7.75
26	Christmas Tree, Needlepoint	7.75

1974

27	VFW	5.25
28	Robert Frost	5.25
29	Expo '74	6.00
30	Horse Racing	8.00
31	Skylab	8.50
32	Universal Postal Union	6.00
33	Mineral Heritage	7.00
34	First Kentucky Settlement	5.25
35	Continental Congress	7.00
35A	Same with corrected logo	—
36	Chautauqua	5.75
37	Kansas Wheat	5.75
38	Energy Conservation	5.00
39	Sleepy Hollow	5.75
40	Retarded Children	5.00
41	Christmas, Currier & Ives	7.50
42	Christmas, Angel Altarpiece	7.50

1975

43	Benjamin West	5.50
44	Pioneer	8.50
45	Collective Bargaining	4.75
46	Contributors to the Cause	6.25
47	Mariner 10	9.00
48	Lexington & Concord	5.50
49	Paul Laurence Dunbar	6.00
50	D.W. Griffith	5.75
51	Bunker Hill	5.75
52	Military Uniforms	5.00
53	Apollo Soyuz	8.25
54	World Peace Through Law	5.00
54A	Same with August 15, 1975 date	—
55	Women's Year	5.75
56	Postal Service Bicentennial	5.50
57	Banking and Commerce	6.25
58	Early Christmas, Card	7.00
59	Christmas, Madonna	7.00

1976

60	Spirit of '76	8.00
61	Interphil 76	7.00
62	State Flags	15.00
63	Telephone	6.75
64	Commercial Aviation	9.25
65	Chemistry	7.00
66	Benjamin Franklin	7.00
67	Declaration of Independence	7.00
68	12th Winter Olympics	7.50
69	Clara Maass	8.00
70	Adolph S. Ochs	9.00
70A	Same with charter logo	—
71	Christmas, Winter Pastime	8.00
71A	Same with charter logo	—
72	Christmas, Nativity	8.75
72A	Same with charter logo	—

1977

73	Washington at Princeton	9.00
73A	Same with charter logo	—
74	Sound Recording	16.00
74A	Same with charter logo	—
75	Pueblo Art	45.00
75A	Same with charter logo	—
76	Solo Transatlantic Lindbergh Flight	45.00
77	Colorado	11.00
78	Butterflies	12.00
79	Lafayette	10.50
80	Skilled Hands	10.50
81	Peace Bridge	10.50
82	Battle of Oriskany	10.50
83	Alta, CA, Civil Settlement	11.00
84	Articles of Confederation	15.00
85	Talking Pictures	13.50
86	Surrender at Saratoga	15.00
87	Energy	12.00
88	Christmas, Valley Forge	18.00
89	Christmas, Mailbox	24.00

1978

90	Carl Sandburg	6.50
91	Captain Cook	12.00
92	Harriet Tubman	9.50
93	Quilts	14.00
94	Dance	10.00
95	French Alliance	10.00
96	Early Cancer Detection	8.25
97	Jimmie Rodgers	11.00
98	Photography	8.00
99	George M. Cohan	12.50
100	Viking Missions	27.50
101	Owls	27.50
102	Trees	26.00
103	Christmas, Madonna	10.50
104	Christmas, Hobby Horse	10.50

1979

105	Robert F. Kennedy	7.25
106	Martin Luther King, Jr.	7.50
107	International Year of the Child	6.50
108	John Steinbeck	6.00
109	Albert Einstein	7.25
110	Pennsylvania Toleware	6.75
111	Architecture	7.50
112	Endangered Flora	7.00
113	Seeing Eye Dogs	6.25
114	Special Olympics	7.50
115	John Paul Jones	7.00
116	15¢ Olympics	8.50
117	Christmas, Madonna	8.50
118	Christmas, Santa Claus	8.50
119	Will Rogers	7.00
120	Vietnam Veterans	9.50
121	10¢, 31¢ Olympics	8.50

1980

122	W.C. Fields	7.50
123	Winter Olympics	7.50
124	Benjamin Banneker	7.25
125	Frances Perkins	5.50
126	Emily Bissell	6.00
127	Helen Keller/ Anne Sullivan	5.50
128	Veterans Administration	6.00
129	General Bernardo de Galvez	5.25
130	Coral Reefs	8.00
131	Organized Labor	5.50
132	Edith Wharton	5.25
133	Education	5.50
134	Indian Masks	8.00
135	Architecture	6.75
136	Christmas, Epiphany Window	8.00
137	Christmas, Toys	8.00

1981

138	Everett Dirksen	6.50
139	Whitney Moore Young	7.00
140	Flowers	7.00
141	Red Cross	7.00
142	Savings & Loans	6.75
143	Space Achievements	11.00
144	Professional Management	5.50
145	Wildlife Habitats	8.00
146	Int'l. Year of the Disabled	5.50
147	Edna St. Vincent Millay	6.00
148	Architecture	6.50
149	Babe Zaharias/ Bobby Jones	20.00
150	James Hoban	5.50
151	Frederic Remington	6.75
152	Battle of Yorktown/ Virginia Capes	5.25
153	Christmas, Madonna	7.00
154	Christmas, Bear and Sleigh	8.00
155	John Hanson	5.50
156	U.S. Desert Plants	8.00

1982

157	Roosevelt	8.25
158	Love	10.00
159	George Washington	9.50
160	State Birds & Flowers	27.50
161	U.S./Netherlands	10.00
162	Library of Congress	10.00
163	Knoxville World's Fair	8.50
164	Horatio Alger	8.75
165	Aging Together	9.50
166	The Barrymores	10.50
167	Dr. Mary Walker	9.00
168	Peace Garden	9.50
169	America's Libraries	8.00
170	Jackie Robinson	30.00
171	Touro Synagogue	9.50
172	Architecture	10.50
173	Wolf Trap Farm Park	10.00
174	Francis of Assisi	10.50
175	Ponce de Leon	10.50
176	Christmas, Madonna	13.50
177	Christmas, Season's Greetings	13.50
178	Kitten & Puppy	14.00

1983

179	Science and Industry	5.25
180	Sweden/USA Treaty	5.25
181	Balloons	6.00
182	Civilian Conservation Corps	5.25
183	40¢ Olympics	6.50
184	Joseph Priestley	5.25
185	Voluntarism	5.25
186	Concord/German Immigration	5.25
187	Physical Fitness	5.25
188	Brooklyn Bridge	6.00
189	TVA	5.25
190	Medal of Honor	8.00
191	Scott Joplin	7.25
192	28¢ Olympics	6.50
193	Babe Ruth	22.50
194	Nathaniel Hawthorne	5.25
195	13¢ Olympics	7.50
196	Treaty of Paris	5.50
197	Civil Service	5.50
198	Metropolitan Opera	6.50
199	Inventors	6.75
200	Streetcars	7.50
201	Christmas, Madonna	8.00
202	Christmas, Santa Claus	8.00
203	35¢ Olympics	8.00
204	Martin Luther	7.00

1984

205	Alaska	4.50
206	Winter Olympics	5.00
207	FDIC	4.75
208	Love	4.00
209	Carter G. Woodson	4.75
210	Soil and Water Conservation	4.75
211	Credit Union Act	4.75
212	Orchids	5.50
213	Hawaii	6.25
214	National Archives	4.50
215	20¢ Olympics	5.25
216	Louisiana World Exposition	5.00
217	Health Research	4.75
218	Douglas Fairbanks	4.75

219	Jim Thorpe	8.25
220	John McCormack	4.75
221	St. Lawrence Seaway	6.25
222	Preserving Waterfowl	9.00
223	Roanoke Voyages	4.75
224	Herman Melville	4.75
225	Horace Moses	4.75
226	Smokey Bear	15.00
227	Roberto Clemente	25.00
228	Dogs	6.25
229	Crime Prevention	5.25
230	Family Unity	4.75
231	Christmas, Madonna	6.75
232	Christmas, Santa Claus	6.75
233	Eleanor Roosevelt	8.50
234	Nation of Readers	4.75
235	Hispanic Americans	4.50
236	Vietnam Veterans Memorial	8.25

1985

237	Jerome Kern	5.75
238	Mary McLeod Bethune	5.75
239	Duck Decoys	10.50
240	Winter Special Olympics	5.00
241	Love	5.00
242	Rural Electrification Administration	5.00
243	AMERIPEX '86	6.75
244	Abigail Adams	5.00
245	Frederic Auguste Bartholdi	6.50
246	Korean War Veterans	6.00
247	Social Security Act	5.00
248	World War I Veterans	5.00
249	Horses	9.00
250	Public Education	5.00
251	Youth	8.25
252	Help End Hunger	5.00
253	Christmas, Madonna	7.00
254	Christmas, Poinsettias	7.00

1986

255	Arkansas	5.25
256	Stamp Collecting Booklet	6.75
257	Love	6.00
258	Sojourner Truth	7.50
259	Republic of Texas	7.50
260	Fish Booklet	6.75
261	Public Hospitals	4.75
262	Duke Ellington	7.50
263	U.S. Presidents' Sheet #1	6.25
264	U.S. Presidents' Sheet #2	6.25
265	U.S. Presidents' Sheet #3	6.25
266	U.S. Presidents' Sheet #4	6.25
267	Polar Explorers	6.75
268	Statue of Liberty	7.50
269	Navajo Blankets	8.00
270	T.S. Eliot	6.25
271	Wood-Carved Figurines	6.75
272	Christmas, Madonna	5.75
273	Christmas, Village Scene	5.75

1987

274	Michigan	5.75
275	Pan American Games	3.50
276	Love	5.75
277	Jean Baptiste Pointe Du Sable	5.75
278	Enrico Caruso	5.50
279	Girl Scouts	7.50
280	Special Occasions Booklet	5.50
281	United Way	4.75
282	#1 American Wildlife	6.50
283	#2 American Wildlife	6.50
284	#3 American Wildlife	6.50
285	#4 American Wildlife	6.50
286	#5 American Wildlife	6.50
287	Delaware	5.75
288	Morocco/U.S. Diplomatic Relations	4.75
289	William Faulkner	4.75
290	Lacemaking	5.50
291	Pennsylvania	5.25
292	Constitution Booklet	5.00
293	New Jersey	5.25
294	Signing of the Constitution	5.00
295	Certified Public Accountants	20.00
296	Locomotives Booklet	7.50
297	Christmas, Madonna	6.25
298	Christmas, Ornaments	5.50

1988

299	Georgia	5.25
300	Connecticut	5.25
301	Winter Olympics	6.25
302	Australia	5.75
303	James Weldon Johnson	5.00
304	Cats	6.50
305	Massachusetts	5.25
306	Maryland	5.25
307	Knute Rockne	9.00
308	New Sweden	5.75
309	South Carolina	5.25
310	Francis Ouimet	14.00
311	New Hampshire	5.25
312	Virginia	5.25
313	Love	6.50
314	New York	5.25
315	Summer Olympics	6.25
316	Classic Cars Booklet	7.00
317	Antarctic Explorers	6.25
318	Carousel Animals	7.00
319	Christmas, Madonna, Sleigh	6.50
320	Special Occasions Booklet	6.50

1989

321	Montana	6.25
322	A. Philip Randolph	8.00
323	North Dakota	6.25
324	Washington	6.25
325	Steamboats Booklet	7.50
326	World Stamp Expo '89	5.50
327	Arturo Toscanini	6.25
328	U.S. House of Representatives	6.25
329	U.S. Senate	6.25
330	Executive Branch	6.25

331	South Dakota	6.25
332	Lou Gehrig	25.00
333	French Revolution	6.50
334	Ernest Hemingway	8.75
335	North Carolina	5.25
336	Letter Carriers	6.50
337	Drafting of the Bill of Rights	6.50
338	Prehistoric Animals	13.50
339	Southwest Carved Figure, Southeast Carved Wood Figure America/PUAS	7.25
340	Christmas, Madonna and Child, Sleigh Full of Presents	8.50
341	Classic Mail Transportation	6.50
342	Future Mail Transportation	8.00

1990

343	Idaho	5.50
344	Love	7.25
345	Ida B. Wells	12.50
346	U.S. Supreme Court	6.00
347	Wyoming	6.25
348	Classic Films	13.00
349	Marianne Moore	5.50
350	Lighthouses Booklet	10.00
351	Rhode Island	5.25
352	Olympians	8.50
353	Indian Headdresses Booklet	10.00
354	Micronesia/ Marshall Islands	7.00
355	Grand Canyon Tropical Coastline America/PUAS	7.50
356	Eisenhower	8.25
357	Creatures of the Sea	11.50
358	Christmas, Traditional and Contemporary	8.00

1991

359	Switzerland	8.00
360	Vermont	6.00
361	Savings Bonds	6.25
362	29¢ and 52¢ Love	8.00
363	Saroyan	8.50
364	Fishing Flies Booklet	10.00
365	Cole Porter	6.00
366	Antarctic Treaty	5.50
367	Desert Shield/ Desert Storm	25.00
368	Summer Olympics	7.50
369	Numismatics	6.50
370	Basketball	12.50
371	World War II Miniature Sheet	12.00
372	Comedians Booklet	9.50
373	District of Columbia	7.00
374	Jan Matzeliger	7.50
375	Space Exploration Booklet	11.50
376	America/PUAS	6.50
377	Christmas, Traditional and Contemporary	9.50

1992

378	Winter Olympics	8.50
379	World Columbian Stamp Expo '92	8.75
380	W.E.B. Du Bois	10.00
381	Love	8.75
382	Olympic Baseball	30.00
383	Columbus' First Voyage	10.00
384	Space Adventures	10.00
385	New York Stock Exchange	11.00
386	Alaska Highway	7.50
387	Kentucky Statehood	6.50
388	Summer Olympics	8.00
389	Hummingbirds Booklet	10.00
390	World War II Miniature Sheet	10.00
391	Dorothy Parker	6.50
392	Theodore von Karman	10.00
393	Minerals	9.50
394	Juan Rodriguez Cabrillo	10.50
395	Wild Animals Booklet	10.00
396	Christmas, Traditional and Contemporary	10.50
397	Columbus Souvenir Sheets	40.00
398	Columbus Souvenir Sheets	40.00
399	Columbus Souvenir Sheets	40.00
400	Wildflowers #1	27.50
401	Wildflowers #2	27.50
402	Wildflowers #3	27.50
403	Wildflowers #4	27.50
404	Wildflowers #5	27.50
405	Happy New Year	15.00

1993

406	Elvis	20.00
407	Space Fantasy	11.00
408	Percy Julian	10.00
409	Oregon Trail	9.00
410	World Univ. Games	9.00
411	Grace Kelly	17.50
412	Oklahoma!	8.50
413	Circus	9.00
414	Cherokee Strip	8.50
415	Dean Acheson	10.50
416	Sport Horses	10.00
417	Garden Flowers	8.50
418	World War II	12.00
419	Hank Williams	15.00
420	Rock & Roll/R&B	20.00
421	Joe Louis	27.50
422	Broadway Musicals	11.00
423	National Postal Museum	9.00
424	Deaf Communication	9.00
425	Country Western	17.50
426	Christmas, Traditional	10.00
427	Youth Classics	10.00
428	Mariana Islands	8.75
429	Columbus Landing In Puerto Rico	10.50
430	AIDS Awareness	10.00

1994

431	Winter Olympics	15.00
432	Edward R. Murrow	9.00
433	Dr. Allison Davis	10.00
434	Year of the Dog	14.00
435	Love	9.50
436	Buffalo Soldiers	13.00
437	Silent ScreenStars	14.00
438	Garden Flowers	11.00
439	World Cup Soccer	12.00
440	World War II	15.00
441	Norman Rockwell	19.00
442	Moon Landing	16.00
443	Locomotives	12.00
444	George Meany	8.00
445	Popular Singers	12.50
446	James Thurber	8.00
447	Jazz/Blues	12.50
448	Wonders of the Sea	11.00
449	Birds (Cranes)	11.00
450	Christmas, Madonna	8.00
451	Christmas, Stocking	8.00
452	Year of the Boar	13.00

1995

453	Florida	10.00
454	Bessie Coleman	14.00
455	Kids Care!	10.00
456	Richard Nixon	15.00
457	Love	14.00
458	Recreational Sports	14.00
459	POW & MIA	12.50
460	Marilyn Monroe	22.50
461	Texas	12.50
462	Great Lakes Lighthouses	14.00
463	United Nations	11.00
464	Carousel Horses	14.00
465	Jazz Musicians	17.50
466	Women's Suffrage	11.00
467	Louis Armstrong	16.00
468	World War II	15.00
469	Fall Garden Flowers	11.00
470	Republic of Palau	11.00
471	Christmas, Contemporary	14.00
472	Naval Academy	14.00
473	Tennessee Williams	12.50
474	Christmas, Traditional	14.00
475	James K. Polk	10.00
476	Antique Automobiles	17.50

1996

477	Utah	10.00
478	Garden Flowers	10.00
479	Ernest E. Just	12.50
480	Smithsonian Institution	10.00
481	Year of the Rat	17.50
482	Pioneers of Communication	14.00
483	Fulbright Scholarships	10.00
484	Summer Olympics	30.00
485	Marathon	13.50
486	Georgia O'Keefe	10.00
487	Tennessee	10.00
488	James Dean	17.50
489	Prehistoric Animals	17.50
490	Breast Cancer Awareness	11.00

491	American Indian Dances	17.50
492	Folk Heroes	17.50
493	Centennial Games (Discus)	11.50
494	Iowa Statehood	10.00
495	Rural Free Delivery	10.00
496	Riverboats	17.50
497	Big Band Leaders	17.50
498	Songwriters	17.50
499	Endangered Species	27.50
500	Family Scenes (4 designs)	14.00
501	Hanukkah	15.00
502	Madonna and Child	13.50
503	Cycling	15.00
503A	F. Scott Fitzgerald	19.00
503B	Computer Technology	19.00

1997

504	Year of the Ox	19.00
505	Benjamin O. Davis	14.00
506	Love	12.00
507	Helping Children Learn	10.50
508	Pacific 97 Triangle Stamps	14.00
509	Thornton Wilder	12.00
510	Raoul Wallenberg	12.00
511	Dinosaurs	20.00
512	Bugs Bunny	16.00
513	Pacific 97 Franklin	40.00
514	Pacific 97 Washington	40.00
515	The Marshall Plan	10.00
516	Classic Aircraft	27.50
517	Football Coaches	17.50
518	Dolls	25.00
519	Humphrey Bogart	14.00
520	Stars and Stripes	13.00
521	Opera Singers	14.00
522	Composers and Conductors	14.00
523	Padre Varela	13.00
524	Air Force	13.50
525	Movie Monsters	16.00
526	Supersonic Flight	16.00
527	Women in the Military	13.00
528	Holiday Kwanzaa	14.00
529	Holiday, Traditional	18.00
530	Holiday Holly	18.00

1998

531	Year of the Tiger	13.00
532	Winter Sports	13.00
533	Madam C.J. Walker	13.00
533A	Celebrate The Century® 1900s	20.00
533B	Celebrate The Century® 1910s	20.00
534	Remember The Maine	13.00
535	Flowering Trees	16.00
536	Alexander Calder	16.00
537	Cinco de Mayo	13.00
538	Sylvester & Tweety	17.00
538A	Celebrate The Century® 1920s	20.00
539	Wisconsin	13.00
540	Trans-Mississippi	20.00
541	Folk Singers	14.00

542	Berlin Airlift	13.00
543	Spanish Settlement of the Southwest	14.00
544	Gospel Singers	13.00
545	Stephen Vincent Benet	13.00
546	Tropical Birds	13.00
546A	Breast Cancer Research	17.50
547	Alfred Hitchcock	13.00
548	Organ Donations	13.00
549	Bright Eyes	13.50
550	Klondike Gold Rush	13.00
551	American Art	20.00
551A	Celebrate The Century® 1930s	20.00
552	Ballet	13.00
553	Space Discovery	13.50
554	Philanthropy	13.00
555	Holiday, Traditional	18.00
556	Holiday, Contemporary	13.00

1999

557	Year of the Hare	15.00
558	Malcolm X	15.00
559	33¢ Victorian - Love	20.00
560	55¢ Victorian - Love	15.00
561	Hospice Care	15.00
562	Celebrate The Century® 1940s	20.00
563	Irish Immigration	15.00
564	Alfred Lunt and Lynn Fontanne	15.00
565	Arctic Animals	15.00
566	Nature of America Sonoran Desert	22.50
567	Daffy Duck	22.50
568	Ayn Rand	15.00
569	Cinco de Mayo	15.00
570	John and William Bartram	15.00
571	Celebrate The Century® 1950s	20.00
572	Prostate Cancer	15.00
573	California Gold Rush	15.00
574	Aquarium Fish	15.00
575	Xtreme Sports	15.00
576	American Glass	15.00
577	James Cagney	15.00
578	Honoring Those Who Served	15.00
579	All Aboard!	16.00
580	Frederick Law Olmsted	15.00
581	Hollywood Composers	16.00
582	Celebrate The Century® 1960s	20.00
583	Broadway Songwriters	16.00
584	Insects and Spiders	22.50
585	Hanukkah	15.00
586	Nato	15.00
587	Holiday Traditional, Bartolomeo Vivarini	15.00
588	Holiday Contemporary, Deer	15.00
589	Kwanzaa	15.00
590	Celebrate The Century® 1970s	20.00
591	Year 2000	16.00

2000

592	Year of the Dragon	15.00
593	Celebrate The Century® 1980s	20.00
594	Patricia Roberts Harris	15.00
595	U.S. Navy Submarines – *Los Angeles* Class	10.00
596	Pacific Coast Rain Forest	25.00
597	Louise Nevelson	10.00
598	Edwin Powell Hubble	10.00
599	American Samoa	10.00
600	Library of Congress	10.00
601	Wile E. Coyote/ Road Runner	10.00
602	Celebrate The Century® 1990s	20.00
603	Summer Sports	10.00
604	Adoption	10.00
605	Youth Team Sports	10.00
606	Distinguished Soldiers	10.00
607	The Stars and Stripes	25.00
608	Legends of Baseball	25.00
609	Stampin' The Future™	10.00
610	Edward G. Robinson	10.00
611	California Statehood	10.00
612	Deep Sea Creatures	10.00
613	Thomas Wolfe	10.00
614	The White House	10.00

2001

615	Love Letters	12.00
616	Lunar New Year— Year of the Snake	12.00
617	Roy Wilkins	12.00
618	American Illustrators	30.00
619	Love Letters (1 oz)	12.00
620	Love Letters (2 oz)	12.00
621	Nine-Mile Prairie	12.00
622	Diabetes Awareness	16.00
623	The Nobel Prize	12.00
624	Mt. McKinley	12.00
625	The Pan-American Inverts	30.00
626	Great Plains Prairie	30.00
627	Peanuts	12.00
628	Honoring Veterans	12.00
629	Frida Kahlo	12.00
630	Baseball's Legendary Playing Fields	30.00
631	Leonard Bernstein	12.00
632	Lucille Ball	12.00
633	The Amish Quilts	12.00
634	Carnivorous Plants	12.00
635	Holiday Celebration: EID	12.00
636	Dr. Enrico Fermi	12.00
637	That's All Folks!	12.00
638	Holiday Traditional: Lorenzo Costa's Virgin and Child	12.00
639	Holiday Contemporary: Santas	12.00

640	James Madison	12.00
641	Holiday Celebration: Thanksgiving	12.00
642	Kwanzas	12.00
643	Hanukkah	12.00
644	Love Letters	12.00

2002

645	Winter Sports	12.00
646	Mentoring a Child	12.00
647	Langston Hughes	12.00
648	Happy Birthday	12.00
649	Year of the Horse	12.00
650	U.S. Military Academy	12.00
651	Greetings From America	40.00
652	Longleaf Pine Forest	30.00
653	Heroes 2001	12.00
654	Masters of American Photography	30.00
655	John James Audubon	12.00
656	Harry Houdini	12.00
657	Andy Warhol	12.00
658	Teddy Bears	12.00
659	Love (1 oz.)	12.00
660	Love (2 oz.)	12.00
661	Ogden Nash	12.00
662	Duke Kahanamoku	12.00
663	American Bats	12.00
664	Women in Journalism	12.00
665	Irving Berlin	12.00
666	Neuter or Spay	
667	Christmas: Gossaert	12.00
668	Hanukkah	12.00
669	Eid	12.00
670	Kwanzaa	12.00
671	Cary Grant	12.00
672	Hawaiian Missionaries	12.00
673	Happy Birthday	12.00
674	Greetings From America	42.50
675	Holiday: Snowmen	12.00

2003

676	Thurgood Marshall	
677	Year of the Ram	
678	Zora Neale Hurston	
679	Special Oylmpics	
680	American Filmmaking: Behind the Scenes	
681	Ohio Statehood	
682	Pelican Island National Wildlife Refuge	—
683	Old Glory	
684	Cesar E. Chavez	
685	Louisiana Purchase	
686	First Flight	
687	Audrey Hepburn	
688	Southeastern Lighthouses	—
689	Arctic Tundra	
690	Korean War Veterans Memorial	—
691	Mary Cassatt	—
692	Early Football Heroes	—
693	Roy Acuff	—
694	District of Columbia	—

695	Reptiles and Amphibians	—
696	Stop Family Violence	—
697	Holiday Music Makers	—
698	Christmas: Gossaert	—
699	Year of the Monkey	—
700	Paul Robeson	—
701	Candy Hearts	—
702	Ted "Dr. Seuss" Giesel	—
703	Weddings (1oz.)	—
704	Weddings (2oz.)	—
705	US Air Force Academy	—

Glossary

Aerophilately – Stamp collecting that focuses on airmail stamps or postage.

Block – A group of unseparated stamps, at least two stamps high and two stamps wide.

Booklet Pane – A small sheet of stamps specially cut to be sold in booklets.

Bourse – A marketplace, such as a stamp exhibition, where stamps are bought, sold, or exchanged.

Cachet (ka-shay´) – A stamp-related design on an envelope.

Cancellation – A mark placed on a stamp by a postal authority to show that the stamp has been used.

Cinderella – Any stamp-like label without an official postal value.

Classic – An early stamp issue.

Commemoratives – Stamps that honor anniversaries, important people, special events, or aspects of national culture.

Compound Perforations – Different gauge perforations on different sides (normally adjacent) of a single stamp.

Cover – An envelope that has been sent through the mail.

Definitives – Regular issues of postage stamps, usually sold over long periods of time.

Denomination – The postage value appearing on a stamp.

Die Cut – Scoring of self-adhesive stamps that allows a stamp to be separated from the liner.

Error – A stamp with something incorrect in its design or manufacture.

Face Value – The monetary value, or denomination, of a stamp.

Fake – A genuine stamp that has been altered in some way to make it more attractive to collectors. It may be repaired, reperfed, or regummed to resemble a more valuable variety.

First Day Cover (FDC) – An envelope or card bearing a stamp cancelled to show its issuance date and place.

Franks – Written, hand-stamped, or imprinted markings on the face of a cover indicating that it is carried free of postage. Franking is usually limited to official government correspondence.

Freak – An abnormal variety of a stamp occurring because of paper fold, over-inking, perforation shift, etc., as opposed to a continually appearing variety or an error.

Gum – The coating of glue on the back of a stamp.

Hinges – Small strips of gummed material used by some collectors to affix stamps to album pages.

Imperforate – Indicates stamps without perforations.

Line Pairs (LP) – Most coil stamp rolls prior to 1981 feature a line of ink (known as a "joint line") printed between two stamps at various intervals, caused by the joining of two or more curved plates around the printing cylinder.

Liner – The backing paper for self-adhesive stamps.

On Paper – Stamps "on paper" are those that still have portions of the original envelope or wrapper attached.

Packet – A presorted group of different stamps, a common and economical way to begin a stamp collection.

Pane – A full "sheet" of stamps as sold by a Post Office.

Perforations – Lines of small holes or cuts between stamps that make them easy to separate.

Philately – The collection and study of postage stamps and other postal materials.

Plate Block (PB) (or Plate Number Block) – A block of stamps with the margin attached that bears the plate number used in printing that sheet.

Plate Number Coils (PNC) – For most coil stamp rolls beginning with #1891, a small plate number appears at varying intervals in the roll in the design of the stamp.

Postal Stationery – Envelopes, aerogrammes, stamped postal cards, and letter sheets with printed or embossed stamp designs.

Postal Cards – See "stamped postal cards."

Postcards – Commercially-produced mailable cards without imprinted postage.

Postmark – A mark put on envelopes or other mailing pieces showing the date and location of mailing.

Precancels – Stamps cancelled by a proper authority prior to their use on mail.

Presort Stamp – A discounted stamp used by business mailers who presort their mail.

Prestige Booklet – A booklet commemorating a special topic and containing stamps, narrative, and images.

Reissue – An official reprinting of a stamp that was no longer being printed.

Reprint – A stamp printed from the original plate after the issue is no longer valid for postage. Official reprints are sometimes made for presentation purposes, official collections, etc., and are often distinguished in some way from the "real" ones.

Revenue Stamps – Stamps issued as proof of payment of certain taxes but not valid for postage.

Rouletting – The piercing of the paper between stamps to facilitate their separation, often giving the appearance of a series of dashes.

Se-tenant – An attached pair, strip, or block of stamps that differ in design, value, or surcharge.

Self-Adhesive Stamp – A stamp with pressure sensitive adhesive.

Selvage – The paper around panes of stamps, sometimes called the margin.

Semipostal Stamp – A First-Class Mail stamp priced to include an additional charge earmarked for a specific charitable purpose.

Series – A number of individual stamps or sets of stamps having a common purpose or theme, issued over an extended period of time (generally a year or more), including all variations of design and/or denomination.

Souvenir Sheet – A small sheet of stamps with a commemorative inscription.

Special Issues – Stamps with a commemorative appearance that supplement definitives and meet specific needs. These include Christmas, Love, Holiday Celebrations, airmail, Express Mail, and Priority Mail stamps.

Stamped Postal Card – The current term for a mailable card with postage imprinted on it.

Stamped Envelope – A mailable envelope with postage embossed or imprinted on it.

Strip – Three or more unseparated stamps in a row.

Surcharge – An overprint that changes the denomination of a stamp.

Sweatbox – A closed box with a grill over which stuck-together unused stamps are placed. A wet, sponge-like material under the grill creates humidity so the stamps can be separated without removing the gum.

Tied On – Describes a stamp whose postmark touches the envelope.

Tongs – A tweezer-like tool with rounded or flattened tips used to handle stamps.

Topicals – A group of stamps with the same theme—space travel, for example.

Unhinged – A stamp without hinge marks.

Unused – The condition of a stamp that has no cancellation or other sign of use.

Used – The condition of a stamp that has been canceled.

Variety – A stamp that varies in some way from its standard or original form. Varieties can include missing colors or perforations, constant plate flaws, changes in ink or paper, differences in printing method or in format.

Watermark – A design sometimes pressed into stamp paper during its manufacture.

Water-Activated Gum – Water-soluble adhesives such as sugar-based starches on the back of an unused stamp.

Organizations

Please enclose a stamped, self-addressed envelope when writing to these organizations.

American Air Mail Society
Rudy Roy
PO Box 5367
Virginia Beach, VA 23471-0367
(p) 757/499-5234
AAMSinformation@aol.com
http://www.americanairmail
society.org

Specializes in all phases of aerophilately. Membership services include Advance Bulletin Service, Auction Service, free want ads, Sales Department, monthly journal, discounts on Society publications, translation service.

American First Day Cover Society
Douglas Kelsey
Executive Director
PO Box 65960
Tucson, AZ 85728-5960
(p) 520/321-0880
520/321-0879
AFDCS@aol.com
http://www.afdcs.org

A full-service, not-for-profit, noncommercial society devoted exclusively to First Day Covers and First Day Cover collecting. Publishes 90-page magazine, First Day, eight times a year. Offers information on 300 current cachet producers, expertizing, foreign covers, translation service, color slide programs and archives covering First Day Covers.

American Ceremony Program Society
John E. Peterson
ACPS Secretary/Treasurer
6987 Coleshill Drive
San Diego, CA 92119-1953
jkpete@pacbell.net
www.webacps.org

The American Ceremony Program Society is a place to learn about First Day and Supplemental (Second Day or later) stamp Ceremonies and Ceremony Programs. The Society publishes a journal, The Ceremonial, can be sent to members in a hard copy format at $2.50 per issue. The Society dues are $7 a year.

American Philatelic Society
Robert E. Lamb
Department PG
PO Box 8000
State College, PA
16803-8000
(p) 814/237-3803
(f) 814/237-6128
apsinfo@stamps.org
http://www.stamps.org
Moving in 2004, check web site for date, address and phone.

America's national stamp society. Membership benefits include various publications, services, and more. Sponsors national stamp exhibitions annually in partnership with the ASDA and USPS. 50,000+ members worldwide.

American Philatelic Research Library
aprl@stamps.org
www.stamplibrary.org

The largest philatelic library in the US, the APRL receives more than 400 periodicals, and houses extensive collections of philatelic literature.

American Society for Philatelic Pages and Panels
Gerald Blankenship
PO Box 475
Crosby, TX 77532-0475
(p) 281/324-2709
asppp134@aol.com
www.asppp.org

The only society with a focus on commemorative cancellations (formerly souvenir pages) and commemorative panels. Free ads, member auction, quarterly publica- *tion sent to all members with reports on new issues, varieties, errors, oddities and discoveries. Active web site.*

American Stamp Dealers Association
Joseph B. Savarese
3 School St., Suite 205
Glen Cove, NY 11542-2548
(p) 516/759-7000
(f) 516/759-7014
asda@erols.com
http://www.asdaonline.com

Association of dealers engaged in every facet of philately, with 6 regional chapters nationwide. Sponsors national and local shows. Will send you a complete listing of dealers in your area or collecting specialty. A #10 SASE must accompany your request.

American Topical Association
Executive Director
PO Box 57
Arlington, TX 76004-0057
(p) 817/274-1181
(f) 817/274-1184
americantopical@msn.com
www.americantopical.org

A service organization concentrating on the specialty of topical stamp collecting. Offers handbooks and checklists on specific topics; exhibition awards; Topical Time, a bimonthly publication dealing with topical interest areas; a slide loan service, and information, translation and sales services.

Ebony Society of Philatelic Events and Reflections
Manuel Gilyard
800 Riverside Drive, Apt. 4H
New York, NY 10032-7412
(p) 212-928-5165
(f) 212-928-1477
gilyardmani@aol.com
http://www.esperstamps.org

Junior Philatelists of America

Jennifer Arnold
Executive Secretary
PO Box 2625
Albany, OR 97321-0643
Exec.sec@jpastamps.org
http://www.jpastamps.org/

Member services include: pen pals, philatelic library, stamp identification, contests, study groups, and other services to young collectors. Members receive a bimonthly newsletter, The Philatelic Observer. Adult supporting membership and gift memberships are available. The JPA also publishes various brochures on stamp collecting.

Mailer's Postmark Permit Club

Charles F. Myers
Central Office
PO Box 3
Portland, TN 37148-0003
(p) 615/325-9478
(f) 615/451-7930
cfmyers@mindspring.com
www.mppclub.org

Publishes bimonthly newsletter, Permit Patter, which covers all aspects of mailer's postmark permits. Also available, an 8-page step by step brochure "How to obtain a Mailer's Postmark Permit...a basic guide."

Plate Number Coil Collectors Club

Thomas McFarland
PNC3 Secretary
PO Box 756
Princeton Jct, NJ 08550-0756
www.pnc3.org

The Plate Number Coil Collectors Club (PNC^3) is an organization that studies the plate numbers and plate varieties of United States coil stamps issued since 1981. The PNC^3 publishes a monthly newsletter, Coil Line. The website includes a membership application and discusses plate number coils and PNC^3 at length.

Postal History Society

Kalman V. Illyefalvi
8207 Daren Court
Pikesville, MD 21208-2211
(p) 410/653-0665
kalphyl@juno.com

Devoted to the study of various aspects of the development of the mails and local, national and international postal systems; UPU treaties; and means of transporting mail.

The Souvenir Card Collectors Society, Inc.

Dana M. Marr
PO Box 4155
Tulsa, OK 74159-0155
(p) 918/664-6724
DMARR5569@aol.com

Provides member auctions, a quarterly journal and access to limited-edition souvenir cards.

Compilation of U.S. Souvenir Cards

United Postal Stationery Society

UPSS Central Office
Cora Collins
Executive Director
PO Box 1792
Norfolk, VA 23501-1792
poststat@juno.com
www.upss.org

Postal stationary is made up of the post office-issued postal cards, envelopes, letter sheets and other postal products having the stamp already printed. The UPSS is the largest society devoted to the collecting and study of postal stationery of the world with members throughout the U.S. and many foreign countries.

19th Century Envelopes Catalog

20th Century Envelopes Catalog

U.S. Postal Card Catalog

U.S. Commemorative Stamped Envelopes, 1867-1965

U.S. Envelope Essays and Proofs Canal Zone Postal Stationery

Universal Ship Cancellation Society

Steve Shay
747 Shard Court
Fremont, CA 94539-7419
e-mail: Shaymur@flash.net
http://www.uscs.org

Specializes in naval ship postmarks and cachets.

U.S. Postal Service Stamp Services

475 L'Enfant Plaza SW
Washington, D.C. 20260-2437

U.S. Stamp Society

Executive Secretary
PO Box 6634
Katy, TX 77491-6634
http://www.usstamps.org

An association of collectors to promote the study of all postage and revenue stamps and stamped paper of the United States and U.S.-administered areas produced by the Bureau of Engraving and Printing and other contract printers.

Durland Plate Number Catalog

Expertisers

American Philatelic Expertizing Service (APEX)

Mercer Bristow
Director of Expertizing
PO Box 8000
State College, PA 16803-8000
Ambristo@stamps.org

Krystal Harter
Expertizing Coordinator
Krharter@stamps.org
(p) 814/237-3803
(f) 814/237-6128
http://www.stamps.org

A service of the American Philatelic Society since 1903, APEX utilizes the outstanding reference collections at APS headquarters in conjunction with the nation's best philatelic scholars to pass judgement on the identification, authenticity and condition of stamps from around the world.

Philatelic Foundation

Attention: Chairman
George J. Kramer
70 W 40th Street 15th Floor
New York, NY 10018
(p) 212/221-6555
(f) 212/221-6208
www.philatelicfoundation.org

A nonprofit organization known for its excellent expertization service. The Foundation's broad resources, including extensive reference collections, 5,000-volume library and Expert Committee, provide collectors with comprehensive consumer protection. Book series include expertizing case histories in Opinions, *Foundation seminar subjects in "textbooks" and specialized U.S. subjects in monographs.*

Professional Stamp Experts, Inc.

PO Box 6170
Newport Beach, CA 92658
(p) 877/782-6788
http://www.psestamp.com
pse@collectors.com

Organization specializing in identification, expertization and grading of U.S. Postage Stamps, Covers, Revenues etc.... PSE issues a Certificate of Authenticity accepted by all auction firms, dealers and collectors.

PSE publishes a Guide to the Grading of U.S. Stamps and The Stamp Market Quarterly Price Guide. Either is free upon request.

Periodicals

The following publications will send you a free copy of their magazine or newspaper upon request.

Global Stamp News

PO Box 97
Sidney, OH 45365-0097
(p) 937/492-3183
jbrandewie@woh.rr.com

America's largest-circulation monthly stamp magazine featuring U.S. and foreign issues.

Linn's Stamp News

PO Box 29
Sidney, OH 45365-0097
(p) 937/498-7273
(f) 937/498-0876
(f) 937/498-0814 (outside US)
linns@linns.com
www.linns.com

Linn's Stamps News, the world's largest weekly stamp newspaper, contains breaking news stories of major importance to stamp collectors, features on a variety of stamp-collecting topics, the monthly U.S. Stamp Market Index, Stamp Market Tips and much more. A sample copy of the weekly newspaper is available upon request.

Linn's U.S. Stamp Yearbook

(p) 937/498-0802
(f) 800/572-6885 (US only)
(f) 937/498-0807 (outside US)
linns@linns.com
www.linns.com

Linn's World Stamp Almanac

Stamp Collecting Made Easy

Mekeel's & Stamps Magazine-fa

John Dunn
175R Proctor Hill Road
Hollis, NH 03049
stampnews@aol.com
http://www.stampnews.com

Weekly magazine for collectors of U.S. & worldwide stamps & covers.

U.S. Stamp News-fb

Monthly magazine for all collectors of U.S. stamps, covers and postal history.

Stamp Collector

Wayne Youngblood
Publisher, Stamps Dept.
700 E. State St.
Iola, WI 54990-0001
(p) 715/445-2214
youngbloodw@krause.com

For beginning and advanced collectors of all ages.

Stamp Wholesaler

For dealers of all levels and those interested in the stamp business. (Published monthly as part of Stamp Collector.*)*

Basic Philately

Stamp Fulfillment Services

U.S. Postal Service
8300 NE Underground Dr
Pillar 210
Kansas City, MO 64144-0001
(p) 1-800-STAMP-24

Scott Specialized Catalogue of U.S. Stamps and Covers

PO Box 828
Sidney, OH 45365-0828
(p) 937/498-0831
(p) 800/572-6885
(f) 937/498-0807
cuserv@amosadvantage.com
www.amosadvantage.com

Scott Standard Postage Stamp Catalogue

Scott Classic Specialized Catalogue of U.S. Stamps and Covers (World from 1840-1940)

Scott Stamp Monthly

Museums, Libraries and Displays

Please contact the institutions before visiting to confirm hours and any entry fees.

The Collectors Club

Irene Bromberg
Executive Secretary
22 E. 35th Street
New York, NY
10016-3806
(p) 212/683-0559
(f) 212/481-1269
collectorsclub@nac.net
http://www.collectorsclub.org

Bimonthly journal, publication of various reference works, one of the most extensive reference libraries in the world, reading and study rooms. Regular meetings on the first and third Wednesdays of each month at 6:30 p.m., except July and August.

National Postal Museum
Smithsonian Institution
Washington, D.C. 20560-0570
(p) 202/633-9360
http://www.si.edu/postal/

*Located in the Old City Post
Office building at
2 Massachusetts Avenue, NE
National Postal Museum
houses more than 16 million
items for exhibition and
study purposes. Collections
research may be conducted
separately or jointly with
library materials. Call the
museum and its library
(202/633-9370) separately to
schedule an appointment.*

**The Postal History
Foundation**
Betsy Towle
PO Box 40725
Tucson, AZ 85717-0725
(p) 520/623-6652
(f) 520/623-6652
phf3@mindspring.com
Hours: M-F 8 a.m.-3 p.m.

*Located at 920 N. First Ave
in Tucson, the Foundation,
established in 1960, has
been a specialist in youth
philatelic education in the
classroom. Regular services
include a library, USPS contract post office, philatelic
sales, archives, artifacts and
collections and a Youth
Department.*

**San Diego County
Philatelic Library**
Al Kish, Library Manager
7403C Princess View Drive
San Diego, CA 92120
(p) 619/229-8813
Hours:
M & T & Th 6:30 p.m.-9:30
p.m. and Sat noon-3 p.m.
Other hours available by
appointment. Please call for
confirmation of hours.

**Spellman Museum of
Stamps and Postal History**
Executive Director
235 Wellesley Street
Weston, MA 02493-1538
(p) 781/768-8367
(f) 781/768-7332
info@spellman.org
www.spellman.org

*America's first fully accred-
ited museum devoted to the
display, collection and
preservation of stamps and
postal history. Exhibitions
feature rarities, U.S., and
worldwide collections.
Philatelic library and family
activity center open with
admission. School and scout
programs by appointment.
Museum store and post
office carries gifts, collecting
supplies, and stamps.*

Western Philatelic Library
PO Box 2219
Sunnyvale, CA 94087-2219
(p) 408/733-0336
stulev@ix.netcom.com
http://www.pbbooks.com/w
pl.htm
http://www.fwpl.org

**Friends of the Western
Philatelic Library**

**Wineburgh Philatelic
Research Library**
Erik D. Carlson, Ph.D.
McDermott Library
University of Texas at Dallas
PO Box 830643
Mailstation: MC33
Richardson, TX 75083-0643
(p) 972/883-2570
http://www.utdallas.edu/libr
ary/special/wprl.html
Hours: M-Th 9 a.m.–6 p.m.;
Fri 9 a.m.-5 p.m.

Exchange Service

Stamp Master
Charles Bergeron
PO Box 17
Putnam Hall, FL 32185-0017
Cbergero@bellsouth.net

*An "electronic connection"
for philatelists via modem
and computer to display/
review members' stamp
inventories for trading purposes, etc.*

Literature

**ArtCraft First Day Cover
Price List**
Washington Press
2 Vreeland Road
Florham Park, NJ 07932-1501
(p) 877/966-0001 (toll free)
info@washpress.com
http://www.washpress.com

*Includes Presidential
Inaugural covers.*

**Legends of the West
Washington Press**
*How some collectors struck
it rich!*

The Hammarskjold Invert
*Tells the story of the Dag
Hammarskjold error/invert.*

**The 24¢ 1918 Air Mail
Invert**
*Tells all there is to know
about this famous stamp.*

**The U.S. Transportation
Coils**
*How some collectors struck
it rich!*

*ALL ABOVE FREE for
#10 SASE.*

**Brookman's 1st Edition
Black Heritage First Day
Cachet Cover Catalog**
Arlene Dunn
Brookman/Barrett &
Worthen
10 Chestnut Drive
Bedford, NH 03110-5566
(p) 603/472-5575
(f) 603/472-8795

*Illustrated 176-page perfect
bound book.*

Brookman's 2nd Edition Price Guide for Disney Stamps
Illustrated 256-page perfect bound book.

2004 Brookman Price Guide of U.S., U.N. and Canada Stamps and Postal Collectibles
Illustrated 408-page catalog.

Postmark Advisory
Paul Brenner
General Image, Inc.
PO Box 335
Maplewood, NJ 07040-0335
Postmark1@earthlink.net
http://home.earthlink.net/
~postmark1
(How-to-do-it is excellent for beginners)

A weekly newsletter is available which provides descriptive information on U.S. pictorial postmarks that you can send away for. A free sample newsletter is available if you send a SASE and ask for a copy. If you are interested in postmarks, you might like to visit the web site.

Fleetwood's Standard First Day Cover Catalog
Fleetwood
Unicover Corporation
1 Unicover Center
Cheyenne, WY 82008-0001
(p) 307/771-3000
(p) 800/443-4225
http://www.unicover.com

Precancel Stamp Society Catalogs
Dick Laetsch
3 Shady Creek Lane
Scarborough, ME 04070
(p) 207/883-2505
precancel@aol.com
www.precanceledstamps.com

Stamp Collecting Made Easy
PO Box 29
Sidney, OH 45365-0097
(p) 937/498-0802
(p) 800/572-6885 (US only)
(f) 937/498-0807 (outside US)

An illustrated, easy-to-read, 96-page booklet for beginning collectors.

International Agents

Japan Philatelic Agency
PO Box 96 Toshima
Tokyo 170-8668
JAPAN

Max Stern
234 Flinders Street
Box 997 H
GPO Melbourne 3001
AUSTRALIA

Harry Allen
PO Box 5
Watford Herts WD2 5SW
UNITED KINGDOM

Nordfrim
DK 5450 Otterup
DENMARK

Georg Roll Stamps LTD
Attn: Tom Schneider
Hafenstrasse 8
D-26931 Elsfleth
GERMANY

Hermann Sieger GMBH
Venusberg 32-34
D73545 Lorch Wurttemberg
GERMANY

Alberto Bolaffi
Via Cavour 17
10123 Torino
ITALY

International House of Stamps
98/2 Soi Tonson
Langsuan Rd
Lumpinee, Pathumwan
Bangkok 10330
THAILAND

**AFINSA
(Centro Distribucion Filatelia)**
Attn: Jordi Casals
Manuel Tovar, 1, 4 izda
28034 Madrid
SPAIN

Philatelic Centers

In addition to the more than 20,000 postal facilities authorized to sell philatelic products, the Postal Service also maintains Philatelic Centers located in major population centers. These Philatelic Centers have been established to serve stamp collectors and make it convenient for them to acquire an extensive range of current postage stamps, postal stationery and philatelic products issued by the Postal Service.

**For questions, location and hours of operation about a Philatelic Center near you, please call 800-275-8777
or visit us online at www.usps.com.**

The numbers listed next to the stamp description are the Scott numbers, and the numbers in parentheses are the numbers of the pages on which the stamps are listed.

G

Postmasters General of the United States

Appointed by the Continental Congress
1775 Benjamin Franklin, PA
1776 Richard Bache, PA
1782 Ebenezer Hazard, NY

Appointed by the President with the advice and consent of the Senate
1789 Samuel Osgood, MA
1791 Timothy Pickering, PA
1795 Joseph Habersham, GA
1801 Gideon Granger, CT
1814 Return J. Meigs, Jr., OH
1823 John McLean, OH
1829 William T. Barry, KY
1835 Amos Kendall, KY
1840 John M. Niles, CT
1841 Francis Granger, NY
1841 Charles A. Wickliffe, KY
1845 Cave Johnson, TN
1849 Jacob Collamer, VT
1850 Nathan K. Hall, NY
1852 Samuel D. Hubbard, CT
1853 James Campbell, PA
1857 Aaron V. Brown, TN
1859 Joseph Holt, KY
1861 Horatio King, ME
1861 Montgomery Blair, DC

1864 William Dennison, OH
1866 Alexander W. Randall, WI
1869 John A.J. Creswell, MD
1874 James W. Marshall, NJ
1874 Marshall Jewell, CT
1876 James N. Tyner, IN
1877 David McK. Key, TN
1880 Horace Maynard, TN
1881 Thomas L. James, NY
1882 Timothy O. Howe, WI
1883 Walter Q. Gresham, IN
1884 Frank Hatton, IA
1885 William F. Vilas, WI
1888 Don M. Dickinson, MI
1889 John Wanamaker, PA
1893 Wilson S. Bissell, NY
1895 William L. Wilson, WV
1897 James A. Gary, MD
1898 Charles Emory Smith, PA
1902 Henry C. Payne, WI
1904 Robert J. Wynne, PA
1905 George B. Cortelyou, NY
1907 George von L. Meyer, MA
1909 Frank H. Hitchcock, MA
1913 Albert S. Burleson, TX
1921 Will H. Hays, IN
1922 Hubert Work, CO
1923 Harry S. New, IN

1929 Walter F. Brown, OH
1933 James A. Farley, NY
1940 Frank C. Walker, PA
1945 Robert E. Hannegan, MO
1947 Jesse M. Donaldson, IL
1953 Arthur E. Summerfield, MI
1961 J. Edward Day, CA
1963 John A. Gronouski, WI
1965 Lawrence F. OíBrien, MA
1968 W. Marvin Watson, TX
1969 Winton M. Blount, AL

Selected by the Presidentially appointed U.S. Postal Service Board of Governors
1971 Elmer T. Klassen, MA
1975 Benjamin Franklin Bailar, MD
1978 William F. Bolger, CT
1985 Paul N. Carlin, WY
1986 Albert V. Casey, MA
1986 Preston R. Tisch, NY
1988 Anthony M. Frank, CA
1992 Marvin Runyon, TN
1998 William J. Henderson, NC
2001 John E. Potter, NY

Acknowledgments

This stamp collecting catalog was produced by Government Relations and Public Policy, Stamp Services, United States Postal Service.

UNITED STATES POSTAL SERVICE
John E. Potter
Postmaster General and Chief Executive Officer

Ralph J. Moden
Senior Vice President, Government Relations and Public Policy

David E. Failor
Executive Director, Stamp Services

Terrence W. McCaffrey
Manager, Stamp Development

Cindy L. Tackett
Manager, Stamp Exhibitions and Products

Sonja D. Edison
Project Manager and Editor

Betty Zelkowitz
Project Assistant

HARPERCOLLINS PUBLISHERS
Nick Darrell
Assistant Editor, HarperResource

Lucy Albanese
Design Director, General Books Group

Jessica Chin
Production Editor, General Books Group

Susan Kosko
Director of Production, General Books Group

PRINTING AND BINDING
Quebecor/World
Taunton, MA 02780

DESIGN SERVICES
Roberta Wojtkowski Design
10992 Thrush Ridge Road
Reston, VA 20191

Night & Day Design
41 River Terrace #2104
New York, NY 10282

Robin Leist
Keystrokes & Design
2616 Hidden Lake Dr N
Sarasota, FL 34237

RESEARCH AND WRITING SERVICES
PhotoAssist, Inc.
7735 Old Georgetown Road
Bethesda, MD 20814

COLOR SEPARATION AND DIGITAL PREPRESS SERVICES
Dodge Color
4827 Rugby Avenue
Bethesda, MD 20814

White *(continued)*
    -fronted Geese, RW11 (483)
    House, 809 (86), 844 (89), 932
        (97), 990 (102), 1208 (125),
        1240 (126), 1338 (137),
        1338A (137), 1338D (137),
        1338F (137), 1338G (137),
        1935–1936 (205), 2219 (238),
        2219e (238), 2609 (285),
        3445 (425)
    House, Little, 931 (97)
    Josh, 3215 (385)
    Minor, 3659t (446)
    Mountain, 2661 (293)
    Oak, 1766 (186)
    Pine, 1765 (186)
    Plains, Battle of, 629 (69), 630
        (69)
    Sanford, 1928 (205)
    -Tailed Deer, 1888 (198)
    William Allen, 960 (98)
    -Winged Dove, 3293c (398)
    -winged Scoters, RW36 (483)
White Cloud, Head Chief of the
    Iowas, 3236k (389)
Whitman, Walt, 867 (90)
Whitney, Eli, 889 (90)
Whittier, John Greenleaf, 865 (90)
Whooping Cranes, 1098 (114)
Widgeons, RW51 (484)
Wightman, Hazel, 2498 (270)
Wigmaker, 1458 (149)
Wild
    Alfalfa, 3506c (433)
    Animals, 2705–2709 (298)
    Pink, 2076 (221)
    Turkey, 1077 (113)
Wildcat, 3142t (358)
Wilder, Thornton, 3134 (353)
Wilderness, Civil War Centennial,
    1181 (122)
Wildflowers, 2647–2660 (293),
    2662–2671 (293), 2672–2696
    (294)
Wildlife, 1757 (186), 1880–1889
    (198), 2476 (269)
    American, 2286–2310 (246),
        2311–2335 (249)
    Conservation, 1077–1078 (113),
        1098 (114), 1392 (141),
        1427–1430 (145), 1464–1467
        (150), 1760–1763 (186)
    Habitats, Preservation of,
        1921–1924a (202)
    and Vegetation, 3802a–j (458)
Wile E. Coyote and Road Runner,
    3391 (414)
Wiley, Harvey W., 1080 (113)
Wilkes, Lt. Charles, 2387 (257)
Wilkins, Roy, 3501 (429)
Willard, Frances E., 872 (90)
Williams
    Hank, 2723 (301), 2771 (306),
        2775 (306)
    Roger, 777 (82)
    Tennessee, 3002 (337)
Willis, Bob, 2774 (306), 2778
    (306)
Willkie, Wendell, 2192 (234)
Willow ptarmigans

bearberry, 3802h (458)
    caribou, 3802f (458)
Willson, Meredith, 3349 (405)
Wilson, Woodrow, 623 (69), 697
    (74), 832 (89), 1040 (106),
    2218i (238), 3183k (369)
Windmills, 1738–1742 (185)
Winfield Hancock, 2975n (330)
Winged
    Airmail Envelope, C79 (470),
        C83 (470)
    Globe, C12 (465), C16–C17
        (465), C19 (465), C24 (466)
Winogrand, Garry, 3649s (446)
Winter
    Olympic Games '84, 2067 (218)
    Olympic Games '94,
        2807–2811 (310)
    Pastime, by Currier, Nathaniel,
        1702 (178)
    Special Olympics, 2142 (229)
    Wren, 3378f (413)
Winter Sports, 3552–3555 (441)
    Skiing, 3180 (366)
Win the War, 905 (93)
Wisconsin, 1662 (170), 2001
    (210), 3609 (442), 3744 (453)
    -Madison, University of, UX301
        (510)
    Statehood, 957 (98), 3206 (382)
    Tercentenary, 739 (78), 755 (81)
    Workman's Compensation Law,
        1186 (122)
Wisdom, 3766 (454)
Witherspoon, John, 1687c (174)
Wizard of Oz, The, 2445 (266)
Wolf
    Gray, 3292 (397), 3802b (458)
    Howlin', 2861 (317)
    Trap Farm National Park, 1452
        (149), 2018 (213)
Wolfe, Thomas, 3444 (425)
Wolf Man, The, 3172 (365)
Woman
    American, 1152 (121)
    Clubs, General Federation of,
        1316 (134)
    with Flag & Sword, 19th
        Century Carving, 3780 (457),
        UX394 (510)
    Suffrage, 1406 (142)
Women
    in Journalism, 3665–3668 (450)
    in Military Service, 3174 (366)
    Support War Effort, 3186e (373)
Women's
    Diving, 3068d (345)
    Gymnastic, 3068g (345)
    Progress of, 959 (98)
    Right's Movement, 3189j (374)
    Running, 3068c (345)
    Sailboarding, 3068h (345)
    Service, 1013 (105)
    Soccer, 3068j (345)
    Softball, 3068o (345)
    Suffrage, 2980 (333)
    Swimming, 3068n (345)
    Voting Rights, 2980 (333)
Wonders of the Sea, 2863–2866
    (317)

Wood
    -Carved Figurines, 2240–2243
        (241)
    Ducks, 2493–2494 (270), RW10
        (483), RW41 (483)
    Grant, *American Gothic*, 3236q
        (389)
Wooden Propeller, Airplane
    Radiator and, C4 (465)
Woodland Habitats, 1924 (202)
Woodpecker
    Gila, 3293j (398)
    Red-Headed, 3032 (341), 3045
        (341)
Woodson, Carter G., 2073 (221)
Woodstock, 3188b (374)
Woody Wagon, 3522 (434)
Wool Industry, American, 1423
    (145)
Woolly Mammoth, 3078 (346)
Workmen's Compensation, 1186
    (122)
World
    Columbian Stamp Expo '92,
        2616 (286), 2624–2629
        (289)
    Cup Soccer Championships,
        1994, 2834–2837 (313)
    of Dinosaurs, 3136a–o (354)
    Exposition, Louisiana, 2086
        (221)
    Forestry Congress, Fifth, 1156
        (121)
    Health Organization, 1194 (122)
    Peace Through Law, 1576 (162)
    Peace Through World Trade,
        1129 (117)
    Refugee Year, 1149 (118)
    Series Rivals, 3187j (373)
    STAMP EXPO '89, 2410 (261),
        2433 (265)
    STAMP EXPO '92, Columbian,
        2616 (286), 2624–2629 (289)
    University Games, 2748 (302)
    War, (313)
    War I, 3183i (369), 537 (62),
        2154 (230)
    War II (10), 899–901 (93), 905
        (93), 907–908 (93), 909–915
        (94), 917–921 (94), 925–926
        (94), 929 (97), 934–936 (97),
        939–940 (97), 956 (98), 969
        (101), 1026 (105), 1289
        (130), 1424 (145), 1869
        (198), 2187 (233), 2191
        (234), 2559a–j (278), 2697
        (297), 2765a–j (305), 2838a–j
        (313), 2981a–j (333), 3186a
        (373), 3420 (422)
    Wide Web, 3191n (378)
World's
    Fair, Expo Seattle '62, 1196
        (125)
    Fair, Knoxville '82, 2006–2009
        (213)
    Fair, New York, 853 (89)
    Fair Expo '74, 1527 (157)
    Fair '64, 1244 (126)
Wreaths, 3245–3252 (390)
Wreath and Toys, 1843 (194)